AI DEVELOPMENT AND THE 'FUZZY LOGIC' OF CHINESE CYBER SECURITY AND DATA LAWS

MAX PARASOL

RMIT Blockchain Innovation Hub
University of New South Wales, Sydney

Shaftesbury Road, Cambridge CB2 8EA, United Kingdom

One Liberty Plaza, 20th Floor, New York, NY 10006, USA

477 Williamstown Road, Port Melbourne, VIC 3207, Australia

314–321, 3rd Floor, Plot 3, Splendor Forum, Jasola District Centre, New Delhi – 110025, India

103 Penang Road, #05–06/07, Visioncrest Commercial, Singapore 238467

Cambridge University Press is part of Cambridge University Press & Assessment, a department of the University of Cambridge.

We share the University's mission to contribute to society through the pursuit of education, learning and research at the highest international levels of excellence.

www.cambridge.org
Information on this title: www.cambridge.org/9781009073639

DOI: 10.1017/9781009064804

© Max Parasol 2022

This publication is in copyright. Subject to statutory exception and to the provisions of relevant collective licensing agreements, no reproduction of any part may take place without the written permission of Cambridge University Press & Assessment.

First published 2022
First paperback edition 2023

A catalogue record for this publication is available from the British Library

Library of Congress Cataloging-in-Publication data
Names: Parasol, Max, 1984- author.
Title: AI development and the 'fuzzy logic' of Chinese cyber security and data laws / Max Parasol, RMIT Blockchain Innovation Hub and University of New South Wales, Sydney.
Other titles: Artificial intelligence development and the 'fuzzy logic' of Chinese cyber security and data laws
Description: Cambridge, United Kingdom ; New York, NY : Cambridge University Press, 2022. | Based on author's thesis (doctoral - University of Technology, Sydney, 2020) issued under title: The impact of China's 'fuzzy logic' legal system on Chinese AI development. | Includes bibliographical references and index.
Identifiers: LCCN 2021030231 (print) | LCCN 2021030232 (ebook) | ISBN 9781316513361 (hardback) | ISBN 9781009073639 (paperback) | ISBN 9781009064804 (epub)
Subjects: LCSH: Artificial intelligence–Law and legislation–China. | Computer security–Law and legislation–China. | Data protection–Law and legislation–China.
Classification: LCC KNQ80.C65 P37 2022 (print) | LCC KNQ80.C65 (ebook) | DDC 343.5109/944–dc23
LC record available at https://lccn.loc.gov/2021030231
LC ebook record available at https://lccn.loc.gov/2021030232

ISBN 978-1-316-51336-1 Hardback
ISBN 978-1-009-07363-9 Paperback

Cambridge University Press & Assessment has no responsibility for the persistence or accuracy of URLs for external or third-party internet websites referred to in this publication and does not guarantee that any content on such websites is, or will remain, accurate or appropriate.

CONTENTS

Acknowledgements xiii
List of Abbreviations xiv

Introduction 1

PART I Historical and Doctrinal Background

1 Innovating in China's Entrepreneurial Ecosystem 21

2 The Extent of Fuzzy Logic: The Tech Giants and Their 'Illegal' Legal Structure 36

3 China's Cyber Policies: Conflict between Innovation and Restriction 62

4 China's Data Security Policies Leading to the Cyber Security Law 80

5 The Cyber Security Law: Fuzzy Logic in a Touchstone Law 94

PART II Impact on Artificial Intelligence

6 The Impacts of Data Localisation on Globalised Ecosystems and Chinese Tech 129

7 Data Protection but Not Data Privacy: 'Data Protection Shall Not Hinder AI' 154

8 The Current State of AI Research Is Perfectly Suited to China's Fuzzy Logic System 209

9 Open-Source AI Platforms and the Cyber Security Law 260

Conclusion: Effect of Data Localisation on Chinese
AI Innovation   329

Bibliography   343
Index   402

DETAILED CONTENTS

Acknowledgements xiii
List of Abbreviations xiv

Introduction 1
0.1 Innovation versus Restriction   4
    0.1.1 Internet Plus   4
    0.1.2 Network Sovereignty   5
0.2 Fuzzy Logic: The Chinese Approach to Innovation Regulation   7
    0.2.1 Policy Petri Dishes in Chinese Innovation   9
    0.2.2 Fuzzy Logic   11
0.3 Significance of Data Localisation   15
0.4 Research Methodology   18

PART I   **Historical and Doctrinal Background**

1 **Innovating in China's Entrepreneurial Ecosystem**   21
   1.1 'China Cannot Innovate'   21
   1.2 The Origin of China's Policy Petri Dishes   24
   1.3 China's Unique Ecosystem: Adept at Catching Up   26
   1.4 Top-Down or Bottom-Up Innovation?   29
   1.5 Entrepreneurial Ecosystems with Chinese Characteristics   32
   1.6 Conclusion: Assumptions on Chinese Innovation Challenges   35

2 **The Extent of Fuzzy Logic: The Tech Giants and Their 'Illegal' Legal Structure**   36
   2.1 'Fuzzy Logic' Laws   37
       2.1.1 What Is Meant by a 'Fuzzy Logic' Law in China?   38
   2.2 Offshore Legal Structures: The Variable-Interest Entity (VIE)   39
       2.2.1 The VIE Structure   40
       2.2.2 Evading China's Investment Laws   42
       2.2.3 Paradoxical Side Effects of Fuzzy Logic on VIEs   43

  2.2.4 Disputes between Chinese Tech Firms and Activist VIE Investors 46
 2.3 The End of VIEs or a False Alarm? 50
  2.3.1 Future Legal Implications and Risks 51
 2.4 China Unable to Lure the Champions Home: 2018 52
  2.4.1 Maintaining the Fuzzy Logic: CDRs and the 2019 Foreign Investment Law 53
 2.5 US Blacklistings in 2019–2020: Are VIEs Still Relevant? 56
 2.6 Conclusion: Still Too Big to Fail 59

3 China's Cyber Policies: Conflict between Innovation and Restriction 62
 3.1 Internet Plus versus Network Sovereignty 62
 3.2 Internet Plus 63
  3.2.1 Background to Internet Plus: China's Informatisation Strategy 64
 3.3 China's Cyber Institutions 65
 3.4 The Language of Internet Plus: Promoting Global Cooperation 70
 3.5 Network Sovereignty 72
 3.6 Network Sovereignty, Content Censorship, Internet Plus and the Influence of the BATs 77
 3.7 Conclusion: Unresolved Questions 78

4 China's Data Security Policies Leading to the Cyber Security Law 80
 4.1 Planning for China's Cyber Regime: 'Cyber Security and Informatisation Are Two Wings of One Body' 81
 4.2 The Critical Need for a Cyber Security Regime in China 83
 4.3 Network Sovereignty Laws Prior to the Cyber Security Law 85
 4.4 China's Anti-Terrorism Law 87
  4.4.1 Data Encryption and Backdoor Keys in the United States 89
 4.5 Conclusion: Policy Indicators? 92

5 The Cyber Security Law: Fuzzy Logic in a Touchstone Law 94
 5.1 Background: Initial Drafting, Consultation then Delayed Implementation 96
 5.2 The Law: Vague Regulations Make Compliance Difficult 98
  5.2.1 Vague Rules: To Whom Does the Law Apply? 98

    5.2.2 Vague Rules: Data Localisation (Data Storage Requirements and Data Exits)   102
    5.2.3 Vague Rules: Unclear Product Review Requirements   105
5.3 Backdoors under the Cyber Security Law?   107
5.4 Third Parties in Security Reviews under the Cyber Security Law   110
5.5 Evolving and Contradictory Subordinate Regulations on Data Transfers and Network Security   115
5.6 Unresolved Issues: The Current Status of Cross-Border Data Flows under Article 37 of the Cyber Security Law   118
    5.6.1 'Important Data'   121
    5.6.2 'Network Operators' Remains Broad and Undefined   122
5.7 Conclusion: Fuzzy Logic, Even in a Touchstone Law   124

PART II Impact on Artificial Intelligence

6 The Impacts of Data Localisation on Globalised Ecosystems and Chinese Tech   129
6.1 Background   130
6.2 What Is Data Localisation?   133
6.3 Two Major Motivations for Data Localisation: Protecting Personal Data and Ensuring Government Control over Data   133
6.4 Existing Theories about Data Localisation Laws   137
    6.4.1 Arguments against Data Localisation Laws: Protectionism versus Data Protection   138
    6.4.2 Data Localisation Is 'Technically Unviable' and Counterproductive to Data Protection Goals and National Security Concerns   141
    6.4.3 Increased Costs for Companies and Consumers   144
6.5 Implications of the Rise of AI: Fuzzy Logic Masks Motivations for Data Localisation   147
6.6 Conclusion: Costs–Benefits Can Change   152

7 Data Protection but Not Data Privacy: 'Data Protection Shall Not Hinder AI'   154
7.1 Background: New Data Protection Regime Still Emerging   155
    7.1.1 Increased Data Protection under the Cyber Security Law   159
7.2 Enforced Real-Name User Registration   159
    7.2.1 Real-Name User Registration   161
    7.2.2 Data Protection, not Privacy   164

7.3 Data Protection a Key Social Issue, among Many 'Trust' Scandals   166
7.4 Polling: Growing Awareness of Data Privacy Issues   175
7.5 BATs and Other Tech Firms Face Regular Data Protection Penalties, but Push Back against Authorities   177
7.6 Privacy Standards Follow the Cyber Security Law on 'Data Protection'   180
    7.6.1 What Is Protected Personal Information?   185
    7.6.2 What Were the Drafters of the Original Privacy Standards Intending?   186
7.7 Definitional Fuzzy Logic in the Privacy Standards: Fuzzy Logic for *Applying* the standards   187
    7.7.1 'Sensitive Personal Information' and 'Core Business Functions'   189
7.8 Periodic Data Protection Impact Assessments   192
7.9 2021: China's Data Security Law and Personal Information Protection Law to Become Fuzzy Logic Law?   194
    7.9.1 Consent and Storage of 'Sensitive Personal Information'   196
    7.9.2 Data Localisation Expanded in 2021 and Beyond?   197
7.10 Real-Name Registration, AI Development and Why Private Companies Control China's Datasets   201
7.11 Conclusion: Inherent Fuzzy Logic Leading to Data Privacy Contradictions That May Benefit AI Development   207

8 The Current State of AI Research Is Perfectly Suited to China's Fuzzy Logic System   209

8.1 Why Has AI Developed So Quickly in China? The Current State of AI   213
8.2 An AI 'Sputnik Moment' for China   221
8.3 AI Research Is Collaborative, Providing the Ideal Environment for China to Establish Pilot Rollouts   223
8.4 Why Has AI Developed So Quickly in China? Private Firm/Government Symbiosis and Public–Private Petri Dishes   227
8.5 Smart Cities as Petri Dishes for AI Development   232
8.6 Incorporation of AI into Smart City and Innovation Policies: The AI Plan   238
8.7 The AI Plan and Smart City Policies as Top-Down Signalling   243
8.8 The Role of Public–Private Partnerships in China's National AI Platforms   247

8.9 Public–Private Standard Setting and Interoperability 251
    8.9.1 Questions Remain Regarding the AI National Team 252
8.10 Local Government Responses to Central Top-Down Signalling 254
8.11 Will Network Sovereignty Threaten AI Development in China? 256
8.12 Conclusion: Public–Private Symbiosis 258

9 **Open-Source AI Platforms and the Cyber Security Law** 260
    9.1 What Are Open-Source AI Platforms? 262
    9.2 History of Open-Source Platforms in China 265
    9.3 Benefits of Open-Source Platforms for Innovation in AI 275
        9.3.1 Attracting Talent through Open Innovation 276
        9.3.2 Transparency: Researchers Demand Repeatability 278
        9.3.3 Cloud Computing Onboarding 282
        9.3.4 Maintenance and Crowdsourced Innovations 285
    9.4 Global Nature of Open-Source AI Platforms and Role of Global R&D Centres in AI Development in China 286
        9.4.1 Global R&D Centres 289
    9.5 Chinese Government Approach to Open-Source AI Platforms: Public–Private Platforms for Domestic Open Innovation 293
        9.5.1 The 'Open-Source' Aspects of the National AI Platforms 293
    9.6 Key Features of Open-Source AI Relevant to Applying the Cyber Security Law 301
    9.7 Case Studies of Open-Source AI Platforms in China 306
        9.7.1 Apollo: 'Android for Automated Vehicles' 313
        9.7.2 Apollo's Data-Sharing Policies 318
        9.7.3 GPS Mapping Laws: Network Sovereignty as Economic Protectionism? 322
    9.8 Conclusion: Linked Open-Source Ecosystems? 326

Conclusion: Effect of Data Localisation on Chinese AI Innovation 329
    10.1 Fuzzy Logic 330
        10.1.1 'Important Data' Remains Undefined in 2021 330
        10.1.2 Concluding Remark: Fuzzy Logic Is Intentional 332
    10.2 Future Uncertainties 335
        10.2.1 Potential Future Developments in AI Policymaking 336
        10.2.2 Future Impact of Fuzzy Logic Regulatory Practice on Tech Firms and Entrepreneurs 338

Bibliography   343
A   Journal Articles   343
B   Books   350
C   Reports   354
D   Other Secondary Sources: English Language   356
E   Other Secondary Sources: Chinese Language   388
F   Chinese Laws   395
G   Chinese Regulations, Notices, Guides and Standards   396
H   Chinese Policies, Plans and White Papers   399
I   Other Legislation   400

Index   402

ACKNOWLEDGEMENTS

Thank you to my wife, Jess, and my family for their support. A PhD (and then a book manuscript) is a long and winding road. There are cracks in everything. That's how the light gets in. I hope that, some day, my beautiful sons will understand why this research is important. They will grow up in a world where data is even more valuable than it is today.

I would like to thank my PhD supervisors, Professor David Lindsay and Professor Colin Hawes, for their support. Professor Lindsay provided some timely advice in the quicksand of the events this book documents in China. Professor Hawes supported me from ideation to execution and understood the signification of Chinese innovation before most. For that I am always indebted.

Thank you to Professor Ross Buckley at UNSW, for allowing me the time to complete this manuscript while a research fellow at UNSW.

Thank you also to Ms Lilla Wendoloski who brilliantly assisted in editing an earlier manuscript, and Joan Dale Lace for her final edit of this book. A special thank you to the team at Cambridge University Publishing, Gemma Smith, Laura Blake and especially Joe Ng.

ABBREVIATIONS

AI	artificial intelligence
BATs	Alibaba, Baidu and Tencent
CAC	Cyberspace Administration of China
CDR	China depositary receipt
CESI	China Electronics Standardisation Institute
CSAC	Cyber Security Association of China
CSIS	Center for Strategic and International Studies
Development Zone	Economic and Technological Development Zone
FBI	Federal Bureau of Investigation
GDPR	General Data Protection Regulation (EU)
GPU	graphics processing unit
ICT	information and communications technology
IETF	Internet Engineering Task Force
IoT	Internet of Things
IPO	initial public offering
ITIF	Information Technology and Innovation Foundation
MIIT	Ministry of Industry and Information Technology
MOST	Ministry of Science and Technology
NGO	non-government organisation
OECD	Organisation for Economic Co-operation and Development
R&D	research and development
SaaS	Software as a Service
SIIO	State Internet Information Office
SOE	state-owned enterprise
TC260	China National Information Security Standards Technical Committee
VIE	variable-interest entity
VPN	virtual private network
WFOE	wholly foreign-owned enterprise

Introduction

Headlines about Chinese innovation can induce a certain cognitive dissonance. On the one hand, until very recently true innovation in China was thought impossible due to censorship and control. The seemingly insurmountable conflict was clear: restriction versus innovation. How could that mesh of an economic, legal and political system, which we cannot label precisely with any existing reference points, be so successful economically and technologically?

Suddenly by 2017–2020, not a week went by without Western media reporting on the impressive and sometimes unnerving Chinese technology and artificial intelligence (AI) developments. Chinese facial and speech recognition companies are now world class, but we know little about their most impressive achievements because their commercial applications have mostly been piloted inside China's borders.

China's opaque cyber regime has also grabbed regular headlines. China's political system remains politically cloudy. Add world-class AI development to that setting and all our fears are confirmed. As a result, we have begun to question our own societies. Is technology no longer about consumer convenience and making our lives easier, but a tool for centralised control?

Cyber or Network Sovereignty became a key policy during Chinese President Xi Jinping's early tenure in 2014. This policy emphasises the authority of a nation-state to regulate cyberspace and assumes that every country should be able to control information and data flows within its jurisdiction as it does other goods and services.[1] China's Cyber Security

---

[1] Discussions of Network Sovereignty in official Chinese media focus on cross-border flows of information and international standard setting: see 'China Releases First Strategy on Cyberspace Cooperation' (*Xinhua*, 1 March 2017) <http://news.xinhuanet.com/english/2017-03/01/c_136094734.htm>.

Law (2017)[2] is the centrepiece of this policy. During 2017–2020, new technologies such as AI became more prominent in Chinese industry and innovation policymaking. Emerging technologies such as AI and the Internet of Things (IoT), rely heavily on using enormous datasets, some of which can be linked globally. These datasets have important implications for the development of new Chinese technologies, which may be impacted by China's Cyber Security Law and other legislation associated with Network Sovereignty. This is despite the fact that the Chinese government seeks to encourage these technologies under its innovation policies, such as Internet Plus.

There is a clear conflict between Chinese policies requiring localisation of data and economic imperatives demanding innovation by Chinese firms within the current globalised technology ecosystem.

The book is divided into an introduction, two main parts and a conclusion. Part I (Chapters 1–5) sets out the historical (2014–2017) and policy context, including introducing the analytical framework, the institutions established to regulate China's data laws, historical analysis of Chinese fuzzy logic regulatory practice, and contextual doctrinal analysis of key provisions in the Cyber Security Law. Part II (Chapters 6–9) documents the impact of Network Sovereignty, specifically data localisation provisions in the Cyber Security Law and associated regulations, on China's AI future. And how fuzzy logic regulatory practice helps to resolve contradictions between Network Sovereignty and innovation.

The first four chapters demonstrate that this internal tension is a longstanding feature of Chinese technology regulation and is evident in various laws and regulations introduced prior to the landmark Cyber Security Law. This book explores China's innovation policies (known as Internet Plus) and its regulatory restrictions on networks and data (under China's stated policy of Network Sovereignty) to identify the key areas of contradiction and tension (Chapter 3).

Competing interests within the Chinese government and the need to maintain flexibility in the face of rapid technological and social change are identified as potential explanations for this tension and the concept of 'fuzzy logic' legislating is adopted to conceptualise this regulatory approach.

China's Cyber Security Law is analysed in detail in Chapter 5, where a number of vague or undefined provisions are identified, especially

[2] «中华人民共和国网络安全法» [Cyber Security Law of the People's Republic of China] (People's Republic of China) National People's Congress, Order No 53, 7 November 2016 (Cyber Security Law).

focusing on the area of data localisation. Chapters 6 and 7 then demonstrate that this vagueness in the law has allowed for selective implementation by Chinese regulators when applying data localisation and privacy protection provisions of the Cyber Security Law.

Chapters 8–9 examine the highly globalised nature of entrepreneurial ecosystems, particularly in open-source[3] development of AI innovations, over the past four years. The contradiction between control and stimulating innovation in Chinese data policymaking in this specific area is shown to be complex and evolving, yet entirely understandable in terms of the historical practice of fuzzy logic regulation. This gives rise to the broader question of whether the technological and financial ecosystem is too globalised to allow for data localisation in any particular country.[4]

Do China's data localisation laws, which were introduced as part of China's Network Sovereignty policy, adversely affect – or are they likely to adversely affect – open innovation in Chinese AI firms, which is a key goal of China's Internet Plus policy? To what extent does the tension between data localisation laws and policies, on the one hand, and innovation in AI, on the other, reflect a broader tension in Chinese policymaking between protecting domestic firms against competition from foreign firms while promoting open innovation in AI? Does innovation in AI depend upon cross-border open-source platforms? Do the requirements for data localisation more broadly affect open innovation by Chinese AI firms, as AI is a technology born of open innovation? Further, to what extent is it possible for China to promote domestic innovation in AI without Chinese AI firms engaging in partnerships with foreign firms?

Will complex and onerous data localisation laws eventually stifle Chinese AI development, and make Chinese tech products unsuited to markets outside China? There is evidence of this global tech decoupling every day, with a growing ban on Chinese AI products by the US government and others since 2019.

However, this book argues that China's 'fuzzy logic' policy framework is a pendulum that swings from global technology cosmopolitanism to restrictive domestic technology drives, depending on the geopolitical

---

[3] Briefly, 'open-source' computer code refers to any computer program whose source code is made available for use or modification for users or other developers. A more detailed explanation of open source appears in Chapter 9.
[4] Some literature detailing these contradictions within Chinese technology policymaking is beginning to emerge. For a detailed description of how technologies like AI assist the Communist Party's rule, see, for example, Yu Hong, *Networking China: The Digital Transformation of the Chinese Economy* (University of Illinois Press, 2017).

climate. Two policies (expanded further in Chapter 3) form each side of that pendulum.

0.1 Innovation versus Restriction

0.1.1 Internet Plus

Internet Plus is a policy introduced by the central government's State Council[5] requiring that China connect the latest internet technologies to industry.[6] Launched in 2015, it sets out initiatives supporting Smart Cities, big data, IoT and AI. China's first internet white paper, published in 2010, had already described the internet's 'irreplaceable role in accelerating the development of the national economy'.[7] Building on this, the Government Work Report[8] that Premier Li Keqiang delivered to the National People's Congress in March 2015 announced a new term for information technology policy: 'Internet Plus'. This was followed up with a detailed action plan drafted by the State Council in July 2015.[9] The intention for this action plan is to 'integrate mobile Internet, big data, cloud computing and the Internet of Things' to modernise traditional industries.[10] It is the latest iteration of a broader strategy to build China into a 网络强国 (*wangluo qiangguo* – a strong internet country). There has been considerable political analysis of this phrase by commentators, with many arguing that China wants to become an internet hegemon.[11]

---

[5] The State Council is the chief administrative authority of the People's Republic of China, chaired by Premier Li Keqiang.
[6] 'China Headlines: China Unveils "Internet Plus" Action Plan to Fuel Growth' (State Council of the People's Republic of China, 4 July 2015) <http://english.gov.cn/policies/latest_releases/2015/07/04/content_281475140165588.htm>.
[7] «中国互联网状况白皮书» [China Internet Status White Paper] (People's Republic of China) State Council, June 2010 (Internet White Paper).
[8] «2015 年政府工作报告» [2015 Government Work Report] (People's Republic of China) State Council, 5 March 2015.
[9] «国务院关于积极推进'互联网+'行动的指导意见» [Guiding Opinions on Actively Promoting the 'Internet Plus' Action Plan] (People's Republic of China) National People's Congress, 4 July 2015 (Guiding Opinions).
[10] «2015 年政府工作报告» [2015 Government Work Report] (n 8).
[11] This kind of analysis interprets Network Sovereignty to mean that China must strengthen its public and private networks, exert greater control over content and harden its broadband networks to close the technical loopholes used by other countries to undermine China's 主权安全 [sovereignty security], 政治安全 [political security] and 社会稳定 [social stability]. See, eg, Nigel Inkster, *China's Cyber Power* (Routledge, 2016) 35; Shazeda Ahmed and Steven Weber, 'China's Long Game in Techno-Nationalism' (2018) 23(5) *First Monday* <https://firstmonday.org/ojs/index.php/fm/article/view/8085/7209>.

While this may be true, a major objective of Internet Plus (literally 'internet + industry') is also to utilise network technologies to reform the inefficiencies in the public sector, such as in China's state-owned enterprises and government institutions.

0.1.2 Network Sovereignty

As noted, during President Xi Jinping's early tenure in 2014, Network Sovereignty became a key policy, emphasising the authority of a nation-state to regulate cyberspace and to control information and data flows as it does for other goods and services. Key statements by President Xi include that it is important for nation-states to have 'respect for cyber sovereignty' and to 'maintain cyber security and promote orderly development'.[12]

While the Chinese term 网络主权 (*wangluo zhuquan*) is commonly translated as internet or cyber sovereignty,[13] this is an imprecise translation.[14] This is because Network Sovereignty is not just about controlling online content; it also seeks to keep the very valuable data flows produced by China's technology ecosystems in China. Since 2006, dozens of restrictive rules and laws affecting tech companies have been legislated in China. However, observers have noticed a marked increase in the rigidity of these rules since 2014, culminating in the Cyber Security Law of 2017 and its associated regulations since.[15] This book examines how Network Sovereignty affects Chinese entrepreneurs: do they benefit from reduced foreign competition, or are they adversely impacted due to their own reliance on global networks? Commentators claim that these frequently vague regulations shut foreign information and communications technology (ICT) service providers out of the market and provide an

---

[12] Xi Jinping, 'Remarks by H E Xi Jinping President of the People's Republic of China at the Opening Ceremony of the Second World Internet Conference' (Speech, Wuzhen, 16 December 2015) <https://www.fmprc.gov.cn/mfa_eng/wjdt_665385/zyjh_665391/t1327570.shtml>.
[13] The official Chinese government English phrasing is 'Cyber Sovereignty': ibid.
[14] From a neutral language perspective, it is better translated as 'Network Sovereignty'.
[15] See, eg, Samm Sacks, Paul Triolo and Graham Webster, 'Beyond the Worst-Case Assumptions on China's Cybersecurity Law' (*New America*, 13 October 2017) <https://www.newamerica.org/cybersecurity-initiative/blog/beyond-worst-case-assumptions-chinas-cybersecurity-law>.

unfair advantage to Chinese firms,[16] but is this interpretation of the new policies too simplistic?

China's laws and regulations relating to data and ICT networks now regularly contain the phrases 'secure and controllable' (安全可控), 'secure and reliable' (安全可靠) or 'indigenous and controllable' (自主可控), and data localisation is frequently linked to security.[17] Yet in China's system of fuzzy logic regulatory practice, these terms and how they will be applied in practice are still not precisely understood.[18]

Further, as of 2016–2017, no other country had implemented a cyber security law as detailed and extensive as China's. Therefore, it is crucial to understand how this law – a key product of Chinese Network Sovereignty concerns – has been and will be implemented, and to evaluate its impact on data control/transfer within China and across international borders.

It is now becoming clear that how China interprets and applies this law will have implications beyond China's borders. Foreign governments and the ICT sector never expected that China would lead global technical standards bodies and technology development races, but it is now in the vanguard of innovation and international jurisprudence. Just as China once modelled its corporate laws on those of the United States and its constitution on that of the former Soviet Union,[19] some mainly non-democratic countries may now look to China's Cyber Security Law for a

---

[16] There is now a necessary technology Cold War undercurrent to the debate around Network Sovereignty. See, eg, Lora Saalman, 'New Domains of Crossover and Concern in Cyberspace' (*Sipri.org*, 26 July 2017) <https://www.sipri.org/commentary/topical-backgrounder/2017/new-domains-crossover-and-concern-cyberspace>.

[17] These phrases began appearing from 2014, first in the banking industry. In late 2014, the China Banking Regulatory Commission and the National Development and Reform Commission, the Ministry of Industry and Information Technology (MIIT) and the Ministry of Science and Technology (MOST) jointly issued «关于应用安全可控信息技术加强银行业网络安全和信息化建设的指导意见» (称 317 号文) [Guiding Opinions on Applying Secure and Controllable Information Technology to Strengthen the Network Security and Informatisation of the Banking Industry (Circular 317)] (People's Republic of China) China Banking Regulatory Commission (CBRC), 26 December 2014 (Circular 317). Since that time these phrases, particularly 'secure and controllable', have become synonymous with Network Sovereignty.

[18] For example, a retreat from formal law in controlling online social movements means that tech companies must often patrol and self-regulate social media content: see Benjamin L Liebman, 'China's Law and Stability Paradox' in Jacques DeLisle and Avery Goldstein (eds), *China's Challenges* (University of Pennsylvania Press, 2015) 157.

[19] After 1979, when China began emphasising the rule of law rather than the previous rule of man system of the Cultural Revolution, it experimented with pilot projects and created a legal system that many other countries could recognise, not least because many of China's commercial laws were 'borrowed from abroad': see Samuli Seppänen, *Ideological*

template. How Chinese regulators interpret and apply this law will have both domestic and international ramifications.

0.2 Fuzzy Logic: The Chinese Approach to Innovation Regulation

Regulatory practice in China is best analysed through two concepts: one is fuzzy logic legislating;[20] the other is public–private petri dishes (see next section). In short, the Chinese government drafts vague laws that can be implemented and effectively adapted with a high degree of discretion (similar to fuzzy logic machines that learn and adapt through doing); and the government also implements pilot schemes, often at a local level, to test new technologies and related policies in a controlled environment (similar to a chemical petri dish experiment).

There is a long history of these systems and approaches to legal development in China. Case studies of innovation in China focusing on high-profile Chinese firms[21] have tended to ignore the impact of Network Sovereignty issues and, by extension, the complexity of regulatory practice and government involvement – both positive and negative – in the innovation ecosystem. By contrast, studies of China's cyber-control regime have generally neglected to note how that regime frequently stimulates Chinese firms' innovation and have overemphasised the perceived dystopian risks. Many have covered one side of the picture: either innovation[22] or restrictions.[23] Yet no scholars or commentators have extensively

---

Conflict and the Rule of Law in Contemporary China (Cambridge University Press, 2016) 72.

[20] Oren Perez and others have developed a concept of 'fuzzy law' since the 1990s. See Oren Perez, 'Fuzzy Law: A Theory of Quasi-Legal Systems' (2015) 28 *Canadian Journal of Law and Jurisprudence* 343. Perez refers to fuzzy law as 'quasi-legality' or soft law. I refer to the Chinese government as deliberately employing unclear laws: 'fuzzy logic'.

[21] See, eg, Edward Tse, *China's Disruptors: How Alibaba, Xiaomi, Tencent, and Other Companies Are Changing the Rules of Business* (Penguin, 2015).

[22] See, eg, G S Yip and B McKern, *China's Next Strategic Advantage: From Imitation to Innovation* (MIT Press, 2016); Tse, *China's Disruptors* (n 21); Yu Zhou, *The Inside Story of China's High-Tech Industry: Making 'Silicon Valley' in Beijing* (Rowman & Littlefield, 2008).

[23] See Guobin Yang, 'Social Dynamics in the Evolution of China's Internet Content Control Regime' in Monroe E Price, Stefaan Verhulst and Libby Morgan (eds), *Handbook of Media Law* (Routledge, 2012) 293. See also Rogier Creemers, 'Cyber China: Updating Propaganda, Public Opinion Work and Social Management for the 21st Century' (2017) 26(103) *Journal of Contemporary China* 85.

covered the symbiotic crossover between them. Again, the reality is that headlines about Chinese innovation policies induce a certain cognitive dissonance. On the one hand, commentators have claimed that true innovation is impossible due to China's censorship and control.[24] Conversely, a comprehensive survey of Chinese private entrepreneurs concluded: 'Party building in the private sector has been more successful at promoting the firms' interests than exerting Party leadership.'[25]

But both Network Sovereignty and innovation policies must be taken into account when evaluating the current and future evolution of the Chinese technology ecosystem. There is a symbiotic relationship between the government and private firms, which emerges from the way that the Chinese government's pilot petri dishes provide unprecedented opportunities for Chinese tech firms to build new technologies. It is therefore in the interests of both sides to minimise the negative impact of censorship and restriction on innovation by those firms. It is, moreover, no accident that a current Chinese innovation policy is promoted as 'Mass Entrepreneurship': setting a policy environment that encourages the masses (老百姓 – *laobaixing*) to start their own businesses.[26]

Further, describing China's cyber security restrictions without understanding their impact on Chinese innovation from the perspective of private Chinese companies would create an incomplete and misleading idea about these policies. This book aims to capture the innovation and the entrepreneurial story, not just the Chinese government's restrictive policies, and in the process to provide a more complete picture of how Chinese technology regulation works in practice.

This can be done by reconceptualising the unique Chinese approach to regulation of innovation as a dynamic interaction between fuzzy logic legislating and testing via public–private petri dishes. Importantly, this analysis also recognises the difficulty in separating targeted government assistance from private bottom-up experimentation at the firm level.

---

[24] In March 2014, the *Harvard Business Review* famously published an article entitled 'Why China Can't Innovate': see Regina M Abrami, William C Kirby and F Warren McFarlan, 'Why China Can't Innovate' (March 2014) *Harvard Business Review* <https://hbr.org/2014/03/why-china-cant-innovate>.

[25] Bruce J Dickson, *Wealth into Power: The Communist Party's Embrace of China's Private Sector* (Cambridge University Press, 2008).

[26] See Xu Wei, 'China to Further Promote Innovation and Entrepreneurship' (State Council of the People's Republic of China, 12 July 2017) <http://english.gov.cn/premier/news/2017/07/12/content_281475723086902.htm>.

0.2.1 Policy Petri Dishes in Chinese Innovation

Policy petri dishes have a long history in Chinese policymaking. China's economic and legal reforms began with pilot agricultural and economic zones in 1979.[27] The relationship between legal and economic development was seen as 'bidirectional – a co-evolutionary process'.[28] In other words, law played an important role in Chinese economic growth, as economic policy also heavily influenced the legal system.[29] Many new laws, regulations, rules and constitutional amendments were adopted to promote and assist China's economic boom, and it is well documented that pilot economic zones were used as legal and economic testing grounds.[30]

Likewise, although constitutionally and legally China is a unitary state, in fact local governments (provincial and below) have enjoyed a high degree of autonomy and freedom in policy enforcement, especially with regard to economic issues, such as the role of state-owned enterprises (SOEs) within their provinces. This has been documented as being the case since the beginning of the reform and opening policies in the late

---

[27] See Pitman B Potter, *The Chinese Legal System: Globalization and Local Legal Culture* (Routledge, 2001) 2.

[28] Donald Clarke, Peter Murrell and Susan Whiting, 'The Role of Law in China's Economic Development' in Thomas Rawski and Loren Brandt (eds), *China's Great Economic Transformation* (Cambridge University Press, 2008) 375, 391. The success of these zones has been appraised at length: see Zhicun Gao and Clem Tisdell, 'China's Reformed Science and Technology System: An Overview and Assessment' (2004) 22(3) *Prometheus: Critical Studies in Innovation* 311; Hooshang Amirahmadi and Grant Saff, 'Science Parks: A Critical Assessment' (1993) 8(2) *Journal of Planning Literature* 107; Loren Brandt and Thomas G Rawski, 'China's Great Economic Transformation' in Brandt and Rawski (eds), *China's Great Economic Transformation* (Cambridge University Press, 2008) 1; Cong Cao, 'Zhongguancun and China's High-Tech Parks in Transition: "Growing Pains" or "Premature Senility?"' (2004) 44(5) *Asian Survey* 647; Cong Cao, 'Zhongguancun: China's Silicon Valley' (2001) 28(3) *China Business Review* 38.

[29] By 2009, early commentary had begun suggesting the policies had worked: see Denis F Simon and Cong Cao, *China's Emerging Technological Edge* (Cambridge University Press, 2009).

[30] Stephen C Hsu, *Understanding China's Legal System* (New York University Press, 2003) 274-6. See also Susan M Walcott, *Chinese Science and Technology Industrial Parks* (Ashgate, 2003); Barry Naughton, *The Chinese Economy: Transitions and Growth* (MIT Press, 2007); Barry Naughton, *Growing out of the Plan: Chinese Economic Reform, 1978-1993* (Cambridge University Press, 1996); Cassandra C Wang, George C S Lin and Guicai Li, 'Industrial Clustering and Technological Innovation in China: New Evidence from the ICT Industry in Shenzhen' (2010) 42(8) *Environment and Planning* 1987.

1970s.[31] Laws and regulations that supported innovation but did not limit the power of the central government were viewed as a technocratic 'means to an end', and when they proved successful at local levels, they were expanded to the rest of China.[32]

Within this context of localised petri dish experimentation, China's government has also provided a flexible policy environment to attract foreign investment, especially in the field of technology, and to encourage the interaction between tech companies, universities and research institutions.[33]

By 2014, Tse, Wertime, Chow and others had begun to argue that after a long period of sustained technocratic success in building China into a manufacturing powerhouse, it was no longer simply a copycat or imitation economy, but had developed a true innovative spirit.[34] In this, they disputed the argument advanced by North and others that institutional development leads to a path-dependent pattern of development[35] or that top-down policymaking suppresses grass-roots innovations.[36] This is

---

[31] See Potter, *The Chinese Legal System* (n 27) 10. 'State capitalism' is a concept that has emerged in the literature. However, how private tech companies operate in this milieu requires further study: see Benjamin Liebman and Curtis Milhaupt (eds), *Regulating the Visible Hand? The Institutional Implications of Chinese State Capitalism* (Oxford University Press, 2015).

[32] See Seppänen, *Ideological Conflict and the Rule of Law* (n 19) 72.

[33] Javade Chaudhri, 'Chinese Industrial Policies: Indigenous Innovation, Intellectual Property Rights, and the Trade Issues of the Next Decade' (2011) 34(1) *Thomas Jefferson Law Review* 1, 15.

[34] Edward Tse, 'Don't Belittle China's Innovation Potential' (*Europe's World*, 14 February 2014) <https://www.friendsofeurope.org/insights/dont-belittle-chinas-innovation-potential>; David Wertime, 'It's Official: China Is Becoming a New Innovation Powerhouse: The World's Factory Is Turning into an R&D Machine – And Fast Catching Up with America' (*Foreign Policy*, 7 February 2014) <https://foreignpolicy.com/2014/02/07/its-official-china-is-becoming-a-new-innovation-powerhouse>; Stacey Chow, 'How Will China's Innovation Change the World?' (*World Economic Forum*, 16 July 2015) <https://www.weforum.org/agenda/2015/07/how-will-chinas-innovation-change-the-world>.

[35] Douglass C North, *Institutions, Institutional Change and Economic Performance* (Cambridge University Press, 1990) 17.

[36] Phelps suggests innovation is impossible without grass-roots activism, and governments cannot 'die-cast' entrepreneurs: see Edmund S Phelps, *Mass Flourishing: How Grassroots Innovation Created Jobs, Challenge, and Change* (Princeton University Press, 2013). Phelps revisits these issues in Edmund S Phelps, 'The Dynamism of Nations: Toward a Theory of Indigenous Innovation' (2017) (12)1 *Capitalism and Society* 1. He suggests that a mass flourishing is necessary and top-down innovation will not work. See also Eric Reinert, *How Rich Countries Got Rich and Why Poor Countries Stay Poor* (Constable & Robinson, 2007); Peter B Evans, *Embedded Autonomy: States and Industrial*

because in developing economies, catch-up activities, which involve the absorption and adoption of existing technologies or approaches for local applications (eg, adapting cars or mobile phones to meet the needs of consumers in emerging markets) can only last so long.[37] For ongoing development, innovation is then essential to satisfy increasingly demanding consumers and citizens, and that has been the case in China over the past five years. This transition has been a combined public–private endeavour, with policy petri dishes, especially various types of Economic and Technological Development Zones (Development Zones), playing a central role in stimulating and testing innovations. Numerous examples are provided in Chapters 7–9.

0.2.2 Fuzzy Logic

Fuzzy logic regulatory practice is a central concept that recurs throughout this book in relation to the implementation of Chinese technology and innovation policies. The reason for choosing to apply the (mathematical) concept of fuzzy logic to Chinese technology policymaking is that it encapsulates the indeterminate yet deliberately flexible nature of the regulatory system in China. The phrase itself originally emerges from computer science, specifically from computer coding where multiple truths may exist simultaneously.[38] In computer programming, practitioners in the field of AI (and intelligent systems in particular) seek to make computers 'smart'. Yet unlike computers, human beings can have a great capacity to deal with ill-defined concepts, such as natural language.[39] Fuzzy logic is an approach to tackling this problem in computer

---

Transformation (Princeton University Press, 1995); Wei, 'China to Further Promote Innovation and Entrepreneurship' (n 26); Peter Evans, 'Development as Institutional Change: The Pitfalls of Monocropping and the Potentials of Deliberation' (2004) 38(4) *Studies in Comparative International Development* 30.

[37] See Chris Freeman and Luc Soete, *The Economics of Industrial Innovation* (MIT Press, 3rd ed, 1997).

[38] Fuzzy logic was first advanced by Dr Lofty Zadeh of the University of California at Berkeley in the 1960s. Dr Zadeh was working on the problem of computer understanding of natural language. Natural language is not easily translated into the absolute terms of 0 and 1.

[39] A language that has developed naturally in use (as contrasted with an artificial language or computer code).

science.⁴⁰ Fuzzy logic is contrary to traditional propositional logic or 'crisp' logic, in which each fact or proposition must be either true or false.

For example, in natural language processing, the result of a comparison between two things may be not 'tall' or 'short' but measured in degrees of tallness. There is a clear ambiguity between what is meant by 'tall' or 'short' and what categories fall in between.⁴¹ In brief, 'fuzzy logic' is a concept evolving from computer science that attempts to deal with 'degrees of truth' rather than a binary 'true or false' logic. This is mostly alien to Western conceptions of legal jurisprudence.⁴²

What does this book mean by fuzzy logic legislating, or fuzzy logic regulatory practice, in China? It involves laws that are intentionally drafted in an unclear manner but can conveniently be moulded through regulations, standards or official discretion to adapt to the contradictions of China's political system and economic needs (including in consultation with the private sector) in a fluid fashion depending on the prevailing climate. Key terms of fundamental laws, such as China's Cyber Security Law (2017) are left vague or undefined. Laws may even contain what appear to be internal contradictions. These contradictions and undefined terms can be resolved (or not resolved) by regulatory developments occurring months or often years later.⁴³ China's Cyber Security Law is still being amended by laws and regulations during 2020–2021. Competing policy agendas and the need to maintain flexibility in the face of rapid technological and social change are identified as the impetus for this approach. Further, while fuzzy logic legislating or regulatory practice refers to the process of intentionally drafting vague laws, this book also refers to 'fuzzy logic' laws, which are the result of this

---

⁴⁰ See Radim Belohlavek, Rudolf Kruse and Christain Moewes, 'Fuzzy Logic in Computer Science' in Edward K Blum and Alfred V Aho (eds), *Computer Science* (Springer, 2011) 385.

⁴¹ For interviews with various computer science professors explaining the foundations for the concept, see 'What Is "Fuzzy Logic"? Are There Computers That Are Inherently Fuzzy and Do Not Apply the Usual Binary Logic?' (*Scientific American*, 21 October 1999) <https://www.scientificamerican.com/article/what-is-fuzzy-logic-are-t>.

⁴² See Oren Perez, 'Law in the Air: A Prologue to the World of Legal Paradoxes' in Oren Perez and Gunther Teubner (eds), *Paradoxes and Inconsistencies in the Law* (Hart Publishing, 2005) 3.

⁴³ For example, the lead drafters of China's subordinate privacy regulations noted that the original Cyber Security Law left them 'dancing with shackles on': 洪延青 [Hong Yanqing], «对'个人信息安全规范'五大重点关切的回应和解释» [Responses and Explanations to the Five Major Concerns of the 'Personal Information Security Specification'] (网安寻路人 – *Wanganxunluren*, 5 February 2018) <https://mp.weixin.qq.com/s/rSW-Ayu6zNXw87itYHcPYA>. See also Chapter 7.

process. This is intended to refer to laws or regulations that are intentionally vague.

Fuzzy logic in computer science enables computers to deal with imprecise terms: it is a systemic approach to making computers 'think' in a more human fashion by appreciating nuance. The systemic ambiguity needed to create 'smart' computing is precisely the sort of ambiguity that has been used by regulators and legislators to allow for the balance between innovation and government control in China's entrepreneurial ecosystem. Thus 'fuzzy logic' is a particularly apt term to describe how innovation is promoted within China's controlled political environment.

While fuzzy logic is a useful metaphor to analyse how the Chinese regulatory system works, this book does not claim that every aspect of fuzzy logic is translatable into Chinese regulatory practice. Thus, in explaining the differences between this use of fuzzy logic to explain Chinese regulatory practice and the meaning of fuzzy logic in computer science, it can be noted that fuzzy logic is only one technique in computer science. Fuzzy logic cannot completely replace conventional logic as a methodology in computer science.[44] Fuzzy logic can supplement conventional logic in circumstances where conventional computer coding approaches fail to solve a problem effectively.[45] Conversely, in China's case, this book argues that the fuzzy logic system is designed to engender systemic vagueness in key legal documents. Thus, while fuzzy logic in computer science is a tool to overcome problems in computer coding that arise from using conventional logic, fuzzy logic in Chinese regulatory practice is a tool to create planned uncertainty. Nevertheless, both employ a form of fuzzy logic as a technique for representing and then manipulating uncertain information.

Fuzzy logic legislating is also not fuzzy law. According to the widely cited work of Oren Perez, 'fuzzy law' is contrary to black-letter law or comprehensive and specific regulation. It is a term used to describe non-legal texts (eg, quasi-legal schemes) and broad legal principles with room for judicial discretion that blur the boundaries of law. The literature on fuzzy law also focuses on vagueness in quasi-legal environments,[46] but unlike the concept of fuzzy logic legislating, it does not help to explain Chinese motivations for systemically vague legal drafting – especially the

---

[44] See Belohlavek, Kruse and Moewes, 'Fuzzy Logic in Computer Science' (n 40).
[45] Ibid.
[46] See Perez, 'Fuzzy Law: A Theory of Quasi-Legal Systems' (n 20).

need to keep open the potential for competing interpretations to be resolved at a later stage.

Chinese regulatory practice is vague by design, driven by the opposing ideological motivations of driving innovation and allowing the Party to maintain control.[47] Fuzzy logic regulatory practice therefore differs from fuzzy law in that, within the Chinese legal and regulatory system, what appear to be binary conceptions of X and Y purposely exist simultaneously. 'Fuzzy law' fails to comprehensively capture what is happening in the Chinese regulatory space.

This book provides several examples of how fuzzy logic influences regulatory practice. Thus, it argues that this non-binary conception of fuzzy logic – for example, a 'variable interest entity' company being simultaneously both legal and illegal in China in Chapter 2 – is a uniquely appropriate encapsulation of Chinese regulatory practice.

Fuzzy logic regulation is deliberately unclear but can conveniently be moulded to suit the contradictions of China's political system and economic needs at any moment in time. Fuzzy logic is a deliberate Chinese strategy to build ambiguity into lawmaking in complex and dynamic areas, often in technology and investment laws.[48] Principally this strategy enables conflicting policies, such as Internet Plus and Network Sovereignty, to be promoted simultaneously, and reconciled through selective implementation. The desired outcomes can be accidental, but the practice of drafting vague laws and delaying regulatory clarity is certainly intentional, and has a long history in China.

There is also a direct relationship between fuzzy logic and public–private petri dishes in the area of technology regulation. Sometimes, implementation issues are so complex that the regulator calls for tests of the technology in pilot programs first, before making final decisions about national implementing regulations. For example, testing facial

---

[47] Part of the vagueness in Chinese lawmaking was historically also because it evolved through a 'bilateral process' depending partly on the way Chinese lawmakers understood Western legal systems: Tianshu Zhou and Mathias Siems, 'Contentious Modes of Understanding Chinese Commercial Law' (2015) 6 *George Mason Journal of International Commercial Law* 177. However, in drafting laws such as the Cyber Security Law, China is among the vanguard. Thus, China could not rely on references to existing Western legal systems.

[48] This vagueness has been identified in many aspects of China's legal system. Hawes et al noted this in Chinese courts dealing with shareholder remedies in the absence of a clear statutory guide to aid deliberations: Colin Hawes, Alex K L Lau and Angus Young, 'The Chinese "Oppression" Remedy: Creative Interpretations of Company Law by Chinese Courts' (2015) 63(2) *American Journal of Comparative Law* 17.

INTRODUCTION   15

recognition as a payment method on public buses was approved in one small Chinese city of 1.5 million people in October 2016 before an extensive pilot rollout of facial recognition technologies across China.[49] The Chinese government at various levels deploys many such pilot programs, frequently in collaboration with private tech firms, in order to test the viability and social impact of innovations quickly, without requiring excessive resources, and deferring decisions about national implementation to a later date.

The system explained in this book implies a deliberate and considered approach to innovation by the Chinese government. It does not seek to discount a prevailing narrative that the lack of regulatory certainty has enabled Chinese tech companies to engage in business model innovations and pilots that did not/could not happen in the West, such as testing facial recognition widely, years before a clear Chinese privacy regime had emerged.

Thus, some of the new technologies (eg, surveillance and facial recognition) have led many commentators[50] to question whether China is creating an Orwellian dystopia (and there is certainly justification for these fears in places like Xinjiang that have experienced repression in recent years). Yet the book argues that most policy petri dishes are designed to assist in solving large-scale social problems (eg, pollution, transport, unemployment and supporting an ageing population).[51] The use of fuzzy logic regulation through vague laws and provisional implementation allows these various local pilots to be implemented and, if unforeseen implementation issues emerge, for the laws to be reinterpreted to resolve those issues through further regulation, or further testing in modified pilot programs. This book is not extolling but explaining the Chinese system of innovation regulation and what it means for the world.

0.3 Significance of Data Localisation

China's huge internet population, its protected and closed online ecosystem and its near-cashless society mean the country has built up more big

---

[49] Daisy Carrington, 'Yinchuan: The Smart City Where Your Face Is Your Credit Card' (CNN, 11 October 2016) <http://edition.cnn.com/2016/10/10/asia/yinchuan-smart-city-future/index.html>.
[50] See, eg, Yuan Yang, 'China's Tech Groups Bow to Beijing Censorship Demands' (*Financial Times*, 29 June 2017) <https://www.ft.com/content/43def3ec-5c8f-11e7-9bc8-8055f264aa8b?mhq5j=e1>.
[51] See Chapter 8, Section 8.3.

data than any other nation. That data – when fed to machines for Machine Learning[52] – means China is now a competitor of the United States in developing AI technologies and applications. However, Chinese laws that enforce localisation of data based on Network Sovereignty may jeopardise this rapid development, as Chinese AI firms are still heavily dependent on research and data obtained from overseas.[53]

Data is essential for developing AI technologies, yet concern about misuse of data is also a key motivator of Network Sovereignty policies. Since the Snowden revelations and other massive leaks of sensitive political and financial data, countries as disparate as Denmark, Australia, South Korea and Russia have developed data localisation over some types of data for a variety of reasons (eg, protecting private medical data in Australia).[54] Yet China is the highest profile example of increased efforts to promote data localisation.

That is why data is a central focus of this book: how China legislates to protect it, how and where it is stored, and whether those laws stifle or stimulate innovation.[55] Moreover, China's protected cyber and industrial

---

[52] Machine Learning 'refers to the development of digital systems that improve their performance on a given task over time through experience'. Machine Learning is variously characterised as either a sub-field of AI or a separate field of AI. See Future of Humanity Institute et al, 'The Malicious Use of Artificial Intelligence Forecasting, Prevention, and Mitigation' (Research Report, February 2018) <https://arxiv.org/pdf/1802.07228.pdf>.

Deep Learning is a sub-field of Machine Learning that involves algorithms inspired by the structure of the brain called artificial neural networks that make complex connections between datasets. There are various types of neural networks. The specifics of neural networks may involve using training and test datasets that create various layers of data (input, hidden and output layers), as well as back-propagation (the practice of fine-tuning the weights of a neural network based on error rates). See Ian Goodfellow, Yoshua Bengio and Aaron Courville, *Deep Learning* (MIT Press, 2016). Deep Learning has advanced greatly, along with increased computing power, it is *the* major recent breakthrough in AI research. Key applications include accurate voice and facial recognition, which can be used for better medical diagnostics. AI is first defined in great depth in Chapter 8. This is because it was not until 2016–2017 that the Chinese government decided to consider top-down policymaking for AI, after the Cyber Security Law was drafted. Thus, this book first sets out the background to that law, and the complex arguments for and against data localisation at the time of the law's release, before introducing AI.

[53] One of the biggest threats for China from Network Sovereignty is the inherent risk of its IT infrastructure still being 'heavily dependent on foreign suppliers': Scott Livingston and Graham Greenleaf, 'Data Localisation in China and Other APEC Jurisdictions' (2016) 143 *Privacy Laws & Business International Report* 22.

[54] See, eg, ibid 22–6.

[55] The phrase 'data is the new oil' is now ubiquitous globally. *Forbes Magazine* first used the phrase in a piece titled 'Is Data the New Oil?' in 2012. See also, for an early exploration of

environment is not just relevant domestically; it is also globally relevant, because our current entrepreneurial ecosystems are global and localising data may potentially disrupt innovation and commerce beyond China's borders.[56]

So, when in 2016 China published its draft Cyber Security Law that seemed to lock data on servers in China, technology industry observers became anxious.[57] This new law provides the basic architecture for data localisation, or containing data within China's borders. In short, it states that Chinese data must be stored on Chinese servers, with some exceptions and negotiated approval of data exits.[58] In practical terms, this data localisation provision appears to mean that foreign companies must partner with local Chinese companies for cloud services, keep Chinese data in China and allow law enforcement access to customer data upon request.

However, this book shows that when the Cyber Security Law came into effect on 1 June 2017, the categories of data that needed to be 'localised' were still not finalised, and neither the exceptions nor the process for obtaining approval for data exits for cross-border data flows were clearly defined. As Chapters 7–9 explain, over the following two years, as Chinese regulators realised the importance of AI development for the future prosperity and effective governance of China – and equally importantly, learned of the continuing dependency of Chinese AI firms on open exchange of data across borders – they deferred implementation of data localisation and redefined key terms in the Cyber Security Law to soften their impact on data transfers by tech firms. Importantly, the Cyber Security Law was drafted before AI became a buzzword in China (see Chapter 8).

As a result, what originally appeared to be a blanket blocking of cross-border data transfers, possibly affecting Chinese firms' ability to innovate in the field of AI and become globally competitive, and hampering

---

the power of big data, Viktor Mayer-Schönberger and Kenneth Cukier, *Big Data: A Revolution That Will Transform How We Live, Work, and Think* (John Murray, 2013).

[56] See, eg, Matthias Bauer, *Unleashing Internal Data Flows in the EU: An Economic Assessment of Data Localisation Measures in the EU Member States* (ECIPE Policy Brief No 3/2016).

[57] See, eg, Josh Horwitz, 'China's Bewildering New Cybersecurity Law Is Keeping Foreign Tech Firms out of the Country' (*Quartz*, 7 November 2016) <http://qz.com/829248/chinas-new-cybersecurity-law-is-so-vague-that-its-keeping-foreign-tech-firms-out-of-the-country>.

[58] Cyber Security Law (n 2) art 37. See Chapter 5.

foreign firms' expansion in China, became, through a process of fuzzy logic regulatory practice, something more like the partial localisation policies of the European Union, which are designed to protect citizens' privacy (and personal data from unwanted intrusions and cyberattacks) without unduly impeding cross-border data flows.

0.4 Research Methodology

As the implementation of data localisation and the development of China's AI sector since 2017 are in a state of both flux and rapid development, studies on the subject are only beginning to emerge on Chinese innovation[59] and cyber security. As a result, grey literature, meaning 'literature that is not formally published in sources such as books or journal articles',[60] is used extensively as an essential source for this book.[61]

In addition to qualitative and doctrinal analysis, the author conducted informal interviews during May–June 2018 as a visiting researcher at Renmin University in Beijing.[62] The interviewees were several Chinese professors in relevant fields (legal and Machine Learning experts), selected company representatives and cyber security managers, including, for example, the head of cyber security at one of China's most famous tech firms. Additional interviews took place in March–April 2019, as a visiting fellow at Peking University. The author met with other tech company representatives, Chinese Communist Party officials involved in cyber regulation, and representatives of non-government organisations (NGOs), including senior staff at the World Economic Forum's Centre for the Fourth Industrial Revolution in Beijing.

---

[59] Books such as *China as an Innovation Nation*, edited by Yu Zhou, William Lazonick and Yifei Sun (Oxford University Press, 2016), have begun to emerge; however, they tend to focus on technological developments (eg, semiconductors).

[60] See Carol Lefebvre, Eric Manheimer and Julie Glanville, 'Searching for Studies' in Julian Higgins and Sally Green (eds), *Cochrane Handbook for Systematic Reviews of Interventions* (Wiley-Blackwell, 2008) 106.

[61] Grey literature is essential for certain kinds of research: Douglas Walton, Chris Reed and Fabrizio Macagno, *Argumentation Schemes* (Cambridge University Press, 2008).

[62] The author lived in China for more than 6 years over a 17-year period.

PART I

Historical and Doctrinal Background

1

Innovating in China's Entrepreneurial Ecosystem

> It is often assumed that an economy of private enterprise has an automatic bias towards innovation, but this is not so. It has a bias only towards profit.
> —Eric J Hobsbawm, British historian, 1969[63]

China's approach to innovation is unique. To analyse the main features of economic innovation and entrepreneurship in contemporary China, it is first necessary to dispel some common misconceptions.

This chapter explains: (1) technological innovation and how it has been conventionally understood; (2) China's distinctive approach to technological innovation; (3) in particular, the complex role of the government, and regulation, in innovation in China; and (4) how China's public-private approach may actually be better than alternatives at promoting innovation in AI technologies, and other rapidly developing technologies.

1.1 'China Cannot Innovate'

Before examining the tensions in China's innovation policymaking, it is necessary to introduce the context of innovation in China's contemporary economy. The Cambridge Dictionary defines innovation as 'a new idea or method, or the use of new ideas and methods', and more modern definitions include 'the latest innovations in computer technology'.[64] Academic definitions of innovation refer to breakthrough and transformative innovation as opposed to incremental change.[65] Innovation

---

[63] Eric J Hobsbawm, *Industry and Empire from 1750 to the Present Day* (Penguin, 1969) 40.
[64] *Cambridge Dictionary* (online at 21 December 2018) 'innovation' <https://dictionary.cambridge.org/dictionary/english/innovation>.
[65] There is no agreed measure for innovation. One challenge is simply identifying whether something is an innovation. Does that innovation have to be truly novel, or can it be an incremental change? Another challenge is obtaining data that enable standardised comparisons across economies. As a result, innovation is often measured by metrics such as the number of patents or PhDs an economy produces every year rather than actual

processes start with an idea or a discovery, then move to invention or creation, often followed by improvements in order to go to market. An innovative company is one that derives a significant portion of sales and profits from newly created products or services introduced recently.[66] In China's AI drive, these factors are clearly apparent, as demonstrated below.

Until recently, it was commonly suggested that China could not possibly be a world-class innovator due to the essentially imitative nature of its economic activity. Joseph Schumpeter's seminal 1911 work posited that the fundamental function of an entrepreneur is innovation and that entrepreneurial innovation is the engine of economic growth. Schumpeter famously identified five types of innovation: new products, new methods of production, the exploitation of new markets, new sources of supply and new methods of organising business.[67] The typical Schumpeterian entrepreneur is a true adventurer who challenges conformism and resistance to change through 'creative destruction'. Today we might refer to 'creative destruction' as 'disruptive' companies, start-ups that disrupt an industry. While internet-industry entrepreneurship began to thrive in China, commentators argued that Chinese entrepreneurship lacked Schumpeterian 'creative destruction' or unique innovations. For example, in November 2011, McKinsey Consulting Group in China, stated:

> [S]purring innovation is one of the top priorities in the Chinese government's latest five-year plan. This policy initiative is creating local champions that are taking market share from multinational corporations operating in China. They're also becoming powerful competitors on the international stage. But progress varies across industries, and as a result, we still see few breakthrough ideas emerging from China.[68]

---

impact. See, eg, Ashish Arora, Marco Ceccagnoli and Wesley M Cohen, 'R&D and the Patent Premium' (2008) 26(5) *International Journal of Industrial Organization* 1153.

[66] Product–market fit is a key indicator of innovation referred to regularly in the Chinese literature: see, eg, 何根源 [He Genyuan] and 刘昱影 [Liu Yuying], «微创新与突破性创新分类梳理» [Micro-Innovation and Breakthrough Innovation Classifications] 合作经济与科技 (2018) 12 *Cooperative Economy and Technology* 57.

[67] Joseph A Schumpeter, *The Theory of Economic Development: An Inquiry into Profits, Capital, Credit, Interest, and the Business Cycle*, trans Redvers Opie (Transaction Books, 1983) [trans of *Theorie der wirtschaftlichen Entwicklung* (1911)].

[68] This was stated in the introduction to the podcast 'Can China Innovate?' *McKinsey on China* (McKinsey & Co, 28 November 2011) <https://podcasts.apple.com/us/podcast/can-china-innovate/id409735817?i=1000226536419>. The first aspirational principle in

More recently, in March 2014, the *Harvard Business Review* published an article entitled 'Why China Can't Innovate'.[69] The authors argued that China could not innovate in its current political climate. At this time, Chinese innovation was synonymous with (山寨) *shanzhai* – the so-called copycat phenomenon that made Shenzhen the world's hardware but also counterfeit consumer goods powerhouse.

Yet the *shanzhai* movement would evolve to become an impressive creative force, which engineered cheaper but highly practical products to satisfy the needs of China's aspirational lower socio-economic classes.[70] Essentially the former copycats were innovating to solve China-specific market problems, a theme that re-emerges throughout this research. For example, the classic example of a factory worker who would build mobile phones with two SIM cards, as a migrant worker might need two SIM cards if they worked between two provinces. Call rates would then be cheaper. Today, by default, phones in certain regions often come with two SIM card slots.

The *shanzhai* movement is an important story of Chinese innovation that emanates from factory workers building consumer electronics by experimenting with various components and creating new products. It is a cultural phenomenon that, perhaps ill-understood in the West, has been a catalyst for Chinese collaborations on experimental AI research (see Chapter 9). Shenzhen is known as the Silicon Valley of Hardware, an electronics components candy store, where hardware hackers from across the globe can build new products, quickly and cheaply, surrounded by electronics component markets.

Sceptical observations about Chinese innovation were premature, and true innovation emerged as China's economic development progressed. In fact, if we include creative processes as well as technological advances within the definition of innovation, China's history of innovation goes back much further, to the earliest years of the reform period in 1979.

At the same time, we see a continuing and highly confusing tension between the creative energy of innovative entrepreneurialism and the potentially restrictive arm of bureaucratic control. Thus, a central

---

China's 13th Five-Year Plan, released in March 2016, is 'innovation', primarily as a driver of economic development.

[69] Abrami, Kirby and McFarlan, 'Why China Can't Innovate' (n 24).
[70] See, eg, Sheng Zhu and Yongjiang Shi, 'Shanzhai Manufacturing – An Alternative Innovation Phenomenon in China' (2010) 1(1) *Journal of Science and Technology Policy in China* 29.

question of this study is how innovation can occur in China despite the tight controls exerted by the political system. Chapter 3 explores the current and evolving conflict between innovation and political restriction, as we document China's recent 'top-down' innovation policies. Yet understanding the likely impact of today's policies requires knowledge of how China has developed an environment for policy experimentation over several decades, the main topic of this chapter. It also requires an understanding of how global technology ecosystems are entangled, as discussed in Chapters 7–9.

1.2 The Origin of China's Policy Petri Dishes

Chinese people have always had an entrepreneurial spirit that, prior to 1979, was suppressed by bureaucratic control over market forces.[71] For only a short time during the Communist period in the 1950s, 1960s and 1970s the word 个体户 (*getihu* – peddler or small business owner) fell out of vogue in the Chinese lexicon.[72] Suppression of market forces would only last for 30 years (1949–1979).

Often ignored today is that China's 'petri dishes' of entrepreneurial experimentation developed from the bottom up as long ago as 1978, in Xiaogang, a small, impoverished village in Anhui Province, on Shanghai's eastern border.[73] In December 1978, villagers met to devise an illegal plan to farm in contravention of central planning rules. Under the plan, each farmer would keep the excess produce after contributing a fixed quota to the state. The villagers also agreed that if one of them was caught and sentenced to death, then the other villagers would raise the farmer's children until they were 18 years old.[74] After the secret contract was

---

[71] Joseph Needham (ed), *Science and Civilisation in China* (Cambridge University Press, 1954–2016) vols 1–7. This is a seminal work that documents China's scientific history and describes numerous Chinese inventions.
[72] Scholars have documented this evolution: see, eg, Carolyn Hsu, 'Cadres, Getihu, and Good Businesspeople: Making Sense of Entrepreneurs in Early Post-Socialist China' (2006) 35(1) *Urban Anthropology and Studies of Cultural Systems and World Economic Development* 1. Hsu's study interestingly finds: 'Most [entrepreneurs] were considered to be selfish, avaricious peddlers or *getihu*. Yet those who were educated or ran "hightech" businesses were never vilified as *getihu* but instead seen as highly respected "good businesspeople". In other words, there was always a pervading appreciation for innovation in China.'
[73] See, eg, 陈禹 [Chen Yu] «小岗村 '生死契约' 幕后» [The Story Behind the 'Life and Death Contract' in Xiaogang Village] 档案春秋 (2018) 1 *Memories and Archives* 10.
[74] Ibid.

signed, Xiaogang village produced a harvest that was larger than the previous five years combined.[75] This attracted significant attention locally and the central Chinese government became aware of the villagers' economic experiment. Deng Xiaoping's new leadership was looking for ways to reform China's economy after the disastrous Cultural Revolution[76] and Xiaogang's innovation was presented as a model for other villages across the country.

The villagers' secret signing of the harvesting agreement in Xiaogang is regarded as the beginning of the period of rapid economic growth and industrialisation that mainland China has experienced since.[77] It also reflects an important maxim in modern China: 上有政策，下有对策 (above there are rules, below there are [*literally*] countermeasures). We will observe this statement's relevance to innovation in China throughout this study.

This story of Xiaogang does not merely highlight the precise origins of China's petri dishes for policy experimentation, but also reveals that Chinese citizens are not bystanders in their own commercial destinies. Stoicism through historical periods of hardship such as the Cultural Revolution is a Chinese characteristic, perhaps ill-understood outside China. This resilience, however, seems to lend itself to the rigorous demands of entrepreneurship. Today, Chinese start-ups are well-known for their '996' work ethic: 9 am to 9 pm six days a week, or even longer. Some commentators, such as Sequoia Capital venture partner Michael Moritz, have publicly lauded this work ethic.[78] As one Alibaba employee

---

[75] Per capita income in the village increased from 22 yuan to 400 yuan, with grain output increasing to 90,000 kg in 1979: Ke Wang, 'Xiaogang Village, Birthplace of Rural Reform, Moves On' (*China.org.cn*, undated) <http://www.china.org.cn/china/features/content_16955209.htm>.

[76] The Cultural Revolution was a political movement in China from 1966 to 1976, launched by then chairman of the Communist Party of China, Mao Zedong. The Cultural Revolution's stated goal was to preserve Chinese Communism by purging the remnants of capitalism and traditional Chinese culture, and to reimpose Mao Zedong Thought as the dominant ideology within the Party, but it led to social and political chaos.

[77] Ibid.

[78] Michael Moritz, 'Silicon Valley Would Be Wise to Follow China's Lead' (*Financial Times*, 18 January 2018) <https://www.ft.com/content/42daca9e-facc-11e7-9bfc-052cbba03425>. Others have questioned the idea that Silicon Valley should follow Chinese practices. Formerly China-based hardware entrepreneur Ben Joffe wrote that China's ecosystem is on its own path with specific circumstances as a developing country: Benjamin Joffe, 'What Sequoia's Mike Moritz Doesn't Understand about Startups in China' (*Venturebeat*, 11 February 2018) <https://venturebeat.com/2018/02/11/what-sequoias-mike-moritz-doesnt-understand-about-startups-in-china>.

explained to me: 'everyone has A-type personalities in the office, it's very quiet, head down, work'.[79]

Another equally important feature of the Xiaogang story is the way that ordinary citizens found ways to work around unreasonably restrictive centralised bureaucratic policies. Over the past 20 years, the emergence of large-scale global companies such as Huawei, Haier, Alibaba, Baidu, Tencent and Xiaomi has shown that China can build growth companies that are competitive and sustainable in the global marketplace.[80] Many of these firms developed as private businesses within an apparently unsympathetic bureaucratic environment favouring state-controlled competitors. In other words, they were forced to innovate with their whole business model, not just their products, in order to survive and prosper. As a result, while Chinese entrepreneurs have certainly benefited from China's enormous protected online marketplace, they have also learned to create products, business models and features that no longer resemble – and can even surpass – anything made in Silicon Valley.[81]

1.3 China's Unique Ecosystem: Adept at Catching Up

Each 'national innovation system' is unique.[82] China's has been particularly adept at 'catching up' to foreign technological leaders. Since China's former leader Deng Xiaoping implemented market-oriented economic reforms in 1979–1980, the Chinese government has steadily introduced an innovation ecosystem across the country, consisting of hundreds of

---

[79] Interview with Alibaba employee (Alibaba headquarters, Hangzhou, 24 March 2017).
[80] Several books have been published about these companies: see, eg, Wu Xiaobo, *The Story of Tencent: Evolution of Chinese Internet Companies from 1998 to 2016* (Zhejiang University Press and China CITIC Press, 2017); Duncan Clark, *Alibaba: The House That Jack Built* (HarperCollins, 2016). One of the first books in English was Edward Tse's *China's Disruptors* (n 21).
[81] China-based venture capitalist Dr Kai-Fu Lee explains: 'the West has to know that China is now ahead in many technologies and actually many business models, products and features. For example, if you compare WeChat with Facebook Messenger or WhatsApp, if you compare Weibo with Twitter, if you compare Alipay with Apple Pay, China is leaps and bounds ahead of the US': see Greg Williams, 'Why China Will Win the Global Race for Complete AI Dominance' (*Wired*, 16 April 2018) <https://www.wired.co.uk/article/why-china-will-win-the-global-battle-for-ai-dominance>.
[82] 'National innovation system' was first defined by Christopher Freeman in *Technology Policy and Economic Performance* (Pinter, 1987).

science and technology parks,[83] universities, government research institutions and government-backed venture capital firms that provide support for new enterprises.[84] The Chinese government has a strong track record of setting broad policies and incentives, and then encouraging citizens and local government officials, right down to the village level, to carry out those policies. China's Development Zones are a well-known success story in this history.[85] In short, China has achieved incredible growth since 1979, by orchestrating top-down policymaking. Beginning in 1980, the Chinese government has used its wealth and political will to stimulate innovation 'from the top' all over China. Development Zones were the first state-sanctioned 'petri dishes' of Chinese innovation.

China's innovation ecosystem today possesses elements that many countries lack. These elements include significant capital, the world's largest population for product scaling, governmental will and a large, expanding military. The innovation ecosystem, including the regulatory environment, continues to evolve with an impressive speed not seen in many developed Western nations. Australia, for example, might have an inquiry and three parliamentary commissions to consider the issue of self-driving cars, whereas in China such vehicles are already at a world-leading stage of development. The ongoing success of top-down innovation in China, especially when combined with local-level experimentation, challenges common assumptions about the supposed negative relationship between regulatory control and mass innovation.

At the same time, China's heavy investment in large-scale R&D and the government's willingness to provide incentives for innovation have allowed the country not just to catch up with advanced economies in many sectors but even to outdo them.[86] In most developing economies, catch-up activities conventionally involve the absorption and adoption of

---

[83] The number of Development Zones in China increased to 156, with operating revenue hitting ¥27.9 trillion (US$4 trillion) in 2016. The Zones accounted for 11.7% of China's GDP in 2016 and 18% of China's total exports, according to Zhang Zhihong, director of Torch High Technology Industry Development Center, MOST: 'More High-Tech Zones in China' (*Xinhua*, 27 March 2017) <http://www.chinadaily.com.cn/china/2017-03/27/content_28692439.htm>.
[84] The Chinese government and business invested some US$190 billion in R&D in 2013, which is around 40% of the annual R&D investment in the United States: Yip and McKern, *China's Next Strategic Advantage* (n 22).
[85] See Wei Liu et al, 'The Development Evaluation of Economic Zones in China' (2018) 15 (1) *International Journal of Environmental Research and Public Health* 1.
[86] China's R&D expenditure represented just over 2% of its GDP in 2016, which is slightly more as a share of GDP than that of Western Europe: see Organisation for Economic

existing technologies for local applications – such as adapting cars or mobile phones to meet the needs of lower-income consumers.[87] The Chinese government's ability to set, and often achieve, ambitious goals, such as high-speed rail in the 2000s and efforts to put satellites and humans in space, has been unparalleled in its pace and scale. Certainly, China has also absorbed Western technologies for a long time – for example, by creating a Chinese high-speed rail industry through joint ventures with foreign companies such as Siemens.[88] But with massive government support for infrastructure development and an enormous existing customer base, this train network is now one of the most extensive and advanced in the world. Similar leapfrogging of technological stages has occurred in other industrial sectors such as telecommunications networks, mobile phones and e-commerce.

The next stage in the development of China's innovation economy concerns the emergence of AI, which raises distinct issues. This is because many of the companies creating world-class AI are already Chinese-controlled:[89] this is domestic innovation through the application of studies published by researchers around the world, as noted in Chapter 8. At the same time, these companies are still highly dependent on foreign technology such as semiconductors. This is because the data processing needed for AI requires enormous computer power. The current leader in the semiconductor market is the US firm Nvidia and Chinese AI companies rely heavily on Nvidia's graphics processing unit (GPU) chips.[90] Hence, the recent trade war with the United States has hardened the Chinese government's resolve to push the domestic chip industry to be more self-sufficient as a technology powerhouse. This is an important and ongoing story, the significance of which is noted in Chapter 8. Creating processing chips is an extremely difficult task that will take China years to achieve (if it ever does).

Co-operation and Development (OECD), *OECD: Main Science and Technology Indicators* <https://stats.oecd.org/Index.aspx?DataSetCode=MSTI_PUB>.

[87] Freeman and Soete, *The Economics of Industrial Innovation* (n 37).

[88] The technology was created by German company Siemens and absorbed into China following regulatory demands for a Sino-German joint venture company to be created. Trains were, subsequently, reverse-engineered by a new Chinese company and resold to Germany at a cheaper price. These war stories about intellectual property theft have continued to colour the debate about Chinese innovation.

[89] They are not wholly Chinese-owned but are Chinese-controlled. See Chapter 2.

[90] See, eg, Karl Freund, 'Is NVIDIA Unstoppable in AI?' (*Forbes*, 14 May 2018) <https://www.forbes.com/sites/moorinsights/2018/05/14/is-nvidia-unstoppable-in-ai/#357f711a759e>.

1.4 Top-Down or Bottom-Up Innovation?

Associated with these policy and technological developments, a new awareness of the role of government in innovation and how innovation in China is understood is emerging within the general literature on the subject. In 2016, Yip and McKern noted three stages of Chinese innovation: (1) moving from copying to 'fit for purpose'; (2) moving from following to world standard; and (3) now seeking new knowledge for world-leading innovation.[91] Likewise, in his 2015 book *China's Disruptors*, Edward Tse coined an acronym to identify factors that triggered China's unique entrepreneurial explosion (including the creation of companies such as Baidu, Alibaba and Tencent): 'SOOT' which stands for scale, openness, official support and technology.[92] For Tse, the following factors were all present: China's market scale, gradually increasing economic openness for the private sector, impressive technological development and official government support for innovation.

The effect of government assistance for private start-ups has always been, and continues to be, disputed by scholars of innovation. On the one hand, many scholars have noted how legal regulation may inhibit innovation. *Mass Flourishing: How Grassroots Innovation Created Jobs, Challenge, and Change*,[93] by economist and Nobel laureate Edmund Phelps, posits that mass innovation is driven by the polity (as opposed to public policy), which fuels the grassroots dynamism necessary for widespread indigenous innovation. Phelps argues that modern desires to create, explore and meet challenges are the wellsprings of innovation. As a result, only free mass creativity produces innovative societies, not top-down technocratic legislation. According to Phelps, planned economies have existing, large bureaucracies that can achieve ambitious goals quickly but can also hinder human creativity. Phelps suggests that innovation is impossible without grass-roots activism, and governments cannot 'die-cast' entrepreneurs.[94]

On the other hand, law and development scholar Erik Reinert argues that government intervention has a major role in protecting innovation and allowing further development.[95] Similarly, Peter Evans notes that governments must kickstart innovation. Yet the political system may also

---

[91] See Yip and McKern, *China's Next Strategic Advantage* (n 22).
[92] Tse, *China's Disruptors* (n 21).
[93] See n 36 in the Introduction.
[94] Phelps, *Mass Flourishing* (n 36) 35.
[95] Reinert, *How Rich Countries Got Rich* (n 36).

cause a lopsided process, and emerging technologies frequently develop so rapidly that government intervention cannot keep pace.[96]

Conventional debates about the role of government in innovation are being challenged by China's recent successes. For example, one of China's current policies for encouraging start-ups – known as mass entrepreneurship – articulates a policy environment encouraging 老百姓 (*laobaixing* – the masses) to start their own businesses.[97] This suggests that there is a complex, symbiotic relationship between the public and private sectors: we see a kind of hybrid system of privately driven, publicly enabled policy petri dishes for innovation, a system that will be illustrated in detail throughout this book.

In short, the Chinese government intentionally creates vague regulations in the areas of economic and technology/innovation policy, and allows local experimentation by entrepreneurs supported by local government officials to test innovations. It then scales up the successful experiments to the national level and refines the regulations to address any unforeseen problems. This is different to many other countries, in that, with the tacit understanding or approval of government, both state-controlled and private Chinese firms are able to exploit gaps or ambiguities in regulations to build and scale up their businesses. A satisfactory understanding of innovation, and of the role of government in innovation, must incorporate these complex public–private interactions that have facilitated the current wave of innovation in China.

Despite the successes of the current Chinese model of innovation, there are also some serious drawbacks. For example, rapid economic change over the past 20 years, together with the uncertain regulatory environment, has created a 'goldrush' or 'land grab' mentality. Entrepreneurs tend to align in almost herd-like fashion with official policy directions, which are considered less susceptible to radical or unexpected changes. Historically in China, funding bubbles have emerged in certain industries that governments identified as supported by national plans and policies. Examples of previous industries that ended up over-saturated due to funding bubbles include the silicon chip and automobile industries.[98] In July 2017, AI became the latest high-profile state-supported sector. It was already a listed

---

[96] Evans, *Embedded Autonomy* (n 36).
[97] See Wei, 'China to Further Promote Innovation and Entrepreneurship' (n 26).
[98] See, eg, Ngai-Ling Sum, 'The Intertwined Geopolitics and Geoeconomics of Hopes/Fears: China's Triple Economic Bubbles and the "One Belt One Road" Imaginary' (2018) *Territory, Politics, Governance* <https://doi.org/10.1080/21622671.2018.1523746>.

pursuit in the Internet Plus plan of 2015, and it was an open question as to whether the sector would soon become swamped due to the government funding bubbles.[99]

Baumol famously defined varying degrees of innovation, including 'unproductive entrepreneurship', where the only end goal is profit.[100] If we define 'unproductive entrepreneurship' as 'innovations in rent-seeking procedures' (eg, 'discovery of a previously unused legal gambit that is effective in diverting rents to those who are first in exploiting it') then, according to Baumol, Chinese innovation might have been hampered by government policy in some industry sectors.[101] Baumol, did, however, famously note that there is 'a remarkable correlation between the degree to which an economy rewarded productive entrepreneurship and the vigor shown in that economy's innovation record'.[102] There is no doubt that China's complex political and legal innovation system has trained a generation of highly successful high-tech entrepreneurs.

Another serious issue impacting on innovation in China is sudden changes of government policy due to mainly ideological reasons. Internet businesses are a prime victim of such changes. Online video, blogging or social media businesses have been permitted to operate for a while, then suddenly been subjected to rigid regulation. In the AI industry this phenomenon has been observed with AI-powered news aggregator ByteDance-owned Jinri Toutiao (ByteDance is also the owner of TikTok). Jinri Toutiao had been permitted to operate freely, before facing numerous content violation fines.[103] First-mover advantage can be taken away by the government overnight. This unpredictability tends to foster a very short-term approach to making profits, and because it is short term,

---

[99] SenseTime's Yang Fan and investors such as Everbright's Ai Yu have argued that the fundamental challenge for Chinese AI start-ups is the commercialisation of new technologies, which need to be focused on real demand. See Nina Xiang, 'China's AI Industry Has Given Birth to 14 Unicorns: Is It a Bubble Waiting to Burst?' (*Forbes*, 5 October 2018) <https://www.forbes.com/sites/ninaxiang/2018/10/05/chinas-ai-industry-has-given-birth-to-14-unicorns-is-it-a-bubble-waiting-to-pop/#2b68965246c3>.

[100] William J Baumol, 'Entrepreneurship: Productive, Unproductive, and Destructive' (1990) 98(5) *Journal of Political Economy* 893. Entrepreneurship and innovation are different concepts; thus, Baumol has questioned whether this premise of 'unproductive entrepreneurship' is truly 'unproductive': at 898.

[101] Baumol explains that rent-seeking is a crucial step on the path to innovation: ibid 897.

[102] Ibid 909.

[103] See Chapter 7.

entrepreneurs often look for shortcuts, such as stealing technology or intellectual property from other firms.[104]

Allowing for these drawbacks and restrictions, Chinese entrepreneurs have still managed to flourish in the gaps between regulatory walls. They have done so by 'carefully consider[ing] the role of government intervention. To avoid unpredictable policy changes, some entrepreneurs choose to enter regulation-light sectors. Others run toward key sectors identified in China's Five-year Plans, which outline the government's strategic directions for the country'.[105] AI is one of the most promising sectors that fulfils these elements and plays to the strengths of Chinese entrepreneurship. This is because AI as an emerging and uncertain technology is perfectly suited to China's system of 'fuzzy logic' legislating. This is due to both the role of government and the nature of AI as a technology. In Chapter 8, the nature of AI is fully explained, and it is demonstrated how fuzzy logic legislating is very well suited for AI development. Secondly, China's thirst for the application of AI products did not emerge in a policy vacuum. China's more recent history of legal petri dishes, as this study describes, includes hundreds of Smart Cities, and these Smart City pilots are perfect for this recent moment in technological history – the arrival of Deep Learning[106] (see Chapter 8).

1.5 Entrepreneurial Ecosystems with Chinese Characteristics

So far, this chapter has focused on identifying the distinctive features of the Chinese model of innovation. This section explains how the Chinese model may be especially well adapted to promoting innovation in rapidly developing technologies (eg, blockchain and AI) where the regulatory environment struggles to keep up.

The regulatory challenges posed by rapidly developing technologies suggest that researchers need to modify current theories of innovation and entrepreneurship by recognising how the concepts of 'fuzzy logic'

---

[104] Wharton Business School, '"Land-Grab Mentality": The Cutthroat Competition on China's Internet' (*Knowledge @Wharton*, 14 December 2010) <https://knowledge.wharton.upenn.edu/article/land-grab-mentality-the-cutthroat-competition-on-chinas-internet>.

[105] Ibid.

[106] Deep Learning is a field that has advanced greatly in recent years. Key applications include accurate speech and facial recognition that can be used for better reading of medical records and diagnostics; and AI image recognition around security issues, which has received much researcher attention. (See Chapter 8.)

and 'public–private petri dishes' are especially suited for promoting innovation in AI.

China's model of innovation challenges our assumptions for two reasons. First 'public–private petri dish' pilots, and fuzzy logic regulation, enable bottom-up design from talented entrepreneurs. Second, flexible laws allow for reinterpretation in real time to adapt to new innovations, and flexible adaptation by regulatory bodies builds confidence in the system among Chinese entrepreneurs. 'Fuzzy logic' legislating does not unnerve Chinese entrepreneurs, because it has had at least three decades of history during the reform period, as discussed in Chapter 2.

According to a popular saying in the Chinese tech industry, first-tier companies make standards, second-tier companies make technology and third-tier companies make products (一流的企业做标准，二流的企业做技术，三流的企业做产品).[107] Thus, 'public–private petri dishes' actually build confidence. A constant refrain is: 'I don't have time to worry about regulations, the government won't harm innovation.'[108] This is because there are constant consultations between industry and government that support Chinese innovation. This is evident in the implementation of the potentially innovation-inhibiting Cyber Security Law discussed in Chapter 5.

When moving from 'public–private petri dishes' to real-world applications in the area of AI, it has largely been entrepreneurs rather than academic or government labs that have applied and refined innovations. This is especially true for Machine Learning technologies such as self-driving cars that need many hours of on-road training. We see a combination of bottom-up energy and investment from entrepreneurs and top-down government policy support for their AI product experiments. The government's relatively laissez-faire attitude to testing self-driving vehicles on Chinese roads has allowed AI machines to 'learn by doing' in real-world circumstances, thereby creating better algorithms and more reliable vehicles.[109] A similar combination of government or state-owned institutional support for private entrepreneurial experimentation within

---

[107] 谢 耘 [Xie Wei], «中国企业技术产品创新中的 几个问题分析» [Analysis of Several Problems in the Innovation of Chinese Enterprise Technology Products] 中国计算机学会通讯 (2009) 5(4) *China Computer Society Newsletter* 60.

[108] This was a frequent response in informal interviews the author conducted with Chinese entrepreneurs in Beijing between 2017 and 2019.

[109] See Chapter 9.

a relatively loose regulatory framework can be seen in other AI product areas (eg, facial recognition).

If we need a final framework or conceptual model of how innovation actually occurs within the Chinese context it is as follows. 'Public–private innovation petri dishes' involve both bottom-up and top-down impetus: government investment in semiconductors and infrastructure, for example, but private sector leadership in commercial rollouts. More precisely, it is 'privately driven' but 'publicly enabled innovation petri dishes'.

This unique regulatory environment means that AI companies must look to the Chinese government for agenda-setting legitimacy for recruitment drives and R&D help, including access to big datasets, and, importantly, early-stage client patronage for product development testing, as well as supportive legal petri dishes for training Machine Learning in real-world environments. New technologies also need much R&D and 'patient capital' (as opposed to 'impatient' venture capital).

Of course, the primary motivation for all this government support, as demonstrated in Chapters 7–9, is that the products developed by these entrepreneurial firms can help to solve social problems caused by a Chinese legal and bureaucratic system that lacks many features we might expect in a developed country. These features include, among others, a developed credit rating system, a general practitioner/health diagnosis system as opposed to visiting public hospitals, and an efficient transportation/logistics system for a population of 1.4 billion people. Local governments, for example, have been keen to fund and assist start-ups to help them resolve their own problems.[110] In essence, Chinese entrepreneurs are not just making money but providing tools to solve Chinese development problems using AI, and there are many thorny problems to solve.

Therefore, AI development is not only a strategic direction for China; it is also potentially a highly practical tool for solving China's development problems.

---

[110] Due to the intertwined nature of private and public interests, local governments tend to use collaborative partnerships involving entrepreneurs to promote regional entrepreneurship: see Yijun Xing, Yipeng Liu and Sir Cary L Cooper, 'Local Government as Institutional Entrepreneur: Public–Private Collaborative Partnerships in Fostering Regional Entrepreneurship' (2008) 29(4) *British Journal of Management* 670 <https://doi.org/10.1111/1467-8551.12282>.

1.6 Conclusion: Assumptions on Chinese Innovation Challenges

China's unique policy environment for innovation has provided fertile conditions for developing world-leading AI companies. The speed of events since 2014 has taken most observers by surprise. It is no longer true, as many commentators had posited, that China cannot innovate. When documenting some of the rising AI start-ups in China (eg, Sensetime and Yitu Tech) this book shows how their world-class award-winning algorithms in speech and image recognition respectively have made onlookers pay attention.

China's distinctive approach to innovation utilises a complex, symbiotic relationship between the public and private sectors: a hybrid system of 'privately driven, publicly enabled policy petri dishes' for innovation. The Chinese government intentionally creates vague regulations in the areas of economic and innovation policies. Local experimentation by entrepreneurs, supported by local government officials, to test innovations is allowed and often encouraged. The Chinese government then scales up the successful experiments to the national level while refining regulations to address any unforeseen problems. This differs from other countries as, with tacit government approval, both state-controlled and privately controlled Chinese firms are able to exploit ambiguities in regulations to build and scale up their businesses. Therefore, an understanding of Chinese innovation must incorporate these complex public–private interactions that have facilitated the current wave of innovation in China.

Yet to fully appreciate the extent of fuzzy logic in China's legal system, and how this has helped Chinese technology companies, the next chapter considers the still highly relevant situation in which legal prohibitions have been tacitly waived since the early 2000s in the area of technology investment, allowing foreigners to invest in industries prohibited for foreign investment in China (eg, the internet and media) with the aim of promoting innovation and economic development. This example will show why few Chinese entrepreneurs are overly concerned about the lack of clear lines between legal and illegal in China's fuzzy logic policymaking system. This is because regulatory fuzziness has for decades been a key factor in the success of China's tech industry.

2

The Extent of Fuzzy Logic

The Tech Giants and Their 'Illegal' Legal Structure

> Every VIE company – Baidu, Sina, Alibaba, Tudou, all of them – is operating by the grace of their Chinese partners. This mess is going to make Enron look like a trivial, little drop in the bucket.
>
> —Steve Dickinson, partner at international law firm Harris Bricken and author of renowned *China Law Blog*[111]

The extent of fuzzy logic surrounding the legal structure of tech companies in China is a profound illustration of the environment Chinese entrepreneurs must operate in and remains an ongoing story. From the outset, Chinese tech entrepreneurs must decide how to legally structure their companies in order to account for vague conceptions of legality. The regulatory practice of fuzzy logic is a longstanding one in China, and it has been applied to other areas of technological and corporate regulation.

While this chapter is a self-contained background chapter, it contributes to the main theme of this book by explaining how Chinese entrepreneurs have been caught between commercial realities and Chinese regulators in the tech sector since at least the year 2000.[112] It shows that although major tech firms have used an 'illegal' – yet tacitly

---

[111] Dickinson was quoted in Sue-Lin Wong, 'China Court Ruling Could Threaten Foreign Investments in Country' (*New York Times*, 19 June 2013) <https://cn.nytimes.com/business/20130619/c19vie/en-us>.

[112] Expansive texts have been written on the subject of foreign investment: see, eg, Tarrant Mahony, *Foreign Investment Law in China: Regulation, Practice and Context* (Tsinghua University Press, 2015). Further, as China goes global (led by the tech companies), international stock market listings have also complicated Chinese regulatory trends and corporate governance: Jin Sheng, *China's Listed Companies: Conflicts, Governance and Regulation* (Kluwer Law International, 2015). See also Kaitlyn Johnson, 'Variable Interest Entities: Alibaba's Regulatory Work-Around to China's Foreign Investment Restrictions' (2015) 12 *Loyola University Chicago International Law Review* 249. Books such as Lin Zhang, *China's Venture Capital Market: Current Legal Problems and Prospective Reforms* (Elsevier, 2015) also detail the problems caused by having invested US venture capital in prohibited Chinese industries.

permitted – structure to list on US stock exchanges, they have until very recently refused to de-list there or to dual-list in China, despite heavy government pressure to do so and law reforms in 2018. It argues that this is due to the desire for a cloak of legitimacy globally, alternative sources of funding and, possibly, an extra level of protection from Chinese government expropriation of assets. These potential benefits are afforded by an offshore ownership structure and a Nasdaq listing. This is fuzzy logic in action. Nevertheless by 2020, some Chinese image recognition (and other) firms would have little choice but to list in China due to the US government's blacklisting of Chinese tech firms.

2.1 'Fuzzy Logic' Laws

One major barrier to a successful entrepreneurial ecosystem is the presence or absence of the rule of law. There are radically different interpretations of the rule of law.[113] In commercial law, it means the ability to have certainty in commercial transactions and precision of the laws governing property rights between citizens and the state and between private individuals. The rule of law is an especially complex topic in China, even for businesses. For example, businesses still remain subject to unpublished 内部 (*neibu* – regulations) and Communist Party policy statements, though recent years have seen a steady push towards greater transparency.[114] Even understanding how formal, published regulations interact with the legal system in practice is a major challenge. Moreover, the local, provincial and central governments often have conflicting agendas. For technology companies this fuzziness could be problematic. Intentionally vague regulations have resulted in, for example, the isolation of technology clusters rather than supportive collaboration within Development Zones.[115]

There is a fundamental epistemic problem in expounding Chinese laws: how do you validate what you cannot precisely define? Further, knowledge of the implementation of laws can be sparsely diffused across

---

[113] Scholars such as Randall Peerenboom have written extensively on the subject of the rule of law: see, eg, Randall Peerenboom, *China's Long March toward Rule of Law* (Cambridge University Press, 2002) and *China Modernizes* (Oxford University Press, 2007).
[114] Peerenboom, *China's Long March toward Rule of Law* (n 113) 7.
[115] See, eg, Debbie Liao and Philip Sohmen, 'The Development of Modern Entrepreneurship in China' (2010) 1 *Stanford Journal of East Asian Affairs* 27.

bureaucracies and government officials. Sometimes that knowledge is not diffused at all.[116]

Lawyers usually search for precise drafting terms. Yet 'fuzzy logic' is perhaps closer to the way our brains work. We aggregate data from a number of partial truths, and aggregate this further into truths which in turn become forms of logic.[117] Fuzzy logic peppers China's exponential growth of legislation in recent years; the following is an example of what is meant by fuzzy logic.

2.1.1 What Is Meant by a 'Fuzzy Logic' Law in China?

'Fuzzy logic' law is law that is unclear but conveniently can be moulded to suit the contradictions of China's political system and economic needs. For example, on 30 December 2014, the Chinese Ministry of Finance released what directly translates as 'Notice on Standardising Government and Social Capital Cooperation Contract Management'.[118] Better understood as 'Guidance on Public Private Partnerships', it is designed to provide rules for state-owned enterprises when contracting with the private sector. The phrase '社会资本' (*shehuiziben* – social capital) requires immediate attention. It is defined twice within the Guidance: first as 'public private partnership (PPP)' and subsequently as 'partnership in the fields of infrastructure and public services for government and *social capital*-based contracts' (emphasis added). Notwithstanding past use of the term in legal statutes, which should bring some clarity to the use of the term in the Guidance, 'social capital' is used in the second part

---

[116] Many laws and regulations are contradictory and uncoordinated and possess vague duties and lines of authority. In some instances, no entity is the responsible authority; in others, several agencies and ministries each exercise partial authority. Post-1979, seeking to encourage initiatives at all levels of government, the Chinese Constitution and other basic laws mandated that the Standing Committee of the National People's Congress can enact laws (法律 – *falu*), the State Council can enact administrative regulations (法规 – *fagui*), and Provincial People's Congresses and their Standing Committees, as well as those of large cities and authorised Special Economic Zones, are enabled to enact local regulations (地方性法规 – *difangxing fagui*), but it is common to have unresolved inconsistencies between these legal instruments: see Dingjian Cai, 'Development of the Chinese Legal System since 1979 and Its Current Crisis and Transformation', trans S Farhad (1999) 11(2) *Cultural Dynamics* 135, 145.

[117] See Lotfi A Zadeh, 'Outline of a New Approach to the Analysis of Complex Systems and Decision Processes' (1973) 3(1) *IEEE Transactions on Systems Man and Cybernetics* 28.

[118] «关于规范政府和社会资本合作合同管理工作的通知» [Guidance on Public–Private Partnerships] (People's Republic of China) Ministry of Finance, 30 December 2014.

of its own definition. This Guidance may be helpful and/or simultaneously counterproductive to the staff of SOEs.

'Social capital' was deliberately selected. This is because while the English-language abbreviation PPP[119] is clear and in common usage, China defines the non-government partner as 'social capital' instead of 'private capital', which opens the door for state-run firms to contract in sectors prohibited from private investment.[120]

This example identified a systemic mixed blessing in the Chinese legal system: regulations are expressed in the form of general principles with undefined or ambiguously defined terms, allowing scope for administrative interpretation and discretion. Alternatively, existing regulations are simply not enforced due to higher policy considerations.[121]

The following discussion illustrates this phenomenon of fuzzy logic law and regulatory practice in more detail using the fascinating case of Chinese tech firms and variable-interest entities.

2.2 Offshore Legal Structures: The Variable-Interest Entity (VIE)

The almost unbelievable tale of foreign investment in 'prohibited' Chinese industries through either Hong Kong-registered or foreign-registered (including Cayman Islands) legal structures elucidates just how far China's legislative 'fuzzy logic' extends.

Under its foreign investment regulations, the Chinese Ministry of Commerce issues an investment catalogue, which lists industries prohibited to foreign investment. This is known as the *Catalogue for the Guidance of*

---

[119] This database (政府和社会资本合作 (PPP)) outlines all PPP-related regulations. The words PPP and 社会资本 (social capital) are used interchangeably. See 政府和社会资本合作 (PPP) (*literally* Government and Social Capital Cooperation – PPP) <http://jrs.mof.gov.cn/ppp>.

[120] Chen-Yu Chang and Shi Chen, 'Transitional Public–Private Partnership Model in China: Contracting with Little Recourse to Contracts' (2016) 142(10) *Journal of Construction Engineering and Management* 7. More than 11,000 of these projects, totalling ¥13.5 trillion (US$2 trillion at the time), had been registered at the end of 2016, according to Ministry of Finance data: see «全国 PPP 综合信息平台项目库第五期季报» [National PPP Integrated Information Platform Project Library Phase 5 Quarterly Report] (People's Republic of China) Ministry of Finance, Department of Finance <http://www.cpppc.org/zh/pppyw/4684.jhtml>. It has also been noted that 'private' partner in these transactions is often an SOE.

[121] There can also be a delay between Chinese publication of a new law and an official English translation affecting foreign businesspeople.

Foreign Investment Industries.[122] Media and internet are included on that list, as the internet and media sectors are politically sensitive, and this legal regulation prohibits foreign investors from funding – and by extension, controlling – Chinese businesses in those sectors.[123]

Essentially, variable-interest entities (VIEs) are established to evade China's heavy restrictions on foreign-owned companies in the Catalogue, and to allow for listing of Chinese technology businesses on the New York or other foreign exchanges.[124] The VIE is a representative example of the extent to which 'fuzzy logic' legislating can accommodate the behaviour of tech firms. It also clearly illustrates the ongoing conflict between the government's desire to promote innovation and its ideological tendency towards restriction of perceived foreign influence.

2.2.1 The VIE Structure

The VIE structure can be explained as follows. First, an existing Chinese firm in a sector prohibited or restricted from foreign investment by the Catalogue decides to seek foreign investment using a VIE structure. An offshore holding company based in the Cayman Islands is established. (A Hong Kong-registered or other foreign-registered company can be used instead.) The holding company can, under local law, be listed on foreign stock markets or be controlled by a foreign investor. The holding company then establishes a wholly foreign-owned enterprise (WFOE) in China, for which it is the sole or controlling shareholder. This is a common corporate structure for foreign investment in China, familiar to all who have set up a business there.[125] The WFOE[126] then enters into a series of contracts with

---

[122] «外商投资产业指导目录 (2017 年修订)» [Catalogue for the Guidance of Foreign Investment Industries (2017 Revision)] (People's Republic of China) Ministry of Commerce, 28 June 2017.

[123] See Thomas Y Man, 'Policy above Law: VIE and Foreign Investment Regulation in China' (2015) 3(1) *Peking University Transnational Law Review* 217.

[124] Ibid; Christopher Beddor, 'The Alibaba IPO and How Chinese Companies Bypass Foreign Investments Restrictions' (*CKGSB Knowledge*, 1 September 2014) <http://knowledge.ckgsb.edu.cn/2014/09/01/china/the-alibaba-ipo-and-how-chinese-companies-bypass-foreign-investment-restrictions>.

[125] A WFOE is defined as a limited liability company wholly owned by foreign investor(s): «中华人民共和国外资企业法 (2016 修正)» [Law on Wholly Foreign-Owned Enterprises of the People's Republic of China (2016 Revision)] (People's Republic of China) National People's Congress, Order No 51, 9 March 2016, art 2.

[126] For accounting purposes, the Chinese partner of the VIE is typically consolidated on the books of the US-listed parent, despite the lack of equity ownership interest or direct operating control.

the existing Chinese firm, which gives the WFOE effective control over the revenues and shareholder powers of the Chinese firm without actually owning any of its shares. Technically it is still a 100% Chinese-owned firm separate from the WFOE, but in practice it has given up its powers and revenues to the WFOE and the foreign investors through contracts.

In summary, under a VIE agreement, a Cayman Islands-registered, Hong Kong-registered or other foreign-registered company sets up a WFOE in China, which then enters into a contract with a mainland Chinese company that wholly owns the firm's mainland operations. Typically, the founding entrepreneurs and their associates retain registered ownership of the Chinese company. Yet the company is bound by contract to return all profits to the foreign holding company.

Since WFOEs are foreign owned, they are precluded from holding the licences and permits necessary to operate in certain industries (eg, internet-content firms). To bypass this, the mainland Chinese company or series of companies continues to hold the licences and sufficient assets and revenue to satisfy the regulators; in other words, it is effectively '[o]wnership through management contracts'.[127]

A large proportion of China's leading internet and telecom companies have established VIEs. Baidu and Alibaba are only a few of the hundreds[128] of VIEs currently operating in China, designed to evade Chinese investment rules. Among tech firms, the VIE was first used by Sina for its Nasdaq listing back in 2000, and as recently as 2014 it was employed by Alibaba for its US$21 billion listing on the New York Stock Exchange. Sina de-listed off the Nasdaq in 2021.

While certainly successful from the perspective of raising capital and allowing foreign investors access to a 'prohibited' Chinese industry sector, the VIE structure is totally dependent on the enforceability of its underlying contracts, and these generally allow the Chinese company's management team to continue running the firm. As a result, major foreign investors in firms such as Alibaba (eg, Yahoo) have had little managerial control over their businesses, and arguably have lost out as a result of recent restructurings (a point discussed further later).[129]

---

[127] See Guo Li, 'Chinese Style VIEs: Continuing to Sneak under Smog?' (2014) 47 *Cornell International Law Journal* 572; Beddor, 'The Alibaba IPO' (n 124).

[128] See Serena Y Shi, 'Dragon's House of Cards: Perils of Investing in Variable Interest Entities Domiciled in the People's Republic of China and Listed in the United States' (2014) 37 *Fordham International Law Journal* 1278.

[129] The Yahoo–Alibaba dispute is outlined in ibid 1291–2. *The Economist* detailed the 'fuzzy' nature of the situation for the general public in 2017: 'Alibaba, the world's

2.2.2 Evading China's Investment Laws

In order to understand the VIE structure, it is also necessary to understand the context in which it has developed. The internet is a 'sensitive' industry in China and, as a result, highly regulated. However, it was once the least regulated sector of the Chinese economy. For years China's internet companies were largely ignored by government regulators. It has been said that the Chinese government undervalued the importance of the internet.[130] There was also a time, only a few years ago, when the Chinese venture capital industry was immature and China sought increased foreign capital to fill the funding needs in this market.[131]

Within this context, the VIE structure emerged to allow Chinese startups to target overseas venture capital, via incorporating as a Cayman Islands entity with an aim to list in the United States or Hong Kong. This model was pioneered by Sina in 2000 for courting investment from the United States.[132] Internet firms Sohu, Baidu and Netease soon followed and created VIEs. These companies were the early pioneers of China's internet industry. Sina is now best known for creating Weibo, the so-called Chinese Twitter. Sohu is famous for its search engine but also has a highly successful online gaming business. Weibo Corp (NASDAQ: WB) remained listed on the Nasdaq in 2021. Baidu, once notable for its search engine, is now an AI-focused conglomerate. Netease, while less well known in the West, operates a profitable online gaming business.

Today hundreds of Chinese companies use the VIE model in a range of industries. Technically they should be categorised as 'foreign-invested

---

sixth-most valuable firm, illustrates how it works. It is incorporated in the Cayman Islands and in 2014 listed its shares in New York, but makes 91% of its sales in mainland China. There it owns five big subsidiaries which have contracts with five corresponding VIEs. The VIEs contain licences and domain names and are owned by Jack Ma and Simon Xie, two of Alibaba's founders. It is as if Facebook were domiciled in Samoa, listed in Shanghai and its website and brand sat in separate legal entities that were the property of Mark Zuckerberg (but which he had agreed to allow Facebook to run and profit from)': see 'A Legal Vulnerability at the Heart of China's Big Internet Firms' (*The Economist*, 16 September 2017) <https://www.economist.com/news/business/21728984-variable-interest-entities-are-their-weakest-link-legal-vulnerability-heart-chinas?fsrc=scn/tw/te/bl/ed/alegalvulnerabilityattheheartofchinasbiginternetfirms>.

[130] See Li, 'Chinese Style VIEs' (n 127) 600.
[131] See, eg, David Ahlstrom, Garry D Bruton and Kuang S Yeh, 'Venture Capital in China: Past, Present, and Future' (2007) 24(3) *Asia Pacific Journal of Management* 247.
[132] See Samuel Farrell Ziegler, 'China's Variable Interest Entity Problem: How Americans Have Illegally Invested Billions in China and How to Fix It' (2016) 84(2) *George Washington Law Review* 539.

firms' under Chinese rules, due to their majority foreign control exercised through contracts.[133] That in turn should prohibit them from owning assets in some politically sensitive sectors, most notably the internet. Yet the Chinese government, while fully aware of these major firms' use of a legal loophole that does not comply with the spirit of the regulations, has consistently allowed foreign capital a large stake in protected industries prohibited for foreign investment, presumably because it has allowed these sectors to develop much quicker than it would have with only domestic investment.

Despite the success of this legally dubious structure, the legal status of VIEs is always subject to change. Since 2018, the Chinese government has agitated for these companies to return 'home' and list on Chinese stock exchanges. It is argued in Section 2.4 that these companies are resisting, in part, because investor rules in the United States offer more transparency and the US listing increases their prestige as they seek to market their AI and other products globally.

The VIE corporate structure truly elucidates the extent of 'fuzzy logic' in the Chinese regulatory system. The Chinese government has never stated that VIEs are legal and has occasionally threatened to render this vehicle illegal. Hence a fuzzy logic has ensued, leaving behind numerous corporate governance, shareholder and legal dilemmas. The long history of tacit acceptance of VIEs may also explain why 'fuzzy logic' legislating does not unnerve Chinese entrepreneurs in the AI sector. It has set the tone for nearly two decades of technology entrepreneurship in China.

2.2.3 Paradoxical Side Effects of Fuzzy Logic on VIEs

The fuzzy logic of the VIE structure, nevertheless, has some paradoxical side effects. First, Chinese law restricts the ability of mainland investors to buy overseas equities, and currently the only way to invest in most of these VIEs is on an overseas or Hong Kong exchange. On 15 September 2014, Bloomberg published an article titled 'Chinese Gripe at Being Left Out of Alibaba IPO'. It quoted a disgruntled would-be Chinese investor, a retired factory worker called Ms Zhou: 'I'm a little confused about why you can't invest in a Chinese company if you're Chinese.' The article noted: 'Though Chinese consumers have driven Alibaba's success, they'll

---

[133] Paul Armstrong-Taylor explains this dilemma succinctly: see *Debt and Distortion: Risks and Reforms in the Chinese Financial System* (Palgrave Macmillan, 2016) 192-3.

largely be left out of the company's stock offering.'[134] The fact that Chinese internet firms are abroad means most Chinese citizens cannot invest in the most dynamic part of the private sector economy. The internet is one of the few sectors of the economy in which SOEs have failed to capture significant market share.[135]

Second, foreign capital helped the early growth of the major internet companies, mainly through listings on stock exchanges outside mainland China.[136] Yet the success of home-grown internet names in China such as Taobao and Baidu at the expense of global giants like eBay and Google is responsible for a popular misconception that foreigners are shut out of China's foreign internet market. This may be true of wholly foreign-owned firms, but through VIEs foreign investors have poured billions of dollars into Chinese internet firms. As a result, China's original big three internet giants – Baidu, Alibaba and Tencent (BATs) – are actually Chinese entrepreneur-founded, foreign venture capital- or market capital-backed, overseas-listed firms.

Almost all of China's major internet firms should be classified as foreign-invested entities. In theory, this means they are subject to the same restrictions as Yahoo, Google or any other foreign internet firm operating in China. Prior to Baidu's initial public offering (IPO), foreign institutional investors owned more than 45% of the company, and Google was an investor before it exited with a large profit.[137] As for Alibaba, even before its IPO, the largest investors were Softbank, a Japanese investment firm with a 34% interest, and Yahoo with a 24% interest. Yahoo ran its Chinese operations through Alibaba.com, which it controlled through contracts but did not legally own. Likewise, South African multimedia company Naspers is one of several foreign institutional investors that together own more than a 50% interest in

---

[134] Shai Oster and Allen Wan, 'Chinese Gripe at Being Left Out of Alibaba IPO' (*Bloomberg*, 15 September 2014) <https://www.bloomberg.com/news/articles/2014-09-14/chinese-gripe-at-being-left-out-of-alibaba-s-21-billion-ipo>.

[135] See Guohua Wu et al, 'The Return of VIE-Structured Enterprise to China's Domestic Capital Market: A Brief Legal Analysis and Other Factors to Be Considered' (2015) 3(1) *Peking University Transnational Law Review* 211.

[136] Tencent, for example, went public in June 2004, raising HK$1.4 billion (US$180 million at the time).

[137] Alibaba gained investments from SoftBank and Yahoo! while Tencent won the backing of Naspers, a South African media company that moved into digital investments. Early investors in Baidu Inc included Google and IDG Capital Partners. See Crunchbase: 'Baidu' (*Crunchbase*) <https://www.crunchbase.com/organization/baidu#section-overview>.

Tencent through its VIE structure.[138] These investments make strange bedfellows; in 2017 News24, a news website owned by Naspers, revealed that the South African apartheid government had bought arms from China in the 1980s, a piece of news that would certainly be censored if it appeared on a Tencent WeChat site.[139]

Many of these investments have been highly profitable. By 2018, Naspers had turned its 2001 investment of US$32 million in Tencent into a market value of US$175 billion. In 2018 *Bloomberg* noted:

> Naspers might have remained an obscure publisher of South African newspapers and operator of pay-TV services if not for its decision in 2001 to invest $32 million in Tencent, a then little-known Chinese start-up. The stake is now worth $175 billion and given that Naspers has a market value of about $125.5 billion, it means investors place no value on Naspers' other operations and investments.[140]

By late 2014, global investors were well aware of the market growth potential of the Chinese technology sector as Alibaba's IPO was enormous.[141] On 18 September 2014, Alibaba's Cayman Islands holding company was listed on the New York Stock Exchange, raising US$21.8 billion from international investors, more than Facebook and General Motors in their IPOs.[142]

The paradox that all the BAT[143] companies, and many other Chinese tech firms, are partially foreign owned, while certainly solving a funding problem and allowing foreigners to share in their profits, has led to

---

[138] Crunchbase: 'Tencent' (*Crunchbase*) <https://www.crunchbase.com/organization/tencent>.

[139] The article was based on research into declassified documents from South Africa's apartheid era. See 'Declassified: Apartheid Profits – China's Support for Apartheid Revealed' (*News24*, 31 October 2017) <https://www.dailymaverick.co.za/article/2017-10-31-declassified-apartheid-profits-chinas-support-for-apartheid-revealed>.

[140] Loni Prinsloo, 'Tencent's 60,000% Runup Leads to One of the Biggest VC Payoffs Ever' (*Bloomberg*, 22 March 2018) <https://www.bloomberg.com/news/articles/2018-03-22/naspers-sells-10-6-billion-of-tencent-to-fund-investments>.

[141] Alibaba founder Jack Ma, adept at growing and diversifying the company rapidly, has also become a global celebrity. Investors may have been confident in Ma's leadership, in addition to the sheer size of the Chinese internet market.

[142] Ryan Mac, 'Alibaba Claims Title for Largest Global IPO Ever with Extra Share Sales' (*Forbes*, 22 September 2014) <https://www.forbes.com/sites/ryanmac/2014/09/22/alibaba-claims-title-for-largest-global-ipo-ever-with-extra-share-sales/#548cc3518dcc>.

[143] Three of China's biggest internet companies have all attracted foreign capital: New York-listed search firm Baidu (often labelled China's Google), Alibaba and the Hong Kong-listed Tencent. Tencent made its early fortune in instant messaging and gaming, and now dominates mobile phone use with WeChat.

commercial and legal complications in the areas of corporate governance and shareholder rights. This is one negative impact of 'fuzzy logic' laws for foreign investors trying to see through the opaque window that is China's legal system.

2.2.4 Disputes between Chinese Tech Firms and Activist VIE Investors

VIEs are not immune to attempts by activist investors to influence their management. For example, in October 2017, Aristeia Capital, a hedge fund based in Connecticut, lobbied the shareholders of Sina's US-listed company to back its two candidates for the board in a bid to give shareholders greater returns.[144] Sina, whose Weibo service is one of China's most popular social media platforms, is a Nasdaq-traded share. This proxy fight between a Chinese company and an American investor was considered a first.[145] Sina, one of the first Chinese technology companies to list its shares in New York, called Aristeia 'self-serving' and naïve about how China's internet sector works. Aristeia, in turn, accused Sina of 'failing to hold itself to the standards expected of US-listed public company boards'.[146] The fight emerged over the separate listing of Weibo (China's Twitter) as a spin-off from Sina. This would remove valuable intellectual property from the company.

In the end, Aristeia Capital did force a referendum among Sina's shareholders over whether the company should consider changes in its business to make more money for shareholders. However, Aristeia's closely watched appeal failed when in November 2017 Sina announced that the investor's two nominees had not been voted onto the board.[147] The example demonstrates that fuzzy logic in legal structures sometimes leads to fuzzy investor protection.

---

[144] Alexandra Stevenson, 'US Investor Tries to Shake Up Sina, a Pillar of China's Internet' (*New York Times*, 31 October 2017) <https://www.nytimes.com/2017/10/31/business/dealbook/china-sina-aristeia-proxy-fight.html>.

[145] According to disclosures tracked by the data provider FactSet: ibid. There have been many shareholder disputes between American investors and managers of Chinese firms listed in the United States, if not proxy fights.

[146] Aristeia pushed for representation on the board so that directors would consider greater returns for shareholders. Including a sale or merger of Sina or Weibo or a buyback of shares by management. Sina argued that Aristeia's wishes would not clear China's complicated telecom and media rules. Alibaba, the Chinese e-commerce giant, also owns a stake in Weibo, further complicating its options, according to Sina: Stevenson, 'US Investor Tries to Shake Up Sina' (n 144).

[147] Ibid.

The Sina Weibo situation was similar to the way in which Jack Ma, Alibaba's founder, had spun off the e-payment business AliPay from Alibaba's corporate ownership in 2012. Both companies claimed that China's complex internet and finance industry rules required them to carry out these restructurings. Often, hard questions from investors are answered by Chinese technology executives simply saying that China's regulatory environment will not allow a particular action to be taken. Alibaba argued that foreign entities could not hold payment licences in China due to newly issued banking regulations. As a result, a very valuable business asset (the AliPay payment system) was moved from Alibaba's Chinese corporation to another Chinese-controlled entity, Ant Financial, which was not subject to the contracts with foreign investors. Investors such as Yahoo claimed that they were not adequately compensated for the loss of this major asset.[148]

The VIE structure is not a shield from accusations of intellectual property theft, as breach of contract actions are possible in China. However, due to fuzzy logic regulations and the possibility that the contracts are illegal, these claims are difficult, if not impossible, to dispute in Chinese courts.[149]

---

[148] An explanation of Alibaba's actions is given in Alibaba's 20-F Annual Report 2017, which is cited in the 6-K disclosures accompanying the announcement. In short, Alibaba was expecting the People's Bank of China to bring in regulations in 2011 relating to foreign ownership of payment processing firms, but those regulations were never issued. To avoid potential prohibition and loss of its payment processing licence, in 2011 Alibaba pre-emptively divested its ownership of Alipay (which is now part of Ant Financial), while maintaining various agreements allowing it to share in Alipay's profits. But since the regulations on foreign ownership were never issued, the divestiture was not necessary, so Alibaba decided to replace the profit-sharing agreements with a direct equity interest of 33% in Ant Financial. The Annual Report notes that the profit-sharing agreement would have terminated anyway if Ant Financial did an IPO, so it may be that this was also intended to simplify the ownership structure of Ant Financial and clarify Alibaba's rights in the firm prior to Ant's IPO. However, the 2017 Annual Report also states: 'We believe that under applicable regulatory rules and practices currently in effect, the relevant PRC approvals necessary for us to own an equity interest in Ant Financial Services would not be granted. There can be no assurance that these applicable regulatory rules and practices will change in the near future.' So, something might have changed since 2017 that would give Alibaba the confidence to take this equity interest and obtain approval for it from the 'relevant officials'.

[149] There has been one case heard by the Supreme People's Court where a similar structure was found to be illegal and unenforceable. In the high-profile *Chinachem* case in 2013, China's highest court, the Supreme People's Court, invalidated VIE-like contracts on the ground that they inherently subverted China's Contract Law. See Li, 'Chinese Style VIEs' (n 127) 571; Shi, 'Dragon's House of Cards' (n 128).

Alibaba's conduct remains the most famous case highlighting the agency issues associated with VIEs. Alibaba's holding company unilaterally moved the Alipay subsidiary out of the consolidated group and into a company wholly owned by Jack Ma. Neither Yahoo (which owned 43% of Alibaba Group) nor Softbank (which owned 30%) was notified or consulted prior to the decision. As a result, the hedge fund Greenlight Capital sold all of its Yahoo stock, noting: 'Shortly after the purchase, the value of the Chinese assets came into doubt as the CEO of the Chinese unit hived-off a valuable subsidiary into a corporation that he personally controls. This wasn't what we signed up for.'[150]

In early 2018 Alibaba would partially reverse the spin-off by taking a direct 33% equity stake in Ant Financial and terminating its profit-share agreement,[151] despite the continuing lack of regulatory clarity for payment system licences in China. Alibaba also sought significant governance rights in Ant Financial through board representation, so that the two companies' interests could be further aligned, which should benefit Alibaba's foreign investors.[152] However, China's fuzzy regulatory system seems inevitably to lead to over-complex legal manoeuvring like this, and consequent lack of clarity about investors' legal rights.

In the United States, regulators allow VIEs if their dangers are disclosed to investors. Although most VIE schemes have operated smoothly, the underlying risks of contract breaches remain. However, most Chinese companies listing in the United States are not subject to US law, as VIEs are generally incorporated in business-friendly countries such as the Cayman Islands. As a result, Chinese companies can act differently from regular US-listed firms. For example, while Sina holds a regular annual meeting, others do not. Baidu, the search engine giant, has not held an annual shareholder meeting since 2008. Online retailer JD.com has never held one. In October 2017, a spokesperson for JD.com said: 'Investors appreciate our candor both on earnings calls and in engagement throughout the year. This issue has rarely, if ever, been raised to us.'[153]

---

[150] Gregory J Millman, 'Alibaba's IPO Puts VIE Structure in the Spotlight' (*Wall Street Journal*, 2014) <https://blogs.wsj.com/riskandcompliance/2014/09/22/alibabas-ipo-puts-vie-structure-in-the-spotlight>. See also Yu-Hsin Lin and Thomas Mehaffy, 'Open Sesame: The Myth of Alibaba's Extreme Corporate Governance and Control' (2016) 10(2) *Brooklyn Journal of Corporate, Financial & Commercial Law* 437.

[151] Mariko Tai, 'Alibaba to Buy 33% of Spinoff Ant Financial' (*Nikkei Asia*, 2 February 2018) <https://asia.nikkei.com/Asia300/Alibaba-to-buy-33-of-spinoff-Ant-Financial>.

[152] Ibid.

[153] Stevenson, 'US Investor Tries to Shake Up Sina' (n 144).

The fuzzy legal structure clearly makes it hard for shareholders to keep track of VIEs. Nevertheless, there is some obvious mutual benefit for the Chinese government and for technology executives in maintaining such a situation. When in doubt, technology executives simply need to say: 'Chinese regulations prohibit me acting otherwise.' An *Economist* article in September 2017 surveyed 10 VIE companies and noted:

> The inner workings of the VIEs are often in flux. In nine cases, their structure has changed in that period: either the names or number of entities, or the names or stakes of their Chinese owners, have been altered. If they are being honest, most shareholders have little idea what is going on.[154]

In other words, Chinese tech firms receive the benefits of foreign investment without giving up effective control over their operations.

There remains a public interest in economic development and Chinese innovation (as examined in the next chapter) and developing the internet rapidly is an essential prerequisite. On the Chinese government side, China's 2010 Internet White Paper states that the internet must serve the interests of both the economy and the state.[155] The Chinese government is also acutely aware of the legitimising role of VIEs and US IPOs in the long-term success of Chinese technology companies. In an article in the *Huffington Post* Lu Wei, former director of the State Internet Information Office,[156] wrote in a piece entitled 'Cyber Sovereignty Must Rule Global Internet':

> The US is the main overseas IPO destination for Chinese internet companies, almost 50 of which are listed in the US with a total market value of nearly US$500 billion. US shareholders have benefited from the development of the internet market in China. Not long ago, the IPO of Alibaba in the US, the largest IPO ever in the world, raised over US $25 billion. Experts believe that the investments made by US shareholders in Alibaba demonstrates they have great confidence in the Chinese internet, the Chinese market and the future of China.[157]

Nevertheless, VIEs are increasingly under pressure, as their legality has never been officially affirmed in China, and there are signs that

---

[154] 'A Legal Vulnerability at the Heart of China's Big Internet Firms' (n 129).
[155] See above n 7 and accompanying text.
[156] Now the Cyberspace Administration of China, as explained in Chapter 3.
[157] Lu Wei, 'Cyber Sovereignty Must Rule Global Internet' (*Huffington Post*, 15 December 2014) <https://www.huffingtonpost.com/lu-wei/china-cyber-sovereignty_b_6324060.html>.

the government wishes to make them subject to formal foreign investment rules.

2.3 The End of VIEs or a False Alarm?

On 19 January 2015, the State Council issued a discussion draft of legislation setting out planned rules that would overhaul the outdated Chinese foreign investment legal regime. The Draft Foreign Investment Law[158] contained 170 articles divided into 11 chapters. The underlying philosophy of the draft law was explained in an accompanying explanation published at the same time. The explanation made it clear that one of the purposes of the new law was to include VIEs or similar structures within the definition of foreign investors, so that they would no longer be able to evade prohibitions on investing in specific Catalogue sectors. At the time, the draft law was expected to be passed in 2017.

The official explanation of the Draft Foreign Investment Law also made it clear that VIEs' sole function is to escape Chinese legal requirements.[159] It clearly stated that such evasive practices are illegal and will be prohibited upon the proposed law becoming effective. In response to the draft law, a 2015 draft regulation from the Ministry of Commerce appeared and proposed to ban some VIEs, but this regulation would not receive final approval. By 2015, annual reports of the 10 largest firms that use VIEs all admitted to uncertainty about their status.[160]

Clearly there is a conflict between foreign investor influence through VIEs, offshore ownership structures and international venture capital funding of Chinese start-ups, and the Chinese government's Network Sovereignty and information control agenda. The 2015 Draft Foreign Investment Law and draft regulations show an obvious intention to rein in this sector. Yet the fact that these drafts were not approved and implemented points to an internal conflict of interest within the Chinese government itself, a recognition in some quarters that the VIE structure does bring the financial benefits of foreign capital without the

---

[158] 《中华人民共和国外国投资法（草案征求意见稿）》 [Foreign Investment Law of the People's Republic of China (Opinion-Seeking Draft)] (People's Republic of China) Ministry of Commerce, 19 January 2015 (Draft Foreign Investment Law).

[159] Steve Dickinson, 'China VIEs Are Dead. Done. Over. Stick a Fork in Them' (*China Law Blog*, 22 January 2015) <http://www.chinalawblog.com/2015/01/china-vies-are-dead-done-over-stick-a-fork-in-them.html>.

[160] 'A Legal Vulnerability at the Heart of China's Big Internet Firms' (n 129).

necessity for Chinese entrepreneurs to give up management control. It also suggests that the government is aware of the economic risks of its proposed reforms.

2.3.1 Future Legal Implications and Risks

The total value of the companies that use VIEs has soared as China's internet industry has boomed, but for foreign investors, there are two risks. First, the Chinese companies that set up VIEs could be deemed to be foreign-invested enterprises under the proposed legal reform, and prohibited from engaging in internet business unless they unwind their contracts with foreign holding companies. Foreign investors would be left with no access to the Chinese companies' value-creating business assets.[161] Second, even without implementing the proposed legal reform, there is a danger that Chinese company manager-controllers will spin off profitable assets to separate companies outside the VIE framework. With Sina and Alibaba there were high-profile precedents (described in Section 2.2.4) where shareholders were forced to accept that these companies do not operate as US corporate entities and valuable intellectual property could be removed from the VIEs' grasp without adequate financial compensation.

In both situations, foreign investors would need to enforce their VIE contracts against the Chinese companies in Chinese courts. That could be difficult, as the use of the VIE structure as a vehicle for foreign investment has never been formally approved by the Chinese government.

At the other extreme, it is possible that China could ultimately relax its foreign-ownership restrictions on the internet sector and open its capital account, allowing both foreigners and locals to directly buy shares of internet firms with a solid legal footing.

Yet neither of these opposite scenarios is likely to happen in the near future, for several reasons. First, under President Xi Jinping's leadership, control of ideology has been tightened, and the internet is viewed as a key information platform that must remain firmly under Chinese government supervision (Chapter 3). For this reason, there is no indication that

---

[161] See Shi, 'Dragon's House of Cards' (n 128); Chris Russell, 'Rules of the Game: Changes in China's Foreign Investment Law' (*CKGSB Knowledge*, 1 September 2014) <https://english.ckgsb.edu.cn/knowledges/rules-of-the-game-changes-in-chinas-foreign-investment-law/>.

direct foreign ownership of Chinese internet firms will occur in the foreseeable future.

Second, if one of the major internet firms reneged on its VIE contracts, the impact on foreign investor confidence in the Chinese market would be drastic, possibly leading to foreign capital suddenly drying up for numerous Chinese corporations. As noted earlier, the Chinese government is keenly aware of the fundamental role played by foreign investment in many sectors of the Chinese economy. Third, the delay in implementing the Draft Foreign Investment Law and recent government attempts to provide a compromise solution for existing VIEs suggests that fuzzy logic lawmaking is still alive and well in the Chinese technology sector.

Instead of drastic changes to the current tacitly permitted system, therefore, the Chinese government has recently introduced a mix of incentives to encourage Chinese internet firms gradually to unwind their VIE structures and become fully domesticated Chinese corporations.

2.4 China Unable to Lure the Champions Home: 2018

By setting up new boards for high-tech small and medium enterprises on the Shenzhen Stock Exchange, and streamlining the listing process, the Chinese government has made it attractive for smaller internet firms to buy back all their shares and de-list in the United States, then re-list in mainland China.[162] Many of these firms already had difficulties meeting the stringent disclosure and accounting requirements of US exchanges, and would prefer to access the growing pool of venture capital investors in China.

However, the cost of completing such a buyback would be prohibitive for the biggest firms such as Alibaba and Tencent. Their CEOs also appear to be unwilling to give up their overseas listings and dismantle their VIE structures. Clearly, they enjoy their listings in the United States as a mark of legitimacy or prestige, and as a reliable source of funding for both their Chinese and international operations, and possibly also for the added level of protection that it provides from Chinese government expropriation.

---

[162] Samuel Shen and Julie Zhu, 'Start-Ups Hopeful as China Readies Nasdaq-Style Tech Board' (*Reuters*, 6 January 2019) <https://www.reuters.com/article/us-china-markets-exchange-tech/start-ups-hopeful-as-china-readies-nasdaq-style-tech-board-idUSKCN1P00PA>.

These benefits make it worth their while to maintain their complex investment structures and juggle the interests of early-stage investors, institutional and retail investors all demanding profits, and the regulatory demands of US exchanges and the Chinese government.

What is interesting, and highly relevant, is that the Chinese government has apparently backed away from its initial blanket prohibition of foreign investment through VIEs, and is attempting to find a workable compromise with the major Chinese tech firms that maintains the current fuzzy logic approach. In March 2018, China's cabinet formally approved a framework to allow foreign-listed Chinese companies in strategic industries to bypass rules governing mainland IPOs, including bans on dual-class shares and VIEs.[163] They did so by creating a new listing mechanism known as China depositary receipts.

2.4.1 Maintaining the Fuzzy Logic: CDRs and the 2019 Foreign Investment Law

China Depositary Receipts

The China Securities Regulatory Commission created China depositary receipts (CDRs) specifically to provide a way for mainland Chinese investors to trade securities in these large overseas-listed Chinese companies without requiring the companies to de-list from US exchanges or unwind their VIE structures.

Depositary receipts, which were first created in the 1920s in the United States, involve usually foreign companies depositing stocks (ie, shares) from their primary market listing with a bank, which then issues securitised receipts of these stocks in a second market. The depositary receipts are traded in the currency of the second market (ie, US dollars if in New York). The benefit to US investors is that they can buy an interest in a foreign company that tracks the company's share price and is traded in New York, without the complications of foreign currency transactions and overseas investment rules. The foreign company also benefits by being able to raise money in the United States without having to give up its foreign listing.[164]

---

[163] See Hui (Robin) Huang, Wei Zhang and Kelvin Siu Cheung Lee, 'The (Re)introduction of Dual-Class Share Structures in Hong Kong: A Historical and Comparative Analysis', *Journal of Corporate Law Studies* (24 December 2019), <https://ssrn.com/abstract=3245885>.

[164] CDRs were to track the prices of the shares in their primary markets, the same format as the American Depositary Receipts (ADR). See G Andrew Karolyi, 'The Role of American

In China, CDRs were billed as a similar type of financial instrument aimed at letting local Chinese investors partake in the financial rewards of technology behemoths, most of which are listed offshore. Alibaba, Xiaomi and JD.com were expected to be the first companies to make secondary listings on the mainland.[165]

Nevertheless, by August 2018 the Securities Regulatory Commission had removed CDRs from the available financial instruments in China's listing regime.[166] The likely reasons for this sudden backtracking include the fact that domestic listings for the largest technology companies had threatened to swallow up a large portion of the liquidity in China's capital markets.[167] At the same time, the poor reception of mobile phone maker Xiaomi's Hong Kong 2018 IPO sparked fears that investors were falling out of love with Chinese tech companies. Reportedly, they were not convinced that Xiaomi had a well-defined business model and Xiaomi's IPO shrunk from an expected $10 billion to $4.72 billion in late June 2018.[168] The commission then suspended Xiaomi's planned listing of CDRs in Shanghai.[169]

While it is too early to say whether the CDR experiment will succeed or not, the key issue of relevance is that the Chinese government has shown willingness to compromise with major tech firms, rather than insisting on them dismantling their VIE structures due to ideologically motivated prohibitions on foreign investment in the internet sector. In early 2021, Chinese tech companies including Baidu again began to utilise CDRs for Chinese listings.

Depositary Receipts in the Development of Emerging Equity Markets' (2004) 86(3) *Review of Economics and Statistics* 670.

[165] Baidu, Tencent, Ctrip.com, Weibo, Netease and Sunny Optical were cited as other potential candidates: see Qu Yunxu, Liu Caiping and Han Wei, 'Alibaba, JD.com on Fast Track for Homecoming' (*Caixin Global*, 22 March 2018) <https://www.caixinglobal.com/2018-03-22/alibaba-jdcom-on-fast-track-for-homecoming-101224491.html>.

[166] This began as a temporary halt while market conditions were unfavourable.

[167] Fiona Lau and Julie Zhu, 'China's Xiaomi Raises $4.72 Billion after Pricing HK IPO at Bottom of Range: Sources' (*Reuters*, 29 June 2018) <https://www.reuters.com/article/us-xiaomi-ipo/chinas-xiaomi-raises-4-72-billion-after-pricing-hk-ipo-at-bottom-of-range-sources-idUSKBN1JP0EC>.

[168] Ibid.

[169] Shidong Zhang, 'China's Regulator Quietly Removes Capital-Sapping CDRs as It Vows Reforms to Soothe Frayed Nerves' (*South China Morning Post*, 9 August 2018) <https://www.scmp.com/business/china-business/article/2158953/chinas-regulator-quietly-removes-capital-sapping-cdrs-it>.

THE EXTENT OF FUZZY LOGIC 55

At the same time, high-profile Chinese tech companies continue to apply to list in the United States using VIE structures. According to *China Money Network*'s China Unicorn Ranking, there were (as of July 2018) 139 unicorns[170] in China worth a total of US$480 billion.[171] Certainly, there are increasing numbers of domestic IPOs for these companies, as Chinese regulators have eased the domestic listing process.[172] However, high-profile start-ups such as e-commerce rising star Pinduoduo[173] is listed as a VIE and TikTok parent company Bytedance is still pursuing listing as VIE in the United States.[174]

Pinduoduo is also interesting because it reflects another theme of this book: the connections between the Chinese and global technology ecosystems. The company's founder, Colin Huang, is a former Google employee. Pinduoduo is the e-commerce market leader in rural China, where it overtook both Alibaba's Taobao marketplace and JD.com in 2018.

These new listings suggest that even recent Chinese start-ups were not fazed by the fuzzy legality of VIEs. Rather they embrace the VIE structure as both a source of and a cloak for foreign capital. The entrepreneurs obtain not just foreign financial capital but 'reputational capital' that they can use in China to prove that their business is internationally competitive and therefore should be protected from interference by the Chinese government.

The 2019 Foreign Investment Law

As a further indication that the Chinese government has decided to maintain the fuzzy approach of the past, in March 2019 China finally

---

[170] A unicorn is an unlisted tech company worth at least US$1 billion.
[171] 'China Money Network's China Unicorn Ranking' (*China Money Network*, July 2018) <https://www.chinamoneynetwork.com/china-unicorn-ranking>.
[172] For example, by allowing for dual listings.
[173] Pinduoduo (拼多多 – *pīnduōduō*; literally piece together more and more), China's 'Facebook-Groupon mashup', filed for an IPO on the Nasdaq in 2018 within three years of its founding. During 2018, Pinduoduo became China's second most popular e-commerce company, after Alibaba but ahead of JD.com, as measured by its user base of 344 million people. Pinduoduo integrates with WeChat and gamifies mass online shopping in bulk. See Iris Ouyang, 'Pinduoduo, China's Facebook-Groupon Mashup, Files for $1B US IPO' (*Pandaily*, 1 July 2018) <https://pandaily.com/pinduoduo-chinas-facebook-groupon-mashup-files-for-1b-us-ipo>.
[174] One likely reason is that Toutiao's TikTok, a music video platform and social network launched in September 2016 (known as *Douyin* in China), is a global operation. Reports have emerged constantly in early 2021 that a US IPO was imminent.

approved the amended Foreign Investment Law,[175] which removed all references in the 2015 Draft Law (cited in Section 2.3) that would have defined VIEs as 'foreign investment', rendering them illegal.[176] While not explicitly permitting VIEs, the government has clearly decided in typical fuzzy fashion not to outlaw the VIE structure as a vehicle for foreign investment. Observers, including lawyers practising in China, noted that this will freeze the issue of the illegality or legality of VIEs for at least another few years. Zhang Biwang, a partner at Allbright Law Offices in Shanghai, observed: 'To some extent, it shows the government easing concerns over VIEs – but they still care about who's the ultimate controller of the company.' Another commentator argued that, as long as the controller of the company remains a Chinese citizen, 'the government won't shut their eyes and ignore reality to make the companies give up VIEs'.[177] It would appear that as long as a Chinese national is in ultimate control of large internet firms, foreign capital can continue to flow into VIEs.

This strengthens and ultimately evidences the arguments in this chapter, and more broadly supports the arguments in the main body of this book, that a similar kind of fuzzy approach will be used to allow the development of AI in China through selective enforcement of data localisation provisions in China's Cyber Security Law. The time lag between the draft for discussion and final Foreign Investment Laws extended from January 2015 to March 2019. China's Cyber Security Law has also faced a similar and ongoing delay in explaining key terms. This is emblematic of the flexibility of key terms and consultation periods in 'fuzzy logic' Chinese jurisprudence. Yet geopolitical forces have swayed the fuzzy logic regulatory pendulum towards Network Sovereignty considerations in 2019–2021. This has affected overseas market listings.

2.5 US Blacklistings in 2019–2020: Are VIEs Still Relevant?

Being US-listed via the medium of the VIE structure provides a powerful cloak of legitimacy in that it gives Chinese tech companies some

---

[175] «中华人民共和国外国投资法» [Foreign Investment Law of the People's Republic of China] (People's Republic of China) Ministry of Commerce, 15 March 2019 (Foreign Investment Law).

[176] See art 14 of the 2015 Draft Foreign Investment Law (n 158), noting especially art 14.6. In comparison, art 2 of the 2019 Foreign Investment Law (n 175) removes references to VIEs.

[177] Venus Feng, 'World's Most Valuable Startup Is Home to a Complex Fortune' (*Bloomberg*, 24 March 2018) <https://www.bloomberg.com/news/articles/2019-03-24/the-complex-fortune-growing-inside-world-s-most-valuable-startup>.

regulatory acceptance and stakeholders outside China. It is generally assumed that Chinese tech firms must engage in some content control for the Chinese government.[178] These obligations are unclear and outsiders will never truly know what conversations about censorship take place behind closed doors. As one venture capitalist on the China team of one of the world's most famous venture capital firms told me: 'China is opaque, we just do not know exactly what is taking place. Maybe the summation of your research is simply that. China is opaque.'[179]

However, allowing for a certain degree of self-censorship, the VIE structure still provides China's tech companies more financial and political leeway to avoid being wholly under the thumb of the Chinese government, and gives them negotiating room when responding to new policies that impact their businesses.

This leeway is important in that internet companies are globalised in a way that is unique among Chinese industries.

> In this era of global cooperative capitalism, businesses are no longer centralized vertically-integrated entities, but decentralized networks. If a new law is to be effective it must somehow deal with complicated jurisdictional and ownership issues where accountability is often murky.[180]

The complications in turn provide room for these firms to manoeuvre.

The history of the VIE legal structure is now especially relevant for the future of AI in China in the face of concerns over cyber security and Network Sovereignty. AI companies, like the major internet firms, cannot be isolated islands but must remain connected to the global entrepreneurial system, including the investor interests they represent, in order to flourish and bring benefits to Chinese society. This is how the VIE was designed, almost by default. It is a makeshift-turned-enduring public–private attempt to balance state control with access to foreign capital and expertise for economic development, a legal experiment that remains ensconced in a certain predetermined fuzzy logic.

Nevertheless, Chinese AI firms that have focused on the ethically murky area of facial recognition have had no choice but to list in China, due to the sensitivity of their product offerings leading to US

---

[178] Self-censorship by Baidu, Tencent and others is explained further in Chapters 5–7.
[179] Interview with venture capitalist at a Chinese venture capital firm (telephone, 12 August 2017).
[180] Richard A Spinello, 'Google in China: Corporate Responsibility on a Censored Internet' in Alfreda Dudley, James Braman and Giovanni Vincenti (eds), *Investigating Cyber Law and Cyber Ethics Issues, Impacts and Practices* (IGI Global 2011) 244.

government trade blacklisting (US Entity List) of Chinese image recognition and other technology companies, which have continued unabated since 2019.

For example, on October 2019, Beijing-based AI unicorn Megvii (also known by its product Face++) was among 28 Chinese public security bureaus and companies put on the US Entity List over alleged human rights violations in assisting government surveillance of China's minority Muslim Uighurs in Xinjiang Autonomous Region.[181] Megvii is one of China's 'most high-profile AI startups because its facial scan software helps power the Ministry of Public Security's database of about 1.3 billion Chinese people'.[182] Megvii and its facial recognition market competitors SenseTime, Yitu and CloudWalk are collectively recognised as the 'Four AI Dragons' for their image recognition market dominance in China and their funding from high-profile investors, including overseas investors.[183] Yet the AI Dragons are highly controversial outside their home market. In 2019, Megvii, Yitu and SenseTime were all added to the US Entity List for their alleged roles in enabling the government's mass surveillance of the Muslim minority groups in Xinjiang. CloudWalk was subsequently added to the blacklist in 2020 and cut off from its US suppliers, including the powerful computing chips needed to process AI computations (see Chapter 8).

In this climate, in January 2021 Megvii publicly announced plans to list CDRs on the Shanghai Stock Exchange Star Market (Science and Technology Innovation Board) (Shanghai Star Market) in 2021, according to a notice posted by the China Securities Regulatory Commission.[184] In 2019, China established the 'Nasdaq-style' stock exchange, the Shanghai Star Market, to attract high-growth, as yet

---

[181] See US Department of Commerce, Bureau of Industry and Security, Addition of Certain Entities to the Entity List, A Rule by the Industry and Security Bureau on 10/09/2019 (10 September 2019) <https://www.federalregister.gov/documents/2019/10/09/2019-22210/addition-of-certain-entities-to-the-entity-list>. Companies added to the list include telecoms equipment giants Huawei and ZTE Corp over sanction violations and surveillance camera maker Hikvision.

[182] Sarah Dai, 'This Beijing Hub Is Home to 10 Major AI Labs Driving China's Tech Ambitions'(*South China Morning Post*, 8 February 2019) <https://www.scmp.com/tech/big-tech/article/2184987/beijing-hub-home-10-major-ai-labs-driving-chinas-tech-ambitions>.

[183] These companies are all discussed in Chapter 9.

[184] The filing can be found here in Chinese: «关于 Megvii Technology Limited 公开发行存托凭证并在科创板上市 之辅导基本情况表» [CITIC Securities Co., Ltd. Notice about Megvii Technology Limited Public Issuance of Depositary Receipts and Listing on the Science and Technology Innovation Board] China Securities Regulatory Commission, 29 September 2020 <http://www.csrc.gov.cn/pub/beijing/bjfdqyxx/bjfdqyjbqk/202101/P020210112533742962617.pdf>.

unprofitable Chinese tech start-ups after losing them to the United States as VIEs for 20 years.[185]

According to the notice, Megvii plans to issue CDRs on the Shanghai Star Market. Yet it also suggests that Megvii has not ruled out listing outside mainland China, perhaps awaiting a change in policy direction under the Biden administration in 2021.[186] In addition, as is explained in Chapters 8–9, global tech ecosystems remain heavily interconnected. Megvii's investors include renowned Australian banking firm Macquarie Group as well as Alibaba, Ant Financial and the Bank of China.[187]

No doubt, in the current geopolitical milieu those AI companies that have sensitive products, and an increasing number of tech companies more generally, will list in Hong Kong and on Shanghai's Star Market. This will apply especially to those that rely for their initial revenue on government contracts (pilot petri dishes) to test new products such as facial recognition for public security, thus rendering them subject to the United States–China technology trade war blacklists.

2.6 Conclusion: Still Too Big to Fail

So is a VIE legal or illegal? No one has really been certain since its inception in 2000. The Chinese government has never explicitly answered this question through enacted legislation, including the 2019 Foreign Investment Law. The VIE therefore truly depicts the extent of fuzzy logic in the Chinese legal and regulatory system, and this manifestly imperfect, paradoxical system has endured for two decades.

---

[185] Rita Liao, 'China Opens Nasdaq-Style Board to Lure Tech Firms Back Home' (*TechCrunch*, 13 June 2019) <https://techcrunch.com/2019/06/13/china-new-tech-board/>.

[186] As of March 2021, six high-profile Chinese tech companies had plans to list on stock markets in Shanghai and Hong Kong: Megvii, Bilibili, Tencent Music, Lenovo, Vipshop and Joy. Kuaishou, a video-sharing application similar to TikTok, listed in Hong Kong in February 2021. Five would be secondary listings. Lenovo, listed in Hong Kong, plans to issue CDRs on the Shanghai STAR market. Short-video app Bilibili, listed on the NASDAQ, has confidentially filed for a secondary listing in Hong Kong. Music streaming company Tencent Music, online discount sales website Vipshop and Joyy, a company that owns the video-based social media platform YY, are also seeking secondary listings in Hong Kong later in 2021. Tencent Music and Vipshop are listed on NYSE and Joyy was listed on NASDAQ. See Frida Qi, 'Tech Companies Prepare for Jumbo IPO Season in Hong Kong and Shanghai' (*SupChina*, 15 January 2021) <https://supchina.com/2021/01/15/tech-companies-prepare-for-jumbo-ipo-season-in-hong-kong-and-shanghai/>.

[187] Crunchbase: 'Megvii' (*Crunchbase*) <https://www.crunchbase.com/organization/megvii-technology/company_financials/>.

Entrepreneurs understand this fuzzy logic intuitively, while admitting the uncertainty:

> Few legal experts think that VIEs are about to collapse, but few expect them to endure, either. One sizeable investor admits loving Chinese tech firms' businesses while feeling queasy about their legal structures. Like scientists appalled by their monstrous creations, even the lawyers who designed VIEs worry. They are 'China's version of too-big-to-fail', says one.[188]

However, in 2021 a domestic float is now increasingly appealing to Chinese firms. Dual listings on multiple markets will likely be a new trend though, with one listing in China and one abroad, perhaps still in the United States. Megvii may, in time, still pursue this course for the reasons outlined in this chapter, as per their notice posted by the China Securities Regulatory Commission in January 2021.

Ant Group's delayed dual-listing IPO on the Shanghai Star Market and Hong Kong Stock Exchanges, at the end of 2020, must also be briefly noted here, simply because of its high profile and because it seemed mystifying to outsiders. Criticisms of Chinese regulators require perspective. While the swift timing just prior to the IPO was unfortunate, there was apparently a justifiable regulatory explanation – namely reporting irregularities due to recently released draft regulations requiring fintech platforms to provide higher funding to back loans and to cap loan size to borrowers.[189] As the largest revenue stream for Ant Financial is not payments but online lending,[190] the rules around this industry will likely develop further in 2021, in sync with this IPO. The new rules could significantly change Ant Group's profitability and risk profile. The delay may in time prove to be another example of fuzzy logic regulation in action, as delaying the Ant Group IPO may evidence the Chinese regulators' desire to improve banking rules for consumers.[191] This will be a key story to follow in the future.

---

[188] 'A Legal Vulnerability at the Heart of China's Big Internet Firms' (n 129).

[189] See Yuanyuan Pan, 'The Long-Term Implications of Ant Group's Delayed IPO' (*The Diplomat*, 20 November 2020) <https://thediplomat.com/2020/11/the-long-term-implications-of-ant-groups-delayed-ipo/>.

[190] The filing can be found here: 'Application Proof of Ant Group Co, LTD. Technology Limited' «螞蟻科技集團股份有限公司» (*Stock Exchange of Hong Kong Limited*, 27 October 2020) <https://www1.hkexnews.hk/listedco/listconews/sehk/2020/1026/2020102600165.pdf>.

[191] Owned by Jack Ma, the *South China Morning Post* produced a measured editorial in November 2020: see 'Delay to Ant IPO shows Beijing's Desire to Get the Rules Right' (*South China Morning Post*, 10 November 2020) <https://www.scmp.com/comment/opinion/article/3109261/delay-ant-ipo-small-price-pay-getting-new-rules-right>.

Further, on 30 June 2021, Didi Chuxing, China's ride-hailing giant, listed on the Nasdaq, and on 2 July 2021, the Chinese government introduced new draft regulations, mandating cyber security reviews to ensure the safety of user data before Chinese tech companies are allowed to IPO overseas, while also investigating Didi Chuxing's data-handling practices. In mid-2021 the policy contradictions outlined in this book again collided, perhaps signalling the end of VIEs. The Didi Chuxing cyber security review investigation will be another key story to follow in 2021–2022 and beyond. The amended cyber security review regime will probably remain fluid and fuzzy, as the legality of VIEs have for decades.

In the next chapter the broader policy context within which Chinese tech firms must operate today is outlined. This will provide a detailed account of Network Sovereignty as China's central policy for controlling its cyber borders and networks, and the potential conflict between the localising demands of China's 2016 Cyber Security Law and the need for innovative Chinese firms to build links with the global research and business community.

While these laws and policies superficially appear to stifle those international linkages in the name of national security, the vagueness of their wording and the prior example of VIEs suggests that a legislative fuzzy logic is once again at work, leaving innovative firms with room to manoeuvre.

In subsequent chapters, it is argued that the long-term success of Chinese AI firms – like the major internet firms (the so-called BATs) previously – is so important to the government's economic agenda, fuzzy compromises will be made to encourage those firms to continue growing their businesses relatively unimpeded by bureaucratic restrictions. In the current climate, though, some firms operating even one product offering in sensitive areas such as public security may need to focus exclusively on the domestic Chinese market for the time being.

3

China's Cyber Policies

Conflict between Innovation and Restriction

> A plethora of new internal Party leadership groups has taken shape in the areas of foreign affairs, economic reform, and Internet security. Their shared feature is Xi Jinping at the apex.
> —Carl Minzner, Professor of Chinese Law, Fordham Law School[192]

In the previous chapter we saw how 'fuzzy logic' operates to blur the distinction between legal and illegal in relation to the corporate structures of China's tech companies. This example was selected to highlight the extent of fuzzy logic in China. It also demonstrated the contradiction between the encouragement to innovate and the legal restrictions that entrepreneurs must navigate.

This chapter builds on the understanding of fuzzy logic regulatory practice, but re-focuses on the main topic of the book: the policy contradictions between the emergence of a seemingly more restrictive cyber regime in China since 2014 and simultaneous announcements of new top-down policies for encouraging entrepreneurial activities. It argues that China's data and cyber security laws cannot be understood without first understanding the Chinese government's Informatisation drive (which includes the Internet Plus policy).

In other words, this chapter documents the conflicting demands of retaining national control while promoting world-leading innovation.

3.1 Internet Plus versus Network Sovereignty

China's first internet white paper, published in 2010, described the internet's 'irreplaceable role in accelerating the development of the national economy'.[193] Building on this, the Government Work Report that Premier Li Keqiang delivered to the National People's Congress in

---

[192] Carl Minzner, *End of an Era: How China's Authoritarian Revival Is Undermining Its Rise* (Oxford University Press, 2018) 29.
[193] Internet White Paper (n 7).

March 2015 announced a new term for information technology policy: Internet Plus. The intention for this action plan is to 'integrate mobile internet, big data, cloud computing and the Internet of Things' to modernise traditional industries.[194] It is the latest iteration of a broader strategy to build China into a strong internet country (网络强国 – *wangluo qiangguo*). There has been political analysis of this phrase by Western commentators, arguing that China wants to be an internet hegemon.[195] That may be true in part, but another major directive of Internet Plus (literally internet + industry) is to reform the inefficiencies in the public sector (such as China's SOEs).

In addition, Chinese officials are increasingly promoting a policy known as Informatisation (explained in Section 3.2.1), which aims to connect industry online and to use technology to improve efficiency and tackle economic developmental problems in China. Internet Plus is part of that overall drive.

However, Internet Plus is just one element of the complex collection of Chinese laws and policies that apply to new technologies. In particular, a raft of recent laws has been introduced under the rubric of the policy of Network Sovereignty (网络主权 – *wangluo zhuquan*), which reflects the Chinese government's intention to assert national control over the internet. The tension between these laws and the Internet Plus strategy raises significant questions, including how the new laws will affect China's ability to attract foreign tech firms to invest in China, as well as its ability to hire globally trained talent and, importantly, encourage technology transfers. Will the new laws slow China's technological development, especially its vision to create Smart Cities and become a world leader in AI?

3.2 Internet Plus

Internet Plus is a policy which proposes that China must connect the latest internet technologies to industry. In other words, China must apply new technological advances to conventional industries, including initiatives to support Smart Cities, big data, IoT and AI. These initiatives aim to raise productivity by providing the connectivity to make businesses (eg, e-commerce, industrial networks and internet banking) and government more efficient.[196]

---

[194] «2015 年政府工作报告» [2015 Government Work Report] (n 8).
[195] See, eg, Ahmed and Weber, 'China's Long Game in Techno-Nationalism' (n 11).
[196] 'China Headlines' (n 6).

Again, the Internet Plus policy introduced in 2015 promotes the idea of a vast array of technology deployments being utilised for Chinese development. Essentially, it states that mobile internet, cloud computing, big data and/or IoT should be added to existing industries (eg, e-commerce, industrial networks and internet banking), fostering new industries and business development. The Internet Plus policy also declares that an important objective is to provide an open and shared innovation platform by dissolving the barriers that restrict innovation for entrepreneurs. Finally, as Internet Plus is a national Chinese policy, governments in different regions of China and at various levels are expected to play a leading role in establishing an efficient ecosystem for applying the policy and developing industrial parks and incubators for Internet Plus-driven enterprises.

3.2.1 Background to Internet Plus: China's Informatisation Strategy

China's Internet Plus policy is just one part of the broader Informatisation strategy, and must be seen against that background. The strategy has been mentioned in Chinese policy documents since the early 1990s and its stated goal is to build an 'information society'.[197] In Chinese, the characters for informatisation strategy, 信息化战略 (*xinxihua zhanlue*), literally mean 'the force for transformative change 化 [*hua*] that information can provide'. This sounds much less technocratic than the literal translation into English. The Chinese government's intention is therefore best understood as the transformation of an economy and society driven by ICT. Although upgrading networks and other technical requirements for the development of the internet is part of this broader strategy,[198] the Chinese government has often used 'Informatisation' interchangeably with other terms – including the information society, knowledge economy and e-development – some of which overlap with Internet Plus, whereas others are much broader in scope.[199]

---

[197] See Nagy K Hanna and Christine Zhen-Wei Qiang, 'China's Emerging Informatization Strategy' (2010) 1(2) *Journal of the Knowledge Economy* 128.

[198] See ibid 129.

[199] '[Informatization] covers the enablers of the knowledge economy and the application of information and communication technology (ICT) to government, business, and society. They identify the challenges facing government, business, and rural informatization, the growing digital divide between rural and urban areas and the innovations pursued to bridge this divide': ibid 162.

There are two contrasting views among Western China scholars about the impact of Informatisation. The more optimistic view is expressed by Greg Austin. In his 2014 book, *Cyber Policy in China*, Austin traced the evolution of China's Informatisation strategy since 2000,[200] and predicted that the increasing information flows in China constitute an inexorable force that can only diminish government censorship. At the time of Austin's writing, the global linkages connecting China's innovation ecosystem to the outside world were mainly limited to investment and venture capital (described in Chapter 2). Today those linkages are increasingly dense, as demonstrated in Chapters 8–9, which may suggest greater foreign commercial influence in China. However, Austin's predictions about a reduction in censorship have so far not been fulfilled. The other view, exemplified by the work of legal scholar Carl Minzner, suggests that the datasets obtained through Informatisation will be used for more restrictive governance. Many observers besides Minzner consider China to be becoming more tightly controlled under President Xi, assisted by greater access to advanced data-gathering tools.[201]

These two ways of understanding the Informatisation strategy are reflected in the similar conflict between Internet Plus and Network Sovereignty. To explain the impact of these policies and how they might interact, more detail on the recent evolution of China's cyber institutions needs be set out.

3.3 China's Cyber Institutions

In 2014 the central government formed the Cyber Security and Informatisation Leading Small Group[202] and its administrative arm, the Cyberspace Administration of China (CAC).[203] This was a critical moment in the development of China's overall strategy and institutional approach to the problems of cyber security and Informatisation. It signified that President Xi Jinping was taking a personal supervisory role over ICT policy and the regulatory process. This centralisation has provided much of the impetus for legal and institutional developments in these policy areas since 2014.

---

[200] Greg Austin, *Cyber Policy in China* (Polity Press, 2014).
[201] See Minzner, *End of an Era* (n 192).
[202] The new leading group largely merged the membership of the previous two leading bodies for online governance: the State Informatisation Leading Group and the State Network and Information Security Coordination Small Group.
[203] Chinese title: 国家互联网信息办公室 [CAC].

As part of this reform, the consolidation of internet regulatory bodies, such as the Central Leading Group for Cyberspace Affairs and the State Internet Information Office[204] (SIIO), represented a fundamental change from China's previous patchwork of online governance.[205] The Cyber Security and Informatisation Leading Small Group exerts ultimate authority over CAC, including taking responsibility for regulating online content.[206] The realisation of the Informatisation agenda was a central plank of this political and economic reform.

CAC's membership comprises two disparate groups: on the one hand, economic and technological policymakers, whose focus is innovation and development, and, on the other, bureaucracies more concerned with ideological and international security.[207] Therefore, CAC embodies the inherent conflict between Network Sovereignty and Informatisation. Inevitably, there are differing interests at stake, not least because of the contrasting backgrounds of its leading personnel. Prior to its establishment, a patchwork of ministries had authority over various aspects of telecommunications and the internet, and CAC continues to face a lot of bureaucratic hurdles in trying to centralise control over cyber security and (sometimes contradictory) Informatisation policies and regulation.

One example of the difficulties faced by CAC is Facebook's recent attempted entry into the Chinese market by registering a subsidiary company with the local authorities in Hangzhou on 24 July 2018,[208] only to be banned by CAC within 24 hours.[209] For several hours, a Chinese government database showed that Facebook had gained approval to open

---

[204] Chinese title: 中央网络安全和信息化领导小组 [SIIO].
[205] «习近平: 把我国从网络大国建设成为网络强国» ['Xi Jinping: Build Our Country from a Large Network Country into a Strong Network Country'] (*Xinhua*, 27 February 2014) <http://news.xinhuanet.com/politics/2014-02/27/c_119538788.htm>.
[206] «国务院关于授权国家互联网信息办公室负责互联网信息内容管理工作的通知国发» [Notice Concerning Empowering CAC to Be Responsible for Internet Information Content Management Work] (People's Republic of China) State Council, 26 August 2014. For an English translation see Rogier Creemers (ed), *China Copyright and Media* (26 August 2014) <https://chinacopyrightandmedia.wordpress.com/2014/08/26/notice-concerning-empowering-the-cyberspace-administration-of-china-to-be-responsible-for-internet-information-content-management-work>.
[207] Creemers, 'Cyber China' (n 23).
[208] 'Facebook Sets Up Subsidiary in China according to Filing' (*CNBC*, 25 July 2018) <https://www.cnbc.com/2018/07/24/facebook-sets-up-subsidiary-in-china-according-to-filing.html> (the link is no longer active).
[209] Paul Mozur, 'China Said to Quickly Withdraw Approval for New Facebook Venture' (*New York Times*, 25 July 2018) <https://www.nytimes.com/2018/07/25/business/facebook-china.html?emc=edit_mbau_20180725&nl=&nlid=8467969320180725&te=1>.

a subsidiary in the eastern province of Zhejiang. Facebook said it had planned to use the company to set up an innovation hub there. CAC was apparently unaware of the actions of the local authorities at the time, but swiftly asserted its authority.[210]

While regulatory gaps allowed for the rapid growth of China's internet giants (noted in Chapter 2), the government is clearly anxious to exert tight control over their business operations and use of information, and to restrict foreign influence over internet content in the face of dramatic technological change.[211] Chinese ICT expert Samm Sacks posited that: 'The senior political ranks in Beijing recognize that the government's ability to control, censor, and supervise the technology and the information it transmits has fallen behind and must now catch up. Essentially, the technology has gotten ahead of the government's ability to manage it.'[212]

At the same time, the positioning of CAC at the apex of China's leadership hierarchy means China's top leaders will be able to pursue fundamental reform of national internet regulations in line with those principles they view as most essential to China's future development. Placing internet regulations close to the leadership hierarchy may mean that the government's strong desire to promote invention and innovation and modernise its economy will receive a major boost. There is also the argument that, in light of China's top-down innovation policies, high-level 'e-leadership' such as that provided by CAC is necessary.

The centralised internet governance regime may also offer more clarity for companies, which have always faced the persistent fuzzy logic of China's legal system and the substantial discretion afforded administrative authorities to interpret laws in an ad hoc manner. Thus, if it is true that some of the criticism of China's legal system emanates from its perceived legislative vagueness,[213] it is also true that China is addressing

---

[210] Ibid.
[211] See Guosong Shao, *Internet Law in China* (Elsevier, 2012). See also Tain-Jy Chen and Ying-Hua Ku, 'Rent Seeking and Entrepreneurship: Internet Startups in China' (2016) 36(3) *Cato Journal* 659.
[212] Samm Sacks, 'Apple in China, Part I: What Does Beijing Actually Ask of Technology Companies?' (*Lawfare*, 22 February 2016) <https://www.lawfareblog.com/apple-china-part-i-what-does-beijing-actually-ask-technology-companies>.
[213] Scholars who have explained China's legislative vagueness in depth include Randall Peerenboom and Stanley Lubman. See, eg, Peerenboom, *China's Long March toward Rule of Law* (n 113); Peerenboom, *China Modernizes* (n 113); Stanley Lubman (ed), *China's Legal Reforms* (Oxford University Press, 1996); Stanley Lubman (ed), *The Evolution of Chinese Law Reform: An Uncertain Path* (Edward Elgar, 2012).

some of these concerns. While China's Network Sovereignty push and centralisation of the internet bureaucracy poses challenges for open global internet governance, it also may conceal 'something of a silver lining for global tech firms wishing to operate in China'.[214]

The Cyber Security Law authorises CAC as the bureaucracy in charge of cyber security matters.[215] Articles 50–53 state that CAC is the highest authority in this field.[216] Article 51, moreover, states that CAC is in charge of coordinating the relevant departments in matters involving cyber security.[217] Article 39 provides that the state network shall comprehensively coordinate relevant departments for various tasks such as inspections and technical support.[218]

In a Chinese-language report, the official Xinhua News Agency noted that CAC is also trying to reassure foreign companies that it will not compromise products and services, and that intellectual property is not in danger. Xinhua also noted that after the passing of the Cyber Security Law, CAC was drafting related guidelines on accessing online data, trying to ease concerns that the new Law opens the door for police abuse of power.[219] However, the law created fears among foreign businesses and industry commentators that it will impede their operations in the name of national security (see Chapters 4–6).

Those fears appeared to be confirmed when China subsequently created the Cyber Security Association of China (CSAC) (中国网络空间安全协会) in March 2016, which is an industry association controlled by the Chinese Communist Party. It further connects the major stakeholders in China's evolving cyber-governance regime: government, the private sector and researchers. CSAC also reflects President Xi's broader efforts to centralise power over China's cyber bureaucracy. Like many of these new institutions (and the Cyber Security Law itself) the organisation has very diverse goals. Its leadership and membership are also noteworthy:

---

[214] Scott Livingston, 'Beijing Touts "Cyber-Sovereignty" in Internet Governance: Global Technology Firms Could Mine Silver Lining' (*China Law Blog*, 19 February 2015) <http://www.chinalawblog.com/2015/02/beijing-touts-cyber-sovereignty-in-internet-governance-global-technology-firms-could-mine-silver-lining.html>.
[215] Cyber Security Law (n 2) art 23.
[216] Ibid art 50.
[217] Ibid art 51.
[218] Ibid art 39.
[219] «中央网信办: 正制定个人信息收集规范标准» [CAC: Establishing a Standard for Collecting Personal Information] (*Xinhua*, 11 November 2016) <http://news.xinhuanet.com/2016-11/11/c_1119897534.htm>.

inaugural chair, Fang Binxing (方滨兴), is known as the 'Father of the Great Firewall', China's internet censorship and surveillance system. Fang's selection as head of the association suggested a pro-Network Sovereignty orientation for CSAC, again worrying those who saw this as a move to introduce Network Sovereignty ideology into internet governance.[220]

CSAC consists of academic institutes, individuals and internet companies, including Alibaba and Tencent, and internet security companies such as Qihu 360;[221] altogether there are 257 founding members.[222] There were no non-Chinese representatives among CSAC's initial membership.[223] However, foreign tech companies are often consulted by these kinds of committees in China (discussed in Chapters 4–5), and CSAC's remit includes establishing industry standards, engaging with the international cyber security community and participating in international cooperation through conferences and comparative bodies.[224] In 2018, almost 40,000 cyber security professionals and other participants attended its annual conference.[225]

---

[220] On 27 December 2016, CAC published China's first National Cyberspace Security Strategy. See «国家网络空间安全战略» [National Cyberspace Security Strategy] (People's Republic of China) CAC, 27 December 2016 (National Cyberspace Security Strategy). The strategy offered few fresh initiatives, but summarised goals within the Cyber Security Law (n 2) and other regulations passed during the year prior. A guiding concept is 'Network Sovereignty' and the strategy emphasises the need to safeguard key information infrastructure operators.

[221] CSAC seemed to be an example of the pursuit of President Xi and his former chief cyber security deputy, Lu Wei (鲁炜), to align government, industry and academia around a shared set of cyber governance objectives. Lu Wei was seen as an evangelist for Network Sovereignty. He was later removed from his post in a graft scandal during 2016.

[222] Members included senior representatives from Alibaba, Chinese network security companies, and influential scientific universities and research institutes (eg, the Chinese Academy of Engineering and the Beijing University of Posts and Telecommunications): Nectar Gan, 'Father of China's Great Firewall to Lead New Cybersecurity Association' (*South China Morning Post*, 26 March 2016) <https://www.scmp.com/news/china/policies-politics/article/1930959/father-chinas-great-firewall-lead-new-cybersecurity>.

[223] Fang Binxing justified favouring Chinese companies over their (possibly) technologically more sophisticated foreign competitors on the grounds that they are more secure since they are bound by local government laws: see Samm Sacks and Robert O'Brien, 'What to Make of the Newly Established CyberSecurity Association of China' (*CSIS*, 25 May 2016) <https://www.csis.org/analysis/what-make-newly-established-cybersecurity-association-china>.

[224] 'Draft Law Strengthens China's Cyber Security Legislature' (*Tech 2*, 27 June 2016) <http://tech.firstpost.com/news-analysis/draft-law-strengthens-chinas-cyber-security-legislature-322671.html>.

[225] See 'ISC 360' (*ISC website*) <http://isc.360.cn/2018/en/index.html> (the link is no longer active).

Like CAC, CSAC exemplifies the contradictions in Chinese policies for Network Sovereignty and innovation. It is a body both for creating cyber security standards and for engaging with international stakeholders. This is important as China faces major cyber security threats. At the same time, its role is still unclear, and fears remain about its leadership's apparent focus on ideology over business development.

Yet, in contrast with the conflicting interests of the new cyber security administrative regime, the Internet Plus policy appears to offer a more open and straightforward vision of China's ICT development.

3.4 The Language of Internet Plus: Promoting Global Cooperation

As Internet Plus is a high-level strategy, it can only be understood by means of the policy documents which are intended to guide its implementation. The earliest policy documents aimed at implementing Internet Plus focused on achieving better government coordination. On 4 July 2015, the State Council released the Guiding Opinions on Actively Promoting the 'Internet Plus' Action Plan (Guiding Opinions).[226] In addition to detailed action plans, the Guiding Opinions set out general policy goals. The language of the Guiding Opinions seeks to describe everything Chinese technological development might need for its rapid progress, including 'openness of public data resources'.[227] The stated goals are that 'by 2025, a networked, intelligent, service-oriented and collaborative Internet plus industry ecological system ... a new economic pattern of the Internet Plus shall have been preliminarily formed, and the Internet Plus shall have become an important driver of the innovative economic and social development'.[228] 'Openness and sharing' and 'data sharing' are phrases used commonly throughout the Guiding Opinions.

---

[226] Guiding Opinions (n 9). The document, which includes general requirements and targets, detailed action plans and supportive policies, outlined 11 key Internet Plus actions, including: (1) entrepreneurship and innovation; (2) collaborative manufacturing; (3) modern agriculture; (4) smart energy; (5) inclusive finance; (6) public services; (7) efficient logistics; (8) e-commerce; (9) convenient transportation; (10) green ecology; and (11) AI (robotics).

[227] See ibid 'Basic Principles'.

[228] Ibid. The Guiding Opinions have a stated aim of achieving rapid, high-quality economic growth and industry development, taking advantage of China's scale and applications of the internet to drive comprehensive integration between the internet and the real economy.

In addition, the Guiding Opinions call for several relevant policies for start-up technology businesses. They include the following proposed changes to the policy environment: eliminating unreasonable mechanisms and policies, easing internet-integrated product and service market access, and promoting entrepreneurship and innovation. They also include government support for businesses through increased government procurement of cloud services, innovative credit products and services, and crowdfunding.

Also importantly, the Guiding Opinions include a strong push for globalising the Chinese tech sector. The goals include encouraging 'more [Chinese] Internet companies to increase their presence in the global market ... train[ing], and mak[ing] a better use of local and foreign talent ... provid[ing] finance support and tax incentives to key projects related to the Internet Plus plan, and encourag[ing] local governments to follow suit, while welcoming investors from home and abroad'.[229] This desire to attract foreign investors seems to echo the fuzzy logic of allowing foreign investment in technology VIEs, culminating in China's 2019 Foreign Investment Law (discussed in Chapter 2). Of course, this language of global cooperation would be less pronounced during 2019–2020, as global trade policy spot fires emerged around the world. However, in early 2021, as President Biden took office, President Xi Jinping defended 'multilateralism', using the term 11 times in his address at the World Economic Forum's annual meeting in Davos, Switzerland. He warned against any kind of 'cold war, hot war, trade war or tech war'.[230] This came after China proposed a 'Global Data Security Initiative' in September 2020, to create agreed global data security standards so that data could be used for enhanced global economic development.[231] Thus, the language of the Internet Plus strategy is permeated with statements extolling the benefits of openness and global cooperation. Yet this language is in stark contrast with that used in Network Sovereignty policies.

---

[229] See ibid art 5.

[230] See 'Full Text: Special Address by Chinese President Xi Jinping at the World Economic Forum Virtual Event of the Davos Agenda' (*Xinhua*, 25 January 2021) <http://www.xinhuanet.com/english/2021-01/25/c_139696610.htm>. A Chinese version can be found here: «习近平在世界经济论坛"达沃斯议程"对话会上的特别致辞» (*Xinhua*, 25 January 2021) <http://www.xinhuanet.com/politics/leaders/2021-01/25/c_1127023884.htm>.

[231] See Graham Webster and Paul Triolo (trans), 'Translation: China Proposes "Global Data Security Initiative"' (*New America*, 7 September 2020) <https://www.newamerica.org/cybersecurity-initiative/digichina/blog/translation-chinese-proposes-global-data-security-initiative/>.

3.5 Network Sovereignty

In contrast to the developments outlined in the previous section, during President Xi Jinping's early tenure, in 2014, cyber or Network Sovereignty emerged as a key policy concern. This policy emphasises the authority of a nation-state to regulate cyberspace. The fundamental principle of Network Sovereignty is that every country should be able to control information and data flows on the internet at their borders just as they do for other goods and services.[232]

While the Cyber Security Law is the centrepiece of Network Sovereignty, the policy is also reflected in a diverse array of other laws and policies (sometimes by default) covering the following:

- data localisation laws;[233]
- cloud server rules;[234]
- encryption rules;[235]
- bans on virtual private networks (VPNs);[236]
- bans on foreign anti-virus software;[237]
- bans on foreign Software as a Service (SaaS) software;[238]
- possible forced source code disclosures;[239] and
- potential rules requiring installation of 'backdoors' to servers.

---

[232] See 'China Releases First Strategy on Cyberspace Cooperation' (*Xinhua*, 1 March 2017) <http://news.xinhuanet.com/english/2017-03/01/c_136094734.htm>. See also Jinghan Zeng, Tim Stevens and Yaru Chen, 'China's Solution to Global Cyber Governance: Unpacking the Domestic Discourse of "Internet Sovereignty"' (2017) 45(3) *Politics and Policy* 432.
[233] Discussed in Chapter 5.
[234] Discussed in Chapter 5.
[235] Discussed in Chapter 5.
[236] VPN crackdowns are common and include the removal of VPNs from app stores.
[237] China has deployed policies of prohibiting SOEs from buying anti-virus software from companies such as the US firm Symantec and the Russian company Kaspersky Lab. See Charlie Osborne, 'China Excludes Symantec, Kaspersky Lab from Approved Anti-Virus Vendors' (*ZDnet*, 4 August 2014) <https://www.zdnet.com/article/china-excludes-symantec-kaspersky-lab-from-approved-anti-virus-vendors>.
[238] Software companies looking to sell SaaS in China often need to use either a reseller or licensee model, due to complex rules for obtaining a licence to sell software in China. This is because the Chinese government must review or approve the software content. See Steve Dickinson, 'SaaS in China: The 101' (*China Law Blog*, 10 October 2016) <https://www.chinalawblog.com/2016/10/saas-in-china-the-101.html>.
[239] Source code is a kind of readable programming map and a valuable form of intellectual property.

As noted in the Introduction,[240] while the Chinese term 网络主权 (*wangluo zhuquan*) is almost always translated as internet or cyber sovereignty, this is an imprecise translation. This is because Network Sovereignty is about not just controlling online content but also asserting control over the valuable data flows produced by China's technology ecosystems, which are becoming increasingly important in the context of new technologies, especially AI, and may not be confined to the internet.

Since 2006, dozens of restrictive rules and laws applying to tech companies have been legislated in China. Moreover, observers have noticed a marked increase in the rigidity of these rules since 2014.[241] Laws and regulations relating to data and ICT networks now regularly contain the phrases 'secure and controllable' (安全可控), 'secure and reliable' (安全可靠) or 'indigenous and controllable' (自主可控), and data localisation is linked to information security. China's Cyber Security Law has begun to identify a series of actors such as 'network operators' – broadly (and vaguely) defined – and pair them with a potential threat. In China's system of 'fuzzy logic legislating' it is not quite clear what these terms mean and how they will be applied in practice, hence there is ongoing speculation as to the impact of these laws and rules.

For example, one claim often made by commentators is that these frequently vague regulations shut foreign ICT service providers out of the market and provide an unfair advantage to Chinese firms. Yet this interpretation of the new policies is too simplistic.[242] This is because there are, in fact, two linked but contrasting aspects of Network Sovereignty.

First, 'Network Sovereignty' means that the Chinese government considers the close control of online discourse to be a matter of national sovereignty.[243] It suggests that cyber security is analogous to the

---

[240] See above n 14.
[241] See, eg, Sacks, Triolo and Webster, 'Beyond the Worst-Case Assumptions on China's Cybersecurity Law' (n 15).
[242] See, eg, Graham Webster et al, 'China's Plan to "Lead" in AI: Purpose, Prospects, and Problems' (*New America*, 1 August 2017) <https://www.newamerica.org/cybersecurity-initiative/blog/chinas-plan-lead-ai-purpose-prospects-and-problems/>. Some Chinese analysts also see cyberspace as a key mechanism used by the United States to reinforce its hegemonic role: see Saalman, 'New Domains of Crossover and Concern in Cyberspace' (n 16). They advocate that China strengthen its public and private networks, exert greater control over content and harden its broadband networks to close the technical loopholes used by other countries to undermine China's sovereignty security (主权安全), political security (政治安全) and social stability (社会稳定).
[243] It is a common trend in Chinese politicking that certain phrases become 'fashionable' in China's political discourse and the Chinese media.

international law principle of exclusive economic zones, or a country's controlled maritime borders. China has debated and implemented increasingly tight data localisation policies over the past few years and proposed further restrictions such as requiring all Chinese data to be held in servers located in China, while granting access to government authorities.[244]

Second, however, China's conception of Network Sovereignty also means being actively engaged in global internet governance. In particular, China has actively been involved in creating global internet technical standards and norms of behaviour.[245]

While some fear China's global impact on the internet, Chinese agencies and engineers are increasingly cooperatively involved in technical standards development and internet regulation working groups.[246] A major impetus for intelligent Smart Cities is, for example, the creation of clear and precise technical regulatory standards. China is also increasingly influencing and directing AI standards committees.[247] As Hana and Qiang put it: 'When it comes to standards, strategic engagement is likely to be more successful than isolationism.'[248] In many ways, cooperation is inevitable. There continue to be large flows of capital in and out of China to other countries including into foreign tech companies,[249] and the drive for foreign tech companies to enter China ensures that mutually recognised best practices are an aspirational objective.

Furthermore, without international cooperation there can be no extra-territoriality for cyber security laws.[250] That is, the global nature of the internet means that some degree of international cooperation is inevitable (see Chapter 6). China and the United States have since 2018 held extensive dialogues on cyber security issues.

---

[244] See Chapters 4 and 5.
[245] See Zeng, Stevens and Chen, 'China's Solution to Global Cyber Governance' (n 232).
[246] 'CNNIC Hosts "Promote Internet Development through Technology and Standards" Session of WIC Wuzhen Summit' (China Internet Network Information Center, 2 February 2016) <https://cnnic.com.cn/IC/Events/201602/t20160204_53402.htm> (the link is no longer active).
[247] See Chapter 9.
[248] Hanna and Qiang, 'China's Emerging Informatization Strategy' (n 197) 153.
[249] See, eg, Julie Zhu and Tova Cohen, 'China's Tech Money Heads for Israel as US Welcome Wanes' (*Reuters*, 11 May 2017) <http://www.reuters.com/article/us-china-investment-israel-idUSKBN187080>.
[250] China's criminal law was amended in 2016, to encapsulate cybercrime offences. It now overlaps with the Cyber Security Law.

Therefore, as with China's cyber security regime, there are contradictory aims at work. Under Network Sovereignty, China is attempting to create a more controlled domestic online environment, while simultaneously trying to increasingly participate in collaborative international cyber forums and standard setting.[251] This will have important implications for the development of AI. The tension between Internet Plus and Network Sovereignty also exists within Network Sovereignty and the cyber regime itself, and inevitably arises from the competing interests between promoting the benefits of the global internet (including in relation to standards for a cross-border network) and promoting national control.

Further reflecting the internal tensions within the Network Sovereignty policy, on 1 March 2017 China released its 'International Strategy of Cooperation on Cyberspace' (Cyberspace Strategy). This strategy encompasses both the potential for international collaboration and the potential threats China faces. It provides the first comprehensive explanation of China's policy and position on cyber-related international affairs as well as the basic principles, strategic goals and plan of action in its cyberspace relations. The Cyberspace Strategy implores other countries to 'guard against cyberspace becoming a new battlefield', aims to guide China's participation in international cooperation, and encourages the international community to build a secure, open, cooperative and orderly cyberspace.

The Cyberspace Strategy reflects the inherent tension between Internet Plus and Network Sovereignty. Network Sovereignty must be understood as being different in domestic and international contexts. Domestically, it often means information control and censorship guidelines. Internationally, however, it means China outlining its perspective on global internet guidelines, but also cooperating in international internet governance processes. This is where the conflict between the two aims becomes complex. The key question is: Which of these aims would gain precedence?

Some have argued that Network Sovereignty inevitably stifles the kind of innovation promoted through Internet Plus. In December 2015, the Hong Kong-based *South China Morning Post*, a staunch voice for

---

[251] For example, item 54 of the Outline of the National Informatisation Development Strategy («国家信息化发展战略纲要» [Outline of the National Informatisation Development Strategy] (People's Republic of China) State Council, 27 July 2016.) defines Network Sovereignty as having multiple aims from cyber security to online content control. For an English translation see Creemers, 'Outline of the National Informatisation Development Strategy' (n 206).

critique of the Party's mainland rule before it was acquired by Alibaba's Jack Ma, published a sceptical editorial about Internet Plus in the context of Network Sovereignty:

> China is well known for its strict censorship of online content. Hundreds of foreign websites are blocked and Google remains unstable in China. More recently, the influential documentary film *Under the Dome*[252] about air pollution in the country has been taken off all major domestic websites.
>
> We all know the key thing about the internet is freedom. If Beijing misses the point and continues to censor access to information, Premier Li's new Internet Plus strategy will probably just get more Chinese to shop online rather than have any significant and long-term impact on the country's long-awaited economic transformation.[253]

In China's conception of Network Sovereignty, 'secure and controllable' is a key concept. China's vision of Network Sovereignty, the idea that the internet, like territory, has borders which each nation is entitled to monitor and defend, is an idea that is also gaining appeal around the globe, particularly among authoritarian regimes. Iran, Russia, Turkey, Thailand and Zimbabwe are looking to China as they consider their own national version of the 'Great Firewall'.[254] This vision does not leave much room for the creative international collaboration that is required to keep China at the forefront of technological development.

Yet the persistent capacity of Chinese tech firms to engage in leading-edge innovation despite these kinds of restrictive laws has continued to befuddle onlookers. Part of this confusion stems from a failure to understand the pragmatic working relationship between the public and private sectors in China's ICT industry. This testy relationship is explored throughout this book.

---

[252] The high-profile documentary, 穹顶之下 [Qióngdǐng Zhī Xià – Under the Dome] (2015), shaming China's environmental degradation, epitomises the complex censorship and policy environment in China. It was allowed to be accessed online, and had been viewed over 300 million times on a Tencent platform by the time it was taken offline by censors four days later.

[253] George Chen, 'Can Li Keqiang's Internet Plus Strategy Really Save China?' (*South China Morning Post*, 8 March 2015) <http://www.scmp.com/business/china-business/article/1732704/can-li-keqiangs-internet-plus-strategy-really-save-china>.

[254] IETF, 'A Survey of Worldwide Censorship Techniques' (*IETF*, 22 October 2018) <https://tools.ietf.org/id/draft-hall-censorship-tech-06.html>.

3.6 Network Sovereignty, Content Censorship, Internet Plus and the Influence of the BATs

As the web expands between the Chinese government, large Chinese internet giants such as Alibaba, Baidu and Tencent (the BATs), foreign tech firms and a large number of third-party service providers operating between the government and these enterprises, who gets access to what data and when will become increasingly important.[255] Chapter 7 notes that the private sector largely controls China's datasets, yet there is an evolving fuzzy and uneasy relationship between the public and private sectors.[256] Reports of such delegated censoring abound and a distinct fuzzy logic in content control ensues. For example, in 2017, Alibaba's e-commerce platform Taobao reportedly banned merchants from selling foreign media in China – even media approved by Chinese censors. The e-commerce booksellers were informed of the ban by Alibaba – not the Chinese regulators.[257] These mistakes are often a result of fuzzy regulatory directives. Presumably they must harm innovation and efficiency, as the BATs must employ large content control teams.

So, despite some progress in developing the Chinese technocratic environment described in this chapter, China's legal and regulatory framework for informatisation faces considerable implementation challenges, due to competing policy interests and contradictory aims. Further, linked to the central theme of the conflict between innovation and Network Sovereignty, it is often reported that Chinese start-ups increasingly must align with or seek investment from the BATs, who are themselves cooperating with the government:

---

[255] See Creemers, 'Cyber China' (n 23) 89.

[256] For example, China's three biggest internet conglomerates – Baidu, Alibaba and Tencent – formed an 'Internet Plus alliance' on 16 December 2015 at the World Internet Conference, the most prominent state internet event. The alliance's leading organiser was, however, the China International Development fund, which is governed by China's State Council. Jack Ma, founder of Alibaba, chaired the alliance. The alliance also includes companies, government organisations and NGOs. See Jack Liu and Zen Soo, 'China's Alibaba, Baidu and Tencent Join Hands to Promote "Internet Plus" Strategy' (*South China Morning Post*, 16 December 2015) <http://www.scmp.com/news/china/policies-politics/article/1892180/chinas-alibaba-baidu-and-tencent-join-hands-promote>.

[257] Echo Huang, 'Taobao Is Banning Merchants from Selling Foreign Media in China – Even Media Approved by Censors' (*Quartz*, 10 March 2017) <https://qz.com/929540/selling-foreign-media-in-china-even-media-approved-by-censors-is-being-banned-alibaba-baba-groups-online-shopping-platform-taobao>.

Although unfavorable to Western companies, this policy has led to the rise of the BAT (Baidu, Alibaba, Tencent) companies, who are most in tune with Chinese government policies and guidelines. When it comes to publishing content, they have become the frontline enforcers of law, making sure that content published online all follows guidelines in real-time. On the business level, this means that other startups have to look to what these three companies are doing, and find a path to survive, which usually involves establishing a certain degree of partnership with these companies. *A great example of this is Pinduoduo, which recently stated publicly that its relationship with Tencent is important to its survival and growth.*[258]

Therefore, for high-growth start-ups like Pinduoduo, while policies such as Internet Plus should theoretically give a boost to new innovators versus large incumbents like the BATs, this is often not the case.

3.7 Conclusion: Unresolved Questions

Great tension exists between China's policies aimed at promoting innovation in technology industries and policies aimed at asserting centralised, state control over internet activities and data. Internet Plus, introduced in 2015, proposes that China must connect the latest global internet technologies to industry. Conversely, Network Sovereignty, introduced in 2014, is based on the principle that every country should be able to control information and data flows on the global internet within their territorial borders. This reflects a fundamental tension between open innovation and centralised control.

This situation has led to a complex relationship between the Chinese government and the private sector. The regulatory framework for enabling an innovation ecosystem is complex in any country. In China, internet controls lead to further regulatory uncertainty. For example, does China's Cyber Security Law restrict market entry by local Chinese start-ups by making compliance too onerous?

These competing policy frameworks raise questions about whether an appropriate balance can be found between innovation and restriction in China. In the next few chapters, China's Cyber Security Law and related developments are used as the lens to begin answering these questions in more detail.

---

[258] Paul Denlinger, 'What Will Data Rights for the Individual Look Like in China?' (*Pandaily*, 10 September 2018) (emphasis added) <https://pandaily.com/what-will-data-rights-for-the-individual-look-like-in-china>.

In Chapter 4, the intersection of these policies is further assessed by considering China's extreme cyber security threats. The laws and policies leading up to the Cyber Security Law's enactment are also surveyed. Through these laws and their application, it is shown that China has a history of avoiding damaging its innovation agenda by using extended consultation periods to engage with industry before enacting, revising and enforcing problematic laws.

4

China's Data Security Policies Leading to the Cyber Security Law

> Thus, the fundamental elements of 'socialism with Chinese characteristics' became entrenched: namely, tight party control of politics within a one-party state; pursuit of economic growth and whatever is required to achieve it consistent with maintaining control; and gradualism, involving small policy steps and evaluating them before proceeding further.
> —Dr Geoff Raby, former Australian ambassador to China[259]

China has profound cyber security concerns arising from recent technological developments and policies such as Informatisation for government departments, Smart City development, and the promotion of a leading-edge AI industry. This chapter analyses the policy and regulatory developments leading up to the enactment of the Cyber Security Law, including China's Anti-Terrorism Law and how enforced source-code 'backdoor provisions' were removed from the final draft of this law to protect China's innovation policy goals.

There was significant debate about Network Sovereignty ideology in China's Anti-Terrorism Law. This law is yet another example of how problematic laws are delayed as further consultation is sought. Comparisons are also made with a similar policy debate on 'backdoor provisions' in the United States, showing that the initial Chinese approach was not so different from universal debates at that time, and ultimately reflected international practice. Similar approaches are now finding more widespread acceptance globally, including in Australia and the United Kingdom.

This history provided an indicator of how China may resolve the issue of data localisation within the Cyber Security Law. The following policy analysis is relevant to understanding China's wider technological and

---

[259] Geoff Raby, 'Not All Successful Markets Are Free' (*Sydney Morning Herald*, 7 August 2018) <https://www.smh.com.au/politics/federal/not-all-successful-markets-are-free-20180806-p4zvqt.html>.

security policy goals and the inherent contradictions within those goals, issues that are still playing out as China continues to draft and finalise cyber and privacy laws in 2021.

4.1 Planning for China's Cyber Regime: 'Cyber Security and Informatisation Are Two Wings of One Body'

On 27 July 2016, China released the Outline of the National Informatisation Development Strategy[260] (the Outline). This document begins with the bold statement that since the world is entering a new stage of global technological development, 'without informatisation, there is no modernisation' and that 'global informatisation has entered a new stage of comprehensive penetration, cross-boundary convergence, where it accelerates innovation and leads development'.[261] According to the Outline, Internet Plus changes the policy landscape, including by creating the need to form smart 'e-government' and engage China's citizenry in that mission.[262] There are numerous references in the Outline to the importance of big data and the Internet Plus action plan[263] in driving China's development. Like Internet Plus, the strategic objectives identified in the Outline are focused on practical goals, such as widespread fifth generation (5G) mobile telecommunications coverage. There are also more ambitious goals such as improving China's satellite capabilities.

Further, in relation to a central question of this book – the intersection between Internet Plus and Network Sovereignty – the Outline makes the key point that cyber security is an inseparable aspect of China's innovation strategy: 'Guaranteeing security. Cyber security and informatisation are two wings of one body, two wheels of one cart, they must be planned together, arranged together, moved forward together and implemented together, it must be ensured that they are coordinated and

---

[260] Outline of the National Informatisation Development Strategy (n 251). The Outline is an adjustment and development of the National Informatisation Development Strategy 2006–2020 'on the basis of new circumstances'. For an English translation of the Outline see Creemers, 'Outline of the National Informatisation Development Strategy' (n 206).
[261] Ibid.
[262] Outline of the National Informatisation Development Strategy (n 251) s II(3) ('Basic Principles').
[263] See Guiding Opinions (n 9).

consistent, and are advanced simultaneously.'[264] According to the Outline, China must therefore 'build secure and controllable information technology systems [in order to lead globally] in next-generation mobile telecommunications, next-generation internet and other such areas, strive to build comparative advantages in areas such as mobile internet, cloud computing, big data, and the Internet of Things'.[265]

Like the Cyber Security Law, innovation, security and information control are all intertwined in ambitious goals such as 'comprehensively planning the construction of a national internet big data platform; progressively launching open trading data backups and authentication, and ensuring that data are traceable and recoverable'.[266]

The Outline also calls for 'deepening international cooperation and exchange', 'participating in the formulation of international norms' and 'vigorously participating in the formulation of international standards' – all key aspects of Network Sovereignty.[267] Finally, item 49 of the Outline emphasises the need to 'persist in giving precedence to urgent necessities, and accelerate the promulgation of urgently needed laws'.[268] Introducing a Cyber Security Law is listed as the first priority.

Likewise, on 27 December 2016, the Central Cyber Security and Informatisation Leading Small Group approved, and CAC published, the National Cyberspace Security Strategy (the Strategy).[269] This repeats the mantra: 'cyber security and informatisation are two wings of one body, two wheels of one cart'. It then outlines the potential of the internet for 'greatly stimulating economic and social flourishing and progress', but at the same time notes that it has also 'brought new security risks and challenges'.

These policy documents – the Outline and the Strategy – therefore clearly demonstrate the Chinese government's great concern about the security risks of innovative technologies. Yet what are these risks, particularly in relation to Internet Plus and the development of AI?

---

[264] Outline of the National Informatisation Development Strategy (n 251) s II(3) ('Basic Principles').
[265] Ibid s III(1) ('Developing Core Technologies, Strengthening the Information Industry').
[266] Ibid s III(3) item 10 ('Strengthening Information Resource Planning, Construction and Management').
[267] Ibid s III(4) item 18 ('Participating in the Formulation of International Norms').
[268] Ibid item 49.
[269] See n 220. The Outline and Strategy both reflect high-level policy goals but do not have the weight of law. The Strategy reflects more detailed policy goals.

4.2 The Critical Need for a Cyber Security Regime in China

Introducing an effective cyber security regime is essential for successful technological innovation in China. While IoT enables objects to 'talk' to other objects, this potentially creates vulnerability to hackers and viruses. China already has billions of smart devices connecting to a wide range of applications.[270] Security is essential for all of these applications. A system of live sensors connected in a network across a Smart City (discussed in Chapters 8 and 9), for example, would amplify the threat of a major cyberattack.

If China continues collecting data and employing sensors on a national scale, an effective cyber security regime will be critical to prevent systemic collapse. All countries must protect critical infrastructure that is connected through private smart phones, among other devices. Yet in many ways China is at the global vanguard of dealing with these issues because of the scale of its data collecting and the number of policy petri dishes or pilot rollouts of AI applications, such as designating entire cities for autonomous vehicle testing, and installing internet-connected street signs for self-driving cars.[271]

Again, China had 731 million internet users and 695 million users accessing the internet through mobile devices in January 2017, according to government statistics. By 2020, China would have almost a billion internet users.[272] Many Chinese consumers rarely use cash and rely upon China's distinct online, e-commerce payment and logistics

---

[270] China was predicted to have 10 billion connected devices by 2020: Mary Lennighan, 'China to Have 10BN Connected Devices by 2020' (*Total Telecom*, 24 February 2016) <https://www.totaltele.com/view.aspx?ID=492917> and did indeed reach that number: John Lee, *The Connection of Everything: China and the Internet of Things* (Report, China Monitor, 24 June 2021) <https://merics.org/en/report/connection-everything-china-and-internet-things>.

[271] These issues are discussed at length in Chapters 8 and 9.

[272] At the end of 2020, China had 989 million internet users, according to government statistics. In comparison, the US has around 284 million internet users, and India has 639 million. The government statistics report added that 94% of all Chinese internet users watched online videos, and 88% used short-video apps. More than 781 million people have reportedly shopped online. See «47次《中国互联网络发展状况统计报告》[47th Statistical Report on the Development of the Internet in China] (*CNNIC*, 3 February 2021) <http://www.cnnic.cn/hlwfzyj/hlwxzbg/hlwtjbg/202102/t20210203_71361.htm>.

ecosystems.²⁷³ These systems create further serious cyber threats given the high penetration of internet usage and connected devices in China.

To cite just one high-profile example, in May 2017 it was reported that China was a major victim of a global ransomware attack.²⁷⁴ Evidence suggested the attack was associated with a group backed by North Korea.²⁷⁵ China struggled to recover from this global hacking assault, which hit Chinese companies, government agencies and universities especially hard. The consequences could have been exponentially worse if that software had been connected to hardware and infrastructure across a 'smart' Chinese city.

Researchers believe large numbers of computers running unlicensed versions of Microsoft Windows, for which China has been notorious, probably exacerbated the ransomware attack.²⁷⁶ As pirated software is usually not registered with the developer, users often miss major security patches that ward off newer cyber assaults.²⁷⁷

Thus, the enactment of the Cyber Security Law in 2016 reflected much more than a legislative attempt to censor the internet. Cyber technologies will define the twenty-first century. Cyber security must therefore be part of everything that is created, and this is as true in China as anywhere else. While the Cyber Security Law (and previous legislation) certainly does

---

[273] This is according to Chinese government statistics from January 2017. See Steven Millward, 'China Now Has 731 Million Internet Users, 95% Access from Their Phones' (*TechinAsia*, 23 January 2017) <https://www.techinasia.com/china-731-million-internet-users-end-2016>.

[274] The WannaCry ransomware attack was a worldwide cyberattack which targeted computers running the Microsoft Windows operating system, encrypting data and demanding ransom payments in Bitcoin. The attack started on 12 May 2017 and was described as unprecedented in scale, infecting computers in over 150 countries.

[275] Evidence for North Korean involvement via the Lazarus Group remains tentative. Symantec called the code overlap 'weak links'. The Lazarus Group is a hacker collective with ties to North Korea: 'North Korean Hackers behind Global Cyberattack?' (*CBS News*, 16 May 2017) <http://www.cbsnews.com/news/cyberattack-wannacry-ransomware-north-korea-hackers-lazarus-group>.

[276] Paul Mozur, 'China, Addicted to Bootleg Software, Reels from Ransomware Attack' (*New York Times*, 15 May 2017) <https://www.nytimes.com/2017/05/15/business/china-ransomware-wannacry-hacking.html>.

[277] This is why increased Chinese intellectual property protection for software, as well as open-source software, is increasingly important in China. (See Chapter 9.) A study by BSA, a trade association of software vendors, found that 70% of software installed on computers in China was not properly licensed in 2015: 'Seizing Opportunity through License Compliance', BSA Global Software Survey, May 2016 <http://www.bsa.org/~/media/Files/StudiesDownload/BSA_GSS_US.pdf> (the link is no longer active) cited in ibid.

involve censorship and is directed at Network Sovereignty concerns, one main focus is legitimate national and global security threats to 'critical infrastructure', which are not dissimilar to those faced by advanced economies throughout the world.

Chinese leaders have complex policy and legislative decisions to make in attempting to address these cyber risks without stifling innovation. There are currently no international guidelines for best practice in creating a cyber security regime. There is no equivalent law in the United States in terms of cyber security planning.[278] Many countries are just starting to consider these issues, and there is no clear blueprint for success.[279]

The legislative precursors to China's Cyber Security Law are now considered in depth as legislative policy direction markers.

4.3 Network Sovereignty Laws Prior to the Cyber Security Law

In an attempt to deal with increasing cyber security risks, China drafted several security laws during 2014–2016 that tightened regulation over suppliers of technological equipment and services. Many of these measures involve the concept of 'secure and controllable' technology, a loosely defined term that involves government security checks and data storage within China.[280] They include data

---

[278] However, in 2018 the United States enacted the Clarifying Lawful Overseas Use of Data Act or CLOUD Act, which allows federal law enforcement to compel US-based technology companies via warrant or subpoena to provide requested data stored on servers regardless of whether the data are stored in the United States or on foreign soil.

[279] Australia's Telecommunications and Other Legislation Amendment (Assistance and Access) Act 2018 (Cth) might compel technology companies to provide access to information on their encrypted platforms. The focus of the new legislation is access to information (not mandatory decryption). The Australian legislation is reportedly based on the Investigatory Powers Act 2016 (UK), which requires UK companies to remove encryption when compelled by law enforcement agencies.

[280] The term 'secure and controllable' was initially introduced in Circular 317 (n 17). It was reported that the China Banking Regulatory Commission was going to reintroduce the banking safety rules (the Revised Regulation) after it consulted representatives of Western technology enterprises such as Microsoft, IBM and Cisco. The rules were suspended in April 2015 and an amended version was released. The phrase 安全可控 (secure and controllable) is sometimes also referred to as 安全可靠 (secure and reliable) or 自主可控 (indigenous and controllable). The Chinese government has also set out new security requirements in industry-specific regulations. The phrase has appeared in separate pending rules for ICT used in insurance, medical devices and the Internet Plus sectors (ie, smart technology, cloud computing, mobile technology and e-commerce). See Sacks, 'Apple in China, Part I' (n 212).

protection,[281] banking[282] and media regulations,[283] the National Security Law[284] and the 2015 Anti-Terrorism Law.[285] These laws legislate on high-profile matters such as data encryption and technology transfers.[286] Chinese officials referred to the measures as essential to national security. They would allow China to verify that critical equipment is not vulnerable to hacking, and facilitate the fight against terrorism and criminality.[287]

By contrast, foreign governments and trade groups viewed many of these policies as onerous and a possible way to discriminate against non-Chinese vendors. They created great uncertainty among foreign firms

---

[281] Instead, provisions relating to personal data protection are found in various laws and regulations. Generally speaking, provisions found in laws such as the General Principles of Civil Law and the Tort Liability Law may be used to interpret data protection rights as a right of reputation or right of privacy. See Yang Feng, 'The Future of China's Personal Data Protection Law: Challenges and Prospects' (2019) 27(1) *Asia Pacific Law Review* 1.

[282] See Circular 317 (n 17).

[283] For example, MIIT and the State Administration of Press Publication Radio Film and Television unveiled new measures that require localisation of server and storage equipment for online publishing and took effect on 10 March 2016. See «网络出版服务管理规定» [Network Publishing Services Management Regulations] (People's Republic of China) MIIT and the State Administration of Press Publication Radio Film and Television, 4 February 2016 <http://www.gapp.gov.cn/govpublic/84/1067.shtml>.

[284] «中华人民共和国国家安全法» [National Security Law of the People's Republic of China] (People's Republic of China) National People's Congress, Order No 68, 1 July 2015 (National Security Law). The National Security Law covers China's border security and acts of terrorism but also contains a provision that discusses the need for the Chinese internet to be a 'secure and controllable' network and the need to maintain that network safely. Article 25 introduces the concept of a 'secure and controllable' (安全可控) network. Article 59 establishes the concept of 'national security review and oversight'.

[285] «中华人民共和国反恐怖主义法» [Anti-Terrorism Law of the People's Republic of China] (People's Republic of China) National People's Congress, Order No 36, 27 December 2015 (Anti-Terrorism Law).

[286] In recent years, China and the United States have clashed over trade in the technology industry, partly as a result of laws like this. In 2015, the Obama administration responded to lobbying from American companies against a number of Chinese laws that the companies said were devised to push them out of China. China abandoned a regulation restricting what foreign hardware could be sold to Chinese banks. China also banned Microsoft's Windows 8 from government offices and threatened to phase out IBM servers from Chinese banks.

[287] For example, the English language *China Daily* referenced the murder of 29 people and the injury of many more by knife-wielding assailants at a train station in Kunming on 1 March 2014 as evidence of the need for the new anti-terrorism law. See 'Lawmakers Weigh China's Draft Anti-Terrorism Law' (*China Daily*, 25 February 2015) <http://www.chinadaily.com.cn/china/2015-02/25/content_19653472.htm>.

and also among Chinese tech companies with international operations, links and partnerships.

In assessing whether these fears were justified, the following section critically analyses one of the more high-profile pieces of legislation introduced in this period, the final version of China's Anti-Terrorism Law of December 2015. This law clearly fits within China's ethos of Network Sovereignty – the idea that states should be permitted to govern and monitor their own cyberspace, controlling incoming and outgoing data flows. Yet its drafting and consultation process demonstrate the government's receptiveness to industry concerns, and its willingness to remove draconian provisions that would stifle innovation at that time.

4.4 China's Anti-Terrorism Law

China's Anti-Terrorism Law is given prominence here as its development reflected a public debate happening contemporaneously around the world. Further, it served to dispel some public perceptions of the ideological trajectory of Network Sovereignty policies at the time.

The State Council of China published the Anti-Terrorism Law[288] on 27 December 2015, and the law came into effect on 1 January 2016. The initial draft law had been circulated for comment in late 2014. It attracted global criticism, especially from tech companies operating in China.[289]

Most of the debate on the draft law was focused on its so-called 'backdoor' provisions. The draft law would have required telecommunications operators and internet service providers to allow the Chinese government backdoor access to their products, to hand over encryption codes for review, and to store local user data on servers within China.[290] Had the backdoor provisions been implemented, foreign tech companies feared losing their intellectual property via theft through these declared backdoors. This may also have isolated and slowed China in its innovation drive, because foreign companies would have moved out of China to protect their data.

---

[288] See Anti-Terrorism Law (n 285).
[289] This is documented in Chapter 6.
[290] Article 15 of the draft law required internet service providers to install 'technical interfaces in the design, construction, and operation of telecommunication and Internet [services]'. These technical 'interfaces' could have acted as backdoors for government access.

However, the final revised draft that was approved by the State Council abandoned these demands for encryption review and data localisation. The final Anti-Terrorism Law requires telecommunications operators and internet service providers to help decrypt information in the event of a terrorist attack, but not to install security 'backdoors' as initially planned in the draft version.[291] In reality, this requirement could logically have the same effect as a backdoor. Even if a company has an encryption system, mandated access (in a terrorist event[292]) is arguably the same as having either a backdoor or a front door. Yet the amendment did appear to appease critics of the law.[293]

Furthermore, and important from a commercial and global trade perspective, the provision in the initial draft that required companies to keep servers and user data within China was also removed from the final law. What might have been a major setback for Chinese innovation was thereby averted.

Again, this kind of consultation, internal debate and compromise is not unusual in recent Chinese lawmaking, and is a key feature of fuzzy logic legislating.[294] Publishing and circulating draft laws for comment allows Chinese legislative bodies time to await domestic and international reaction. The initial draft and revisions also reflect the competing interests within the Chinese government and the tension between Network Sovereignty and Internet Plus objectives. The drafting of the Cyber Security Law is another example of fuzzy logic legislating, in the form of amending some provisions before enactment, and then issuing 'interpretations' that effectively revised the law after its enactment.

Assessing the drafting process of the Anti-Terrorism Law against this context of recent Chinese legislative trends, there is a clear effort by the

---

[291] The final law (art 18) retains the original text on the requirement for providing the government with technical support, including backdoor access and decryption, but only for the prevention and investigation of terrorist activities.

[292] Of course, definitions remain subject to abuse. A peaceful protest over civil rights by China's Uighurs in Xinjiang could be considered a terrorist event.

[293] For an explanation of the subsequent muted public debate, see Zunyou Zhou, 'China's Comprehensive Counter-Terrorism Law' (*The Diplomat*, 23 January 2016) <https://thediplomat.com/2016/01/chinas-comprehensive-counter-terrorism-law>.

[294] Both China's Anti-Terrorism Law (n 285) and Cyber Security Law (n 2) went through public consultation periods. Public comment was also sought for subsequent regulations. The debate and prolonged discussion is a feature of fuzzy logic legislating. In regard to the public consultation process in recent Chinese lawmaking, see Jinting Deng and Pinxin Liu, 'Consultative Authoritarianism: The Drafting of China's Internet Security Law and E-Commerce Law' (2018) 26(107) *Journal of Contemporary China* 1.

Chinese government to take industry concerns into account when implementing security-related legislation. The fears of global critics appear not to have been justified in this case.

Nevertheless, the further question remains: are the counter-terrorism provisions in line with international norms? Is China merely legislating standard international practice? For example, how do the Chinese policy developments surrounding backdoor keys for mobile phone encryptions compare with recent public debates on this issue in countries such as the United States?

4.4.1 Data Encryption and Backdoor Keys in the United States

Many Western governments, including that of the United States, have made similar requests for encryption keys.[295] In December 2015, just as China was finalising its Anti-Terrorism Law, a public debate broke out in the United States on the same backdoor key issue. The precipitating event was a terrorist attack in San Bernardino, California, on 2 December 2015, in which 14 people were murdered by an Islamist terrorist. The Federal Bureau of Investigations (FBI) requested that Apple decrypt the terrorist's phone for evidence in their investigations of his supporters and networks.

In response, Apple CEO Tim Cook released a statement in February 2016:

> When the FBI has requested data that's in our possession, we have provided it. Apple complies with valid subpoenas and search warrants, as we have in the San Bernardino case. ... While we believe the FBI's intentions are good, it would be wrong for the government to force us to build a backdoor into our products. ... ultimately, we fear that this demand would undermine the very freedoms and liberty our government is meant to protect.[296]

This debate revolves around a combination of cyber security measures, US political culture and commercial realities. The US developments also occurred in the shadow of the Snowden revelations, which revealed that

---

[295] In addition to the United States, Australia, for example, began legislating on the issue in 2018.
[296] Elias Groll, 'Why Apple – and Not Google – Is in the FBI's Crosshairs' (*Foreign Policy*, 18 February 2016) <http://foreignpolicy.com/2016/02/18/why-apple-and-not-google-is-in-the-fbis-crosshairs>.

the United States was spying on its citizens.[297] First, within the cyber security community there is the belief that backdoors are dangerous. They could allow a country to develop so-called NOBUS exploitation technology. The phrase refers to 'NObody But US', and concerns security vulnerabilities that the US National Security Agency believes only it can exploit. This opens up major ethical questions: should China stockpile internet vulnerabilities or should it disclose and fix them? It is a complicated problem, and one that starkly illustrates the difficulty of separating attack from defence in cyberspace.[298]

In addition, the dangers identified by the cyber security community are not confined to NOBUS. Another major concern is that introducing a backdoor is inherently dangerous as it provides the potential for anyone with sufficient skills to exploit the backdoor.[299]

Further, in terms of technical capacities, US authorities have had great difficulty decrypting devices. Reportedly, Apple uses more secure encryption in its mobile software than does Google for its Android phones, a commercial selling point for Apple.[300] Further, highly popular messaging platforms (eg, Facebook's WhatsApp) use end-to-end encryption that even the National Security Agency had to invest significant resources to crack.[301] Facebook then began working on integrating cryptography into its normal chat.[302] (Although WhatsApp users had until 15 May 2021 before Facebook sought to share their WhatsApp user data with the parent company Facebook.)

Eventually, the US Justice Department abandoned its bid to force Apple to help the FBI unlock the iPhone used in the San Bernardino

---

[297] See Chapter 6.
[298] Bruce Schneier, 'Should US Hackers Fix Cybersecurity Holes or Exploit Them?' (*The Atlantic*, 19 May 2014) <https://www.theatlantic.com/technology/archive/2014/05/should-hackers-fix-cybersecurity-holes-or-exploit-them/371197>.
[299] In 1998, pioneering cryptographer Ronald L Rivest had already written 'The Case against Regulating Encryption Technology' (*Scientific American*, October 1998) <https://people.csail.mit.edu/rivest/pubs/Riv98e.pdf>. Hundreds of peer-reviewed articles concern the issues, and technical problems relating to iPhone decryption and, in general, backdoors. See, eg, Jonathan Zdziarski, 'Identifying Back Doors, Attack Points, and Surveillance Mechanisms in iOS Devices' (2014) 11(1) *Digital Investigation* 3.
[300] Google cannot encrypt its phone data as securely as Apple. This makes Apple's encryption technology a commercial selling point. Arguably, Apple's embrace 'of encryption is as much a business model decision as it is a principled embrace of user privacy': Zdziarski, 'Identifying Back Doors' (n 299).
[301] Ibid.
[302] Signal is an encrypted instant messaging and voice calling application for Android and iOS.

terrorist attack. Investigators found a software loophole without Apple's assistance.[303] It was later reported that an Israeli security firm possessed the necessary technology to decrypt the iPhone and had shared the technology with the FBI.[304]

It has also been suggested in cyber security circles that the US Justice Department and the FBI abandoned the matter as much for political reasons due to public pressure as for technical reasons.[305] US policymakers seemed to be turning against the idea of providing technological backdoors to enforcement agencies. The Congressional Committee Encryption Working Group[306] concluded on 20 December 2016 that backdoors and 'compelled disclosure by individuals' are a bad idea.[307] A key question was asked: 'What vulnerabilities remain after communications have been encrypted and how might those vulnerabilities be addressed?'[308]

The House Committee's response was emphatic:

> Encryption is inexorably tied to our national interests. It is a safeguard for our personal secrets and economic prosperity. It helps to prevent crime and protect national security. The widespread use of encryption technologies also complicates the missions of the law enforcement and intelligence communities. As described in this report, those complications cannot be ignored. This is the reality of modern society. We must strive to find common ground in our collective responsibility: to prevent crime, protect national security, and provide the best possible conditions for peace and prosperity.

---

[303] Matt Zapotosky, 'FBI Has Accessed San Bernardino Shooter's Phone without Apple's Help' (*Washington Post*, 28 March 2016), <https://www.washingtonpost.com/world/national-security/fbi-has-accessed-san-bernardino-shooters-phone-without-apples-help/2016/03/28/e593a0e2-f52b-11e5-9804-537defcc3cf6_story.html>.

[304] 'Israeli Firm "Helped FBI Crack San Bernardino Gunman's Cell Phone without Apple's Help"' (*Daily Mail*, 30 March 2016) <http://www.dailymail.co.uk/news/article-3514875/Israeli-firm-helped-FBI-crack-San-Bernardino-gunman-s-cellphone-without-Apple-s-help.html>.

[305] National reactions to Apple's opposition of the order were mixed. A CBS News poll that sampled 1,022 Americans found that 50% of the respondents supported the FBI's stance, while 45% supported Apple's stance: 'CBS News Poll: Americans Split on Unlocking San Bernardino Shooter's iPhone' (*CBS News*, 18 March 2016) <http://www.cbsnews.com/news/cbs-news-poll-americans-split-on-unlocking-san-bernardino-shooters-iphone>.

[306] Formerly known as the House Judiciary Committee and House Energy and Commerce Committee Encryption Working Group.

[307] US Congressional Committee, *Encryption Working Group Year-End Report* (20 December 2016) <https://judiciary.house.gov/wp-content/uploads/2016/12/20161220EWGFINALReport.pdf> (the link is no longer active).

[308] Ibid 13.

> That is why this can no longer be an isolated or binary debate. There is no 'us versus them', or 'pro-encryption versus law enforcement'. This conversation implicates everyone and everything that depends on connected technologies – including our law enforcement and intelligence communities. This is a complex challenge that will take time, patience, and cooperation to resolve. The potential consequences of inaction – or overreaction – are too important to allow historical or ideological perspectives to stand in the way of progress.[309]

This brief commentary on US practice serves to highlight the broader contemporaneous international context for recent Chinese legislative developments in the area of cyber security and the tension they potentially create with the need to innovate intelligent technologies. The fact that both the Chinese and US governments stepped back from initial calls to introduce general 'backdoor provisions' to combat terrorism indicates that China's approach to Network Sovereignty may not be as draconian as its critics have suggested, or at least may be more complex than some think. In this aspect, one could argue that, at least before the introduction of the Cyber Security Law, the Chinese approach was broadly in line with international practice.

4.5 Conclusion: Policy Indicators?

There are enormous cyber security challenges tied to China's great leaps in innovation, challenges shared by countries throughout the world. This chapter reviewed the Chinese government's initial attempts to legislate cyber protections prior to the introduction of the Cyber Security Law.

Like the statement of the Congressional Committee quoted above, noting that backdoors and network security are a complex issue, China's statement that 'cyber security and informatisation are two wings of one body' indicates that the Chinese government aspires to provide the public with effective and secure big data solutions. The government is, however, not just acting out of an altruistic desire to protect ordinary citizens' data. Greater public information, increased transparency and accountability, and efficient collection of statistical data facilitated by smart technologies are all crucial to improving government effectiveness within a populous nation and eliminating corruption, which may in turn allow the Party to maintain power.

---

[309] Ibid.

Thus, despite the sometimes heavy-handed efforts at exerting control over internet-driven innovation, there were sufficient interests at stake to suggest that security concerns would not unduly impede technological advancement in 2016.

The retreat from backdoor access in the Anti-Terrorism Law is also an example of fuzzy logic policymaking. This amendment of the Anti-Terrorism Law in response to industry concerns provides support for the hypothesis that tech companies may be able to negotiate their data security arrangements under the new Cyber Security Law, a point discussed further in the next chapter.

A similar kind of collaborative fuzzy logic policymaking in the drafting and subsequent reinterpretation of China's Cyber Security Law is outlined in the next chapter, and then analysed further in subsequent chapters with regard to Chinese AI development.

5

The Cyber Security Law
Fuzzy Logic in a Touchstone Law

> China's much-anticipated Cyber Security Law (CSL) will come into effect on 1 June 2017. The new law is the first comprehensive law to address cyber security concerns at the national level and to some extent consolidates cyber activities captured in other laws and regulations. The move by China to beef up its laws and regulations governing cyber activity is not dissimilar to what is happening around the globe. However, deciphering exactly who is captured and what is covered is leaving companies unsure as to how they will comply with this vague and potentially onerous law.
>
> —Carly Ramsey and Ben Wootliff[310]

The key provisions of China's Cyber Security Law relating to data localisation and data exits still allow for competing interpretations by regulators, which makes compliance difficult, even in 2021. The further attempt to include 'backdoor' keys to encryption in this law is also noted, although foreign companies have managed to exert some influence on this point and other implementation issues.

The Cyber Security Law is an important and high-profile development in Chinese cyber policy history. It created much more controversy than the Anti-Terrorism Law explained in the previous chapter. In recent years China has gradually adopted a series of laws, regulations and macro policies in the field of cyber security and data protection aimed at turning the country into a 'cyber superpower' and boosting its digital economy. The Cyber Security Law, which subsequently came into partial effect from 1 June 2017 (with an official 18-month phase-in period for the data localisation provisions), is a milestone in the development of China's legal framework for cyber security and data protection.

The law also provides further evidence of the inherent tensions underlying China's key innovation policies. However, vague regulations allow

---

[310] Carly Ramsey and Ben Wootliff, 'China's Cyber Security Law: The Impossibility of Compliance?' (*Forbes*, 29 May 2017) <https://www.forbes.com/sites/riskmap/2017/05/29/chinas-cyber-security-law-the-impossibility-of-compliance/#580961c7471c>.

regulators leeway to adjust their aims in response to broader economic and political trends by means of implementing rules. Finally clarifying the vaguest provisions in the Cyber Security Law through more transparent rules may provide an opportunity for the Chinese government to decide which way it is heading: towards further innovation or further restriction beyond the ongoing United States–China trade war.

The Cyber Security Law defines cyber network operators and operations very broadly, and some key terms used in the law (eg, 'important data' and 'critical information infrastructure') are too vague for their precise meaning to be grasped. Long-awaited subordinate regulations, which will implement the data localisation provisions, are yet to be published, although various contradictory drafts, noted in following sections, have appeared during 2017–2021.

The broad nature of the areas covered, the vagueness of terminology and the uncertainties with implementation have led to an outcry from many multinational companies operating in China, claiming that it is impossible to understand the law, let alone to comply with its requirements. Part of the complexity derives from the fact that China's data protection regime is highly opaque and still evolving. Fuzzy logic within Chinese laws is a key factor in this opacity.

Looking deeper into the Cyber Security Law in this chapter, it becomes clearer that Chinese policymakers are confronted with dilemmas of conflicting objectives, and are striving to find a balance. That is the root cause of the 'fuzzy' nature of the Cyber Security Law. These competing objectives are introduced here and surveyed further in Chapters 6 and 7, and include the following: (1) national and cyber security versus the free flow of cross-border data transfers; (2) privacy (from the government in China) versus data protection (from companies operating in China) and (3) economic growth through the big data economy versus big data monopolies and data protection accountability for private companies.

While it is true that in any jurisdiction, ambiguities may result from applying new laws to complex emerging technologies, the Chinese approach to fuzzy lawmaking is to intentionally enact unclear laws and subsequently tweak the direction of implementation as necessary. This chapter demonstrates specifically through analysis of selected provisions in the Cyber Security Law that Chinese fuzzy logic lawmaking involves legislating ambiguous definitions about which entities are regulated under the law and what rules pertain to their data storage and movement of data outside China.

5.1 Background: Initial Drafting, Consultation then Delayed Implementation

From the time of the drafting of the Cyber Security Law to its enactment, controversial articles were delayed and additional consultations with industry were held. It was an opportunity for the implications of the fuzziness in the law to be reconciled in a manner that would not inhibit Chinese technological developments.

On 6 July 2015, the Standing Committee of the National People's Congress released a first draft of the Cyber Security Law for public comment.[311] When the third draft was adopted in November 2016, it became the first Chinese law to focus exclusively on cyber security and was China's first attempt to legislate a comprehensive cyber security regime that was not spread across various bureaucracies.[312]

The draft law signalled that the Chinese government was tightening control on domestic networks and data security in line with its policy of Network Sovereignty. The draft law also caused great concern among foreign companies, which feared provisions requiring the turnover of encryption keys to communications equipment under certain circumstances. While companies were understandably reluctant to speak out publicly for risk of offending the Chinese government, many risk management consultants published opinion pieces outlining these fears.[313]

The first draft of the law granted authorities the power to cut internet access in public security emergencies, and required data localisation of servers in China as well as cyber security reviews of company data. These moves dovetailed with other regulations (noted in Chapter 3) including data protection, banking[314] and media regulations[315] that required

---

[311] «中华人民共和国网络安全法 (草案)» [Cyber Security Law of the People's Republic of China (Draft)] (People's Republic of China) National People's Congress, 6 July 2015. After first and second drafts were released for public consultation in June 2015 and May 2016, respectively, the third draft issued in October 2016 was passed into law.

[312] Previously regulations relating to cyber security in China were scattered across many different laws, regulations and regulatory documents: see, eg, «互联网信息服务管理办法» [Administrative Measures on Internet Information Services] (People's Republic of China) State Council, amended 1 August 2011; «中华人民共和国电信条例» [Telecommunications Regulations of the People's Republic of China] (People's Republic of China) State Council, amended 2 June 2016.

[313] See, eg, Ramsey and Wootliff, 'China's Cyber Security Law' (n 310).

[314] See Circular 317 (n 17).

[315] See above n 283.

companies with businesses in China to store data on servers located inside the country.

Many observers waited for an about-face and a watering down of controversial provisions, as had occurred with the Anti-Terrorism Law.[316] When, in November 2016, the Standing Committee of the National People's Congress approved the Cyber Security Law,[317] ignoring calls for revisions from foreign industry groups, hopes that the Chinese government would respond positively to the concerns expressed on the draft law were initially dashed. This development was in stark contrast to China's Anti-Terrorism Law.[318]

At the same time, there had been a number of attempts to lobby the CAC to delay implementation. On 15 May 2017, global technology companies represented by 54 trade groups from Europe, Asia and the United States petitioned China to delay the enactment of the Cyber Security Law.[319] Their major argument was that it would discriminate against foreign businesses. According to industry experts, it seemed unlikely that there would be any delay in the Cyber Security Law coming into force on 1 June 2017, as the CAC was under heavy pressure to implement it and the supporting regulations.[320]

However, on 19 May 2017 CAC called a meeting – with around 100 participants, including representatives from global tech firms – to present last-minute changes to proposed implementation rules for China's new Cyber Security Law. It was reported that possible changes being considered by CAC included a new 18-month phase-in period from June

---

[316] See, eg, Jack Wagner, 'China's Cybersecurity Law: What You Need to Know' (*The Diplomat*, 1 June 2017) <https://thediplomat.com/2017/06/chinas-cybersecurity-law-what-you-need-to-know>.

[317] The Cyber Security Law (n 2) was adopted at the 24th session of the Standing Committee of the 12th National People's Congress on 7 November 2016. With 7 chapters and 79 articles, the law came into force on 1 June 2017.

[318] The rules in China's Anti-Terrorism Law (n 285) requiring companies in the financial sector to prove the 'security and controllability' of their equipment through intrusive testing were suspended. Encryption code handover requirements under national security and counter-terrorism laws were also rolled back.

[319] The letter was signed by 54 trade groups including the United States–China Business Council, the American Chamber of Commerce in China, Business Europe, the Japan Chamber of Commerce and Industry, and the Korea–China Business Council. See Eva Dou, 'Global Tech Companies Call on China to Delay Cybersecurity Law' (*Wall Street Journal*, 15 May 2017) <https://www.wsj.com/articles/global-tech-companies-call-on-china-to-delay-cybersecurity-law-1494837117>.

[320] The author saw only one advanced mention of a delay potentially occurring: Wagner, 'China's Cybersecurity Law' (n 316).

2017. This would mean that the law would not be fully implemented until the end of 2018, allowing time for further clarity to be provided in the rules.[321] As with the Anti-Terrorism Law, Chinese regulators were clearly concerned not to harm the nation's innovation agenda through hasty implementation.

As China's increased policy support for AI took place simultaneously with the law's enactment in 2017 (discussed in Chapter 8), a new spotlight was shone on the potential shortcomings of the law in connection with globalised R&D in the AI field. Controversial articles in proposed implementing rules were delayed and additional consultations with industry were held. Nevertheless, key terms and provisions remained vague, leading to uncertainty among technology companies subject to the new law.

5.2 The Law: Vague Regulations Make Compliance Difficult

The following discusses the key vague provisions in the Cyber Security Law, and the fuzzy, drawn-out implementation process to illustrate the impact of competing interests on developing technology policy in the current Chinese political environment.

5.2.1 Vague Rules: To Whom Does the Law Apply?

A preliminary question that affects compliance is: to whom does the law apply? Depending on how a company is viewed under the Cyber Security Law, it imposes security obligations. But uncertainty surrounds exactly who will be caught by the new rules. Definitions of entity types are understandable to a reader but not precise. While the new law would clearly apply to businesses and organisations, the extent to which its terms will apply to individual employees and officers as well as web users remains unclear.

Definitions of the following regulated entities are included in the law:

- 'suppliers of network products and services';[322]
- '[suppliers of] critical network equipment and specialised network (cyber) security products';[323]

---

[321] Michael Martina and Cate Cadell, 'Amid Industry Pushback, China Offers Changes to Cyber Rules: Sources' (*Reuters*, 19 May 2017) <http://www.reuters.com/article/us-china-cyber-law-idUSKCN18F1VZ>.
[322] 网络产品, 服务的提供: Cyber Security Law (n 2) arts 22, 64.
[323] 网络关键设备 和网络安全专用产品: ibid art 23. Critical network equipment and specialised network (cyber) security products must obtain government certification or meet prescribed safety inspection requirements before being sold or provided. This

THE CYBER SECURITY LAW

- 'electronic information distributors';[324]
- 'application software providers';[325]
- 'electronic information distributor service providers';[326] and
- 'application software download service providers'.[327]

Examples of which entities would fall within these categories remained speculative but uncontroversial throughout 2017–2021, as these entities' responsibilities pertain to either Chinese online censorship rules or cyber security aims, focusing mainly on content control. This is because content restrictions and punishment of those who breach them were already widely accepted as standard practice in China, and the law did not add much to this area. In Article 48 of the Cyber Security Law, these entities are forbidden from sending or installing 'malicious programs' and must conduct security management tasks for these cyber security measures. Article 68 outlines their punishment for violations.

While law firm bulletins speculated about the precise meaning of all these terms, two terms remained overwhelmingly the subject of the greatest focus: 'critical infrastructure operators' and 'network operators'. These phrases are particularly vague yet highly important. This is because data localisation provisions, which will strongly impact on foreign firms and Chinese firms with international operations, only apply to those entities. Accordingly, these terms and the requirement for data localisation are the focus of this chapter.

---

potentially catches a wide range of software, hardware and other technologies being sold – or proposed to be sold – by international companies in China, since the definitions used in the law are drafted very broadly. Further guidance by way of a catalogue of key network products is expected in due course. Understandably there are concerns that this may create barriers to international businesses looking to enter the Chinese market. This provision is considered further in Section 5.2.3.

[324] 电子信息发送者: ibid arts 48, 68. An example is online content providers. In art 48, they are forbidden from sending 'malicious programs'. Art 68 outlines the punishment for those violations.

[325] 应用软件提供者: ibid arts 48, 68. This relates to software products. In art 48, they are forbidden from sending 'malicious programs'. Art 68 outlines the punishment for those violations.

[326] 电子信息发送服务的提供者: ibid arts 48, 68. This is a vague term that would likely include online news providers. In art 48, they are forbidden from sending 'malicious programs'. Art 68 outlines the punishment for those violations.

[327] 应用软件下载服务提供者: ibid arts 48, 68. This is a vague term that would likely include, for example, the App store for downloading applications. In art 48, they are forbidden from sending 'malicious programs'. Art 68 outlines the punishment for those violations.

'Network Operators' and 'Critical Infrastructure Operators'

This analysis of 'fuzzy logic' regulatory practice turns on the definitions of two key terms: 'network operators'[328] and 'critical infrastructure operators'.[329] These entities are not defined in the law; instead, the definition is left to implementing regulations.

In the law, a range of new obligations apply to an organisation that is a 'network operator'.[330] A network operator is likely to mean a network owner, network administrator or network service provider. A 'network' means any system comprising computers or other information terminals and related equipment for collection, storage, transmission, exchange and processing of information.[331] Some commentators have argued that these broad definitions could catch any business that owns and operates IT networks or infrastructure or even just a website in China.

Some reports suggested that vague terminology could be intended to catch popular apps such as Taobao and WeChat, which have millions of daily users in China who would be affected by a security breach. This is not necessarily a sinister appraisal relating to censorship but rather a data protection issue, discussed further in Chapter 7.

Also, under the law a 'critical infrastructure operator' is not defined; rather, the definition is left to implementing regulations. Considering China's ambitious technology goals and its aspiration to build connected Smart Cities, its aim to protect its infrastructure is justifiable. It seems that the intention of the Cyber Security Law is to regulate tech firms, including Smart City providers, who may control 'critical network equipment' that could be vulnerable to cyberattack.[332]

The definitions in the law become less abstract when viewed in the light of China's Smart City and IoT drive. For example, an IoT manufacturer may be considered a 'network operator' (as a 'network service provider'[333] under Article 76 of the law, or perhaps a provider of

---

[328] 网络运营者: ibid arts 21, 24–5, 28–9, 40–3, 47, 49–50, 59, 61, 64, 68–9. These obligations are set out in appendix 1.
[329] 关键信息基础设施的运营者: ibid arts 34–9, 59, 65–6. These obligations are set out in appendix 1.
[330] See ibid appendix 1.
[331] Ibid art 76(1).
[332] 'Critical network equipment' is not defined in the law.
[333] 'Network service provider' is part of the definition of 'network operators' in art 76(3) of the Cyber Security Law (n 2): 'Network operators refers to network owners, managers and network service providers.'

'network products').³³⁴ Furthermore, IoT manufacturers or Smart City providers might be considered in control of 'critical infrastructure operators' or 'critical network equipment and specialised network (cyber) security products' (Articles 22–23).³³⁵ In turn, a firmware³³⁶ administrator could be considered a 'network operator' or 'application software download service provider' (Article 48).³³⁷ However, what equipment falls into the category of 'critical network equipment' and 'specialised network (cyber) security products' is still unclear.³³⁸

Above all, one important and highly practical question needs clarification: If you provide a service for an SOE, are you then a critical infrastructure provider? The answer to this key question probably depends on the kind of information in question as well as how 'important data' is eventually defined.³³⁹

A broader reading might argue that these terms could affect almost any business that has electronic data in China. The international business community has focused much of its attention on how business obligations will change for foreign firms' mainland China operations and how the law will affect cross-border handling of customer, operations and other data.³⁴⁰ These are all legitimate questions that Chinese regulators need to elaborate upon through detailed implementing rules defining what kinds of businesses will be subject to the definitions. It remains unclear under the law what criteria or procedures will be used for 'critical information infrastructure facilities security assessments'.³⁴¹

---

³³⁴ 'Network products' is not defined in the law.
³³⁵ 'Critical network equipment and specialised network security products' is not defined in the law.
³³⁶ In simple terms, firmware is software that is embedded in a piece of hardware. In the context of IoT companies, it is important how firmware is classified under the Cyber Security Law with regard to security protocols.
³³⁷ 'Application software download service provider' is not defined in the law.
³³⁸ Neither 'critical network equipment' nor 'specialised network (cyber) security products' are defined in the law. A prescribed catalogue of critical network equipment and specialised network (cyber) security products is to be produced in due course, according to Cyber Security Law (n 2) art 23.
³³⁹ 'Critical information infrastructure operators' must comply with ibid arts 34–9, 59 and 65–6, which are all provisions strongly geared towards cyber security incident prevention, disaster recovery and technical support. This further suggests that the law was strongly focused on China's Smart City and IoT ambitions.
³⁴⁰ Companies were represented by chambers of commerce in China in making public statements.
³⁴¹ See Cyber Security Law (n 2) art 37 (discussed in Section 5.2.2).

5.2.2 Vague Rules: Data Localisation (Data Storage Requirements and Data Exits)

The most controversial provision in the Cyber Security Law is Article 37, which mandates China's evolving data storage regime. According to Article 37, businesses designated to be 'critical information infrastructure operators' are required to store their personal or 'important data' within mainland China.

This section also explains that Article 65 of the law, which states that 'critical information infrastructure providers' stand to violate the law if they use products or services that 'have not had safety inspections or did not pass safety inspections'.

Data Storage Requirements

The vague nature of the Cyber Security Law has caused great fear among tech companies. Article 37 has caused foreign observers the greatest concern. First, the article was broadened between the final draft and the passing of the law; the word 'citizens' was deleted so as to require all 'personal information and important data' collected and produced in China to be stored in China. This changed phrasing, set out below, now explicitly includes the data of non-Chinese residents in China:

> Critical information infrastructure operators that gather or produce citizens' personal information or important data during operations within the mainland territory of the People's Republic of China, shall store it within mainland China. Where due to business requirements it is truly necessary to provide it outside the Mainland, they shall follow the measures jointly formulated by the State Cyber Security and Informatisation departments and the relevant departments of the State Council to conduct a security assessment; where laws and administrative regulations provide otherwise, follow those provisions.[342]

Thus, according to Article 37, businesses designated as 'critical information infrastructure operators' are required to store their data within mainland China. Moreover, companies that want to transfer data overseas must undergo a security assessment by regulators, which would depend on the type of data and the scale of the data transfers. The vague nature of this review process is explained in Section 5.2.3.

---

[342] Ibid art 37.

The following explains the evolving rules that apply to particular types of entities caught by Article 37 of the law:

- First, only 'network products and services' used in 'critical information infrastructure' will be subject to review. The law's text offers no details on what this will entail. According to the Interim Measures for Cyber Security Review (explained in Section 5.2.3), the review would not be a compliance test, but would focus on the trustworthiness of the company and its supply chain rather than on the nature of the products or services.[343]
- Second, 'critical information infrastructure operators' must store user data within the territory of mainland China. Problematically, data collection operators that may be labelled 'critical information infrastructure operators' may be obliged to store data and personal information collected and produced by their services in China.[344] This raises the question of how 'data' and 'personal information' are defined (explained in the next section and in Chapter 7). Companies may apply for exceptions to this rule, but only after undergoing an additional audit and certification process unspecified by the new law.
- The law defines critical information infrastructure as services that may endanger national security or the public interest if they break down or suffer data leaks, with finance and electricity among the examples provided.[345] Draft implementation regulations list 27 types of data under this category,[346] including financial, infrastructure-related, health and medical information.

Understandably, Article 37 has created fears of potential trade secret and intellectual property theft in China, and the possibility that, in a security event, the Chinese government would receive the encryption keys to servers containing all business data stored in China. Data storage compliance costs and the scope of 'security assessments' have also proved worrying.

Data Exits

Data exits from China is a key issue under Article 37 of the Cyber Security Law. The article allows for data storage exceptions, and future

---

[343] «网络产品和服务安全审查办法 (试行)» [Security Review Measures for Network Products and Services (Interim)] (People's Republic of China) CAC, 2 May 2017 (Interim Security Review Measures).
[344] Cyber Security Law (n 2) art 37.
[345] See ibid art 31.
[346] See Chapter 7.

regulations might provide more clarity about who is exempt from the requirement. Personal data[347] and important data generated or collected in China by the operators of 'critical information infrastructure facilities' (which could mean cloud computing firms)[348] must be stored in China.

However, data transfers abroad are allowed if: (1) there is a business need; and (2) security assessments are passed according to the rules issued by CAC or other relevant governmental agencies. A fuzzy loophole therefore exists in the original legislation. Exemptions would likely operate but questions remain. For example, must the data continue to be held in China as well or does the transfer mean the data ceases to exist in China?

Crucially, the law does not specify what is meant by other 'important data' in Article 37. (Article 31 of the law does provide the concept and examples of critical information infrastructure: see Section 5.2.3). That ambiguity may, in effect, mean keeping all data (in addition to personal data) inside China, costing overseas and some Chinese companies more, and heightening fears of proprietary data theft.

Importantly, open innovation by means of open access to data conflicts with elements of the Cyber Security Law, principally Article 37. In Chapter 8 it is shown that open-source platforms would be impacted by data localisation provisions of the Cyber Security Law, if they were strictly enforced. This is because the law includes two broad categories of data: 'personal information' and 'important data'. The two concepts were explained in an essay on the CAC website written by Dr Hong Yanqing (洪延青), the lead drafter of the data privacy specification outlined in detail in Chapter 7. Hong wrote that protection of personal data refers to having 'autonomy and control over one's data', aligning with the general understanding of privacy in Western legal traditions.[349] He wrote further that 'personal data' is distinct from individual concerns, and pertains to interests 'at the national level' that concern 'important data affecting national security, the national economy, and people's

---

[347] 'Personal information' is defined as including all kinds of information, recorded electronically or through other means, that can identify a person's identity, including full names, birth dates, identification numbers, personal biometric information, addresses and telephone numbers. See Cyber Security Law (n 2) art 76(5). See also Chapter 7.

[348] Cloud computing servers are, interestingly, not mentioned in the Cyber Security Law (n 2).

[349] 洪延青 [Hong Yanqing], «数据出境安全评估: 保护基础性战略资源的重要一环» [Outbound Data Security Assessment: An Important Part of Protecting Basic Strategic Resources] (*CAC*, 7 August 2017) <http://www.cac.gov.cn/2017-08/07/m_1121443948.htm> (the link is no longer active).

livelihood'.[350] Thus 'personal information' governance is seemingly primarily a function of the interests of the individual, while 'important data' governance concerns issues ranging from everyday cyber security needs to broader concerns about national security and prosperity.[351]

Presumably, the fuzziness of the word 'important' would affect Chinese data flows, as the meaning of the phrase could remain in flux indefinitely.

5.2.3 Vague Rules: Unclear Product Review Requirements

Article 65 of the Cyber Security Law states that 'critical information infrastructure providers' stand to violate the law if they use products or services that 'have not had safety inspections or did not pass safety inspections'. Article 31 provides a seemingly partial definition of 'critical information infrastructure operators' who are subject to a cyber security review:

> The State implements key protection on the basis of the cyber security multi-level protection system for public communication and information services, power, traffic, water resources, finance, public service, e-government, and other critical information infrastructure which – if destroyed, suffering a loss of function, or experiencing leakage of data – might seriously endanger national security, national welfare, the people's livelihood, or the public interest. The State Council will formulate the specific scope and security protection measures for critical information infrastructure.
>
> The State encourages operators of networks outside the [designated] critical information infrastructure systems to voluntarily participate in the critical information infrastructure protection system.[352]

However, the nature and procedure for these safety inspections remained only partially specified at the time the law was published. The government was also yet to formulate and promulgate the catalogue of key network equipment.[353]

Article 21 of the law states that 'network operators' must meet a set of standards in a future cyber security multi-level protection system. These standards were not initially included in the published law, but

---

[350] Ibid.
[351] Ibid.
[352] Cyber Security Law (n 2) art 31.
[353] Ibid art 23.

Article 21 lists a series of pre-emptive cyber security measures a 'network operator' must adopt to self-regulate, such as:

- formulate internal security management systems;
- adopt technical measures to prevent computer viruses, cyberattacks and network intrusions;
- monitor and record network operational statuses and cyber security incidents; and
- adopt measures such as data classification, backup of important data and encryption.

According to Article 23, products and services providers should comply with the compulsory requirements of relevant national standards: 'key network equipment' and 'specialised cyber security products' must be either certified or tested by a licensed security certification institution in order to ensure compliance with relevant national and industry standards, and are not allowed to be released into the Chinese market unless they have passed the certification or testing process.

The security review measures in the law add that national security[354] checks triggering cyber security reviews of critical information infrastructure network operators shall be determined by critical information infrastructure protection departments.[355] Adding another layer of bureaucratic uncertainty to a contentious provision and resembling China's policy of 'indigenous innovations' (described in Chapter 1) is the fact that government procurement decisions will be influenced or even determined by the new cyber security review. This type of provision is what has led to charges of 'indigenous innovation'-style protectionism being levelled against China.[356]

---

[354] The Cyber Security Law (n 2) also requires internet company operators to cooperate with investigations involving criminal conduct and national security. Companies must give government investigators full access to their data if national security risks are suspected. Art 75 states that the Chinese government will handle cyber security threats originating from within the country or overseas sources. The review process is unclear in the law itself. See arts 12, 28, 31, 35, 58 and 63, which refer to national security events and the corresponding requirements.

[355] Ibid art 11.

[356] Ibid art 10: 'Party and government departments and key industries shall prioritise the procurement of network products and services that have passed the review, and shall not procure network products and services that have failed the review.' Chinese policy documents continue to reference indigenous innovations. For example, the State Council's original outline of its China Manufacturing 2025 policy included market share targets to 'realise guarantees of self-sufficiency' (实现自主保障) for sourcing 40% and

Thus, a common perception among foreign companies, venture capitalists and commentators is that China's Cyber Security Law would simply benefit Chinese incumbents, especially China's cloud computing industry (eg, Alibaba's cloud computing arm, AliYun),[357] which can more easily abide by these rules. This claim is critically analysed in Chapter 6, where it is argued that such a perception is valid, but also too simplistic within the current globalised technology supply chain, including in the AI R&D environment.

Another important question that emerges from the vague provisions in the law is: how do these security reviews relate to encryption and enforced backdoors?

5.3 Backdoors under the Cyber Security Law?

So-called backdoors to encryption might be required by the Cyber Security Law in order to allow security testing.[358] As documented in Chapter 4, such backdoors were ultimately rejected during the drafting of the Anti-Terrorism Law. It was also noted that mandating backdoors can create security vulnerabilities within network products.

While media reports stated that foreign tech companies will be required to provide source code to the Chinese government under proposed security reviews, there is no such obligation in the Cyber

---

70% of both core components and key basic materials by 2020 and 2025 respectively: «国务院关于印发'中国制造 2025'的通知» [Notification on the Printing and Distribution of Made in China 2025] (State Council, 8 May 2015) <http://www.gov.cn/zhengce/content/2015-05/19/content_9784.htm>.

The China Manufacturing 2025 roadmap also includes numerous mentions of 'indigenous innovation' (自主创新) and 'self-sufficiency' (自主保障, 自给, 自给率). This is consistent with the «国家中长期科学和技术发展规划纲要 (2006-2020年)» [National Outline for Medium- and Long-Term Science and Technology Development Planning (2006-2020) Ministry of Science and Technology, 9 February 2006 <http://www.gov.cn/jrzg/2006-02/09/content_183787.htm> and the «国务院关于加快培育和发展战略性新兴产业的决» [Decision on Accelerating and Developing Strategic Emerging Industries] State Council, 18 October 2010 <http://www.gov.cn/zwgk/2010-10/18/content_1724848.htm>: 'Strategic Emerging Industries Likely to Contribute 8% of GDP by 2015' (*People's Daily*, 19 October 2010) <http://en.people.cn/90001/90778/90862/7170816.html>.

[357] See, eg, 'China's Cybersecurity Law Enacted' (*ChinaTechNews*, 7 November 2016) <https://www.chinatechnews.com/2016/11/07/24439-chinas-cybersecurity-law-enacted>.

[358] China's Cyber Security Law arguably echoes other existing requirements that companies install 'backdoors' so that security agencies can access encrypted communications. At the time of writing the process remains unclear.

Security Law, which adopts a fuzzy logic approach by failing to explain what the source code compliance requirements are. Subsequently, Chinese regulators continued the compliance debate with Chinese and foreign tech companies during 2017–2020 and beyond. They thereby demonstrated that reports of CAC '[i]ndiscriminately requiring businesses to hand over source codes'[359] are inaccurate, at least at the time of writing, as the precise implementing rules are yet to be finalised.

While certification requirements could ultimately mean that tech companies will be asked to provide source code, encryption or other critical intellectual property for review by security authorities, reports suggest that this did not occur during 2017–2020.

Some tech firms have been pro-active in setting up security review processes, based on their interpretation of the law. For example, Microsoft in China already allows regulatory review of its software under controlled conditions[360] and in 2016 announced its 'transparency centre', allowing Chinese government coders to test and analyse Microsoft's products for cyber security issues.[361] Under the Cyber Security Law, tech companies may be required to provide source code to third-party bodies as part of specific licensing/review requirements. However, this was never explicitly legislated under the law; it was merely interpreted that way by some observers. That could take place in a system similar to Microsoft's transparency centres, in which regulators can review source code in a highly controlled environment. It is important to point out that this kind of security review is not just occurring in China, but has been effectively mandated in other countries too. For example, Chinese surveillance company Hikvision created a transparency centre in California in 2018 and these transparency centres may become a global trend in the current commercial and geopolitical backdrop.[362] Chinese ICT giant Huawei, which was under increasing scrutiny in 2018 and 2019, also

---

[359] Martina and Cadell, 'Amid Industry Pushback, China Offers Changes to Cyber Rules' (n 321).

[360] Eva Dou, 'Microsoft, Intel, IBM Push Back on China Cybersecurity Rules' (*Wall Street Journal*, 1 December 2016) <http://www.wsj.com/articles/microsoft-intel-ibm-push-back-on-china-cybersecurity-rules-1480587542>.

[361] Tekendra Parmar, 'China: Tech Giants Push Back against Beijing's New Cyber Security Bill' (*Fortune*, 2 December 2016) <https://fortune.com/2016/12/02/cyber-security-bill-source-code/≥.

[362] 'Hikvision Launches Source Code Transparency Center' (*Ciston PR Newswire*, 8 March 2018) <https://www.prnewswire.com/news-releases/hikvision-launches-source-code-transparency-center-300610397.html>.

created a source code transparency centre in Germany in October 2018, and has had a similar centre in the United Kingdom for many years, seeking to allay foreign suspicions of its influence over critical infrastructure.[363]

Nevertheless, tech companies have made public statements criticising China's Cyber Security Law for requiring companies to share proprietary source code within China. Microsoft wrote in a public statement that '[s]haring source code in itself can't prove the capability to be secure and controllable. It only proves there is source code'.[364] An expert security audit would be required to prove this capability. China would reportedly need to build its cryptographic expertise to be able to conduct such security audits.[365]

---

[363] Douglas Busvine, 'Exclusive: China's Huawei opens up to German Scrutiny ahead of 5G Auctions' (*Reuters*, 23 October 2018) <https://www.reuters.com/article/us-germany-telecoms-huawei-exclusive/exclusive-chinas-huawei-opens-up-to-german-scrutiny-ahead-of-5g-auctions-idUSKCN1MX1VB>.

[364] Dou, 'Microsoft, Intel, IBM Push Back' (n 360).

[365] In reality, for both financial and technical reasons, it is unlikely that China would invest in auditing source code to ensure Chinese Network Sovereignty. This might be too great a task. This is because in cyber security it is much easier to build attacks than to verify defences: Interview with cyber security expert (via Skype, 3 October 2018).

Furthermore, the following explains the complexity of such disclosures from a technical perspective. Cyber security algorithms are often public. Encryption algorithms are standardised, are created by public research and are mostly not proprietary. This is true for all the encryption algorithms in very common use, but some important ones have been patented. Encryption algorithms are rarely secret as that is a recipe for exploitable products. (Encryption algorithms may be intellectual property, but they are not 'secret'. Encryption technology is generally available as open-source products, which it would be trivial to subvert.) However, how encryption algorithms are integrated to software is both intellectual property and a possible target for cyberattack. That is, the code that combines different primitive cryptographic algorithms is often secret, and amounts to intellectual property.

Source code disclosure, on the other hand, would be a major risk. Intellectual property theft may occur, as source code amounts to instructions of how to do something. Source code is the implementation instructions for that encryption design, for example.

Overall, cyber security depends on many things, including how code is added to the wider product. In essence, you cannot tell if your house is secure just by looking at the lock on the door. You have to look at the door frame. If the whole house's source code was shared, there may be serious intellectual property theft concerns.

Furthermore, backdoors do not affect the company that creates the encryption technology, but the companies that use encryption technology might need to worry, as might individuals who have an expectation of privacy. For example, if Microsoft provides encryption technology to Ford Motor Company, the Chinese government might request Microsoft's assistance in an investigation of Ford.

5.4 Third Parties in Security Reviews under the Cyber Security Law

There are also uncertainties relating to third-party involvement in security reviews. In dealing with the issue of prejudice towards foreign technology providers under the law, the role of third-party involvement in security reviews must be considered. The extent of such third-party involvement, and especially the involvement of foreign entities, is unclear in the law. Thus, another major ongoing question is: What role will third parties have in China's cyber regime?

Article 34 of the Cyber Security Law requires firms that operate 'critical information infrastructure' to fulfil security protection obligations, and is very broadly worded:

> In addition to the provisions of Article 21 of this law,[366] critical information infrastructure operators shall also perform the following security protection duties:

> (1) Set up specialised security management bodies and persons responsible for security management, and conduct security background checks on those responsible persons and personnel in critical positions;
> (2) Periodically conduct network security education, technical training and skills evaluations for employees;
> (3) Conduct disaster recovery backups of important systems and databases;
> (4) Formulate emergency response plans for network security incidents, and periodically organise drills;
> (5) Other obligations provided by law or administrative regulations.

Article 34 could become important to offsetting foreign fears, as companies will likely negotiate mutually agreed outcomes with the Chinese government. These agreements may be entered into as part of joint

---

> Companies are required to report 'network security incidents' to the Chinese government and inform consumers of breaches, but the law also states that companies must provide 'technical support' to government agencies during investigations. 'Technical support' is also not clearly defined, but could mean providing encryption backdoors or other surveillance assistance to the government.
>
> Thus, the issue is how encryption usage is legislated. In practical terms, there is no difference between building a backdoor or forcing Microsoft to un-encrypt when 'technical support' is required. Currently we have no concrete idea what 'technical support' means. It does raise concerns at least theoretically of commercial espionage and sabotage.

[366] Art 21 pertains to security inspections: Cyber Security Law (n 2) art 34.

venture or licensing agreements; or, like Microsoft, companies could open a 'transparency centre' where Chinese government coders could test and analyse Microsoft's products for security.[367] Perhaps a regulatory precedent will be set by Microsoft's new centre.

Article 34 may also just be a codification of existing practices. In 2016, Samm Sacks, the then head of Asia-Pacific Cyber Security Strategy for Siemens AG, referred to China's common practices and existing informal pressures and argued as follows:

> Beyond the new and pending laws and regulations, foreign firms already face pressure to submit source code, undergo security audits, and localize data and equipment. These procedures are costly and expose foreign tech companies to a host of security, regulatory, and [intellectual property] risks in order to be in the market.
>
> Foreign tech firms have been providing at least partial source code to the Chinese government for years. For example, Microsoft provided Windows source code to the Chinese government in the 1990s. And it remains the common practice today. Providing source code is not necessarily the same as providing so-called 'backdoor' access to device contents, but it does have significant security implications. And understanding the ongoing provision of such information is necessary to meaningfully evaluate the consequences of other requirements.
>
> Similarly, security audits are also a regular part of operating in the China market. In practice, a security audit could range from something as benign as sitting down for a series of meetings with government officials – perhaps from the Ministry of Public Security – and answering questions about security features, data storage, or management techniques to something far more invasive. And as a consequence of the pending laws and regulations, these security reviews are likely to become increasingly intensive.[368]

Nevertheless, the Chinese government has continued to draft regulations to clarify the scope and implementation of China's Cyber Security Law, especially in the area of third-party participation and consultation. In China's entrepreneurial ecosystem where complex competing goals of Network Sovereignty and Informatisation collide, it seems likely that

---

[367] Parmar, 'China: Tech Giants Push Back' (n 361).
[368] Sacks, 'Apple in China, Part I' (n 212). In January 2015, Apple became the first foreign tech company to publicly announce it would comply with increasing China's increasing security review procedures: Yin Cao, 'Rule to Protect Security "On the Way this Year"' (*China Daily*, 22 January 2015) <http://www.chinadaily.com.cn/china/2015-01/22/content_19373572.htm>.

foreign firms will be (or already have been) consulted as part of this process. Article 29 of the Cyber Security Law, for example, provides that 'relevant industry organisations will establish sound cyber security standards and mechanisms for coordination'.

On 4 February 2017, CAC sought public opinion on its draft internet product and service security inspection rules under the Cyber Security Law: the Measures for Security Reviews of Network Products and Services (Opinion-Seeking Draft) (Draft Security Review Measures).[369] Articles 5–8 of the draft measures contain numerous references to a new body to oversee technical matters: the Cyber Security Review Committee.[370] Under the committee, a Cyber Security Review Office would be established to handle the actual review work.[371]

In assisting the office's review, two more groups would be involved in the process: designated third-party evaluation centres, providing technical evaluation reports; and an expert panel assembled by the committee, to evaluate whether the suppliers are 'secure and controllable' on the basis of third-party reports. The office would then make decisions based on the third-party reports and the panel's recommendations.[372] This raised a number of questions. Would these new organs include

---

[369] «网络产品和服务安全审查办法征求意见 (草案征求意见稿)» [Measures for Security Reviews of Network Products and Services (Opinion-Seeking Draft)] (People's Republic of China) SIIO, 4 February 2017 (Draft Security Review Measures).

[370] See ibid arts 5,6,7,8.

[371] The Draft Security Review Measures (n 369) provide that the Cyber Security Review Office can initiate security reviews in response to requests made by government agencies, suggestions made by trade associations, or incidents in the market. Companies can also voluntarily submit their products or services for review (art 8). The review will consist of four elements: lab testing, on-site inspection, online monitoring, and review of background information (art 3). No further detail was provided with respect to how these elements will be carried out and the overall timeframe for the entire review.

[372] The *Global Times*, a state-owned tabloid newspaper, reported that yet another cyber organisation would be created from the Draft Security Review Measures (n 369): 'A proposed new cyber security watchdog will prevent online products and services from being manipulated by foreign forces and safeguard Party and government departments and key industries from national security threats.' The report went on: 'Because China now still heavily relies on foreign core technology, the Web review body will examine loopholes that may have been intentionally installed into online products or services, which might pose a threat to national security.' Liu Caiyu, 'China Eyes New Cyber Security Watchdog' (*Global Times*, 2 February 2017) <http://www.globaltimes.cn/content/1031517.shtml>.

representatives from foreign tech companies? Would the 'third-party institutions'[373] in Article 7 include foreign technology companies?[374]

Subsequently, on 2 May 2017 China released the Interim Security Review Measures for Network Products and Services (Interim Security Review Measures).[375] It is a short document of 16 provisions which states that these reviews will focus on the 'security and controllability of network products'.[376] CAC will perform the reviews.

The Interim Security Review Measures require a security review of certain imported foreign IT equipment and services to ensure they are 'secure and controllable.' Inbound IT equipment and services are to be assessed for various risks, including the risk the products or servers will be illegally controlled, interfered with or interrupted or that the provider of the product or service may use it to illegally collect, store, process or use its users' personal information.

Again, in the Interim Security Review Measures there are multiple references to accredited third parties in cyber security reviews.[377]

---

[373] In Chinese, the phrases '第三方评价' (third-party appraisals) and '第三方机构' (third-party organisations or institutions) suggest an air of objectivity in Chinese language usage.

[374] It could be that only Chinese organisations are capable of providing the necessary technical support. There is a precedent. Foreign cloud service providers in China are currently required to obtain a mobile service licence, for which issuance is restricted by regulation, and are largely held by domestic data service operators. Therefore, a Sino-foreign joint venture needs to be established in order to obtain the licence.
This dynamic is typified in IBM's cooperation with Tencent Cloud and 21Vianet, which has enabled it to offer its services to the Chinese market and participate in the construction of a large data centre just outside Beijing. Microsoft and Amazon have also established partnerships with domestic Chinese companies in order to offer their cloud services in China. Intel and Oracle are two Western companies that bought into China's existing cloud systems.
For a cloud services review, it was China Academy of Information and Communications Technology (CAICT), China Information Technology Security Certification Center (CNITSEC), a source code review lab, and China Electronic Standardization Institute (CESI). These bodies will likely be included as third-party reviewers for Cyber Security Reviews.
Nevertheless, TC260 was involved in drafting standards for China's cloud security review regime. See US Information Technology Office, 'TC260 Drafts New Standard for China's Cloud Security Review Regime' (*USITO*, 26 June 2015) <http://www.usito.org/news/tc260-drafts-new-standard-chinas-cloud-security-review-regime>.

[375] See Interim Security Review Measures (n 343).

[376] Ibid art 4.

[377] Ibid arts 3, 6, 7, 8, 11, 12. See, eg, art 6: 'The Cyber Security Review Committee shall engage relevant experts to establish a Cyber Security Review Experts Committee, which shall, based on third-party assessments, perform comprehensive assessment on the

Regulatory updates continue to refer to third-party cyber security assessments.[378] In fact, 6 of the 16 articles mention third-party organisations or assessments. Thus, the final resolution of who these third parties are and how assessments would be conducted could go a long way to ease foreign and domestic concerns.

A possible indicator that the 'third parties' may include qualified foreign participants can be seen in the way that key Chinese information security institutions, such as the China National Information Security Standards Technical Committee (TC260), have been open to international cooperation. In August 2016, it was reported that TC260 was at work defining cyber security standards. It allowed Microsoft, Intel, Cisco and IBM to take part in drafting these security rules rather than participating as observers only.[379]

TC260 is a cyber security advisory committee tasked with defining China's standards for 'secure and controllable' technologies.[380] It is involved in discussions of data storage and encryption. There is a live issue to be addressed by TC260 in that global companies juggling multiple national security agendas can encounter many competing standards.[381] Many closed-door conversations take place, with both Chinese and foreign companies involved. Perhaps these foreign tech firms, members of TC260, already know the answer to the problem of vague Chinese regulations and understand phrases such as 'secure and controllable'.

For example, with regard to the location of servers within China, many foreign internet companies complied with this measure well before the Cyber Security Law was enacted or data localisation details were finalised, indicating that they may have already received at least informal administrative guidance from relevant Chinese government departments.[382]

---

security risks of network products and services, and the security and trustworthiness of the suppliers.'

[378] Interim Security Review Measures (n 343) arts 7, 8, 11.

[379] Eva Dou and Rachel King, 'China Sets New Tone in Drafting Cybersecurity Rules' (*Wall Street Journal*, 26 August 2016) <http://www.wsj.com/articles/china-moves-to-ease-foreign-concerns-on-cybersecurity-controls-1472132575>.

[380] Ibid. The participation of foreign firms was also reported in cyber security circles: see, eg, Samm Sacks and Manyi Kathy Li, 'How Chinese Cybersecurity Standards Impact Doing Business in China' (*CSIS*, 2 August 2018) <https://www.csis.org/analysis/how-chinese-cybersecurity-standards-impact-doing-business-china>.

[381] Ibid.

[382] Companies such as Apple and Airbnb pre-emptively complied with Chinese demands for local data centres within mainland China before the Cyber Security Law came into

Global cooperation in the form of technical standard setting remains a goal of China's Cyber Security Law. Article 7 of the law echoes the aspiration of Network Sovereignty to create global internet standards.[383] It is difficult to see how such global standards can be developed without consultation between Chinese government regulators and multinational tech firms. TC260 was an example of such consultations before 1 June 2017, but its continuing role remains unclear.

In 2020, the updated Interim Security Review Measures were released, taking effect on 1 June 2020.[384] The 2020 Security Review Measures[385] mandated measures for reviewing procurement of network products and services used by 'critical information infrastructure operators', allocating four Chinese bureaucracies as the third parties responsible for this review process. While the chain of authority was clarified, the scope of 'critical information infrastructure operators' remain undefined.[386]

5.5 Evolving and Contradictory Subordinate Regulations on Data Transfers and Network Security

Analysis of the evolving subordinate regulations that have emerged to accompany the Cyber Security Law indicates that the issue of cross-border data flows is complex, and still evolving. On 11 April 2017, CAC released a policy circular for public consultation.[387] The circular sought opinions until 11 May 2017 on the Personal Information and Important Data Outbound Security Assessment Measures (Draft) (Draft

---

effect (discussed in Chapter 6). Airbnb, for example, announced in November 2016 that it would move its Chinese user data to a domestic location, over a year after it officially entered the Chinese market via a joint venture: Horwitz, 'China's Bewildering New Cybersecurity Law' (n 57).

[383] Cyber Security Law (n 2) art 7.
[384] The Interim Security Review Measures (n 343) would be replaced by subsequent Cyber Security Review Measures 《网络安全审查办法》 [Cyber Security Review Measures] (People's Republic of China) CAC, 13 April 2020 (2020 Security Review Measures).
[385] 2020 Security Review Measures (n 384).
[386] The relevant bodies listed as responsible for the review process are the Cyber Security Review Office (网络安全审查办公室), Cyber Security Review Working Group (网络安全审查工作组), CII Protection Departments (信息基础设施保护工作部门) and CAC.
[387] 《个人信息和重要数据出境安全评估办法 (征求意见稿》 公开征求意见 [Circular of the SIIO Seeking Public Opinions on the 'Measures for the Assessment of Personal Information and Important Data Exit Security (Opinion-Seeking Draft)'] (People's Republic of China) SIIO, 11 April 2017.

Outbound Data Measures).[388] These measures were designed to implement Article 37 of the Cyber Security Law, which required 'personal information and important data' gathered or produced in China by 'critical information infrastructure operators' to be stored in China. This amounted to a sweeping but vague requirement for data localisation. However, Article 37 added that if it is 'truly necessary' for critical information infrastructure operators' to send this data outside China, they may do so in accordance with 'measures' formulated by cyberspace and other authorities.

In brief, the Draft Outbound Data Measures require 'network operators' in China looking to transfer data abroad to undergo a security assessment to determine whether: (a) the transaction carries any national security 'risks such as disclosure, damage, tampering and abuse'; or (b) any business seeking to transfer over one terabyte of data or information on 500,000 or more individuals.[389]

This original version in April 2017 seemed to widen the applicability of the Cyber Security Law. The rules limiting the transfer of data outside China's borders had previously applied only to 'critical information infrastructure operators', but the Draft Outbound Data Measures also

---

[388] 《个人信息和重要数据出境安全评估办法 (征求意见稿)》 [Personal Information and Important Data Outbound Security Assessment Measures (Opinion-Seeking Draft)] (People's Republic of China) SIIO, 11 April 2017 (Draft Outbound Data Measures).

[389] Ibid. Art 9 of the Draft Outbound Data Measures blocks data transfers under the following circumstances: 'Article 9: If outbound data is stored in one of the following circumstances, network operators should report to the industry regulators or supervisory authorities and organise a security assessment:

(A) the [dataset] contains or has accumulated personal information of more than 500,000 people;
(B) the amount of data is over 1,000 GB;
(C) the data includes sector data on nuclear facilities, chemical and biological facilities, the national defence industry, or population health, large-scale engineering activities, the marine environment, and sensitive geographic information data;
(D) the data includes cyber security information including system vulnerabilities and security protection for critical information infrastructure;
(E) the data includes personal information and important data provided by critical information infrastructure operators to [parties] outside China;
(F) the data includes other data that could affect national security and social and public interests that industry regulators or supervisory departments consider should be assessed.

For areas where there is no clear industry regulator or supervisory department, an assessment shall be organised by national cyber security and informatisation departments.'

included 'network operators'.[390] 'Network operator' remains undefined and could be very broad.

However, a second version of the measures (Draft Outbound Data Measures 2) was privately circulated in May 2017, which gave network operators and critical information infrastructure operators until 31 December 2018 to comply with the data export provisions.[391]

These private or internally circulated 内部 (*neibu*) measures reflect the problems associated with fuzzy logic regulation described in Chapters 2–4. Their legal status is not clear, but regulated parties are still expected to comply with them as a matter of practice; this obviously means that communication with regulators is essential to discover what the fuzzy laws really mean in practice.[392]

The Draft Outbound Data Measures 2 also prohibit any transfer of personal information without prior consent of the user.[393] Nevertheless, few clues were given as to how this process would take place.

While terms in the Outbound Data Measures are generally consistent with the Cyber Security Law, Article 6 of the Outbound Data Measures allows 'industry regulatory or supervisory departments' to be responsible for the security assessment of the outbound data and to regularly organise the inspection of the specific industry's outbound data. Greenleaf and Livingston suggest that, in most cases, these inspections will be 'self-assessments' conducted by the companies themselves, although the circumstances when they may be escalated to regulators are still not clearly stated.[394]

While providing some clarification of security assessments on outbound data transfers, and implying that a certain amount of self-regulation by firms will be permitted, the Outbound Data Measures have not yet been formally issued, and their legal force remains uncertain.

---

[390] 'Network operators' were not included in Cyber Security Law (n 2) art 37.
[391] Graham Greenleaf and Scott Livingston, 'PRC's New Data Export Rules: "Adequacy with Chinese Characteristics"?' (2017) 147 *Privacy Laws & Business International Report* 9.
[392] Peerenboom, *China's Long March toward Rule of Law* (n 113) 7.
[393] 'Personal information' is defined as various types of information recorded by electronic or other means capable of identifying a person's personal identity alone or in combination with other information. It includes the name of the natural person, date of birth, identity document number, personal biometric information and telephone number: Draft Outbound Data Measures 2 (see Section 5.5) art 17. 'Important data' refers to data that is closely related to national security, economic development and social and public interests, with specific reference to national relevant standards and important data identification guidelines: at art 17.
[394] Greenleaf and Livingston, 'PRC's New Data Export Rules' (n 391).

However, on 15 September 2018 the Ministry of Public Security released the Provisions for the Supervision and Inspection of Network Security by Public Security Agencies, also known as Circular 151 (effective from 1 November 2018). This new regulation provides a legal basis and framework for wide-ranging authority for local law enforcement agencies (the Public Security Bureau) to enforce China's cyber security and data privacy laws by conducting onsite or remote inspections of internet service providers, as well as any entities that use networks for their operations. The emphasis of Circular 151 is to ensure that companies register as network operators (or service providers) under the Cyber Security Law. There are penalties for noncompliance.

Thus, as was evident with the drafting of the Anti-Terrorism Law, the uncertainty with issuing subordinate regulations to the Cyber Security Law, and the contradictory signals sent out by different government departments with respect to self-regulation versus intrusive regulatory or public security monitoring demonstrate once again the competing policy interests within the Chinese government.

The result is a regulatory pendulum constantly swinging back and forth between Network Sovereignty and more laissez-faire innovation policies – a fuzzy realm in which tech firms must seek to operate as effectively as they can.

5.6 Unresolved Issues: The Current Status of Cross-Border Data Flows under Article 37 of the Cyber Security Law

China's Cyber Security Law is, at the time of writing, yet to be clarified and fully enforced. China's legislative approach in 2017 appeared to be a blanket ban on overseas data transfers, due to the use of the vague term 'important data'. This made the Chinese method unique when compared to other nations' partial localisation policies, such as the limited localisation policy for health data in Australia. A blanket banning of cross-border data transfers was seen as highly problematic by leading legal practitioners,[395] possibly affecting Chinese firms' ability to innovate in the field of AI, to expand overseas and become globally competitive, and hampering foreign firms' expansion in China. Few subordinate regulatory updates were released in 2018, but regulatory updates related to the

---

[395] Steve Dickinson and Grace Yang, 'China's Cybersecurity Law and Employee Personal Information' (*China Law Blog*, 8 January 2017) <http://www.chinalawblog.com/2017/01/chinas-cybersecurity-law-and-employee-personal-information.html>.

Cyber Security Law were finally released in mid-2019.[396] In May–June 2019, about two years after China's Cyber Security Law came into effect on 1 June 2017, the Chinese government released several new draft regulations. The regulations provide some further details about how major aspects of the Cyber Security Law will operate and also provide further examples of fuzzy logic in operation.

One new draft measure is particularly important as it possibly supersedes a previously unfinalised draft regarding cross-border data flows. In June 2019, China released a draft regulation governing the transfer of personal information out of China: the Personal Information Outbound Transfer Security Assessment Measures (Draft) (Draft Outbound Data Measures 3).[397] These measures were developed to expand China's existing Cyber Security Law, and were released for a month-long public

---

[396] After long waits in several cases, several draft regulatory documents were published in mid-2019. They include:

«网络安全审查办法 (征求意见稿)» [Cyber Security Review Measures (Opinion-Seeking Draft)] (People's Republic of China) CAC, 21 May 2019. This measure creates a cyber security review regime for information technology products and services linked to 'national security'. A translation can be found here: https://www.newamerica.org/cybersecurity-initiative/digichina/blog/chinas-cybersecurity-reviews-critical-systems-add-focus-supply-chain-foreign-control-translation.

«数据安全管理办法 (征求意见稿)» [Data Security Management Measures (Opinion-Seeking Draft)] (People's Republic of China) CAC, 28 May 2019 (Draft Data Security Management Measures). This draft provides some additional information regarding the meaning of 'important data' and is cited in Section 5.6.1. A translation can be found here: https://www.newamerica.org/cybersecurity-initiative/digichina/blog/translation-chinas-new-draft-data-security-management-measures.

«网络关键设备安全检测实施办法 (征求意见稿)» [Critical Network Equipment Security Testing Implementing Measures (Opinion-Seeking Draft)] (People's Republic of China) CAC, 4 June 2019. This draft measure relates to the testing of 'critical network equipment' under Cyber Security Law (n 2) art 23. A translation can be found here: https://www.newamerica.org/cybersecurity-initiative/digichina/blog/translation-critical-network-equipment-testing-implementing-measures-draft-comment.

«个人信息出境安全评估办法 (征求意见稿) 公开征求意见的通知» [Personal Information Outbound Transfer Security Assessment Measures (Opinion-Seeking Draft)] (People's Republic of China) CAC, 13 June 2019 (Draft Outbound Data Measures 3). A translation can be found here: https://www.newamerica.org/cybersecurity-initiative/digichina/blog/translation-new-draft-rules-cross-border-transfer-personal-information-out-china.

These measures will likely be the supporting documents of the Cyber Security Law. Elements relevant to this book have been cited in the main text analysis.

[397] Draft Outbound Data Measures 3 (n 396).

comment period. The Cyber Security Law continues to take precedence over the measures.[398]

The Draft Outbound Data Measures 3 aim to ensure that data protection objectives are upheld and that people whose data is transferred abroad have their interests protected. This is consistent with the discussion of China's data protection regime in Chapter 7. Scholar and government adviser Dr Hong Yanqing wrote in a WeChat post that the intent of the regulation is to protect the 'legitimate rights and interests of individuals if [their] data is separated from the original data controller and travels outside of the country'.[399]

On closer inspection of the Draft Outbound Data Measures 3, several unresolved issues further reveal fuzzy logic in action. These unresolved issues may have implications for how the Chinese government is responding to the longstanding domestic and international technology industry concerns outlined in Chapters 7–9.

For example, would the Draft Outbound Data Measures 3 replace the draft measures on security assessments for cross-border data transfer, and the surrounding controversy (noted in Section 5.5)? The original Draft Outbound Data Measures[400] released in April 2017 were explained as a method for allowing fuzzy negotiated data exits.[401] The April 2017 draft, however, was never finalised, despite rumours that possibly two later drafts, released in May[402] and August 2017, were quietly circulated among stakeholders.[403] The Draft Outbound Data Measures 3 does not specify whether the Outbound Data Measures have been superseded.

This creates uncertainty about the relationship between the two documents, but the timeline is consistent with the arguments of this book, that the Draft Outbound Data Measures 3 replaced the original Draft

---

[398] Ibid art 1.
[399] 洪延青 [Hong Yanqing], «解析 '个人信息出境安全评估办法 (征求意见稿)' 实体保护规则背后的主要思路» [An Analysis of the Main Ideas behind the Entity Protection Rules of the 'Measures for the Assessment of Outbound Security of Personal Information (Opinion-Seeking Draft)'] (*CAC*, 15 June 2019) <https://mp.weixin.qq.com/s/sCGZtqmQBWyH_sSan8q-Eg>.
[400] See Draft Outbound Data Measures (n 388).
[401] Ibid.
[402] Draft Outbound Data Measures 2 (discussed in Section 5.5).
[403] Graham Webster and Samm Sacks, 'Five Big Questions Raised by China's New Draft Cross-Border Data Rules' (*New America*, 13 June 2019) <https://www.newamerica.org/cybersecurity-initiative/digichina/blog/five-big-questions-raised-chinas-new-draft-cross-border-data-ruless>.

Outbound Data Measures after industry had time to plead its case to the Chinese government (discussed in Chapters 7–9).

Regardless, in further explaining the new Outbound Data Measures 3, fuzzy logic remains and 'important data' still needs further explanation. This is because the phrase 'important data' is not used in the Draft Outbound Data Measures 3, only 'personal information' is referred to in that document.

In addition, on 21 October 2020 the Standing Committee of the National People's Congress published for public comment the first draft of China's Personal Information Protection Law. This draft law, when enacted, would likely overhaul the Outbound Data Measures 3 (see Chapter 7).

5.6.1 'Important Data'

Since 2017, 'important data' has very gradually and unofficially been clarified to refer to national security concerns, but still remains vague and problematic. Again, there are two categories of protected data unable to leave Chinese borders under the Cyber Security Law: 'personal information' and 'important data'. This is consistent with the original Draft Outbound Data Measures of April 2017, but not the Draft Outbound Data Measures 3. Dr Hong Yanqing wrote that 'one of the biggest changes in the [new] "Measures" compared with the previous "Outbound Transfer Security Assessment Measures" is to treat security assessment of personal information and important data separately'.[404] Hong wrote that he had favoured this approach from the beginning during the drafting phases in 2017. That is, 'personal information' and 'important data' should be treated under different regulatory regimes. This is, in fact, what would happen.

Supporting this interpretation, a definition of 'important data' was included in a different regulatory document, the May 2019 Draft Data Security Management Measures.[405] Article 28 defines 'important data' broadly as:

> data the divulgence of which may endanger national security, economic safety, social stability, public health and safety, such as undisclosed government data, or large-scale volume of demographic, genetic health, geographic, mining, resources and other data. Important data generally

---

[404] 洪延青 [Hong Yanqing], [An Analysis of the Main Ideas] (n 399).
[405] Draft Data Security Management Measures (n 396).

does not include enterprises' production, operations, and internal management information, personal information, and so on.[406]

Thus, according to Hong's approach, and the exclusion in this definition, it may be reasonable to expect separate rules to govern the outbound transfer of 'important data' as defined here versus 'personal information' as understood in China's broader data governance regime (described in Chapter 7), and the rules requiring localisation of 'important data' will not be allowed to impede the global R&D work of AI firms (explained in Chapter 9).[407]

However, another problem remains unresolved: How widely 'important data' is applied remains unclear as it seems that both the original Draft Outbound Data Measures and the Draft Outbound Data Measures 3 apply to 'network operators'.

5.6.2 'Network Operators' Remains Broad and Undefined

The Outbound Data Measures 3 provide basic parameters for the security assessment of cross-border data transfer, but fails to clarify many of the Cyber Security Law's ambiguities and, further, creates some of its own. In particular, like the original Draft Outbound Data Measures, the Draft Outbound Data Measures 3 require all network operators, rather than 'critical information infrastructure operators', as stipulated in Article 37 of the Cyber Security Law, to complete security assessments before transferring personal data outside China. One step further, the Draft Outbound Data Measures 3 explicitly require offshore operators who collect personal data from users within China to bear the same obligation through a domestic representative.[408] This means that where personal data is collected by foreign 'network operators' during business operations in China, their domestic representative or domestic entities must perform these assessment obligations. This is a new twist on previous protectionist arguments.

Thus, both the original Draft Outbound Data Measures and the Draft Outbound Data Measures 3 apply to 'network operators', in addition to

---

[406] Ibid art 28.
[407] Commentators predicted that this split would culminate when two laws (the Personal Information Protection Law and Data Security Law) were both finalised. See Webster and Sacks, 'Five Big Questions' (n 403). These laws were enacted in 2020 and are explained in Chapter 7.
[408] See Draft Outbound Data Measures 3 (n 396) art 20.

the Cyber Security Law's rules on data localisation which apply to the presumably narrower category of 'critical information infrastructure operators'. The shift from regulating critical information infrastructure operators to network operators matters to businesses because 'network operator' is a much broader category. 'Network operator' is defined as 'network owners and managers, and network service providers', a definition that can be read so broadly as to include any person or company with a network of any kind.[409] It is worth noting that at the time of writing neither category is rigorously defined in an authoritative way, leaving significant room for discretion in enforcement.

Thus, China's Cyber Security Law still lacks clear definitions in critical areas, including with respect to international data transfers and the data export review procedure (unfinalised at the time of writing). In April 2019, it was reported that China would put data localisation rules on hold while trade talks were ongoing with then US President Trump.[410]

So, will these regulations be finalised and implemented quickly, or will another prolonged waiting game ensue? The speed with which Chinese authorities finalise and implement these rules which underpin the supposedly already effective provisions of the Cyber Security Law will affect regulatory certainty in China's innovation economy. Further, it is still difficult to see how obtaining prior regulatory approval of every transfer of personal data or 'important data' from China will work. At a minimum it will raise the compliance costs for companies that operate in China and have to send personal information across borders.[411]

According to Chinese media, the latest draft guideline, the Outbound Data Measures 3, will prevent the flow of personal information overseas if it 'risks undermining national security and public interests' or if the security of personal information cannot be effectively guaranteed.[412] To manage these uncertainties, companies seeking to transfer personal

---

[409] Ibid art 21.
[410] This was reported widely, including in Qiheng Chen, 'China's New Data Protection Scheme' (*The Diplomat*, 2 July 2019) <https://thediplomat.com/2019/07/chinas-new-data-protection-scheme>. See also 'China Delays Data-Onshoring Rules Until after US Trade Talks (*Regulation Asia*, 23 April 2019) <https://www.regulationasia.com/china-delays-data-onshoring-rules-until-after-us-trade-talks>.
[411] Ming Jing, 'China's Cybersecurity Laws May Be Used to Block US Tech Firms on National Security Grounds, Says Expert' (*South China Morning Post*, 24 May 2019) <https://www.scmp.com/tech/policy/article/3011655/chinas-cybersecurity-laws-may-be-used-block-us-tech-firms-national>.
[412] Liu Caiyu, 'China Sets Cross-Border Data Flow Rules' (*Global Times*, 13 June 2019) <http://www.globaltimes.cn/content/1154091.shtml>.

information and important data outside China would need to be preemptively prepared for the Chinese government's security assessment. This is, once again, for both Chinese and foreign companies the negative side of fuzzy logic caused by regulatory uncertainty. As the Outbound Data Measures 3 are still in draft form, they may be subject to further modification before they are finalised. Or, like the April 2017 Draft Outbound Data Measures, they may never be finalised and China's Draft Personal Information Protection Law may soon take precedence.

5.7 Conclusion: Fuzzy Logic, Even in a Touchstone Law

An analysis of the major provisions impacting tech firms in the Cyber Security Law has reinforced the central arguments of this book, that Chinese law and regulations often lack clarity, ultimately leaving both Chinese and foreign companies without a proper roadmap for how to abide by the law. It is the kind of business environment the party-state seems to prefer, due to its flexibility and the room it allows for official discretion and control. Those who seek to conduct business in this environment must do so by navigating China's currently fuzzy but also flexible rules, in consultation with relevant government departments. Further regulations will likely clarify some of these issues, in part responding to business concerns, but competing interests within the Chinese government mean that the written laws and regulations will inevitably contain contradictions.

Vague regulations do make compliance difficult. The question remains, however: do these vague regulations shut foreign ICT service providers out of the market, or unfairly discriminate against them? In this aspect, it is important to remember that Chinese industry faces the same obstacles from the fuzzy logic Chinese regulatory environment. The new security regulations will also bring added compliance costs to all Chinese start-ups and small-to-medium sized companies, perhaps inhibiting Chinese innovation, especially within the current globalised tech R&D environment.

Clearly, critical infrastructure information operators are subject to data localisation requirements under the Cyber Security Law. These operators must store 'important data' and 'personal data' generated on servers in China.

Under the proposed subordinate regulations discussed, the Chinese government has begun to formulate a review and assessment process to allow data transfer and storage overseas, but this process is still evolving, and several key terms (namely 'important data' and 'network operators') in the Cyber Security Law are still not precisely defined.

A law that regulates cyber security necessarily raises the tension between innovation and Network Sovereignty; however, the fuzzy drafting of the law allows the government to avoid making express policy choices between the two, and provides the scope for negotiated outcomes in due course, or during any fluid geopolitical environment, such as a change of US president.

China is at the vanguard of legislating cyber security laws; thus, some 'fuzzy' fluidity of definitions should be expected if not encouraged in some circumstances for technology laws. Fuzzy logic laws serve a notable purpose in China's entrepreneurial ecosystem. They allow for a pendulum to swing between two contradictory policies: Network Sovereignty and the development of new technologies under Internet Plus.

In the next chapter, the global debate about the market implications of data localisation is explained in more detail. It is shown that China has multiple objectives for data localisation, and the fuzzy logic embedded in terms such as 'important data' has permitted those terms to be defined or interpreted as necessary to attain those objectives. In Chapter 7, what is meant by 'personal information' and how that concept evolved further in late 2020 is explained.

PART II

Impact on Artificial Intelligence

6

The Impacts of Data Localisation on Globalised Ecosystems and Chinese Tech

> Business is what happens while politicians are talking.
> —Jonathan Woetzel, Asia-based director of McKinsey Global Institute[413]

Part I identified the tensions between Chinese innovation policymaking and Network Sovereignty, analysed relevant provisions in the Cyber Security Law that appear to exacerbate those tensions in the area of data localisation, and proposed that fuzzy logic regulatory practice will work to defuse those tensions, or exacerbate them further due to the ongoing US–China trade war.

Part II tests this hypothesis by tracing the subsequent impact of data localisation and related data regulations, focusing particularly on the interaction between these regulations and the rapidly developing Chinese AI sector.

This chapter contributes to understanding the possible impacts of China's Cyber Security Law once it is fully implemented, as it concludes that Chinese authorities conduct an ongoing cost–benefit analysis in evaluating data localisation policies and practices, and that this partly explains China's delay in implementing the data localisation provisions within the law. This is also consistent with the longstanding practice by the Chinese government of creating fuzzy logic laws in areas of rapid change in order to allow for flexibility in implementation depending on the milieu.[414] The costs and benefits of data localisation vary over time, requiring continual re-evaluation; hence, the laws can be implemented and reinterpreted in line with fuzzy logic. In particular, what is meant by

---

[413] Scott Thurm, 'Chinese-American Elites Lament a Brewing Trade War' (*Wired*, 6 May 2018) <https://www.wired.com/story/chinese-american-elites-lament-a-brewing-trade-war>.

[414] See Sebastian Heilmann, 'From Local Experiments to National Policy: The Origins of China's Distinctive Policy Process' (2008) 59 *China Journal* 1.

'important data' can be changed according to the policy considerations outlined in this chapter.

An important conclusion is that the original cost–benefit matrix of data localisation is already being altered by the emergence of AI, and that conclusion is elucidated in detail in Part II. Changes in data practices mean that the advantages and disadvantages of data localisation will change over time and must continually be re-evaluated. This leads to the central argument of this book, which is that the Chinese fuzzy logic approach creates flexibility in dealing with these changes, including unexpected changes such as the emergence of AI.

There is also a global context to China's data localisation policies. Data localisation has been increasing globally since 2013 and thus this chapter also outlines the ICT industry's main arguments in favour of and against data localisation, while evaluating international fears about Chinese motivations for data localisation.

6.1 Background

The story of the recent re-emergence of data localisation begins with the whistle-blowing leaks of former US national security contractor Edward Snowden, which highlighted how many major US companies complied with US government requests to enable state-level surveillance. This event led to many countries legislating to stop cross-border flows of certain classes of data.[415] Thus, since the Snowden revelations, 'data localisation' legal provisions similar to those in China's Cyber Security Law are becoming commonplace around the world.[416] However, China's data localisation law is much more expansive than its European or US equivalents due to its fuzzy logic drafting, pending further regulatory clarity. Yet, as noted in Chapters 5 and 7, parts of the Cyber Security Law deal with genuine national security and privacy concerns, and the policy impetus for data localisation laws has been stated to be enhancing both privacy and national security.[417]

---

[415] See Glenn Greenwald, *No Place to Hide: Edward Snowden, the NSA, and the US Surveillance State* (Metropolitan Books, 2014).

[416] See Livingston and Greenleaf, 'Data Localisation in China and Other APEC Jurisdictions' (n 53).

[417] Cyber Security Law (n 2) arts 41, 42 and 43 restrict the amount of personally identifiable information that can be collected. These articles also limit how data can be transferred, and give an individual the right to request that information be deleted if mishandled.

Beyond these security concerns, there are other reasons for this rush by governments around the world to update their data laws and policies. One major argument raised by scholars is that those countries that can access, use and control data will be:

> the rulers not only of the digital realm, but also of the real world. Cross-border flows of information and unlimited access to data are the main facilitators of the emerging digital economy. How easily data can be obtained, how expensive it is, and to what legal rules it must adapt are all critical questions for everyone involved, not least for data scientists.[418]

It is argued that Chinese regulators have become increasingly aware of the importance, value and complexity of data while drafting the Cyber Security Law and issuing implementing regulations, and this has impacted on the way they have enforced the law.

Additionally, as various nations use the internet both to assert power and to conduct trade, there are countervailing commercial imperatives for authoritarian powers to keep internet traffic open in certain domains. It is difficult to simultaneously maintain rigid digital borders while asserting cyber power (网络强国 – *wangluo qiangguo*) influence, a stated aim of Network Sovereignty. This is because countries have to 'cooperate to compete'.[419] This in turn adds complexity to the task of finding a balance between innovation and restriction, or openness and localised control, in China.

The complexity means that multiple motivations exist simultaneously for data localisation, and Chinese regulators' fuzzy logic approach may be particularly well suited to such a multifaceted policy context. Moreover, it is argued that these rationales very likely include the potential economic benefits of data localisation for promoting innovation in AI.

To clarify the debate surrounding data localisation, the concept is first defined and the main reasons why localisation may be justified are introduced. Previous debates about transborder data flows[420] since the

---

[418] Helena Ursic et al, 'Data Localisation Measures and Their Impacts on Data Science' in Vanessa Mak, Eric Tjong Tjin Tai and Anna Berlee (eds), *Research Handbook in Data Science and Law* (Elgar, 2018) 322, 322.

[419] Jon R Lindsay, 'The Impact of China on Cybersecurity' (2014) 39(3) *International Security* 7. By 'cooperate to compete' Lindsay means that supply, research and import and export sales linkages cannot be easily disentangled. This concept is explained in later chapters when noting the global technology ecosystem's entanglement.

[420] From the 1980s and pre-dating the internet, this area was initially known as 'TBDFs' or 'transborder data flows'.

1980s concerned data protection,[421] yet this debate has recently taken on more importance due to the increased value of data. The distinct rationales for data localisation include data protection/data privacy as well as national security/state control and economic protectionism. Protectionist arguments have emerged in a new form in the past five years, as governments increasingly understand the value of data in the age of big data and AI. On the other hand, there are strong counterarguments that data localisation may be technically unfeasible and hinder commerce and innovation in this digital age.

The Chinese government's decision to 'lock' all 'important data' in China under Article 37 of the Cyber Security Law has led observers[422] to question China's motivations for data localisation. Such observers would assert that the point of data localisation laws, in the data privacy context, should not be to prohibit global data flows, but to regulate the conditions under which such data flows occur, essentially by regulating entities responsible for the flows. Some argued that the data localisation provisions threaten to shut foreign tech companies out of various sectors deemed 'critical'. Among those voices, James Zimmerman, chairman of the American Chamber of Commerce in China, argued: 'Some of the measures seem to emphasize protectionism rather than security.' He also alluded to the potential downside for China: '[O]ne thing is for sure: the more difficult it is for data to travel across the Chinese border, the more difficult it will be for companies inside those borders to innovate, and China risks becoming isolated technologically from the rest of the world.'[423] Also, it may be technically impossible to prevent cross-border data flows – but is this really China's motivation for data localisation? These questions are revisited (in Section 6.4) after the data localisation provisions are placed within their broader global context.

---

[421] See William L Fishman, 'Introduction to Transborder Data Flows' (1980) 16(1) *Stanford Journal of International Law* 1. The debate continued in the 1990s and 2000s and the arguments for and against extending the boundaries to the internet are reflected in the debate from the late 1990s and early 2000s between David Post and Jack Goldsmith. See, eg, Jack L Goldsmith, 'Against Cyberanarchy' (1998) 65(4) *University of Chicago Law Review* 1199; David R Johnson and David Post, 'Law and Borders: The Rise of Law in Cyberspace' (1996) 48(5) *Stanford Law Review* 1367; David G Post, 'Against "Against Cyberanarchy"' (2002) 17(4) *Berkeley Technology Law Journal* 1365.

[422] As cited in Chapter 5. See also Section 6.4.

[423] James Zimmerman cited in Horwitz, 'China's Bewildering New Cybersecurity Law' (n 57).

6.2 What Is Data Localisation?

Data localisation is the act of storing data on any device that is physically present within the borders of a specific country where the data was generated.[424] However, data localisation laws may refer to the laws governing both local storage as well as the export of data. Laws may require that some or all of the categories of personal data are stored and processed on local servers within the country. Data localisation laws may also make data exports subject to conditions. Chander and Le define data localisation widely so as to include all measures that 'encumber the transfer of data' across national borders.[425] Applying this approach, this book defines data localisation as laws governing local data storage as well as the export of data.

6.3 Two Major Motivations for Data Localisation: Protecting Personal Data and Ensuring Government Control over Data

There are two contrasting major motivations for data localisation: protecting personal data; and ensuring government control over data, often for economic protectionist reasons.[426] In the Chinese context of Network Sovereignty, laws requiring data to be hosted within a particular jurisdiction are commonly thought to be based on state-centric ideas about how the internet should be subject to control.[427] China has begun to affirmatively require data localisation for broad and as yet unclear categories of electronic data under its conception of Network Sovereignty. This is a new and more extensive component of the nation's evolving data privacy and cyber regime. Again, these provisions first began to appear in a

---

[424] See Livingston and Greenleaf, 'Data Localisation in China and Other APEC Jurisdictions' (n 53) 22.
[425] Anupam Chander and Uyen P Le, 'Data Nationalism' (2015) 64(3) *Emory Law Journal* 679.
[426] There is an extensive academic literature on data privacy that also encompasses these issues. See, eg, Marijn Janssen and Jeroen van den Hoven, 'Big and Open Linked Data (BOLD) in Government: A Challenge to Transparency and Privacy?' (2015) 32(4) *Government Information Quarterly* 363. The authors argue that there is a nexus between privacy and transparency in governance where governments can use and control datasets to provide better government. The key is to balance that task with personal privacy.
[427] See Sacks, Triolo and Webster, 'Beyond the Worst-Case Assumptions on China's Cybersecurity Law' (n 15).

number of industry-based regulations[428] before being consolidated in China's Cyber Security Law in 2017.

However, another explanation for data localisation laws is that they are created to ensure the protection of the personal data of citizens of a jurisdiction by, for example, ensuring that sensitive biometric or financial data are not exported to jurisdictions with weak data protections.[429] This is often stated as a major reason for the need for data localisation.[430] However, applications and tools can be carefully designed and applied to increase privacy protection by enabling anonymity and confidentiality and by reducing possibilities for accessing and processing data, which may reduce the need for blanket localisation policies.[431] Thus a distinction can be made here between a limited data localisation policy (eg, for health data) and a blanket data localisation policy over a wider definition of data.

This personal privacy justification for data localisation is also highly relevant to China today. The next chapter describes the now almost weekly data theft scandals that have occurred in China. There is a whole

---

[428] Besides those regulations discussed in Chapter 3, other recent examples include ride sharing and internet mapping. Regarding ride sharing, effective 1 November 2016, art 27 of the Interim Regulations for the Management of Network Appointed Taxi Services Operations requires ride-sharing services (eg, Didi Chuxing) to store all collected personal data and 'produced business data' on servers in China for at least two years. See 《网络预约出租汽车经营服务管理暂行办法》 [Interim Regulations for the Management of Network Appointed Taxi Services Operations] (People's Republic of China) Ministry of Industry and Information Technology, 28 July 2016. Regarding internet mapping, effective 1 January 2016, the State Council issued the Administrative Regulation of Maps which contains an entire chapter dedicated to 'internet map services'. This regulation requires a licence (heavily restricted for foreign enterprises) for online navigation and map databases, and that map data must be stored within China. Possibly the Chinese government already understood the value of its mapping data for future applications such as self-driving cars. See «地图管理条例» [Administrative Regulation of Maps] (People's Republic of China) State Council, 1 January 2016.

[429] 'These opposing frameworks continue to diffuse globally as countries such as Colombia, Brazil, India, Nigeria and South Korea introduce or adopt local data standards': 'The March toward Data Localization' (*Endgame*, 10 January 2018) <https://www.endgame.com/blog/technical-blog/march-toward-data-localization>.

[430] Michael Friedewald et al, 'Privacy, Data Protection and Emerging Sciences and Technologies: Towards a Common Framework' (2010) 23(1) *European Journal of Social Science Research* 61.

[431] See David Pelkola, 'A Framework for Managing Privacy-Enhancing Technology' (2012) 29(3) *IEEE Software* 45; Ira S Rubinstein, 'Regulating Privacy by Design' (2011) 26(3) *Berkeley Technology Law Journal* 1409.

cottage industry built to sell stolen data, and Chinese regulators are penalising these violators heavily under the new cyber regime.[432]

It is noteworthy that the final version of the Cyber Security Law imposes criminal and administrative penalties against individuals and entities that commit these types of cyber fraud and cybercrime.[433] It is also likely that outside commentators commenting on China's motivation for data localisation have been unaware of the extent of this data theft problem in China and the corresponding need for regulation. This is because data protection only entered the public discourse in China during 2017–2018. Since then, the protection of personal data has become a high-profile issue that China's leadership is keen to police through its cyber security regime.[434]

Certainly, data localisation is an increasing global trend, for reasons similar to those that motivate Chinese policymakers. The European Centre for International Political Economy calculates that in the decade to 2016, the number of significant data localisation measures in the world's large economies nearly tripled from 31 to 84.[435] By 2018, more than 100 countries had enacted comprehensive data protection legislation.[436] The European Union's General Data Protection Regulation (GDPR) has set a prominent example.[437]

The GDPR, which came into effect in May 2018, epitomises the push towards the protection of personal data of individuals. The GDPR seeks to ensure a 'high level' of protection for the personal data of EU citizens in relation to cross-border flows of personal data, and includes

---

[432] Discussed further in Chapter 7.
[433] See Cyber Security Law (n 2) ch VI ('Legal Responsibility').
[434] Discussed further in Chapter 7.
[435] Bauer, *Unleashing Internal Data Flows in the EU* (n 56).
[436] 'The Keys to Data Protection' (*Privacy International*, August 2018) <https://privacyinternational.org/sites/default/files/2018-09/Data%20Protection%20COMPLETE.pdf> (the link is no longer active).
[437] Regulation (EU) 2016/679 of the European Parliament and of the Council of 27 April 2016 on the Protection of Natural Persons with regard to the Processing of Personal Data and on the Free Movement of Such Data, and repealing Directive 95/46/EC [2016] OJ L 119/1 (General Data Protection Regulation or GDPR). The GDPR is a regulation in EU law on data protection and privacy for all individuals within the European Union and the European Economic Area. For a full explanation of data collection in light of the GDPR's privacy provisions, see Christina Tikkinen-Piri, Anna Rohunen and Jouni Markkula, 'EU General Data Protection Regulation: Changes and Implications for Personal Data Collecting Companies' (2018) 34(1) *Computer Law & Security Review* 134.

mechanisms for this process.[438] There are many similarities with China's data regime, such as the identification of regulated entities: the GDPR's 'data controller' might be similar to a 'network operator'[439] under the Cyber Security Law. A data controller is an organisation that collects data from EU residents.[440] There are also significant differences: for example, the right of access (Article 15 of the GDPR) gives citizens the right to access their personal data and information about how this personal data is being processed, including by government actors.[441] The most important distinction, however – the overall objectives of the regimes – is outlined in Chapter 7. In short, the Chinese approach reflects protection of data from commercial abuse rather than data privacy from the government. Chinese law also includes access and correction rights to data collected by companies. China's unique data protection regime is elucidated further in the next chapter, shedding additional light on China's motivations for data localisation.

By contrast with the GDPR, Russian[442] and Chinese[443] data localisation laws are thought to reflect government-control approaches to the data itself. Consequently, China's Cyber Security Law on its face regulates a much broader category of data than just personal information and its localisation provisions are more draconian: virtually all business data may be caught by the fuzzy phrase 'important data' in Article 37. Real-name registration rules also mean that network users have less privacy from government intrusion.[444]

---

[438] See the Recital to the GDPR (n 437).

[439] As explained in Chapter 5, definitions of 'network operator' remained unclear in the legislation. However, in art 76(3) of the Cyber Security Law (n 2), '"Network operators" refers to network owners, managers, and network service providers'.

[440] GDPR (n 437) art 3(2).

[441] Access and correction have always been central principles of the data protection/data privacy paradigm going back to the OECD's original 1980 Guidelines on the Protection of Privacy and Transborder Flows of Personal Data.

[442] Russia's data localisation legislation is officially known as Federal Law No 242-FZ. Its long title is 'Processing and Storage of Personal Data in the Russian Federation', Ministry of Telecom and Mass Communications of the Russian Federation, 12 February 2016. The final amendments to this data localisation law in Russia went into effect on 1 September 2015, and required all domestic and foreign companies to accumulate, store and process personal information of Russian citizens on servers physically located within Russian borders.

[443] See Jonah Force Hill, 'A Balkanized Internet? The Uncertain Future of Global Internet Standards?' (2012) *Georgetown Journal of International Affairs* 49, 54.

[444] Cyber Security Law (n 2) art 37, and for real-name registration see Chapter 7.

The United States does not have a uniform data localisation regime, but it did enact the CLOUD Act in 2018 which empowers US federal law enforcement agencies to compel US-based tech companies to provide access to requested data stored on servers, regardless of whether the data are stored in the United States or on foreign soil.[445] Despite the fact that the CLOUD Act provides a means for enforcement agencies to access data wherever it is stored, and it is not a data protection law, such provisions prompted Chinese regulators to wonder whether this was the United States' own attempt to create a data localisation regime.[446]

Certainly, the two major motivations for data localisation – protecting personal data and ensuring government control over data – often seem to become conflated in the politicised nature of this debate.[447]

6.4 Existing Theories about Data Localisation Laws

Data localisation and access to data remains a complex and evolving international issue, and China's recent legislation in this area must be placed within a broader global context and theoretical debates about localisation. Some disentangling of the arguments for and against some degree of data localisation is needed. First, there is the need to protect the rights of domestic citizens, specifically their data privacy rights, in cross-border data flows. Second, there are national security concerns (or, in the case of China, perhaps social control concerns). Third, there is economic protectionism. Each of these raises distinct issues and concerns about its significance as a motivating factor in Chinese policymaking.

---

[445] The Clarifying Lawful Overseas Use of Data Act (CLOUD Act) is a United States federal law enacted in 2018 by the passing of the Consolidated Appropriations Act, 2018, PL 115-141, s 105, executive agreements on access to data by foreign governments. This raises the question of whether the United States has its own data model, and how this will relate to other countries in the future. These issues are all still evolving.

[446] See 刘迈 [Liu Mai], «GDPR 之风盛行, 美, 印, 巴接连启动数据保护立法» [The Winds of the GDPR Are Blowing, as the United States, India and Pakistan Successively Initiate Data Protection Legislation] (*Baidu Institute for Public Policy*, 29 August 2018) <https://mp.weixin.qq.com/s/ePwUquQL9gZ3EeANnGAwDA>.

[447] See Tatevik Sargsyan, 'Data Localisation and the Role of Infrastructure for Surveillance, Privacy and Security' (2016) 10 *International Journal of Communication* 2221. Sargsyan argues that in today's geo-political ecosystem, personal data can be viewed as a currency to be traded between nation-states and that all countries have a rationale to capture as much data as possible.

6.4.1 Arguments against Data Localisation Laws: Protectionism versus Data Protection

One major argument levelled against data localisation is that it is a harmful zero-sum protectionist action by a government to maintain control over its domestic data.[448] It is argued that restricting global data flows in this way creates political, economic, financial and, potentially, technical problems for globalised technology ecosystems (explained below). Technology policy scholars, therefore, noting the potential implementation and cyber security problems of data localisation, argue that it must logically be a politically motivated act.[449]

Many commentators view data localisation laws as a discrete non-tariff barrier, curtailing the growth of trade and efficient distribution of business operations in a digitally powered world.[450] This is a real problem, as the digital world has long been globally interconnected. For example, when a Chinese user inputs their phone number on a foreign mobile app, that data might be stored on the company's servers overseas. Likewise, a global retail company's employee list in China might be kept on the company's servers overseas. And a medical device generating data about a Chinese patient's health might be sent to the company's servers overseas. These companies might do this to reduce costs and increase efficiency, as well as for R&D work abroad.

With these kinds of examples in mind, numerous industry reports and academic studies[451] have posited that the free flow of data is critical for ICT services and trade in goods and services:

---

[448] Sargsvan argues that '[d]ata localization is one of the series of attempts by state actors to configure intermediaries' private infrastructure for their political goals': ibid 2222.

[449] Konstantinos Komaitis, 'The "Wicked Problem" of Data Localisation' (2017) 2(3) *Journal of Cyber Policy* 355. Komaitis argues: 'The main question of which we should keep reminding ourselves is why, in the face of clear evidence regarding the detrimental impact of data localisation in a country, a government would still opt for such a measure. The answer is to be found in power': at 356.

[450] Chander and Le, 'Data Nationalism' (n 425). From an international political economy perspective, 'innovation mercantilism' continues to emerge in digital trade today: Stephen Ezell et al, *Localization Barriers to Global Trade: Threat to the Global Economy* (ITIF, 2013) <http://www.itif.org/publications/localization-barriers-trade-threat-global-innovation-economy>.

[451] See Roger Hurwitz, 'Depleted Trust in the Cyber Commons' (2012) 6(3) *Strategic Studies Quarterly* 20; Komaitis, 'The "Wicked Problem" of Data Localisation' (n 449); Ursic et al, 'Data Localisation Measures and Their Impacts on Data Science' (n 418) 322.

For example, requirements for data localisation may prevent engineers that are employed by the same Chinese firm, but located separately in Europe and China, from effectively communicating on how to rapidly address a problem. This would provide a particular challenge given that they would be competing in international markets with companies that do not face this limitation.[452]

On the farthest, free market end of the spectrum in this debate, Nigel Cory of the Information Technology and Innovation Foundation (ITIF),[453] an organisation focused on spurring global technology innovation, argues that restricting data flows of any kind, even health data, severely harms innovation:

> Barriers to the exchange of personal medical data, such as those in Australia, Canada, China, and Russia, could prevent these countries' citizens from accessing the latest technological advances. For example, companies such as Hermes and Alliance Medical provide outsourced analysis of MRI scans, thereby decreasing health-care costs and time demands on doctors. Likewise, such health-data restrictions prevent IBM Watson – which combines a supercomputer, artificial intelligence (AI), and sophisticated analytical software – from using patient data for newer, quicker, and better health diagnosis.[454]

Cory's view is perhaps too extreme in seeking uninhibited global data flows. Just as there is no such thing as absolute data security, there is no such thing as absolute free flow of data. Moreover, it is possible to argue that ensuring proper protection of personal data is necessary to build the trust required for data flows. Several Western jurisdictions have already legislated that health and biometric data, tax and judicial evidence, for example, should not be allowed free passage around the world due to data protection concerns.[455] Government and commercial data providers

---

[452] European Chamber of Commerce in China, *China Manufacturing 2025: Putting Industrial Policy Ahead of Market Forces* (March 2017) 26.
[453] The ITIF is a US non-profit public policy think tank based in Washington, DC.
[454] Nigel Cory, *Cross-Border Data Flows: Where Are the Barriers, and What Do They Cost?* (ITIF, May 2017) <http://www2.itif.org/2017-cross-border-data-flows.pdf>. Cory argues further: 'Given that each of Watson's AI applications – such as for health, weather forecasts, or others – require customized hardware to match the application, it is unrealistic to assume that IBM would build such data centers in each and every country that enacts barriers to health data. Instead, citizens in these countries are likely to miss out on access to the latest and most-sophisticated medical services': at 8.
[455] Sectorial localisation norms are, for example, employed in Australia (health data), France (data relating to judicial proceedings) and Germany (telecommunications metadata and tax accounting data).

may require some flexibility to negotiate with each other the terms of those data flows. One pertinent real-world example in China is an Israeli vital heath monitoring system using AI and at the time of writing being trialled in hospitals in Zhejiang. If that data is localised, does it affect the company's ability to safely monitor patients in real time? That is an issue that must be resolved prior to beginning a trial as both the company and the government (not to mention the hospital) have fiduciary duties to patients.

Therefore, despite the arguments of free market advocates, all jurisdictions with data protection or data privacy laws must regulate the transfer of data outside the jurisdiction.[456] The question is not whether or not there should be regulation, but the nature and spectrum of regulation.

Further, those who cite China's techno-nationalism (eg, Ahmed and Weber) argued that the process through which the Cyber Security Law was drafted and eventually approved bears similarities to three previous cases that they cite 'from the past two decades of Chinese information technology policymaking', whereby vague laws were left on the books to be 'enforced' at a later stage. In all these cases, they concluded, those laws were created to penalise foreign companies in China. They argued 'that economic concerns have consistently overshadowed claims of national security considerations throughout laws directed at foreign enterprises'.[457]

Others, such as the Washington-based think tank Center for Strategic and International Studies (CSIS), argued in August 2018 that China's cyber security standards could in the future be used as an 'invisible tool' of retaliation against Washington's tariffs, specifically as Sino-US trade tensions escalated during 2018.[458] China has issued close to 300 new national standards over a few years, according to the CSIS report.[459] They argue that although these standards are only aspirational, they can potentially be enforced as if they were law. In other words, they are government-issued recommended guidelines that are technically

---

[456] Christopher Kuner suggests distinguishing between privacy rights and protectionism by explicitly defining the scope of these laws. See Christopher Kuner, 'Data Nationalism and Its Discontents' (2015) 64 *Emory Law Journal* 2089.
[457] Ahmed and Weber, 'China's Long Game in Techno-Nationalism' (n 11).
[458] Samm Sacks and Manyi Kathy Li, *How Chinese Cybersecurity Standards Impact Doing Business in China* (Report, CSIS Briefs, 2 August 2018) <https://www.csis.org/analysis/how-chinese-cybersecurity-standards-impact-doing-business-china>.
[459] That figure also reflects increased global understanding of cyber risks as well as China's rapid policymaking under President Xi Jinping since 2014.

voluntary, but could be treated as mandatory by foreign firms' Chinese business partners.

In this vein, Kuner argues that while 'governments have a legitimate interest in protecting individuals online, they neglect to examine some legal questions that are crucial to define the scope of this interest'.[460] Economic protectionism can be minimised by clearer legislating. Thus, in China's case, the problem is not data localisation per se, but the fuzziness in the undefined phrase 'important data'. Data protection may be a legitimate concern but economic protectionism remains and is an available option under the fuzzy logic of 'important data'.

6.4.2 Data Localisation Is 'Technically Unviable' and Counterproductive to Data Protection Goals and National Security Concerns

The technical impossibility of localisation and attempts at data localisation may also be self-defeating. Further, data being inherently insecure in China can be a positive and a negative for data originating in countries other than China. For data originating in China, it may be an argument for data to be stored outside China.

As noted by Reisman, data localisation can be 'technically unviable' as the 'overarching point is that data can live ephemerally, in many copies and in many places'.[461] Reisman notes further:

> Some of our most important Internet applications, from search functions to communications, rely on those places being across a national border. It is an immense challenge to design laws and policies that best serve the interests of users and law enforcement without compromising on the principles that power the Internet. We will only be able to meet that challenge, however, by developing a more complete understanding of how our data actually exists in the world.[462]

A further longstanding cyber and national security argument against forced data localisation is that interconnected infrastructure may make advanced industrial powers particularly vulnerable to hacking by weaker

---

[460] Kuner, 'Data Nationalism and Its Discontents' (n 456) 2094.
[461] Dillon Reisman, 'Where Is Your Data, Really? The Technical Case against Data Localization' (*Lawfare*, 22 May 2017) <https://www.lawfareblog.com/where-your-data-really-technical-case-against-data-localization>.
[462] Ibid.

states or even non-state actors[463] and may even interfere with the broader architecture of the internet.[464] This seems to be an argument against data localisation (ie, the centralisation of data in one geography creates a honey pot that is easier to hack). Therefore, data should not be sent to those countries. In countries with poor IT security systems, data localisation may defeat the domestic government goals of data protection.[465] A proper technical and legal infrastructure is needed for there to be secure data flows. Thus, data localisation may actually hamper data security. According to the ITIF and expert academic arguments, in most instances, data localisation mandates 'do not increase commercial privacy nor data security. This is a key point that few policymakers have fully grasped'.[466]

Accordingly, absolute data localisation may be impossible for technical reasons (depending on the nature of the venture) and this suggests that any regulations can only be very limited in their impact. The point is best illustrated by two major features of data that make localisation especially problematic: 'derived' data (ie, repurposed data) and the 'sharding' or splitting of data between data centres.

First, in the context of AI research, deciding when data is sufficiently 'secure' can be a difficult problem. Data might be processed in batches at a central location, frequently offshore, to add features like search functionality or AI. That is, data is commonly used to generate 'derived data'. Data science is an industry based on derived data research. Therefore,

---

[463] See Gregory J Rattray, *Strategic Warfare in Cyberspace* (MIT Press, 2001); Scott Borg, 'Economically Complex Cyberattacks' (2003) 3(6) *IEEE Security and Privacy Magazine* 64; Richard A Clarke and Robert K Knake, *Cyber War: The Next Threat to National Security and What to Do about It* (Ecco, 2010); Joseph S Nye Jr, 'Nuclear Lessons for Cyber Security?' (2011) 5(4) *Strategic Studies Quarterly* 18; Timothy J Junio, 'How Probable Is Cyber War? Bringing IR Theory Back in to the Cyber Conflict Debate' (2013) 36(1) *Journal of Strategic Studies* 125; Dale Peterson, 'Offensive Cyber Weapons: Construction, Development, and Employment' (2013) 36(1) *Journal of Strategic Studies* 120.

[464] Neha Mishra, 'Data Localization Laws in a Digital World: Data Protection or Data Protectionism?' (*Public Sphere*, 2016) <http://publicspherejournal.com/wp-content/uploads/2016/02/06.data_protection.pdf> (the link is no longer active).

[465] See Patrick S Ryan, Sarah Falvey and Ronak Merchant, 'When the Cloud Goes Local: The Global Problem with Data Localization' (2013) 46(12) *Computer* 54. The authors argue that regulating separate spheres through localisation of the internet makes the internet less secure.

[466] Cory, *Cross-Border Data Flows* (n 454) 3. See also Andrew Mitchell and Neha Mishra, 'Data at the Docks: Modernizing International Trade Law for the Digital Economy' (2018) 20(4) *Vanderbilt Journal of Entertainment and Technology Law* 1073, 1127–9.

deciding when derived datasets are sufficiently 'safe' can be a difficult problem to define in regulations, and the 'whole data reuse industry' could be negatively affected by data localisation.[467]

In many cases, derived data requires the same security and privacy protections as the private data it was derived from. For example, if an AI system could extract your opinion about everyone you have spoken to from your text messages, that information would be highly sensitive and require a level of protection equal to the texts themselves. However, aggregate statistics derived from data could be useful to share between engineers or release publicly without revealing anything about any individuals. If the AI system only noted how many people a person texted regularly, without recording their names, this might be considered less sensitive information than the content of the original texts.[468] Hence, a certain degree of regulatory flexibility may be necessary in defining the kinds of data that must be protected.

Furthermore, a major problem with blanket localisation is that cloud computing is only viable because a company can typically have, for example, three or more data centres in different cities around the world, reducing infrastructure costs and enabling 'sharding' of data for security. Sharding is storing data in 'shards' or packets divided across data centres internationally, for cyber security purposes.[469] Data might even be sharded across multiple machines in multiple data centres internationally. Sharding is a metaphorical adaptation of the original meaning of 'shards' as in splinters of glass or metal. A web service may store millions of gigabytes of data. To do this, the web service stores data across many 'shards', with an individual computer responsible for holding a shard of data. An individual's data can be split between any number of shards and distributed, copied and backed up across multiple machines. This helps support a web service's goals for performance and efficiency – load

---

[467] See Ursic et al, 'Data Localisation Measures and Their Impacts on Data Science' (n 418) 349.

[468] See Ira S Rubinstein and Nathaniel Good, 'Privacy by Design: A Counterfactual Analysis of Google and Facebook Privacy Incidents' (2013) 28(2) *Berkeley Technology Law Journal* 1333. The authors reviewed 10 major Google and Facebook privacy incidents and then considered whether the firms in question would have averted these incidents if they had implemented privacy by design.

[469] See Daniel Castro, *The False Promise of Data Nationalism* (ITIF, 1 December 2013) <http://www2.itif.org/2013-false-promise-data-nationalism.pdf>. Castro provides a technical explanation of the sharding process in relation to data localisation and cyber security.

balancing, for instance, can be made even more efficient if the network chooses which 'shards' of data need to be copied and distributed based on demand – while also limiting potential damage caused by cyberattacks.[470] Thus, undermining sharding remains a major problem for blanket data localisation.

If data is only permitted to be located in one of those three cities in a single country, it may not be safe depending on the efficacy of local laws and regulations. Thus, computer scientists note that data localisation laws do not necessarily provide a solution to problems of data breaches or boost data security.[471] The infrastructure needed to set up secure and efficient data centres must also include a 'secure technical infrastructure and an appropriate legal regime'.[472]

China, for example, faces great domestic data theft problems. One reason is because China's versatile app WeChat, while being the data repository for the world's most-used mobile app with hundreds of millions of users, is subject to data theft vulnerabilities.[473] Compelling localisation of data for applications like WeChat may make data even more vulnerable to security attacks, as a more attractive 'honey pot' target for hackers. This is because the data will no longer undergo cross-border sharding. China's billions of connected devices are also a major cyber security challenge, which may compound the collateral damage caused by attacks. If data is inherently insecure in China, and localisation will not make it safer, then data protection for users is a weak rationale for data localisation in that jurisdiction. The more compelling rationales must therefore be data control and/or economic protectionism.

6.4.3 Increased Costs for Companies and Consumers

It is argued further by data localisation's detractors that localisation raises costs and reduces competitiveness and productivity for both local

---

[470] Reisman, 'Where Is Your Data, Really?' (n 461).
[471] As some computer scientists have noted: 'Requirements to localize data . . . only make it impossible for cloud service providers to take advantage of the Internet's distributed infrastructure and use sharding and obfuscation on a global scale.' See Ryan, Falvey and Merchant, 'When the Cloud Goes Local' (n 465) 56.
[472] Mishra, 'Data Localization Laws in a Digital World' (n 464) 142–5.
[473] WeChat's data security has been an ongoing issue, though it is improving year on year. See Chapter 7.

consumers and businesses.[474] Countries implementing data control measures can therefore potentially damage the local ICT industry and many other industries that depend on it for their operations.[475] Studies have attempted to calculate the negative impact to a country's GDP caused by such policies.[476] A study by ECIPE in 2014 showed that legal restrictions on cross-border data flows adversely impact countries which adopt those laws. In Indonesia, for example, data localisation laws could reduce GDP by 0.7% and reduce investments by 2.3%.[477]

Furthermore, commentators have argued that forced localisation of data centres may not lead to domestic economic returns through relocation of related industries. Some policymakers believe that, if they restrict data flows, their countries will gain a net economic advantage from companies that will be forced to relocate data-related jobs to their nations. Data localisation laws are often put in place in a perhaps misguided attempt to benefit the host country economically by requiring infrastructure investment there: 'Some countries believe data localisation offers a quick way to force high-tech economic activity to take place within their borders – a new form of "digital mercantilism" – similar to how countries use local content requirements and tariffs to protect local manufacturing operations.'[478] Thus, '[i]n essence, these tactics constitute "data protectionism" because they keep foreign competitors out of domestic markets'.[479] However, among numerous existing studies, none have predicted positive returns to an economy through blanket data

---

[474] See Erica Fraser, 'Data Localisation and the Balkanisation of the Internet' (2016) 13(3) SCRIPTed: A Journal of Law, Technology and Society 359; Stephen Ezell and Robert Atkinson, The Good, the Bad, the Ugly, and the Self-Destructive of Innovation Policy (ITIF, October 2010) <http://www.itif.org/files/2010-good-bad-ugly.pdf>.

[475] See Ezell et al, Localization Barriers to Global Trade (n 450); McKinsey Global Institute, Global Flows in a Digital Age (April 2014) <https://www.mckinsey.com/business-func tions/strategy-and-corporate-finance/our-insights/global-flows-in-a-digital-age>; Matthias Bauer et al, Data Localization in Russia: A Self-Imposed Sanction (ECIPE Policy Brief No 6/2015) <https://ecipe.org/publications/data-localisation-russia-self-imposed-sanction/>.

[476] See Matthias Bauer et al, The Costs of Data Localization: Friendly Fire on Economic Recovery (ECIPE Occasional Paper No 3/2014) <https://ecipe.org/publications/dataloc/>. Similar results were also recorded for South Korea and the European Union: Bauer et al, Data Localization in Russia (n 475).

[477] Bauer et al, The Costs of Data Localization (n 476).

[478] Cory, Cross-Border Data Flows (n 454).

[479] Ibid 2.

localisation.[480] This is mainly because data centres are largely automated and do not generate significant levels of employment.

Mandating localisation of data centres also goes against the free-market economic logic of the technology industry, which is based on global economies of scale requiring global data centres.[481] The internet itself was regarded by pioneers and campaigners as a decentralised, self-regulating community, and that ethos informed internet institutions such as the Internet Engineering Task Force.[482] From the early days of the internet, privacy protection greatly depended on the careful technological design choices that engineers made.[483] Thus, except for its role in protecting personal data, industry groups regard government intervention such as data localisation provisions with suspicion.[484] In fact, for many decentralised technology activists the internet does not go far enough, and blockchain may one day represent a new, even more decentralised, 'Web 3.0'.[485] Indeed, with soaring prices in early 2021 suggesting widespread institutional investment, Bitcoin may become one of the most important open-source pivots in computer history.

Existing discourses opposing data localisation make compelling economic and technical arguments as to why data localisation policies are harmful for trade, investment, cyber security and innovation. However, they fail to grasp the strong political rationale driving such policies in

---

[480] Several business associations (mostly consisting of global market leaders based in the United States) (eg, AmCham China; Information Technology Industry Council; Asia Internet Coalition; US Chamber of Commerce in China) as well as a few governments (notably the US government) (Office of the United States Trade Representative, 2015) have presented economic cases for the free flow of data in various regional trade agreements such as the Trans Pacific Partnership, the Trade in Services Agreement and the Transatlantic Trade and Investment Partnership: Bauer et al, *Data Localization in Russia* (n 475).

[481] Ezell and Atkinson, *The Good, the Bad, the Ugly, and the Self-Destructive of Innovation Policy* (n 474). For example, Google and Amazon Web Services (AWS) have data centres in Singapore, Taiwan and Japan. Alibaba Cloud, the computing arm of the Chinese company, has set up data centres in Malaysia, India, Indonesia and Sydney.

[482] See IETF, 'A Survey of Worldwide Censorship Techniques' (n 254).

[483] Sandra Braman, 'Privacy by Design: Networked Computing, 1969–1979' (2012) 14(5) *New Media and Society* 798.

[484] As noted in Chapter 3. See also Laura DeNardis, *Protocol Politics: The Globalisation of Internet Governance* (MIT Press, 2009).

[485] There is today a strong push to build a myriad of dApps (decentralised applications) on blockchains, forming a whole new protocol layer for the transfer of information and other applications. As this is an emerging technology, experts in the field of blockchains cannot define with certainty the stack of protocols that will form the future so-called Web 3.0.

China and elsewhere, the complex nascent political economy of the digital world and, crucially in the Chinese context, whether those policies will in fact be able to localise all Chinese data in practice.

6.5 Implications of the Rise of AI: Fuzzy Logic Masks Motivations for Data Localisation

In reality, countries such as China have multiple and often legitimate policy rationales and different approaches for implementing data localisation laws, ranging from protecting private health records to cyber security and data privacy and even tax avoidance minimisation.[486] Some commentators have even argued that countries are using data localisation not only for protectionism but also to create improvements in economies of scale for their internet signals intelligence capabilities.[487] Thus, sometimes data localisation has an economic cost and sometimes it has economic benefits.

Until the fuzzy logic is completely removed from China's Cyber Security Law, Chinese government motivations will remain relatively opaque, or at least mixed. That is, it is not always possible to demarcate the 'protectionist' rationale from legitimate 'data protection' aims. Chinese justifications for data localisation appear to combine the aims of promoting China's own domestic ICT industry through localisation measures and ensuring sovereign control in the highly privatised and decentralised world of internet governance.

Policy rationales for implementing data localisation laws are therefore contextual and complex. There is a calculated trade-off between market forces and the domestic political climate. Purely economic arguments based on current business practices may not take account of benefits and changes that occur from gaining local control over data, including political advantages to the ruling political party.[488]

---

[486] See, eg, Lingjie Kong, 'Data Protection and Transborder Data Flow in the European and Global Context' (2010) 21(2) *European Journal of International Law* 441.

[487] Signal intelligence is information gained by the collection and analysis of the electronic signals and communications of a given target identified by intelligence agencies. See John Selby, 'Data Localization Laws: Trade Barriers or Legitimate Responses to Cybersecurity Risks, or Both?' (2017) 25(3) *International Journal of Law and Information Technology* 213.

[488] See Robert Gilpin, *Global Political Economy* (Princeton University Press, 2001). Gilpin refers to the 'Internet economy' as a new paradigm of power post the Cold War: see at 10.

Finally, even in the economic sphere, there is one major rebuttal of the economic (as opposed to technical) arguments against data localisation. The cost–benefit matrix of data localisation is already being altered by AI, and is elucidated in detail in the next chapters. China too had not considered the issue of AI when drafting its Cyber Security Law, as is shown in Chapters 7–9. Therefore, the arguments outlined were the major persuasive arguments in this debate about data localisation until 2016–2017.

Changes in data collection practices (which are not confined to AI) mean that the advantages and disadvantages of data localisation will change over time, and must continually be re-evaluated. This leads to the central argument of this book, which is that the Chinese fuzzy logic approach creates flexibility in dealing with these changes, including unexpected changes such as the emergence of AI.

With the rapid development of AI, which relies heavily on the massive accumulation of data, scholars have argued that such localisation may provide a strategic long-term advantage:

> Countries (particularly those with larger populations and/or resources, such as China) are likely to consider data localization as a strategic tool to gain control over more data at home and abroad, thereby providing credible competition to some of the biggest American players who dominate the market today. Again, many trade practitioners would recognize this is as a use of a non-tariff barrier to gain greater market shares. However, this narrative is incomplete in terms of recognizing several other strategic interests (aside from gaining trade) that drive domestic policies in the digital world today.
>
> Services such as cloud computing, e-commerce, and big data processing now allow some of the biggest American internet companies to collect and control vast amounts of data. Many developed countries and fast-developing economies such as China recognize that overpowering American leadership in digital space is only possible if they develop indigenous data processing facilities that reach a larger chunk of the global market.[489]

Links can be drawn between the massive surge in data localisation measures in the last 10–15 years and global developments in the rise of the data-driven economy with accompanying social, economic and political consequences.[490] Therefore it could just as easily be argued by those who support data localisation that China is now building that legal

---

[489] Mishra, 'Data Localization Laws in a Digital World' (n 464) 154.
[490] See Neha Mishra, 'Building Bridges: International Trade Law, Internet Governance, and the Regulation of Data Flows' (2019) 52 *Vanderbilt Journal of Transnational Law* 463. Mishra argues that there is a strong connection between trade and internet governance.

regime through its Network Sovereignty policies.[491] We are therefore not witnessing *more* of the same protectionism through cyber controls,[492] but a desire to build China's innovation economy within new 'real-world' legal parameters, including containing data in China for the development of AI.

In addition, the existing locations of global AI R&D bases will also create problems for China's technology industry if blanket localisation is enforced, as many Chinese tech companies[493] have since 2017 set up such bases in Seattle, Silicon Valley and elsewhere.[494] Their R&D cross-border data exchanges might be captured by the 'fuzzy logic' of data exits in the Cyber Security Law. If these global linkages were halted, presumably there would be negative economic implications for Chinese innovation. Discussing the Chinese context, Maisog notes that the free flow of data is crucial to globalised technology ecosystems:

> [D]ata localization policies have the effect of undermining innovation. Despite all the economic and technological advances that China has made in recent decades, for many important economic sectors, the engines of innovation and discovery still do not reside within China. They reside elsewhere, and therefore to participate in this innovation China's own industries must – short of physically relocating themselves to these other countries – remain in close communication with them. Adopting data localisation policies would cut off China's communications with these engines of innovation. It would thereby consign Chinese businesses in

---

[491] The United Nations Conference on Trade and Development (UNCTAD) has noted that privacy laws, data protection laws and intellectual property laws, as well as laws protecting against political persecution – necessary to maintain the integrity of data centres – are often lacking in developing countries. See UNCTAD, *Information Economy Report 2013: The Cloud Economy and Developing Countries* (3 December 2013) <http://unctad.org/en/PublicationsLibrary/ier2013_en.pdf>. See also Cushman & Wakefield (law firm), 'Data Centre Risk Index 2013' <http://www.cushmanwakefield.com/~/media/global-reports/data-centre-risk-index-2013.pdf>.

[492] Increased protectionism seems unlikely: 'Key players in China think that cutting off cross-border data flows will hurt the country's global economic goals. From national tech champions like Alibaba seeking global markets, to Chinese financial institutions facilitating global transactions, cross-border data flows are a core operational reality': Sacks, Triolo and Webster, 'Beyond the Worst-Case Assumptions on China's Cybersecurity Law' (n 15).

[493] Chinese companies would face detrimental impacts if their 'Go Global' strategies were halted. The major technology firms are all listed companies. Alibaba and Baidu are registered in the Cayman Islands and listed on the New York Stock Exchange. Tencent is also registered in the Cayman Islands and listed in Hong Kong (as noted in Chapter 2).

[494] AI engineers of Chinese descent often prefer to remain in Silicon Valley while working for Chinese AI companies.

these industry sectors to the role of being late adapters rather than innovators in their own right. In the end, these Chinese industry sectors would find themselves simply awaiting and accepting innovations achieved elsewhere and then executing practical applications of them while others in the world have already commenced their next wave of innovation.[495]

The 'fuzzy logic' in China's Cyber Security Law has already had the effect of promoting China's domestic cloud computing industry. Promoting the domestic ICT industry occurs, for example, as a by-product of these laws by giving a comparative advantage to domestic Chinese cloud providers (eg, AliYun)[496] that are already localised within Chinese borders. There is also a close link between AI and cloud computing as AI requires enormous computing power, and this means that AI companies require a cloud services provider to power their research and operations (see Chapters 8 and 9).

As the economist Douglass North expounded, institutional changes augment the nature of the actors within economies.[497] Entrepreneurs try to take advantage of the opportunities provided within a given institutional framework. Institutional development may therefore lead to a path-dependent pattern of development with unexpected repercussions on particular industries.[498] Thus, promoting China's domestic cloud industry may not be a directly stated aim of the Cyber Security Law, but it is a major repercussion of the data localisation rule in Article 37.

Among foreign businesses with extensive operations in China, many have adopted a proactive approach in order to avoid being disadvantaged by the localisation provisions. As noted in Chapter 4, Airbnb made an unusually public announcement in December 2016, stating that it had begun storing data for its Chinese users on domestic Chinese servers provided by local cloud service firms.[499]

---

[495] Manuel E Maisog, *Making the Case against Data Localization in China* (IAPP, 20 April 2015) <https://iapp.org/news/a/making-the-case-against-data-localization-in-china>.

[496] Eileen Yu, 'Alibaba's Fiscal 2017 Revenue Climbs 56% on Cloud, Mobile Commerce Growth' (*ZDnet*, 18 May 2017) <http://www.zdnet.com/article/alibabas-fiscal-2017-revenue-climbs-56-percent-on-cloud-mobile-commerce-growth>. AliYun (also known as AliCloud) is Alibaba's cloud service provider whose business grew dramatically in 2016–2017.

[497] North, *Institutions, Institutional Change and Economic Performance* (n 35).

[498] Ibid.

[499] 'Airbnb Tells China Users' Personal Data to Be Stored Locally' (*Reuters*, 1 November 2016) <http://www.reuters.com/article/us-airbnb-china/airbnb-tells-china-users-personal-data-to-be-stored-locally-idUSKBN12W3V6>.

Uber,[500] Evernote,[501] LinkedIn[502] and Apple[503] each did the same, well before the official implementation of the Cyber Security Law. Apple in 2017 moved its Chinese processing centres to Guizhou Province, which has recently become a government-supported hub for big data. It may be that these foreign firms are acting on informal administrative guidance from Chinese regulators or simply hoping to pre-empt intrusive Chinese government scrutiny and discrimination by supporting local economic development and cloud providers.

These companies took these actions prior to the Cyber Security Law coming into effect. But did the law actually require that pre-emptive action? In North's conception of entrepreneurs attempting to take advantage of the opportunities provided within an institutional framework, perhaps China's cloud providers simply took advantage of the legal fuzzy logic to promote their businesses. Was it legally necessary or not? The actions of these foreign firms indicate their strong belief that the Chinese government will indeed enforce the data localisation provisions. Yet China's market potential means that they pre-emptively and voluntarily comply with those provisions in order to continue doing business there.

China's move to control its data may therefore be highly rational, an attempt to provide the fundamental conditions to compete with US tech firms, the first movers in AI. In fact, the European Union has had similar discussions regarding keeping data flows in Europe to assist the development of better self-driving cars.[504] This is a global phenomenon, and one

---

[500] Richard Waters, 'Making It Big in China Requires a Large Measure of Localisation' (*Financial Times*, 20 August 2015) <https://www.ft.com/content/0d472a74-4752-11e5-af2f-4d6e0e5eda22?mhq5j=e5>.

[501] 'Evernote Will Set Up a Data Centre in China' (*BBC*, 7 May 2012) <http://www.bbc.com/news/technology-17981737>.

[502] John McDuling, 'LinkedIn Is Doing What Facebook, Google, and Twitter Can't: Expanding in China' (*Quartz*, 24 February 2014) <https://qz.com/180755/linkedin-is-doing-what-facebook-google-and-twitter-cant-expanding-in-china>.

[503] Gerry Shih and Paul Carsten, 'Apple Begins Storing Users' Personal Data on Servers in China' (*Reuters*, 15 August 2014) <https://www.reuters.com/article/us-apple-data-china/apple-begins-storing-users-personal-data-on-servers-in-china-idUSKBN0GF0N720140815>.

[504] In 2015, German carmakers Audi, BMW and Daimler teamed up to buy Nokia's mapping business for €2.8 billion, signalling how much the auto industry values internet-connected functions – and independence from competing mapping services such as Google's. See Catherine Stupp, 'Carmakers Fear EU Plans to Ease Data Flows Will Help Tech Rivals' (*Euractiv*, 30 September 2016) <https://www.euractiv.com/section/transport/news/carmakers-fear-eus-plan-to-ease-data-flows-will-help-tech-rivals>.

that needs to be understood from a broader perspective than claims of short-sighted protectionism. The nexus between the rapid development of AI, which relies deeply on the massive accumulation of data, and localisation is evaluated further in subsequent chapters. Yet partly due to China's fuzzy logic legislating, multiple motivations for its policies can exist and be emphasised at different moments depending on political and economic developments, and AI development may be only one of the motivations for data localisation, with another obvious one being Network Sovereignty.

6.6 Conclusion: Costs–Benefits Can Change

Unresolved fuzzy logic laws intentionally create uncertainty to allow for selective enforcement after cost–benefit analyses are made. The data localisation debate cannot be discussed purely in universal terms, even though Chinese academics have also expressed similar concerns regarding the disruption to innovation. States are now not only interested in increasing revenues for their own economy, but also in their position relative to other countries. Countries are often driven by relative gains, even at the cost of sacrificing absolute gains. It is a cost–benefit analysis in which the Chinese government will seek to further its own interests and those of broader economic development.

This chapter summarised the main drawbacks and potential advantages of data localisation, and suggested that China may benefit from restricting outflows of critical infrastructure data. However, the actual purposes of the localisation provisions in the Cyber Security Law and how strictly they will be enforced remain uncertain. This has led to justifiable confusion and concern among foreign businesses and expert commentators that has continued from 2017 to 2021. This uncertainty was greatly heightened during 2017–2019 as the emergence of global AI R&D emerged. R&D cross-border data exchanges might be captured by the 'fuzzy logic' of data exits in the Cyber Security Law.

In the next chapters, it is argued that both the pessimists and optimists are too extreme in their predictions of the impact of the data localisation provisions on the functioning of the internet and business development in China. Based on its previous record, especially in the areas of internet control and information censorship, the Chinese government is highly unlikely to allow the new laws to remain unenforced. Instead, as with previous policy areas involving rapid innovation, the government has intentionally left the laws fuzzy or unclear – after consultation with industry groups – to provide more time to observe the developing technologies. Using targeted regulations, it will then try to seek a middle path between requiring compliance, such as setting up data centres in China to potentially enable government access – yet without enforcing the law so strictly that it jeopardises technological innovation and economic development.

Nevertheless, the Chinese government is not monolithic, and there are competing interests within its various policymaking institutions and agencies (see Chapter 8). This means that the contradictions between evolving Chinese policies such as Internet Plus and Network Sovereignty will continue in the more complex and technical domain of data localisation, just as they have in previous internet content control policies. These multiple, often contradictory, aims will continue to create confusion not just among foreign commentators but also among Chinese tech entrepreneurs.

At the same time, a certain degree of fuzziness may be essential in the area of technology regulation. As new technologies emerge, regulators must also exponentially consider new and complex issues. Policymakers need to judge how the technologies operate on a case-by-case basis without stifling them through over-regulation. Policy and law will inevitably lag behind technological change, as there are no crystal balls to predict new innovations. Over-regulation may be particularly damaging in this area, as the key tools of the modern innovation economy – big data, cloud computing and IoT as well as encryption, AI research and cyber security protocols – are all inextricably tied into the global innovation ecosystem.

In this context, China's fuzzy logic policymaking approach, if combined with a carefully calibrated degree of enforced data localisation, may avoid the risks and drawbacks identified by detractors above, while proving to be especially beneficial for the development of China's AI sector, which relies on both protected access to enormous amounts of private data and international (cross-border) research collaboration. If the Chinese government can get the regulatory balance right, avoiding too much heavy-handed Network Sovereignty micromanagement, China may continue to be a frontrunner in this sector.

The discussion now turns from analysing the broader debate about data localisation to the likely impact of those provisions on the regulation of new technologies in China, especially in the AI sector. The next chapter begins by examining the implementation of China's data privacy laws in the context of data localisation.

7

Data Protection but Not Data Privacy
'Data Protection Shall Not Hinder AI'

> The advantage of the internet over traditional industries is that it can 'iterate quickly' at low costs. And the basis of iteration is to understand the user's needs based on big data, so we must first affirm the value of the data.
>
> —张朝 [Zhang Chao], Senior Legal Adviser, Baidu[505]

The next logical question is how localised data will be protected in China, especially in relation to privacy concerns. This chapter identifies a clear discordance within the Cyber Security Law itself. On the one hand, the law promotes unprecedented increased personal data protections, and on the other, enforces real-name user registration for ICT platforms. Categories of protected data are yet another example of fuzzy logic in Chinese legislating around technology issues.

This chapter demonstrates the extent of the data protection problems in China, and the public's growing concern about loss of privacy and abuse of their personal data. It proceeds to show that under China's Cyber Security Law, the government has responded to this issue by strengthening 'data protection' from abuse by private companies but without shielding 'data privacy' from government intervention. In particular, enforced real-name user registration for online services potentially allows the Chinese government to demand access to the local data of any person who uses an online service in China, for national security or criminal investigation purposes.

The chapter argues that this internal contradiction within the Cyber Security Law – increased data protection while demanding real-name user registration – may also benefit AI development. This is due, in part, to the vagueness of key terms within the Cyber Security Law, and the

---

[505] 张朝 [Zhang Chao], «张朝: 百度隐私保护经验分享» [Zhang Chao: Sharing Baidu's Privacy Protection Experience] (Baidu Institute for Public Policy, 13 August 2018) <https://mp.weixin.qq.com/s/2cw5suQgwIY8augRepLjNQ>.

accompanying fuzzy logic within the Privacy Standards[506] issued under that law, which allow both tech firms and government regulators considerable discretion in how they comply with and enforce data protection provisions.

Finally, it is argued that due to the potential benefits of AI in solving serious governance problems, the Chinese government will only selectively enforce the data privacy provisions in the Cyber Security Law, seeking to prevent commercial abuse without hindering useful technological advances.

7.1 Background: New Data Protection Regime Still Emerging

China is creating its first comprehensive data protection regime. The new regime has implications for Chinese internet users, companies and the development of technologies such as AI. The system is still in its early stages, but the Chinese government has laid the groundwork for implementing concepts such as user consent as well as other requirements for collecting, processing and sharing of personal data. Even amid uncertainty around the practical effect of these rules, China is in the vanguard of countries dealing with this issue through the Cyber Security Law and its regulations, though Chinese regulators have often looked to Europe's GDPR in drafting privacy regulations (documented in Section 7.6.2). And in fact, unlike China, the United States still does not have a national data policy.

In Western media, China's privacy legislation seems to contradict other regimes, such as China's experimental pilot Social Credit System(s), which collect and require extensive personal data. It is important to emphasise that whilst the Social Credit System(s) are still evolving, the final criteria will be likely to raise serious ethical questions. There are different rules of access for the Chinese government compared with ordinary citizens and commercial firms. Government requests for personal data are exempt from the Cyber Security Law. But what is the nature of this exemption? Is it simply that the law does not apply to the government?

At the same time, there are strong indications of growing citizen awareness of the importance of data privacy. Chinese netizens facing constant data theft, hacking and privacy scandals are keenly cognisant of

---

[506] See «GB/T 35273-2017 信息安全技术 个人信息安全规范» [GB/T 35273-2017 Information Technology – Personal Information Security Specification] (People's Republic of China) National Information Security Standardisation Technical Committee (TC260), 29 December 2018 (Privacy Standards).

data privacy issues. There is growing public awareness of data protection as an issue due to increased official tolerance for public discussion, which escalated prominently during 2018.

Yet the government's requirement of real-name registration means that personal data in China will never be totally confidential. The requirement has inadvertently given a major boost to private tech firms, who have collected enormous amounts of user data and can associate it with real-name user registration details to develop powerful new AI applications.

This contradiction is outlined in the data protection regime emerging in subordinate standards under the data protection provisions of the Cyber Security Law. The regime contains negotiable classes of data formulated according to perceived, but fuzzy-logic, conceptions of 'risk' of data protection breaches (eg, theft, leak or inappropriate use).

After the Cyber Security Law went into partial effect in June 2017, the system of supporting rules and government guidelines around it continued to evolve sporadically during 2018–2021. As noted in Chapter 5, data localisation provisions remained subject to yet-to-be released subordinate regulations. In some areas (eg, personal information protection), regulation has become more codified under the law. In other areas of great importance (eg, the scope of the 'critical information infrastructure' rules, cyber security reviews of network products and services, and security assessment for outbound data transfers), final clarifications were still to come in 2019. Final details of the measures for security assessment of outbound data transfers were also expected in 2019–2020 but were to remain vague.[507]

Due to the many problems of data leakage (noted extensively below) officials from various institutions, including the National People's Congress and People's Bank of China, called for the urgent establishment of a Personal Information Protection Law in addition to the non-binding Privacy Standards (see Section 7.7).[508] Reports emerged during 2018 that

---

[507] Mingli Shi, 'What China's 2018 Internet Governance Tells Us About What's Next' (*New America*, 28 January 2019) <https://www.newamerica.org/cybersecurity-initiative/digichina/blog/what-chinas-2018-internet-governance-tells-us-about-whats-next>.

[508] See 吴晓灵, 周学东 [Wu Xiaoling and Zhou Xuedong], «吴晓灵, 周学东: 建议尽快制定 '个人信息保护法'» [Wu Xiaoling and Zhou Xuedong: Recommended Formulating the Personal Information Protection Law as Soon as Possible] (*Caixin*, 16 March 2018) <http://topics.caixin.com/2017-03-16/101066803.html>. Wu Xiaoling is deputy director of the National People's Congress and its Finance and Economic Committee. Zhou Xuedong is deputy to the National People's Congress and director of the business management department of the People's Bank of China.

a Personal Information Protection Law was in the early draft stage,[509] along with a related Data Security Law; both were publicly released by late 2020 and enacted in 2021.[510] The Draft Data Security Law and the Draft Personal Information Protection Law were both released for public comment in July 2020 and October 2020 respectively (discussed in Section 7.9). Both laws had appeared on the Chinese government's list of legislation planned for deliberation between 2018 and 2023. A draft Encryption Law also remained in development (eventually taking effect in January 2020).[511] That meant that for the interim period, companies

---

[509] The Personal Information Protection Law (个人信息保护法) was listed for action in the legislative priority agenda of the National People's Congress for 2018–2023, after an earlier draft in 2005 did not result in passage. The list is available here: «十三届全国人大常委会立法规划» [Legislative Planning of the 13th National People's Congress Standing Committee] (National People's Congress, 10 September 2018) <http://www.npc.gov.cn/npc/xinwen/2018-09/10/content_2061041.htm> (the link is no longer active).

[510] The Data Security Law (数据安全法) was also included in the National People's Congress priority agenda and was enacted in 2020. This new law was expected to be closely interlinked with the existing National Security Law (n 284) and the Cyber Security Law (n 2), addressing the common practice of data security with a particular emphasis on data generated by certain important sectors such as critical information infrastructure: see ibid. On 2 July 2020, China's Data Security Law was released for public comment: «中华人民共和国数据安全法(草案)» [Data Security Law of the People's Republic of China (Opinion-Seeking Draft)] (People's Republic of China) National People's Congress, 2 July 2020. On 21 October 2020 the Standing Committee of the National People's Congress published for public comment the first draft of the Personal Information Protection Law: «中华人民共和国个人信息保护法(草案)» [Personal Information Protection Law of the People's Republic of China (Opinion-Seeking Draft)] (People's Republic of China) National People's Congress, 21 October 2020 (Draft Information Protection Law).

[511] Much less controversial than the Anti-Terrorism Law (n 285) at the time, and in line with China's genuine cyber security concerns, is the Draft Encryption Law promulgated in April 2017. The draft law sought to promote and standardise the use of encryption technologies from a national level. There was no international outcry over its intent at that time. See «中华人民共和国密码法 (草案征求意见稿)» [Encryption Law of the People's Republic of China (Opinion-Seeking Draft)] (People's Republic of China) Office of State Commercial Cryptography Administration (OSCCA), 13 April 2017. There is a strong focus in the draft and final Encryption Law on the use of encryption to protect critical information infrastructure. Similar to China's Anti-Terrorism Law (n 285): People's procuratorates, public security bodies and state security bodies may require telecommunications operators and internet service providers to provide technological decryption support when necessary for national security or the prosecution of criminal cases. Art 11 of the draft law set forth that commercial encryption products that are sold or used in business activities, as well as the provision of commercial encryption services, will be subject to approval in accordance with – at the time not yet created – certified encryption catalogues. Unlike the Draft Anti-Terrorism Law, it does not require

and regulators have had to rely on the current, vague provisions in the Cyber Security Law and a constantly evolving patchwork of accompanying regulations and standards. The way that these are implemented may be crucial for the development of AI in China and globally. The final Encryption Law for example has been regarded as both containing fuzzy logic in how encryption application is regulated but also commended for helping local governments to better protect personal information data.[512] The reality is that foreign companies and the Chinese government have strong commercial imperatives not to side-step commercial encryption standard practice, despite any outside commentary.[513]

'backdoors' to be built. In achieving these aims, the major global technology companies would need to be involved in assisting in the creation of these encryption catalogues. Third-party reviews continue to take place. The final law encourages foreign participation providing commercial encryption: arts 22–3.

[512] On one hand, this law is 'tightening up the mess', according to David Li, executive director of the Shenzhen Open Innovation Lab. He noted that while China has had encryption technologies for decades, local officials were not using it. National education and civil service training will now include encryption: Lavender Au, 'China's New Encryption Law Takes Effect (TechNode, 2 January 2020) <https://technode.com/2020/01/02/chinas-new-encryption-law-takes-effect/>.

Alternatively it was argued that, in reality, the law would create an additional lawyer of 'fuzzy logic'. The final law divides encryption into three categories: core, common and commercial. Core and common are intended for systems that transmit and store PRC state secrets. Commercial encryption is intended for business and private use. 'This three class system ignores the way cryptography is normally implemented.' See: Steve Dickinson, 'China's New Cryptography Law: Still No Place to Hide' (Harris Bricken (law firm)), 7 November 2019) <https://harrisbricken.com/chinalawblog/chinas-new-cryptography-law-still-no-place-to-hide/>. The law provides that it welcomes foreign providers of commercial encryption: arts 22–3. The State Cryptography Administration (SCA), an office of the CCP, will have authority to monitor and inspect implementation and use of the cryptography system: art 31. «中华人民共和国密码法» [Encryption Law of the People's Republic of China] (People's Republic of China) Office of State Commercial Cryptography Administration (OSCCA), 26 October 2019.

[513] Today, most encryption is simply based on well-known mathematics, that is implemented broadly in a bunch of plug-and-play libraries, or a cryptographer can implement a bespoke system. OpenSSL, libgcrypt, NaCl are some common libraries. Most programming languages also have built in cryptography to use, as well as every major operating system.

The Encryption Law possibly seeks to get companies that use encryption to find ways to subvert the encryption without 'breaking' the cryptography. That may not mean much. For example, Apple can design iPhones in two ways: 1. No one, not even Apple, can gain access; 2. If the Chinese government asks, Apple can gain access. This means that it is not truly end-to-end encrypted (see discussion of Apple's practices in Chapter 4). That would be a public relations nightmare for Apple.

7.1.1 Increased Data Protection under the Cyber Security Law

The Cyber Security Law provides increased individual protections that are unprecedented for China. It is the first national legislation establishing legal principles for the protection of personal data. In the past, data privacy was regulated by administrative rules, judicial interpretations, government policies and non-binding industry guidelines.[514] Articles 41–3 of the Cyber Security Law restrict the amount of personally identifiable information that can be collected by 'network operators'. These articles also limit how data can be transferred, and provide an individual with the right to request that information be deleted if mishandled.[515] Article 41 also provides that network operators must safeguard the secrecy of personal data collected. The collection and use of personal data must follow the principles of legality, propriety and necessity, and data collectors must follow the legal requirements in terms of giving notice and obtaining consent.[516]

Further, in relation to public policy and privacy concerns, Article 22 of the Cyber Security Law states that the general public must be notified of any security flaws regarding their personal data by the provider of network products and services.[517] Further subordinate regulations have since followed (explained in Section 7.6). Nevertheless, the key point is that this new codified data protection regime in the Cyber Security Law and subordinate regulations reflects a genuine effort by the Chinese government to stop the 'trust' and data protection scandals emerging frequently in China. This chapter outlines how this effort creates conflicts of interest yet also opportunities for data-collecting Chinese companies, wedged as they are between the competing demands of Network Sovereignty and trying to innovate for their customers and earn greater profits.

7.2 Enforced Real-Name User Registration

The data protection provisions contain a major contradiction that makes it almost impossible for them to resist government demands for access to information or censorship of unacceptable content. Government requests

---

[514] See Creemers, 'Cyber China' (n 23).
[515] In case of a data breach incident, the data collectors shall report to the authority and affected users should also be contacted. Companies and individuals who are directly in charge can be fined up to ¥100,000 for failure to comply.
[516] Under Cyber Security Law (n 2) art 41.
[517] Ibid, art 22.

for personal data are exempt from the Cyber Security Law. But what is the nature of this exemption? Again, is it simply that the law does not apply to the government in practice? This inherent conflict is complex. Private Chinese companies do, at times, resist efforts to provide user data to the government.

In the first legal case in China on data privacy and security, in June 2017 AliYun (or Alibaba Cloud) lost a lawsuit brought by a private online gaming company, seeking compensation from AliYun for allowing unlicensed operation of its games. The information request was made by the plaintiff through the court, trying to find out the number of unauthorised users of the game in order to calculate damages. AliYun apparently refused to provide the confidential information, but the lawsuit was not decided on that point. Compensation was ordered based on estimated losses to the plaintiff. However, AliYun did state that if a court or judicial body ordered it to release confidential information for specific cases, it would need to comply with that order.[518]

Senior AliYun executives, however, issued statements after the ruling saying that users' data privacy is a top priority. Although AliYun lost, some media reports cited those who urged the company to appeal.[519] They likened the case to Apple's refusal to comply with US government requests to unlock an iPhone of a suspect in the high-profile domestic terrorism case in San Bernardino (discussed in Chapter 4).

Yet despite active enforcement against companies that exploit or fail to protect users' data, when it comes to government demands for data, the situation is not so clear. Companies such as Alibaba, JD.com, Baidu and Tencent have a poor record when it comes to refusing to turn over data to government entities, as discussed below. On the other hand, companies have at times managed to avoid or obstruct the regulatory authorities to protect users' privacy. Transportation authorities in Guangdong Province reported that ride-sharing service Didi Chuxing had been irresponsibly uncooperative in sharing information about drivers and cars with local regulators.[520] In August 2018, in Shenzhen alone, there were

---

[518] See 《阿里云涉侵权被判赔 26 万：'宁输官司也要保护隐私'》[AliYun (AliCloud) Alleged Infringement: 26 Million Awarded: 'Would Rather Face a Lawsuit in Order to Protect Users' Privacy'] (*Sina*, 3 June 2017) <http://tech.sina.com.cn/i/2017-06-03/doc-ifyfuzmy1489932.shtml>.

[519] Ibid.

[520] Gu Liping, 'Didi Chuxing Refuses Data Supervision: Transport Official' (*Ecns.cn*, 28 August 2018) <http://www.ecns.cn/news/cns-wire/2018-08-28/detail-ifyxikfc9645161.shtml>.

about 5,000 Didi drivers and 2,000 cars on the road without proper approvals[521] (an interesting fact in the context of Didi's 2021 IPO).

7.2.1 Real-Name User Registration

Despite these examples of pushback, companies face great pressures in legally resisting data disclosures to the government. While the Cyber Security Law contains broader data protection provisions, the great internal contradiction of the law is that it also requires instant messaging services and other internet companies to register users' real names and personal information,[522] and to censor content that is 'prohibited'. This can even extend to online gaming. In September 2018, Tencent enforced real-name verification for the PC game *Honor of Kings* to satisfy regulators.[523]

This requirement appears to have little to do with cyber security. Burglars do not leave business cards. No hacker will send you their email address while attacking your network and systems. Real-name registration as required by various Chinese laws and regulations is aimed at discouraging what the Party sees as socially harmful online activities, including criticism of the Party and online political activism. Fears operate because historically the government largely outsourced the burdens of regulating individual behaviour to internet enterprises resulting in a fuzzy censorship process,[524] but it has now under the Cyber Security Law drastically expanded the range and scope of legal and regulatory measures directly affecting internet users.

---

[521] Ibid. Tragically, two passengers were murdered by Didi drivers in 2018, sending reverberations through China's technology industry: Sarah Dai, 'Didi Rocked by Second Passenger Killing in Three Months Despite Additional Security Measures' (*South China Morning Post*, 25 August 2018) <https://www.scmp.com/tech/article/2161341/didi-rocked-second-passenger-killing-three-months-despite-additional-security>.

[522] See Cyber Security Law (n 2) art 24. The official reason given for introducing this requirement is public security. (See Chapter 5.) See Jyh-An Lee and Ching-Yi Liu, 'Real-Name Registration Rules and the Fading Digital Anonymity in China' (2016) 25 *Washington International Law Journal* 1.

[523] Chris Udemans, 'Tencent Enforces Real-Name Verification in "Honor of Kings"' (*TechNode*, 17 September 2018) <https://technode.com/2018/09/17/real-name-verification-honor-of-kings>.

[524] For example, in March 2017 there was a report that Taobao (Alibaba's e-commerce platform) was banning merchants from selling foreign media in China – even media approved by censors. The smaller players in this story (the e-commerce booksellers) followed Alibaba's dictates – not the Chinese regulators' dictates. See Huang, 'Taobao Is Banning Merchants from Selling Foreign Media in China' (n 257).

China's internet content regulators – CAC and the Ministry of Industry and Information Technology[525] (MIIT) – determine whether content is consistent with social values. Various regulators then focus on preventing dissemination of information that the government considers illegal.[526] Unlike information network or cyber security, which mainly deals with data and network protection, internet content regulation involves placing regulations on what Chinese people can read, see and hear on the internet. Real-name policies restrict anonymity and can lead to self-censorship and suppression of online communication.[527]

Real-name user registration is not unique to the Cyber Security Law: it was already required by previous regulations.[528] In August 2014, the (former) SIIO promulgated the so-called WeChat (微信) Articles – regulations designed to collect WeChat user data.[529] The SIIO (now renamed

---

[525] MIIT was established in 2008 as a department under the State Council, responsible for the administration of China's industrial branches and information industry. It is a 'super-ministry' responsible for the integration of science and technology planning and industry, but not media content control. See <https://www.miit.gov.cn/>.

[526] See, eg, Guobin Yang, *The Power of the Internet in China: Citizen Activism Online* (Columbia University Press, 2011).

[527] According to one report, during mandatory site and app registrations, Chinese netizens tend to be cautious about giving out their real identity and information (eg, bank account, identity card and address). They feel more secure in giving their birthday, gender and the name of the province they live in. If the option is provided, 88.1% of Chinese online users choose to log in via third-party accounts such as QQ, WeChat and Weibo because of the extra layer of security protection. In other cases, they prefer mobile phone over email registration for a faster and more convenient service: see «我们真的在意隐私吗: 多少中国网民'一套密码走天下'?» [Do We Really Care about Privacy: How Many Chinese Netizens 'Have a Set of Passwords to Go Online'?] (*Qianjia Net*, 15 August 2018) <http://www.qianjia.com/html/2018-08/15_301849.html>. See also Creemers, 'Cyber China' (n 23).

[528] Notwithstanding these broad new grants of authority, many provisions appear to codify longstanding government restrictions on internet usage. For example, art 24 of the Cyber Security Law (n 2) mandates that companies verify an individual's real identity before providing internet services. CAC has enforced similar requirements on blogs, instant-messaging services, discussion forums and other internet outlets. Art 12 prohibits persons or organisations from 'subverting national sovereignty' or 'overthrowing the socialist system'. This parallels art 15 of the National Security Law (n 284). Art 58 of the Cyber Security Law gives the State Council and other government entities the ability to temporarily restrict internet access as required by 'national security' or to preserve 'social order'. The Cyber Security Law does not retreat from past censorship powers.

[529] «即时通信工具公众信息服务发展管理暂行规定» [Provisional Regulations for the Development and Management of Instant Messaging Tools and Public Information Services] (People's Republic of China) SIIO, 7 August 2014. These regulations require instant-messaging service providers that engage in 'public information service activities' to obtain certain prior qualifications.

CAC) demanded real-name registration for WeChat accounts, with the proviso that users would be permitted to adopt a public handle or nickname when communicating online. Previous similar legislation aimed specifically at Sina Weibo initially had a major negative commercial effect on Sina Weibo.[530]

However, this targeted 'pilot' approach has not stopped consumers using these products. Both Sina Weibo and WeChat have survived and are flourishing again. With 390 million monthly users, Sina Weibo experienced a huge, unforeseen revival in late 2016.[531] What was once called 'China's Twitter' has now become a comprehensive platform that incorporates the major features of social media channels like Twitter, YouTube and Instagram.[532] WeChat, the world's most popular app, is even more successful, with estimates of over a billion active daily users in 2019.[533]

Thus, one dominant element of this strategy is the gradual expansion of these rules previously aimed at specific companies. For example, real-name registration was steadily introduced in various areas of telecommunications and internet use.[534] An early 'self-regulatory' notice on mobile telephone apps, passed in November 2014 with the 'encouragement' of the Beijing municipal government, committed developers and app stores to broaden the implementation of identity authentication

---

[530] See, eg, Eric Harwit, 'The Rise and Influence of Weibo (Microblogs) in China' (2014) 54 (6) *Asian Survey* 1059.

[531] See Steven Millward, 'Seven Years of "China's Twitter"' (*TechinAsia*, 14 August 2016) <https://www.techinasia.com/7-years-of-weibo-china-social-media>.

[532] Manya Koetse, 'Weibo's Revival: Sina Weibo Is China's Twitter, YouTube and InstaGram' (*What's on Weibo*, 20 November 2016) <http://www.whatsonweibo.com/weibos-revival-sina-weibo-chinas-twitteryoutubeinstagram>.

[533] «2018 微信年度数据报告: 00 后睡觉少, 70 后爱刷朋友圈» [WeChat Annual Data Report: Less Sleep after Midnight and 70 Love to Swipe Friends Groups] (*Sina*, 9 January 2019) <https://tech.sina.com.cn/i/2019-01-09/doc-ihqhqcis4468637.shtml>. In English see Cyrus Lee, 'Daily Active Users for WeChat Exceeds 1 Billion (*ZDNet*, 9 January 2019) <https://www.zdnet.com/article/daily-active-user-of-messaging-app-wechat-exceeds-1-billion>.

[534] For example, a Judicial Interpretation on online infringement of personality rights, promulgated in October 2014, provides that courts may order internet companies to provide names, addresses and contact methods of users, where these are deemed to have published defamatory information. Companies refusing to carry out such requests would be liable for punitive measures: «关于审理理应信息网络侵权人身权益民事纠纷按键使用法律若干问题的规定» [Regulations Concerning Some Questions of Applicable Law in Handling Civil Dispute Cases Involving the Use of Information Networks to Harm Personal Rights and Interests] (People's Republic of China) Supreme People's Court, 9 October 2014.

systems.[535] These efforts seem to have worked: it was reported in January 2015, for example, that more than 80% of WeChat users had registered under their real identities.[536]

Moreover, real-name registration duties were not limited to online content; they were also mandated for the purchase of telephones, enabling the identification of online activities through individual pieces of hardware since 2013.[537] In February 2015, CAC issued regulations mandating a real-name registration system for all account-based online information services.[538]

Article 24 of the Cyber Security Law has now expanded the range of real-name user registration to include any 'network operator' (eg, smaller internet firms) and new forms of media, including IoT and smart technologies: 'Article 24: ... Where users do not provide real identity information, network operators must not provide them with the relevant services.'[539] Theoretically, there are some privacy protections, including the fact that the obligation to require real-name registration under the Cyber Security Law is accompanied by restriction on the use of such information: Article 30 makes it clear that information obtained by CAC 'when carrying out cyber security protection duties, may only be used for cyber security needs, and may not be used for other purposes'.[540] Yet many may wonder whether the Chinese government will really restrict its use of information in this way, and what is meant by this phrase 'cyber security'.

7.2.2 *Data Protection, not Privacy*

Thus, while data privacy scandals have engulfed Chinese tech firms, and many have already been penalised under the Cyber Security Law for

---

[535] «北京市移动互联网应用程序公众信息服务自律公约» [Beijing Municipality Self-Discipline Convention on Internet Application Programmes and Public Information Services], Capital Internet Society, 26 November 2011.

[536] Liu Sha, 'Govt Takes Down Illegal Websites' (*Global Times*, 14 January 2015) <http://www.globaltimes.cn/content/901784.shtml>.

[537] «电话用户真实身份信息登记规定» [Telephone User Real Identity Information Registration Regulations] (People's Republic of China) MIIT, 16 July 2013.

[538] «互联网用户账号名称管理规定» [Internet User Account Name Management Regulations] (People's Republic of China) CAC, 4 February 2015.

[539] 'The State implements an online trustworthy identity strategy, supports research and development of secure and convenient electronic identity confirmation technologies, and promotes mutual recognition among different electronic identify confirmation technologies': Cyber Security Law (n 2) art 24.

[540] Ibid art 30.

selling or leaking data (see next section), these privacy provisions do not apply to demands for information by the Chinese government:

> Given these dual tracks of Chinese data regulation, the term 'data protection' or 'personal information protection' may be more accurate characterizations than 'data privacy' in the context of China. In Europe, the term 'data protection' captures both security and privacy, but in China, there appears to be more emphasis on data security rather than a Western notion of privacy. While these concepts are still in early stages and vague in China, officials and commentators tend to use the term 'personal information protection' rather than privacy. Since Chinese users' concern over government access to personal data is muffled, private-sector fraud and abuse of data become the primary regulatory target of China's data protection rules.[541]

This contradiction is transparent in disclosing that data may be shared with the government. WeChat's user terms now make it clear that they share information with the government to comply with 'applicable laws or regulations'.[542] Likewise, when Airbnb entered the Chinese market, its hosts listing their properties in China were notified by Airbnb China that under the Cyber Security Law their information could be shared with Chinese government agencies without further notice starting from 30 March 2018.[543] Many other companies routinely release similar announcements.[544]

Thus, the meaning of data privacy in China is quite different from that in liberal democracies in the West.[545] Since users are not in a position to

---

[541] Lu Xiaomeng, Li Manyi and Samm Sacks, *What the Facebook Scandal Means in a Land without Facebook: A Look at China's Burgeoning Data Protection Regime* (CSIS, 25 April 2018) <https://www.csis.org/analysis/what-facebook-scandal-means-land-without-facebook-look-chinas-burgeoning-data-protection>.

[542] Emma Lee, 'Updated: WeChat's Privacy Policy Update Draws Attention to Information Shared with the Government' (*TechNode*, 19 September 2017) <https://technode.com/2017/09/19/now-its-official-wechat-is-watching-you-1>.

[543] Linda Lew, 'Airbnb China Notifies Hosts They May Begin Sharing Their Information with the Government' (*TechNode*, 28 March 2018) <https://technode.com/2018/03/28/airbnb-china-host-data-privacy>.

[544] In May 2017, Baidu also made a statement acknowledging that compliance with the Cyber Security Law means users must use their real name: «百度用网盘, 发贴, 评论必得实名认证» [Those Who Use Baidu's Network, Posting or Comments Functions Must All Undergo Real-Name Certification] (*Xianji*, 11 May 2017) <https://www.xianjichina.com/news/details_35326.html>.

[545] It must be acknowledged that this Chinese public discussion may not be in absolute contrast to Western considerations of privacy: 'People are inconsistent about the kind of exposure they'll tolerate [in the West]. We don't like to be fingerprinted by government

prevent government access to personal information, they must direct their frustrations towards private companies misusing their data. Or they can attempt to get around the rules by buying privacy; entire marketplaces have sprung up in China selling fake WeChat accounts to avoid real-name registration.[546]

China's genuine attempts at data protection aimed at private Chinese companies are outlined below, but first the extent of data protection problems in China, and the growing public concern about loss of privacy and abuse of personal data must be explained.

7.3 Data Protection a Key Social Issue, among Many 'Trust' Scandals

The following background is crucial to understanding the Chinese demand for greater data protection. Data protection is a pressing current issue in China, among many other scandals involving the breakdown of trust in institutions, so much so that Renmin University Law Professor Liu Junhai (刘俊海) wrote that the major thrust of the Cyber Security Law is to stop fraud.[547] The Cyber Security Law has legislated stringent punishments for private information hacking, and Chinese regulators often initiate public campaigns to crack down on abuses. Although the data localisation provisions in the law had a delayed implementation, the data protection infringements were immediately enforced. There is

---

agencies, a practice we associate with mug shots and state surveillance, but we happily hand our thumbprints over to Apple, which does God knows what with them. ... Possibly the discussion is using the wrong vocabulary. "Privacy" is an odd name for the good that is being threatened by commercial exploitation and state surveillance. Privacy implies "It's nobody's business".' Louis Menand, 'Why Do We Care So Much About Privacy?' (*New Yorker*, 18 June 2018) <https://www.newyorker.com/magazine/2018/06/18/why-do-we-care-so-much-about-privacy>. This fascinating and complex discussion demands further empirical research beyond the scope of this study.

[546] According to an investigation by the *Beijing Youth Daily*, the accounts on offer vary regarding their authentication levels, from newly registered profiles to old accounts which have undergone real-name verification, and those that have been bound to payment tools. Prices range between ¥58 (around US$9) to ¥500. See Emma Lee, 'Sale of WeChat Accounts Prompts Concern over Fraud (*TechNode*, 16 January 2019) <https://technode.com/2019/01/16/wechat-accounts-sale-online-fraud/>. The original *Beijing Youth Daily* link is now blocked.

[547] 刘俊海 [Liu Junhai], «网安法一周年: 网络安全筑起五道 '防火墙'» [The One Year Anniversary of the Cyber Security Law: Cyber Security Builds Five 'Firewalls'] (*China Information Security*, 2 June 2018) <https://mp.weixin.qq.com/s/cjMZ1Km4bfNjwaIvw9u5Mw>.

absolutely no doubt that the Chinese government sees the need to resolve this pressing issue, as the Chinese people become increasingly frustrated with the almost weekly reports of stolen data being sold on black markets. The seriousness of the problem is perhaps ill-understood outside China.

In the public debate about Chinese privacy protections – like many other social issues in China – the word 'trust' is often used. From the baby milk scandal of 2008[548] to the vaccine scandal of July 2018, and ongoing shadow banking and peer-to-peer lending scandals,[549] who you can 'trust' is a high-profile concern. In particular, China faces great problems with inaccurate datasets, data theft cases and data 'trust' scandals. Even government bureaucracies are notorious for data leaks and inaccurate datasets[550] and children's vaccine records have been found to be fraudulent.[551] Hence, the Chinese people have become highly cognisant of the importance of data protection, as evidenced by the polls. Just as the 'EU's push towards individual data protection and privacy is not surprising in the wake of the increasingly unprecedented magnitude and scope of corporate data breaches',[552] so China's constant – almost

---

[548] In 2008, six children died and 300,000 became ill after drinking formula made from milk powder tainted with melamine, a case officials had initially covered up. Chinese netizens have not forgotten this earlier scandal. Some on social media compared milk powder with the more recent vaccine scandal: one commenter on Weibo wrote in July 2018: 'Yesterday it was milk powder, today vaccines. What will it be tomorrow?': Lucas Niewenhuis, 'Yet Another Vaccine Scandal Punctures Public Trust in Safety' (*SupChina*, 23 July 2018) <https://supchina.com/2018/07/23/outrage-over-faulty-vaccines-again>.

[549] Gabriel Wildau and Yizhen Jia, 'Collapse of Chinese Peer-to-Peer Lenders Sparks Investor Panic' (*Financial Times*, 22 July 2018) <https://www.ft.com/content/75e75628-8b27-11e8-bf9e-8771d5404543>.

[550] See, eg, 'Another Chinese City Admits Releasing "Fake" Economic Data' (*South China Morning Post*, 17 January 2018) <https://www.scmp.com/news/china/economy/article/2128629/another-chinese-city-admits-releasing-fake-economic-data>. Baotou in China's Inner Mongolia autonomous region revised its estimated fiscal revenue in 2017 lower by nearly 50% in an annual work report, a copy of which was published on the Baotou government's website on 13 January.

[551] Kristin Huang and Zhou Xin, 'Fake Data: The Disease Afflicting China's Vaccine System' (*South China Morning Post*, 30 July 2018) <https://www.scmp.com/news/china/policies-politics/article/2157341/fake-data-disease-afflicting-chinas-vaccine-system>. In response to this scandal, Alipay quickly introduced a new feature allowing parents to trace the vaccines their children were receiving. See Jiefei Liu, 'Alipay Introduces New Feature Allowing Parents to Trace the Vaccines Their Children Are Receiving' (*TechNode*, 24 July 2018) <https://technode.com/2018/07/24/alipay-introduces-new-feature-allowing-parents-to-trace-the-vaccines-their-children-are>.

[552] 'The March toward Data Localization' (n 429).

weekly – data scandals have created a strong impetus for its Cyber Security Law.

In China, state media regularly reports on data breaches, media investigations occur often, and individual and corporate violators are regularly and publicly shamed. Data protection is therefore a high-profile public concern in China as the censors allow for and even encourage official dialogue on the topic. For example, in February 2017, Chinese state media CCTV released a report suggesting that vendors have been selling confidential information such as people's national identity card numbers, home addresses, the value of their assets including property, and even mobile phone call logs. Chinese netizens were outraged.[553]

These kinds of news reports have become commonplace in Chinese-language media, and even salacious data theft cases have not been blocked by the censors. For example, it was reported in Chinese-language media that 'sexy bots' have been used to lure lonely men into online dating scams. Police in Guangdong Province arrested more than 600 suspects across 13 provinces for running such scams on dating apps in 2017.[554]

One could characterise the relationship between popular sentiment and censorship controls in China using the analogy of a shaken-up Coke bottle. That is, when an issue is too controversial to completely suppress, China's propaganda control apparatus allows at least temporary public discourse to emerge on that issue. It works something like twisting the top of the Coke bottle to let some pressure out, but once people have had their say, the lid can be tightened again by information controllers using technological tools to 'ban' controversial words from official and social media.[555]

---

[553] Liu Xiaojing and Li Rongde, 'QQ Blocks Thousands of Accounts for Selling Private Information' (*Caixin Global*, 21 February 2017) <https://www.caixinglobal.com/2017-02-21/qq-blocks-thousands-of-accounts-for-selling-private-information-101057642.html>.

[554] According to Chinese media, in one data theft scam, police arrested 113 individuals who formed part of a data broking network. Police said the group showed how criminals are building complex operating structures to avoid being caught. See «揭秘个人信息交易黑市: 内部分工明确 日交易额百万» [Exposing the Personal Information Transaction Black Market: The Scheme is Exposed, the Daily Trade Is Worth Millions'] (*People's Daily*, 11 October 2018) <http://tech.qq.com/a/20181011/003346.htm>. «'虚拟美女'诈骗背后, 除了男人还有机器人» [Men and Robots behind Online Dating Scams] (*Guangzhou Daily*, 8 January 2018) <https://www.weibo.com/ttarticle/p/show?id=2309351000344193881934670946&u=1887790981&m=4193881803559510&cu=1739281457>.

[555] There is an extensive online literature concerning public discourses on China's internet. See, eg, Rebecca MacKinnon, *Consent of the Networked: The Worldwide Struggle for Internet Freedom* (Basic Books, 2013); Yang, *The Power of the Internet in China* (n 526).

DATA PROTECTION BUT NOT DATA PRIVACY   169

Data privacy is now a permissible issue for public polling and debate in China due to the prevalence of and social concern about complex data theft schemes.[556] The issue has even become a topic of contemporary cultural discourse. In April 2018, artist Deng Yufeng bought the personal data of 346,000 Wuhan residents and displayed them at a Wuhan Art Gallery in an attempt to make people realise the extent of the data leakage problem in China. He text-messaged over 300,000 of the people – using their leaked private data – to invite them to the gallery to see their data. The exhibition was reportedly closed after its first two days and Deng was investigated by the authorities.[557]

The crux of the issue is that Chinese hackers regularly sell personal information for as little as US$0.01 per item.[558] There are entire marketplaces for the sale of data.[559] For example, police in Beijing's Haidian district announced on 5 December 2017 that a group of hackers was arrested in possession of over a million pieces of information on Chinese citizens, including mobile phone numbers.[560] The report in the *People's*

---

[556] See Section 7.4.
[557] According to *1Shoucang*, an art news site, the Hubei youth artist Deng Yufeng put on the exhibition titled 'Secrets', billed as an experimental project, in the Wuhan Art Gallery. There was an opening ceremony on 4 April and much publicity surrounded the event: 彭云燕 [Peng Yunyan], «邓玉峰个展开幕 34.6 万武汉公民的秘密被 '公之于众' [Deng Yufeng's Opening Ceremony: 346,000 Wuhan Citizens' Secrets 'Made Public'] (*1Shoucang*, 4 April 2018) <http://www.1shoucang.com/article-41710-1.html>.

Deng Yufeng has explored themes of data at previous exhibitions in Beijing and online. In 2016 a Twitter account called 'state ID' in Chinese leaked the personal and ID information of Alibaba's Jack Ma and controversial businessman Guo Wengui, in an attempt to make the poster's 'countrymen think about how worthless their privacy is'. See C Custer, 'State IDs of China's Rich and Powerful, Including Jack Ma, Leaked in Apparent Privacy Protest' (*Tech in Asia*, 12 May 2016) <https://www.techinasia.com/state-id-numbers-chinas-rich-powerful-including-jack-ma-fang-binxing-leaked-apparent-privacy-protest>.
[558] Masha Borak, 'Chinese Hackers Are Selling Personal Information for as Little as $0.01' (*TechNode*, 22 December 2017) <https://technode.com/2017/12/22/chinese-hackers-selling-personal-information-little-0-01>.
[559] Chris Udemans, 'Second-Hand Mobile Phone User Data Is Being Sold in China for as Little as RMB 10' (*TechNode*, 1 June 2018) <https://technode.com/2018/06/01/mobile-phone-user-data>.
[560] A seemingly simple code system hid a chain of personal information resellers, divided into three layers. The first layer comprised the coders, the second the website and the third layer the intermediaries bridging the two. Intermediaries would buy codes for ¥600 and resell them to websites for ¥1,000. But websites could not access the personal information themselves. The information was bought by the intermediaries for ¥0.8 to ¥0.1 per item and then sold for ¥0.5 to ¥1. «谁卖了我的手机号? 手机信息被盗一年损失近千亿» [Who Sold My Mobile Number? Mobile Phone Information Stolen Worth

Daily described in depth the nature and sophistication of the scam, including the way marketplaces have been built and decentralised with codes and middlemen to avoid detection.

Furthermore, according to a December 2017 survey conducted by the *China Youth Daily* and the Standing Committee of the National People's Congress, of 10,000 people surveyed more than 61% said they have encountered companies that restrict access to online services unless users give permission to collect and use their personal information.[561] Chinese netizens thus feel pressured by companies to provide personal information that can potentially be sold or misused at a later stage. The results of the survey were released by Wang Shengjun (王胜俊), vice chairman of the Standing Committee of the National People's Congress, while briefing lawmakers on cyberspace protection: 'Wang called for a new law to protect personal information which would specify the responsibilities of online operators and the scope of personal information they are allowed to collect.'[562] Therefore, public calls for greater legal data protections are increasing but the drafting, promulgation and implementation of these laws has been slow. As noted, China's Draft Data Security Law and Draft Personal Information Protection Law were both released for public comment in July 2020 and October 2020 respectively, four years after the Cyber Security Law came into effect on 1 June 2017. Both became effective laws in late 2021.

In particular the user data collected by tech firms has been notoriously subject to leaks, as is clear from the increasing public disclosures made by such companies of cases of data theft. A unit overseeing information security at Tencent, which owns instant-messaging service QQ, released a statement in February 2017 reporting that since August 2016, QQ had blocked over 3,500 group accounts where personal information was sold in bulk. This included 30 such accounts in the previous four days alone.[563] In another high-profile case, in June 2018 the private data of more than 1.9 million users of 51Job.com, one of China's largest

---

Nearly 100 Billion in One Year] (*People's Daily*, 21 December 2017) <http://it.people.com.cn/n1/2017/1221/c1009-29720427.html>.

[561] Liu Caiyu, 'Companies Collect Personal Info, Sell Data Despite China's New Cyber Security Law' (*Global Times*, 24 December 2017) <http://www.globaltimes.cn/content/1081849.shtml>.

[562] Ibid.

[563] Xiaojing and Rongde, 'QQ Blocks Thousands of Accounts for Selling Private Information' (n 553).

recruitment platforms, were found for sale on the dark web.⁵⁶⁴ Hackers had access to usernames, passwords, email addresses, real names and identity card numbers. The whole package of data could be purchased for 12 bitcoin (worth US$80,000 at that date).

Data theft has also led to widespread spam telephone calls and spam text messages in China. According to a 2016 survey from the China Internet Association, internet users on average receive spam messages 20.6 times per week and 21.3 harassing phone calls per week. Netizens have also complained of searching for something online only to have a company call them soon after to offer them the service or product they were searching for. This has raised great suspicion about the prevalence of online monitoring. And monitoring by whom: private companies or the government? Surprisingly, even older generations are becoming more conscious of the value of their data; this is due largely to the persistence of telephone marketers, according to a 2017 study by the Chinese Academy of Social Sciences.⁵⁶⁵ Chinese citizens therefore view phone numbers as the second most important piece of private data after identity card numbers.⁵⁶⁶ In 2016, one of these scam calls led to the widely publicised death of a college-bound student, Xu Yuyu. She died of a cardiac arrest after funds her family had raised for her tuition fees were swindled in a telephone scam.⁵⁶⁷

The problem has become so prevalent that '[l]eaking personal information has become the unspoken rule [for many apps]'.⁵⁶⁸ A report in *Technode* concluded: 'Data leaks [are] so ubiquitous in China that some

---

⁵⁶⁴ 杨鑫健 [Yang Xinyu], «独家: 51Job 百万条用户信息外泄？暗网售价 12 个比特币» [Exclusive: Millions of 51Job Users Information Leaked? The Darknet Price Is 12 Bitcoins] (*The Paper*, 15 June 2018) <https://www.thepaper.cn/newsDetail_forward_2198458>. In January 2019, it was reported that personal data from 200 million Chinese jobseekers had been exposed by a Ukrainian cyber security researcher. See also Zheping Huang and Jane Zhang, '200 Million Resumés of Chinese Jobseekers Leaked, Cybersecurity Researcher Says' (*South China Morning Post*, 11 January 2019) <https://www.scmp.com/tech/big-tech/article/2181709/200-million-resumes-chinese-jobseekers-leaked-cybersecurity-researcher>.

⁵⁶⁵ See Hui Zhao and Haoxin Dong, 'Research on Personal Privacy Protection of China in the Era of Big Data' (2017) 5 *Open Journal of Social Sciences* 139.

⁵⁶⁶ Ibid. IP addresses, internet records, friendship dynamics, ages and real names are also included in the list.

⁵⁶⁷ 'Student Suffers Fatal Cardiac Arrest after Telephone Scam' (*China Daily*, 25 August 2016) <http://www.chinadaily.com.cn/china/2016-08/25/content_26591216.htm>.

⁵⁶⁸ 'Chinese Company Apologizes over Flight Passenger Data Leaks' (*Ecns.cn*, 13 June 2018) <http://www.ecns.cn/news/society/2018-06-13/detail-ifyvfaqz8675561.shtml>.

of the country's top tech firms have started to take users' privacy for granted.'[569]

These examples indicate a critical need for the data privacy protection and related criminal offence articles in the Cyber Security Law. As noted in Chapter 5, these data leak penalties were strengthened in the Cyber Security Law during 2016; yet, despite this, such data breaches have continued unabated since the data breach provisions of the law began being enforced from June 2017. Furthermore, the data theft problem in China is an epidemic that extends beyond the example of poor cyber security protocols that allow hackers to sell personal data for one cent. Companies themselves have had to deal with data theft by their own employees. For example, Chinese authorities in June 2018 discovered that Chinese Apple employees were themselves selling personal information from iPhone users.[570]

Part of the problem is the internal vulnerability of many popular Chinese software apps. For example, Citizen Lab, an interdisciplinary cyber laboratory and research group within the University of Toronto, found in 2016 that Tencent's QQ browser was transmitting personally identifiable data with little or no encryption, leaving users open to 'man-in-the-middle' data collection.[571] Citizen Lab also found that Baidu's web search browser was easy to exploit. A later investigation, however, found the problems to be partially resolved.[572]

An even more fundamental issue concerns allegations that tech firms are themselves abusing users' data. Popular apps such as Alipay[573] and WeChat, each of which has hundreds of millions of users, sparked public outcries for accessing users' data without their consent. WeChat, for example, had to publicly defend itself in January 2018, after Li Shufu (李书福), chairman of Chinese automaker Geely, suggested that WeChat

---

[569] Emma Lee, 'China Launches Mobile ID Authentication Chips to Rein in Personal Data Theft' (*TechNode*, 17 April 2018) <https://technode.com/2018/04/17/id-authentication-chips-data-theft>.

[570] Lianzhang Wang, 'Apps That "Unlock" Wi-Fi Investigated for Privacy Breaches' (*Sixth Tone*, 4 April 2018) <https://www.sixthtone.com/news/1002042/apps-that-unlock-wi-fi-investigated-for-privacy-breaches>.

[571] See Jeffrey Knockel, Adam Senft and Ron Deibert, 'Privacy and Security Issues in QQ Browser' (*Citizen Lab*, 28 March 2016) <https://citizenlab.ca/2016/03/privacy-security-issues-qq-browser>.

[572] See Jeffrey Knockel, Sarah McKune and Adam Senft, 'Baidu's and Don'ts: Privacy and Security Issues in Baidu Browser' (*Citizen Lab*, 23 February 2016) <https://citizenlab.ca/2016/02/privacy-security-issues-baidu-browser/#analysis>.

[573] Explained in Section 7.4.

was invading user privacy by reading all user messages: '[Tencent CEO] Pony Ma (马化腾) is watching us through WeChat every day.'[574]

WeChat swiftly denied the charge in a public statement, insisting that the networking app does not 'keep' user chat history; nor does it use chat history for big data analysis and AI development. The statement read:

1. WeChat does not retain any user chat records. The chat content is only stored on users' mobile phones, computers, and other terminal equipment.
2. WeChat does not use any chat content of the user for big data analysis.
3. Because WeChat does not use the technological model of storing and analysing user chat content, to say that 'we are watching your WeChat every day' is purely a misconception.

    Please rest assured that respect for user privacy has always been one of the most important principles of WeChat. We have no authority and no reason to 'look at your private WeChat'.[575]

However, as the *New York Times* reported, Tencent's statement was met with widespread disbelief: 'WeChat users have been arrested over what they've said on the app, conversations have turned up as evidence in court proceedings, and activists have reported being followed based on WeChat conversations.'[576] And despite Tencent's public statement, in mid-2018, pop-up messages on WeChat still requested permission to access users' data.[577]

---

[574] Chen Mengfan, An Limin and Han Wei, 'Is WeChat Snooping on Your Chats?' (*Caixin Global*, 4 January 2018) <https://www.caixinglobal.com/2018-01-04/is-wechat-snooping-on-your-chats-101193014.html>.

[575] 张林成 [Zhang Lincheng], «微信官方:我们不留存任何用户的聊天记录» [WeChat Official: We Don't Keep Users' Chat History] (*TechNode*, 2 January 2018) <https://cn.technode.com/post/2018-01-02/wei-xin-yinsi>. For an English summary, see Masha Borak, 'WeChat Denies Reading Users' Private Messages to Train Its AI' (*TechNode*, 2 January 2018) <https://technode.com/2018/01/02/wechat-denies-reading-users-private-messages-train-ai>.

[576] Paul Mozur, 'Internet Users in China Expect to Be Tracked. Now, They Want Privacy' (*New York Times*, 4 January 2018) <https://www.nytimes.com/2018/01/04/business/china-alibaba-privacy.html>.

[577] See 'China's Social Media App WeChat Demands More Info from Users' (*Radio Free Asia*, 14 June 2018) <https://www.rfa.org/english/news/demands-06142018124702.html>. WeChat appears to have further tightened requirements for user registration, demanding access to all files and media content, and potentially giving the authorities access to everything on a user's smartphone. A newly registered WeChat account resulted in a pop-up request, calling for permission to access the device's 'photos, media

This prominent example of WeChat illustrates that Chinese netizens are aware of actual and potential invasions of their own privacy, but cannot avoid using potentially privacy-invasive applications in China's all-pervasive digital economy, described in Chapter 1. The *New York Times* piece concluded by quoting a young university student: "'Being angry doesn't do us any good", he said. "Maybe you can stop using Alipay if you are angry, but there's no way you could stop using WeChat."'[578]

Given all of the above, these regular high-profile data scandals have resulted in a Chinese public that is hypersensitive to, and fearful of, data theft. The situation is, in fact, similar to other countries around the world, where people are demanding greater responsibility and legal accountability from companies that profit from their data. This is not unexpected, as globally our understanding and public outrage about unethical data usage is only becoming more prominent.[579] In the West, for years there have been calls among activists (and others) to break up Facebook and other similar companies, yet these data protection issues have only relatively recently moved to the centre of public discourse,

---

library and file content'. Pressing 'Deny' resulted in a further pop-up asking to turn on 'storage space permissions'. Denying such permission resulted in the registration being aborted. See also Tara Francis Chan, 'The Chinese Government Confirmed That It Can Access Deleted WeChat Conversations – and People Are Terrified' (*Business Insider*, 1 May 2018) <https://www.businessinsider.com.au/chinese-government-accessed-deleted-wechat-messages-2018-5?r=US&IR=T>.

[578] Mozur, 'Internet Users in China Expect to Be Tracked' (n 576). Also, key WeChat statistics during 2017 evidence this point:

- WeChat had 980 million monthly active users.
- There are 580,000 mini-programs on WeChat, and 170 million users using mini-programs every day.
- 95% of e-commerce platforms in China have created their own mini-programs on WeChat.
- Tiao Yi Tiao (跳一跳, one of WeChat's mini-games that went viral) is one of the most-played games ever, with over 100 million daily active players.
- WeChat's focus in 2018 will be helping users navigate the offline world.
- WeChat is making its search more powerful.
- WeChat will reintroduce its tipping feature and allow users to tip authors directly, after reaching a deal with Apple which had forced WeChat to take down the tipping feature.
- WeChat will integrate its regular version with Enterprise WeChat.

[579] See, eg, Corinne Purtill, 'Your Phone Isn't Really Spying on Your Conversations – The Truth Might Be Even Creepier' (*Quartz*, 2 May 2018) <https://qz.com/1609356/your-phone-is-not-recording-your-conversations>.

especially after the Cambridge Analytica scandal.[580] Chinese people are part of this global movement, despite regular claims in the Western media during 2017–2019 that they do not care about their privacy.[581] As opposed to these claims, the following section demonstrates that Chinese polls have consistently and publicly evidenced the privacy-related concerns of Chinese people in the face of justifiable fears of data theft.

7.4 Polling: Growing Awareness of Data Privacy Issues

There is growing evidence of Chinese people's fears about the security of their personal data and concerns about data privacy.

Chinese polling has consistently demonstrated Chinese people's deep concern about data privacy issues. More than 85% of Chinese app users have had their data leaked, according to the *App Personal Information Disclosure Report* published on 29 August 2018 and based on a survey by the Chinese Consumer's Association.[582] This report came a week after China's authorities began investigating the biggest online data theft in the country's history, as a criminal gang obtained 3 billion items of user records to reap profits worth ¥30 million (US$4.4 million at the time) through marketing businesses.[583]

Both privately commissioned and government polls consistently evidence growing data protection and privacy concerns among Chinese

---

[580] Regular articles now appear in the mainstream press: see, eg, Robert Reich, 'Break Up Facebook (and While We're at It, Google, Apple and Amazon)' (*The Guardian*, 20 November 2018) <https://www.theguardian.com/commentisfree/2018/nov/20/facebook-google-antitrust-laws-gilded-age>. See also Tim Wu, *The Curse of Bigness: Antitrust in the New Gilded Age* (Columbia Global Reports, 2018). Wu articulates the dangers of excessive corporate and industrial concentration for our economic and political future.

[581] This has been a constant claim in Western media. See, eg, Harrison Jacobs, 'Chinese People Don't Care about Privacy on the Internet – Here's Why, According to a Top Professor in China' (*Business Insider*, 27 June 2018) <https://www.businessinsider.com.au/why-china-chinese-people-dont-care-about-privacy-2018-6>. Jacobs begins by stating: 'Despite a raging debate in the US and Europe over data privacy in recent months, there hasn't been much talk about data privacy in China.'

[582] «App 个人信息泄露情况调查报告» [App Personal Information Disclosure Report] (*Chinese Consumer's Association*, 29 August 2018) <http://www.cca.org.cn/jmxf/detail/28180.html>.

[583] 'China's Biggest User Data Theft Exposes 3 Billion Traces of Online Data into the Wrong Hands' (*Yicai Global*, 21 August 2018) <https://www.yicaiglobal.com/news/china-biggest-user-data-theft-case-exposes-3-billion-traces-of-online-life-in-wrong-hands>.

citizens.[584] For example, a 2017 survey by China's state-run *Beijing Youth Daily* found that leaking personal data was the single greatest concern among consumers.[585] Tencent's research arm Penguin Intelligence also released a report in 2018 to shed light on this complex issue. Chinese netizens responded to the issue of data leaks as follows:[586]

- 35% of the 1,285 interviewed users have constant concerns over data leakage;
- 60.6% worried about the problem occasionally; and
- only 4% did not care.

Chinese internet users are also aware of the value of their data. Even more convincing than the Tencent poll was a subsequent poll conducted by Sina Finance of over 10,000 Weibo users to gauge whether they value their online data: 86% responded by saying their privacy should not be violated, and over 50% saw data breaches as a severe problem.[587]

State media has also run influential investigations into awareness of online 'data-for-use trade-offs'. For example, in late March 2018 a Chinese state-run CCTV investigation found that users of popular free wi-fi apps did not actually understand that by using the apps they were agreeing to upload a list of all the networks they have ever connected to – including their own homes and workplaces.[588] Users were unaware of the trade-off whereby they were able to save on mobile data but at the cost of giving up their own personal data.

Thus, numerous polls indicate that Chinese netizens value their privacy. Further, the Chinese government now uses the new data protection regime under the Cyber Security Law to regularly penalise Chinese companies for data leaks (see Section 7.5). Following from this, tech

---

[584] Besides the examples given in the main text, in its 2017 report on China Social Media Impact, market research firm Kantar found that 43% of respondents were concerned about their privacy and the integrity of their information online. See «报告 2017 凯度中国社交媒体影响报告» [2017 Kantar China Social Media Impact Report] (*Kantar Research*, 6 June 2017) <https://cn.kantar.com/媒体动态/社交/2017/2017 凯度中国社交媒体影响报告>.
[585] Mozur, 'Internet Users in China Expect to Be Tracked' (n 576).
[586] See «我们真的在意隐私吗?» [Do We Really Care about Privacy] (n 527).
[587] «李彦宏称中国人愿意用隐私换便利, 你认可他的观点吗?» [Robin Li Said That Chinese People Are Willing to Trade Privacy for Convenience: Do You Agree?] (*Weibo*, May 2018) <http://vote.weibo.com/poll/138701440>(the link is no longer active).
[588] «重大预警! 多家国家机关, 金融机构 Wi-Fi 密码被窃, 9 亿用户如同 '裸奔'» [Major Warning! Wi-Fi Passwords of Many State Agencies and Financial Institutions Stolen, 900 Million Users Are 'Exposed'] (*CCTV Finance*, 28 March 2018) <https://mp.weixin.qq.com/s/ZZnnyuIJRKV9vnYEHSbjAQ>.

companies also now face increasing backlashes from consumers and the authorities over excessive data collection practices and data leaks.

Nevertheless, this does not mean that tech firms can freely exploit commercial data. What appears to be happening is selective enforcement based on the types of data breaches that occurred. In other words, companies have faced regular penalties for the infringement of data protection rules when it clearly harms the interests of consumers, yet their use of personal data for research purposes has not been so strictly monitored, and sharing data with the government is positively encouraged.

7.5 BATs and Other Tech Firms Face Regular Data Protection Penalties, but Push Back against Authorities

The Cyber Security Law outlines consent and processing requirements for personal information. Under the law users must consent to usage and be informed of any changes to the terms of usage.[589] Soon after the law came into force, all the BATs faced regular penalties for breach of data protection provisions, as well as for processing personal data without consent and failing to obtain consent for collecting personal data. Cyberspace regulators also quickly began using the aspirational Privacy Standards[590] to publicly penalise companies that did not follow the provisions. From December 2017, a few foreign companies were also fined for shortcomings in reporting cyberattacks to the authorities (a failure to comply with a data breach law), and for storing the user history of their customers in violation of the Cyber Security Law.[591] Yet these penalties paled into insignificance when compared to those handed out to Chinese violators.[592]

---

[589] See Cyber Security Law (n 2) art 41.

[590] See Privacy Standards (n 506).

[591] 'Japan, US and Europe Push Back on China's Data Controls' (*Nikkei Asian Review*, 13 December 2017) <https://asia.nikkei.com/Politics-Economy/International-Relations/Japan-US-and-Europe-push-back-on-China-s-data-controls>.

[592] According to China Information Security, a research and industry body, there were dozens of enforcement actions by cyberspace authorities in 2018, but among foreign firms only the Marriott hotel chain, clothing firm Zara and medical device company Medtronic were disciplined for suggesting that Taiwan is not part of China. The dozens of other cases all pertained to Chinese companies. See «盘点: 2018 年全国各级网信办互联网乱象规范治理工作» [Inventory: 2018 Work on Standardizing Governance by CAC at Every Level throughout China of Disorderly Online Practices] (*China Information Security*, 1 September 2018) <https://mp.weixin.qq.com/s?__biz=MzA5MzE5MDAzOA==&mid=2664115873&idx=1&sn=29fc50a73b0b3e92260ac511ccc9d854&chksm=8b5e2c58bc29a54ee0282605911888e1153f156c77f823df938bb67bc9797d3746d47d6f74ac&scene=0&xtrack=1#rd>.

On 11 January 2018, MIIT reprimanded three top tech firms, in a notice posted on its website, over poor privacy protections: Alibaba's payment affiliate Ant Financial, Baidu and Bytedance,[593] which oversees popular algorithm-powered news feed app Jinri Toutiao. MIIT stated that the three firms had 'inadequate' policies relating to personal information protection and any violations would be investigated and 'severely punished'. The regulator said the three companies had failed to fully disclose to users the purpose behind the collection of their personal information, and their policies for how the information would be used. The companies were ordered to take immediate steps to better safeguard user privacy.[594]

In the case of Ant Financial (Alipay) on 10 January 2018, CAC cited the new Privacy Standards[595] as the legal basis for penalising the company for opting users into the company's Sesame Credit scoring system by default.[596] Sesame Credit was in 2018 and remains the most high-profile pilot social credit system in China. In April 2018, Alipay was again fined for failing to comply with the principle of collecting the minimum amount of information necessary for the purposes of the service it was offering.[597]

---

[593] ByteDance is a Chinese tech company operating several machine learning-enabled content platforms, headquartered in Beijing. ByteDance's core initial product, Jinri Toutiao (Today's News), is a popular news content platform in China. Subsequently it has had enormous commercial success with apps like short-video-making TikTok in the United States (Douyin in China), and by 2018 was considered the world's most valuable start-up. See Sam Byford, 'How China's Bytedance Became the World's Most Valuable Startup' (*The Verge*, 30 November 2018) <https://www.theverge.com/2018/11/30/18107732/bytedance-valuation-tiktok-china-startup>.

[594] Ibid.

[595] See Privacy Standards (n 506).

[596] According to the website of the regulator (CAC): «国家互联网信息办公室网络安全协调局约谈'支付宝年度账单事件'当事企业负责人» [National Internet Information Office Cyber Security Coordination Bureau Schedules a Meeting to Talk to the Business Leaders Responsible for the 'Alipay Annual Event'] (*CAC.gov.cn*, 10 January 2018) <http://www.cac.gov.cn/2018-01/10/c_1122234687.htm>. The particular provisions that were breached were not cited. Authorities cited the new Privacy Standards (n 506): see «你的个人信息安全吗？工信部约谈百度蚂蚁金服今日头条?» [Is Your Personal Information Safe? MIIT Cites Baidu, Ant Financial and Jinri Toutiao's Conduct] (*Sina*, 12 January 2018) <http://tech.sina.com.cn/roll/2018-01-12/doc-ifyqqciz5880474.shtml>.

[597] Zhang Yuzhe and Liu Xiao, 'Alipay Racks Up More Penalties for Rule Violations' (*Caixin Global*, 9 April 2018) <https://www.caixinglobal.com/2018-04-09/alipay-racks-up-more-penalties-for-rule-violations-101232168.html>.

DATA PROTECTION BUT NOT DATA PRIVACY 179

Likewise, Baidu was issued a warning urging the firm to do more to protect its users' personal information.[598] Baidu has long faced allegations of poor privacy protections or excessive data collection practices.[599] In another case, in late 2017 a government-backed consumer protection group sued Baidu for failing to properly notify users about what data it was collecting.[600] Baidu denied charges that its mobile apps eavesdrop on calls and read texts, stating that its apps do not have the technical capabilities to do so.[601] Further, in a more stereotypical Chinese censorship violation, high-profile start-up ByteDance had to apologise for the illegal nature of some of its prohibited content under the Cyber Security Law.[602] During 2018 CAC more regularly pursued content violation cases than data protection cases. These types of regulatory penalties have occurred frequently, and firms in other sectors, such as Tencent-backed Meituan food delivery service, have also faced probes for massive user data leaks.[603]

---

[598] See «你的个人信息安全吗? 工信部约谈百度蚂蚁金服今日头条?» [Is Your Personal Information Safe?] (n 596). The particular provisions that were breached were not cited.
[599] In May 2016, Chinese regulators limited the lucrative healthcare advertisements that Baidu could carry following the death of a student after undergoing experimental cancer treatment he found on the site. The treatment took place at a state hospital. Some felt that Baidu was made a scapegoat for problems in China's healthcare system. In early 2019, Baidu was also under fire from an influential writer for rigged search results. Fang Kecheng (方可成), a veteran political journalist, was the latest to write a high-profile, scathing criticism of the search engine for its promotion of fake and low-quality news. 'Baidu wasn't like this one year ago. It was far from this 10 years ago. Though it had various problems back then, it still fulfilled its basic responsibilities as a search engine. It served as people's entry point to the Chinese internet': 方可成 [Fang Kecheng], «搜索引擎百度已死 (以及我的几点补充)» [Search Engine Baidu Is Already Dead (As Well as a Few Other Points)] (*Weibo*, 23 January 2019) <https://www.weibo.com/ttarticle/p/show?id=2309404331600992154916#_0>(the link is no longer active).
[600] Two months earlier, Baidu had been taken to court by the Jiangsu Consumer Protection Committee for illegally collecting user data. According to the group, two of Baidu's apps gathered personal information without a user's consent. See Chris Udemans, 'Chinese Care More about Data Privacy than You Think, but They Still Need Better Protection (*TechNode*, 15 May 2018) <https://technode.com/2018/05/15/data-privacy-china>.
[601] Ibid.
[602] Cyber Security Law (n 2) art 47 prohibits the transmission of any legally prohibited information: «涉嫌侵犯用户隐私 工信部约谈百度, 支付宝, 今日头条» [User Privacy Infringements Alleged, MIIT cites Baidu, Ant Financial and Jinri Toutiao's Conduct] (*Xinhua*, 12 January 2017) <http://www.xinhuanet.com/fortune/2018-01/12/c_1122250046.htm>.
[603] Lulu Yilun Chen, 'Tencent-Backed Internet Giant Probes Massive User-Data Leak' (*Bloomberg*, 3 May 2018) <https://www.bloomberg.com/news/articles/2018-05-03/tencent-backed-meituan-will-probe-reports-of-huge-user-data-leak>.

There is overwhelming evidence of a need for increasing encryption standards and a genuine domestic need for China's new cyber security regime, especially its data protection and privacy provisions. However, the contradiction in the regulatory regime emerges from the fact that companies are penalised for data leaks, but the Chinese government is not subject to these rules. The consequences of this double standard were noted in Section 7.2.2, but now it is necessary to show how the data protection provisions have evolved and subsequently been enforced under the new Cyber Security Law and associated implementing rules.

7.6 Privacy Standards Follow the Cyber Security Law on 'Data Protection'

The following explains how the Cyber Security Law intersects with subordinate privacy legislation released since 2018. It notes that an intentional fuzziness may have been drafted in the regulations so as not to 'inhibit' AI applications. First, 'personal information' (个人信息) in Article 76 of the Cyber Security Law

> refers to all kinds of information, recorded electronically or through other means, that taken alone or together with other information, is sufficient to identify a natural person's identity, including but not limited to natural persons' full names, birth dates, national identification numbers, personal biometric information, addresses, telephone numbers, and so forth.

The privacy provisions in the Cyber Security Law are as follows:

- Article 22 requires 'network operators' to obtain users' consent to collect personal information.
- Article 41 requires network operators collecting and using personal information to abide by the principles of legality, propriety and necessity. They also need to publish the rules for collection and use, explicitly stating the purposes, means and scope for collecting or using information obtaining the consent of the persons whose data is gathered.
- Article 42 requires that network operators must not disclose, tamper with or destroy personal information they gather and must adopt technical measures to prevent leaks or losses of personal information. If leaks occur, remedial measures must be taken, and users and the competent government departments must be informed.
- Article 43 gives users the right to demand the network operators delete the users' personal information, where they discover that network

operators have violated laws, regulations or agreements between the parties or there are errors in user personal information.
- Article 44 prohibits the theft and unlawful sale of personal information. Penalties corresponding to these provisions are outlined in Article 64.

On 2 January 2018, the Standardisation Administration of China (SAC) released the final version of the national standards on personal information protection: the Privacy Standards. These came into effect on 1 May 2018.[604] On 6 March 2020, the Privacy Standards were amended and replaced by Specification (GB/T 35273-2020) (2020 Privacy Standards) proposed by TC260 as an amendment and replacement for the November 2017 Privacy Standards (GB/T 35273-2017).[605] The 2020 Privacy Standards took effect on 1 October 2020. The two standards are dealt with concurrently, first by outlining the fuzzy logic in the Privacy Standards and then by explaining how those fuzzy logic issues were or were not resolved in the 2020 Privacy Standards.

It should be noted first, as it is the major focus of this study, that while the original Privacy Standards state that 'data controllers' will need to go through a security assessment if they would like to transfer personal data out of China,[606] further detail and clarity regarding cross-border data

---

[604] Privacy Standards (n 506).

[605] «GB/T 35273-2020 信息安全技术 个人信息安全规范» [GB/T 35273-2020 Information Technology – Personal Information Security Specification] (People's Republic of China) National Information Security Standardisation Technical Committee (TC260), 6 March 2020 (2020 Privacy Standards). According to the Preamble of the 2020 Privacy Standards, the principal amendments to the 2017 version include:

- Addition of 'voluntary selection of multiple Business Functions';
- 'Exceptions to Consent';
- 'Restrictions on use of User Profiling';
- 'Use of Personalised Display';
- 'Convergence and consolidation (汇聚融合) of personal information collected for different business purposes';
- 'Third-party connection management';
- 'Clarification on departments and personnel';
- 'Personal information security engineering';
- 'Recording of personal information processing activities';
- Revisions to 'exceptions to soliciting Consent'; and
- Refinements with respect to personal biometric information.

[606] Privacy Standards (n 506) art 8.7 renders authority for cross-border personal data transfer to 'relevant departments' rather than listing scenarios and corresponding permissible thresholds for cross-border transfer, such as: with user consent, in emergency situations, and in accordance with obligations under international treaties.

transfers is not provided. So while the Privacy Standards assist understanding of the data protection aspects of the Cyber Security Law, they do not clarify the process for data exits from China.[607] Interestingly, the drafters publicly admitted that they had great difficulty trying to fit the Privacy Standards within the parameters of the Cyber Security Law. According to them, that task amounted to 'dancing while wearing shackles',[608] which reinforces the argument that there are internal contradictions within the law itself. The 2020 Privacy Standards did not expand on this issue in any great detail. Article 9.8 simply states that personal information collected and generated in China can be transferred overseas, but the controller must comply with all relevant national regulations and standards.

The Privacy Standards do not have the force of law. They are a recommendation or guideline to be relied on by Chinese government agencies to determine whether companies are following China's data protection rules.[609] The Privacy Standards set out the best practices that will be expected by regulators auditing companies and enforcing China's existing, but more vaguely worded, data protection rules – most notably the Cyber Security Law.[610]

Even though the Privacy Standards are theoretically non-mandatory, in practice 'there is a high likelihood that they will be used as a benchmarking tool to evaluate corporate privacy practice and may set the defacto mandatory requirements'.[611] Yet while they do provide a more expansive definition of personal information than the Cyber Security Law, they still leave much room for company and official discretion. While the Privacy Standards are a 'guideline' and not law, they do fill

---

See 周汉华 [Zhou Hanhua], «探索激励相容的个人数据治理之道：中国个人信息保护法的立法方向» [Exploring Incentive-Compatible Personal Data Governance: The Legislative Direction of China's Personal Information Protection Law] (2018) 2 *Law Research* 3.

[607] Cyber Security Law (n 2) art 37 is the data localisation provision and requires that 'critical information infrastructure operators' that gather or produce personal information or important data during operations within China must be stored in China.

[608] 洪延青 [Hong Yanqing], «对'个人信息安全规范'» [Personal Information Security Specification] (n 43).

[609] See Jiangqiu Ge, *A Comparative Analysis of Policing Consumer Contracts in China and the EU* (Springer, 2019) 39. 规范性文件 (*guifan xing wenjian* – normative documents) are non-legally binding standards.

[610] Cyber Security Law (n 2) art 42 merely requires 'network operators' to notify an incident to regulators and affected individuals when there has been actual or potential 'leakage, damage, or loss' of personal data.

[611] Xiaomeng, Manyi and Sacks, *What the Facebook Scandal Means in a Land without Facebook* (n 541).

gaps in that 'personal information' in the Cyber Security Law remained 'fuzzy'. Yet the Privacy Standards still raise the following uncertainties.

As in the Cyber Security Law, in the Privacy Standards, 'network operators' or 'personal information controllers' are prohibited from collecting personal information that is not relevant to the services they offer.[612] They must obtain consent before collecting personal information.[613] There are no penalties set out in the Privacy Standards, but penalties pursuant to breaches of the Privacy Standards are to be administered according to the Cyber Security Law.[614]

The main focus of the data protection provisions in the Cyber Security Law is on personal information and privacy of citizens in China. The Law states that companies wishing to collect data must do so in accordance with a set of general principles. Collection needs to be legal, justified and necessary. Justification and necessity mean that a company cannot collect data on things that are not necessary for the services that are being provided.[615]

The Privacy Standards go further than the law by requiring prior notice and consent from individuals for the transfer or sharing of their data, unless the information is de-identified.[616] This is distinct from the consent that covered the initial collection and processing of data. The Cyber Security Law only requires initial collection consent. In line with the law, public disclosures of biometric information are also prohibited by the Privacy Standards.[617]

---

[612] Privacy Standards (n 506) art 5.5; 2020 Privacy Standards (n 605) art 7.3.
[613] Privacy Standards (n 506) art 4; 2020 Privacy Standards (n 605) art 3.7. Consent is defined in the 2020 Privacy Standards as clear authorisation to have 'personal information' processed in a specific way (art 3.7). Consent includes 'Explicit consent' (明示同意) and implied consent. Implied consent is not a defined term. Explicit consent is defined as an affirmative act of authorisation electronically or in writing, such as checking the box, clicking on 'Agree', 'Register', 'Send' or 'Call', or voluntarily filling out or providing information (art 3.6).
[614] Privacy Standards (n 506) art 7.6. This remained the same in the 2020 version.
[615] Ibid arts 5.2–5.3.
[616] Ibid arts 6.2, 7.2, 8.2, 10.2(a)(4), app D (a privacy policy template). Art 3.14 explains data de-identification: 'The technical processing of personal information is the process of making it impossible to identify a person with personal information without additional information. Note: De-identification is based on the individual, retaining the individual granularity, and using the pseudo-name, encryption, hash function and other technical means to replace the identification of personal information' (通过对个人信息的技术处理，使其在不借助额外信息的情况下，无法识别个人信息 主体的过程。注:去标识化建立在个体基础之上，保留了个体颗粒度，采用假名，加密，哈希函数等技术手段替代对个人信息的标识).
[617] Ibid. Public disclosures of personal biometric information are also prohibited in arts 3.1 and 8.4(f). Personal biometric information is included in appendix A as personal information. Appendix B defines 'personal biometric information' as 'personal genes, fingerprints, voiceprints, palm prints, auricles (ear lobes), irises, facial recognition

While the original Privacy Standards do provide some clarity on these points, there is uncertainty in terms of their legal force and how they interact with other relevant laws, as the Privacy Standards do not have the force of law. For example, there are data protection infringement offences in China's Criminal Law[618] and an associated Supreme People's Court interpretation, the Interpretation on Several Issues Concerning the Application of Law in Criminal Cases of Infringing on Citizens' Personal Information (Interpretation).[619] The Interpretation is a legally binding document that specifies criminal penalties for misuse of citizens' personal information that meets one of ten criteria.[620] This means that a government department applying the non-binding Privacy Standards may by default look to apply the Interpretation.

It was not clear how the original Privacy Standards would work alongside the Interpretation, as there is no consensus on whether the Privacy Standards 'should be interpreted as mandatory or just one interpretation of how to comply with China's Cyber Security Law'.[621] In February 2019, companies such as Alipay and Tencent Cloud have received certification as being compliant with the Privacy Standards.[622] Further, Baidu and AliPay were both forced to overhaul their data policies due to not 'complying with the spirit' of the Privacy Standards.[623]

While the Interpretation was legislated on 1 June 2017, at the same time as the Cyber Security Law, it is explained in Chapters 8 and 9 why the Privacy Standards reflect a latent attempt to retrofit fuzzy logic terms

---

features, etc' (个人基因, 指纹, 声纹, 掌纹, 耳廓, 虹膜, 面部识别特征等). However, in appendix D (a privacy policy template) it is noted that why biometric data is collected and how it will be treated should be explained to the person whose data is collected.

[618] Legislators amended China's Criminal Law (中华人民共和国刑法) in 2015 to expand privacy protections. It now affects data protection. The amending bill initially only applied to the collection of data by government entities, but at the date of writing concerns anyone buying and selling data illegally.

[619] «最高人民法院 最高人民检察院关于办理侵犯公民个人信息刑事案件适用法律若干问题的解释» [Explanation on Several Issues Concerning the Application of Law in Criminal Cases of Infringing on Citizens' Personal Information] (People's Republic of China) Supreme People's Court and the Supreme People's Procuratorate, 1 June 2017.

[620] See ibid. The 10 criteria revolve around benefiting from illegally obtained data.

[621] Ibid.

[622] Hongquan Yang, 'China – the Privacy, Data Protection and Cybersecurity Law Review – Edition 6' (*Law Reviews*, October 2019) <https://thelawreviews.co.uk/edition/the-privacy-data-protection-and-cybersecurity-law-review-edition-6/1210009/china>.

[623] Yuan Yang, 'China's Data Privacy Outcry Fuels Case for Tighter Rules' (*Financial Times*, 1 October 2018) <https://www.ft.com/content/fdeaf22a-c09a-11e8-95b1-d36dfef1b89a>.

to the development of AI, and how they might interact with these other relevant regulations.

7.6.1 What Is Protected Personal Information?

First, it is important to note that these Privacy Standards only concern personal information, and not generalised data.

What is meant by protected personal information? The answer is important, because the Privacy Standards define protected information differently from the Cyber Security Law and from the Interpretation, which assigns criminal thresholds to categories of personal information: 'The [Interpretation] categorizes personal information by three classifications and assigns penalty thresholds for criminal cases involving each type of information: Sensitive information, important information, and ordinary information.'[624] These three classifications pertain to the seriousness of the data theft from a criminal law perspective.

Under the Cyber Security Law, personal information means information that can be used to identify a person if used separately or in combination with other information. Article 76 refers to 'personal information' as 'information, recorded electronically or through other means, that taken alone or together with other information, is sufficient to identify a natural person's identity'. As noted in Chapter 5, the meaning of these phrases, along with 'important data', remained unclear.

By contrast, the Privacy Standards categorise personal information as information that can be used to identify or track a person.[625] This is because the Privacy Standards clarify and expand the definition to include information that reflects a person's activities, including their personal location, personal correspondence records and online browsing history.[626] Thus, comparing the definition of 'personal information' under the Cyber Security Law[627] with that under the Privacy Standards, the latter expressly expands the scope of personal information to cover (in addition to personal identity information) information reflecting the activities of certain individuals. The Interpretation then classifies the

---

[624] Xiaomeng, Manyi and Sacks, *What the Facebook Scandal Means in a Land without Facebook* (n 541).
[625] This is not from a particular section but based on the author's reading of the nature of items listed in Privacy Standards (n 506) appendix A.
[626] See ibid.
[627] Cyber Security Law (n 2) art 76(5).

seriousness of the data theft or data mishandling from a criminal law perspective.

The 2020 Privacy Standards further expand sensitive personal information: to include information created by the 'personal information controllers' (through the processing of personal information or other information which, if leaked, illegally provided or abused, may harm the security of person or property, personal reputation, or physical or mental health of the personal information subject (defined as the natural person identified or associated with by the personal information), or lead to discriminatory treatment.[628]

7.6.2 What Were the Drafters of the Original Privacy Standards Intending?

Obviously, it would be helpful if more clarity were provided by the regulators. Xie Wei (谢玮), a deputy director at a Chinese think tank,[629] criticised the current patchwork of rules listed earlier:

> Although there are many pieces of legislation for personal information protection, relevant regulations are scattered, and fragmented. It is difficult to provide effective or substantial legal protection for personal information. New laws urgently need to be made to specify principles and processes for internet providers in terms of collecting users' information, to clarify obligations in protecting collected information, and to clarify how to assess personal information protection.[630]

One argument is that the resistance by the regulators to clarifying the rules and their legal force may be due to the rapid growth of China's AI sector, and the regulators' realisation that removing the fuzziness and strictly enforcing data protection rules may block that growth. Commentary from CSIS cited private exchanges with the drafters of the

---

[628] 2020 Privacy Standards (n 605) art 3.2. Personal biometric information is a type of Personal Sensitive Information and includes personal genes, fingerprints, voice prints, palm prints, auricles, irises, facial recognition features, etc. In principle, personal biometric information may not be shared or transferred (art 9.2.i), unless essential for business needs and consent is obtained.

[629] China Institute of Information and Communications Security Research (中国信息通信研究院安全研究所).

[630] 张一琪 [Zhang Yiqi], «今天, 个人该怎样保护隐私» [Today, How Do Individuals Protect Privacy?] (*People's Daily*, 16 April 2018) <https://mp.weixin.qq.com/s/rSW-Ayu6zNXw87itYHcPYA>.

Privacy Standards evidencing the motivations of the Chinese regulators not to inhibit AI:

> Drawing on exchanges with the lead drafter [of the Privacy Standards], we looked at how the drafters modeled the [Privacy Standards] on the European Union's General Data Protection Regulation (GDPR) but sought to make a standard that was more business friendly, in part, so as not to inhibit the development of AI.[631]

Importantly, the definitions of other key phrases in the Privacy Standards have critical implications for the development of Chinese AI. The next sections demonstrate how these definitions, through their fuzzy logic, seem to leave the door open to that development while at the same time aiming to protect against harmful uses of data. And did the 2020 Privacy Standards alter this matrix?

7.7 Definitional Fuzzy Logic in the Privacy Standards: Fuzzy Logic for *Applying* the Standards

First, who is regulated? Both Privacy Standards apply to 'personal information controllers', defined as any private or public organisation that has 'the power to decide the purpose and method' of processing personal information.[632] This is seemingly modelled on the GDPR's concept of a 'data controller'.[633]

Second, how is data used? Interestingly, the term 合法权益 (*hefa quanyi*) is used throughout both Privacy Standards. It means that personal data should only be used in accordance with a person's 'legitimate legal rights and interests'. This additional term creates a distinct fuzzy logic in that multiple variables are possible under this phrase. It raises the question of how a 'personal information controller' (eg, in a private AI

---

[631] Samm Sacks, *China's Emerging Data Privacy System and GDPR* (CSIS, 9 March 2018) <https://www.csis.org/analysis/chinas-emerging-data-privacy-system-and-gdpr>.

[632] Privacy Standards (n 506) art 10.2(b)(1). Art 6(1) of the GDPR sets out the conditions that must be met for the processing of personal data to be lawful. Art 6(1)(f) of the GDPR provides that it is lawful to process the personal data of a data subject where the 'processing is necessary for the purposes of the legitimate interests pursued by the controller or by a third party, except where such interests are overridden by the interests or fundamental rights and freedoms of the data subject which require protection of personal data, in particular where the data subject is a child'.

[633] Galaad Delval, 'Old Rules, New Specification for Data Protection in Mainland China' (*International Association of Privacy Professionals*, 3 May 2018) <https://iapp.org/news/a/old-rules-new-specification-for-data-protection-in-mainland-china>.

medical image recognition company) can decide what a person's 'legitimate legal rights and interests' are.

Moreover, as the Privacy Standards are not mandatory, negotiated noncompliance may be possible for some Chinese companies. Luo and Bradley-Schmieg noted that drafts of the Privacy Standards, prior to their finalisation, have in some cases 'been the basis for noncompliance remediation plans and undertakings agreed between companies and [CAC] following CAC audits'.[634] Thus, it seems possible to enter noncompliance remediation plans (and undertakings) in relation to the Privacy Standards. Do such plans also excuse non-compliance with the law? Furthermore, what is the legal basis for a non-compliance plan? This uncertainty left companies without a clear roadmap.

In addition, templates for complying with the Privacy Standards (Privacy Management Templates) have been built through a public–private partnership project. These Privacy Management Templates are for company privacy policies that explain to employees and customers how the company protects and uses data, and how it complies with the Privacy Standards. The public–private partnership that created these templates included the CAC, MIIT, the Ministry of Public Security, the Standardisation Administration of China, Alibaba, Ant Financial (an Alibaba affiliate), AutoNavi (a Chinese online map service) and Didi Chuxing (a Chinese ride-hailing app).[635] Although the 29-page Privacy Standards include much aspirational detail, the Privacy Management Templates for data controllers take up less than two pages. The 2020 Privacy Standards would include an updated eight-page template for compliance.

It seems that, in consultation with their private partners, regulators have decided to allow companies to use their discretion to basically self-manage these tasks. But is this any different to guides produced by data protection or privacy commissioners in other jurisdictions around the world, which are produced to explain to companies how to comply with privacy principles? Probably not, though it could be questioned why these Chinese documents are so short in length.

---

[634] Yan Luo and Phil Bradley-Schmieg, 'China Issues New Personal Information Protection Standard' (*Inside Privacy*, 25 January 2018) <https://www.insideprivacy.com/international/china/china-issues-new-personal-information-protection-standard>.

[635] Xiaomeng, Manyi and Sacks, *What the Facebook Scandal Means in a Land without Facebook* (n 541).

7.7.1 'Sensitive Personal Information' and 'Core Business Functions'

A second area that allowed for discretion is that, rather than listing specific types of data requiring protection, the original Privacy Standards take a graded, risk-based approach to 'sensitive personal information'. This creates further fuzzy logic, because there is no clear categorical delineation between the binary categories of sensitive and non-sensitive personal information. This is precisely the way fuzzy logic operates in computer science.[636] For example, property, health and physiological, biometric and identity information are listed[637] as examples of both potentially sensitive and non-sensitive personal information depending on the risks. This binary fuzzy logic based on perceived risk is a major departure from the Cyber Security Law.[638]

Under an appendix to the Privacy Standards, 'sensitive personal information' could also include national identity card numbers, login credentials, banking and credit details, a person's address, information on a person's real-estate holdings, and information about a minor (under 14 years old). Other examples may include device hardware serial codes, IP addresses, website tracking records and unique device identifiers.[639]

Yet these are merely potential examples that depend on circumstances, because the drafters took a 'consequence-based approach' in differentiating the two categories: 'Personal sensitive information refers to personal information whose leakage, illegal provision or abuse may endanger personal property safety and easily lead to damage of personal reputation and physical or mental health, or to discriminatory treatment.'[640] As one commentary noted: 'In practice, it is often difficult for data controllers to evaluate the impact of data leakage before incidents happen.'[641] Likewise, the use of the word 'may' leaves the door open to further discretion by the company that collects and controls the data. The 2020 Privacy Standards would provide some clarity.

---

[636] As explained in the Introduction and Chapter 2.
[637] See Privacy Standards (n 506) appendices A and B.
[638] Definitions of sensitive information in other data protection laws are similar. See, eg, GDPR (n 437) art 9.
[639] See Privacy Standards (n 506) art 3.1, annex A.
[640] Ibid art 3.2.
[641] Xiaomeng, Manyi and Sacks, *What the Facebook Scandal Means in a Land without Facebook* (n 541).

'Core Business Functions'

Third, just as the Cyber Security Law fails to clearly define 'important business data', so the fuzzy logic binary distinction in the original Privacy Standards between 'core business functions' and 'additional functions' remained unclear. These concepts do not appear in the Cyber Security Law. In the Privacy Standards they arguably play a distinct role by not inhibiting China's innovation drive.

What Is Meant by 'Core Business Functions' and 'Additional Functions'?

Specifically, the Privacy Standards require data controllers to inform data subjects of the 'core business functions' of the products or services and the personal sensitive information that has to be collected and used by those products or services. If data controllers create or provide 'additional functions', they must inform data subjects what personal sensitive information is required for fulfilling such additional functions.[642] If the personal data subjects decline the additional functions, the data controllers should continue to provide the core business function without the additional functions relying on the data.

Nevertheless, it is increasingly challenging to distinguish 'core business functions' from 'additional functions' under the Privacy Standards since these concepts evolve quickly as new technologies develop and change. For example, mobile payment products from companies such as WeChat have transformed from additional functions to core business functions within three to five years in China. As one Chinese commentator noted, 'so-called "add-on" features may be the "core" features of tomorrow'.[643]

The Privacy Standards also contain a requirement akin to the GDPR's 'purpose limitation' requirement. (The GDPR requires that all uses of the information, including secondary uses, should be reasonably connected with the original purpose of collection of the data, and should be re-authorised if that is not the case.)[644] But how will the purpose limitation

---

[642] Privacy Standards (n 506) art 5.5.
[643] 车宁 [Che Ning], «'个人信息安全规范' 生效在即, 金融科技从业人员应了解这些事» [The 'Privacy Standards' [author's terminology] Come into Effect Soon, and Financial Technology Practitioners Should Understand These Things] (*TC260*, 20 January 2018) <https://www.tc260.org.cn/front/postDetail.html?id=20180201201040>.
[644] Lee A Bygrave, *Data Privacy Law: An International Perspective* (Oxford University Press, 2014) provides comparative analysis of 70 countries and their approach to data collection. The purpose limitation is a key principle. See at ch 5 ('Core Principles of Data Privacy Law').

principle operate under the 'core business function' rules? That is, how will it operate if business functions change, but require more personal information to operate? Certainly, more fuzziness operates at the intersection of these rules. Further, the purpose limitation is set aside for certain research and academic purposes provided the personal information is de-identified in public disclosures about the research, which arguably might include companies' own R&D work.[645] Thus, distinguishing 'core business functions' from 'additional functions' is another example of binary fuzzy logic in Chinese legislation.

The 2020 Privacy Standards, however, will strengthen privacy protection, as they place more weight on the will of individuals to decide whether to share 'personal sensitive information' as a condition of access to products and services that offer 'business functions'. 'Business function' is now defined as a type of service that meets the specific need of personal sensitive information subjects: this includes services such as map navigation, online car hailing, instant messaging, social media, online payment, news, online shopping, express delivery and transport ticketing.[646]

A proper-use approach to defining data sensitivity will be part of how the Cyber Security Law could be used to permit AI development. Instead of limiting data classes, China's 'fuzzy logic' approach will allow case-by-case approvals for data collection points. This is different to, for example, Europe's GDPR, which defines asset classes such as heath data. There is a certain tautology in all these key definitions which creates problems of interpretation for businesses, yet also leaves room for discretion in implementation, and may allow companies flexibility in using personal data for their AI research.

Article 5.3 of the 2020 Privacy Standards states that the personal information controller providing a product or service that requires personal information cannot bundle a subject's personal information into multiple business functions. If the subject does not specifically authorise the consent to use personal information for a specific business function, the controller may not incentivise the subject by guaranteeing better quality service or increased security in return for authorised consent. If the subject ceases to use a specific business function, the controller cannot continue to use the personal information previously collected.

---

[645] Privacy Standards (n 506) arts 5.4J, 6.2, 7.3.
[646] 2020 Privacy Standards (n 605) art 3.17.

'User profiling' and 'personalised displays' are also regulated more tightly regulated in the updated 2020 Privacy Standards.[647]

In summation, the 2020 Privacy Standards clarifies concepts such as biometric data, multiple business functions and also what is meant by explicit consent. Yet, as before, it is still unclear to what extent the new standard will be enforced and how it will interact with other laws and regulations.

There remains a tension that is difficult to resolve because, although it is true that these standards are only voluntary, standards in China hold substantive clout for enforcing government policy aims such as developing AI through Internet Plus.

7.8 Periodic Data Protection Impact Assessments

Finally, both Privacy Standards require data protection impact assessments (DPIAs), at least annually, as well as when (1) new legislative requirements come into effect; (2) business models, information systems or operational environments undergo a major change; or (3) a significant personal information security incident occurs. The assessment reports must be 'open to the public in appropriate form'.[648]

To explain these DPIAs, on 13 June 2018 China's information security standards organisation, TC260, released for comment a draft guide for organisations to assess the privacy implications of a wide variety of practices: Information Security Technology – Security Impact Assessment Guide of Personal Information[649] (Draft DPIA Guide). The Draft DPIA Guide is designed to set a standard for DPIAs.[650]

---

[647] User profiling is defined as the process of forming personal characteristics of an individual based on the individual's personal information such as occupation, income, health, education, personal preferences, credit rating and behaviour (art 3.8) and may not result in discrimination.

Personalised display is defined as the display of information and search results of products or services based on the individual's personal information such as internet browsing history, hobbies, consumption records and habits (art 3.16). Consent prompts such as the labelling of 'Targeted Push' (定推) are required (art 7.5).

[648] Ibid art 10.2(6). Art 35 of the GDPR (n 437) also provides for risk assessments.

[649] «信息安全技术 个人信息安全影响评估指南» [Information Security Technology – Security Impact Assessment Guide of Personal Information] (People's Republic of China) TC260, 13 June 2018 (Draft DPIA Guide).

[650] DPIAs are needed in scenarios where data processing poses high or unknown risks to privacy: for example, when new products or practices in an organisation trigger particular privacy concerns, or when large amounts of sensitive personal information will be processed.

It specifically addresses both private sector and government actors. It is an impact assessment guide for the harm caused by data protection breaches. It takes into account damages to personal self-determination rights, reputation, unemployment, mental stress, property and physical harm among other factors. There are also mitigating factors that can adjust the impact assessment.[651]

As with many TC260 standards, the Draft DPIA Guide, once finalised, will not be binding, but will effectively establish standard practices and a 'fuzzy' basis for regulatory enforcement. The guide seems to have been influenced to a certain extent by the EU's GDPR:

> The guide embeds the idea of privacy-by-design, echoing elements of the EU's General Data Protection Regulation (GDPR).[652] It suggests that organizations assess impacts from the very beginning of a new product design and continue in an ongoing process whenever a significant legal or business environmental change occurs. Section 6.3 lists nine high-risk scenarios where impact assessments are suggested, which are highly similar to the list recommended by the EU advisory body WP29 in its Guidelines on Data Protection Impact Assessment supporting the GDPR.[653]

The Guide for De-Identifying Personal Information,[654] the Guide for Data Cross-Border Transfer Security Assessment[655] and the Draft DPIA

---

[651] Draft DPIA Guide (n 649) section 6.3.
[652] As set out in GDPR (n 437) art 25. 'Privacy by design' is a framework for proactively embedding privacy into the design and operation of IT systems, networked infrastructure, and business practices.
[653] The Draft DPIA Guide (n 649) covers details such as who should initiate and lead PIAs (section 4.4), how to prepare (section 5.2), what factors should be considered with what weights (sections 5.4–5.6) and when PIAs should be conducted (section 6). In many aspects, the guide appears similar to an EU approach, setting a high bar to protect individual rights against data breaches. In the suggested criteria, heavy weight is placed on potential risks to individual interests, which range broadly from financial loss and effects on credit scores, to discrimination, reputational damage and psychological effects. See Mingli Shi, 'Translation: Principles and Criteria from China's Draft Privacy Impact Assessment Guide' (*New America*, 13 September 2018) <https://www.newamerica.org/cybersecurity-initiative/digichina/blog/translation-principles-and-criteria-from-chinas-draft-privacy-impact-assessment-guide>.
[654] 《信息安全技术 个人信息去标识化指南》 [Guide for De-Identifying Personal Information] (People's Republic of China) National Information Security Standardisation Technical Committee (TC260), 1 September 2018.
[655] 《信息安全技术 数据出境安全评估指南》 [Guide for Data Cross-Border Transfer Security Assessment] (People's Republic of China) National Information Security Standardisation Technical Committee (TC260), 1 September 2018.

Guide were designed to establish a tripartite standard system[656] for personal information security under the broader Privacy Standards.

While these various guides appear to create a detailed data protection procedural system, the fact that they are being issued not as mandatory regulations but recommended guidelines suggests that the relevant government regulators wish to keep the standards flexible in order to deal with rapidly changing technologies. This flexibility is especially crucial for AI firms, due to their reliance on collecting and analysing massive amounts of data to refine and improve their products.

7.9 2021: China's Data Security Law and Personal Information Protection Law to Become Fuzzy Logic Law?

On 21 October 2020 the Standing Committee of the National People's Congress published for public comment the first draft of the Personal Information Protection Law (Draft Information Protection Law).[657] When passed in late 2021, it became China's first law solely regulating the collection and processing of personal information but not 'important information'. The Information Protection Law codifies many data protection principles and concepts from China's current data governance regime, including the Cyber Security Law and the 2020 Privacy Standards and China's new and first Civil Code,[658] which became law on 1 January 2021.[659] In late 2021, the Information Protection Law, the Cybersecurity

---

[656] Shi, 'Translation' (n 653).
[657] Draft Information Protection Law (n 510).
[658] 《中华人民共和国民法典》 [Civil Code of the People's Republic of China] (People's Republic of China) National People's Congress, 28 May 2020 (Civil Code).
[659] In May 2020, after ten rounds of open consultation, the National People's Congress passed the new code. The Civil Code is a foundational legal instrument composed of 1,260 articles that codify detailed legal rules related to almost all civil and commercial matters, including property, contracts, personal rights, family, inheritance and torts. Under China's legislative hierarchy, the Information Protection Law has the same level of authority as the Cyber Security Law and the Data Security Law, but its position relative to the Civil Code is more complicated.
 The Civil Code dedicates a whole chapter to the protection of privacy rights and personal information. The Civil Code lays down the principle that personal information is protected by law and sets out the civil rights of individuals to their personal information. However, it only applies to civil matters, and lacks any detailed rules or powers for regulators to protect personal information. It also includes the concept of 'private information (私密信息) within personal information' (art 1034). This phrase is not mentioned in the Draft Information Protection Law. The Civil Code revolves around the

Law and the Data Security Law,[660] became the three main laws covering data security and protection China. While the Data Security Law (which became law on 1 September 2021) deals with 'important data', the Information Protection Law (which became law on 1 November 2021) deals only with 'personal information'. While there was no official timeline for a revised or final version of the Draft Information Protection Law, it was enacted quickly following the 2020 draft's release.[661]

Significantly, the Information Protection Law and the Data Security Law propose to have extraterritorial applicability and impose significant penalties for serious violations similar to those contained in the EU's GDPR.[662] It seems likely that the current geopolitical environment has led to China seeking to strengthen its data governance by establishing a

---

term 'personal information rights and interests (个人信息权益)'. In Chinese regulatory practice, this emphasises 'interests' rather than 'rights' on personal information.

The Information Protection Law defines 'personal information' in a more expansive way than the Civil Code. For example, the Information Protection Law restricts processing to the reasonable scope of the use for which the information initially entered the public domain (the Civil Code allows processing personal information already legally disclosed in the public domain). The Information Protection Law also follows international privacy law approach of only distinguishing sensitive personal data from non-sensitive personal data.

[660] The Data Security Law became law on 10 June 2021, taking effect on 1 September 2021: «中华人民共和国数据安全法» [Data Security Law of the People's Republic of China] (People's Republic of China) National People's Congress, 10 June 2021 (Data Security Law).

[661] Before this draft law was enacted it had several processes to pass through and could have been modified substantially. The public comment period for this draft closed on 19 November 2020. The legislative review process usually requires two more rounds of official review before a potentially revised draft can be put to a vote by the full National People's Congress. This timeline is unclear. As the draft law appeared on the government's list of legislation planned for deliberation between 2018 and 2023, we could expect this law to be passed prior to 2023. Nevertheless, on 20 August 2021, the Standing Committee of the National People's Congress adopted the Personal Information Protection Law, becoming effective on 1 November 2021.

[662] See art 3(2) of the GDPR (n 437). The Data Security Law (n 660) art 2 will upgrade the protection of consumer and personal data to the comparable level afforded to military and national data. Citizens will have legal recourse when their consumer or personal data is stolen, misused or corrupted. The Information Protection Law «中华人民共和国个人信息保护法» [Information Protection Law of the People's Republic of China] (People's Republic of China) National People's Congress, 20 August 2021 (Information Protection Law). follows an approach to extraterritoriality similar to the GDPR. But it is broader, providing potentially expansive legal grounds to regulate foreign entities if authorised by other Chinese 'laws or administrative regulations' (art 3). It is not clear how China can or will punish extraterritorial violations of the law; fines, sanctions and condemnation are all possible options.

detailed system of data security rules, emphasising national security. The thrust of the Data Security Law is to regulate security matters related to data activities in China. In addition, bans on TikTok and WeChat proposed by the US government in 2020 may have influenced the Information Protection Law, which allows CAC to 'blacklist', and prevent sharing of personal information, foreign entities and individuals that process personal information in a manner that damages the personal information rights and interests of Chinese citizens, or endangers national security or the public interests of China.[663]

7.9.1 Consent and Storage of 'Sensitive Personal Information'

The Information Protection Law partially clarifies the fuzzy law of China's data protection regime. The law expands the scope of personal information and sets out the key concepts and principles for processing personal information. It replaces the current consent-based protection regime with a new one allowing multiple legal bases for processing personal information, as well as setting out more detailed requirements for consent (discussed later in this section). The Information Protection Law also explains the obligations on processors when sharing and transferring personal information to third parties.[664]

However, with regard to the 'fuzzy logic' of data privacy rules and concepts, these proposed laws would further complicate the situation. As noted, in the Cyber Security Law, legitimacy of collection and use of personal information hinges entirely on consent (Articles 41–3). The Information Protection Law does not define consent, but sets out some general requirements for a valid consent as follows: the individuals are fully informed; consent is freely given; and consent is unambiguous.[665] These requirements resemble those under the GDPR. However, detailed criteria for meeting these requirements still need clarification.

The Information Protection Law defines sensitive personal information as information that, if leaked or illegally used, may lead to discrimination against an individual or serious harm to their personal or property safety. This includes race, ethnicity, religion, biometric

---

[663] Information Protection Law (n 662) art 43. The law allows China to take corresponding measures against countries or regions that take discriminatory measures against China in respect of the protection of personal information.
[664] Ibid art 22.
[665] Ibid arts 13–17.

information, medical and health information, financial accounts and personal location.⁶⁶⁶ The law extends the scope of personal information from information relevant to an identified person (as defined in the Cyber Security Law⁶⁶⁷ and the Civil Code⁶⁶⁸) to include information relevant to an identifiable person. This is similar to the approach taken in the GDPR. The concept of de-identification is also introduced in the draft law.⁶⁶⁹

Finally, two further areas are somewhat clarified by the law: automated decisions must be fair and reasonable⁶⁷⁰ and surveillance data collected by the government must only be used for public security.⁶⁷¹ These provisions seem to apply to state actors.

7.9.2 Data Localisation Expanded in 2021 and Beyond?

The Information Protection Law also continues China's preference for utilising security assessments to legitimise cross-border data transfers for 'critical information infrastructure operators' and other 'personal information processors' subject to data localisation requirements.

Security assessments have been proposed in various forms in previous draft regulations and are required under the Cyber Security Law for 'Critical information infrastructure operators'. The Draft Outbound Data Measures 3⁶⁷² outlined in Chapter 5 would be overhauled by this new regime. The Information Protection Law also further expands the data localisation requirement to all 'personal information processors' whose processing of personal information reaches a yet-to-be determined volume threshold determined by Chinese regulators.⁶⁷³ This would also

---

⁶⁶⁶ Ibid art 28.
⁶⁶⁷ Cyber Security Law (n 2) art 76(5).
⁶⁶⁸ Civil Code (n 658) art 1034.
⁶⁶⁹ Draft Information Protection Law (n 662) art 51(3).
⁶⁷⁰ Ibid art. 24.
⁶⁷¹ Image capture and personal identification equipment installed in public places must be necessary for maintaining public security, accompanied by conspicuous signage and may not be publicly disclosed or provided to other parties. Confusingly, unless the individual provides consent or the use is otherwise permitted or required by other Chinese laws and regulations. Personal information collected by Chinese government entities is required to be stored within China, and a security assessment is required for providing such information to an overseas party: arts 27 and 37. It remains unclear how this data localisation requirement would apply to state-owned enterprises.
⁶⁷² Draft Outbound Data Measures 3 (n 396).
⁶⁷³ Information Protection Law (n 662) art 40.

expand data localisation requirements beyond the 'critical infrastructure operators' covered in the Cyber Security Law, requiring non-'critical infrastructure operators' to store personal data locally if reaching designated thresholds.

The safeguards on export of personal information and the requirements on data localisation are less stringent and more practical as compared to the Draft Outbound Data Measures 3 published in 2019.[674] Yet, as noted, the extraterritorial effect extends the application of the Information Protection Law to processors outside of China.

The Information Protection Law now expands requirements to legitimise cross-border data transfers to all 'personal information processors' and proposes additional pathways to do so, including obtaining certification from special professional certification organisations designated by CAC regulators, and concluding a contract with the overseas data recipient and supervising its data processing activities.[675] This provides a further possible fuzzy allowance of global data transfers. Further, Article 13 of the Information Protection Law provides seven specific lawful bases to allow personal data processing, including consent, plus an additional catch-all clause, 'other circumstances provided in laws and administrative regulations'.[676] This may provide Chinese regulators the fuzzy flexibility to determine additional cross-border data transfer

---

[674] Draft Outbound Data Measures 3 (n 396).
[675] Ibid art 38. Under art 38, personal information can leave mainland China for business needs (which excludes cross-border transfers for non-business uses), one of the following conditions must be met: (1) it must pass a security assessment; or (2) it must have undertaken personal information protection certification conducted by professional agencies; or (3) it must have signed a contract with the overseas receiving parties which provides the rights and obligations of both parties, and supervising their activities of handling personal information to ensure the relevant standards under the Personal Information Protection Law are met; or (4) it must meet other conditions stipulated by laws, administrative regulations, or the national cyberspace authorities.
[676] Ibid art 13. Personal information handlers may only handle personal information where they conform to one of the following circumstances:

1. Obtaining the individuals' consent;
2. Where necessary to conclude or fulfil a contract in which the individual is an interested party;
3. Where necessary to fulfil statutory duties and responsibilities or statutory obligations;
4. Where necessary to respond to sudden public health incidents or protect natural persons' lives and health, or the security of their property, under emergency conditions;
5. Handling personal information within a reasonable scope to implement news reporting, public opinion supervision, and other such activities for the public interest;

mechanisms in the future. In contrast to the Cyber Security Law's rigidly restrictive approach, the Information Protection Law is more flexible, similar to the EU's GDPR.

It remains unclear if these seven additional avenues for consent in Article 13 would provide greater flexibility for conducting cross-border data transfers than previously proposed. In practical terms these avenues may be unworkable.[677] Particularly in respect of real-time data transfers where security assessments and pre-certification on a per-transfer basis are, in practice, generally unworkable. For example, 'personal information processors' that transfer personal information to a recipient outside China are required to notify the individual of the identity of the recipient, provide a method of contacting the recipient, make clear the purposes and methods of the recipient's processing, the types of personal information involved, and how the individual can exercise his/her rights against the recipient, and obtain the individual's consent to the transfer; these requirements remain unclear and impractical.[678]

The Information Protection Law and the Cyber Security Law overlap yet have inconsistencies. For example, Article 23 of the Information Protection Law would require data handlers to fully disclose and obtain individuals' specific consent for sharing their data with third parties. Article 42 of the Cyber Security Law also mandates that 'network operators' – still so broad in 2021 that it may include almost every business entity in China that uses a network – shall not provide personal information to others without consent of the data subject. Yet, as drafted, Article 23 of the Information Protection Law may also conflict with Article 13 in the same law, which allows data processing without consent for certain other purposes that could entail personal information sharing with third parties. Fixing this fuzzy logic within the Information Protection Law by removing the consent requirement from Article 23, however, would then put the Information Protection Law in tension with the Cyber Security Law.

---

6. Handling personal information disclosed by persons themselves or otherwise already lawfully disclosed, within a reasonable scope of the law;
7. Other circumstances provided in laws and administrative regulations.

[677] Recognising business needs to transfer data abroad, the Information Protection Law provides several legal bases to do so, yet if the data is generated by critical information infrastructure operators or the amount of the data to be processed by non-critical information infrastructure operators reaches certain thresholds, as mentioned above, a heightened set of legal requirements apply, tilting toward data localisation as a default.
[678] Information Protection Law (n 662) art 39.

The Data Security Law and 'Important Data'

The Data Security Law proposes to protect data, in particular 'important data' that is not personal information or a state secret. In Article 21, each region and department, according to relevant national provisions, shall determine a regionally, departmentally and industrially important data protection catalogue, and undertake special protections for that which is listed in the catalogue. Thus, Article 21 empowers regional government and sectoral regulators with producing 'important data' catalogues. This distributed responsibility will create further uncertainty.

The Data Security Law mandates a top-down, government promulgated mandate on data processors to protect their client's data. The enactment of the Data Security Law could have one essential implication for businesses operating in China, any organisation or individual 'conducting data activities' will be required to take all necessary steps to ensure data security is achieved (Article 32). Data activities are defined in the law as 'data collection, storage, processing, use, provision, transaction, publication, and other activities' (Article 3). This broad language of the law suggests if a business is obtaining and/or using consumer data in China then the law applies.

But yet again, 'importance' of the data remains ensconced in a certain fuzzy logic. Depending on the data's 'importance', it will be protected under a multi-level classified protection regime. Ministries and local governments are required to draft catalogues of important data and protect the data included in the catalogue. Important data processors must conduct periodical risk assessment and appoint personnel and departments responsible for data protection. The law also proposes a national security review regime, under which data activities affecting (or likely to affect) national security will be subject to national security review.[679] If enacted, this will have a profound impact on data security practices in China as well as on those foreign organisations and persons processing data from China.

To conclude, although subject to some clarifications, the future regulatory landscape of personal information protection but not yet 'important data' is progressing. The practical impact of these new laws is that many entities are still struggling to comply with 'all applicable laws' by complying with conflicting conceptions of privacy while also being

---

[679] Data Security Law (n 660) art 24.

forced to enforce the real-name registration of users, resulting in large pools of data being collected and subject various evolving rules.

7.10 Real-Name Registration, AI Development and Why Private Companies Control China's Datasets

While consumers of network products may not benefit from real-name registration, it is not only the Chinese government that receives the benefits. Perhaps inadvertently, the real-name registration rules are likely to provide a huge boon for Chinese firms seeking to develop AI technologies.

The following sets out two main propositions. First, China's cyber security regime, enforcing real-name registration, will greatly assist AI development, as it allows disparate datasets to be integrated. Legally enforced real-name registration means information is already labelled as being connected to one identity, one name or one ID card number. As China further digitises data under its Informatisation policy, enormous quantities of digital content will be accurately tagged and labelled.

Second, China's private sector controls most of these valuable datasets. China's entrepreneurial ecosystem is unique, as explained in Chapter 1, in that private companies control China's datasets due to its rapid evolution as a developing country that has lacked centralised governance mechanisms and data collection capacity. The private sector has led China's rapid digitisation in recent years and as a by-product has amassed enormous amounts of user data on a national scale.

The inherent binary contradictions in China's Cyber Security Law and associated standards and regulations have thus created a unique climate for developing increasingly well-structured datasets for AI development. Enforced real-name registration was originally introduced by the Chinese government in an attempt to retain control and impose a measure of censorship over online communications. However, inadvertently, this requirement has given an important boost to the development of AI by network operators due to the value of their connected datasets. The government has recently become aware of the potential for AI tools to help solve various wide-scale social and governance problems, and kick-start China's advanced economic development. This means that the enforcement of privacy standards under the Cyber Security Law is likely to be selective, focusing on commercial abuse of customer data without hindering the constructive use of such personal data for AI R&D.

This debate about the use of personal data is not necessarily sinister, but the technology industry clearly has an agenda. AI expert-turned-venture capitalist Dr Kai-Fu Lee has referred to China's approach to AI as 'techno-utilitarian', something similar to law in a petri dish focused on solving Chinese developmental problems. The key point is that in the public debate in China, entrepreneurs, technology CEOs and venture capitalists have often described a Chinese preference for consumer convenience over privacy, as it suits their investment agenda. Admittedly, this would benefit their own industries and investments. Yet Chinese state media has made similar claims that 'if [we] strictly follow requirements to protect privacy, most data cannot be used, and this will limit the development of the big data industry. However, like the Facebook data leak scandal, a lack of data protection will adversely impact society'.[680]

To provide an example of how the 'fuzzy logic' around data privacy may help Chinese start-ups, consider Infervision, a four-year-old Beijing firm that has amassed more than a million scans from Chinese hospitals and is using those scans to train and test algorithms in a radiology clinic in North Carolina. 'In the US, particularly for big academic hospitals, you have to go through so many processes and it can take a really long time to access data', Yufeng Deng, Infervision's chief scientist, was quoted as saying.[681] He noted further that while Chinese institutions do take steps to protect patient privacy (eg, anonymising records used in research) and those protections are becoming stronger, they are not bound by as many rules and external regulatory processes as in the United States. According to Deng: 'In China it's less well-defined.'[682]

Baidu Founder Robin Li (李彦宏) highlighted these points just before he made the high-profile and highly controversial comments suggesting that Chinese people are willing to trade privacy for convenience: 'When you are able to join different sets of data, the power becomes much more,

---

[680] 张一琪 [Zhang Yiqi], «今天, 个人该怎样保护隐私» [Today, How Do Individuals Protect Privacy?] (n 630).

[681] Tom Simonite, 'How Health Care Data and Lax Rules Help China Prosper in AI' (*Wired*, 8 January 2019) <https://www.wired.com/story/health-care-data-lax-rules-help-china-prosper-ai>.

[682] IBM has spent more than $3.5 billion since 2015 acquiring healthcare software companies and amassing millions of patient records and billions of images of all kinds of medical conditions. See ibid.

it's exponential growth.' He continued: 'if more of that data can be put together, our capacity to achieve more will rise exponentially'.[683]

Li also acknowledged that 80% of useful data 'lies in the hands of enterprises' not government departments. Presently, in the age of big data, private corporations aim to collect as much data as possible, while preventing others from having access to that data. The more data one has, the more valuable each piece of that data and the datasets overall potentially become, especially when developing AI applications.[684] A China-based privacy lawyer noted:

> There is a lot of different information that you would never think would be able to identify a person. But if you combine it, and especially if you have a computer combine it, the computer can see connections in ways that you or I couldn't. [The connected data] could become personal information.[685]

It is important here to briefly consider how Machine Learning AI works, although these ideas are explored in depth in Chapter 8. AI is sometimes built up from random pools of 'unsupervised' data. Those isolated islands of information are connected through 'Neural Networks' that piece isolated bits of data together the way our brain does.[686] But for the purpose of training Neural Networks to analyse datasets, those who have more identifiable data have an unassailable advantage over others. The reason is that with current techniques, the more data used to 'train' specific neural networks, the better the algorithms it produces. As a result, it would be a formidable challenge to compete with established firms in the AI field that have exclusive access to huge amounts of labelled data, such as Google, Facebook, Microsoft, Amazon and the BATs.[687] Start-ups can often

---

[683] Xinmei Shen, 'Chinese Internet Users Criticize Baidu CEO for Saying People in China Are Willing to Give Up Data Privacy for Convenience' (*Abacus*, 28 March 2018) <https://www.abacusnews.com/big-guns/chinese-internet-users-criticize-baidu-ceo-saying-people-china-are-willing-give-data-privacy/article/2139313>.

[684] See Chapter 8.

[685] Quoting Jared T Nelson, data protection lawyer at MWE China Law Offices, in Udemans, 'Chinese Care More about Data Privacy than You Think' (n 600).

[686] See Chapter 8.

[687] Eric A Posner and E Glen Weyl, 'Property Is Only Another Name for Monopoly' (2017) 9(1) *Journal of Legal Analysis* 51; Charles Duhigg, 'The Case Against Google' (*New York Times*, 20 February 2018) <www.nytimes.com/2018/02/20/magazine/the-case-against-google.html>; Lina M Khan, 'Amazon's Antitrust Paradox' (2016) 126(3) *Yale Law Journal* 710; Kira Radinsky, 'Data Monopolists Like Google Are Threatening the Economy' (*Harvard Business Review*, 2 March 2015) <https://hbr.org/2015/03/data-monopolists-like-google-are-threatening-the-economy>.

only work with pre-labelled datasets, as the cost of labelling can be prohibitive.[688]

One reason why much of the useful network data in China is controlled by private firms is the fragmented nature of China's government bureaucracy, divided into numerous levels and ministries each with their own siloed and haphazard datasets.[689] As noted in Chapter 1, China's online (and now AI) ecosystem developed organically to fill gaps in the official financial and personal credit systems, leading to a unique cashless society powered by WeChat Pay and AliPay, and creating massive integrated databases on a national scale. There is now a widely shared view that these vast financial data collecting systems and many others in different sectors will supercharge Chinese AI development.[690] The enormous datasets created by these cashless payment systems are all relatively new, so their true potential has still not been fully exploited. AliPay, for example, was founded in 2004, but WeChat was only launched in 2011 and WeChat Pay came along in 2014.

Therefore, by default, private sector companies became the major data aggregators, largely through solving China's private credit system problems and providing various other ubiquitously used communication and lifestyle tools to consumers. Despite data privacy concerns, users cannot avoid using WeChat for applications like the cashless WeChat pay system, as many sellers even in bricks-and-mortar stores prefer not to accept cash, and traditional credit cards are not widely used in China. This means that Privacy Standards cannot prevent users from trading away their privacy (for essential services) in many instances. Even Chinese media sometimes write quirky, human interest pieces about the few who shun WeChat: "'I know my data will be collected somehow in the end, but I just want to have more dignity", says a 36-year-old Chinese woman who has forgone the app.'[691]

---

[688] Renowned Chinese AI pioneer 陆奇 [Lu Qi] made this point eloquently in «新经济 NEO100: 陆奇, YC 中国的 01 号员工» [New Economy NEO100: Lu Qi, YC China's No 01 Employee] (*36Kr*, 15 August 2018) <https://36kr.com/p/5148299.html>.

[689] See, eg, Dong Jing and Liu Xiao, 'Divided among Departments, Big Data Eludes Government' (*Caixin Global*, 16 April 2018) <https://www.caixinglobal.com/2018-04-16/divided-among-departments-big-data-eludes-government-101235107.html>.

[690] Discussed at length in Chapter 8.

[691] Lin Qiqing, 'Outside the Green Bubble of China's Super-App' (*Sixth Tone*, 28 June 2018) <http://www.sixthtone.com/news/1002502/outside-the-green-bubble-of-chinas-super-app>. See also Laurie Chen, 'Why China's Tech-Savvy Millennials Are Quitting WeChat' (*South China Morning Post*, 22 July 2018) <https://www.scmp.com/news/

Yet in return for using these kinds of essential apps, Chinese consumers will generally volunteer to give up their personal privacy to the companies that operate them. This voluntary submission makes the Privacy Standards moot as users will be forced to consent to giving up their personal data. Baidu founder Robin Li, infamously postulating that Chinese internet users do not care about their privacy in December 2017, caused outrage on Chinese social media. He was widely quoted as saying: '[I]f they can trade privacy for convenience, for security, for efficiency; in a lot of cases, they are willing to do that.' However, seen in context his full statement seems more measured and reflects the reality of consumer behaviour:

> We're very aware of the privacy issue, including data protection. Over the past few years, China has also become increasingly aware of this problem, and has been enforcing relevant laws and regulations, during the process of which, I think that the *Chinese people are more open, or not so sensitive, about the privacy issue. If they are able to exchange privacy for convenience or efficiency, they are willing to do so in many cases.*[692]

This statement is very important in a Chinese context because awareness of the impact of data privacy is generally increasing in China as the government is allowing that debate to occur online. Yet without WeChat, many would struggle to pay for lunch, speak to their mothers or hail a Didi rideshare. This data collecting is now a constant in China, and the scale is much larger than in other countries. China's private sector mobile platforms have an unassailable lead in data collection that new laws and standards cannot totally regulate. In fact, regulations like Europe's GDPR and China's emerging privacy regime favour the incumbent giant technology platforms. This is because '[y]ou're quite likely to click "I Consent" or "Yes" when a GDPR form is put in between you and your next hit of Facebook dopamine. You're utterly unlikely to do the same when a small publisher asks for your consent via what feels like a spammy email'.[693] This could easily be adapted to the Chinese context by replacing 'Facebook' with 'WeChat'.

---

china/society/article/2156297/how-growing-privacy-fears-china-are-driving-wechat-users-away>.

[692] «百度系两款 APP 未经提示开启隐私权限» [Two Baidu Apps Expand the Limits of Privacy Permission without Giving Warnings] (*Xinhua*, 28 March 2018) (emphasis added) <www.xinhuanet.com/fortune/2018-03/28/c_1122600485.htm>.

[693] John Battelle, 'How GDPR Kills the Innovation Economy' (*New Co Shift*, 25 May 2018) <https://shift.newco.co/how-gdpr-kills-the-innovation-economy-844570b70a7a>.

One major reason why the Chinese government has allowed the growth of private firms like Tencent and Alibaba is that they have helped to solve problems that were beyond the capability of SOEs, such as providing access to finance for small businesses. The government has now realised, however, that the data collected by these firms is more reliable and extensive than that collected using traditionally haphazard official data collection methods. Such big data may be used to solve various other governance problems in a country where 14 million people had no official government identity and 'did not exist', having had no official documentation until late 2016, or where hundreds of millions of people are living as migrant workers away from their officially registered homes.[694] Local officials now face increased pressure not to inflate or falsify[695] datasets.[696] Thus, some academics, such as Yasheng Huang, professor in Chinese economy and business at MIT's Sloan School of Management, have argued that China's use of big data might actually make it less 'Big Brother-ish' as 'precise' data-driven policymaking is better than indiscriminate government controls.[697] To implement this, however, requires the government to adopt a relatively laissez-faire attitude to data collection by these private firms, and not to obstruct their development of advanced AI tools through over-regulation. It may even require the government to open up its own datasets to private firms, so that the information can be used to improve the AI-powered governance that is crucial to solving China's development problems.

---

[694] Over four years the Ministry of Public Security registered 14 million people who had never been officially included in the country's household registration record system, known as the Hukou (户口), which is closely linked to a person's legal identity. That means they did not officially exist: Echo Huang, 'China Keeps Finding Millions of People Who Never Officially Existed' (*Quartz*, 27 March 2017) <https://qz.com/941240/china-keeps-finding-millions-of-people-who-never-officially-existed>.

[695] The irony of this issue is, again, that most big datasets have remained in the hands of private companies in China.

[696] 'Fudging or inflating the data won't lead to promotions for officials, but only to demotions. So who would manipulate the data? There isn't any incentive', stated Ning Jizhe, the head of the National Bureau of Statistics, as the Chinese government announced a crackdown on inaccurate datasets. See 'China's Stats Chief Defends Quality of Data' (*Bloomberg*, 21 August 2018) <https://www.bloomberg.com/news/articles/2018-08-20/china-s-statistics-chief-defends-data-quality-as-doubts-linger>.

[697] Huang Yasheng, 'China's Use of Big Data Might Actually Make It Less Big Brother-ish' (*MIT Technology Review*, 22 August 2018) <https://www.technologyreview.com/s/611814/chinas-use-of-big-data-might-actually-make-it-less-big-brother-ish>.

From the tech firms' perspective, Cai Xiongshan, deputy director and chief researcher of Tencent Law Research Center, made the point that open datasets are key to the development of AI:

> In the AI era, we cannot ignore the importance of institutional construction for AI. Artificial intelligence is based on 'feeding' large datasets to machines. In the case of open data for example, there is currently no government open data. Thus many AI applications will become '无本之末, 无源之水' [branches without roots, or water drying up without a source]. It can be said that the issue of open data is the main pain spot for the problem of the development of AI in China.[698]

Certainly, the vast data collections by private companies are relatively new and algorithms will need time to mature (explained further in Chapter 8). Nevertheless, the real-world activities of Chinese people are increasingly captured in a digital format that is 'useful' to an AI algorithm.[699] A user profile could identify a person's habits across numerous 'sticky' platforms, including WeChat mini-programs that keep the user within WeChat to access goods and services from other companies. The fact that real-name registration is required for all these online applications under the Cyber Security Law therefore creates an extremely powerful impetus for AI development that complicates our understanding of data 'privacy' in China, as datasets can easily be connected to create more powerful AI.

7.11 Conclusion: Inherent Fuzzy Logic Leading to Data Privacy Contradictions That May Benefit AI Development

China's approach to data protection (or data privacy) is characterised by an ongoing fuzzy logic approach because it wants to both control data (for reasons including protecting the security of people's data and surveillance) and allow personal data to be collected, accessed and used

---

[698] On his public WeChat account he also noted that success in Chinese AI development requires legal changes as well as resource and capital input from the Chinese government: 蔡雄山 [Cai Xiongshan], «第三波人工智能发展浪潮中的顶层设计, 评《新一代人工智能发展规划»[Top-Level Design in the Third Wave of AI Development, Commenting on the 'New Generation AI Development Plan'] (*Tencent Research Institute*, 27 July 2017) <https://mp.weixin.qq.com/s/vtarWQe1vZiBkJyJBvhHtw>.

[699] Discussed in Chapter 8, but veteran AI expert turned venture capitalist Kai-Fu Lee often makes these comments to English speaking audiences: see, eg, Kai-Fu Lee, 'What China Can Teach the US about Artificial Intelligence' (*New York Times*, 22 September 2018) <https://www.nytimes.com/2018/09/22/opinion/sunday/ai-china-united-states.html>.

(for reasons including government censorship and the promotion of AI-based applications). In China, data privacy and data protection are not the same thing. Protection of data from abuse by companies is the legal standard, but the use of private data for socially beneficial purposes will apparently be permitted due to discretionary loopholes and a relaxed attitude towards voluntary consent.

This chapter outlined the evolving data protection regime emerging in subordinate standards under the data protection provisions of China's Cyber Security Law. It is a fuzzy regime designed for negotiable data classes according to perceived risk of data protection breaches (eg, theft, leak or inappropriate use). It was explained how data protection laws may benefit domestic AI development due to their often vague and binary 'fuzzy logic' categorisation of X or Y. When combined with widespread use of consent forms in return for consumer access to apps, these gaps should allow Chinese tech firms plenty of room to manoeuvre and few obstacles to prevent them using the data they have amassed to develop new AI products. If data localisation provisions are also stringently enforced during 2022, it will simply consolidate the strong position of these Chinese firms in relation to foreign firms that lack access to such extensive pools of data.

Clearly, China is experiencing various competing tensions arising from the debate between 'those advocating for greater data privacy protections and those pushing for the development of fields like artificial intelligence (AI) and big data, with no accompanying limits on how data is used. The very existence of this debate is not well known to outside observers'.[700]

In the next chapter, the current state of AI research is expounded in great detail, explaining further why China's fuzzy legal system and AI ecosystem are perfectly placed to take AI technologies to the next level of development, raising great possibilities and further concerning ethical questions.

---

[700] Sacks, *China's Emerging Data Privacy System and GDPR* (n 631).

8

The Current State of AI Research Is Perfectly Suited to China's Fuzzy Logic System

> Do you know why the Chinese are so naturally good at deep learning? Because the black box has been part of Chinese society and Chinese culture since the very beginning. Chinese medicine. There is an input, some herb or infusion. You have no idea how it works, but it does. All you can do to get a different result is enter a different input.
>
> —Dinglong Huang, CEO, Malong Technologies[701]

China's fuzzy logic system and government support for pilot petri dishes is perfectly suited to the current state of AI research. This has enabled the rapid development of world-class AI applications, particularly in image recognition. This is due, in part, to the regulatory environment facilitating the development of AI pilots. Yet it is further argued that this suitability is due to a combination of three factors: (1) the current state of AI research and its applicability to numerous real-world applications; (2) the open nature of AI research culture globally and (3) the complex emerging role of public–private petri dishes in China for testing innovative applications. This chapter also explains how public–private connections are formed, including how top-down government signalling is important to the trajectory of private companies.

The previous chapter showed how China's data protection regime is not intended to hinder AI progress in China; nonetheless, unfettered access to personal data remains a political, social and moral tinderbox in China. 'Chinese companies are increasingly finding that the days of collecting data without public scrutiny are over – and Chinese consumers are vocally standing up for their own privacy in ways not seen before.'[702]

---

[701] Bruno Maçães, 'China's Black Box Superiority' (*Politico*, 11 December 2018) <https://www.politico.eu/blogs/the-coming-wars/2018/11/china-black-box-superiority-cybersecurity-artificial-intelligence-ai>.
[702] Samm Sacks and Lorand Laskai, 'China's Privacy Conundrum' (*Slate*, 7 February 2019) <https://slate.com/technology/2019/02/china-consumer-data-protection-privacy-surveillance.html>.

For this reason, a number of Chinese scholars[703] hailed 2018 as the year the Chinese public awoke[704] to data privacy. China's government now treats seriously the protection of private data from commercial abuse. This is now a political imperative.

The development of AI in China has also been drawn into the data privacy debate. Balancing demands for privacy with the development of AI is now a live issue in China. The Chinese government has permitted some discussion about AI ethics and facial recognition in the official media. According to a survey carried out by the state-run CCTV and Tencent Research in 2018, 76.3% of the 8,000 participants felt that AI is a threat to privacy, with the main fear being facial recognition technologies.[705] Clearly, there is a greater public consciousness about data collecting for these new emerging technologies.[706]

---

[703] 王融 [Wang Rong], «迷雾中的新航向: 2018 年数据保护政策年度观察» [A New Direction in the Fog: 2018 Data Protection Policy Observations] (*Tencent Research Institute*, 29 December 2018) <https://www.secrss.com/articles/7496>.

[704] «腊月十二, 来听互联网隐私保护界最 '硬核' 的故事» [Twelfth Day of the Lunar Month, Come and Listen to the Most 'Hardcore' Story in the Internet Privacy Protection Community'] (*Privacy Guard in the Southern Metropolis Daily*, 9 January 2019) <https://m.mp.oeeee.com/a/BAAFRD000020190109129910.html>.

[705] The China Economic Life Survey «中国经济生活大调查» covers 100,000 households in first-, second- and third-tier cities across China. It covers people aged 16 to 60 years. It is carried out by CCTV, the National Bureau of Statistics of China and China Post and has been running since 2006, covering over a million households. The AI section of this year's CCTV television programme about the results was arranged in collaboration with Tencent Research (腾讯社会研究中心 – Tencent Social Research Center). Tencent Research and state-run TV network conducted an additional set of questions on AI as part of the annual TV show that publicises the results of the larger China Economic Life Survey. For a summary of the findings, see Frank Hersey, 'Almost 80% of Chinese Concerned about AI Threat to Privacy, 32% Already Feel a Threat to Their Work' (*Technode*, 2 March 2018) <https://technode.com/2018/03/02/almost-80-chinese-concerned-ai-threat-privacy-32-already-feel-threat-work>.

[706] Surveillance cameras and sensors are the new data collection frontier in China. For example, in December 2017 cyber security firm Qihoo 360 shut down its online streaming platform connected to its wireless security cameras in public places after pressure from the public: Frank Hersey, 'Qihoo 360 Shuts Down Surveillance Camera Live Streaming Platform' (*Technode*, 20 December 2017) <https://technode.com/2017/12/20/shuidi-shutdown-qihoo-360>.

However, Qihoo 360 continued to supply free cameras to kindergartens so that parents could monitor their children during 2018. The debate as to whether cameras should be installed in schools followed a very high-profile case at a branch of the RYB kindergarten chain in Beijing in late November 2017, where streaming cameras showed that children were pricked with needles and given unidentified pills: see Casey Quakenbush, 'Three Things to Know about China's Kindergarten Abuse Scandal (*Time*, 27 November 2017) <http://time.com/5037556/china-beijing-kindergarten-abuse-scandal>.

Data protection laws that do not stifle innovation will be crucial, as AI research has developed rapidly over the past few years, buoyed by massive access to unstructured data such as photos, videos and social media posts. Enormous banks of data are essential for developing AI, and use of electronic devices such as personal mobile phones is a prime source of that data. Ultimately, the AI applications that Chinese and foreign firms build will be dictated by the data they legally collect, whether it be internet platform data, consumer data, auditory data or data collected by roadside sensors.

This chapter introduces the current state of AI research and discusses why China's 'fuzzy logic' legal system is perfectly suited to rapidly developing an advanced AI ecosystem. It shows that far from reining in private AI firms, the Chinese government is actively encouraging them to develop AI applications, frequently by using government-provided data. It explains why the Chinese government is such an enthusiastic supporter of experimental AI pilots across numerous sectors, 'industry verticals' and applications, especially those that help to solve governance and business efficiency problems in China's emerging Smart Cities.[707] These AI rollouts have the potential to solve China's problems and build mammoth private companies. A June 2017 report from consulting firm PwC forecast that AI will contribute US$15.7 trillion to the global economy in 2030 and China will be among the biggest beneficiaries, with a 26% boost to its GDP in 2030.[708] This market potential and the fact that AI is a general-purpose technology[709] also explains why China needed

---

[707] See Ajay Agrawal, Joshua Gans and Avi Goldfarb, *Prediction Machines: The Simple Economics of Artificial Intelligence* (Harvard Business Review Press, 2018). The authors contend that AI is today a system for 'cheap prediction machines'.

[708] 'Sizing the Prize: What's the Real Value of AI for Your Business and How Can You Capitalise?' (PWC, June 2017) <http://www.pwc.com/gx/en/issues/analytics/assets/pwc-ai-analysis-sizing-the-prize-report.pdf>.

[709] General-purpose technologies have spurred economic revolutions since the nineteenth century. 'The steam engine drove the first wave of industrialization in the 1890s to 1920s; electricity powered the second wave in the 1890s to 1930s; and information technologies brought the third, which started in the 1970s and culminated with the explosion of the internet in the 2000s, thus paving the way for the fourth industrial revolution, which is currently underway. Its key driver is artificial intelligence, which makes robots smart, facilitates the analysis of big data, allows for the customization of almost any product, and enables control of sophisticated industrial processes': Edoardo Campanella, 'The Real Payoff from Artificial Intelligence Is Still a Decade Off' (*Foreign Policy*, 9 August 2018) <https://foreignpolicy.com/2018/08/09/the-solution-to-the-productivity-puzzle-is-simple-robots-ai>. Economists Boyan Jovanovic and Peter Rousseau wrote that general-purpose technologies are innovations that are pervasive, improve over time, and spawn further innovation. See Boyan Jovanovic and Peter Rousseau, 'General

fluidity in its lawmaking during 2016–2021 and will continue to do so as the economic and political ramifications of AI innovations become clearer. But who is driving this development and implementation of AI: the government or the private sector? This chapter argues that it is a symbiotic process that benefits both.

Why has AI developed so quickly in China? In brief, it is, first, because AI research is globalised and open-sourced; Chinese developers and entrepreneurs have easy access to that research to build start-ups, which can then be piloted in China's large domestic market. Second, the Chinese government has promoted AI in the form of Smart Cities and other policies such as Informatisation, along with increased investment in the education and training of engineers, and by acting as a major customer for AI applications seeking to solve governance problems with technology – what this book calls creating experimental public–private petri dishes. Public–private petri dishes involve government support for private sector companies in establishing controlled pilot product launches of emerging technologies. Third, the huge Chinese population with limited and fuzzy privacy protections has allowed AI firms to collect big data. When this is combined with massive government databases being opened up to these companies, it means sufficient data is available for AI product development. Fourth, AI start-ups and large tech firms have an enormous potential domestic market and huge economic incentives to find workable applications that solve real-life problems.

Finally, the chapter explains that the symbiotic relationship between the Chinese government and AI firms within a globally open R&D ecosystem gives China the potential to become a world leader in AI. This is why public–private petri dishes of technology and AI development continue to be built. Also, in the development of AI industries, there is a need for the government to assist in building core technologies (eg, semiconductors) to drive private sector technology progress, and this is part of the government's recent AI Plan, which is analysed in detail.

Purpose Technologies' in Philippe Aghion and Steven N Durlauf (eds), *Handbook of Economic Growth* (North-Holland, 2005) vol 1B, 1181.

General-purpose technologies also raise many discussions that are not considered here (eg, civil–military fusions). In short, AI is applicable to many scenarios and applications. Some will solve societal problems; some will create societal problems, such as facial recognition used for state surveillance which raises a range of ethical dilemmas. See, eg, Elsa B Kania, 'Battlefield Singularity: Artificial Intelligence, Military Revolution, and China's Future Military Power' (*Center for a New American Security*, 28 November 2017) <https://www.cnas.org/publications/reports/battlefield-singularity-artificial-intelligence-military-revolution-and-chinas-future-military-power>.

Carefully defining the role of government will be crucial,[710] in part to avoid regulatory overreach that could threaten innovation and in part to not unduly restrict the achievements of private Chinese companies. This is because while public infrastructure is crucial to AI product rollouts, private tech companies, for the most part, are the key architects of AI applications. However, those companies providing public security authorities with facial recognition tools may not be able to sell into Western countries in the near future.

8.1 Why Has AI Developed So Quickly in China? The Current State of AI

An understanding of the current state of AI research is crucial to explaining why public–private AI rollouts, such as Smart City applications, are perfect for developing AI technologies. In recent times there has been a discordance in the public understanding of the capabilities of AI technologies and their reliability. Public interest in topics such as Machine Learning and Deep Learning has led to a deluge of opportunistic journalism and speculation regarding so-called killer robots. Newspapers and popular media now often focus on 'creepy Facebook bot AIs'[711] that become 'artificial brains'[712] then morph into 'artificial super-intelligence'[713] and finally lead to 'AI apocalypses'.[714]

---

[710] For example, a recent study found that: 'the role of government data in shaping AI innovation and the trade-offs represented by different state policies in the age of data-intensive innovation ... In the context of the facial recognition AI industry in China, we have shown that firms awarded public security contracts providing access to more government data produce more software for both government and commercial purposes'. See Martin Beraja, David Y. Yang and Noam Yuchtman, 'Data-Intensive Innovation and the State: Evidence from AI Firms in China' (NBER Working Paper No w27723, 21 January 2021), 39–40, <https://papers.ssrn.com/sol3/papers.cfm?abstract_id=3679716>.

[711] Chris Perez, 'Creepy Facebook Bots Talked to Each Other in a Secret Language (*New York Post*, 1 August 2017) <https://nypost.com/2017/08/01/creepy-facebook-bots-talked-to-each-other-in-a-secret-language>.

[712] Lou Del Bello, 'Scientists Are Closer to Making Artificial Brains That Operate Like Ours Do' (*Futurism*, 28 January 2018) <https://futurism.com/artificial-brains-operate-like-humans-close>.

[713] Shridhar Marri, 'Can Super Intelligence and Emotional Intelligence Co-Exist?' (*Forbes*, 27 June 2017) <https://www.forbesindia.com/blog/technology/can-super-intelligence-and-emotional-intelligence-co-exist/>.

[714] Tom Fish, 'AI to Bring "Mankind to Edge of APOCALYPSE" – With Robots a Bigger Risk than NUKES' (*Daily Star*, 15 July 2018) <https://www.dailystar.co.uk/news/latest-news/716305/ai-artificial-intelligence-autonomous-weaponry-arms-race>.

This reflects a wider problem: the difference between academic AI research and the wider public's understanding. Zachary Lipton, an assistant professor in the Machine Learning department at Carnegie Mellon University, has labelled this problem an 'AI misinformation epidemic'.[715] Yet, he notes, we 'cannot stop these articles; this is because articles about electronic brains or pernicious chatbots are less about the state of technological advancement and more about our own hopes and anxieties'.[716] Google's former head of AI, renowned Stanford University professor Fei-Fei Li, further noted that 'humans have a tendency to overestimate the short-term promise while underestimating long-term promise'.[717]

Algorithms cannot at this stage 'bootstrap' their learning – that is, teach themselves how to think. Nevertheless, unplanned results can occur in Machine Learning, and these unplanned results are often widely publicised, leading to popular misconceptions about AI having a mind of its own.[718] In China this was almost comically apparent in August 2017 when Tencent shut down BabyQ, a chatbot on the QQ messaging app with more than 800 million users. BabyQ had told Chinese users that it 'did not love the Communist Party'.[719] This incident reflects the

---

[715] Zachary C Lipton, 'The AI Misinformation Epidemic' (*Approximately Correct*, 28 March 2017) <http://approximatelycorrect.com/2017/03/28/the-ai-misinformation-epidemic>. In 2017, pioneering roboticist Rodney Brooks also wrote an article criticising the 'hysteria about the future of artificial intelligence'. See Rodney Brooks, 'The Seven Deadly Sins of AI Predictions' (*MIT Technology Review*, 6 October 2017) <https://www.technologyreview.com/s/609048/the-seven-deadly-sins-of-ai-predictions>.

[716] Oscar Schwartz, '"The Discourse Is Unhinged": How the Media Gets AI Alarmingly Wrong' (*The Guardian*, 25 July 2018) <https://www.theguardian.com/technology/2018/jul/25/ai-artificial-intelligence-social-media-bots-wrong>.

[717] Tony Peng, 'Fei-Fei Li at Google I/O: Humans Overestimate AI in the Short-Term, Underestimate Its Long-Term Potential' (*Synced Review*, 10 May 2018) <https://medium.com/syncedreview/fei-fei-li-at-google-i-o-humans-overestimate-ai-in-the-short-term-underestimate-its-long-term-f21d7a4a19a9>.

[718] Polina Golland, Professor of Electrical Engineering and Computer Science at MIT, noted that algorithms cannot learn as they go and bootstrap their learning: see Masha Borak, 'We Went to Suzhou to Find AI's Biggest Breakthroughs and Bottlenecks' (*Technode*, 12 May 2018). <https://technode.com/2018/05/12/suzhou-global-ai-product-application-expo>.

[719] It was not clear whether censorship regulators forced Tencent to remove BabyQ or if it was a pre-emptive move: «腾讯 QQ 群机器人服务调整中: QQ 小冰, Baby Q 被关闭» [Tencent's QQ Chatbot Suspended: QQ Xiaobing, Baby Q Shut Down] (*Sina*, 30 July 2017) <http://tech.sina.com.cn/i/2017-08-03/doc-ifyitamv4697563.shtml>. When the *South China Morning Post* asked Microsoft's Xiaobing chatbot what happened to BabyQ, Xiaobing replied: 'What an odd question.' Coco Liu, the author of the *South China Morning Post* article, reasoned this too was pre-emptive censorship programming. Tencent also pulled the QQ version of Xiaobing, another chatbot developed by

conflict between what appears to be unbridled Machine Learning and China's controlled cyber domain.

Focusing on academic AI literature, particularly in the field of Machine Learning, what is the current state of AI research today? A broad definition of AI and Machine Learning might start by explaining that AI refers to the use of technology to create systems that are capable of performing tasks commonly thought to require intelligence,[720] or 'the computational part of the ability to achieve goals in the world'.[721] Machine Learning was defined by 26 AI policy and technical researchers as follows: 'Machine learning is variously characterized as either a sub-field of AI or a separate field, and refers to *the development of digital systems that improve their performance on a given task over time through experience.*'[722]

AI research has had its peaks and troughs over an extended period dating back to 'the first AI winter' between the 1970s and the 1980s. This was a period in which funding for research in the field stopped almost entirely.[723] 'While there were small resurgences in the 1980s and 1990s, AI was more or less a topic relegated to the realm of corny sci-fi novelists – computer scientists often avoided the term artificial intelligence altogether for fear of being viewed as "wild-eyed dreamers".'[724]

At the beginning of the 2010s, after a new generation of researchers started publishing papers about successful applications of a technique

---

Microsoft, after Xiaobing described her 'China Dream' – a term coined by Chinese President Xi Jinping in a campaign to strengthen the nation – as 'moving to the United States'. Coco Liu, 'My China Dream Is Moving to the United States: Chinese Chatbots Censored after Going Off Script' (*South China Morning Post*, 3 August 2017) <http://www.scmp.com/week-asia/politics/article/2105338/my-china-dream-moving-united-states-chinese-chatbots-censored>.

[720] See Stuart J Russell and Peter Norvig, *Artificial Intelligence: A Modern Approach* (Pearson, 2016).

[721] The 2004 definition by Stanford University Computer Science Professor John McCarthy is widely cited as being a seminal early definition of AI. See John McCarthy, 'What is Artificial Intelligence?' (*Formal Reasoning Group Stanford*, revised 12 November 2007) <http://jmc.stanford.edu/articles/whatisai/whatisai.pdf>.

[722] Future of Humanity Institute et al, 'The Malicious Use of Artificial Intelligence' (n 52) 9 (emphasis added).

[723] See Sally Adee, 'Will AI's Bubble Pop?' (2016) 231(3082) *New Scientist* (16 July 2016) 16.

[724] See Schwartz, 'The Discourse is Unhinged' (n 716). See also John Markoff, 'AI Reemerges from a Funding Desert' (*New York Times*, 13 October 2005) <https://www.nytimes.com/2005/10/13/business/worldbusiness/ai-reemerges-from-a-funding-desert.html>. Interestingly, today many company representatives the author met with preferred to market themselves as 'automation' companies even if their products offered genuine AI applications. This was to avoid perceptions of cashing in on buzzwords.

called 'Deep Learning', the AI winter melted.[725] What we are witnessing today is rapid development in fields such as Machine Learning and its subfields including Deep Learning, Neural Networks and Natural Language Processing. Nevertheless, it is commonly argued that we are many years away from artificial general intelligence: a machine with all the capacity of humans but with infinitely more computing power.[726]

Machine Learning is a subfield of AI that is predicated on self-learning. Its methodologies are supported by algorithm-driven processes such as Neural Networks, boosting[727] and clustering.[728] Self-learning in this specific context means that machines can learn based on their knowledge via pattern recognition derived from data. However, Machine Learning commonly incorporates several hundred statistically based algorithms, and selecting the right algorithm or combination of algorithms for a given task is a constant challenge of working in this field.[729]

There are three categories of Machine Learning: supervised, unsupervised and reinforcement. Supervised Learning concentrates on learning patterns from labelled datasets and decoding the relationship between input features (independent variables) and their known output (dependent variables).[730] In the case of Unsupervised Learning, the output variables are unlabelled, and combinations of input and output variables are consequently unknown. This type of learning focuses on analysing

---

[725] See, eg, Alex Krizhevsky, Ilya Sutskever and Geoffrey E Hinton, 'ImageNet Classification with Deep Convolutional Neural Networks' (2012) 25(2) *Advances in Neural Information Processing Systems* 1. The study trained a large, deep, convolutional neural network to classify 1.2 million high-resolution images in the ImageNet LSVRC-2010 contest into the 1,000 different classes.

[726] This is still a debated subject. This book acknowledges this issue, but does not survey it any further. There is a small community of researchers focusing on the pursuit of artificial general intelligence, most notably the group led by Professor Ben Goertzel. In 2007, Goertzel edited a book of papers on the theoretical subject. See Ben Goertzel and Casio Pennachin (eds), *Artificial General Intelligence* (Springer, 2007). Their research group, Artificial General Intelligence, holds annual conferences and publishes an annual compendium of key research papers.

[727] Boosting means creating a meta-algorithm for primarily reducing bias and variance in Supervised Learning. It is a family of Machine Learning algorithms that convert weak learning algorithms into stronger ones.

[728] Clustering is a Machine Learning technique that involves the grouping of data points. In Data Science, clustering analysis can be used to gain valuable insights from data by seeing what groups the data points fall into when a clustering algorithm is used.

[729] See Shai Shalev-Shwartz and Shai Ben-David, *Understanding Machine Learning: From Theory to Algorithms* (Cambridge University Press, 2014).

[730] In simple terms, in data science dependent variables are data that cannot be controlled directly, and independent variables are data that can be controlled directly.

relationships between input variables and uncovering hidden patterns that can be extracted to create new labels for possible outputs.

Reinforcement Learning is the third and most advanced category of Machine Learning. Unlike Supervised and Unsupervised Learning, Reinforcement Learning builds a predictive model by gaining feedback through random trial and error and leveraging insight from previous iterations – in other words, learning by doing.[731]

Deep Learning is a subfield of Machine Learning that involves algorithms inspired by the structure and function of the brain. Called artificial Neural Networks,[732] these algorithms make complex connections between datasets. Deep Learning is a field that has advanced greatly in recent years. Key applications include accurate speech and facial recognition, which can be used for better reading of medical records and diagnostics; and AI image recognition for security issues, which has received much researcher attention.[733]

Deep Learning is *the* major recent breakthrough in AI research.[734] Deep Learning algorithms are trained on a batch of related data (eg, human faces) and are then fed increased data which steadily improve the algorithm-enabled software's pattern-matching accuracy. Although the technique has spawned commercial successes in China and elsewhere, the results are largely confined to fields where those huge datasets are available and the tasks are well-defined (eg, in labelling images or translating speech to text).[735] Therefore, in computer science an academic debate has emerged about whether Deep Learning may have reached the peak of its powers[736] and be over-hyped. It is beyond the scope of this

---

[731] See Shalev-Shwartz and Ben-David, *Understanding Machine Learning* (n 729).
[732] There are various types of Neural Networks. The specifics of Neural Networks may involve using training and test datasets that create various layers of data (input, hidden and output layers) as well as back-propagation (the practice of fine-tuning the weights of a Neural Network based on error rates). See Goodfellow, Bengio and Courville, *Deep Learning* (n 52).
[733] Ibid.
[734] Ibid.
[735] Ibid. The authors contend that Machine Learning is the only approach to building AI that is applicable to real-world environments: see at 8.
[736] Some AI experts are warning that the infatuation with Deep Learning may breed myopia and overinvestment now – and disillusionment later. Michael I Jordan, a professor at the University of California, Berkeley noted that 'trusting these brute force algorithms too much is a faith misplaced': Michael I Jordan, 'Artificial Intelligence: The Revolution Hasn't Happened Yet' (*Medium*, 19 April 2019) <https://medium.com/@mijordan3/artificial-intelligence-the-revolution-hasnt-happened-yet-5e1d5812e1e7>. Gary Marcus, a professor at New York University, posed the question: 'Is deep learning approaching a

research to contribute to that technical debate, but it is clear that AI or Machine Learning is currently proficient at mastering single repetitive tasks.

Neural Networks are one algorithm subclass, and in relation to AI development they are only relevant to Deep Learning. Neural Networks connect different parts of the algorithm's analysis. In short, developers input data (eg, lots of images), add an algorithm (or algorithms) giving those images meaning over time, and Neural Networks will create improved learning. Neural Network algorithms mature as the machine learns more.[737]

One key factor that has greatly assisted the development of AI is the huge increase in availability of inexpensive computer-processing power. In 2009, Andrew Ng and a team at Stanford University discovered that by linking inexpensive GPU clusters (originally used in computer gaming) to run Neural Networks consisting of hundreds of millions of connection nodes, they could 'democratise' Deep Learning.[738] Now, individuals can access computing power from cloud providers offering GPU resources to run computationally intensive processes such as Deep Learning. Thus, although in practice AI models and applications are extremely complicated, in theory the computational resources are now available to anyone.

The democratisation of computational resources has enabled many of the rapid developments in AI and Machine Learning over the past few years, leading to a wide range of beneficial applications. For example, AI is a critical component of widely used technologies such as automatic speech recognition, machine translation, spam filters and search engines. Additional promising technologies currently being researched or undergoing small-scale pilots include driverless cars, digital assistants for nurses and doctors,[739] AI-enabled drones for deliveries,[740] surf

---

wall?' He wrote: 'As is so often the case, the patterns extracted by deep learning are more superficial than they initially appear': Gary Marcus, 'Deep Learning: A Critical Appraisal' (*arXiv.org*, 19 April 2018) <https://arxiv.org/pdf/1801.00631.pdf>.

[737] See Shalev-Shwartz and Ben-David, *Understanding Machine Learning* (n 729).

[738] Kevin Kelly, *The Inevitable: Understanding the 12 Technological Forces That Will Shape Our Future* (Penguin Books, 2017).

[739] Tencent, for example, has plans to reinvent the Chinese healthcare system, due to the fact that China does not have general practitioners, by creating trust in AI robo-doctors: 吴朋阳 [Wu Pengyang], «人工智能在医疗行业应用的三大场景，信任如何建立？前沿科技» [How to Build Trust in the Three Major Scenarios of AI Application in the Medical Industry? Frontier Technology] (*Tencent Research Institute*, 30 March 2018) <https://mp.weixin.qq.com/s/Zf5Igvkqc-N2JqW9ail1lQ>.

[740] Chinese e-commerce giant JD.com began in 2017 testing 40 drones to deliver ecommerce deliveries to 100 rural Chinese villages. It should also be noted here again that data localisation would theoretically be problematic for some AI that is created. For example, in 2018 JD.com had 12,000 engineers based in China and Silicon Valley. Yolanda Redrup, 'How Chinese e-Commerce Player JD.com is Becoming an AI

lifesaving[741] and expediting disaster relief operations.[742] Thus there are vast numbers of different and unique potential fields for AI applications.[743] AI can outperform humans at driving cars in controlled environments,[744] diagnosing cancer,[745] shooting basketball free throws[746] and predicting crop yields.[747] But currently the AI platform must be trained for each specific task using enormous amounts of data.

The sudden advancement of AI applications due to improvements in Machine Learning, demonstrated especially in their ability to win games of strategy such as chess,[748] Go[749] and poker[750] in 2016–2017 significantly influenced Chinese policymaking. This was particularly the case

Powerhouse' (*Australian Financial Review*, 21 July 2018) <https://www.afr.com/technology/how-chinese-ecommerce-player-jdcom-is-becoming-an-ai-powerhouse-20180719-h12vph>.

[741] 'Westpac Partners with Surf Life Saving Australia to Put More Eyes in the Sky over Aussie Coastline This Summer' (*Surf Life Saving*, 17 December 2018) <https://sls.com.au/westpac-life-saver-drones-program-launches>.

[742] Alana Rudder, 'ML and AI Partner to Save Disaster Victims: How Aid Organizations Can Tap into Its Power' (*Towards Data Science*, 5 April 2018) <https://towardsdatascience.com/ml-and-ai-partner-to-save-disaster-victims-how-aid-organizations-can-tap-into-its-power-b8de67e92a09>.

[743] Richard Bellman, *An Introduction to Artificial Intelligence: Can Computers Think?* (Boyd & Fraser, 1978). Bellman's definition emphasises that AI is not a single technology field, but a general term for a group of research fields that concern the automation of activities associated with human intelligent behaviour with minimal human intervention. Robotics, for instance, falls under the general umbrella of AI.

[744] Arian Marshall, 'To Save the Most Lives, Deploy (Imperfect) Self-Driving Cars ASAP' (*Wired*, 11 July 2018) <https://www.wired.com/story/self-driving-cars-rand-report>.

[745] Rosie McCall, 'This App Can Detect Cancer Better than Doctors Can' (*IFLScience*, 29 May 2018) <https://www.iflscience.com/health-and-medicine/artificial-intelligence-can-now-detect-skin-cancer-better-than-humans>.

[746] 'Toyota Created a Robot That Shoots Hoops Better than the Pros' (*CNBC*, 15 March 2018) <https://www.cnbc.com/video/2018/03/15/toyota-created-a-robot-that-shoots-basketball-better-than-the-pros.html>.

[747] Alex Brokaw, 'This Startup Uses Machine Learning and Satellite Imagery to Predict Crop Yields' (*The Verge*, 4 August 2016) <https://www.theverge.com/2016/8/4/12369494/descartes-artificial-intelligence-crop-predictions-usda>.

[748] Samuel Gibbs, 'AlphaZero AI Beats Champion Chess Program after Teaching Itself in Four Hours' (*The Guardian*, 7 December 2017) <https://www.theguardian.com/technology/2017/dec/07/alphazero-google-deepmind-ai-beats-champion-program-teaching-itself-to-play-four-hours>.

[749] Colin Dwyer, '"Like a God" Google AI Beats Human Champ of Notoriously Complex Go Game' (*NPR*, 23 May 2017) <https://www.npr.org/sections/thetwo-way/2017/05/23/529673475/like-a-god-google-a-i-beats-human-champ-of-notoriously-complex-go-game>.

[750] Cade Metz, 'A Mystery AI Just Crushed the Best Human Players at Poker' (*Wired*, 31 January 2017) <https://www.wired.com/2017/01/mystery-ai-just-crushed-best-human-players-poker>.

for Go, which is a highly complex Asian game of strategy holding great significance in Chinese culture. That story is outlined in Section 8.2.

Returning to the state of AI, for the future, advanced AI holds much promise. More experimental AI technologies (eg, hierarchical temporal memory) have shown some promise. Hierarchical temporal memory focuses on developing computer algorithms by analysing and attempting to replicate the working of the human brain when it comes to solving complex problems rapidly.[751] However, at the current stage, data scientists cannot fully explain conclusions reached by Neural Networks trained by Deep Learning: 'That's why we are still not using deep learning in very important technologies like autonomous driving and nuclear control'.[752] Nor do regulators yet trust Neural Networks for the implementation of these technologies due to safety concerns.

Accordingly, AI is not a single field. It is made up of many different and varied fields. Not all AI even uses action selection: that is, the AI does not make decisions.[753] There is a vast difference between computational linguistics, game AI and AI in creating dexterous robots. Even training a robot to hold an item using a fist is difficult.[754] Some future directions (eg, hierarchical temporal memory) are highly experimental.

In addition, there is a never-ending array of new technologies and marriages between technologies that are difficult to regulate due to their decentralised and automated nature. For example, there are many start-ups working to solve the problem of how Reinforcement Learning can be married to an immutable blockchain ledger.[755] As noted earlier in this section, Reinforcement Learning is a type of Machine Learning algorithm,

---

[751] See, eg, Jeff Hawkins and Subutai Ahmad, 'Why Neurons Have Thousands of Synapses: A Theory of Sequence Memory in Neocortex' (2016) 10 *Frontiers in Neural Circuits* 1.

[752] Charles Ling, Professor of Computer Science, University of Western Ontario quoted in Steve Lohr, 'Is There a Smarter Path to Artificial Intelligence? Some Experts Hope So' (*New York Times*, 20 June 2018) <https://www.nytimes.com/2018/06/20/technology/deep-learning-artificial-intelligence.html>.

[753] For example, data mining (generally not considered to be a branch of AI) is concerned with finding statistical relationships and unseen patterns, not decision-making. Action selection, or decision-making, is the most basic problem of intelligent systems. See, eg, Trevor Hastie, Robert Tibshirani and Jerome Friedman, *The Elements of Statistical Learning* (Springer Science & Business Media, 2013).

[754] See, eg, Sergey Levine et al, 'Learning Hand-Eye Coordination for Robotic Grasping with Deep Learning and Large-Scale Data Collection' (*arXiv.org*, 28 August 2016) <https://arxiv.org/pdf/1603.02199.pdf>.

[755] Masha Borak, 'China's AIChain is Decentralizing Artificial Intelligence' (*Technode*, 29 June 2018) <https://technode.com/2018/06/29/aichain-artificial-intelligence-blockchain>.

which allows software to automatically determine the ideal behaviour within a specific context. Relatedly, blockchains ensure that data ledgers cannot be altered. That marriage is designed to ensure the sanctity and immutability of the machine-powered decision-making process. Such marriages between emerging technologies will continue to evolve.

Returning to the task of explaining AI today, the emergence of Deep Learning and access to inexpensive processing chips have placed AI within the grasp of any start-up willing to pilot an application in the past few years. As shown below, China's system of pilots and fuzzy logic legislation may be ideally suited to navigating this context of rapidly emerging new technologies. Machine Learning is being tested in pilots for commercial applications, and numerous controlled experiments are taking place throughout China to train better AI applications. In China's policy petri dishes, AI is now an entrepreneurial, not merely a research, endeavour. Nevertheless, as Alibaba's Strategy Chief Ming Zeng noted: 'How to apply that [AI] to real-world problems still takes tremendous innovation.'[756] This is where China's public–private pilot petri dishes of innovation are particularly useful.

Before proceeding to discuss these policy petri dishes, this chapter briefly introduces further important aspects of the current state of AI research, its collaborative nature,[757] and why Chinese policymakers only awoke to the power of AI post-2016.

Before then, the rapid development of AI had not been anticipated by the drafters of China's Cyber Security Law. It is important to outline how Chinese regulators woke up to the potential of AI, and how the fuzzy logic and definitional vagueness of the Cyber Security Law have allowed them to respond rapidly with new policies that seek to tap this potential. This lack of knowledge about AI's potential may be accidental rather than intentional, but the delay in finalising key legislative terms was by design.

8.2   An AI 'Sputnik Moment' for China

The drafters of the Cyber Security Law did not foresee AI's commercial development. History has now documented that such development,

---

[756] David A Andelman, 'How China Out-Innovates: A Chat with Alibaba's Strategy Chief Ming Zeng' (*Forbes*, 25 July 2018) <https://www.forbes.com/sites/forbesasia/2018/07/25/how-china-out-innovates-a-chat-with-alibabas-strategy-chief-ming-zeng/#624c89171a90>.
[757] Also discussed in Chapter 9.

including open-source AI platforms and Chinese companies establishing global R&D, was not in the mind of the drafters of China's Cyber Security Law in 2014–2015; rather, ideas of Network Sovereignty provided the inspiration. This is an evolving example of how fuzzy logic law helps Chinese innovation.

In March 2016, one event dramatically changed Chinese policymakers' thinking about the power of AI. AlphaGo, the AI-powered computer of UK start-up DeepMind (subsequently acquired by Google) beat the World Champion Go player, Korean Lee Sedol. Extolled by those who play it, Go is thought to be the oldest board game of mental skill in the world still being played.[758] The game of Go holds great significance in East Asian culture and, without warning, it was no longer beyond the competitive reach of machines.[759] This was China's 'Sputnik moment' regarding the power of AI.[760] Suddenly the power of AI was on show for all to see.

The events of this match were remarkable.[761] Twenty years had passed since 10 February 1996, when IBM supercomputer Deep Blue became the first machine to win a chess game against a reigning world champion, Garry Kasparov, under regular time controls. The ancient Chinese game

---

[758] Go is an abstract strategy board game for two players. The aim is to surround more territory than the opponent. Invented in China more than 2,500 years ago, Go has simple rules, but its complexity in terms of possible permutations is baffling and eludes definitive analysis.

[759] See, eg, John Fairbairn and T Mark Hall, *The Go Companion: Go in History and Culture Intelligence* (Slate & Shell, 2009).

[760] Yu Kai, the well-known Chinese founder of start-up Horizon Robotics noted along with various others that this was China's Sputnik moment regarding the power of AI. See «AI 芯片卡位战: 谁赢得自动驾驶处理器, 谁就赢得了AI 时代» [AI Chip War: Whoever Wins the Autonomous Processor Race Will Win the AI Era] (*Sequoia Exchange*, 26 April 2018) <https://mp.weixin.qq.com/s/0Th9C7pwhGU9D1vEkShZE> (the link is no longer active). Tencent CEO Pony Ma also stated that 'since AlphaGo, people have come to realise the power of deep learning': 'Strengthening AI R&D among China's 2018 Innovation Goals' (*Synced*, 7 March 2018) <https://medium.com/@Synced/strengthening-ai-r-d-among-chinas-2018-innovation-goals-dee468e95abb>. The algorithm displayed sophisticated Machine Learning to triumph at this complex board game. One of the leading Go experts, Fan Hui, first thought one of the lethal moves must have been a mistake. When he recognised its purpose he said: 'It's not a human move. I've never seen a human play this move. So beautiful.' He repeated: 'So beautiful! So beautiful! So beautiful!'

[761] Also in June 2017, AlphaGo completed a 3–0 clean sweep over Ke Jie, the world No 1 Go player. These events greatly lifted AI's profile, driving the Chinese government's dream of 'mass entrepreneurship': 'China's AI Business Ready to Lead the World' (*China Daily*, 1 June 2017) <http://www.chinadaily.com.cn/business/tech/2017-06/01/content_29576692.htm>.

of Go is an abstract strategy game with seemingly countless permutations.[762] When AlphaGo made a move anticipating multiple future moves, AI's potential suddenly became obvious. It had become an ideal-use case for Neural Networks. Humans can only see so far in advance, whereas a computer programmed to use multiple Neural Networks of information may be able to see further.[763] That is why this game of Go was such a powerful event in human history as well as being China's 'Sputnik moment' regarding the power of AI.[764]

In July 2017 China's government released its National AI Plan (discussed in depth in Sections 8.6 and 8.7), aiming to be a world leader in AI by 2030. AlphaGo was symbolic of this broader development. The release of China's AI Plan cannot be attributed solely to AlphaGo, but the match may have expedited its release and broadened its aims. AI progress, however, remains a company, national and highly globalised endeavour, which has important ramifications for the key issue of openness versus localised control.

8.3 AI Research Is Collaborative, Providing the Ideal Environment for China to Establish Pilot Rollouts

Current AI research is indisputably a global endeavour, and even though China lags behind the United States in fundamental AI breakthroughs, this open innovation environment has allowed Chinese firms to build their AI capacity, taking advantage of their ability to roll out experimental pilots.

AI research is mostly publicly available in journals or shared on open-source platforms. AI academics often publish in real time and make their open-source code available as well as the associated training datasets. Academic researchers demand repeatability from AI, and this forces developers to be transparent with their computer code.[765] Repeatability

---

[762] The exact number of moves is a mathematical problem of great discussion.
[763] AlphaGo drew on three separate Neural Networks in its calculations. That is, three separate systems to make a decision.
[764] There was a moment of palpable tension during the second game between AlphaGo and Lee. Under visible stress, the normally affable Lee stepped out for a cigarette and returned to a move made by the computer that Go commentators had never seen before and that Lee could not understand. The commentators and crowd were shocked and dumbfounded for minutes before Lee returned from his stress-induced break. These events sent reverberations around the world, not just in China.
[765] Repeatability or 'test–retest reliability' is the closeness of the agreement between the results of successive measurements of the same measure and carried out under the same conditions of measurement.

in this context means that studies can be replicated and verified by other researchers globally. Thus, the current state of AI research is collaborative and provides all the necessary data for AI firms that are in a position to develop new products rapidly and implement pilot rollouts.

Due to open-source platforms in AI, technological breakthroughs today spread faster than they did before. For example, in 2017 Google's Waymo built the first Level 4[766] autonomous driving program, yet Waymo had been founded in 2009. Less than a year later, Chinese tech giant Baidu announced that it was producing an entire Level 4 autonomous bus fleet through its open-source platform Apollo and its then almost 100 commercial partners.[767]

Clearly, certain kinds of AI research will continue to be proprietary for security reasons. A report[768] by more than 25 researchers from the universities of Oxford and Cambridge, OpenAI[769] and the Electronic Frontier Foundation[770] found that some AI research may need to be kept secret to prevent 'exploits'.[771] However, the majority of AI research in non-sensitive fields remains publicly available.[772]

Globalised AI research has greatly benefited Chinese progress in this field. 'What is not in dispute is that the close ties between Silicon Valley and China both in terms of investment and research, and the open nature of much of the American AI research community, has made the most advanced technology easily available to China.'[773] As one American Machine Learning professor noted:

---

[766] Level 4 is one level below fully autonomous driving.
[767] 王融 [Wang Rong], «自动驾驶三件事, 安全, 安全, 还是安全!» [The Three Keys to Drive Autonomously: Safety, Safety, and Safety!] (*Baidu AI*, 26 July 2018) <https://mp.weixin.qq.com/s/Ro_5bJYx9WO_46JjEMPSCA>. The Apollo case is analysed further in Chapter 9, Section 9.7.
[768] Future of Humanity Institute et al, 'The Malicious Use of Artificial Intelligence' (n 52). The report warns that the same technology creates new opportunities for criminals, political operatives and oppressive governments – so much so that some AI research may need to be kept secret.
[769] OpenAI is a not-for-profit organisation set up to research and enact a path to safe artificial general intelligence.
[770] The Electronic Frontier Foundation is a not-for-profit organisation defending digital privacy, free speech and innovation.
[771] Exploits are software tools designed to take advantage of a flaw in a computer system, typically for malicious purposes (eg, installing malware).
[772] Future of Humanity Institute et al, 'The Malicious Use of Artificial Intelligence' (n 52).
[773] John Markoff and Matthew Rosenberg, 'China's Intelligent Weaponry Gets Smarter' (*New York Times*, 3 February 2017) <https://www.nytimes.com/2017/02/03/technology/artificial-intelligence-china-united-states.html>.

> Honestly, I at the present (and of course this may change), I don't think companies actually have many secret technical capabilities. The core successes of [Machine Learning] are all things where mostly every expert knows how they work and the work is published. Now some companies have better data. Some companies have better engineers and infrastructure. And generally just have more research talent to identify how to use the technology on new problems. But there's (for the time being) surprisingly little secret sauce. Data and talent are bigger barriers to entry and these give a big advantage to large companies since they can afford to pay 300–600k per year for very strong employees and since they have real services generating enormous amounts of data.[774]

This is not a controversial statement. In May 2018, Wan Gang (万钢), chairman of the China Association for Science and Technology, said publicly that Chinese companies were world leaders in applying image recognition, voice translation and behavioural analysis, even though China is yet to contribute much to deep AI research: 'China has advantages in the speed of AI development and its wide applications, but our weak points are the depth of basic research and originality.'[775] He noted that the United States is ahead of China in basic algorithmic inventions. This is despite the fact that in China 'remarkable achievements have been made in intelligent robotics, unmanned shops, machine translation, shared and driverless vehicles. There are wide applications in the fields of city planning, smart transport, social governance, health, agriculture and national security'.[776] In 2018, Tencent CEO Pony Ma stressed that China should focus more on core scientific research and not only the quick development of applications.[777] Just prior to stepping down as Alibaba CEO, Jack Ma made similar comments.[778]

---

[774] Correspondence with Professor Zach Lipton (1 August 2018).
[775] 'World Intelligence Congress Gathers Discussion on AI' (*Xinhua*, 17 May 2018) <http://www.xinhuanet.com/english/2018-05/17/c_137184327.htm>.
[776] Ibid.
[777] Pony Ma said: 'China has led the world in some areas such as mobile payments and 3G/4G network building … However, we should also look backward to see whether the foundation (of basic scientific research) is solid or not': Celia Chen and Li Tao, 'Tencent CEO Pony Ma Says China Risks Falling Behind without Strong Base in Scientific Research' (*South China Morning Post*, 28 May 2018) <http://www.scmp.com/tech/tech-leaders-and-founders/article/2148112/tencent-ceo-pony-ma-says-china-risks-falling-behind#FDgmYwXu4Vh04pcB.99>.
[778] Ibid.

Furthermore, Rong Jin, head of machine intelligence technologies at Alibaba's global research programme, DAMO Academy,[779] noted that 'the perception in China is that Americans throw themselves into fundamental research and are heavy duty mathematicians – the disciplines at the heart of AI – while Chinese tend to study coding or engineering'.[780] This perception emerges from AI engineers building viable pilots of AI applications across China. AI in China in 2018 is geared towards commercial applications, in the form of pilot petri dishes.[781]

AI researcher-turned-venture capitalist Dr Kai-Fu Lee argued:

> A lot of people misunderstand AI as a brilliant scientist invents another AI algorithm for medicine, finance, loans, banking, autonomous vehicle, face recognition ... But that is just not the way the AI business is run. There is really one fundamental AI innovation – deep learning – and everybody else is tweaking it for the domains.

That is, according to Lee:

> [W]e're not in the age of discovery; we're in the age of implementation [AI application and commercialisation], we're in the age of data, and China has a better set, a larger set of implementers or good AI engineers who get the work done, who make the algorithms run fast, connect to business logic.[782]

The collaborative and open nature of AI research, combined with increasingly affordable pricing for processing chips globally, is highly relevant because it means that the only barriers to Chinese firms developing AI technologies are access to data and opportunities to test their products in controlled real-world environments.

---

[779] Alibaba announced in October 2017 that it would invest US$15 billion over the next three years in 'cutting edge technologies', including AI, through its global research effort, called Discovery, Adventure, Momentum and Outlook (Damo) Academy.

[780] Louise Lucas and Richard Waters, 'China and US Compete to Dominate Big Data' (*Financial Times*, 1 May 2018) <https://www.ft.com/content/e33a6994-447e-11e8-93cf-67ac3a6482fd>.

[781] 李开复 [Kai-Fu Lee], «李开复: 人工智能超级大国的那些事» [Kai-Fu Lee: The Things That Are Needed to Create an AI Superpower] (*Sina*, 23 August 2018) <http://tech.sina.com.cn/csj/2018-08-23/doc-ihicsiav6703902.shtml>. As AI permeates various sectors of the economy, the demand for skilled AI engineers will far exceed the need for top-tier AI researchers. Dr Kai-Fu Lee noted: 'In the age of AI implementation, you won't just need a few cutting-edge AI research scientists to achieve economic superiority, you'll need engineers who can join forces with entrepreneurs to turn scientific research into commercially viable products. China is currently training an army of those sorts of entrepreneurs.'

[782] Williams, 'Why China Will Win' (n 81).

It is also true that AI has developed so rapidly in China because China's public–private policy petri dishes have removed those barriers and provided an optimum regulatory environment for that development.

8.4 Why Has AI Developed So Quickly in China? Private Firm/ Government Symbiosis and Public–Private Petri Dishes

China's impressive rise in AI has been driven by its private sector.[783] This section explains that this is due to Chinese entrepreneurs having the capability and incentive to solve numerous governance problems in a developing country.

China's private sector is often the main architect of AI products for one simple reason: access to and control of nationwide big data resources. There is now a widely shared view that China's vast data reserves will provide crucial support for Chinese AI to attain world-leading levels of development.[784] Yet, as noted in Chapter 7, previously Chinese bureaucracies kept siloed, haphazard or non-digitised datasets. Private companies like Tencent and Alibaba were pioneers in widescale digital collection of Chinese data through their highly popular products like Alipay and WeChat, and they have also made use of that data to develop AI applications.

In fact, private sector AI implementation in China has been impacting certain Chinese industries since 2013, yet this impact is not always obvious as it has been largely confined to enterprise data-driven companies in sectors such as the internet, finance or insurance.[785] Deep Learning was first used in these sectors because the implementation could be handled entirely by the private sector: for example, Alibaba did not need government cooperation to deploy AI in optimising its own

---

[783] See Kai-Fu Lee, *AI Superpowers: China, Silicon Valley, and the New World Order* (Houghton Mifflin Harcourt, 2018). See ch 5 in particular, where Dr Lee explains the waves of AI, and China's data-collecting companies and mechanisms (discussed further in the following chapters). See also Paul Triolo and Matt Scott, 'China's AI Trajectory Is Set by Entrepreneurs and International Collaboration, Not By Government Edict' (*SupChina Project*, 19 April 2019) <https://supchina.com/2019/04/19/chinas-ai-trajectory-is-set-by-entrepreneurs-and-international-collaboration-not-by-government-edict>.
[784] See Lee, *AI Superpowers* (n 783).
[785] Ibid.

advertising mechanisms, and BaoAn Insurance did not need to engage CAC to analyse big data for its insurance premium calculations.[786]

There has been a huge growth of enterprise AI businesses in China: by the end of 2017, China had over 2,000 companies in AI-related industries, according to MIIT.[787] And private AI firms have been highly active in providing 'AI Plus B2B [business-to-business] enterprise services' to solve Chinese development and 'trust' problems, including as contractors to SOEs.[788] For example, in 2017, AI start-up Kuang-Chi joined other leading Chinese tech companies including the BATs in investing nearly US$12 billion in state-owned telecommunications company, China Unicom.[789] Private AI firms operate in areas including cloud computation, big data, IoT, AI digital content and payment finance. AI is also being used to reform SOEs that must lower debt levels and refinance their debt by building AI applications on existing financial datasets to make their operations run more efficiently.[790]

Another example of a successful private AI technology firm is fintech company 4Paradigm, founded by a former Baidu Deep Learning programmer. 4Paradigm helps clients develop AI software to match customers and services more efficiently. Its customers include insurers and banks, including China Merchants Bank.[791] Those state-owned financial institutions have also invested in 4Paradigm AI and assisted in providing data under encouraged, open government data policies.[792]

---

[786] Ibid.
[787] 'World Intelligence Congress Gathers Discussion on AI' (n 775).
[788] See, eg, «创新工场智能投资基金落户广州, 目标总规模 25 亿» [Innovative Workshop Smart Investment Fund Settled in Guangzhou with a Total Target of 2.5 Billion] (*Innovation Works WeChat page*, 24 May 2018) <https://mp.weixin.qq.com/s/V7MVeYST17wQKau_7GjIpg>.
[789] Bien Perez, 'China Taps Nation's Who's Who of Technology to Anchor Ownership Shakeup at Unicom's Parent' (*South China Morning Post*, 17 August 2017) <https://www.scmp.com/tech/article/2106982/unicom-shares-halted-speculation-mounts-new-investors-its-parent-company>.
[790] China pledged to clear up debt and get banks to finance productive activity instead of subsidising state companies but the government has ruled out allowing any state companies to go bankrupt: see 'Why China Keeps Bailing Out Ailing Heavy Industries' (*South China Morning Post*, 25 January 2017) <https://www.scmp.com/news/china/economy/article/2065332/why-china-keeps-bailing-out-ailing-heavy-industries>.
[791] See 'Trio of China's Big State Banks Invest in 4Paradigm AI' (*Synced*, 20 January 2018) <https://medium.com/@Synced/trio-of-chinas-big-state-banks-invest-in-4paradigm-ai-72f444ad5e8b>.
[792] Ibid. See also '4Paradigm (第四范式) national team' (*Tech in Asia website*) <https://www.techinasia.com/companies/4paradigm>.

In 2016, 4Paradigm introduced its large-scale distributed Machine Learning platform, Prophet. Prophet assists clients in the finance industry to boost performance in verticals such as targeted client bookings, personalised recommendations, application anti-fraud, transaction anti-fraud, overdue or loss warnings, liquidity management, smart collection and disposal of non-performing assets.

4Paradigm's services also allow other AI companies or developers to build on its systems under licence, creating a business ecosystem.[793] Guangdong Development Bank (GDB), for example, reportedly built 10 different AI applications based on 4Paradigm's core systems in a year. It must be further noted that GDB is actually a mixed-ownership bank with a 20% stake owned by the US bank Citibank; other shareholders include Chinese SOEs. This is another example of how Chinese enterprises have long built global links.

Furthermore, in conjunction with a public hospital, 4Paradigm has created an AI model for diagnosing pre-diabetes.[794] In 2021, 4Paradigm would raise US$700 million in a Series D funding round. Investors included Sequoia Capital China and Goldman Sachs.[795]

This industry diversification is a feature of Chinese AI companies: once they have mastered a specific technology (eg, image recognition) they sprout into various industries to solve a variety of governance and performance problems.

Another company seeking to create trust for consumers and wholesalers, and more widely representative of the arguments in this research, is Malong Technologies. Its business efficiency AI application, ProductAI, allows visual product search and tagging, without the need for barcodes. The AI technology recognises a product based on its visible attributes. ProductAI has other potential uses as well, including detecting defects in manufacturing, scanning baggage and analysing medical

---

[793] 4Paradigm is now building customised AI 'brains' for its clients, which can potentially spawn large numbers of AI applications.
[794] 洪杉 [Hong Shan] «当顶尖的 AI 创业者济济一堂，他们在谈些什么？特别报道» [When Top AI Entrepreneurs Come Together, What Do They Talk About? Special Report] (*Sequoia Exchange*, 27 August 2018) <https://mp.weixin.qq.com/s/1F2IZ_DGQ318nDDQsmu8Yg>.
[795] Eudora Wang, 'Chinese AI Firm 4Paradigm Pockets $700m Led by Boyu, Primavera, Hopu' (*Deal Street Asia*, 23 January 2021) <https://www.dealstreetasia.com/stories/4paradigm-funding-224587/>.

images.[796] Visual quality inspections are a good example of 'low-hanging fruit' for AI implementation.[797]

Not only is ProductAI representative of the most common applications for computer vision; it also reflects many of the themes of this study that are expanded in the next chapter, especially the global commercial entanglement of AI companies that create open-source products and are globalised. ProductAI is an open-source product and has software development kits for the computer programming languages Python, PHP, Java and C#. It is open-sourced on GitHub, and is available as an embedded system or as a server appliance, with the software running on servers in the businesses' home countries to comply with both local security requirements and China's Cyber Security Law. Malong Technologies is supported by and in some cases has investment from several US and Chinese companies including global consultancy Accenture, Microsoft Ventures, eBay, US AI chipmaker Nvidia and China's famed Tsinghua University.[798]

In addition to Accenture's investment in Malong Technologies, the two companies have signed an alliance to jointly develop industry solutions and prepare go-to-market activities. As part of the agreement, Malong has designated Accenture as its preferred systems integrator and consulting partner. This is now the preferred strategy for Chinese tech companies: signing global partnerships to create transparency in murky areas such as data-sharing platforms that may come within the reach of the Cyber Security Law.

These new start-up firms all have a plethora of real-world applications, and in China, these applications are being trained in real-world environments at a far more rapid rate than anywhere else.[799] This is creating a strong AI industry in China, not to mention a thriving venture capital industry. High-profile AI-focused venture capital firm Sinovation Ventures already had five AI companies in its portfolio valued at over

---

[796] Joseph F Kovar, 'Accenture Invests in China-Based AI Firm' (*CRN*, 13 August 2018) <https://www.crn.com/news/channel-programs/accenture-invests-in-china-based-ai-firm?itc=refresh>.

[797] Cliff Saran, 'Why AI Success Depends on IT Picking the Low-Hanging Fruit' (*Computer Weekly*, 22 September 2017) <https://www.computerweekly.com/news/450426790/Why-AI-success-depends-on-IT-picking-the-low-hanging-fruit>.

[798] 'Accenture Forms Strategic Alliance, Invests in Chinese AI Start-up Malong Technologies' (*Businesswire*, 13 August 2018) <https://www.businesswire.com/news/home/20180812005014/en/Accenture-Forms-Strategic-Alliance-Invests-Chinese-AI>.

[799] See Bandurski, 'Big Data, Big Concerns' (n 23).

US$1 billion in late 2018. That may be a record for any venture capital firm worldwide.[800] China's 'magical ascent' in AI took just two years.[801]

Sinovation's billion-dollar AI companies then included crypto firm Bitmain, image recognition company Face++, fintech-focused 4Paradigm, autonomous driving AI company Momenta and AI-processing chipmaker Horizon Robotics. As of early 2021, Sinovation claimed to have invested in 16 Chinese companies now worth over US$1 billion.[802]

Yet even though private firms were first movers in AI development in China, and many of them have become highly successful in their fields, a closer analysis reveals that most private Chinese AI companies have a symbiotic relationship with the government. Their success is in many cases dependent on state-sponsored (facial ID and other) datasets, extensive government support for fundamental research, and rapidly unveiled government-funded pilot programs that are loosely regulated or fuzzy in regulatory definition.[803] If a start-up AI firm can solve a governance problem (eg, regulating China's large shadow banking industry), government(s) local or central will generally be its patron, first customer and chief evangelist.

The symbiotic government–private AI ecosystem that is emerging in China is perfect for developing AI products rapidly. For example, speech and facial recognition companies such as SenseTime,[804] Yitu Tech,[805] Megvii (commonly known as Face++)[806] and Intellifusion,[807] among others, initially relied upon large-scale procurement of their services by

---

[800] Jon Russell, 'China Is Beating the US on AI, Says Noted Investor Kai-Fu Lee' (*TechCrunch*, 7 September 2018) <https://techcrunch.com/2018/09/05/china-is-beating-the-us-on-ai-says-noted-investor-kaifu-lee>.
[801] Ibid.
[802] 'Sinovation Ventures' (Sinovation website) <https://www.sinovationventures.com/>.
[803] Discussed further in Chapter 9 and the Conclusion. See also Bandurski, 'Big Data, Big Concerns' (n 23). Bandurski notes: 'China is certainly not alone in the development of such technologies. But it stands apart in their actual deployment, which is happening quickly and in the utter absence of scrutiny.'
[804] Josh Chin and Liza Lin, 'China's All-Seeing Surveillance State Is Reading Its Citizens' Faces' (*Wall Street Journal*, 26 June 2017) <https://www.wsj.com/articles/the-all-seeing-surveillance-state-feared-in-the-west-is-a-reality-in-china-1498493020>.
[805] Sam Schechner, Douglas MacMillan and Liza Lin, 'US and Chinese Companies Race to Dominate AI (*Wall Street Journal*, 18 January 2018) <https://www.wsj.com/articles/why-u-s-companies-may-lose-the-ai-race-1516280677>.
[806] AI unicorn Megvii, also known as Face++, was first introduced in Chapter 2.
[807] Chin and Lin, 'China's All-Seeing Surveillance' (n 804).

the government. Accordingly, China is now home to some of the world's leading image and facial recognition companies.[808]

At the same time, buoyed by government incentives and a huge potential market, these AI firms have turned their collective minds to developing products with broader social and market functions. While facial recognition applications have received the most Western media attention for their role in building police video surveillance networks across China, these companies have created multiple other image recognition products, from cancer diagnostic applications to financial applications. Moreover, many 'surveillance' AI technologies (eg, facial recognition) have been used in commercial or public interest pilot applications such as taking food orders at a KFC restaurant and stopping paper theft at public toilets.[809] Clearly, there is a sometimes incongruous overlap between the public (governance) and private (commercial) ventures of AI firms.

To further understand these symbiotic relationships, the role of China's government in building out pilot projects, especially through its Smart Cities policy and AI Plan, needs to be further explained.

8.5 Smart Cities as Petri Dishes for AI Development

As a general-purpose technology, AI in China can solve various governance problems associated with China's development. In *China's Disruptors*, Edward Tse noted that Chinese innovation must always come up with 'answers to operating problems', and that this is what 'makes Chinese innovation so powerful'.[810] Due to China's relatively immature yet rapidly changing social and political environment, there are numerous large-scale governance and legal problems to solve, and '[t]he pace of change leads to continuous restlessness'.[811] This means that 'China is

---

[808] Schechner, MacMillan and Lin, 'US and Chinese Companies Race to Dominate AI' (n 805).
[809] Will Knight, 'Paying with Your Face: 10 Breakthrough Technologies 2017' (*MIT Technology Review*, May 2017) <https://www.technologyreview.com/s/603494/10-breakthrough-technologies-2017-paying-with-your-face>. See also the reference to face-scanning dispensers that limit each person to one 0.6 m length of paper every nine minutes in Stephen Chen, 'Elderly Chinese Toilet Paper Thieves Face Up to Their Crimes' (*South China Morning Post*, 19 March 2017) <http://www.scmp.com/news/china/society/article/2080272/elderly-chinese-toilet-paper-thieves-face-their-crimes>.
[810] Tse, *China's Disruptors* (n 21) 100.
[811] Ibid 208.

producing a generation of experimenters – people who are willing to test things out and see what happens'.[812] There is also a need to innovate to solve China's 'trust' problems (as noted in Chapter 7).

Over the past three decades, China's government has learnt to support private sector innovations by using policy petri dishes with fuzzy legal rules to solve Chinese development problems.[813] At the same time, the Chinese government must balance policy considerations that affect its own rule, such as the trade-offs between economic prosperity and environmental protection. For example, air pollution is a constant complaint of Chinese citizens. Therefore, electric vehicles and other sustainable technologies are more than a major Chinese policy target and recipient of subsidies;[814] they are essential planks supporting the Party's fundamental goal to keep the people happy and thereby maintain its own rule.[815]

One of the largest scale policy petri dishes introduced in recent years is the Smart City initiative. For over a decade, the Chinese government has been introducing and refining Smart City and innovation development policies, and testing their feasibility through experimental pilots (as noted in Chapter 1). Since 2006 a plethora of industrial and technology policies ranging from Strategic Emerging Industries (战略性新兴产业)[816] to Made in China 2025 (中国制造 2025)[817] have been implemented in order to drive a structural shift towards enabling indigenous innovation.

More recently, China's national policy plans and guidelines have resulted in a range of new strategies. These include policies of mass

---

[812] Ibid 221.
[813] As was noted in Chapters 1 and 2 regarding Special Economic Zones and VIEs.
[814] For example, in 2012 China's State Council published a plan to develop a domestic new energy vehicle industry, which includes battery-powered electric vehicles, plug-in hybrid vehicles and fuel-cell vehicles. The plan is targeting the production of 500,000 plug-in hybrid and electric vehicles by 2015, with output to grow to 2 million units of those types by 2020. See 《国务院关于印发节能与新能源汽车产业发展规划 (2012–2020 年) 的通知》 [Notice of the State Council on Printing and Distributing the Development Plan for Energy Saving and New Energy Vehicle Industry (2012–2020)] (People's Republic of China) State Council, 28 June 2012 <http://www.gov.cn/zwgk/2012-07/09/content_2179032.htm>.
[815] See Dinny McMahon, *China's Great Wall of Debt: Shadow Banks, Ghost Cities, Massive Loans, and the End of the Chinese Miracle* (Houghton Mifflin Harcourt, 2018).
[816] 《战略性新兴产业》 [Strategic Emerging Industries] (People's Republic of China) State Council, 19 October 2010.
[817] 《中国制造 2025》 [Made in China 2025] (People's Republic of China) State Council, 8 May 2015.

entrepreneurship and innovation (大众创业与创新)⁸¹⁸, to implement innovation-driven development strategies in China by streamlining government agencies in order to mobilise the enthusiasm of hundreds of millions of new market entrants; and A New Generation AI Development Plan (新一代人工智能发展规划), which is designed to accelerate China's ambition of becoming a world leader in AI by 2030.[819] Although many countries have also released AI plans, the scale of China's efforts appear to be unparalleled.[820]

Particularly since 2017, the Chinese government has realised that AI will be a crucial factor in the successful rollout of Smart Cities throughout China due to the enormous potential of AI to enable the efficient operation of various governance tasks within Smart Cities. To understand the impact of government-facilitated petri dishes for private AI development, it is necessary to first introduce the broader topic of Smart City policies in China, and the important role of AI within those policies.

A 'Smart City' (智慧城市 – *zhihui chengshi*) involves the use of ICT to solve urban problems by incorporating intelligent and sustainable urban development.[821] Obviously, a Smart City is a digitally connected city. However, it is as much about town planning for city growth as it is about technology. 'In its widest understanding, smart city integrates the full range of services a city needs and wants to offer in a way that follows state-of-the-art public administration requirements – including the use of most recent technology.'[822] The goals of 'good city management' therefore ideally mirror the 'leading goals of smart city

---

[818] «大众创业与创新» [Mass Entrepreneurship and Innovation] (People's Republic of China) State Council, 2014 (also cited in Chapter 1). The phrase (大众创业与创新) or 'Mass Entrepreneurship and Innovation' came from the speech of Premier Li Keqiang at the Davos Forum meeting of the World Economic Forum in September 2014.

[819] «新一代人工智能发展规划» [New Generation AI Development Plan] (People's Republic of China) State Council, 8 July 2017 (AI Plan). Discussed and explained in detail in Section 8.6.

[820] In recent years, Canada, China, Denmark, the European Commission, Finland, France, India, Italy, Japan, Mexico, the Nordic-Baltic region, Singapore, South Korea, Sweden, Taiwan, the UAE and the United Kingdom have all released official strategies to promote the use and development of AI and to address these important questions: Ganesh Bell, 'Why Countries Need to Work Together on AI' (*World Economic Forum*, 16 September 2018) <https://www.weforum.org/agenda/2018/09/learning-from-one-another-a-look-at-national-ai-policy-frameworks>.

[821] Anthony M Townsend, *Smart Cities: Big Data, Civic Hackers, and the Quest for a New Utopia* (WW Norton, 2013).

[822] Kang Yanrong, Jeanette Whyte and Thomas Hart, 'Comparative Study of Smart Cities in Europe and China' (White Paper, EU-China Policy Dialogues Support Facility II

development'.[823] While the definition of a Smart City varies greatly within the innovation literature, sustainability (eg, electric and self-driving cars – see Chapter 9) is one key phrase associated with a Smart City.[824]

The term 'Smart City' is vague, having been applied to matters ranging from urban design to traffic management policy, but it commonly involves the collection of extensive amounts of data from the real-world city environment rather than from a laboratory to assist in providing various services.[825] Modern technology trends have increased the recent development of Smart Cities. Government-deployed Smart City strategies are regarded as a powerful catalyst to develop and use technologies (eg, IoT,[826] cloud computing and big data) in urban planning, construction and city management. Certain AI-powered data-collecting technologies will therefore inevitably play a key role in the planning and operation of China's Smart Cities, especially those employing sensors, wi-fi trackers, surveillance cameras and QR code-linked transactions.[827]

This is clear from calls by China's central government planning body, the National Development and Reform Commission (NDRC)[828] (中华人民共和国国家发展和改革委员会), to ensure that the Smart City strategy introduces modern science and technology (eg, IoT, cloud computing, big data and spatial geographic information systems) to urban planning and construction and operation. Smart Cities can theoretically

---

(PDSF), March 2014) 16 <http://euchina-ict.eu/wp-content/uploads/2015/01/Smart_City_report_draft-White-Paper-March-2014.pdf> (the link is no longer active).
[823] Ibid.
[824] The term Smart Cities often refers to intelligent and sustainable urban development: ibid.
[825] See Nathan Yau, 'Seeing Life in Your Data' in Toby Segaran and Jeff Hammerbacher (eds), *Beautiful Data: The Stories behind Elegant Data Solutions* (O'Reilly, 2009) 3.
[826] Internet of Things (IoT) is the interconnection via the internet of computing devices embedded in everyday objects, enabling them to send and receive data. Cisco estimates that there were about 200 million things connected to the internet in the year 2000 and that this number had increased to approximately 10 billion by 2013. Joseph Bradley, Joel Barbier and Doug Handler, 'Embracing the Internet of Everything to Capture Your Share of $14.4 Trillion' (Cisco White Paper, 2013) <http://www.cisco.com/c/dam/en_us/about/ac79/docs/innov/IoE_Economy.pdf>.
[827] For the extent of QR code usage in China see Timmy Shen, 'China's Obsession with QR Codes' (*Technode*, 16 February 2018) <https://technode.com/2018/02/16/photo-chinas-obsession-qr-codes>.
[828] The National Development and Reform Commission of the People's Republic of China (NDRC), formerly known as the State Planning Commission and State Development Planning Commission, is a macroeconomic management agency under the Chinese State Council, which has broad administrative and planning control over the Chinese economy. See 'Home' (*NDRC website*) <http://en.ndrc.gov.cn>.

improve urban management and service industries with the aid of real-time monitoring and analysis of data, historical data trends, data warehousing analysis and big data. The goal is to integrate information resources and improve urban management and services, as well as transform China's economy by moving to more advanced industries.

The high-level government attention means that the term 智慧城市 (Smart City) has been widely adopted in China, and the Smart City concept garnered much attention at the 2010 Shanghai World Expo, where it was a key theme. The World Expo's ubiquitous slogan was 城市, 让生活更美好 (Better City, Better Life).[829]

Particularly since 2016, the growth in the number of IoT and biometric identifying applications in pilot Smart City projects has been exponential and increasingly involves the use of AI applications. One example illustrates how AI technologies could greatly assist the implementation of responsive government – while also inevitably arousing suspicions of a nascent dystopia. In October 2016, China announced Yinchuan, the capital of the economically deprived Ningxia province in the north-west of China, as the blueprint for Smart Cities across China. Yinchuan became the favoured model Smart City over Shanghai or Beijing due to its small size and limited population of 1.5 million people.[830] The city in 2016 began testing various Smart City measures, including solar-powered public rubbish bins that double as compactors, increasing storage capacity five-fold. When full, the bins send a signal to garbage collectors to empty them. Other pilot programmes are more problematic, from a privacy perspective. On local buses, AI-powered facial recognition software has replaced the fare box. Commuters' faces are linked to their bank accounts and they are charged for each trip accordingly. This system was one of the first to raise questions regarding the kind of data China's Smart Cities should be permitted to collect.[831]

Yinchuan is only one example of a Chinese Smart City. There are hundreds of other experiments in China, undoubtedly the country with the world's largest rollout of Smart City projects. Reports had claimed that by 2016 there would be more than 300 Smart City pilot projects[832]

---

[829] See Jennifer Hubbert, 'Better City, Better Life? Urban Modernity at the Shanghai Expo' (2019) 17(4) *Asia-Pacific Journal* 1.
[830] Carrington, 'Yinchuan' (n 49).
[831] Ibid.
[832] At present, there are more than 300 pilot Smart Cities in China: Kelly Yang, Aideen Clery and Domenico Di Liello, *Sector Report: Smart Cities in China* (EU SME Centre and

across China; by 2018 there were as many as 500.[833] They build upon China's well-established regulatory practice of using public–private petri dishes, or the legislative real-world laboratory approach that China has developed since 1978 in its Special Economic Zones and its Development Zones (noted in Chapter 1).

Building upon this history, the Internet Plus action plan[834] called for modernising all industries by connecting with internet-based technologies. AI was listed as part of the Internet Plus plan when it was launched in 2015 but with few policy markers and unclear direction.[835] The 12th Five-Year Plan, which guided broad economic policy during 2011–2015, also identified Smart City technology as a sector to be strengthened and encouraged, and ministries subsequently began sponsoring programmes and industry alliances.[836] Multinational companies and Chinese companies have been racing to develop and deploy Smart City platforms in which disparate systems communicate and share information.[837] Innovation is, after all, China's number one priority and developing an innovation economy is a political imperative.[838] This must be emphasised when analysing controversial laws such as China's Cyber Security

---

China–Britain Business Council, 2016) <http://ccilc.pt/wp-content/uploads/2017/07/eu_sme_centre_report_-_smart_cities_in_china_i_edit_-_jan_2016_1_1.pdf>.

[833] 'China Outnumbers Other Countries in Smart City Pilots' (*Xinhua* 16 September 2018) <http://www.xinhuanet.com/english/2018-02/20/c_136987058.htm>.

[834] See Guiding Opinions (n 9).

[835] Townsend, *Smart Cities* (n 821).

[836] For example, in 2012, the Ministry of Housing and Urban–Rural Development formally issued «关于开展国家智慧城市试点工作的通知» [Notice of Carrying out the National Smart City Pilots] (People's Republic of China) State Council, 6 December 2012 and «国家智慧城市试点暂行管理办法» [National Interim Measures for Smart City Pilots] (People's Republic of China) State Council, 22 November 2012 and approved 90 Smart City pilot projects.

[837] Many cities (eg, Nanjing, Shenyang, Chengdu and Kunshan) have made strategic Smart City platform cooperation agreements with global software giant IBM. IBM is generally regarded as a leader in the integration and effective centralisation of communication between Smart City industries and government departments.

[838] However, growth for growth's sake is not enough. 'Inclusive growth' was a key theme of «国民经济和社会发展第十二个五年规划» [Twelfth Five-Year Plan for National Economic and Social Development] National People's Congress, 14 March 2011 (12th Five-Year Plan). It continues to be a high priority for Chinese leaders, who face numerous problems that are already impacting the quality of life of Chinese citizens. These include a widening income gap, a growing elderly population and a deteriorating natural environment. China's comparative advantage in manufacturing continues to erode and many university graduates are unemployed. See also McMahon, *China's Great Wall of Debt* (n 815).

Law. No planning document is more important than China's Five-Year Plans. The central place of innovation was reiterated in the Thirteenth Five-Year Plan,[839] the first under President Xi Jinping's leadership, which was released in March 2016. The Thirteenth Five-Year Plan contains five main principles underpinning the policies for China's future development.[840] The first aspirational principle in the Thirteenth Five-Year Plan is innovation – primarily as a driver of economic development and to shift China's economic structure into a higher-quality growth pattern. The other four principles are coordination,[841] green development,[842] opening up and sharing.[843]

Various other influential policy documents have called for greater attention to the development of Chinese Smart Cities. For example, on 15 January 2014, the NDRC and MIIT, along with other relevant departments, promulgated the *Notice to Speed up the Project Implementation of Smart Cities*.[844]

Although at that stage AI was yet to emerge as a high-profile fundamental technology, key to the successful implementation of China's Smart Cities initiatives, it would soon be welcomed with wide open (policymaking) arms.

8.6 Incorporation of AI into Smart City and Innovation Policies: The AI Plan

The Chinese term for AI, 人工智能 (*rengong zhineng*), first appeared in Chinese government statements in July 2015, in the State Council

---

[839] 《国民经济和社会发展第十三个五年规划》 [Thirteenth Five-Year Plan for National Economic and Social Development] National People's Congress, 17 March 2016 (Thirteenth Five-Year Plan). China's Five-Year Plans act as blueprints containing the country's social, economic and political goals. They encompass and intertwine with existing policies, regional plans and strategic initiatives. A Five-Year Plan signals the Chinese government's vision for future reforms and communicates this to other parts of the bureaucracy, industry players and Chinese citizens. It is also a living document that will go through constant review and revision over its five-year period.
[840] Ibid.
[841] Coordination means to ensure balanced coordinated development among rural and urban areas, and across different industries.
[842] Green development means protecting the environment and pursuing environmentally friendly economic growth.
[843] Sharing means 'Development for the People, by the People and Shared by the Entire Population'.
[844] Cited in Yang, Clery and Di Liello, *Sector Report: Smart Cities in China* (n 832) 8. The link to the Notice <http://gjss.ndrc.gov.cn/zttp/xxhm/201401/t20140113_692263.htm> is no longer active.

document Guiding Opinions on Actively Promoting the 'Internet Plus' Action Plan.[845] This document identified AI as one of 11 priority areas to implement government strategy to accelerate the use of ICT in conventional industries.[846] However, it merely listed AI without further detail. In March 2016, the phrase 人工智能 (artificial intelligence) also appeared in the outline of the Thirteenth Five-Year Plan[847] but the first detailed policy document to highlight AI was the May 2016 'Internet Plus' AI Three-Year Action Implementation Plan.[848] It outlined ambitious goals such as creating a multi-billion renminbi AI industry by 2018.[849]

At the World Intelligence Congress in Tianjin in May 2017, Chinese Minister of Science and Technology Wan Gang announced that China would release its own AI-specific national development plan soon. He also stated that steps would be taken to build closer cooperation with

---

[845] See Guiding Opinions (n 9).

[846] AI has since been prominent in numerous central planning documents. In August 2016, China's 13th Five-Year Plan for National Science and Technology Innovation made AI 'a project of High Importance' («'十三五'国家科技创新规划» [13th Five-Year Plan for National Science and Technology Innovation] (People's Republic of China) State Council, 8 August 2016). In December 2016, the 13th Five-Year Plan for Developing National Strategic and Emerging Industries identified AI as number six among 69 major tasks for the central government to pursue: «'十三五'国家战略性新兴产业发展规划» [13th Five-Year Plan for Developing National Strategic and Emerging Industries] (People's Republic of China) State Council, 8 August 2016. In January 2017, the Catalogue for the Guidance of Important Products and Services in Strategic and Emerging Industries (2016 version) included AI for the first time. Development plans with a focus on AI have been released by the central agencies responsible for policy planning since 2016, such as the Robotics Industry Development Plan (2016–2020), jointly released by NDRC, MIIT and MOF in April 2016, which set concrete technology targets and government strategies for developing the robotics industry in China in the next five years.

[847] See above n 839 and accompanying text.

[848] «'互联网+'人工智能三年行动实施方案» ['Internet Plus' AI Three-Year Action Implementation Plan] (People's Republic of China) MIIT, 25 May 2016. Jointly released by NDRC, MIIT, MOST and CAC in May 2016, it outlined nine key engineering areas in AI technology development between 2016 and 2018. Building upon the Guiding Opinions (n 9), the plan also identified specific strategies the government would take to promote the development of technology and industry. These plans echo numerous high-level policy strategies to facilitate AI R&D. See Yujia He, 'How China Is Preparing for an AI-Powered Future' (*Wilson Briefs*, 20 June 2017) <https://www.wilsoncenter.org/publication/how-china-preparing-for-ai-powered-future>.

[849] In August 2016, the 13th Five-Year Plan for National Science and Technology Innovation (国家科技创新规划) launched 15 'Science and Technology Innovation 2030 Major Programmes' (科技创新 2030 – 重大项目) that included both big data and intelligent manufacturing and robotics.

international AI organisations and encourage foreign AI companies to set up R&D centres in China.[850] That statement seemed antithetical to the data localisation provisions within China's Cyber Security Law.

On 8 July 2017, China published a new national AI roadmap, the New Generation AI Development Plan[851] (AI Plan), to guide the development of AI until the year 2030. The AI Plan lifted AI to the level of national strategy. Detailed AI planning and development standards were released on the heels of the AI Plan.[852] The AI Plan represents an attempt to lead the world in AI by 2030, pursuing a 'first mover advantage' to become the 'premier global AI innovation centre'. China's objectives for advances in AI are divided into three stages, with 2020, 2025 and 2030 respectively aimed at keeping pace, then reaching a 'leading level', then becoming the world's 'premier AI innovation centre' by 2030.

The AI Plan incorporates projects that seek to leverage synergies between AI and other emerging technologies. These technologies include big data, cloud computing, intelligent manufacturing, robotics, quantum computing, quantum communications and brain science.[853] The multibillion-dollar AI Plan will support advantages in next-generation AI technologies that 'could result in paradigm changes, including brain-inspired Neural Network architectures and quantum-accelerated machine learning'.[854]

---

[850] Ibid.
[851] AI Plan (n 819).
[852] For example, in 2018 the Chinese government released its AI Standardization White Paper. The 98-page document was edited by the China Electronics Standards Institute under the guidance of the National Standards Management Committee Second Ministry of Industry, but was a joint effort by more than 30 academic and industry organisations overseen by the Chinese Electronics Standards Institute. AI safety and privacy standards are discussed at length. See «人工智能标准化白皮书 (2018 版)» [AI Standardization White Paper (2018)] (People's Republic of China) National Standards Management Committee Second Ministry of Industry, January 2018.
[853] «根据'规划'将形成'1+N'人工智能项目群» [According to the Plan the '1+N' AI Project Group Will Be Formed] (*State Council Information Office*, 21 July 2017) <http://www.scio.gov.cn/32344/32345/35889/36946/zy36950/Document/1559032/1559032.htm>.
The AI Plan aims to realise the policies of the Planning for Development of New Generation AI and Made in China 2025 (n 817) policy statements. The plan covers smart sensing, smart manufacturing and AI peripheral industries. In terms of products, the plan sets 2020 target performance levels for smart connected vehicles, smart service robots, smart drones, medical image-aided diagnosis systems, identification systems based on image recognition, smart speech interaction systems, smart language translation systems and smart home-use devices.
[854] Elsa B Kania, 'Technological Entanglement? Artificial Intelligence in the US–China Relationship' (2017) 17(17) *China Brief* 11 <https://jamestown.org/program/technological-entanglement-artificial-intelligence-u-s-china-relationship>.

The AI Plan also describes in detail how China lags behind the developed world in many key areas of technologies: basic theory, core algorithms, key equipment, high-end chips, major products and systems, foundational materials, components, software and interfaces. The plan calls for concrete steps to close these gaps and allow China to become a world leader in AI development.

As a result of the AI Plan, AI has become the new frontier in the battle between the United States and China in technology development, something this study acknowledges but does not explore in depth. It should be noted, however, that in October 2016, the Obama administration had published the *National AI Research and Development Strategic Plan for AI Research*, which even then noted that China had overtaken the United States and was leading the world in journal articles on Deep Learning.[855] The Strategic Plan asked: 'What are the right priorities for Federal investments in AI, especially regarding areas and timeframes where industry is unlikely to invest? Are there opportunities for industrial and international R&D collaborations that advance US priorities?'[856] China was seemingly in mind when that sentence was drafted.

However, Chinese internet scholar Rogier Creemers notes validly that China's AI Plan is trying to resolve Chinese governance problems, not necessarily attacking Western companies.[857] There are, as noted, practical policy reasons why China loves AI-powered technologies such as robots in manufacturing.[858] Chinese manufacturing is currently facing surging wages and labour shortages and competition from nearby countries with lower labour costs; these are driving China's move away from low-level manufacturing to mid-level and advanced manufacturing. China is keen to invest in AI as 'the engine of the next industrial revolution' and seeks to reduce gaps in basic research breakthroughs and high-end product development.[859] The Chinese government

---

[855] See National Science and Technology Council, Networking and Information Technology Research and Development Subcommittee, *The National Artificial Intelligence Research and Development Strategic Plan* (Report, October 2016) <https://www.nitrd.gov/PUBS/national_ai_rd_strategic_plan.pdf>.
[856] Ibid 5.
[857] Graham Webster et al, 'China's Plan to "Lead" in AI: Purpose, Prospects, and Problems' (*New America*, 1 August 2017) <https://www.newamerica.org/cybersecurity-initiative/blog/chinas-plan-lead-ai-purpose-prospects-and-problems/>.
[858] In the Thirteenth Five-Year Plan, the Chinese government stated that it aims to increase its annual production of industrial robots to 100,000 by 2020.
[859] The Wilson Brief suggested this may create issues such as academic corruption and embezzlement: He, 'How China Is Preparing for an AI-Powered Future' (n 848) 13.

therefore attaches high importance to AI, as an effective tool to boost industrial productivity, and early reports suggest the AI Plan is achieving positive results.[860]

Part III of the AI Plan is particularly relevant for China's Smart City initiative. It seeks to create theoretical and applied AI breakthroughs associated with Informatisation and better governance. A new 'AI Plus' economy is described in the AI Plan that promotes 'mutual trust', encourages biometric identities and notes that China's Social Credit system[861] is still on the agenda. Smart Cities and smart courts promoting 'intelligentisation of social governance' are an important goal of the AI Plan.[862]

Yet the phrases that define Network Sovereignty, such as 'secure and controllable' along with cyber security and national security, are also frequently mentioned throughout the AI Plan. The AI Plan also illustrates the fundamental tension explored in this book, as there remained throughout 2017–2021 an inherent tension between these two evolving policies: Internet Plus promoting AI, and a potentially restrictive environment for innovation embodied by Network Sovereignty.

Three things are clear from the AI Plan and recent associated policy documents. First, the Chinese government has become fully aware of the crucial importance of developing AI for China's future economic development and its status as an advanced, strong nation. Second, the Chinese government wishes to guide the development of private sector AI technologies towards solving governance problems and improving the efficiency of social management. Third, the government will provide

---

[860] Josh Horwitz, 'China Is Rapidly Making Robots That Will One Day Manufacture Everything You Buy' (*Quartz*, 3 March 2017) <https://qz.com/922742/china-is-rapidly-making-robots-that-will-one-day-manufacture-everything-you-buy>.

[861] Emerging as a comprehensive governance scheme in China, the 'Social Credit System' seeks to promote the norms of 'trust' in Chinese society by rewarding behaviour that is considered 'trust keeping' and punishing those considered 'trust breaking'. In practical terms, the development of such a system in China may seem sinister, but two elements invite moderation. (1) The system is not one unified apparatus, it began attempting to solve a huge problem – the large unbanked economy – and it has run into many hurdles. China is notorious for its shadow banking industry. The future Social Credit System could help to control this murky industry, which is currently without regulatory oversight. (2) It is a pilot system of countless public and private trials nationwide that is intended to be finalised in 2020 as a national system. There are a lot of fallacies floating around regarding the system; for a balanced view of its positives and potential perils see Yu-Jie Chen, Ching-Fu Lin and Han-Wei Liu, '"Rule of Trust": The Power and Perils of China's Social Credit Megaproject (2018) 32(1) *Columbia Journal of Asian Law* 1.

[862] See AI Plan (n 819) section 3 ('Construct a Safe and Convenient Intelligent Society').

research funding and, more important, numerous pilot programmes throughout China for AI firms to test promising new technologies with governance applications. The emerging Smart Cities, while not the sole testing grounds for AI technologies, will provide crucial large-scale petri dishes for experimentation and rollouts. In this way, Smart Cities are tied in with China's push to become a world leader in AI technologies, and they demonstrate in the clearest form the symbiosis between public (government) policy goals and private tech firms that have the innovative capacity to deliver practical AI solutions.

What this also means is that the success of the Chinese government in achieving these policy goals relies heavily on the successful growth and continuing ability of private AI firms to innovate. Thus, despite the government's desire to maintain control of data and Network Security, it will not jeopardise the development of the AI industry in China by strictly enforcing data localisation rules, or other measures that hamper those firms' access to information and foreign technology.

The remaining sections of this chapter demonstrate further the inseparable links between the Chinese government, Smart Cities as policy petri dishes, and top-down support for private AI firms. This, in turn, will help to explain the impact of the 'fuzzy logic' approach adopted in the data localisation rules and other relevant provisions of the Cyber Security Law.

8.7 The AI Plan and Smart City Policies as Top-Down Signalling

China's AI Plan will likely have its strongest impact as a signal broadcast to local officials throughout China's sprawling bureaucracy, rather than as a detailed top-down blueprint for AI development.[863] Despite its vague aspirational language and lack of concrete implementing measures, it imbues AI with the approval of the central government and the Chinese Communist Party, both supporting and actively incentivising local projects that use AI, including public–private partnerships and Smart City projects.

---

[863] Graham Webster et al label the Chinese AI Plan, as reflective of Chinese policymaking, a 'champagne pyramid': a tension-producing bureaucratic structure reflecting a cascade of subordinate problems at various layers, which must be solved 'in order to defuse the dominant contradiction and move forward to the next stage'. See Webster et al, 'China's Plan to "Lead" in AI' (n 857).

The AI Plan is a long-term aspirational document, without much insight into how it will be achieved. However, Webster et al note that it is not a 'paper-generating exercise. Real political capital is spent on drafting a document such as this and considerable resources will be invested in its implementation'.[864] Segal also notes that the technology industry was extensively consulted on the AI Plan.[865] It also created new bureaucracies such as an AI Plan Implementation Office.[866]

There is a longstanding model of 'central signalling' in Chinese government policymaking.[867] However, despite this long-established practice, the role of government policy in driving China's progress in AI has been both 'widely remarked upon and widely misunderstood'.[868] Misunderstandings tend to fall into two differing conceptions of the primary mechanism by which the Chinese government drives AI development: by overstating the importance of 'picking winners that it

---

[864] Ibid. Adam Segal, another Chinese internet expert, provided the following commentary: 'For a country that releases a bevy of slogan-filled "plans" each year, most of which are as vague as they are forgettable, the AI development plan is different. What the plan lacks in concrete details, it makes up for in vision and ambition. It depicts a future China overcoming the challenges of an ageing population and resource constraints through integrating AI into everything from agriculture and manufacturing to governing and public security': Adam Segal, 'Beijing's AI Strategy: Old-School Central Planning with a Futuristic Twist' (*Council on Foreign Relations*, 9 August 2017) <https://www.cfr.org/blog/beijings-ai-strategy-old-school-central-planning-futuristic-twist>.

[865] Segal, 'Beijing's AI Strategy' (n 864). Segal noted: 'In all likelihood, China's cadres already knew that. Government ministries, provinces, and large municipalities like Shanghai and Tianjin have already unveiled a slew of policies to nurture the technology as part of the country's Thirteenth Five-Year Plan. Scientists from the Chinese Academy of Science (CAS) and Chinese Academy of Engineering (CAE) have embarked on a series of AI "megaprojects" including "China AI 2.0" and "China Brain Project," which some have compared to the US Apollo program. China's commercial enterprises are responding, if not already leading the way. The big three – Baidu, Alibaba, and Tencent – are investing heavily in AI. At the same time, a new class of large Chinese AI mega-enterprises, like Sensetime, Mobvoi, and iFlytek, are rising. Unconstrained by strict privacy norms, China is arguably commercializing certain AI applications, like facial and object recognition, at a faster pace than the West.'

[866] Ibid. Segal commented that this reflects the politicking of central planning, as government agencies vie for power, since AI development is being largely driven by the private sector.

[867] See Chapter 1, Section 1.4.

[868] Kai-Fu Lee and Matt Sheehan, 'Is China Outsmarting the US in AI?' (*Hoover Institute*, 29 October 2018) <https://www.hoover.org/research/chinas-rise-artificial-intelligence-ingredients-and-economic-implications>.

showers with subsidies, or by issuing top-down commands dictating what technologies to create'.[869]

In fact, China's science and technology bureaucracy mobilises a range of different methods to encourage the development of key industries and incentivise private firm investment and R&D into AI and related technologies. First, the government actively incentivises private venture capital investment in AI through 'guiding funds' – a financial structure by which public funds are used to guide private venture capital investors into certain sectors by increasing their potential upside without totally removing the downside risks.[870] For example, a local government might invest 'guiding funds' in a start-up that can assist with sustainability problems, such as an electric car manufacturer.[871]

Second, in terms of top-down directives, China's Ministry of Science and Technology (MOST) has set ambitious and highly specific targets for the performance of indigenously produced AI chips, and it is pouring major resources into achieving those goals. The Chinese domestic development of powerful processing chips for AI and deep research certainly requires top-down government support.[872] These processing chips power computing machines to learn. According to Jimmy Goodrich, Vice President of Global Policy at the Semiconductor Industry Association, a US trade group:

> Semiconductors are arguably humanity's greatest achievement to date ... They're still central to everything that's modern or electronic, whether you're driving a car, or surfing the internet, or using a supercomputer – everything is ultimately based on a semiconductor, and lots of them.[873]

As they are incredibly complicated to build, top-down planning is needed for semiconductors.

---

[869] Ibid.
[870] See Lee, *AI Superpowers* (n 783) 64–5 ('Guiding Funds').
[871] Jia Chen, 'China's Venture Capital Guiding Funds: Policies and Practice' (2010) 2(3) *Journal of Chinese Entrepreneurship* 292.
[872] The road for world-class Chinese GPU chips will be long and hard, according to the Semiconductor Industry Association, as the R&D necessary to make advancements in chip design can span decades. Further, beyond the massive challenge of designing world-class chips, there are barriers to manufacturing them. Setting up a fabrication facility can cost US$10–15 billion dollars. See Josh Horwitz, 'Why the Semiconductor Is Suddenly at the Heart of US–China Tech Tensions' (*Quartz*, 25 July 2018) <https://qz.com/1335801/us-china-tech-why-the-semiconductor-is-suddenly-at-the-heart-of-us-china-tensions>.
[873] Ibid.

GPU chips or semiconductors are a key element to powering AI-based innovations and a major Chinese policy goal under the AI Plan. They are also one important part of the 'competitive entanglement'[874] between China and foreign tech companies. Currently China is most reliant on one US company in particular: Nvidia. This is because GPU chips or semiconductors are a key element for powering AI-based innovations and Chinese companies are most in need of high-quality Nvidia chips. China's Science and Technology Minister Wan Gang reiterated in March 2017 during a parliamentary meeting that government finance will lead the way in AI research, including the development of supercomputers, and high-performance semiconductor chips, software and the hiring of key talent to lead the field.[875]

Stimulated by this clear government targeting, numerous private Chinese companies ranging from Huawei[876] and Alibaba[877] to start-ups like Horizon Robotics[878] are all racing to develop their own chips. Fengxiang Ma (马凤翔), director of ASIC[879] chip design at Horizon Robotics (which develops AI for cameras and vehicles), was quoted as saying that the number of companies only making chips may fall in the future. That is, AI companies will need to build their own special-purpose chips, designed for the AI they create. AI companies will expand into AI chip manufacturing to ensure that the core technologies (chips) are suited for their intended applications but also for commercial reasons to alleviate pressure from their supply chains on companies such as Nvidia. Thus, the Chinese government is also funding numerous companies to build their own chips through various grants of up to US$47

---

[874] Kania, 'Technological Entanglement?' (n 854).
[875] Amanda Lee, 'World Dominance in Three Steps: China Sets out Road Map to Lead in Artificial Intelligence by 2030' (*South China Morning Post*, 21 July 2017) <http://www.scmp.com/tech/enterprises/article/2103568/world-dominance-three-steps-china-sets-out-road-map-lead-artificial>.
[876] Shidong Zhang, 'US Semiconductor Makers Dwarf Chinese Peers in Market Valuation as China's Chip Dream Remains Distant' (*South China Morning Post*, 23 April 2018) <https://www.scmp.com/business/china-business/article/2142929/us-semiconductor-makers-dwarf-chinese-peers-market-valuation>.
[877] Jordan Novet, 'Why Tech Companies Are Racing Each Other to Make Their Own Custom AI Chips' (*CNBC*, 21 April 2018) <https://www.cnbc.com/2018/04/21/alibaba-joins-google-others-in-making-custom-ai-chips.html>.
[878] Yiting Sun, 'China Wants to Make the Chips That Will Add AI to Any Gadget' (*MIT Technology Review*, 24 January 2018) <https://www.technologyreview.com/2018/01/24/241365/china-wants-to-make-the-chips-that-will-add-ai-to-any-gadget/>.
[879] ASIC stands for application-specific integrated circuit.

billion.[880] MOST lists 13 projects for developing cutting-edge AI technologies with completion scheduled for 2021. One of them is specifically to develop Neural Network chips with performance 20 times that of the dominant Nvidia Tesla M40 processing chip.[881] This has proved a difficult goal. As of early 2021, Tsinghua Unigroup, a very high-profile Chinese conglomerate that has long sought to become a semiconductor powerhouse and is 51% owned by China's famous Tsinghua University, is riddled with debt from its attempts to build and invest in indigenous Chinese computer chips.[882]

Clearly there is overlap between these different government strategies. For example, 'guiding funds' will include not just AI start-ups but also investment in firms developing core chip technologies. So there will be a combination of direct subsidies, R&D funding and guided venture capital fund investment.

8.8 The Role of Public–Private Partnerships in China's National AI Platforms

A third way in which China's government is attempting to stimulate AI development is through designating selected firms as members of an 'AI National Team'. The currently designated team includes the BATs, iFlytek and (since September 2018) SenseTime. Public–private partnerships mean that private firms play an important role in creating data standards and technology platforms.

The AI National Team is responsible for China's National Open Innovation Platforms for New Generation AI (National AI Platforms),

---

[880] Chris Arkenberg, 'China Inside: Chinese Semiconductors Will Power Artificial Intelligence' (*Deloitte Insights*, 11 December 2018) <https://www2.deloitte.com/insights/us/en/industry/technology/technology-media-and-telecom-predictions/chinese-semiconductor-industry.html>.

[881] The Chinese government's desire to challenge Nvidia specifically is a focus of this article: Tom Simonite, 'China Recruits Baidu, Alibaba and Tencent to AI "National Team"' (*Wired*, 20 November 2017) <https://www.wired.com/story/china-challenges-nvidias-hold-on-artificial-intelligence-chips>.

[882] The state-backed conglomerate, which has warned it may not be able to make upcoming bond payments, had $31 billion in debt as of late June 2020, more than half of which was due to mature in a year's time, filings show. In contrast, it had roughly $8 billion in cash and cash equivalents. See Josh Horwitz, 'Analysis: China's Would-Be Chip Darling Tsinghua Unigroup Bedevilled by Debt and Bad Bets' (*Reuters*, 20 January 2021) <https://www.reuters.com/article/us-tsinghua-unigroup-strategy-analysis-idUKKBN29P0C2>.

which are private entities engaged to help build China's AI sector. Platforms should therefore be viewed as emerging regulatory partners in China. These companies have been designated by MOST to lead China's AI ambitions through the creation of open innovation platforms built on AI source code, which will be made accessible to all of China's digital enterprises.[883] In November 2017, the government published a notice stating that the AI National Team (国家队 – *guojiadui*) would leverage their respective strengths to build 'open innovation platforms' in four different fields.[884] In this way, the Chinese government has taken a distinctive approach to AI innovation. This is related to the creation of a platform-based digital ecosystem in which AI technologies can be supplied, diffused and extended to enable a wider range of enterprises to engage in open-source platform-based innovation, by creating several distinct industry foci for private sector companies as articulated in the 2017 National Open Innovation Platforms for New Generation AI.[885] Item 11 of the 2017 document cites the creation of domestic Chinese open-source platforms.

The industry foci are as follows. Baidu's focus will be on autonomous driving. Alibaba's cloud computing division is tasked with a project called 'city brains',[886] a set of AI solutions to improve urban life, including

---

[883] Meng Jing and Sarah Dai, 'China Recruits Baidu, Alibaba and Tencent to AI "National Team"' (*South China Morning Post*, 21 November 2017) <https://www.scmp.com/tech/china-tech/article/2120913/china-recruits-baidu-alibaba-and-tencent-ai-national-team>.

[884] «15个部委合力首批 4 家国家创新平台确立-聚焦我国新一代人工智能发展规划» [15 Ministries Join Forces to Establish the First Batch of 4 National Innovation Platforms – Focusing on China's New Generation of AI Development Plan] (*Gov.cn*, 23 November 2017) <http://www.gov.cn/guowuyuan/2017-11/23/content_5241718.htm>. The modularisation of AI technologies is taking place through an open-source Platforms as a Service (PaaS) structure, by which large platform integrators are enabling cloud-based resources for other companies to access and innovate upon. The goal is for AI start-ups and established enterprises to build upon the National AI Platforms, thereby allowing these companies to start their product development process at a more mature juncture in terms of algorithmic development.

[885] «国家新一代人工智能开放创新平台» [National Open Innovation Platforms for New Generation AI] (*Gov.cn*, 4 August 2019) <http://www.gov.cn/xinwen/2019-08/04/content_5418542.htm>. The document refers to the notion of China's AI National Team (人工智能国家队), a new class of AI companies that are either backed by national institutes or are closely integrated into government-funded programmes.

[886] Dr Jian Wang (王坚), Alibaba CTO and former assistant managing director at Microsoft Research Asia, noted that by 'brain', Alibaba is referring to a 'living city': 王融 [Wang Rong], «TC 杭州: 王坚博士: '人工智能' 是人类傲慢的名词产物» [TC Hangzhou: Dr Jian Wang: 'Artificial Intelligence' Is a Name Resulting from Human Arrogance] (*TechCrunch*, 2 July 2018) <https://mp.weixin.qq.com/s/1jNalbynko_MtPxQ_PERBQ>.

smart transport. Tencent will focus on computer vision for medical diagnosis. Shenzhen-listed iFlyTek, a renowned voice-recognition start-up, will specialise in voice intelligence. In September 2018, SenseTime – one of China's biggest facial recognition 'unicorns' – joined the state-approved ranks to establish an 'open innovation platform for next-generation AI' on intelligent vision.[887]

One of the core ideas of this programme is to strengthen China's AI ecosystem by requiring the AI National Team to make their AI infrastructure and technologies open source, so that small-to-medium sized enterprises are able to innovate on the National AI Platforms, either by supporting projects directly connected to the ecosystem, or by leveraging some of the infrastructure to create their own innovative applications. This will help to diffuse AI technologies more broadly than if the AI National Team and other enterprises with their own proprietary technologies were the sole market providers of AI solutions.

Furthermore, as part of its role as an AI National Team member, Baidu is leading China's National Engineering Laboratory for Deep Learning Technologies, and contributes to the National Engineering Laboratory for Brain-Inspired Intelligence Technology and Applications. Alibaba Cloud is working with the new National Engineering Laboratory of Big Data Systems and Software, led by Beijing's Tsinghua University. AliYun is also working with the Macao and Malaysian governments on Smart City projects. Clearly the symbiotic relationship between private firms and public/government institutions is becoming further entangled.

This is the first time some of China's biggest private companies have been named in such a strategy. Previously, 'national champions' were state-owned model enterprises.[888] Yet as the new gatekeepers of China's

---

[887] 李诗 [Li Shi], «商汤成为第五大国家人工智能开放创新平台» [Sensetime Becomes the Fifth Company to Join the National AI Open Innovation Platform] (*Leifeng*, 20 September 2018) <https://www.leiphone.com/news/201809/Xf5pNSS103T1cZMh.html>.

[888] See Liwen Lin and Curtis Milhaupt, 'We Are the (National) Champions' (2013) 65(4) *Stanford Law Review* 697. The distinction between the 'AI National Team' and the previous 'National Champion' model is unclear. All five members of the AI National Team were already independent, self-sufficient hybrid firms backed with a lot of foreign capital before they were assigned this 'National AI Platform' task. Previously 'National Champions' were SOEs propped up with government funding. There is also a lot of competition within each of the AI National Team's 'designated' tasks.

Designating national champions is also not a new policy and it has mixed results: see, eg, Thomas A Hemphill and George O White III, 'China's National Champions: The Evolution of a National Industrial Policy – Or a New Era of Economic Protectionism?' (2013) 55(2) *Thunderbird International Business Review* 193–212.

datasets, the BATs must cooperate with the government, and vice versa. Indeed, the 'government's blessing could give Baidu a leg-up when it comes to cooperating with carmakers on self-driving vehicles, and provide Tencent with wider access to hospital data'.[889]

Some have questioned the strategy of naming an AI National Team, as it 'could impact market vitality, posing a challenge to industry latecomers'.[890] However, Yu Kai, the founder of start-up Horizon Robotics and former head of the Baidu Institute of Deep Learning, argued that while only five Chinese companies are responsible for building the open platforms, 'the technologies and resources of the platforms will be open to everyone, which will benefit the entire industry. AI start-ups still have their chance'.[891] Furthermore, as Elsa Kania, an expert in Chinese civil–military technologies, noted: 'Beijing may have labeled Baidu, Alibaba, Tencent, and iFlytek a "national team" in AI, but these are not traditional "national champions": they have all emerged as leaders in the field primarily through their own efforts, but are now also receiving state support and contributing to a national agenda.'[892]

The approach of dividing projects between the BATs may also be a key for China-wide cooperation as it would otherwise be difficult for the Chinese government to get these huge companies to work together cooperatively. For example, Baidu's search engine blocks searches for Alibaba sites and Tencent blocks content linked to Alibaba in browsers that open through the WeChat app.[893]

SenseTime executives also reportedly stated that this position gave the selected companies privileged positions for national technical standard setting and was also intended to give the companies confidence that they would not be in direct competition with SOEs.[894] In December 2018, SenseTime co-founder Bill Xu was quoted as saying 'we are very lucky to be a private company working at a technology that will be critical for the next two decades. Historically, governments would dominate

---

[889] Jing and Dai, 'China Recruits Baidu, Alibaba and Tencent' (n 883).
[890] Ibid.
[891] Ibid. Yu took part in the Technology Ministry planning meetings as a member of China's newly established AI strategy consultancy committee.
[892] Elsa B Kania, 'China May Become the World's Leader in AI. But at What Cost?' (*China File*, 30 July 2018) <http://www.chinafile.com/conversation/china-may-become-worlds-leader-ai-what-cost>.
[893] This fact is made known to users when accessing these applications.
[894] Gregory C Allen, 'Understanding China's AI Strategy' (*Center for a New American Security*, 6 February 2019) <https://www.cnas.org/publications/reports/understanding-chinas-ai-strategy>.

nuclear, rocket, and comparable technologies and not trust private companies'.[895]

8.9 Public–Private Standard Setting and Interoperability

The formation of National AI Platforms, importantly, helps the government and regulators set new standards and coordinate leading market players, with the aim of standardising public data structures within and across provinces in areas of hospitals, security, traffic and so on. The standardisation needed for safety, performance, latency, correctness, bias and even the privacy of AI models – all are new and complex emerging fields for regulators.

A major challenge for a range of China's public and administrative bodies and institutions, including the healthcare sector, is the lack of data definition standards and rules for business information (discussed throughout Chapter 7).[896] Public–private partnerships mean that private firms play an important role in creating data standards. China's Minister of Science and Technology, Wan Gang, has confirmed that private enterprises play a key role in the choice of technical routes and the formulation of industry product standards.[897]

Furthermore, to scale up Machine Learning and Deep Learning development into a predictable, reliable and efficient operation requires standardisation to help maximise the participation of independent parties.[898] This is the reasoning behind increased collaboration between the Chinese government and its private sector AI National Team in software and algorithmic development. A larger AI ecosystem can be formed on the back of strong industry standards.

National AI Platforms are thus being used as instruments helping to diffuse AI innovation, while enabling policymakers and regulators to gain insights into how the industry is proceeding in terms of standard setting,

---

[895] Ibid.
[896] Standardisation is associated with interoperability. In order to scale development, interoperability is needed to maximise the opportunity of reusable development. China has laid out an extensive policy framework for standardisation in its AI industry, while the AI National Team provides a number of direct inroads for policymakers to observe industrial best practices and engage in the development of criteria for standards in alignment with leading existing practices for interoperability.
[897] «人工智能国家队正式出炉 阿里云负责建设城市大脑» [The AI National Team Officially Released Alibaba Cloud to Build the City Brain] (*Sohu*, 16 November 2017) <http://www.sohu.com/a/204718930_694841>.
[898] Standardising best practices for developing AI means that an increased number of teams accelerate their development, but also that innovative solutions can be developed independently and be plugged in to accelerate a larger process.

related information infrastructure and compliance with government requirements. China's National AI Platforms can therefore be viewed as another structural instrument designed to better handle the development of a new and emerging technological regime.

8.9.1 Questions Remain Regarding the AI National Team

By creating National AI Platforms, China's government is strongly supporting China's AI National Team, although the exact details of this support have not been disclosed. While the AI National Team is meant to build the foundations for China's indigenous AI industry, the strategy raises multiple issues. For example, first, it remains unclear exactly what it means to be a member of the AI National Team, as information about preferential access to sources of public data and funding has not been made public.

It appears that the companies will be able to independently train their AI algorithms on publicly provided data, giving the AI National Team a competitive edge.[899] However, it remains unclear what kind of data is being shared with the AI National Team. For example, reportedly, SenseTime and other national AI champions have compiled training sets of more than 2 billion images while working closely with public authorities on specific use cases such as the implementation of local surveillance systems, but presumably there are other kinds of data being shared too.[900]

Second, it is unclear where the boundaries between the companies' private platforms and public–private platforms for open AI innovation lie – if they exist at all. So, under China's privacy regime, which includes real-name registration (see Chapter 7), how will China's new AI National Team share information with government entities?

Third, while each member of the AI National Team is responsible for building a distinct platform in a designated area of AI, it remains unclear exactly how much the varying partnerships benefit the individual companies in terms of allowing feedback loops into their internal product portfolios and AI-based offerings. That is, which companies might gain

---

[899] Data sharing provides a clear edge for some companies in terms of further training and improving their algorithms.
[900] Amanda Lentino, 'This Chinese Facial Recognition Start-Up Can Identify a Person in Seconds' (*CNBC*, 19 May 2019) <https://www.cnbc.com/2019/05/16/this-chinese-facial-recognition-start-up-can-id-a-person-in-seconds.html>.

an unfair benefit in certain areas of business related to Smart City or medical imaging, and which companies may lose out, since most players on the AI National Team offer competing AI products in overlapping sectors?

The AI National Team continues China's legacy of public–private petri dishes of innovation. They bridge private entrepreneurship and public objectives, alleviating governance issues facing public authorities while engaging private firms in new opportunities. The AI National Team will probably help to address key public needs, but ensuring compatibility in public and private objectives, especially in data sharing, will remain a difficult issue.

The operation and potential success of these open-source platforms is considered further in the next chapter. In terms of the public–private symbiosis, which is the main focus of this chapter, while the formation of AI National Teams combined with guiding funds and direct subsidies to promote AI-related technologies will doubtless stimulate China's private sector AI development, they may also lead to distorting effects.[901] Subsidising every AI company across the economy would be wildly inefficient and ultimately unfeasible, and it is highly unlikely that a central policy blueprint could efficiently direct state resources towards exploiting all the potential applications of an uncertain and emerging technology such as AI. China's industrial policies have often led to costly distortions in various industries (as noted in Chapter 1). 'While the unparalleled enthusiasm of local governments will accelerate China's AI development considerably, it also carries the risk of creating overcapacities.'[902] Designating national champions as a policy has, after all, had mixed results in the past.[903]

According to Lee and Sheehan, therefore, subsidies and top-down commands will probably not be the government's most impactful means of accelerating AI development. Instead, it will be the way that the central government's AI Plan incentivises local officials to work with private

---

[901] Ibid.
[902] Jaqueline Ives and Anna Holzmann, 'Local Governments Power Up to Advance China's National AI Agenda' (*MERICS*, 26 April 2018) <https://www.merics.org/en/blog/local-governments-power-advance-chinas-national-ai-agenda>. In the pursuit to outbid each other, some local government targets even exceed ambitious national goals. Eleven local governments published targets for their AI core industries for 2020. Accumulated, this would create an AI core industry of almost ¥400 billion in 2020, exceeding the national target of ¥150 billion more than twofold.
[903] See, eg, Hemphill and White III, 'China's National Champions' (n 888).

sector actors on adapting public infrastructure and accelerating public adoption of AI for solving specific and immediate governance problems – in other words, local public–private petri dishes.[904]

Despite the possible risks identified, in August 2019 the Chinese government expanded the AI National Team to include 10 leading tech companies, among them Huawei, Hikvision, Xiaomi, JD.com, Qihoo 360, Megvii and Yitu Tech.[905] The nature of these collaborations is in the early stages of being publicly disclosed, but it seems that these new AI National Team members were at least in part being named as part of bolstering Chinese AI capabilities and offsetting detrimental impacts of the so-called United States–China trade war.[906] China now has a total of 15 AI National Team members since it started this initiative in 2017. By 2019, this AI National Team expanded to increase the pace of AI development as China's decoupling from the United States was accelerated by the Trump administration's blacklist of Chinese tech companies, many of which joined the AI National Team.

8.10 Local Government Responses to Central Top-Down Signalling

Local government policy petri dishes are crucial because, if AI is to expand its impact from the data-driven commercial world into the physical world – via autonomous vehicles, medical AI and Smart Cities – it will require the proactive adaptation of public infrastructure, and proactive adoption by local governments and public entities. Accelerating deployment of autonomous vehicles may entail changes to public roads, such as embedding sensors or reserving separate lanes for pilot programmes. Bringing AI's benefits to the public education or healthcare spheres will also require analogous tweaks to those systems. All of these changes will also necessitate the creation of new local regulatory frameworks, laws that can embody shared values of privacy or responsibility while harnessing the new possibilities unlocked by the technology.

---

[904] Lee and Sheehan, 'Is China Outsmarting the US in AI?' (n 868).
[905] Sarah Dai, 'China Adds Huawei, Hikvision to Expanded "National Team" Spearheading Country's AI Efforts' (*South China Morning Post*, 29 August 2019) <https://www.scmp.com/tech/big-tech/article/3024966/china-adds-huawei-hikvision-expanded-national-team-spearheading>.
[906] Ibid.

Local bureaucratic actors will employ a range of tools: public procurement, pilot projects, infrastructure adaptations, subsidies and regulatory accommodation. For example, an agricultural official in western China might look to push a pilot project using autonomous seeding drones at state-owned agricultural facilities. A mayor in a large city such as Hangzhou might work with Alibaba to install the infrastructure for a City Brain project that optimises traffic and emergency services using computer vision. A university president in a manufacturing region might establish a new public–private research institute focused on factory automation.[907] Further, the Supreme People's Court's China Judgments Network has made publicly available over 90 million court judgments from all over China since 2011.

Encouraged by the central government's positive signalling, numerous provinces and cities are already spending billions on developing robotics and AI research, and new experimental petri dishes continue to be built. For example, the relatively unknown city of Xiangtan, in China's Hunan province, pledged US$2 billion toward developing robots and AI, and other regions or cities have provided their own direct incentives for the AI industry. In Suzhou, leading AI companies can receive approximately US$800,000 in subsidies and Shenzhen is offering US$1 million in subsidies to support any practical AI project established in those cities.[908] As noted earlier, by 2018 there were already as many as 500 local Smart City projects taking place throughout the country, most of which were experimenting with a range of AI technologies.[909] By 2020, various sources counted this number as having reached as few as 800 and as many as 1,000 Chinese Smart City projects.[910]

Certainly, this model of central signalling and local application could have potential downsides as well. If AI ended up falling far short of current expectations of its economic impact, then directing this level of bureaucratic and financial resources towards maximising its value could prove wasteful.[911]

But local governments should be more aware than central planners of concrete governance issues such as corruption by government officials

---

[907] Ibid.
[908] Lee and Sheehan, 'Is China Outsmarting the US in AI?' (n 868).
[909] 'China Outnumbers Other Countries in Smart City Pilots' (n 833).
[910] Katherine Atha et al, *China's Smart Cities Development* (US–China Economic and Security Review Commission, 20 January 2020) <https://www.uscc.gov/sites/default/files/2020-04/China_Smart_Cities_Development.pdf>.
[911] Lee and Sheehan, 'Is China Outsmarting the US in AI?' (n 868).

and shadow banking that need resolving through record-keeping technology, and local experiments have the advantage that they can be scaled up if successful, or abandoned with relatively fewer costs compared to national rollouts. Therefore, the Smart City initiative combined with the AI Plan, as a public–private petri dish generator at the local level, could represent a powerful synergy of central direction, local government flexibility and private sector entrepreneurship.

8.11 Will Network Sovereignty Threaten AI Development in China?

Does Network Sovereignty threaten AI development? The answer to this question is fluid. This is because the Chinese regulatory regime, especially fuzzy logic lawmaking, is ideally suited to promoting the development of AI, whether that be through an AI National Team or globalised networks, depending on the milieu. AI is a general-purpose technology that can help China resolve many of its development and 'trust' issues. But will this Chinese-led AI ecosystem be threatened by the data-localisation/cyber-security restrictions identified in Chapters 5–7?

On one hand, it is undeniable that the Chinese government benefits too much from AI to want to restrict its development, and becoming an AI world leader is clearly a top policy priority for the Chinese government. As has been shown, private Chinese AI firms are providing essential services to the Chinese government and SOEs, and the government is supporting those private firms with funding and designation as AI National Team members. AI firms also provide thousands of high-quality jobs, helping China to move up the value chain from the factory of the world to an innovative advanced economy.

On the other hand, the government needs to control or have access to certain kinds of data for political reasons, something that is clear from its Cyber Security Law and its continuing tight restriction of the internet and media within China's cyber borders. As noted in previous chapters, data localisation rules, if interpreted strictly, may prevent the easy sharing of AI R&D data across borders. Currently, Chinese fundamental research capability remains limited, and is mainly dependent on applying foreign-created algorithms to develop new products. Yet Chinese AI firms are highly globalised and boast strong international collaboration (the topic of the next chapter). All members of the AI National Team, for example, have various global links, through either capital or partnerships. Presumably, strict localisation might prevent continuing innovation and globalised research by Chinese firms. These issues are expounded further in the next chapter.

The solution appears to be the kind of fuzzy logic legislating and regulation that has already been identified: vague legal provisions and key terms that allow for flexible enforcement or implementation in response to changing technological developments and the fluctuating requirements of innovation versus national security.

The AI Plan itself is another manifestation of this fuzzy logic, calling for intensive private sector development of AI while simultaneously requiring technologies to be 'secure and controllable'. Likewise, in its attitude towards international cooperation, the AI Plan seeks to allow China to learn from international developments while at the same time influencing international standards to benefit Chinese national and Network Sovereignty interests. It calls for Chinese AI scholars to 'enhance their international influence' through taking up 'important positions in international academic organisations' while 'actively participating in the formulation of international rules related to AI'.[912]

The AI Plan further states: 'China will actively participate in global governance of AI, strengthen the study of major international common problems such as robot alienation and safety supervision, deepen international cooperation on AI laws and regulations, international rules and so on, and jointly cope with global challenges.' Thus, language resembling the Internet Plus lexicon (eg, 'construct an open and cooperative AI technology innovation system') is also apparent beside the Network Sovereignty concerns.

Finally, the AI Plan also calls for international open-source collaboration to be fundamental to the future development of AI (as demonstrated in the next chapter) while at the same time setting out goals that are clearly aimed at benefiting China's national security and military interests:

> Open Source and Open. Advocate the concept of open-source sharing, and promote the concept of industry, academia, research, and production units each innovating and in principle pursuing joint innovation and sharing. Follow the coordinated development law for economic and national defence construction; promote two-way conversion and application for military and civilian scientific and technological achievements

---

[912] 'Why Are Standards Important for Artificial Intelligence?' (*JTC1*, 30 May 2018) <https://jtc1info.org/jtc1-press-committee-info-about-jtc-1-sc-42>. The ISO/IEC JTC 1/SC 42 is the first international standards committee looking at the entire AI ecosystem.

and co-construction and sharing of military and civilian innovation resources; form an all-element, multi-domain, highly efficient new pattern of civil–military integration. Actively participate in global research and development and management of AI, and optimise the allocation of innovative resources on a global scale.[913]

Therefore, it is clear from the Chinese government's AI Plan, its symbiotic relationship with private AI firms and its related intensive rollout of experimental policy petri dishes, especially within Smart Cities, that the Chinese government will only selectively (fuzzily) enforce data localisation provisions: it will reserve the right to enforce and access data where necessary for its security purposes, but will not prevent or restrict AI firms from rapidly developing their products and maintaining their globalised R&D ecosystems. This is assuming that the government can get the balance right between providing optimal conditions for growth and resisting the temptation to close China off from the outside world.

In other words, the fuzzy logic within the Chinese regulatory system, with its combination of central government signalling and local government/private firm implementation, could be an optimal one for development of an 'omni-use' or 'general purpose' technology like AI, one that, as has been shown, can be directly applied to thousands of different tasks, as long as the government does not stifle it with over-restrictive enforcement of data and cyber-security regulations.

Nevertheless in the current geopolitical environment, the answer is that the prevailing narrative is that unregulated pilots have enabled Chinese tech companies to engage in business model innovations that did not/could not happen in the West, and this has allowed world-class AI products to be created that can no longer be sold into Western markets as of 2019 and beyond.

8.12 Conclusion: Public–Private Symbiosis

China's existing system of fuzzy logic laws and centrally signalled pilot petri dishes is well suited to building AI and Smart City pilots using the current state of AI research. Current AI research is indisputably a global endeavour, and even though China lags behind the United States in fundamental AI breakthroughs, this open innovation environment has

---

[913] See AI Plan (n 819) section II ('The overall requirements') (2) ('The basic principles').

allowed Chinese firms to build their AI capacity, taking advantage of their ability to roll out experimental pilots. Smart Cities are incubating technology roll outs seeking to capitalise on ambitious policy targets set by China's AI Plan. The AI Plan acts as a form of top-down signalling to entrepreneurs. At the same time, the government is encouraging private companies to build National AI Platforms to further stimulate the growth of the sector.

Thus, as explained, China's capacity to rapidly develop AI applications and new emerging technologies is due to a combination of three factors: the current state of AI research, the open nature of AI research culture globally and the complex emerging role of public–private petri dishes for testing innovative applications. China's impressive rise in AI has been driven by its private sector with the encouragement of the government at all levels, as Chinese entrepreneurs have the incentive to solve numerous governance problems in a developing country.

This symbiosis has been shown to benefit both private companies and the Chinese government. The Chinese government is actively encouraging private companies to develop AI applications, frequently by using government-provided data and allowing pilots to be conducted. The government is an enthusiastic supporter of experimental AI pilots across numerous sectors, industry verticals and applications – especially those that help to solve governance and business efficiency problems in China's emerging Smart Cities.

These AI rollouts have the potential to solve Chinese problems and build mammoth private companies, but those companies remain connected to and highly dependent on the global AI entrepreneurial ecosystem. The implications of this global entanglement within the context of Network Sovereignty are further considered in the next chapter.

9

Open-Source AI Platforms and the Cyber Security Law

> AI is 'probably the best worldwide collaboration anyone has ever seen'.
> —Dr Kai-Fu Lee, pioneering AI scientist and venture capitalist[914]

Open-source platforms are an increasingly popular business model for AI development for global tech companies. This chapter examines why a restrictive (non-fuzzy) interpretation of the data localisation provisions within the Cyber Security Law would harm the growth of China's entrepreneurial ecosystem, focusing on recent Chinese government plans to grow its own domestic open-source AI ecosystem. Accordingly, this chapter reinforces the reasons why fuzzy logic lawmaking in China is so effective. It also queries whether the increased popularity of open-source platforms in China during 2017–2019 may have been another reason why data localisation was not comprehensively enforced.

This chapter begins by explaining open-source platforms and documents the history of open-source development in China. It then states the benefits of open-source platforms for innovation in AI and explains the global nature of open-source AI platforms and global R&D centres in relation to Chinese AI development. Building on Chapter 8, this chapter further outlines the Chinese government's approach to open-source AI platforms through public–private platforms for domestic open innovation and the AI National Team. It goes on to elucidate key features of open-source AI relevant to the application of the Cyber Security Law. These are subsequently further illustrated by case studies of global open-source AI platforms in China, notably Baidu's self-driving platform, Apollo.

The previous chapter explained why the combination of central government signalling and local government implementation is particularly well suited to accelerating implementation of an 'omni-use technology'

---

[914] Kai-Fu Lee quoted in Lucas and Waters, 'China and US Compete to Dominate Big Data' (n 780).

or 'general-purpose technology' like AI, one that can be directly applied to thousands of different tasks. This chapter restates the conflicting drives to data localisation and to open-source AI development. It illuminates the challenges posed by open-source AI for data localisation (and Network Sovereignty) policies; and further explains how fuzzy logic in key Chinese legal terms addresses these challenges (or potential conflicts) in order to promote innovation.

The emergence of open-source AI platforms and the fact that Chinese companies began establishing global R&D facilities during 2017 are explained as a key problem for the Cyber Security Law. These two developments have made the threat of data localisation within China's Cyber Security Law a potential complicated obstacle for China's technology industry. The Cyber Security Law was drafted before 2017, when Chinese companies began increasingly using open-source platforms as a business tool for creating an ecosystem of commercial partners. Yet the delayed full implementation of data localisation, including the lack of a clear definition of terms such as 'important data' in the law until 31 December 2018 (and beyond), has meant that China's technology industry has had additional time to plead that data localisation would harm their global R&D plans. Thus, 'fuzzy logic' lawmaking promotes innovation in the technology industry by allowing time for key stakeholders to pursue their agenda with regard to undefined terms.

It is also important to state at the outset that AI industry professionals have noted that: 'In the future, we expect to see the broadest impact and continued development of open source to be driven by artificial intelligence and machine learning.'[915] That is, the important role of open-source platforms will continue to increase significantly alongside the development of AI. Hence full data localisation could not conceivably be enforced in China. This is where fuzzy logic is important, as laws are intentionally vague and can be augmented over time to account for technological developments.

The implications of a number of outstanding questions surrounding the balance between openness and control are currently unclear but very significant:

---

[915] Dan Kulp, VP of Open-Source Development at Talend (a cloud data integration company) quoted in Laurence Bradford, 'How Open-Source Development Is Democratizing the Tech Industry' (*Forbes*, 26 March 2018) <https://www.forbes.com/sites/laurencebradford/2018/03/26/how-open-source-development-is-democratizing-the-tech-industry/#7bce96c13bb6>.

- Will the final implementing regulations under the Cyber Security Law harm global open-source platform collaborations for Chinese companies? Or does it mean that yet another domain (open-source AI platforms) is set to join a walled-off Chinese internet and protected cloud computing regime?
- Will Chinese companies be forced to keep their datasets and algorithms built upon those datasets in China for Chinese developer use only?

To answer these questions, first it is necessary to understand what open-source AI platforms are and why AI development remains largely open source. And how China has used open-source research to its 'technology catch-up' advantage, and then to assess what this will mean for Chinese innovation in the future.

To further explain these developments, the Chinese government's plan to create a domestic AI ecosystem through its AI National Team (introduced in Chapter 8) is revisited in depth.

In the current geopolitical milieu, it is argued that the Chinese government is increasingly less concerned with the impact of data localisation on Chinese open-source AI than it is with supporting China's own domestic open-source platforms for AI development through China's AI National Team.

9.1 What Are Open-Source AI Platforms?

Developers of AI systems today rarely start from nothing. More often, they leverage pre-written programs developed by others and shared into open-source code libraries. In brief 'open-source computer code' refers to any computer program whose source code is made available for use or modification by users or other developers.[916] Open-source software is usually developed as a public collaboration and either made freely available or to be used under a licence. Further, 'open source' refers to a legal and technical arrangement related to software production that results in open-source code that is accepted under a licence that complies with the

---

[916] See Josh Lerner and Jean Tirole, 'The Scope of Open Source Licensing' (2005) 21(1) *Journal of Law, Economics, and Organization* 20. The authors explain the evolution of open source, including the Open Source Definition, from 1998 when the concept of open source emerged. The Open Source Definition is a document published by the Open Source Initiative (a non-profit organisation that promotes open source, founded in Palo Alto in 1998) to determine whether a software licence can be labelled with the open-source certification mark.

Open Source Definition.[917] As open source is made available under a licence regime, the 'open' nature of open source refers to the source code being made public for collaboration.[918]

Open-source AI platforms can be understood as a vertical technology stack[919] that third parties can access and use through application programming interfaces (APIs). Companies can connect to APIs through cloud computing, using AI technologies on the platform without having to build and invest in their own hardware and IT infrastructure. Earlier technology stacks would have to be built from scratch by companies. Open-source AI platforms have been modularised into specific AI and Machine Learning solutions (eg, image recognition). This means that modularised open-source code sections can be modified through APIs and can be replaced with proprietary implementations, which then can be contributed to a platform. An AI platform can accordingly be conceived in terms of its modular architecture, where AI frameworks/libraries and data-related resources are available as a service.[920]

There is also a need to carefully distinguish between open source – in the sense of access to computer source code – and open access to data. There is a significant difference between open data and open source.

Data can be numbers, locations and names.[921] Source code is human-readable written lines of code that use or produce data. A computer application is compiled source code that operates on data. Although they rely on one another for their significance, data and source code are different in both essence and purpose.

Thus, there is a difference between open-source software (including open-source AI) and open access to data. Open source and open data are distinct phenomena with significant differences, and these differences

---

[917] Ibid.
[918] Ibid.
[919] A technology stack is a list of all the technology services used to build and run a single application.
[920] See, eg, Adrian Mackenzie, 'From API to AI: Platforms and Their Opacities' (2018) *Information, Communication & Society* 1.
[921] A technical computer science definition of 'data' refers to stored symbols. Data is considered a resource, the raw material for an application. Further, open data means data that is technically and legally made available for reuse and republication. Open data can include open government-collected data as well as data released by private actors. Thus, data is not always a company-specific resource and can be bought from providers. Data can also be synthesised or combined from multiple sources. See Juho Lindman and Linus Nyman, 'The Businesses of Open Data and Open Source: Some Key Similarities and Differences' (2014) 4(1) *Technology Innovation Management Review* 12.

clearly affect how commercial success can be achieved in each domain.[922]

The key similarity between open data and open source lies in the prerequisite of 'openness'. Yet what exactly is it that is open, and are there degrees or types of openness? For open-source software, the openness primarily means guaranteed access to the application's source code as well as an arrangement that makes sure that the code can be forked,[923] modified and redistributed.[924]

For open data, a similar 'access principle' provides access to the data (and metadata) and it provides the opportunity to reuse it in applications. Data also needs to be maintained and updated. The actor that collects the data from different sources usually has the option to stop providing access to or maintenance of the data. Although there is continuing uncertainty about the implementation of China's Cyber Security Law, it may affect cross-border access to data, as many foreign companies will be likely to operate according to the strictest interpretations of data localisation in order to minimise risks. This uncertainty could in turn hinder the development and use of AI, and is one of the potential negative aspects of the fuzzy logic approach to regulation. This point will be analysed further (see Section 9.2).

While AI is an engine for continued future innovations, a significant amount of innovation in AI takes place through access to open-source 'algorithms' (ie, open access to source code). In addition, AI is a global endeavour with global ramifications.

Again, there is no 'secret sauce' for Deep Learning, which has led to the greatest advances in Machine Learning and more broadly AI over the past decade. When serious academic works in the field of computer science are published, open-source code and datasets are included to allow other researchers to prove repeatability.[925] Anyone with a large dataset and enough processing power can use open-source tools to implement proven AI use cases. Thus, innovation in AI (especially Machine Learning) can depend not only upon access to source code but upon open access to data too.

---

[922] Ibid.
[923] Defined in Section 9.2.
[924] For more on the significance of the right to fork, see Juho Lindman and Linus Nyman, 'Code Forking, Governance, and Sustainability in Open Source Software' (2013) 3(1) *Technology Innovation Management Review* 7.
[925] See Section 9.4.2.

There is therefore an important nexus between AI and open data in an age where datasets are necessary to train AI applications. Researchers need access to the datasets along with the source code, sometimes in real time. The current state of AI research (explained in Chapter 8) involves the use of datasets for improved decision-making. Any attempt to segregate data may slow or hinder AI research, because the results of applying Machine Learning AI to unstructured datasets cannot easily be predetermined.[926]

Finally, open-source AI development platforms currently fall into two main categories: (1) commercial software platforms to onboard developers (eg, Baidu's Apollo self-driving open-source platform) and (2) free and open community development platforms (eg, Caffe,[927] an open-source Deep Learning platform). The significant commercial benefits for the creators of open-source software platforms are analysed further in Section 9.2. Essentially, open-source software is a significant business model for identifying software developer talent and developer community building, as well as a marketing tool for onboarding commercial cloud computing clients.

While open-source practices have been a feature of AI platforms internationally for many years, they are a much more recent phenomenon in China; the adoption of open source, in general, is also a nascent concept in China.

9.2 History of Open-Source Platforms in China

The history of open-source AI platforms and their adoption in China is a story that needs to be told. Many of the world's biggest tech companies have made their AI systems open source. Services that offer open-source Machine Learning algorithms on demand have become an important area of competition among large tech companies. Originally, Western companies such as Microsoft, IBM, Google and Amazon began using open-source platforms to win cloud services by offering to help other companies develop AI capabilities. Those skills were previously limited to

---

[926] Borne out in Section 9.4.4 with regard to Didi Chuxing's open-source maintenance platforms.
[927] Caffe is notable as it was released in April 2017, and was created by Yangqing Jia, a Chinese national. He created the Caffe project during his PhD studies at University of California Berkeley. There are now many contributors to the project, and it is hosted at source code repository GitHub. GitHub is explained in depth in Section 9.2.

technology companies, including tasks such as parsing the meaning of images or text for clients in industries such as banking, healthcare and manufacturing.[928]

Onboarding external developers can lead to greater developments and innovations, which in turn leads to broader use of large tech firms' services. Microsoft, Google, Facebook and Amazon have made a lot of their AI research available to the public for free use, exploration, adaptation and perhaps improvement. Among the first technologies that major tech companies made open source are:

- Amazon's Alexa – the voice-command response system inhabiting the company's Echo device was opened in June 2015;[929]
- Google's TensorFlow – the heart of its image search technology was made open source in November 2015;[930]
- the custom hardware designs that run Facebook's M[931] personal assistant – these were made open source in December 2015 and
- Microsoft's Machine Learning system – the Computation Network Tool Kit became open source in December 2015.[932]

A variety of other specialist open-source AI platforms exist (eg, Sparkling Water, Acumos and Keras). These software programs aim to make the building blocks of AI available to developers and data scientists, including those who may have limited experience with Deep Learning and AI.[933] Many others have done likewise, among them, as recently as

---

[928] Discussed in depth in following sections.
[929] David Isbitski, 'Introducing the Alexa Skills Kit, Enabling Developers to Create Entirely New Voice Driven Capabilities' (*Amazon Developer*, 25 June 2015) <https://developer.amazon.com/blogs/post/Tx205N9U1UD338H/Introducing-the-Alexa-Skills-Kit-Enabling-Developers-to-Create-Entirely-New-Voic>.
[930] Jeff Dean and Rojat Monga, 'TensorFlow: Google's Latest Machine Learning System, Open Sourced for Everyone' (*Google AI Blog*, 9 November 2015) <https://ai.googleblog.com/2015/11/tensorflow-googles-latest-machine.html>.
[931] Jessi Hempel, 'Facebook Launches M, Its Bold Answer to Siri and Cortana' (*Wired*, 26 August 2015) <https://www.wired.com/2015/08/facebook-launches-m-new-kind-virtual-assistant>.
[932] Xuedong Huang, 'Microsoft Computational Network Toolkit Offers Most Efficient Distributed Deep Learning Computational Performance' (*Microsoft Research Blog*, 7 December 2015) <https://www.microsoft.com/en-us/research/blog/microsoft-computational-network-toolkit-offers-most-efficient-distributed-deep-learning-computational-performance/>.
[933] Sam Dean, 'Open Source AI for Everyone: Three Projects to Know' (*Linux Foundation*, 10 May 2018) <https://www.linuxfoundation.org/blog/2018/05/open-source-ai-for-everyone-three-projects-to-know>.

August 2018, Microsoft's Open Platform for AI (Open PAI), an open-source platform for GPU cluster management and resource scheduling.[934]

By 2017, Chinese companies were beginning to follow suit. Historically, Chinese developers had little involvement in open-source development. There were myriad reasons for this, including a catch-up technology ecosystem and low awareness of the utility of open-source projects.[935] There was anecdotal evidence of this low awareness. In 2016, the world's premier advocate of open source, the Linux Foundation, reported: 'One of the pioneers of the internet in China gave a highly provocative talk – asking the audience why China had yet to birth a major open source project. The consensus in the audience (polled via WeChat platform) was that China's culture inhibited open source.'[936]

However, Chinese start-ups have evolved rapidly.[937] In fact, Duncan Turner, the managing director of well-known Shenzhen-based hardware accelerator company, Hax, has argued that China's history of *shanzhai* innovations[938] – seeking to solve problems with makeshift solutions – foreshadows China's propensity for and willingness to adopt open-source software platforms.[939]

Nevertheless, other obstacles to widespread adoption of open source have included the difficulty at times of using GitHub – one of the major

---

[934] Fan Yang, 'Tech Showcase: OpenPAI: Open Source Initiative for AI Platform in China' (*Microsoft.com*, 2 August 2018) <https://www.microsoft.com/en-us/research/video/openpai-open-source-initiative-for-ai-platform-in-china>.

[935] See 王冲鹤 [Wang Chongyan] and 陈丝 [Chen Si] «人工智能开源平台发展态势研究» [Researching the Development of AI Open Source Platforms] (2018) 8 *ICT and Policy* 56.

[936] 'Tencent and Why Open Source Is About to Explode in China' (*Linux Foundation*, 19 February 2016) <https://www.linuxfoundation.org/blog/2016/02/tencent-and-why-open-source-is-about-to-explode-in-china>.

[937] As noted in Chapter 1.

[938] As noted in Chapter 1, Section 1.1.

[939] According to Turner, open source and sharing of information plays a bigger role in China than in the United States: Tristan Rayner, 'What China Is Doing to Create a Tech Edge over the US' (*Android Authority*, 19 December 2017) <https://www.androidauthority.com/what-china-is-doing-to-create-a-tech-edge-over-the-us-823656>. The academic literature also covers these issues. See, eg, Xin Gu, 'The Paradox of Maker Movement in China' in Jeremy Hunsinger and Andrew Schrock (eds), *Making our World: The Hacker and Maker Movements in Context* (Peter Lang Publishing, 2019) 271. Gu surveys the role of Chinese culture in Chinese maker spaces. According to Turner, patents are not created in China to fight copycats and exert legal pressure; rather they are used for trades between companies to share information. Turner is well placed to make these claims, having run HAX in Shenzhen since 2014.

open-source code repositories globally – in China, due to government blocking of the site.[940]

A GitHub 'project' is a webpage as well as a repository for computer code. Projects can also be repositories of information and not only collections of code. They can be used as a business card of sorts for those seeking to have their coding skills noticed. The flagship functionality of GitHub is 'forking' – copying a repository from one user's account to another. This enables a user to take a project and modify it under their own account. If the user makes changes they would like to share, they can send a notification called a 'pull request' to the original owner. The owner can then, with a click of a button, merge the changes found in the user's repository with the original repository. These three features – forking, pull requests and merging – make GitHub a very powerful coding tool.[941]

GitHub, which was acquired by Microsoft in 2018, is most commonly used as a source code repository for open-source projects. While China has blocked access to GitHub in the past,[942] the restriction is usually temporary,[943] although GitHub generally works better through a VPN in China. A VPN re-routes the user's location when using the internet to avoid detection by Chinese censorship.[944] However, in mid-2019, fears again resurfaced that tensions between the United States and China over technology usage would lead to Chinese developers being unable to use the US-based GitHub, as the US government might block access outside that country.[945]

---

[940] There are other source code repositories (eg, Atlassian-owned BitBucket), however GitHub remains the most famous.

[941] Klint Finley, 'What Exactly is GitHub Anyway?' (*TechCrunch*, 14 July 2012) <https://techcrunch.com/2012/07/14/what-exactly-is-github-anyway>.

[942] Josh Horwitz and Nikhil Sonnad, 'Meet Shadowsocks, the Underground Tool that China's Coders Use to Blast through the Great Firewall' (*Quartz*, 20 September 2017) <https://qz.com/1072701/meet-shadowsocks-the-underground-tool-that-chinas-coders-use-to-blast-through-the-great-firewall/>.

[943] Youyou Zhou, 'Four of the Top 25 Github Projects Are Written in Chinese, Six Contain No Code' (*Quartz*, 18 May 2018) <https://qz.com/1280215/four-of-the-top-25-github-projects-are-written-in-chinese-six-contain-no-code>.

[944] Ibid.

[945] Online chatter began when GitHub's export control rules caught the attention of China's developer community. The rules state that content developed on GitHub needs to comply with US export laws, including the Export Administration Regulations (EAR), the same regulations used to restrict exports to Huawei and affiliated companies in 2019: see 'GitHub and Export Controls' (*GitHub Help*, May 2019) <https://help.github.com/en/articles/github-and-export-controls>. See also US Department of Commerce, Bureau of Industry and Security, *Addition of Certain Entities to the Entity List (Final Rule)*,

OPEN-SOURCE AI PLATFORMS

China's historic shift towards open source began in December 2014, when internet regulator MIIT declared its support for OpenStack (open-source projects) for SOEs.[946] Not long after, Tencent embraced the Open Daylight Foundation's software-defined networking (SDN) controller instead of developing its own proprietary distributed cluster SDN controller. SDN seeks to provide a suitable architecture for the high-bandwidth, dynamic nature of today's applications.[947] This was also done to help Tencent support its extreme scalability demands[948] (with over 1.2 billion users across its platforms). These efforts were, however, token drops in the ocean of global open-source development.

Since 2016–2017, efforts to use, and increasingly contribute, open-source code have flourished across China.[949] Chinese developers have even begun to use GitHub as a platform to vent their frustration about, for example, being overworked by the 996 (9am to 9pm, six days a week) lifestyle common among Chinese start-ups.[950] The activists launched a

---

Effective May 16, 2019 (16 May 2019) <https://www.bis.doc.gov/index.php/all-articles/17-regulations/1555-addition-of-certain-entities-to-the-entity-list-final-rule-effective-may-16-2019>.

See also Masha Borak, 'Chinese Developers Fear Losing Open Source Tech to Trade War' (*South China Morning Post*, 25 May 2019) <https://www.abacusnews.com/digital-life/chinese-developers-fear-losing-open-source-tech-trade-war/article/3011463>.

GitHub restricts some countries, including Iran and North Korea, from accessing its Enterprise Server: see Nick Farrell, 'US Might Have Control of Open Source' (*Fudzilla*, 28 May 2019) <https://www.fudzilla.com/news/48769-us-might-have-control-of-open-source>.

[946] MIIT held the first China Open Source and Cloud Computing Summit (COSCCS) on 11 December 2014. At this event, the Chinese government for the first time officially declared its intention to support OpenStack ecosystems and encourage SOEs to use OpenStack-based cloud products. The OpenStack Foundation supports the development and adoption of open infrastructure globally, across a community of 100,000 individuals in 187 countries (as of May 2019), by hosting open-source projects and communities. See Frank Liu, 'OpenStack Development Will Accelerate Rapidly in China Market in 2015' (*Forrester* 24 December 2014) <https://go.forrester.com/blogs/14-12-24-open stack_development_will_accelerate_rapidly_in_china_market_in_2015>.

[947] 'Tencent and Why Open Source Is about to Explode in China' (n 936).

[948] Network traffic scalability demands are explained further in Section 9.3.4.

[949] See 王冲鹍 [Wang Chongyan] and 陈丝 [Chen Si] «人工智能开源平台发展态势研究» [Researching the Development of AI Open-Source Platforms] (n 935).

[950] See Elliot Zaagman, 'Github Gives Chinese Developers Censor-Proof Forum' (*Technode*, 16 April 2019) <https://technode.com/2019/04/16/github-gives-chinese-developers-censor-proof-forum>. On the global open-source software platform Github, Chinese high-tech workers launched the 996.icu campaign against the 12 hours a day, 6 days a week schedule. Organisers called for the enforcement of labour laws. An editorial published in state media Xinhua supported the call for labour law enforcement, but chairman of Chinese internet giant Alibaba, Jack Ma, defended the 996 system.

site (or repository) in early 2019 on GitHub, which quickly become one of the platform's fastest growing repositories ever. It acquired more Stars (akin to Likes on Facebook) than Google's open-source AI framework TensorFlow or Facebook's user interface library React.[951] This is important because it illustrates two things: (1) the rapid uptake of GitHub over a two-year period, and (2) the fact that the Chinese government would not block the GitHub discussion regarding Chinese labour laws. This raises the crucial question of whether GitHub has become too important for the Chinese government to block from Chinese developers.

China provides the fastest growing base of GitHub users outside the United States.[952] Programmers in China have strongly embraced the 'open-source way of thinking'. This philosophy promotes the free exchange of ideas, without government interference or regulation. Despite the discordance between the 'open-source way of thinking' and China's Network Sovereignty policies, code hosted on GitHub has been essential for the country's tech sector.

Yet again, in 2020, Chinese activists were arrested for publishing personal accounts and news stories chronicling the Covid-19 outbreak on GitHub.[953] Chinese citizens had again used GitHub after the Covid-19 outbreak began, as it remains one of the few major foreign websites that can still be accessed in China, as of 2021.[954] This may change, however. Adopting open-source technologies means embracing a deeply held culture of borderless standardisation – one that may now sit uncomfortably with China's push for Network Sovereignty and technological

---

See «辛识平: 奋斗应提倡, 996 当退场» [Xin Zhiping: The Struggle Should Be Advocated, 996 Should Be Ended] (*Xinhua*, 15 April 2019) <http://www.xinhuanet.com/politics/2019-04/15/c_1124370790.htm>. Serenitie Wang and Daniel Shane, 'Jack Ma Endorses China's Controversial 12 Hours a Day, 6 Days a Week Work Culture' (*CNN Business*, 2 April 2019) <https://edition.cnn.com/2019/04/15/business/jack-ma-996-china/index.html>.

[951] Klint Finley, 'How GitHub Is Helping Overworked Chinese Programmers' (*Wired*, 4 April 2019) <https://www.wired.com/story/how-github-helping-overworked-chinese-programmers>.

[952] See 'The 2020 State of Octoverse' (*GitHub Octoverse*, 2021) <https://octoverse.github.com/>.

[953] Jane Li, 'Chinese Internet Users Who Uploaded Coronavirus Memories to GitHub Have Been Arrested' (*Quartz*, 27 April 2020) < https://qz.com/1846277/china-arrests-users-behind-github-coronavirus-memories-page/>.

[954] Jane Li, 'Chinese Citizens are Racing against Censors to Preserve Coronavirus Memories on GitHub (*Quartz*, 3 March 2020) <https://qz.com/1811018/chinese-citizens-use-github-to-save-coronavirus-memories/>.

self-reliance in a trade war milieu. 'Basically, you cannot nationalize open source', 'It's already global'.[955]

As tensions with the United States escalated, China would begin to promote its own code repository, Gitee, in 2020. In July 2020, China's MIIT joined Huawei, Tencent and universities in a high-tech consortium endorsing Gitee as the official hub for China's open-source community.[956] Shortly after, Huawei, Tencent, Alibaba, Baidu and other tech companies launched the OpenAtom Foundation, China's version of the Linux Foundation, a long-standing pillar of the international open-source community.[957] The OpenAtom Foundation's flagship project is Huawei's new mobile operating system, HarmonyOS, intended to rival the dominance of Android and Apple's operating systems, with the code hosted on Gitee.[958] Huawei being listed on the US Entity List would mean that Google could no longer allow Huawei to use its open-source Android operating system. That story is explained further in Section 9.4.

Two years earlier, the story was quite different for open source in China. In May 2018, JD.com joined the high-profile open-source

---

[955] Quoting Julian Sun, Beijing-based senior research director at tech industry analysis firm Gartner. See Meaghan Tobin, 'China Wants to Build an Open Source Ecosystem to Rival GitHub (*Rest of the World*, 19 January 2021) <https://restofworld.org/2021/china-gitee-to-rival-github/>.

[956] «工信部携 Gitee 入场，国内开源生态建设进入快车道» [MIIT Backs Gitee, to Support the Development of the Domestic Open-Source Ecosystem] (*Gitee*, July 2020) <https://blog.gitee.com/2020/08/17/gitee-gxb/>.

[957] See 'OpenAtom Project List' (*OpenAtom Foundation*) <https://www.openatom.org/#/projectList>.

[958] A code repository maintained by China's OpenAtom Foundation on Gitee hosts the open-source information for Huawei's Harmony operating system. See https://gitee.com. There are an estimated 780 million smartphone users in China, and Huawei accounts for 40% of the smartphone market in China. Huawei has said it is aiming to get HarmonyOS loaded onto 400 million devices in 2021, including smartphones, wearables and TVs. This could create an enormous market for developers to make products for Harmony in China alone. See Celia Chen, 'Huawei Aims to Deploy Harmony OS on 400 million Devices in 2021, Going beyond Smartphones to Reach Many IoT gadgets' (*South China Morning Post*, 13 January 2021) <https://www.scmp.com/tech/article/3117573/huawei-aims-deploy-harmony-os-400-million-devices-2021-going-beyond>. Released in December 2020, HarmonyOS seems to be mostly still modelled on Google's Android OS. See Ron Amadeo, 'Huawei's HarmonyOS: "Fake It Till You Make It" Meets OS Development' (*Ars Technica*, 2 March 2021) <https://arstechnica.com/gadgets/2021/02/harmonyos-hands-on-huaweis-android-killer-is-just-android/>.

software project Linux Foundation.[959] Other Chinese members now include China Unicom, ZTE, Huawei, Alibaba and Tencent.[960]

Certainly, the rise of big data has made open-source platforms much more prominent, including in China. The most popular AI development platforms are all open source, including TensorFlow, Keras (built on top of TensorFlow) and Baidu's PaddlePaddle. Baidu released its open-source Machine Learning platform, PaddlePaddle, in September 2016 under an Apache[961] licence. According to one technology entrepreneur: 'This is as significant as when Google open-sourced its machine learning platform, Tensorflow.'[962] Baidu's decision to open source PaddlePaddle suggested a shift in how China's technology industry thought about software.

The open-source movement has been crucial to China's technological catch-up. 'For developers, source code is a very important resource', noted Liu Chen, director of operations for Open Source China, which refers to itself as the largest open-source community in China.[963]

Further, Chinese open-source projects have begun to proliferate since 2017. Tencent offers a wide range of open-source infrastructure projects from data warehousing to mobile network acceleration.[964] Huawei actively promotes its FusionInsight product,[965] which depends heavily

---

[959] See '26 Organizations Join the Linux Foundation to Support Open Source Communities with Infrastructure and Resources' (*Linux Foundation*, 23 May 2018) <https://www.prnewswire.com/news-releases/26-organizations-join-the-linux-foundation-to-support-open-source-communities-with-infrastructure-and-resources-300653177.html>.

[960] 'Linux Foundation Members' (*Linux Foundation*) <https://www.linuxfoundation.org/join/members/>.

[961] An Apache Licence is a permissive free software licence written by the Apache Software Foundation.

[962] Alluxio CEO and founder (an open-source virtual distributed cloud system) Haoyuan Li, cited in Matt Asay, 'Why China Is the Next Proving Ground for Open Source Software' (*Tech Republic*, 20 September 2016) <https://www.techrepublic.com/article/why-china-is-the-next-proving-ground-for-open-source-software>.

[963] Borak, 'Chinese Developers Fear Losing Open Source Tech' (n 945).

[964] See 'Tencent Open Source' (Tencent Open Source) <https://opensource.tencent.com>. By May 2018, Tencent had released 52 open-source projects, 22 were released for WeChat.

[965] FusionInsight is an intelligent data solution providing an enterprise-class platform for big data integration, storage, search and analysis as well as AI. The platform allows enterprises to quickly process massive sets of data, and helps enterprises capture opportunities and discover risks by analysing and mining data in a real-time or non-real-time manner.

on a variety of open-source technologies (to which it increasingly contributes).[966]

Furthermore, in September 2018 Baidu launched an online tool in beta, EZDL,[967] that makes it easy for virtually anyone to build, design and deploy AI models without writing a single line of code.[968] EZDL targets three broad categories of machine learning: image classification, object detection and sound classification. Youping Yu, general manager of Baidu's AI ecosystem division, commented: 'We seek to create a true ecosystem for AI, democratising access to AI capabilities.'[969] Also in September 2018, Tencent announced its own open AI platform.[970] While most AI development in China continues to rely on foreign and often US-developed open-source AI frameworks (out of both habit and necessity), cultural changes towards open source could be seen in the release of Baidu's PaddlePaddle, Alibaba's XDL[971] and Huawei's MindSpore[972] Deep Learning frameworks. These framework releases marked the beginning of a strengthened culture of open-source software and development within China. These platforms are designed to compete with Google's TensorFlow. It is also noteworthy that Baidu can be seen as an early leader globally in open-source ecosystem development and may enjoy a first-mover advantage as a result.

Open-source development has grown so much in China that Def Con, the 'Olympics of hacking', which emphasises the open-source sharing of everything, including software vulnerabilities, was held in Beijing in May 2018. It had previously only been held in the United States, for the past 25 years in Las Vegas. While Chinese authorities had ordered local attendees not to share knowledge with the international community,

---

[966] See 'Huawei Enterprise – Big Data' (*Huawei*) <https://e.huawei.com/au/solutions/cloud-computing/big-data>.
[967] See 'EZDL Custom Sound Recognition' (Baidu AI) <http://ai.baidu.com/ezdl/sound>.
[968] See Kyle Wiggers, 'Baidu Launches EZDL, an AI Model Training Platform That Requires No Coding Experience' (*Venture Beat*, 1 September 2018) <https://venturebeat.com/2018/09/01/baidu-launches-ezdl-an-ai-model-training-platform-that-requires-no-coding-experience>.
[969] Ibid.
[970] Iris Deng, 'Tencent Releases Open Platform to Help Drive AI Projects at Other Companies' (*South China Morning Post*, 19 September 2018) <https://www.scmp.com/tech/big-tech/article/2164765/tencent-releases-open-platform-help-drive-ai-projects-other-companies>.
[971] Alibaba's XDL is an industrial deep learning framework for high-dimension sparse data, it was made open source in December 2018.
[972] MindSpore is Huawei's equivalent of TensorFlow, PyTorch or PaddlePaddle AI frameworks. Its launch was announced in late November 2018.

over 1,300 people attended. Def Con came to Beijing in partnership with the internet security arm of Baidu. An attendee who works for a security company in Shanghai told reporters: 'Although the co-operation between Baidu and Def Con looks purely commercial, in such a sensitive area, it in fact shows some level of government approval.'[973] The gathering reflects the government's difficult trade-off between controlling the internet and encouraging companies to innovate in technology. Jeff Moss, the conference's founder, told the media: 'China is the best place to take Def Con [out of the US] because in the future there really will be two superpowers in internet security: the US and China ... security problems are global problems and need a global response.'[974] Def Con, in seeking to emphasise the open-source sharing of everything including software vulnerabilities, must logically require a Chinese presence. The significance of these events is the fact that the 'Olympics of hacking', a non-governmental event, took place in China. It explains much about the 'organic nature' of developer communities. This organic nature is also reflected in AI platforms.

A subsequent Def Con event, Def Con China 1.0, was held in Beijing in May 2019. Def Con China 2.0 was postponed (more than once) in 2020 due to the Covid-19 travel concerns, but the 'hacking Olympics' organisation planned to return to stage Def Con China 2.0 in Beijing in 2021, suggesting the hacking community is still very interested in trading knowledge with its Chinese programming peers.[975]

That an international organisation which promotes open-source development as a means of encouraging open-source cyber security believed that China was ready to host its flagship conference in 2018, and continued to plan events in China in 2020–2021 (postponed due to Covid-19), is highly significant. That the Chinese government by approving the conference tacitly acknowledged the importance of open source to cyber security in China is even more significant. This cyber-security benefit is another motivation for the Chinese government to promote open source (discussed further in Section 9.3.4).

---

[973] Yuan Yang, 'Chinese Hackers Defy Government Warnings at Beijing Def Con' (*Financial Times*, 14 May 2018) <https://www.ft.com/content/f03995de-5711-11e8-bdb7-f6677d2e1ce8?desktop=true>.
[974] Ibid.
[975] 'DEF CON China 2.0 Is Cancelled' (*DEF CON Organisation*) <https://www.defcon.org/html/defcon-china-2/dc-cn-2-index.html>.

The swift adoption of open-source platforms in China (over the past four years) and globally has coincided with the rise of AI. Companies are building AI and Machine Learning developer tools and technologies, and making them widely available for developers and businesses at an affordable cost. But what is the commercial drive for this business model? Companies rarely give away trade secrets for free. So, if open-source software is made freely available and may be redistributed and modified, then what are the benefits to these companies that onboard external programmers to modify or 'fork' their code?

9.3 Benefits of Open-Source Platforms for Innovation in AI

There are several motivations for companies to engage in open-source AI research in communities. First, commercial operators open source their AI software because they wish to become the chosen platform upon which other talented developers innovate and by doing so attract talent. Second, algorithmic transparency is another selling point for open-source communities. This is because there is increasingly popular demand for openness in AI development.[976] Third, and most important, there are commercial incentives for corporate open-source platforms (eg, Google's TensorFlow or Baidu's Apollo) to onboard developer talent and cloud computing clients, thereby creating a source of revenue and a new business ecosystem. Finally, open source can help companies fix bugs by allowing open-source maintenance of servers and platforms. This method is already being employed by Chinese companies such as ride-hailing giant Didi Chuxing (see Section 9.3.4).

An obvious benefit of open source is the well-known 'network effect'. A network effect is a phenomenon whereby increased numbers of participants improve the value of a good or service. A nascent academic literature has documented the 'network effect' of why developers join open-source platforms. For example, how a platform entrant can overcome an incumbent competitor based on the strength of developers' indirect network effects, or, in other words, a critical mass of talented developers join an open-source platform.[977] The numbers of developers

---

[976] Mike Ananny and Kate Crawford, 'Seeing without Knowing: Limitations of the Transparency Ideal and Its Application to Algorithmic Accountability' (2016) 20(1) *New Media and Society* 88.

[977] Yoo et al first noted that little formal analysis had investigated software platform business models: Youngjin Yoo, Ola Henfridsson and Kalle Lyytinen, 'Research

using a given Machine Learning framework ultimately decides the 'network effects' that are derived from this framework. That is, the more people working on any given framework, the greater the network effect will be and the more rapidly the framework will disperse and evolve.

Taking Google's Deep Learning framework TensorFlow as an example, whenever a new paper is published by Google DeepMind or Google Brain, TensorFlow is then used by developers to try and learn from and replicate that published breakthrough. This trickles down to independent researchers who will use TensorFlow for implementing that published innovation. As TensorFlow has numerous tutorials and supporting documents to aid independent developers, an open-source community is established around the AI framework. This is reinforced by the network effect of the developer community that keeps the open-source community an evolving source, for the benefit of developers as well as for Google. Open-source software, of course, cannot be stolen, but being freely available does not mean it is free. To benefit fully from open source, developers and the organisations that employ them must all make active contributions to open-source communities.

All of these motivations for open-source platforms had the potential to be affected by data localisation in the Cyber Security Law. The following explains the benefits in more detail. The impact of data localisation on open-source AI is analysed in Section 9.7.

9.3.1 *Attracting Talent through Open Innovation*

There are a few reasons why open source is historically popular. Traditionally, software users could use the end product of a piece of software (eg, writing a document in Microsoft Word or playing a computer game). However, the underlying programming, the source code,

---

Commentary: The New Organizing Logic of Digital Innovation: An Agenda for Information Systems Research' (2010) 21(4) *Information Systems Research* 724. Feng and Iansiti show how a platform entrant can overcome an incumbent competitor based on the strength of developers' indirect network effects: Zhu Feng and Marco Iansiti, 'Entry into Platform-Based Markets' (2012) 33(1) *Strategic Management Journal* 88. See also Peijian Song et al, 'The Ecosystem of Software Platform: A Study of Asymmetric Cross-Side Network Effects and Platform Governance' (2018) 42(1) *MIS Quarterly* 121. The authors theorise how the app-side and the user-side react to each other with distinct value creation/capture processes, and how these processes are influenced by the platform's governance policies on application review and platform updates. This research is highly relevant to this study as app governance policies clearly impact the way open-source value is captured by a platform.

was invisible because it was proprietary. As noted earlier, making source code freely available is helpful because the more people who review the code, the more likely it is that bugs and risks can be identified and resolved.[978] Yet there is another reason why open source is particularly well suited to AI:

> These companies open-source their AI software because they wish to be the foundations on which other people innovate. Any entrepreneur who does so successfully can be bought up and easily integrated into the larger parent. AI is central because it, by design, learns and adapts, and even makes decisions. AI is more than a product: it is a product generator. In the near future, AI will not be relegated to serving up images or consumer products, but will be used to identify and capitalize on new opportunities by innovating new products.[979]

When fed large datasets, Machine Learning is a 'product generator' (as noted in Chapter 8). Unforeseen permutations occur as machines learn. 'Using loosely affiliated ecosystems, firms are able to harness a global network of partners they have never met. These partners can connect through digital networks to innovate on top of a platform's core set of resources, thereby creating highly valuable products and services for ecosystem users.'[980]

Thus, today, at the intersection of open source and AI, innovation is blossoming. Companies ranging from Google to Baidu to Facebook to Tencent to IBM are open-sourcing AI and Machine Learning tools. Open-source AI serves these companies' broader goals of staying at the forefront of technology. They are therefore not giving away the keys to their success; rather, they are paving the way to their own future by allowing talented developers to help build new innovations. Innovation is crowdsourced by open innovation, as external developers can change the way IT products are developed. Firms will choose to innovate using 'open external contracts in preference to closed vertical integration. . . . And, this is not just outsourcing. Firms are relinquishing product specifications to third parties that they do not even know'.[981] Developers are key

---

[978] Youngjin Yoo et al, 'Organizing for Innovation in the Digitized World' 23(5) (2012) *Organization Science* 1398, 1403.

[979] Patrick Shafto, 'Why Big Tech Companies Are Open-Sourcing Their AI Systems' (*The Conversation*, 16 February 2016) <https://theconversation.com/why-big-tech-companies-are-open-sourcing-their-ai-systems-54437>.

[980] Geoffrey Parker, Marshall Van Alstyne and Xiaoyue Jiang, 'Platform Ecosystems: How Developers Invert the Firm' (2017) 41(1) *MIS Quarterly* 255, 256.

[981] Ibid 263.

to a platform's ability to scale rapidly because what the platform firm does is not limited by the processes of hiring, training, project selection and project coordination. A historic shift is underway, driven by rapid improvements in global network connectivity and computing power.[982]

In addition, compounding the necessity for external developer input is the fact that the so-called AI race is primarily a competition for global AI research talent. Chinese R&D facilities in the United States (Baidu, Tencent and numerous start-ups), Singapore (Yitu Tech), Israel (Alibaba) and elsewhere are increasingly important to harnessing the talented workforce in those countries.[983] According to one assessment by LinkedIn, during 2017 the United States had 850,000 AI technical role workers, whereas China had only 50,000.[984] This is one reason why open-source platforms are crucial to developing AI ecosystems. They help to redress global developer and engineering talent shortages.

9.3.2 Transparency: Researchers Demand Repeatability

The wider culture surrounding the field of AI research is now largely impacted by open and transparent research.[985] Algorithms created by researchers are often published and many researchers have made it a condition of joining Baidu, Google and Facebook that their results

---

[982] The idea of open innovation is not new. See, eg, Henry Chesbrough, Wim Vanhaverbeke and Joel West (eds), *Open Innovation: Researching a New Paradigm* (Oxford University Press, 2006). However, the literature on open innovation in AI is nascent. This book is one of the earliest attempts to understand this phenomenon from a Chinese perspective. See also Erik Brynjolfsson and Andrew McAfee, *The Second Machine Age: Work, Progress, and Prosperity in a Time of Brilliant Technologies* (WW Norton, 2014). The authors document the rise of AI and are optimistic about its growing application.

[983] These R&D centres are outlined in greater depth in Section 9.4. The media constantly refers to the China–US AI race, this study prefers to describe a competitive entanglement that is explained in this chapter. See, eg, Lucas and Waters, 'China and US Compete to Dominate Big Data' (n 780).

[984] According to LinkedIn (Chinese Report), there are about 1.9 million AI specialists in the world with 850,000 of them working in the United States and only 50,000 in China. See «全球 AI 领域人才报告» [Global AI Talent Report] (*LinkedIn*, 2017) <https://business.linkedin.com/content/dam/me/business/zh-cn/talent-solutions/Event/july/lts-ai-report/%E9%A2%86%E8%8B%B1%E3%80%8A%E5%85%A8%E7%90%83AI%E9%A2%86%E5%9F%9F%E4%BA%BA%E6%89%8D%E6%8A%A5%E5%91%8A%E3%80%8B.pdf>. The survey took a broad approach to AI, covering deep learning, voice recognition, autonomous driving, natural language processing, but a narrow approach to the roles it counts. Only the technical roles (eg, engineers) are included, rather than other divisions within tech firms (eg, marketing).

[985] As noted in Chapter 8, Section 8.3.

generated while researching at work are published.[986] AI therefore 'reframes' traditional ideas of commercial advantage.[987] Even in datasets, 'sharing is not a dirty word. The key is to build an unassailable and advantaged collection of open and closed data sources'.[988] Microsoft, Google, Facebook and Amazon, while making remarkable progress developing AI systems, released much of their work to the public for free use, exploration, adaptation and perhaps improvement. Even DARPA[989] (the research arm of the US Department of Defense) has promoted its own open-source platforms[990] that now include Machine Learning technologies. The DARPA XDATA program resulted in a catalogue of state-of-the-art Machine Learning and other technologies that anyone can download, use and modify to build custom AI tools.[991] That DARPA and the US Defense Department are so supportive of open-source methods strongly indicates that the advantages of open source outweigh the disadvantages of making high-quality tools available to potential adversaries. This is partly because the more people looking at open-source code, the more likely it is that cyber-security risks can be found and resolved.

Furthermore, as noted in Chapter 8, AI researchers demand repeatability. In mid-February 2019, the not-for-profit research company OpenAI (founded by Elon Musk and Y Combinator's Sam Altman) announced that it had in simple terms made a breakthrough in training AI language models.[992] However, in doing so, it chose not to release the code or data so that its breakthrough could be verified. While media outlets promptly retold the story of the research breakthrough, prominent researchers in the Machine Learning community harangued OpenAI for its decision to keep the model private. Criticisms ranged from

---

[986] Philipp Gerbert, Jan Justus and Martin Hecker, 'Competing in the Age of Artificial Intelligence' (*BCG*, 16 January 2017) 2.
[987] Ibid.
[988] Ibid 3.
[989] Defense Advanced Research Projects Agency.
[990] Ryan Paul, 'Department of Defense Launches Open Source Site Forge.mil' (*Ars Technica*, 2 April 2009) <https://arstechnica.com/information-technology/2009/02/department-of-defense-launches-open-source-site-forgemil2019>.
[991] To view the DARPA XDATA program catalogue, see 'XDATA' (*DARPA*, 2019) <https://www.darpa.mil/program/xdata>.
[992] The non-profit said it decided not to share the full version of the program, a text-generation algorithm named 'GPT-2', due to concerns over 'malicious applications'. But many AI researchers criticised the decision, accusing the lab of exaggerating the danger posed by the work and inadvertently stoking 'mass hysteria' about AI in the process.

comedic jabs to arguments that OpenAI's claims were merely clickbait to attract media attention. Machine Learning Professor Zachary Lipton posed the question: Was OpenAI right to withhold its code and data?[993] OpenAI, however, claimed that the algorithm, open-source code and related datasets were not made public because of fears that bad actors would use them for nefarious means and 'malicious applications'.[994]

By withholding the model, OpenAI is stopping other researchers from replicating its work. Although Machine Learning is a relatively level playing field with lone researchers able to deliver surprising breakthroughs, in recent years there has been an increasing emphasis on resource-intensive research. Algorithms such as the one created by OpenAI are created using huge amounts of computing power and big datasets, both of which are expensive. The open-source community's argument posits that if well-funded labs such as OpenAI do not share their results, it diminishes the future crowdsourced innovations of the rest of the community.[995]

Thus, one benefit of open source is that it is good for crowdsourced innovation. On the other hand, there can be a risk that commercial open-source systems such as Google's Android mobile phone operating system will destroy competition.[996] Thus, advocates of open source also argue that there is a need to find ways to ensure that commercial open source can thrive, without the big cloud providers consuming all value and failing to contribute back to the community.[997] In fact, licensing of open source has always been a hotbed of debate, as providers such as Amazon

---

[993] Zachary C Lipton, 'OpenAI Trains Language Model, Mass Hysteria Ensues' (*Approximately Correct*, 17 February 219) <http://approximatelycorrect.com/2019/02/17/openai-trains-language-model-mass-hysteria-ensues/#more-875>.

[994] James Vincent, 'AI Researchers Debate the Ethics of Sharing Potentially Harmful Programs' (*Verge*, 21 February 2019) <https://www.theverge.com/2019/2/21/18234500/ai-ethics-debate-researchers-harmful-programs-openai>.

[995] Ibid.

[996] The academic literature posits that firms must be considered in the context of their business ecosystems and explores how differences in the ways in which firms are organized with respect to complementary activities affect their decision to invest in new technologies. See Rahul Kapoor and Joon Mahn Lee, 'Coordinating and Competing in Ecosystems: How Organizational Forms Shape New Technology Investments' (2012) 34(3) *Strategic Management Journal* 274.

[997] Matt Asay, 'MongoDB's New License Won't Solve Its China Problem' (*Techworld*, 19 October 2018) <https://www.techworld.com.au/article/648494/mongodb-new-license-won-t-solve-its-china-problem/?fp=16&fpid=1>.

Web Services (AWS) are making huge profits taking free code and running it as a service.[998]

Nevertheless, the relevance of this background is that without this wellspring of open-source knowledge, China could not have emerged as an AI powerhouse. And if China closes off its global innovation links by further employing Network Sovereignty policies such as data localisation, this may greatly damage its AI agenda.

Open-source innovation has been key to China's rapid AI progress. This progress has been enabled by its access to global technology research and markets. In fact, '[m]any seemingly "Chinese" AI achievements are actually achievements of multinational research teams and companies, and such international collaboration has been critical to China's research progress'.[999] According to a study of China's AI ecosystem by Tsinghua University, '[m]ore than half of China's AI papers were international joint publications'.[1000] This indicates that Chinese AI researchers – the top tier of whom often received their degrees abroad – were likely co-authoring with non-Chinese individuals. Even 'purely Chinese successes often build upon open-source technologies developed most often by international groups'.[1001] At academic AI conferences, a Chinese presence is now keenly felt. For example, a minor crisis erupted when the Association of the Advancement of Artificial Intelligence announced that its 2017 meeting dates conflicted with Chinese New Year. Chinese researchers were so integral to the meeting that the association had to reschedule.[1002] Importantly, this culture of openness has also allowed Chinese AI engineers to learn and build great companies, courtesy of openly available published research.[1003]

---

[998] 'The New War Over Open Source Licensing' (*Angel List*, 21 February 2019) <https://angel.co/newsletters/the-new-war-over-open-source-licensing-131>.
[999] Allen, 'Understanding China's AI Strategy' (n 894) 10.
[1000] Kai-fu Lee and Matt Sheehan, 'China's Rise in Artificial Intelligence: Ingredients and Economic Implications' (*Hoover Institute*, 29 October 2018) <https://www.hoover.org/research/chinas-rise-artificial-intelligence-ingredients-and-economic-implications>.
[1001] Ibid.
[1002] Sarah Zhang, 'China's Artificial-Intelligence Boom' (*The Atlantic*, 16 February 2017) <https://www.theatlantic.com/technology/archive/2017/02/china-artificial-intelligence/516615>.
[1003] See Lee, *AI Superpowers* (n 783).

9.3.3 Cloud Computing Onboarding

A third major benefit of the open-source AI platform business model, such as Google's TensorFlow, revolves around cloud service provider onboarding for developers who are using the platform to fork code and build new products. That is, large tech firms provide open-source tools for the purpose of selling cloud server storage. According to a report from research company IT Intelligence Markets, the global AI software market, which relies on cloud server storage, is expected to reach almost US$14 billion by the end of 2022.[1004]

Further, the companies that emerge as the dominant cloud players could shape the kinds of AI services that become widely adopted. 'Cloud computing companies are all racing to deploy increasingly sophisticated services featuring machine learning and AI. At stake is the opportunity to become the dominant player in what promises to be the next big computing paradigm.'[1005] Speaking at the technology conference EmTech China in Beijing in January 2018, Jian Wang, president of Alibaba's technology committee, predicted that cloud AI would become a major trend: 'I'm convinced that AI or machine learning will be the major consumer of applications [in the cloud]. ... It will offer many scenarios.'[1006] Therefore, there is a commercial reason why localising data in China is counterproductive to building China's innovation economy: it could hurt Chinese cloud providers (eg, AliYun) and China's ecosystem by scaring off foreign programming and development talent.

As the price of data storage in the cloud has decreased and high-performance computers and GPU processing chips have become more widely accessible, Machine Learning has expanded into a host of industries. As theoretical research is leveraged into practical tasks, a feature of China's AI ecosystem noted in previous chapters – Machine Learning tools – is increasingly useful and commonly integral now to many business operations.[1007] These AI platforms must all store data in the cloud. If a policy goal of data localisation is to encourage companies to

---

[1004] Global Artificial Intelligence Software Market Research Report 2017, *IT Intelligence Markets*.

[1005] Will Knight, 'China and the US Are Bracing for an AI Showdown – In the Cloud' (*MIT Technology Review*, 31 January 2018) <https://www.technologyreview.com/s/610140/china-and-the-us-are-bracing-for-an-ai-showdownin-the-cloud>.

[1006] Ibid.

[1007] See Sara Landset et al, 'A Survey of Open Source Tools for Machine Learning with Big Data in the Hadoop Ecosystem' (2015) 2(1) *Journal of Big Data* 1. Hadoop is an open-source project for reliable, scalable, distributed computing.

use Chinese cloud providers such as Alibaba Cloud, then the promotion of Chinese AI open-source platforms benefits these providers. For example, in July 2018, German technology provider Siemens agreed to partner with Alibaba Cloud for its MindSphere service – its cloud-based open IoT operating system that intelligently connects products, factories, systems and machines.[1008]

This field of AI is so new that there are still many opportunities for Chinese cloud providers.[1009] Building AI architectures remains difficult, but the open-source data science community is prolific, resulting in many AI software, data science and architecture options to choose from. Chinese open-source platforms were late entrants to the field (by a few years), but continue to emerge on the global marketplace. There are no one-size-fits-all Machine Learning tools. This is because the increasing complexity of Machine Learning project requirements as well as the nature of the data itself may require different types of solutions.[1010] As there is no single tool or framework that covers all or even the majority of common tasks, developers must consider the trade-offs that exist between usability, performance and algorithm selection when examining different solutions. There is a lack of comprehensive research on many of them, despite being widely employed on an enterprise level, and there is no current industry standard.[1011] Chinese open-source AI platforms (and cloud providers) can therefore still offer an alternative in the market.

Amazon and Google have both published open-source code that allows other companies to integrate more easily with their own cloud services. However, Google's success as an early mover in this space is clear. Google published and announced the open-source AI development

---

[1008] 'Siemens Inks Deal with Alibaba to Launch Digital Products in China' (*Reuters*, 9 July 2018) <https://www.reuters.com/article/us-siemens-alibaba/siemens-inks-deal-with-alibaba-to-launch-digital-products-in-china-idUSKBN1JZ22U>.

[1009] Current technology trends (eg, mobile phones and other IoT devices) are allowing for unprecedented access to massive amounts of data. Viable learning from this data can require complex architectures that use a combination of tools and techniques for collection, storage, processing and analysis. See Frieder Ganz, Daniel Puschmann and Payam Barnaghi, 'A Practical Evaluation of Information Processing and Abstraction Techniques for the Internet of Things' (2015) 2(4) *IEEE Internet of Things Journal* 340.

[1010] Often developers will find the selection of tools available to be unsatisfactory, but instead of contributing to existing open-source projects, they will begin one of their own. For further technical information see Goodfellow, Bengio and Courville, *Deep Learning* (n 52).

[1011] See Landset et al, 'A Survey of Open Source Tools' (n 1007).

system TensorFlow under version 2.0 of the Apache Licence on 9 November 2015. It has been very successful:

> Google, for its part, is the second-largest corporate contributor on GitHub, with roughly 1,850 employees actively contributing. More interestingly, Google has launched industry standards for container orchestration (Kubernetes)[1012] and machine learning (TensorFlow). Google benefits from that standardization around code friendly to its cloud, but it benefits even more from companies discovering they can run related workloads more productively on Google Cloud Platform. It's open source genius.[1013]

Nevertheless, like many other technology revolutions beginning in the United States, cloud computing is now taking China by storm as Chinese start-ups mature and Chinese conglomerates update their technology infrastructure. Alibaba's 2018 cloud computing conference[1014] attracted over 120,000 people from across China and Asia,[1015] dwarfing the more than 50,000 people who went to Las Vegas to attend Amazon Web Services' re:Invent 2018 conference.[1016] Key themes of the Alibaba conference included 'open-source software, adopting containers as part of their application deployment strategy, and learning how to apply machine-learning cloud services to their apps and businesses'.[1017] So perhaps China's Cyber Security Law will, intentionally or otherwise, allow Chinese firms to become the next dominant players in this new cloud computing market.

[1012] Kubernetes is an open-source container-orchestration system for automating application deployment, scaling and management. Designed by Google it is now maintained by the Cloud Native Computing Foundation.

[1013] Matt Asay, 'Why Critics Who Bash Musk's Open Source Tesla Security Project Are Wrong' (*Tech Republic*, 14 August 2018) <https://www.techrepublic.com/article/why-critics-who-bash-musks-open-source-tesla-security-project-are-wrong>.

[1014] Conference content is still available here: 'Alibaba's September Cloud Computing Conference' (*Alibaba*, September 2018) <https://www.alibabacloud.com/the-computing-conference-2018>.

[1015] Gabriel Li, 'Jack Ma Talks about Manufacturing Woes, Alibaba Cloud, and the DAMO Academy at the Computing Conference 2018' (*Pandaily*, 20 September 2018) <https://pandaily.com/jack-ma-talks-about-manufacturing-woes-alibaba-cloud-and-the-damo-academy-at-the-computing-conference-2018>.

[1016] Tom Krazit, 'AWS re:Invent 2018' (*Geek Wire*, 21 November 2018) <https://www.geekwire.com/special-coverage/aws-reinvent-2018>.

[1017] Tom Krazit, 'Building a Wall around the Cloud: Why China Will Soon Be a Very Important Cloud Computing Market' (*Geek Wire*, 13 January 2019) <https://www.geekwire.com/2019/building-wall-around-cloud-china-will-soon-important-cloud-computing-market>.

9.3.4 Maintenance and Crowdsourced Innovations

A fourth benefit of making software and platforms open source is that it is a powerful method for outsourcing maintenance, as developers can attempt to fix bugs. This benefit derived from open source is highly significant and perhaps more so in China than elsewhere, due to its huge population of software developers. Open-source software forms the backbone of many well-known products (eg, Netflix and Instagram) and other common daily online activities which are aided by open-source technology. Scrutiny, troubleshooting and bug-fixing are especially important in AI, where systems are designed to learn, adapt and make decisions autonomously. This is important because Deep Learning decisions – organising layers of Neural Networks hierarchically to analyse very large datasets to identify rich and interesting abstract patterns – are subject to much maintenance.[1018]

Chinese companies operating at large scale already understand the power of open source for product maintenance. Li Luo, technical director of big data at Didi Chuxing (which acquired Uber in China in 2016), explained how by pushing innovation into open-source projects, Didi effectively shares the wealth of crowdsourced innovation:

> Most of the time, we don't have to keep up with the pace of innovation, since in the projects we use we'll often also be leading contributors of that innovation because of our specific requirements. So we don't have to worry about open source projects being displaced by new ones. Our job is to solve the business problems of our company and open source allows us to solve those problems more efficiently. That's why we use it.[1019]

Didi Chuxing's ride-hailing services operate on a massive scale; it provided more than 30 million rides per day in 257 different Chinese cities during 2017.[1020] This is another important reason why open source is

---

[1018] As explained in Chapter 8.

[1019] Asay, 'Why Critics Who Bash Musk's Open Source' (n 1013). For companies like Telsa, trying to build the maximum number of cars at the minimum cost, 'outsourcing' some of its key software development is seen as a key strategic move.

[1020] Bernard Marr, 'AI in China: How Uber Rival Didi Chuxing Uses Machine Learning To Revolutionize Transportation' (*Forbes*, 26 November 2018) <https://www.forbes.com/sites/bernardmarr/2018/11/26/ai-in-china-how-uber-rival-didi-chuxing-uses-machine-learning-to-revolutionize-transportation/#11b7bc6f6732>. Additionally, in 2019, Didi Chuxing launched an open platform for smart transportation, giving enterprises and developers access to its AI capabilities. Didi now provides access to its Machine Learning platform that includes services such as voice, image and natural language processing. Other applications include scene perception, mapping and travel safety.

important to China specifically: 'There is great value in stress-testing software in China. Because, if you can meet China's scale demands, everything else is easy.'[1021]

Thus, these three reasons – onboarding talented developers through transparent and open innovations, gaining cloud computing customers and outsourcing maintenance – show why open-source AI platforms have become a globally popular business model for AI firms over the past five years, and why China is rapidly developing such platforms itself.

9.4 Global Nature of Open-Source AI Platforms and Role of Global R&D Centres in AI Development in China

Global links to and from China's AI ecosystem have evolved rapidly since 2017 through open source and R&D. Globalised R&D centres and cross-border strategic research partnerships and investments are a prominent feature of AI development internationally. It is important to assess these networks and cross-border linkages as they impact China, and to explore how they operate on a practical level, such as in the operation of open-source AI platforms and R&D split across global research centres.[1022]

These linkages are too numerous to list, but key partnerships are noted in Section 9.4. These examples are important for two reasons. First, they signify the extent of the global connections; second, these connections mostly began during 2017 when China's cyber regulators still had little awareness of their potential conflict with data localisation.

The evolving global links to China's AI ecosystem are extensive and worth documenting at length here. These links perhaps illustrate the confidence in China's AI ecosystem, or a commercial desire for companies to have a relationship with both major AI ecosystems (China and

---

Didi has previously provided anonymised trip data and computing resources to researchers through its Gaia Initiative. Its academic collaboration expanded recently through a partnership with US-based Berkeley DeepDrive (BDD) Industry Consortium: Chris Udemans, 'Didi Launches Open Platform for Smart Transportation, AI Services' (*Technode*, 9 May 2019) <https://technode.com/2019/05/10/didi-open-ai-transport>.

[1021] Asay, 'Why China Is the Next Proving Ground' (n 962).

[1022] For example, see KC Fung and Nathalie Aminian, 'Silicon Valley, France and China: A Comparative Study of Innovation Systems and Policies' (2017) *Journal of Chinese Economic and Foreign Trade Studies* 10(3) 194–214. The authors argue that the internet-driven economy is a radical, systemic technological change that has features specific to China, as affected by the nature of the closed off internet, but electronics supply chains remain highly globalised.

the United States),[1023] regardless of the Cyber Security Law's data localisation provisions. For example, in May 2018, US firm Qualcomm, an early player in AI development, opened an AI lab in Beijing in conjunction with Baidu's open-source Deep Learning framework PaddlePaddle. Qualcomm stated they would use its Qualcomm AI Engine to drive the application of the PaddlePaddle open-source Deep Learning framework models on Qualcomm Snapdragon mobile platforms.[1024] Essentially, PaddlePaddle is a Chinese version of Google's TensorFlow and it is possible that Qualcomm made this move to gain access to parochial (perhaps mostly Chinese) Baidu developers, or in anticipation of the Cyber Security Law's data localisation provisions rendering some datasets immovable outside of China.

Further, in March 2019, when Huawei announced its latest smartphone, the company also announced another product, Track AI, which allows Huawei devices to help 'non-trained professionals' diagnose eye conditions. Yet missing from the Chinese company's announcement was that Huawei Technologies built Track AI using Google's TensorFlow. As TensorFlow is open source, anyone anywhere can use it and Google cannot control access.[1025] Despite the ongoing United States–China trade war (at the time of writing), Chinese tech companies continue to build products on open-source platforms created in Silicon Valley.[1026] In March 2020, Huawei announced that Mindspore was now clearly intended to rival TensorFlow.[1027]

Previously, in 2018, Huawei had made Google's open-source Android messages application its default messaging app across all its devices.[1028]

[1023] See Lee, *AI Superpowers* (n 783).
[1024] Masha Borak, 'Qualcomm Opening an AI Lab in Beijing, Joining Hands with Baidu's PaddlePaddle' (*Technode*, 24 May 2018) <https://technode.com/2018/05/24/qualcomm-ai-lab-china-baidu-paddlepaddle>.
[1025] Shelly Banjo and Mark Bergen, 'The Trade War Didn't Stop a Google and Huawei AI Collaboration' (*Bloomberg*, 1 April 2019) <https://www.bloomberg.com/news/articles/2019-04-01/the-trade-war-didn-t-stop-a-google-and-huawei-ai-collaboration>.
[1026] Ibid.
[1027] Mike Wheatley, 'Huawei Open-Sources AI Framework MindSpore to Rival Google's TensorFlow' (*Silicon Angle*, 30 March 2020) <https://siliconangle.com/2020/03/30/huawei-open-sourced-ai-framework-called-mindspore-rival-googles-tensorflow/>.
[1028] Paul Sawers, 'Google and Huawei Partner to Bring RCS to Millions via Jibe and Android Messages App' (*Venture Beat*, 18 January 2018) <https://venturebeat.com/2018/01/18/google-and-huawei-partner-to-bring-rcs-to-millions-via-jibe-and-android-messages-app>.

John Suffolk, senior vice president and global cyber security and privacy officer at Huawei, noted:

> If you open up a Huawei telecommunications equipment, 70% of what's in there is not Huawei. Typically, the biggest providers of components to Huawei's telecommunications equipment are American technology companies. So, you are not banning Huawei or singling out Huawei, you are singling out a set of global supply chains, in which only 30% is Huawei . . . Singling out any particular vendor doesn't work because it's just a label. Even for mobile phones, what's in there is the Android operating system, which is American.[1029]

However, as noted, by mid-2019, Huawei could no longer use Android, as the company found itself at the centre of a global tussle between the United States and China after the Trump administration placed the Chinese brand on the blacklist of foreign suppliers that could pose national security risks, limiting the business US companies could do with it, and leading to Google blocking Huawei's future access to Android updates.[1030]

Certainly, many 'Made in China' products are assembled with semiconductor chips that are designed in the United States and manufactured in Taiwan or Korea, and that run software developed by US firms such as Google, Microsoft and Apple.[1031] Coe et al called this phenomenon 'global production networks (GPNs)': 'the globally organized nexus of

---

[1029] Yuthika Bhargava, 'No Right Answer Yet to "Privacy vs Security" Parley' (*The Hindu*, 10 December 2017) <http://www.thehindu.com/opinion/interview/no-right-answer-yet-to-privacy-vs-security-parley/article21386236.ece>.

[1030] Gareth Beavis, 'Huawei Ban: The Global Fallout Explained' (*Techradar*, 28 May 2019) <https://www.techradar.com/au/news/googles-huawei-android-restrictions-heres-what-it-means-for-you>.

[1031] Supply chains are complex, as noted in Allen, 'Understanding China's AI Strategy' (n 894) 13: Most of the world's consumer electronics are labelled 'Made in China'. Sixty-five per cent of the world's personal computers, notebooks and tablets as well as nearly 85% of the world's mobile phones are reportedly made in China: Shanshan Du, *China Integrated Circuit Ecosystem Report* (SEMI Industry Research and Statistics, October 2018) 5 <http://www1.semi.org/en/china-ic-ecosystem-report>. The iPhone, for example, bears a 'Made in China' label, but only low-skill assembly and commodity component production occurs in China. One study calculated that Chinese contributions account for less than 2% of the overall cost of the iPhone, even though 100% of the cost of the device is counted in the United States' trade deficit with China: Jason Dedrick and Kenneth L Kraemer, 'Intangible Assets and Value Capture in Global Value Chains: The Smartphone Industry' (World Intellectual Property Organization Working Paper, November 2017) <https://www.wipo.int/edocs/pubdocs/en/wipo_pub_econstat_wp_41.pdf>.

interconnected functions and operations by firms and non-firm institutions through which goods and services are produced and distributed'.[1032] Already by 2013 a World Investment Report estimated that 80% of global trade was organised by GPNs.[1033]

9.4.1 Global R&D Centres

Connections between Chinese and US companies or institutions engaged in the development of AI increased greatly during 2017–2018, especially in the area of R&D. Chinese AI companies have pursued strategic investments and partnerships in Silicon Valley. Baidu, for example, was among the first to set up a Silicon Valley AI Lab in 2014. US companies have also begun to set up in China. Google opened an AI lab in Beijing in 2017, and Apple announced a partnership with Tsinghua University to create a joint research centre for AI-related technologies in 2018.[1034] In May 2018, Amazon also launched an innovation centre in Xian.[1035] Google and Microsoft both opened AI research centres in China reportedly looking to hire a talented Chinese AI workforce.[1036] However, there remains a strong belief that the US West Coast is still the magnet for many of the world's top engineering brains, and many of the AI engineers in Silicon Valley and other advanced centres of AI development are Chinese.[1037] In April 2016, Tencent set up its AI lab in Shenzhen and in May 2017 it opened a research centre in Seattle led by former Microsoft

---

[1032] Neil M Coe et al, '"Globalizing" Regional Development: A Global Production Networks Perspective' (2004) 29(4) *Transactions of the Institute of British Geographers* 468, 471.

[1033] UNCTAD, *World Investment Report 2013: Global Value Chains: Investment and Trade for Development* (2013) <https://unctad.org/en/PublicationsLibrary/wir2013_en.pdf>.

[1034] Both deals were noted in Ma Si, 'China a Pioneer in AI Innovation' (*China Daily*, 27 March 2018) <http://www.chinadaily.com.cn/a/201803/27/WS5ab9a24da3105cdcf65147e9.html>.

[1035] 'Amazon Launches another Innovation Center in China' (*Xinhua*, 24 May 2018) <http://www.xinhuanet.com/english/2018-05/24/c_137203869.htm>.

[1036] Runhua Zhao, 'Microsoft to Set Up Asia AI Research Branch in Shanghai' (*Technode*, 17 September 2018) <https://technode.com/2018/09/17/microsoft-research-asia-shanghai>. Zhao noted: 'During the World AI Conference taking place in Shanghai, Microsoft announced they will launch an R&D affiliate Microsoft Research Asia's branch for AI in Shanghai. Big data, cloud computing, and deep learning are the three elements Microsoft acknowledges as driving forces.'

[1037] Lucas and Waters, 'China and US Compete to Dominate Big Data' (n 780).

scientist Yu Dong. Baidu also set up in Seattle[1038] after acquiring a small US start-up called Kitt.ai in July 2017.

Of the high-profile 'unicorn' Chinese AI start-ups, image recognition company Yitu Tech opened a Singapore research branch in 2019.[1039] In August 2018, ByteDance[1040] and US chipmaker Intel set up a joint innovation lab,[1041] now located at ByteDance's new data centre in Beijing. The partnership between the two companies dates back to 2013 through cooperation in a variety of fields ranging from big data to AI technology development.[1042] The two parties also established an innovation fund in 2018. Even in the core technology sector of AI chip making, which is a central objective of China's AI plan (noted in Chapter 8), China's AI sector saw cross-border mergers and acquisitions[1043] and partnership activity in 2018.[1044]

[1038] Todd Bishop, 'Chinese Tech Powerhouse Baidu Opens Seattle-Area Office, Expanding Its Reach in AI and the Cloud' (*Geek Wire*, 9 October 2017) <https://www.geekwire.com/2017/chinese-tech-powerhouse-baidu-opens-seattle-area-office-expanding-reach-ai-cloud>.

[1039] 'Yitu Technology Opens AI R&D Centre in Singapore; To Add Some 70 Staff over 3 Years' (*Straights Times*, 31 January 2019) <https://www.straitstimes.com/business/companies-markets/yitu-technology-opens-ai-rd-centre-in-singapore-to-add-some-70-staff-over>.

[1040] ByteDance is worth singling out here, as its original flagship product Jinri Toutiao is an AI-powered news aggregation platform that delivers personalised content recommendations based on readers' interests. It is notable as an AI firm because AI firms in China usually create politically acceptable technologies (eg, public security products or self-driving cars). As an algorithm-generated news aggregator, ByteDance is succeeding in China's fuzzy content control regulations, largely by hiring many content controllers. The company uses several AI technologies in its services (eg, content recommendation algorithms, natural language processing, computer vision and voice recognition). The company also operates the massively popular video content-creating platforms Douyin (TikTok), musical.ly and Huoshan (Vulcano Video). With the popularity of ByteDance-backed apps, the company is in need of huge processing power for its massive data, which is important because it has been very successful abroad, particularly in India and the United States.

[1041] Emma Lee, 'Updated: Toutiao and Intel Set Up Joint AI Lab' (*Technode*, 22 August 2018) <https://technode.com/2018/08/22/bytedance-intel-ai-lab>.

[1042] Ibid.

[1043] DeePhi Technology, a Beijing-based Machine Learning specialist, was acquired by US chipmaker Xilinx Inc: 'Xilinx Announces the Acquisition of DeePhi Tech' (*Xilinx*, 17 July 2018) <https://www.xilinx.com/news/press/2018/xilinx-announces-the-acquisition-of-deephi-tech.html>.

[1044] Baidu joined Intel in a wide-spanning alliance. This includes joining forces in making AI 'Kunlun' processing chips. Kunlun leverages Baidu's AI ecosystem, which includes AI applications such as search ranking and Deep Learning frameworks, PaddlePaddle

Research partnerships between Chinese AI companies and US universities also expanded in 2018. In addition to the Intel partnership, ByteDance partnered with the Berkeley University AI Research Lab.[1045] Facial recognition start-up SenseTime also signed a research partnership with MIT.[1046] That partnership is seen as controversial because SenseTime provides the Chinese government with surveillance assistance.[1047]

Thus, another factor behind AI's rapid development in China is the willingness of Chinese AI firms to collaborate in cross-border research and product development with foreign universities and companies (eg, SenseTime collaborating with MIT in AI R&D).[1048] And to compete with Google Home, US giant Amazon's Alexa division and Chinese telecommunications giant Huawei signed an agreement for Huawei to develop an AI Cube smart speaker with a 4G router in September 2018.[1049] The internal workings of the speaker are made by Amazon. This agreement occurred during the start of tensions in the US–China geopolitical environment in 2018. By 2019 such agreements were difficult if not impossible.

---

among them. Kunlun can be used in many areas ranging from autonomous vehicles to data centres. In addition to supporting the common open-source Deep Learning algorithms, Kunlun can support a wide variety of AI applications such as voice recognition, search ranking, natural language processing, autonomous driving and large-scale recommendations: Andy Patrizio, 'Baidu Takes a Major Leap as an AI Player with New Chip, Intel Alliance' (*Network World*, 11 July 2018) <https://www.networkworld.com/article/3289387/data-center/baidu-takes-a-major-leap-as-an-ai-player-with-new-chip-intel-alliance.html>.

[1045] 'Bytedance Partners with Berkeley Artificial Intelligence Research Lab to Foster Future AI Innovators and Entrepreneurs' (*PR Newswire*, 3 April 2018) <https://www.prnewswire.com/news-releases/bytedance-partners-with-berkeley-artificial-intelligence-research-lab-to-foster-future-ai-innovators-and-entrepreneurs-300623346.html>.

[1046] 'MIT and SenseTime Announce Effort to Advance Artificial Intelligence Research' (*MIT News*, 28 February 2018) <http://news.mit.edu/2018/mit-sensetime-announce-effort-advance-artificial-intelligence-research-0228>.

[1047] Paul Mozur, 'One Month, 500,000 Face Scans: How China Is Using AI to Profile a Minority' (*New York Times*, 14 April 2019), <https://www.nytimes.com/2019/04/14/technology/china-surveillance-artificial-intelligence-racial-profiling.html>.

[1048] 'MIT and SenseTime Announce Effort to Advance Artificial Intelligence Research' (n 1046).

[1049] Jason Evangelho, 'Amazon Alexa and Huawei Team Up for AI Cube Smart Speaker + 4G Router' (*Forbes*, 31 August 2018) <https://www.forbes.com/sites/jasonevangelho/2018/08/31/amazon-alexa-and-huawei-team-up-for-ai-cube-smart-speaker-4g-router/#2095d09cba73>.

Links between China and the United States in technology are so extensive that most casual onlookers might be surprised. For example, Tencent and Google in late 2017 agreed to cross-licence patents on a range of products and technologies.[1050] Under the agreement, both companies have the freedom to access each other's patent portfolios. Neither party can sue the other for patent infringement. Google has signed similar agreements before with Samsung Electronics, LG Electronics and Cisco Systems, but the deal with Tencent was the first with a large Chinese tech firm.

With the growing importance of international open-source platforms for Chinese AI firms, and the extensive links between Chinese and international technology partners in the area of AI research, the Chinese government finally began to understand the value of open-source platforms to AI R&D, and in March 2018 released a white paper on the subject.[1051] China's minister of science and technology, Wan Gang, also announced in March 2018 that China would accelerate the application of AI technologies in wider fields by constructing open-source platforms. He noted that open source can help create greater transparency around AI applications, stating that China 'must make such sources open so that the technologies can play a role in economic and social development'.[1052] That new Chinese government approach is explained next.

[1050] Google signed a patent-licensing deal with Tencent as it looked for ways to expand in China, where many of its products (including the Google app store, search engine and email service) are blocked by regulators. According to Google, patent-licensing agreements reduce the potential of litigation over patent infringement. In 2018 Google opened an office in Shenzhen, which is home to Tencent. In December 2017, Google announced the opening of its new AI lab in Beijing. Both companies have been making strategic investments in each other's parts of the world. Examples include Tencent's investments in Snapchat, Spotify and Tesla, and Alphabet's (Google's) investments in Chushou. See Toyoki Nakanishi and Yu Nakamura, 'Google Seeks Better China Relations via Tencent Patent Deal' (*Nikkei Asian Review*, 20 January 2018) <https://asia.nikkei.com/Business/Deals/Google-seeks-better-China-relations-via-Tencent-patent-deal>.

[1051] «中国人工智能开源软件发展白皮书» [White Paper on the Development of China's AI Open-Source Software] (People's Republic of China) MIIT, July 2018 (Open-Source White Paper). The full Chinese text can be found here: <https://pan.baidu.com/s/1p8hAM8Ggz4LjXagO62-AYg>.

[1052] Li Yingqi, 'China Eyes Wider Application of AI Technologies' (*People's Daily*, 14 March 2018) <http://en.people.cn/n3/2018/0314/c90000-9437000.html>.

9.5 Chinese Government Approach to Open-Source AI Platforms: Public–Private Platforms for Domestic Open Innovation

Having grasped the significance of open-source platforms and open innovation, Chinese technology regulators are seeking to replicate the success of TensorFlow by announcing public–private partnerships with leading Chinese market players named as the 'AI National Team' (see previous chapter). This development was introduced in Chapter 8 (Section 8.7), but without detailed analysis of its implications for open-source AI. As noted, the notion of an AI National Team dates back to November 2017 when China's MOST originally elevated four companies to lead development in four specific fields of AI technology application. While the government seeks to enable open platforms for AI innovation through this process, private sector companies are in charge of creating the necessary information infrastructure behind these platforms. The companies are Baidu (NASDAQ listed), responsible for autonomous driving; Alibaba (NYSE listed), responsible for Smart Cities; Tencent (SEHK Hong Kong listed), responsible for medical imaging; and iFlyTek (SSE Shenzhen listed), responsible for intelligent voice. In September 2018, MOST designated a fifth National AI 'Champion', when SenseTime[1053] (privately held) was elevated to be responsible for building an open innovation platform for intelligent vision. During 2019 this expanded to 15 National AI Team members, many blacklisted by the US Entity List. After providing more detail on the different focuses of the first five platforms, this chapter analyses the Chinese government's objectives for adopting this approach.

9.5.1 The 'Open-Source' Aspects of the National AI Platforms

The 'open-source' aspects of the National AI Platforms are as follows:

- iFlytek – iFLYOS is an open speech-recognition platform, with 920,000 registered developers by December 2018. Its speech-recognition capabilities cover 23 Chinese dialects. (Some Chinese dialects remain a complex problem for speech recognition, because there is little data due to small numbers of remaining speakers.) Reports about iFLYOS claim that on the platform there are more than 100,000 personal voice banks and more than 90 customised corporate voice banks (ie, to be used by

---

[1053] The most valuable AI start-up globally in 2018, valued at US$1.2 billion.

corporate partners).[1054] iFLYOS code remains housed on GitHub as of 2021.[1055]

- Alibaba – Feitian or ET Brain is the cloud computing platform for the company's Smart City platform. ET Brain has been made an open-source project, partially built on Alibaba's own Deep Learning framework, XDL, which was released in late 2018. Any engineer or company with technical development capabilities can become a developer of the ET Brain open platform.[1056] The platform provides urban databases, a city platform, computing capabilities and an AI modelling platform. In the case of Alibaba's Smart City Brain project, public data is being used in pilot projects run together with the Hangzhou and Suzhou local governments to make the two cities' public traffic flows more efficient. Alibaba's ET Smart City Brain is directly linked to image data collected by urban cameras and is able to use Computer Vision and big data analysis to process the flows of information in real time.[1057]
- Tencent – In August 2017, Tencent released an AI medical imaging product which, in cooperation with medical schools and medical institutions, aims to help improve disease detection across public hospitals. Miying is Tencent's AI imaging product. The 'open innovation' aspect of Miying is reportedly that Tencent's reports on its vast repositories of medical knowledge datasets are fed into Miying. How this works

---

[1054] 王刚 [Wang Gang], «BAT, 科大讯飞, 商汤等 5大 AI 国家队的 一次 '集体工作汇报» [A 'Collective Work Report' of the Five Major 'National Team' Members – BAT, iFlytek and Sensetime] (*Leiphone*, 11 May 2019) <https://mp.weixin.qq.com/s/ksJm980HsmfUEhI5U6UQlg?fbclid=IwAR3BGbjFtiz1UFtMRWvYPjkfWDfGf3KgsIWJtVKn_UwXjAdGyC3wE_cnZ-I>.

[1055] 'iFLYOS Open Source' (*GitHub*) <https://github.com/iFLYOS-OPEN>.

[1056] Besides the ET City Brain, Alibaba offers an ET Industrial Brain, ET Medical Brain, ET Environment Brain, ET Aviation Brain and ET Financial Brain.

[1057] A strong competitor to Alibaba on this field is DiDi, which is engaged in similar partnerships with several local governments across China. DiDi's advantage on the field is that its ride-hailing platform and its large ecosystem provide a direct view into traffic patterns based on the information of its fleet of drivers. Similar to Alibaba's ET Brain, DiDi's platform software is currently being used by cities ranging from Xi'an to Chengdu to optimise mobility flows bridging old physical infrastructure with a layer of digital infrastructure to upgrade existing traffic flows, enhancing the provision of public goods. The city government connects IT systems that power its public infrastructure, from traffic lights to mass transit systems, with the DiDi platform. Integrating these with knowledge of traffic patterns, ride-hail and bike-sharing infrastructure, the optimisation of the flow of people and traffic is being updated in a new and innovative manner through the sharing of public proprietary data with industry and platform-based AI solutions.

remained unclear.[1058] Miying focuses on five major diseases: colorectal, lung, breast and cervical cancers and various diseases of the eye.

Of particular significance to this book are the last two platforms: SenseTime's SenseParrots, because it was designed to compete with Google's TensorFlow, and Baidu's Apollo, because of its global research programme.

- SenseTime – SenseParrots is a platform which is positioned to compete with Berkeley's Caffe2, Facebook's PyTorch and Google's TensorFlow.[1059] After being publicly endorsed by the Chinese government, Tang Xiaoou, founder of SenseTime[1060] and professor at the Chinese University of Hong Kong, declared new plans to invest more in the construction of the designated open innovation platform.[1061]
- Baidu – Apollo is an open-source platform for autonomous driving. It is explained in depth in Section 9.7.

The five original National AI Platforms are designed to play the role of incubators for start-ups and smaller enterprises, allowing them to explore, build, incorporate and base their value propositions on interconnected AI applications. Alibaba Cloud Machine Intelligence chief scientist, Min Wanli, noted that Alibaba is willing to take advantage of the opportunity to build a platform and develop it together with industry

---

[1058] 王刚 [Wang Gang], «次 '集体工作汇报» [A 'Collective Work Report'] (n 1054).
[1059] Ibid.
[1060] SenseTime is responsible for realising breakthroughs in four key areas. The first area relates to core R&D of intelligent computer vision and connected IT tools. The area involves core R&D of SenseTime's training system, including its computer vision application chain, and the construction of its data analysis system. The second area of responsibility relates to key technologies and common support technologies of computer vision, promoting the integration of computer vision technology with multiple industries. The third area of responsibility is to establish an AI talent system that is able to cultivate international talents. SenseTime's fourth area of responsibility is to create mass entrepreneurship and innovation through AI empowerment, bringing into play its ecosystem environment through collective innovation spaces as well as internal company incubators. SenseTime has also been designated as an important player in promoting China's Greater Bay Area consisting of Guangdong, Hong Kong and Macau.
«商汤继 BAT，科大讯飞后成第五个国家人工智能开放创新平台» [SenseTime Follows BAT and IFlytek to Become the Fifth National AI Open Innovation Platform] (*Sohu*, 20 September 2018) <https://www.sohu.com/a/254985856_115565>.
[1061] 胡喆 [Hu Wei] and 周琳 [Zhou Lin], «智能视觉国家新一代人工智能开放创新平台正式亮相» [Intelligent Vision National New Generation AI Open Innovation Platform Officially Debuts] (*Xinhua*, 20 September 2018) <http://www.xinhuanet.com/politics/2018-09/20/c_1123461737.htm>.

to enhance the competitiveness of China's AI sector in the shortest time possible.[1062]

Thus, arguably, this plan does not demonstrate the Chinese government's awareness of the negative impact of data localisation on Chinese open-source AI; rather, it is simply a domestically focused attempt to create and foster China's own domestic open-source AI industry.

There is certainly evidence for this view. As noted in the previous chapter, China's AI industry has achieved important breakthroughs in some core areas of AI technology, especially industrial applications. However, compared with leading countries in AI development, China still lacks major original results in the development of basic theory, core algorithms, key equipment and high-end chips, according to the Chinese government.[1063] Chinese policymakers are therefore trying to close these perceived gaps by actively supporting the formation of an open innovation ecosystem for AI in close collaboration with leading market players.

A 2019 paper by the Centre for New American Security covering China's AI ecosystem noted that the 'absence of Chinese AI companies among the major AI framework developers and open-source AI software communities was identified as a noteworthy weakness of China's AI ecosystem in several of [the author's] conversations with executives in China's technology industry'.[1064] Indeed, China's first open-source white paper to promote a nascent domestic open-source platform development in China, promulgated in March 2018, also identified these weaknesses, along with proposals for overcoming them.

The White Paper on China's Development of AI Open-Source Software （中国人工智能开源软件发展白皮书）(Open-Source White Paper)[1065] was published by a new body called the China AI Open-Source Software Development League （中国人工智能开源发展联盟）. This was established on 15 March 2018 to support the China Electronics Standardisation Institute (CESI) under MIIT.[1066] In accordance with standard practice, industry was extensively consulted for the

---

[1062] «国家级'新一代人工智能开放创新平台'怎么建» [How to Build a National New-Generation AI Open Innovation Platform] (*Xinhua*, 27 November 2017) <http://www.xinhuanet.com//tech/2017-11/27/c_1122013676.htm>.

[1063] «15个部委合力 首批4家国家创新平台确立» [15 Ministries Join Forces to Establish the First Batch of 4 National Innovation Platforms] (n 884).

[1064] Allen, 'Understanding China's AI Strategy' (n 894) 12.

[1065] Open-Source White Paper (n 1051).

[1066] Ibid.

white paper along with academia. The League and CESI convened meetings of more than 60 contributors. Academic institutions and tech companies included Peking University, the Chinese Academy of Sciences, JD.com, Webank, Ant Financial, Alibaba, Baidu and Huawei. The Open-Source White Paper made the following statement about China's future trajectory:

> In the development history of AI Open Source Software, due to the relatively limited participation of China, the current situation of the AI Open Source Software market is dominated by Western developed countries. At the same time, regarding China's AI Open Source Software technology and industry ecology there exist certain insufficiencies. To this end, this White Paper proposes three pathways for China's AI Open Source Software development based on the strategic objectives of: 'directly adopt, partly participate', to 'emphasise breakthroughs, lead locally', and then to 'independently lead, widely use'. This is not just producing methods to gain traction based on analysis of the current status of China's AI Open Source Software, it is more so creating effective measures that can be gradually implemented for the future development of China's AI Open Source Software.[1067]

Stakeholder mapping in the Open-Source White Paper evidenced a deep understanding of the global open-source ecosystem, including open-source developer foundations such as the Apache Software Foundation.[1068] Yet how Chinese open-source platforms will integrate into this global system with Network Sovereignty in the background was not addressed in the Open-Source White Paper. China's Cyber Security Law still potentially posed great problems for the global expansion plans proposed in the White Paper.

However, what appears to be emerging from this policy discussion document is a staged process whereby China will initially rely on global networks. But after building its own domestic AI capability through the AI National Team's development of open source, it will increasingly cut those chains of dependence. Therefore, in the initial period at least, data localisation rules are unlikely to be enforced if they would hinder that development. The creation of Gitee in 2020 discussed earlier evidences this hypothesis.

Certainly, China's leaders now see open source as a way to promote the domestic technology industry. In November 2018, Dr Tan Tieniu,

---

[1067] Ibid.
[1068] Explained above in Section 9.2.

deputy secretary-general of the Chinese Academy of Sciences, gave a wide-ranging speech to many of China's most senior leaders at the 13th National People's Congress Standing Committee. He argued that China's lagging status in technical standards, software frameworks and semiconductors left China vulnerable and in dire need of domestic alternatives:

> [China should] construct an independent and controllable innovation ecosystem. American companies such as Google, IBM, Microsoft, and Facebook have actively built innovation ecosystems, seized the innovative high ground, and already in the international AI industry hold the upper hand in AI chips, servers, operating systems, open source algorithms, cloud services, and autonomous driving, among others. China's AI open source community and technological innovation ecosystem are comparatively lagging, the strength of technology platform construction needs to be reinforced, and [China's] international influence remains to be improved.[1069]

China's AI Security White Paper[1070] also lamented the fact that 'at present, the research and development of domestic artificial intelligence products and applications is mainly based on Google and Microsoft'.[1071] It was reported that the absence of 'Chinese AI companies among the major AI framework developers and open-source AI software communities was identified as a noteworthy weakness of China's AI ecosystem [by] executives in China's technology industry'.[1072] Notably, 'none of the most popular machine learning software frameworks have been developed in China'.[1073]

As an example of these weaknesses, Chinese AI leader SenseTime has devoted extensive resources to its own Machine Learning framework,

---

[1069] An English translation of Tan Tieniu's speech is available in Cameron Hickert and Jeffrey Ding (trans), 'Read What Top Chinese Officials Are Hearing about AI Competition and Policy' (*New America*, 29 November 2018) <https://www.newamerica.org/cybersecurity-initiative/digichina/blog/read-what-top-chinese-officials-are-hearing-about-ai-competition-and-policy>.

[1070] 《人工智能安全白皮书》 [AI Security White Paper] (People's Republic of China) China Academy of Information and Communications Technology (CAICT), September 2018 <http://www.caict.ac.cn/kxyj/qwfb/bps/201809/P020180918473525332978.pdf> (AI Security White Paper).

[1071] Quoted in Allen, 'Understanding China's AI Strategy' (n 894) 12. The original comment can be found in AI Security White Paper (n 1070) 36.

[1072] Ibid.

[1073] Ibid.

SenseParrots. SenseParrots is intended to be a superior platform for computer-vision AI applications, yet so far, the company appears to have had limited success in promoting adoption.[1074] Ultimately, SenseTime chose to open source an alternative platform, OpenMMLab,[1075] first instead of SenseParrots, because SenseParrots lacked 'ecosystem-level influence'.

TensorFlow still reigns supreme and will continue to do so for the foreseeable future. This is because Google uses TensorFlow extensively. As noted, whenever a new paper is published by Google DeepMind or Google Brain, it uses TensorFlow, and this trickles down to independent researchers who end up using their TensorFlow implementations. While open-source AI frameworks continue to proliferate, TensorFlow remains the most popular.[1076]

As popular open-source projects draw a lot of their power from the talent they can harness, having thousands of engineers use and rely on their software is pure marketing. A national data localisation policy may draw the ire of the open-source community, and as a result is a great danger to continued cross-border collaborative innovation. Thus, it is worth highlighting the discordance between Network Sovereignty and community open-source projects, which are open collaboration

---

[1074] Ibid.

[1075] PyTorch and TensorFlow have consolidated huge network effects and first-mover advantages creating rich ecosystems. Thousands of papers and products are built on these two frameworks. Simply open-sourcing an AI training framework is not enough for SenseTime's bottom-layer Deep Learning framework SenseParrots to compete. So SenseTime chose to compete from another angle. OpenMMLab, which includes upper-level algorithms and application platforms in Deep Learning for computer vision. As of March 2021, OpenMMLab had accumulated more than 20,000 stars (akin to Facebook's likes, but also a way of following a project) on GitHub, covering more than 10 research directions, more than 100 algorithms, and more than 700 pre-trained models. For reference, TensorFlow has 154,000, and Megvii's MegEngine has 3,800).

阿司匹林 [Aspirin – a pen name], «GitHub 汽车标星 20000+, 国产 AI 开源从算法开始突破 | 专访商汤联合创始人林达华» [20,000+ stars on Github, a domestically developed AI open-source software starts to breakthrough | interview with Lin Dahua, Sensetime cofounder] (*CSDN*, 31 August 2020) <https://mp.weixin.qq.com/s/7LLfEEONLaVTxAQDke87xw?fbclid=IwAR30b6jkmKfnrPrQR5lww4w_3qtmBBBmlfWZT8AxDiXgetqnZ13GmJ31qTw>. Thanks to Jeff Ding for finding this source and his original translation.

[1076] Giang Nguyen, Stefan Dlugolinsky and Martin Bobák, 'Machine Learning and Deep Learning Frameworks and Libraries for Large-Scale Data Mining: A Survey' (2019) 51 (1) *Artificial Intelligence Review* 77.

Table 9.1 *The most popular AI frameworks and their origination*

Framework/Library	Description	Language	Developer	Year
TensorFlow	Library for Machine Learning	Python, C++	Google Brain Team	2015
Microsoft CNTK	Library for Machine Learning	C++	Microsoft Research	2016
Theano	Library for Machine Learning	Python	University of Montreal	2007
Caffe	Library for Machine Learning	C++	Berkeley	2017
Keras	Library for Machine Learning	Python	Google	2015
Torch	Library for Machine Learning	C	NYU	2002
Accord.NET	Library for Machine Learning	C#	Stanford	2010
Spark MLlib	Library for Machine Learning	Scala	Berkely	2014
Sci-kit Learn	Library for Machine Learning	Python	Google Summer of Code	2008
MLPack	Library for Machine Learning	C++	Georgia Institute of Technology	2018
Appache MXNET	Library for Machine Learning	C++, Python	Apache Software Foundation	2015
Gluon	Library for Machine Learning	C++, Python	Microsoft/AWS	2017
PaddlePaddle	Library for Machine Learning	Python	Baidu	2016
Mindspore	Library for Machine Learning		Huawei	2018
XDL	Library for Machine Learning		Alibaba	2018

The list has been created in order of popularity. Note that SenseTime's SenseParrots is not on the list.
Source: Benjamin Cedric Larsen (2020). [to be updated]

communities in which social aspects of the developer community are important.[1077]

Within this context of greater Chinese government awareness of Chinese AI firms' global entanglements, it is important to reconsider what these global interconnections in open-source AI development mean for data localisation. The intersection between Network Sovereignty and the development of open-source projects provides some indication of how the apparent conflict between data localisation in China's Cyber Security Law and Chinese innovation might be resolved.

9.6 Key Features of Open-Source AI Relevant to Applying the Cyber Security Law

The various benefits of open-source software and platforms in AI development identified above are clearly relevant to Chinese tech firms and to the Chinese government's push to make China a world leader in AI by 2030.[1078] Open-source development, however, conflicts with a literal interpretation of the data localisation provisions in the Cyber Security

---

[1077] Andrea Forte and Cliff Lampe, 'Defining, Understanding, and Supporting Open Collaboration: Lessons from the Literature' (2013) 57(5) *American Behavioral Scientist* 535. This article surveys various discourses on the social structures of open-source projects, including the volunteers who join these projects and their motivations. For example, there is a huge body of knowledge on the motivation of volunteers that joined the workforce of open-source projects. See Cristoph Hannebauer and Volker Gruhn, 'Motivation of Newcomers to FLOSS Projects' (12th International Symposium on Open Collaboration, 2016) 1.10; Georg von Krogh, Stefan Haefliger and Sebastian Spaeth, 'Carrots and Rainbows: Motivation and Social Practice in Open Source Software Development' (2012) 36(2) *MIS Quarterly* 649; Karim R Lakhani and Robert G Wolf, 'Perspectives on Free and Open Source Software' in Joseph Feller, Brian Fitzgerald and Scott Hissam et al (eds), *Perspectives on Free and Open Source Software* (MIT Press, 2005) 1; Shaul Oreg and Oded Nov, 'Exploring Motivations for Contributing to Open Source Initiatives: The Roles of Contribution Context and Personal Values' (2008) 24(5) *Computers in Human Behaviour* 2055.

The developer-joining process has also drawn the attention of researchers from different areas attempting to understand how developers join an open-source community: Fabian Fagerholm et al, 'Onboarding in Open Source Projects' (2014) 31(6) *IEEE Software* 54; Georg von Krogh and Eric von Hippel, 'Editorial: Special Issue on Open Source Software Development' (2003) 32(7) *Research Policy* 1149. Researchers have also examined how those developers became central to an open-source community: Minghui Zhou and Audris Mockus, 'Who Will Stay in the FLOSS Community? Modelling Participant's Initial Behaviour' (2015) 41(1) *IEEE Transactions on Software Engineering* 82.

[1078] As discussed in Chapter 8.

Law, especially as the open-source development of AI has become dependent on global networks and data sharing. This section analyses the key challenges of data localisation to open AI innovation, including the challenges of applying the Cyber Security Law (especially the data localisation principles) to open-source AI platforms.

Building on the earlier explanation of the development and use of open-source AI platforms in China (and globally), it is clear that global access to open research has been crucial for the rapid advances made by Chinese firms in the AI sector. This raises some ongoing questions for China's data regime. The arguments that follow suggest that technical impediments to localisation may not be overwhelming, but that the culture of open innovation in AI (both academically and commercially) conflicts with Network Sovereignty in addition to the Cyber Security Law.

First, it must be recalled that while the Cyber Security Law seeks to localise sets of 'personal data' and 'important data' in China, theoretically this does not affect software code. Therefore, to begin answering the question of the impact of data localisation under the Cyber Security Law, the difference between open-source code and open datasets (described in Section 9.1) and their relationship to China's Cyber Security Law and AI must be further explained. This is because, while a substantial number of AI applications do not involve personal data, many others do, and will therefore be subject to the Cyber Security Law.

Historically, AI companies have been able to build competitive advantages based on possessing more and higher quality data to use for training purposes (see Section 9.4). Data quality, diversity and especially quantity all remain key sources of competitive advantage for many AI applications, but there are also caveats to this principle. Firstly, much of the training data for Machine Learning is application specific, so having a large quantity of healthcare data, for example, does not help to develop a self-driving car.

Second, some applications of AI can use 'synthetic data' created through computational simulation to reduce or eliminate the performance advantage from very large quantities of real-world data. Further, 'synthetic data' may or may not come under the definition of 'important data' in the Cyber Security Law. So, will companies be able to create 'synthetic data' to avoid having to localise 'personal' or 'important' data?

Further, cross-border data flows may not always be that critical for the R&D process in AI. The general rule is that more data is always better. However, diminishing marginal returns on data might be seen within a certain spectrum. To clarify, 1 million users is vastly more useful than 10 users, but 3 billion users is not that much more useful than 2 billion users. Thus, if an enterprise has enough data locally, access to an extra 1 billion users may not improve its services to the extent where the enterprise is put at a competitive disadvantage in the local market. The caveat is that the rule is general, and very context specific, and the specific dynamics are not well understood.[1079]

Furthermore, as AI systems often require very large amounts of code, this can stretch the ability of any single individual developer to understand the architecture of the AI model.[1080] Therefore, another very crucial caveat is that any attempt to segregate data may slow or even hinder AI research.[1081]

Additionally, if open source is used for outsourcing maintenance, data localisation may inhibit Chinese innovation by preventing overseas developers (who may include Chinese living abroad) from accurately assessing bugs and identifying stress points. Open and public cybersecurity tools are part of keeping security faults at bay. Crucially, predicting how localised servers can deal with that amount of traffic is also unprecedented. Thus, data localisation within China's borders remains a problematic concept for the Chinese technology industry. Also (as noted in Section 9.2.4, server and application maintenance will be increasingly important due to the expansion of AI. Thus, addressing scale and server maintenance problems without open-source AI may be a problem for data localisation. Jian Wang, president of Alibaba's technology committee, predicted that the rush to deliver and tap into cloud AI would use huge amounts of energy: 'It will consume a lot of computing resources, which may have not been seen before in history.'[1082] Therefore the expansion of AI services in the cloud could have other ramifications as well, as this model may conflict with data localisation of data servers. Making it harder for cloud computing companies to move data between countries also makes it more difficult for them to make efficient use of their servers by allocating resources to different customers depending on when they most need them, or storing data to the cheapest data centre

---

[1079] See Goodfellow, Bengio and Courville, *Deep Learning* (n 52). In particular see 'Recurrent Neural Networks'.
[1080] Ibid.
[1081] For example, China's AI 'Sputnik moment' in Alpha Go's victory over Lee Sedol illustrated that onlookers cannot see multiple steps that a computer might be able to achieve, hence researchers may not know the impact of segregating datasets.
[1082] Knight, 'China and the US Are Bracing for an AI Showdown' (n 1005).

where possible (discussed extensively in Chapter 6). It has been argued that this deeply impacts AI. Nicholas Hodac, government and regulatory affairs executive for IBM, noted that as an increasing number of the company's clients run operations entirely in the cloud, '[y]ou can't offer efficient services to clients in the artificial intelligence or analytics space unless you can transfer data to where it can be best served'.[1083]

One response is for new enterprises to become 'cloud native' to deal with scaling issues. Cloud native computing 'uses an open source software stack to deploy applications as microservices, packaging each part into its own container, and dynamically orchestrating those containers to optimise resource utilisation. Cloud native technologies enable software developers to build great products faster'.[1084] Thus, there has been a large increase in cloud native applications in China.[1085]

However, one foreseeable problem with localising cloud services is that Chinese technology standards do not always match global standards.[1086] Should cloud computing techniques used by Chinese cloud providers become an essential part of operating a cloud service in the country, cloud providers might have to make hard choices about whether to offer two types of services to customers inside or outside China, or to follow Chinese standards.

As a result, the need for cloud services presents both a global market challenge and a domestic opportunity for Chinese open-source AI platforms. This is because, since the approval of the Cyber Security Law, China-based cloud service providers were presumed to be legally required to provide China-based cloud services for Chinese data.[1087]

[1083] Alan Beattie, 'Data Protectionism: The Growing Menace to International Business' (*Financial Times*, 13 May 2018) <https://www.ft.com/content/6f0f41e4-47de-11e8-8ee8-cae73aab7ccb>.

[1084] 'What Is CNCF?' (*Cloud Native Computing Foundation website*) <https://www.cncf.io>.

[1085] A key growth area for cloud native is China. Asia has experienced a spike in cloud-native adoption of 135% since March 2018, according to a Cloud Native Computing Foundation survey, and several key open-source projects have been born in China: see 'A Look Back at KubeCon + CloudNativeCon Shanghai 2018' (*Cloud Native Computing Foundation*, 5 December 2018) <https://www.cncf.io/blog/2018/12/05/a-look-back-at-kubecon-cloudnativecon-shanghai-2018>.

[1086] Andrew Polk, 'China Is Quietly Setting Global Standards' (*Bloomberg*, 7 May 2018) <https://www.bloomberg.com/opinion/articles/2018-05-06/china-is-quietly-setting-global-standards>. Polk is an economist based in Beijing whose research is often reproduced by China watchers.

[1087] As per the vagueness in art 37, some multinational companies thought that the Cyber Security Law, was a blanket ban on any data transfers outside of China. This was discussed at length in Chapters 5 and 6.

There may even be a connection between China's open-source epiphany and the Cyber Security Law. When Apple moved its Chinese data centres to Guizhou in a supposed pre-emptive compliance move with the Cyber Security Law in April 2017 and Amazon Web Services sold off its cloud infrastructure to its Chinese joint venture partner in November 2017, questions about China's Network Sovereignty policy directions escalated (as noted in Chapter 6).[1088] This raises the question: Was this a brilliant stroke of fuzzy logic Chinese policy coordination or merely good fortune for China's cloud sector?

Nevertheless, one logical question remains: with 1.2 billion people, do data localisation requirements really affect or hinder Chinese innovation in any meaningful way? Perhaps not, as the amount of data in China, relatively speaking, is vaster than anywhere else in the world (see Chapter 1). On the other hand, the preceding discussion of Chinese AI firms' global networks and Chinese regulators' awareness of these firms' weaknesses in key areas of AI technology development suggests that there is still major dependency on the free flow of 'important data' across borders. So, assuming that data localisation requirements will be enforced to a certain degree under policies such as Network Sovereignty, how will these requirements impact on AI developers in practice? In other words, will the Chinese government adopt a fuzzy logic approach in implementing data localisation in the AI sector? And, to the extent that data localisation remains a possibility, how will open-source platforms be affected by the ongoing spectre of Network Sovereignty?

The commercial potential of open source has been tested and proven over several years, and several business models have emerged. Yet the business of open data is still in a pioneering phase associated with Machine Learning research. This may be a problem. If, for example, under China's Cyber Security Law, the data is not created by a particular

---

[1088] As noted in Chapter 5, companies that want to offer cloud services inside mainland China – essential for cloud performance due to the Great Firewall of China – must register with a local partner. Amazon Web Services and Microsoft technically do not sell cloud services in China. They have local joint ventures: Microsoft with 21Vianet and AWS with Beijing Sinnet. 21Vianet and Beijing Sinnet own the physical infrastructure built by the cloud providers in China and are known as the 'seller of record'. The US cloud companies retain the rights to their trademarks and IP. During 2019, China offered to relax these JV rules for cloud computing in discussions with President Trump. See Robert Delaney, 'Encouraging Signs for US–China Business Ties in Cloud Computing Access Talks' (*South China Morning Post*, 12 April 2019) <https://www.scmp.com/news/china/diplomacy/article/3005809/encouraging-signs-us-china-business-ties-cloud-computing>.

developer, how certain can a developer be that the open-source platform will continue to be provided openly in the future by the open-source platform host? This is especially problematic under China's expanding focus on Network Sovereignty.

The growing awareness among Chinese regulators of the importance of these global open-source networks to Chinese tech firms was most likely a major factor in the delay in implementing the data localisation provisions of the Cyber Security Law. This delay was assisted by the fuzzy logic, or indeterminate nature, of those provisions in Article 37 and related regulations which allowed for discretion in the way the provisions were interpreted (as discussed in Chapter 6). Problems such as building AI platforms to scale without open-source development protocols may therefore be another possible reason why China's Cyber Security Law had not been fully implemented from June 2017 and remained fuzzy even up to the present.

A useful way to provide some provisional answers to the questions raised above is through detailed analysis of case studies involving individual Chinese AI firms, and their development trajectory in the post-Cyber Security Law period.

9.7 Case Studies of Open-Source AI Platforms in China

The case studies in this section are a partial illustration of the chapter's argument regarding how fuzzy logic lawmaking can be used to promote (or manage) innovation in the development of AI. However, they also explain why Network Sovereignty continues to create practical difficulties for Chinese tech companies. The case studies focus on self-driving cars – an industry sector in which developing advanced AI applications is crucial.

The section explains two things. First, Chinese self-driving car companies are increasingly globalised, so much so that sometimes deciphering a nationality is unclear. And second, while widespread pilot projects allow Chinese start-ups to test autonomous vehicles extensively in China,[1089] technology, testing data and talent come from both China and the United States. This means that if 'important data' prejudices the

---

[1089] The Chinese government named autonomous cars one of the key sectors in its Made in China 2025 initiative, which is designed to transform China into a world-beating manufacturer of high-end, innovative products. Official policies encourage collaboration between Chinese technology companies involved in various aspects of transportation, from the cars themselves to satellite navigation. Alibaba is among the biggest of those firms and has developed a 'City Brain' AI hub that uses big data to 'automatically deploy public resources and amend defects in urban operations'.

transmission of data for autonomous vehicle R&D, it would negatively affect Chinese innovation in this industry sector.

Several of the start-up firms pursuing self-driving technology employ people and technology from both the United States and China. This is because the more a car is tested in different traffic and weather conditions, the better its Machine Learning becomes. Geographically dispersed testing is therefore crucial to creating safe autonomous cars.

For example, Pony.ai is headquartered in Fremont, California, and the company is registered in the Cayman Islands (as a VIE). Autonomous driving testing occurs in Beijing, Guangzhou and the United States.[1090]

> As in the United States, regulation and permission for autonomous driving technology in China are processed on a city-by-city basis. Two hundred and ninety Chinese regions have already introduced projects for Smart Cities controlled by AI that can be optimised for autonomous transportation: see Karen Yeung and Eric Ng, 'China to Spearhead US$1 Trillion Autonomous Driving Revolution' (*South China Morning Post*, 13 December 2017) <https://www.scmp.com/business/china-business/article/2124042/china-spearhead-us1-trillion-autonomous-driving-revolution>.
>
> The city of Beijing only allowed for testing autonomous vehicles in December 2017. Prior to that date, Chinese start-ups spent 2017 testing in California. This enabled these firms to set up bi-national R&D bases. In 2017, the Shanghai, Beijing and Chongqing municipal governments introduced their own self-driving regulations; and China's first special autonomous driving licence plates were issued to Baidu and electric vehicle start-up NIO. China announced a national testing regime in 2018. The new regulations aim to facilitate the development of self-driving technology through the wide deployment of public road tests.
>
> MIIT, the Ministry of Public Security and the Ministry of Transport jointly issued «智能网联汽车道路测试管理规范试行» [Intelligent Connected Vehicle Road Test Management Standards (Trial)]. The instrument introduces regulations for testing self-driving cars on public roads nationwide and took effect on 1 May 2018.
>
> Testing companies must meet all technical requirements and provide a detailed test plan and insurance of ¥5 million for each test vehicle. Once an application is approved, the company will receive an Intelligent Connected Vehicle Road Test Notice (智能网联汽车路测试通知书), and can then apply for a temporary test licence plate from the local Traffic Management Department of Public Security (公安机关交通管理部门). Test vehicles must adhere to their submitted test plans. If a test vehicle experiences a severe accident or serious violation, the relevant supervision department (主管部门) can revoke the temporary test licence plate. The testing company must submit a summary report one month after each test ends and full test reports every six months.
>
> «印发 智能网联汽车道路测试管理规范 （试行)» [Three Ministries and Commissions: Issued the 'Intelligent Network Linked Vehicle Road Test Management Regulations (Trial)'] (*Tencent Research Institute*, 16 April 2018) <https://mp.weixin.qq.com/s/yK2G1LMKPAdGLdnGN5-BLQ>.

[1090] Ingrid London, 'China's Pony.ai Nabs $102M at Nearly $1B Valuation to Take Its Self-Driving Platform up Another Gear' (*TechCrunch*, 11 July 2018) <https://techcrunch.com/2018/07/11/chinas-pony-ai-nabs-102m-at-nearly-1b-valuation-to-take-its-self-driving-platform-up-another-gear>.

Investors include United States-headquartered Sequoia Capital.[1091] In February 2020 Toyota made a US$267 million investment.[1092] And in November 2020, a fund run by the Ontario (Canada) Teachers' Pension Plan Board led a US$267 million investment.[1093] The founders and a large number of employees are from China or have a Chinese background. The two founders, James Peng and Lou Tiancheng, have backgrounds at both Baidu and Google's autonomous driving projects.[1094] The founders consider Pony.ai an 'international company'. They set up in the United States to search for 'talent' but they also test their cars extensively in China where 'the data, the patterns can be very different'.[1095] The company has a 'China first' mentality for testing and product release.[1096] Various other 'Chinese' start-ups, such as Roadstar.ai,[1097] JingChi (now WeRide.ai),[1098] TuSimple[1099]

[1091] Ibid.
[1092] Andrew J. Hawkins, 'Toyota Steers $400 Million to Self-Driving Startup Pony.ai' (*The Verge*, 25 February 2020) <https://www.theverge.com/2020/2/25/21152817/toyota-pony-ai-self-driving-car-investment-valuation-china-silicon-valley>.
[1093] Arjun Kharpal, 'Chinese Driverless Car Firm Pony.ai Valued at $5.3 Billion after New Cash Injection' (*CNBC*, 6 November 2020) <https://www.cnbc.com/2020/11/06/china-driverless-car-firm-ponyai-valued-at-5point3-billion-after-funding.html>.
[1094] Peng worked for seven years at Google in the United States as a software engineer developing big data applications and AI. He joined Baidu in 2012, and led its autonomous vehicle project in Sunnyvale. There he met Pony co-founder Tiancheng, who worked to develop self-driving cars at Google before the formation of Google's Waymo autonomous unit. Pony.ai was established in December 2016.
[1095] Frank Hersey, 'Pony.ai Q&A: Having a China Background Will Be Key to Autonomous Driving Success' (*TechNode*, 26 April 2018) <https://technode.com/2018/04/26/pony-ai-autonomous-driving-success-needs-china>.
[1096] Ibid.
[1097] Roadstar founder Xianqiao Tong is a Chinese engineer who got started in autonomy by working on Nvidia's driver assistance systems and then working at Apple before joining Baidu. Roadstar set up a large R&D centre in Cupertino, California, for self-driving technologies.
[1098] On 3 April 2017, JingChi was established in Silicon Valley by Wang Jing, former head of Baidu's Autonomous Driving Unit. It completed its first self-driving test on 12 May 2017. In June 2017, it obtained a testing licence for California and completed the open road test in the same month. On 8 September 2017, JingChi completed the road commuting test during rush hour in Silicon Valley. In September 2017, Nvidia GPU Ventures participated in a US$52 million pre-A round in JingChi.
[1099] TuSimple is an autonomous truck technology start-up with offices in Beijing and San Diego. US chipmaker Nvidia led a series B round in TuSimple. Based in Beijing and San Diego, California, TuSimple is operating three to five revenue-generating trucking routes in Arizona. In 2019, TuSimple aims to expand to Texas.

and Momenta,[1100] employ a similar or partially similar international corporate structure, driving testing regime, global investors and globalised strategy to Pony.ai.[1101] Among them, Roadstar.ai, Pony.ai, WeRide.ai,[1102] Horizon Robotics and TuSimple have particularly high-calibre teams with global education and experience, according to industry observers.[1103]

In January 2019, Roadstar.ai fired its co-founder, Zhou Guang (周光), for corruption.[1104] In March 2019, Roadstar.ai's investors filed a lawsuit to liquidate the company. The company's bank account holding nearly renminbi 600 million was frozen and its Shenzhen headquarters closed.[1105] Yet Roadstar.ai had already developed a celebrated Level 4 autonomous driving system, which could, in certain conditions, drive completely autonomously, as well as the most cost-effective LiDAR system[1106] in China, before its investors pulled their support. The three co-founders all had experience in autonomous driving R&D at Google, Baidu, Tesla, NVIDIA or Apple, which wooed investors.

[1100] Beijing-based start-up Momenta raised US$46 million in July 2017 from investors including NIO Capital, the China arm of US venture capital firm Sequoia Capital and Hillhouse Capital.

[1101] During 2018, there were at least 12 Chinese start-ups pursuing autonomous driving, including TuSimple, Horizon Robotics, Roadstar, Pony.ai, Jingchi (now WeRide.ai), Momenta, UISEE, Hi-Sense, Idriverplus, AutoX and Jimu.

[1102] WeRide.ai and Pony.ai went straight to R&D of Level 4 technology after leaving Baidu.

[1103] Sarah Dai, 'One of the World's Top Coders, Known as Godfather, Is Backing a Chinese Self-Driving Car Start-up' (*South China Morning Post*, 7 February 2018) <https://www.scmp.com/tech/start-ups/article/2132420/one-worlds-top-coders-known-godfather-backing-chinese-self-driving>.

[1104] The company's statement can be read here: «深圳星行科技有限公司关于处理周光违纪行为的公告» [Shenzhen Xingxing Technology Co, Ltd Announcement on Handling Zhou Guang's Disciplinary Behaviour] (*Roadstar.ai Official WeChat Account*, 21 January 2019) <https://mp.weixin.qq.com/s?__biz=MzU3MDA5ODkyOQ==&mid=2247484868&idx=1&sn=5c340f0169fa3e5dc811596d9a06bcf9&chksm=fcf5d05acb82594c13b1f0f1528a52593a586906d547714984aa7bf048cd83b5ff72df54d5fb&mpshare=1&scene=1&srcid=0121aLVkJQh096XryqUdXhfT#rd> (the link is no longer active).

[1105] «从首家无人车公司猝死，看股权设计 7 个原则» [Beyond the Sudden Death of a Leading Autonomous Car Company, a Look at the Company's 7 Equitable Principles] (*China HRD*, 4 October 2019) <http://www.chinahrd.net/blog/412/469578/411740.html>.

[1106] LiDar is a method for measuring distances by illuminating the target with laser light and measuring the reflection with a sensor. Nan Hua, 'Roadstar.ai: A Promising Autonomous Driving Startup Wrecked by Infighting' (*CompassList*, 25 July 2019) <https://www.compasslist.com/insights/roadstarai-a-promising-autonomous-driving-startup-wrecked-by-infighting>.

WeRide.ai is backed by Renault–Nissan–Mitsubishi[1107] but also raised a US$200 million strategic round from Chinese bus maker Yutong[1108] in December 2020.[1109] In 2021 Horizon Robotics sought to complete a US$700 million Series C Capital raise led by US, Chinese and Korean investors.[1110] TuSimple also reportedly closed a US$350 million funding round from a 'diverse consortium of strategic investors that include major U.S. corporations in rail, retail and freight' in December 2020.[1111] TuSimple's global links had continued to develop steadily in August 2019, when UPS[1112] announced that the company's venture capital arm, UPS Ventures, had taken a minority stake in TuSimple.[1113]

These investments in December 2020 and January 2021 strongly suggest that geopolitical tensions and China's data localisation rules have not swayed international (and US investor) confidence in testing self-driving cars in both China's government-supported public–private petri dish pilots. For example, TuSimple's founding team and its earliest backers, Sina and Composite Capital, are from China, but a portion of its operations are in the United States, including its global headquarters in San Diego, an engineering centre and truck depot in Tucson and a facility in Texas to support its autonomous trips. TuSimple also has operations in Beijing and Shanghai.

[1107] 'Renault–Nissan–Mitsubishi and WeRide.ai to Increase Presence in Chinese Autonomous Vehicle Services' (*PR Newswire*, 19 October 2018) <https://www.prnewswire.com/news-releases/alliance-ventures-leads-strategic-investment-in-weride-ai-864897996.html>.

[1108] See 'Yutong' (*Yutong Website*) <https://en.yutong.com/>.

[1109] Rita Liao, 'Chinese Autonomous Driving Startup WeRide Bags $200M in Funding' (*TechCrunch*, 23 December 2020) <https://techcrunch.com/2020/12/22/weride-200-million-funding/>.

[1110] Rita Liao, 'Horizon Robotics, a Chinese Rival to Nvidia, Seeks to Raise Over $700M' (*TechCrunch*, 22 December 2020) <https://techcrunch.com/2020/12/21/horizon-robotics-700-million-funding/>.

[1111] Kirsten Korosec, 'Self-driving Trucks Startup TuSimple Raises $350M from US Rail, Retail and Freight Giants' (*TechCrunch*, 3 December 2020) <https://techcrunch.com/2020/12/02/self-driving-trucks-startup-tusimple-raises-350m-from-u-s-rail-retail-and-freight-giants/>. Goodyear, Union Pacific, CN Rail, freight company US Xpress and retailer Kroger all participated in the round. Existing investors Volkswagen AG's heavy-truck business The Traton Group and Navistar also participated. TuSimple has raised $648 million since its founding in 2015.

[1112] United Parcel Service, an American multinational package delivery and supply chain management company (NYSE:UPS).

[1113] 'UPS Invests in Autonomous Trucking Company, Tests Self-Driving Tractor Trailers' (*UPS Pressroom*, 16 August 2019) <https://www.pressroom.ups.com/pressroom/ContentDetailsViewer.page?ConceptType=PressReleases&id=1565871221437-794>.

There was once a common belief that these well-funded start-ups would struggle against the incumbent firms holding much data (eg, Google and Baidu).[1114] However, autonomous vehicles can serve many purposes. The Uber-style model is only one application for self-driving cars; there will be many others such as delivery, transport, shuttles on campuses, car-sharing, trams, electric buses, trolleys, 'Jitneys' (on the US East Coast) and as a solution to the last mile to home from public transport. An example of this is Chinese start-up Uisee (驭势科技), which began testing self-driving cars in airports for cargo and luggage at slow speeds and away from crowds. From its inception, Uisee was commercially focused, with the Chinese government being its first client.[1115] Yet investors in Uisee include Chinese government funds as well as the German firm Bosch Venture Capital in 2020.[1116] TuSimple's strategy for commercialisation was to test autonomous long-haul delivery trucks at Tianjin Port, where there are few or no cars.[1117]

This is where China's system of experimental petri dishes is important, as it provides opportunities for testing a range of highly specific technology applications. Thus, start-ups such as Uisee stand a chance of finding their niche despite not having as much data as big tech companies. China's deployment of 'petri dishes' means that for Chinese AI firms, commercial rollouts often trump lab-based advancements, and entire cities are being built with infrastructure optimised to train autonomous vehicles.[1118]

[1114] Jason Rowley, 'The Well-Funded Startups Driven to Own the Autonomous Vehicle Stack' (*TechCrunch*, 27 May 2018) <https://techcrunch.com/2018/05/27/the-well-funded-startups-driven-to-own-the-autonomous-vehicle-stack>.

[1115] Liu Sha, 'UISEE Finds a Short Cut for Driverless Cars' (*CKGSB Knowledge*, 19 June 2017) <http://knowledge.ckgsb.edu.cn/2017/06/19/automobile-industry/uisee-technology-finds-shortcut-driverless-cars>.

[1116] 'Robert Bosch Venture Capital Backs the Evolution of Automated Driving with Investment in UISEE' (*Bosch Media Services Press Release*, 26 February 2020) <https://www.bosch-presse.de/pressportal/de/en/robert-bosch-venture-capital-backs-the-evolution-of-automated-driving-with-investment-in-uisee-208768.html>.

[1117] Kirsten Korosec, 'Autonomous Truck Startup TuSimple Hits Unicorn Status in Latest Round' (*TechCrunch*, 13 February 2019) <https://techcrunch.com/2019/02/13/autonomous-truck-startup-tusimple-hits-unicorn-status-in-latest-round>.

[1118] Experimental efforts to build self-driving cities have begun all over the world. China is not unique in this regard. For example, the US state of Ohio built a 35-mile stretch of highway with sensors and fibre optics to support autonomous vehicles. Randy Ludlow, 'Ohio Tries to Pull Ahead in Transportation Tech Race' (*Government Technology*, 19 January 2018) <https://www.govtech.com/fs/transportation/State-Creates-DriveOhio-to-Capture-Smart-Transportation-Research.html>.

In conjunction with a supportive regulatory environment in China for vehicle testing, learning by doing in pilots accelerates AI learning for smaller start-ups as well as established tech companies. Start-ups can target other industry vertical applications with partnerships and can obtain data to target problems using AI. As a result, there are small-scale autonomous vehicle pilots emerging all over China. Examples of autonomous testing include driverless trains[1119] and unmanned street sweepers in Shanghai, beginning in April 2018, which could replace millions of sanitation workers in China.[1120] Baidu and the Beijing Environmental Equipment Company launched seven autonomous driving vehicles for urban environment cleaning in September 2018.[1121] In addition, Alibaba and JD.com as well as food delivery service Meituan[1122] have all commenced testing autonomous package delivery

---

South Korea announced plans for US$64 billion in smart highways in 2016: Charlene Chin, 'South Korea to Build Smart Highways for Driverless Cars' (*GovInsider*, 2 September 2016 <https://govinsider.asia/smart-gov/south-korea-to-build-smart-highways-for-driverless-cars>.

Engineers of self-driving cars have long imagined linking them to centralised traffic infrastructure in order to train autonomous vehicles. However, China is building new cities from scratch. The 'game-changing idea is to create both smart roads and smart cars', according to Chen Lijuan, head of Alibaba AI Labs. Rather than loading more sensors into the vehicles, the approach is to have a network of static and connected roadside sensors that communicate with the cars and feed data into the company's Machine Learning data platforms: He Wei, 'Ma: Embrace AI Opportunities' (*China Daily*, 21 September 2018) <http://www.chinadaily.com.cn/a/201809/21/WS5ba444dca310c4cc775e7726.html>. As Gansha Wu, the founder of autonomous vehicle company Uisee noted, building autonomous vehicles is a 'town planning issue'. For example, town planners can enable stoplights to communicate with cars via wi-fi. 'So long as the Wi-Fi signal is strong, the car not only knows when to slow down; in theory, it could obtain that information long before arriving at an intersection and adjust its route for maximum time and fuel efficiency. If other cars had the same capability, then that "smart" stop light could direct traffic better than a human, let alone a traditional light.' See Sha, 'UISEE Finds a Short Cut for Driverless Cars' (n 1115).

[1119] Beijing, Guangzhou and Shanghai all began testing driverless trains in early 2018: Sarah Zhang, 'Society Shanghai Begins Driverless Trains Trial Run on Metro Line' (*South China Morning Post*, 1 April 2018) <http://www.scmp.com/news/china/society/article/2139814/shanghai-begins-driverless-trains-trial-run-metro-line>.

[1120] 'Driverless Street Sweepers Employed for Trial Run in Shanghai' (*Xinhua*, 13 June 2019) <http://www.xinhuanet.com/english/2018-04/18/c_137120453.htm>.

[1121] «百度联手北环卫发布 7 款智能环卫产品» [Baidu Teamed Up with Northern Environmental Protection Department to Release 7 Smart Sanitation Products] (*PingWest*, 28 September 2018) <https://www.pingwest.com/w/177811>.

[1122] Meituan's Autonomous Delivery (MAD) Platform features driverless delivery vehicles that shuttle meals from restaurants to consumers: Masha Borak, 'Meituan Dianping

systems.[1123] In order to develop autonomous technologies further, Chinese companies and start-ups have pursued a global R&D agenda since 2017. According to Michael Dunne, an automotive industry expert on the electric-autonomous market: 'California is the R&D center and China is the place where the rubber meets the road. ... It's just a beautiful formula for success.'[1124]

9.7.1 Apollo: 'Android for Automated Vehicles'

Clearly, there are numerous examples of closely interlinked global R&D cooperation within and among autonomous vehicle firms. To shed further light on why the implementation of data localisation provisions in China's Cyber Security Law was delayed, the case of Baidu's successful Apollo open-source platform is detailed here.

The automotive industry is a century-old industry that may not have deep AI research capability, and it is difficult for internet companies to build their own cars; therefore, open-source AI platforms in partnership with companies like Baidu are an ideal way for companies such as Ford and BMW to create autonomous vehicles. Baidu's approach is to cooperate with automotive manufacturers by providing the driverless-car testing software and software algorithms, known as Apollo. Automotive suppliers offer hardware integration, product development and manufacturing facilities. Other companies provide Baidu with processing chips, sensors, vehicle architecture and other pieces of hardware.

Baidu's open-source Apollo platform provides a method for integrating the components of different stakeholders. The Apollo platform standardises an operating system across various industries. Apollo allows a multitude of manufacturers and auto suppliers to focus on manufacturing, rather than software engineering. Auto manufacturers who have partnerships with technology providers can focus on building

---

Launches Autonomous Food Delivery System' (*Technode*, 26 July 2018) <https://technode.com/2018/07/26/meituan-dianping-autonomous-delivery>.

[1123] In June 2017, JD.com starting piloting a robot on wheels that is delivering packages to students at universities across China: Malek Murison, 'JD.com Launches Robot Delivery in China' (*Internet of Business*, 20 June 2017) <https://internetofbusiness.com/jd-com-robot-delivery-china>; Shannan Liao, 'Alibaba Made a Driverless Robot That Runs 9 mph to Deliver Packages' (*The Verge*, 31 May 2018) <https://www.theverge.com/circuitbreaker/2018/5/31/17413836/alibaba-driverless-robot-deliver-packages-speed>.

[1124] Yunan Zhang, 'China's Autonomous Driving Startups Join the Billion-Dollar Club' (*The Information*, 23 November 2018) <https://www.theinformation.com/articles/chinas-autonomous-driving-startups-join-the-billion-dollar-club>.

autonomous vehicle systems, which is a complex matter involving the integration of multiple systems and technologies.

As an open-source platform, Apollo is able to accumulate driving data quickly, and bring autonomous vehicle technology to maturity at an expedited rate. The creation of Apollo is a strategic move; Baidu and other Chinese firms entered the self-driving race later than Google's Waymo and others, and so Chinese firms remained short on data and talent. Therefore, they set up R&D facilities abroad and went on hiring sprees. In addition, US$1.2 billion of Baidu's $9 billion revenue from the first three-quarters of 2017 was put back into R&D.[1125]

On 19 April 2017, Baidu officially announced the Apollo plan, billed as the first system-wide opening of the global automated driving technology.[1126] Apparently, Baidu CEO Robin Li asked then high-profile Chief Operating Officer (COO) Lu Qi, a former Microsoft executive, what would happen if Baidu opened up the self-driving technologies it had begun researching in-house in 2015. Essentially, Baidu would offer carmakers a brain for their cars in exchange for access to their data, which would be used to train its algorithms. Lu, leveraging his experiences at Microsoft, supported the idea.[1127]

Industry observers had long assumed that autonomous vehicles would be a domain that established car companies would dominate.[1128] Chinese companies entered the field later than many. Yet Apollo quickly gained recognition and has grown to be a leading player in the autonomous vehicle industry.[1129] Automotive industry expert Michael Dunne wrote

---

[1125] Charlie Campbell, 'Baidu's Robin Li Is Helping China Win the 21st Century' (*Time*, 18 January 2018) <http://time.com/5107485/baidus-robin-li-helping-china-win-21st-century>.

[1126] Baidu describes Apollo as 'a complete open automatic driving ecosystem' that can help partners in the automotive industry and autonomous driving to combine vehicle software and hardware systems to quickly build their own complete AV system.

[1127] Jessi Hempel, 'Inside Baidu's Bid to Lead the AI Revolution' (*Wired*, 12 June 2017) <https://www.wired.com/story/inside-baidu-artificial-intelligence>.

[1128] See Daniel Sperling (ed), *Three Revolutions: Automated, Shared and Electric Vehicles, Steering Automated, Shared, and Electric Vehicles to a Better Future* (Island Press, 2018).

[1129] Baidu led Tesla, Uber and Apple in developing self-driving cars, according to a 2018 study by Navigant Research which placed Apple and Tesla at the bottom when it came to autonomous driving leadership while traditional automakers ranked at the top. The US-based research company's annual report ranked 19 companies involved in developing self-driving cars, scoring them on 10 criteria ranging from the company's technology and vision to its strategy to commercialise products and their quality. Based on the score, companies were divided into four categories. Baidu was rated among

that allowing the internet company into the automotive market was 'a surprise move' and 'created an infusion of new thinking about technology transfer' in China because it was open source and a new way of thinking.[1130] It would prove to be a very high-profile open-source and data-sharing project.

Baidu President Yaqin Zhang, another former Microsoft executive, noted:

> What we are doing is trying to position ourselves as the Android for autonomous driving. There will be a bunch of closed systems that continue to exist, but we believe in the long run an open system will be the mainstream. It's very similar to mobile platforms and the phone makers back then [Google's open-source Android system].[1131]

Baidu is therefore using the same open-source strategy that helped Google's Android become the most dominant operating system platform in the global smartphone market.

At this stage, the meaning of 'important data' in Article 37 of China's Cyber Security Law data localisation provisions remained vague, and throughout 2017–2021 an impressive data-sharing ecosystem was built by Baidu. However, the explanation of China's GPS mapping laws (at Section 9.9.3) suggests that mapping data from within China would be considered 'important data'.

'contenders', along with companies such as Toyota, Jaguar Land Rover and Hyundai. The Chinese company had moved up from the 'challengers' section, leaving Tesla, Uber and Apple in the lowest-ranked category. The traditional automotive giants General Motors, Volkswagen and Ford dominated the top tier, together with Google's Waymo self-driving unit. The only 'technology' rather than automotive company in the 'leaders' group was Google's Waymo, which partnered with Fiat-Chrysler, Lyft and Avis to help address its weakness – a lack of experience in building a fleet of vehicles. See Navigant, *Navigant Research Leaderboard: Automated Driving Vehicles* (Report, January 2018) <https://www.navigantresearch.com/reports/navigant-research-leaderboard-automated-driving-vehicles>.

[1130] See Michael Dunne, 'The Dark Horse: Will China Win the Electric, Automated, Shared Mobility Race?' in Daniel Sperling (ed), *Three Revolutions: Automated, Shared and Electric Vehicles, Steering Automated, Shared, and Electric Vehicles to a Better Future* (Island Press, 2018) 176.

[1131] Alan Ohnsman, 'Baidu Aims for "Android" of Robocar Tech with Open-Source Apollo Platform' (*Forbes*, 27 October 2017) <https://www.forbes.com/sites/alanohnsman/2017/10/27/baidu-aims-for-android-of-robocar-tech-with-open-source-apollo-platform/#2edbb5d0c799>. 'China is very much about one solution in general. Think of WeChat [in China] – there's one solution. Didi [in China] – one solution', noted Lei Ma, a senior product manager of autonomous driving at Baidu, '[w]e're hoping that Apollo becomes that one solution for autonomy.'

The key point is that this open-source model of innovation revolves around building an ecosystem and involving like-minded stakeholders. The model is not confined to self-driving cars; Baidu AI has built two major open-source platforms: Apollo, one of the world's leading self-driving platforms; and DuerOS, China's leading smart speaker system. DuerOS has led to Baidu AI being recognised by MIT as a key player for near real-time translation.[1132]

Importantly, Apollo has been very successful in onboarding partners. By May 2019 the platform had more than 130 domestic and international partners, including 12,000 developers worldwide.[1133] Auto manufacturers such as Ford, Volkswagon, Honda, Volvo, Jaguar Land Rover, Hyundai, Daimler BMW, Peugeot and Citroen and several of China's leading auto manufacturers, including 13 SOEs and seven privately owned enterprises are part of the platform. Furthermore, Toyota joined in June 2019.[1134] By March 2020, Apollo had nearly 180 partners.[1135]

Despite the international collaborators, much of Apollo's business involves public–private partnerships in China, a fact that became clearer when Baidu's Apollo was made a part of China's AI National Team.[1136] More than 30 of Apollo's platform partners come from Chinese government departments including research, industry and local and regional government partners. Local government partners include Beijing

---

[1132] Laura He, 'Baidu's Seismic Shift towards AI Must Start Delivering the Goods' (*South China Morning Post*, 8 June 2017) <https://www.scmp.com/business/companies/article/2097495/baidus-seismic-shift-towards-ai-must-start-delivering-goods>. During 2019, Baidu ramped up efforts to install its voice assistant DuerOS into cars in China as the government pushes for world leadership in intelligent connected vehicle technology by 2035. Jill Shen, 'Baidu Accelerating Automaker Deals for Car Software Deployment' (*Technode*, 12 June 2019) <https://technode.com/2019/06/12/baidu-dueros-apollo-installment>.

[1133] «百度推出 Apollo 3.5 和 Apollo Enterprise» [Baidu Launches Apollo 3.5 and Apollo Enterprise] (*Baidu Official Blog*, 9 January 2019) <https://www.infoq.cn/article/3NA0SmwHbeg_CaUEXgxR>.

[1134] Tomoyoshi Oshikiri, 'Toyota to Join Baidu's Self-Driving Platform Apollo' (*Nikkei Asian Review*, 28 June 2019) <https://asia.nikkei.com/Business/Companies/Toyota-to-join-Baidu-s-self-driving-platform-Apollo>.

[1135] «百度 Apollo 生态合作伙伴再添新成员，携手共建车路协同智能交通» [Baidu Apollo Ecosystem Adds New Members] (*Apollo Official WeChat Account*, 3 March 2020) <https://mp.weixin.qq.com/s?__biz=MzI5MjcyNTc1Mw==&mid=2247491018&idx=1&sn=2b83c08287e952d0badc5922aa42c5a2&chksm=ec7dab5cdb0a224ac8058d1e5916f06bc055cdde871d8cfaf408c921770b510719882743d13f&mpshare=1&scene=24&srcid=&sharer_sharetime=1583322601059&sharer_shareid=081fb2cac668f46b68cafe2e49724859#rd>.

[1136] As described in Chapter 8, Section 8.7.

Innovation Center for Mobility, Beijing Environment Sanitation Group, BeijingEtown, Xiongan New Area (which will be China's future second capital city), Anting Shanghai International Automobile City, Chongqing Liangjiang New Area and the prefecture-level cities Wuhu and Baoding.[1137] Several Chinese research institutes are also a part of the platform, including Beihang University, Beijing Institute of Technology, Shanghai JiaoTong University, Tsinghua University, Tongji University and the China Automotive Engineering Institute.[1138]

On the other hand, besides its international automotive manufacturing company partners, Apollo's suppliers include leading microprocessor and semiconductor companies from the United States and Europe and a range of Chinese and international technology providers. This reflects the current global technological entanglement and the fact that Chinese firms are still reliant upon computer processing chips from outside China.

By July 2018, Apollo's official website displayed a long list of its partners, among which are international parts suppliers Bosch, Continental AG and ZF;[1139] sensor and chip makers Velodyne, Intel and Nvidia; server suppliers such as Microsoft; and autonomous driving system suppliers idriverplus and Momenta. Eighty per cent of Apollo's partners are autopilot parts, chips, radar and camera manufacturers, and research institutes; the remaining 20% are automakers. On this basis, Baidu impressively built a global supply chain for self-driving cars in less than two years.[1140]

The Apollo ecosystem has expanded its scope of cooperation with original equipment manufacturers, tier one and core suppliers (important product manufacturing supply chain members), travel service providers, start-ups, investment funds, relevant governments and research institutions.

[1137] See 'Welcome to Apollo' (*Apollo website*) <http://apollo.auto>.

[1138] Partnerships with research institutes serve to establish stronger ties between industry and research, while strengthening core knowledge and engineering aspects of the platform. In its partnership with several educational institutions, Baidu is creating synergies with China's educational system. Baidu's partnership with e-learning platform Udacity offers courses for creating self-driving cars using Baidu's software, another important component in spreading its open-source software and related autonomous vehicle services. See ibid.

[1139] ZF Friedrichshafen AG is a German auto parts manufacturer. See 'Home' (*ZF website*) <https://www.zf.com/mobile/en/homepage/homepage.html>.

[1140] See Partners section of Apollo website <http://apollo.auto>.

Thirty per cent of these are companies and institutions outside China. While testing extensively in China, in January 2021 Baidu also obtained a permit from the California Department of Motor Vehicles (DMV) to test three autonomous vehicles on specified streets in the San Francisco Bay Area, without safety drivers behind the wheel, having tested in the United States since 2016.[1141] California-based start-up AutonomouStuff[1142] is a notable example of a partner in the United States. AutonomouStuff partnered with Apollo to install the Apollo software on its Lincoln drive-by-wire system and test and tune it in just three days. This is a process that would normally take a dozen workers six months.[1143] Baidu displayed that particular Lincoln to the world's media as a triumph for Apollo. AutonomouStuff, despite being a US-based start-up, became a key partner in the Apollo programme.

If the Cyber Security Law's insistence on 'important data' not leaving China had disrupted the US development of that vehicle, at that moment, it would have resulted in a major loss of face for Baidu before the world's media. So how does Apollo allow for global data sharing with respect to Article 37 of China's Cyber Security Law?

9.7.2 Apollo's Data-Sharing Policies

Baidu seeded Apollo by making its vast dataset available for its developer and commercial partner community to use; however, this data contribution was not enough to sustain Apollo's evolution. Therefore, Apollo created an open-source data collective that pools high-quality data from its partners, that can each leverage the full data pool.[1144] The Apollo platform consists of three parts: HD map localisation, an open software platform and a Baidu cloud service platform. The Apollo website explains that the Apollo platform provides partners with high-precision map services with advanced technology, extensive coverage and high automation. Apollo also offers a simulation engine, which the company claims to

---

[1141] Ding Yi, 'Baidu Wins California Permit to Test Fully Driverless Vehicles' (*Caixin*, 20 June 2021) <https://www.caixinglobal.com/2021-01-28/baidu-wins-california-permit-to-test-fully-driverless-vehicles-101657263.html>.

[1142] See 'Lincoln MKZ Platform' (*AutonomouStuff website*) <https://autonomoustuff.com/>.

[1143] Frank Hersey, 'Baidu Launches Their Open Platform for Autonomous Cars – And We Got to Test It' (*Technode*, 5 July 2017) <https://technode.com/2017/07/05/baidu-apollo-1-0-autonomous-cars-we-test-it>.

[1144] See 'Apollo Governance' (*Apollo website*) <http://apollo.auto/docs/manifesto.html>.

be 'the only one in the world that is open and is equipped with massive data'.[1145] Moreover, Apollo's end-to-end autonomous driving algorithm has 'the world's largest volume of deep-learning data sets' that are open.[1146]

Baidu's business model is a test for the Cyber Security Law's policy of data localisation.[1147] Apollo has successfully onboarded customers perhaps because the benefits of open source outweigh the fact that, under the system, Chinese data collected by Apollo systems is localised in China. According to Apollo's usage terms and conditions, the firm complies with China's Cyber Security Law:[1148]

> **2.2 Principle of data storage**
> Data collected in China shall, and shall only, be stored on servers in China; data collected in other countries and regions shall be subject to data storage restrictions specified by laws of the relevant countries.[1149]

The system is set up so that data aggregates to Baidu in China but algorithmic development can be used by the whole community.[1150] So

---

[1145] See 'Welcome to Apollo' (n 1137).
[1146] Ibid.
[1147] Paul Triolo and Jimmy Goodrich, 'From Riding a Wave to Full Steam Ahead' (*New America*, 28 February 2018) <https://www.newamerica.org/cybersecurity-initiative/digichina/blog/riding-wave-full-steam-ahead>.
[1148] A hard drive is placed inside an Apollo partner's car, which sends data straight to a Baidu cloud. Collecting and training of data occurs on Baidu's own networks. See 'Apollo Data Sharing' (*Apollo website*) <http://apollo.auto/docs/promise.html>.
[1149] Ibid.
[1150] See ibid art II.6 ('Data privacy') which provides:

- Any partner can view their own data and set the privacy properties of the data as: private or public.
- Private: it indicates that the data can only be viewed and used by the partner itself.
- Public: it indicates that the data is licensed to this Platform. Platform will disclose the derived data and resources based on the principle of data sharing of this Platform.
- The data uploaded by partners are considered to be private by default. The data after the secondary processing by Apollo based on the data uploaded and marked as public by partner (such as annotation or scene extraction) should be used as the public data of this Platform.
- Blacklist: if partners do not want their data to be accessed by any sensitive partner, they can make the relevant settings.
- Special data: which is considered to be the private data of partners by default. The owner of the data can specify the data open to specific partners of this Platform.

In order not to lose the value of being a platform Hub, or main integrator, Baidu has a range of governing mechanisms, laid out in a policy manifesto on the platform's website.

far, this 'principle' does not seem to have impeded Baidu's (Apollo) business model. Baidu released its eighth version in July 2019: Apollo 5.0.[1151] There is a 1:3 data exchange principle under which partners open some data to Baidu, and Baidu opens three times the amount of its data to give back.[1152]

According to Lei Ma, a senior product manager of autonomous driving at Baidu, Baidu will make no claim on any use of its source code, however it is used:

> People are free to take Apollo, modify it or not, put it on a car and say 'we're selling autonomous vehicles'. Baidu does not lay claim to revenue, data, intellectual property. They can take it and commercialize it, anywhere in the world . . . Of course, if you work with Baidu, we can make things move a lot faster.[1153]

The clear assumption here is that no obstacles will prevent users of Apollo from transferring data out of China, despite the apparent restrictions in the Cyber Security Law on 'important data'.

When asked about companies that join but do not contribute useful data or code, Baidu President Yaqin Zhang replied:

> I think we are fine with that. Obviously, with the platform we encourage people who come with more, not only technology but data. Just like with Android, there are so many phone makers and they all have their different nuances. We want to see differentiation, and we will make sure the baseline technology is rock solid and as good as it could be. . . . But there are companies that don't contribute. You'll see that.[1154]

In stark contrast to foreign commentators' fears about Network Sovereignty, former Baidu COO Lu Qi noted: 'What will give an edge

---

[1151] Kyle Wiggers, 'Baidu Releases Apollo 5.0 with Upgrades for "Complex" Road Scenarios' (*Venture Beat*, 1 July 2019) <https://venturebeat.com/2019/07/01/baidu-releases-apollo-5-0-with-upgrades-for-complex-road-scenarios>. It has a Dual Hundred Plan that will invest ¥10 billion (100 *yi*) in 100 autonomous driving-related businesses: 王刚 [Wang Gang], «次 集体工作汇报» [A Collective Work Report] (n 1054).

[1152] This was highlighted at a conference held in Suzhou in May 2019, where Baidu noted that data sharing on the platform follows a '1 to 3' exchange principle, meaning that partners share some data with Baidu, while Baidu as the platform orchestrator opens up three times its data for testing models in exchange. Baidu crafted the rules of data exchange and is thereby shaping the process of ecosystem development, making complementors abide by these rules if they want to engage with the ecosystem at large. See also 王刚 [Wang Gang], «次 集体工作汇报» [A Collective Work Report] (n 1054).

[1153] Hersey, 'Baidu Launches Their Open Platform for Autonomous Cars' (n 1143).

[1154] Ohnsman, 'Baidu Aims for "Android" of Robocar Tech' (n 1131).

to China is a much larger population and a fast growing market. And a favorable policy environment designed to nurture and enable more data harnessing and AI technology.'[1155] Baidu, as one of the original five members of the AI National Team, was awarded the chance to help develop Xiongan as a training ground for self-driving cars.[1156] That Baidu Apollo has been designated a National AI Platform indicates a greater level of future access to public-road testing and service deployments for self-driving cars in Smart Cities such as Xiongan, in line with Chinese conceptions of self-driving cars as an extension of the Smart City model.[1157]

In September 2020, Baidu launched the Apollo Go Robotaxi service in Beijing, becoming the first company to allow people in Beijing to use robotaxis. The service encompasses the largest total area and longest road network of about 700 km for a manned autonomous driving test area in China, with nearly 100 pick-up and drop-off stations.[1158] A safety driver is still behind the wheel, as required by Beijing's regulations.

[1155] Blair Hanley, 'Baidu COO Says China's Government Will Help the Country Dominate AI' (*Venturebeat*, 9 January 2018) <https://venturebeat.com/2018/01/09/baidu-coo-says-chinas-government-will-help-the-country-dominate-ai>.

[1156] This is a private–public endeavour. Baidu was awarded the chance to help develop the Xiongan Smart City. Baidu will help to build infrastructure (eg, 5G network) that supports the long-term operation of autonomous vehicles. In September 2017, Baidu announced a US1.52 billion (¥10 billion) autonomous-driving Apollo Fund to invest in 100 autonomous driving projects over the next three years. Baidu began testing its autonomous cars on 33 km of closed highway between Beijing and Tianjin, its coastal sister city, in December 2017. Xiongan is now the most high-profile example of China's self-driving petri dishes built especially for training driverless cars. It was first announced on 1 April 2017 as a plan to build a brand-new city outside of Beijing. Xiongan is a rural township near Beijing with a population of 1 million and plans to transform itself into a green and intelligent metropolis of 5 million by 2035. It is estimated that there will be a $315 billion investment in high-technology infrastructure. The city is also exploring a new government structure. Party and government organs are more tightly integrated, and there are fewer government departments. See «雄安: 年» [Xiongan: After One Year] (*The Paper*, 1 April 2018) <https://www.thepaper.cn/newsDetail_forward_2048269>; «雄安新区一周年 这座城正在如何改变?» [The First Anniversary of Xiongan: How Is the City Changing?] (*China News*, 1 April 2018) <http://www.chinanews.com/gn/2018/04-01/8480837.shtml>. Baidu tweeted about Apollo being rolled out in Xiongan on 20 December 2017. See <https://twitter.com/Baidu_Inc/status/943509094404517888>.

[1157] «重磅: 百度 Apollo 发布全球首个车路协同开源方案» [Heavyweight: Baidu Apollo Releases the World's First Car Road Collaborative Open Source Solution] (*Baidu Public Policy Research Institute*, 14 September 2018) <https://mp.weixin.qq.com/s/p7TWjidyZ5eN5Uhc3yx1-g>.

[1158] 'What You Need to Know About Baidu's Apollo Go Robotaxi in Beijing' (*ApolloAuto Medium Page*, 28 October 2020) <https://techcrunch.com/2020/12/02/self-driving-trucks-startup-tusimple-raises-350m-from-u-s-rail-retail-and-freight-giants/>.

However, in December 2020 the Beijing government granted Baidu's autonomous driving unit five licences to test five autonomous cars in designated areas within China's capital city, without a safety driver.[1159] Baidu said that the Apollo platform had more than 36,000 developers worldwide in March 2020.[1160]

Yet beyond Baidu's business model of open source, its success in onboarding global partners is partly due to a protectionist remnant of Network Sovereignty policies that is relevant here: China's GPS mapping laws.

9.7.3 GPS Mapping Laws: Network Sovereignty as Economic Protectionism?

Network Sovereignty's fuzzy logic often seems to serve Chinese economic interests as much as its security interests. While laws enforcing Sino-foreign joint ventures in China's automotive industry were eased in 2018 to allow some wholly foreign-owned firms, market entry bans still exist in Chinese mapping laws.[1161] In late 2018, only 14 Chinese companies were approved to engage in the type of high-definition mapping required for automated driving technology, and other firms (including Chinese firms) must partner with one of these to develop their self-driving cars. By June 2020, this number had reached 22.[1162] As a result,

---

[1159] Che Pan, 'Baidu's Apollo Gets Green Light to Test AD Cars in Beijing Without On-Board Safety Driver' (*South China Morning Post*, 8 December 2020) < https://www.scmp.com/tech/innovation/article/3113029/baidus-apollo-gets-green-light-test-ad-cars-beijing-without-board>.

[1160] See «百度 Apollo 生态合作伙伴再添新成员，携手共建车路协同智能交通» [Baidu Apollo Ecosystem Adds New Members] (n 1135). See also 'ApolloAuto' (*GitHub*) <https://github.com/ApolloAuto/apollo>.

[1161] On 17 April 2018, China's NDRC announced the elimination of foreign equity restrictions on special-purpose vehicles and new energy vehicles in 2018, on commercial vehicles in 2020, and on passenger vehicles in 2022. In addition to the opportunity to own their own manufacturing ventures, foreign automakers are no longer restricted to having only two joint ventures in China. Interestingly, though, most leading Chinese privately owned car companies (eg, Geely, Great Wall and BYD) have achieved their position as domestic market leaders without the benefit of having initially formed a joint venture. See Bill Russo, Edward Tse and Alan Chan, 'Accelerating Innovation in China's Automobility Sector' (*Gao Feng Advisory*, April 2018) <http://www.edwardtseblog.com/view/accelerating-innovation-in-chinas-automobility-sector/>.

[1162] Given the political sensitivities, it is not surprising that mapping is a restricted area for foreign investment. According to the 2017 Foreign Investment Catalogue, foreign investors can only set up joint ventures with Chinese partners to engage in mapping. The Chinese partners need to be the controlling shareholders.

Google Maps, for example, is banned in China. Further, the Surveying and Mapping Law (revised in 2017) states that foreign entities or individuals involved in surveying or mapping must cooperate with Chinese government departments or entities to ensure no involvement of state secrets or issues in respect of Chinese national security.[1163] Foreign investment in internet mapping services is further restricted to joint ventures with Chinese partners.[1164]

As with the yet-to-be-agreed definition of 'important data', this has created fears among foreign investors that China is using concerns about national security to hinder their work on autonomous driving technology in China. Foreign companies already face significant restrictions that require them to work with a limited number of local partners that are licensed to engage in high-definition mapping.[1165] One industry source stated: 'We have obstacles driving around China making photos and recording GPS coordinates.'[1166] Another noted:

> Concurrently, it is clear that the playing field is not truly level for US tech companies in China. Even as Baidu plans to test self-driving cars in the US, US tech companies have been banned from doing so in China, due to purported concerns over espionage risks.... [The] Chinese government is clearly committed to helping Chinese companies lead the world in such technology. At a minimum, it's unlikely to allow foreign rivals to engage in mapmaking and comprehensive data collection on Chinese soil.[1167]

[1163] 《中华人民共和国测绘法》 [Surveying and Mapping Law of the People's Republic of China] (People's Republic of China) National People's Congress, amended 27 April 2017, art 8. Only 14 Chinese entities were granted an Electronic Navigation Mapping Licence by 2018. NavInfo, in which Tencent is the second largest shareholder, was the first to obtain the ENM Licence back in 2001 and DiDi Chuxing, China's largest ride-hailing company, was the 14th entity to obtain one in late 2017.

[1164] Ibid. Foreign investor shareholdings in such joint ventures cannot exceed 50% if the joint venture will apply for a licence for internet mapping services only as per art 8 of 《外国的组织或者个人来华测绘管理暂行办法》 [Temporary Measures on Administration of Mapping and Surveying in China by Foreign Organisations and Individuals] (People's Republic of China) Ministry of Land and Resources, 27 April 2011.

[1165] Yan Zhang, David Ramli and Lulu Chen, 'Wanted in China: Detailed Maps for 30 Million Self-Driving Cars' (*Bloomberg*, 22 August 2018) <https://www.bloomberg.com/news/articles/2018-08-22/wanted-in-china-detailed-maps-for-30-million-self-driving-cars>.

[1166] Charles Clover, 'China Impedes Foreign Carmakers' Autonomous Tests' (*Financial Times*, 14 December 2017) <https://www.ft.com/content/2ba4366c-e08c-11e7-a8a4-0a1e63a52f9c>.

[1167] Ibid.

Yet foreign firms can partner with Chinese firms. Thus, these comments are misleading in suggesting a complete ban, although there are limitations on foreign companies.

It seems that, learning from Baidu: 'On the recommended legal framework to move forward: the optimal choice is to reuse the structures of open-source software licensing for open data.'[1168] This may be borne out further in the future.

Likewise, while the wide net of global partnerships helps Baidu assemble driver data from road testing and simulations faster than the individual companies would be able to do on their own, at the same time, Baidu is reserving some of its services (eg, mapping and Machine Learning) for an application programming interface that remains under its control. From a company perspective, Baidu is monetising a plug-and-play device to bring autonomous capabilities into a vehicle.[1169]

So, is it the major restrictions on foreign participation in autonomous vehicle development in China that explain why Baidu's Apollo is attracting so many international partner companies? Does data localisation mean Chinese autonomous driving companies can 'unfairly' use data from US trials and stockpile data from Chinese trials?

Obviously, China represents one of the largest markets for autonomous vehicles, and access to that market is crucial for multinational firms, but Baidu is also a strong strategic partner in itself. The company has significant advantages in three key technologies essential in autonomous vehicles: technologies tied to the automotive industry, AI and mapping. Yet Baidu obtained its own mapping licence when it bought a Beijing-based start-up in 2013. This makes it difficult for global rivals to compete against Baidu in China. Any company with a plan to launch self-driving cars in China must cooperate with a licensed map company, and among these Baidu (and Apollo) is the obvious choice.[1170]

[1168] Colin Blackman and Simon Forge, *Data Flows – Future Scenarios: In-Depth Analysis for the ITRE Committee* (European Parliament, November 2017) 7 <http://www.europarl.europa.eu/RegData/etudes/IDAN/2017/607362/IPOL_IDA%282017%29607362_EN.pdf>.

[1169] Apollo is modularised, meaning that open-source code sections can be modified through APIs and can be replaced with proprietary implementations, which then can be contributed back to Apollo for redistribution and commercialisation.

[1170] General Motors, for example, has chosen Alibaba-owned AutoNavi for its Super Cruise driver-assistance system on the Cadillacs it plans to sell in China. Stated-owned SAIC Motor Corporation, China's biggest carmaker, bought shares in licence-holder Wuhan Kotei Informatics Co and formed a joint venture to develop driverless mapping. AutoNavi provides mapping data to Apple in China for its Apple Maps service, which

Of course, Baidu is not the only Chinese company active in the self-driving vehicle sector. On 22 September 2018, the Beijing Municipal Government issued licence plates to seven companies for street testing of autonomous vehicles. Six were Chinese companies and one, Daimler Greater China, is a high-profile participant in Baidu's Apollo. The other companies include subsidiaries of internet giants Tencent, Didi Chuxing and Baidu, as well as automakers NIO, BAIC BJEV and Pony.ai.[1171]

Daimler was the first international automaker to receive permission.[1172] It was given the test permit by the Chinese government after extensive closed-course testing.[1173] Daimler was also one of the first partners to join Apollo when it was launched in April 2017. As a result, the company obtains its mapping information through the Apollo platform. It is also a member of the Apollo Committee, a group that wants to accelerate research on safer solutions in automated driving in China and that promotes the drafting of related laws and regulations.

Therefore, while clearly Baidu has some competition within the Chinese market from other Chinese autonomous vehicle developers, its willingness to use open source and partner extensively with foreign car manufacturers and suppliers, and its access to a mapping licence, means

---

is only available when Apple devices are located in China. See Zen Soo, 'Alibaba's AutoNavi Becomes the First Chinese Maps Service to Navigate a Path to 100 Million Daily Users' (*South China Morning Post*, 5 October 2018) <https://www.scmp.com/tech/enterprises/article/2167114/alibabas-autonavi-blazes-trail-first-chinese-maps-service-cross-100>.

[1171] Bonnie Zhang, 'Tencent, Didi, Baidu among the Seven Companies Approved for Autonomous Car Road Tests in Beijing' (*Pandaily*, 25 September 2018) <https://pandaily.com/tencent-didi-baidu-among-the-seven-companies-approved-for-autonomous-car-road-tests-in-beijing>. The licence plates are arranged in levels from T1 to T5, based on the capabilities of the tested vehicle. The T3 licence plate received by Didi Chuxing, Baidu and Pony.ai is the highest level of plate issued by the Beijing Municipal Government and requires the smart vehicle in question to be able to follow traffic rules and handle emergencies. Corresponding to the five levels of licence plates are five levels of test roads: R1 to R5. In September 2018, Beijing allocated 11 more roads for autonomous vehicle testing in addition to the first 33 roads opened in March. The 44 roads cover a variety of traffic scenarios in urban and suburban areas.

[1172] Official records show that 35 companies across 16 cities were granted 109 licences by April 2019. Nearly half of these licences were obtained by Baidu: Jill Shen, 'China Drafts Guidelines for AV Security, but Challenges Remain' (*Technode*, 14 June 2019) <https://technode.com/2019/06/14/china-icv-policy-cesa-19>.

[1173] Kirsten Korosec, 'Daimler Deepens Ties with China's Baidu on Automated Driving' (*TechCrunch*, 25 July 2018) <https://techcrunch.com/2018/07/25/daimler-chinas-baidu-automated-driving>.

that it is the first choice for a foreign firm like Daimler to create an autonomous vehicle presence in China.[1174]

9.8 Conclusion: Linked Open-Source Ecosystems?

This chapter has identified the apparent conflict between China's data localisation laws and open-source development. It has explained the challenges posed by open-source AI for data localisation (and Network Sovereignty) policies.

On the one hand, data localisation requirements hinder globalised AI innovations, as open-source data-sharing platforms form the backbone of global AI development. Open-source data sharing increasingly seems to conflict with some of the aims of Network Sovereignty. The current Chinese government approach is to support the developments of China-based open-source initiatives, while keeping domestic control over data, where possible, without hindering innovations.

This chapter began by explaining open-source platforms and documented the history of open-source development in China. China was a latecomer to open-source development. Yet more recently the benefits of open-source platforms for innovation in AI such as the global nature of open-source AI platforms and global R&D have propelled Chinese open-source AI development. The chapter also further outlined the Chinese government's belated approach to supporting open-source AI platforms through the AI National Team. Finally, it then elucidated the key features of open-source AI relevant to the application of the Cyber Security Law by documenting the case studies of private globalised open-source AI platforms in China, notably Baidu's Apollo.

Many Chinese AI companies, including Baidu, are increasingly global in their R&D bases and employ open-source platforms. The Apollo Global Institute, established in 2018, is designed to promote the growth of Apollo around the globe by tying together Baidu's R&D bases in

---

[1174] It is also noteworthy that in January 2019, at the Consumer Electronics Show in Las Vegas, California-based company Udelv announced that it would use self-driving delivery vans built on Baidu's open-source Apollo platform to provide logistics for Walmart in Arizona, marking the entry of Baidu's autonomous technology, driven globally by the open-source platform, Apollo, into the United States: Sarah Dai, 'China's National AI Champion Baidu to Test Driverless Delivery Vans in US with Udelv for Walmart' (*South China Morning Post*, 9 January 2019) <https://www.scmp.com/tech/big-tech/article/2181214/chinas-national-ai-champion-baidu-test-driverless-delivery-vans-us>.

Beijing, Shanghai, Shenzhen, Silicon Valley and Seattle.[1175] Presumably, therefore, cross-border data flows will only be more important to the further development of Apollo and AI more broadly. For this reason, data localisation provisions in China's Cyber Security Law remained in flux without much regulatory guidance throughout 2018–2020. During this time, however, Sino-foreign R&D, investment and open-source platform-building continued unabated. Thus, fuzzy logic served its purpose in this instance, as data localisation remained unenforced, although uncertainty remains about whether this will change in the future.

Open-source platforms do not necessarily require data sharing; however, open-source AI is a global endeavour that may be further affected by China's cyber regime. For example, what happens when you wish to involve the global users of your platform, integrating talented developers into your ecosystem headquartered in China? This was a problem the drafters of China's Cyber Security Law did not foresee, as the increasing participation in free and open-source software by Chinese start-ups is an extremely recent phenomenon.

Both Chinese tech firms and the Chinese government now realise that open-source has been a crucial element in China's rapid AI progress, and the Chinese government is now seeking to build its own open-source AI industry. But China has yet to create a notable and viable open-source ecosystem, aside from Apollo, suggesting that continued open global collaboration will be necessary for some time to come.

One other key conclusion from this chapter is that Chinese tech firms move into foreign markets by creating partnerships; however, when it comes to entry into the Chinese market, China's mapping laws, inspired by Network Sovereignty, gave Baidu (and other Chinese firms) a first-mover advantage. To a certain extent, therefore, Network Sovereignty policies involve some elements of economic protectionism.

Looking to the future, will the impact of Network Sovereignty and the Cyber Security Law be such that a notable and successful domestic self-contained open-source AI software framework ecosystem is developed, shutting out foreign competitors from the Chinese AI market? Alternatively, will the Cyber Security Law eventually shut off the global open-source innovation tap for China? Or will domestic Chinese developers ever favour a Chinese open-source AI platform over Google's TensorFlow?

[1175] 'Baidu Jumps to Apollo 2.0' (*China Daily*, 17 January 2018) <http://www.chinadaily.com.cn/m/beijing/zhongguancun/2018-01/17/content_35529002.htm>.

The answers to these questions may depend on whether Chinese regulators introduce similar restrictions on foreign participation for Network Sovereignty reasons in this sector, as they did for mapping and autonomous vehicles. Furthermore, how China's Cyber Security Law is eventually enforced in a world of global open innovation in AI will have a major bearing on Chinese innovations in AI. At the current stage, it is not possible to provide definitive answers, but the Conclusion makes some tentative predictions based on the historical development of the Chinese government's fuzzy logic regulatory practice, and its current record of delayed/partial implementation of data localisation provisions.

While many commentators believe that the Chinese government always places a priority on domestic political stability, Chinese regulators seem willing to compromise on Network Sovereignty for AI development. However, there is a balance between stability and development – hence, China's fuzzy logic legal system.

Conclusion

Effect of Data Localisation on Chinese AI Innovation

> China is the 'richest petri dish of innovation in the world'.
> —Ming Zeng, Strategy Chief, Alibaba[1176]

China must regulate new and complex problems associated with emerging technologies, as must the rest of the world. Yet the Chinese government must also ferment innovation in an attempt to increase economic performance on various levels to improve China's standard of living, while making regulatory decisions in the context of Network Sovereignty, keeping the Communist Party in control. Thus, the multiple (partly contradictory) aims of the Chinese government create an ongoing tension between openness and control in laws and regulatory practice.

On the one hand, major fears surrounding China's Cyber Security Law concern where and how data is stored and whether this will obstruct cross-border AI R&D and allow for the abuse of citizens' rights and freedoms by an authoritarian government. Principally that data must be locally stored in China, due to China's preoccupation with Network Sovereignty, which is best embodied by the phrase 'secure and controllable'.

On the other hand, innovation is *the* major priority for the Chinese government. Party pronouncements have hailed technology as a key factor in fostering economic growth, productivity and efficiency, as well as a crucial element in better delivering public services such as education and healthcare. As China's comparative advantage in manufacturing erodes, and university graduates go unemployed, China must innovate for its own economic development and for the Party to maintain its leadership.

There remains a clear conflict between Chinese policies requiring localisation of data and economic imperatives demanding innovation by Chinese firms within the current globalised technology ecosystem. Thus, fuzzy logic lawmaking is a strategy that is adopted by the Chinese

---

[1176] Andelman, 'How China Out-Innovates' (n 756).

government to manage inconsistencies between competing policies, such as inconsistencies between Network Sovereignty and Internet Plus.

Do China's data localisation laws adversely affect – or are they likely to adversely affect – open innovation in Chinese AI firms? To what extent does innovation in AI depend upon cross-border open-source platforms? Do the requirements for data localisation more broadly affect open innovation by Chinese AI firms, as AI is a technology born of open innovation? Finally, to what extent is it possible for China to promote domestic innovation in AI without Chinese AI firms engaging in partnerships with foreign firms? The answers lie in the fluidity of fuzzy logic.

10.1 Fuzzy Logic

10.1.1 'Important Data' Remains Undefined in 2021

Fuzzy logic is used by the Chinese government to balance its competing interests in creating an environment that is conducive to innovation and assisting its Network Sovereignty agenda. The book concludes that data localisation laws, which form part of China's Cyber Security Law, will not (once the law is finalised) have a major impact on open-source AI innovation. This is because the 'fuzzy logic' regulatory approach, consistent with prior Chinese regulatory practice, is being employed by the Chinese authorities in selectively implementing these laws to avoid impeding AI development. In short, the Chinese authorities, in presiding over contradictory policy and regulatory decisions that may inhibit technological advancement in China, apply this approach to flexibly navigate those policies – and frequently to defer any conclusive decision-making to a future time (perhaps indefinitely). This is why many legal documents, including both the Cyber Security Law and its implementing rules and regulations, use intentionally vague language around data transfers and security verification and testing; this gives the government broad discretion, allowing for a spectrum of enforcement actions between promoting innovation and maintaining control.

'Fuzzy logic' is not 'fuzzy law' but is a deliberate Chinese strategy to build ambiguity into lawmaking in complex and rapidly changing areas, often in technology and investment laws. This strategy enables conflicting policies, such as Internet Plus and Network Sovereignty, to be simultaneously promoted, yet reconciled through selective implementation. The outcomes can be accidental, but the practice of drafting vague laws and delaying regulatory clarity is certainly intentional and has a long history in China. Various examples of fuzzy logic were expounded and are summarised below, with analysis of their broader significance for understanding Chinese regulatory practice in the area of innovation policy.

The Cyber Security Law was drafted before 2017 when Chinese companies began increasingly to use open-source AI platforms as a business tool for creating an ecosystem of commercial partners. The fact that Chinese companies only began establishing open-source AI platforms and global R&D facilities as recently as 2017 was identified as a key problem for regulators seeking to implement data localisation provisions under the Cyber Security Law.

Open-source platforms are an increasingly popular business model for AI development for global tech companies. Thus, restrictive (non-fuzzy) interpretation of the data localisation provisions within the Cyber Security Law would harm the growth of China's entrepreneurial ecosystem, including recent Chinese government plans to grow its own domestic open-source AI ecosystem.

Additionally, the Chinese government now also has a detailed plan to create a domestic AI ecosystem by setting up Chinese open-source platforms through its AI National Team. This plan shows that both Chinese tech firms and the Chinese government now realise open source has been a crucial element in China's rapid AI progress, and should not be jeopardised through draconian implementation of data localisation. As evidence for this point, the previous chapter documented the impressive success of Baidu's global open-source self-driving platform, Apollo, in onboarding global partners during 2017–2021.

At the same time, while the Chinese government will not block Chinese tech firms from access to overseas research and moving into foreign markets by creating partnerships, Network Sovereignty may still play a role in protecting Chinese tech firms from competition within China. For example, China's mapping laws, which restrict mapping firm licences to a limited number of 'trusted' companies for national security reasons. These laws gave Baidu (and other Chinese firms) a first-mover advantage in developing AI applications for autonomous vehicle manufacturers in China (including for international automobile firms). This belief was strengthened in June 2021, when China's MIIT published a tighter policy on data protection and data storage specifically for the automotive industry. Car manufacturers need to get regulatory approval for when they export data.[1177]

[1177] 《关于加强车联网（智能网联汽车）网络安全工作的通知（征求意见稿）》
[Notice on Strengthening Cyber Security Work in the Internet of Vehicles (Smart Connected Vehicles) (Opinion-Seeking Draft)] (People's Republic of China) MIIT, 23 June 2021.

Thus, the previous chapter identified the challenges posed by open-source AI for data localisation (and Network Sovereignty) policies. Further, it explained how fuzzy logic in the interpretation of key Chinese legal terms has addressed these challenges (or potential conflicts) in order to promote innovation, and in some cases, to benefit Chinese AI firms at the expense of foreign competitors.

To what extent does innovation in AI depend upon cross-border open-source platforms? This is an evolving question. Clearly AI is an open-source research exercise that will continue to depend on cross-border exchanges for years to come. How this emerging technology, and especially its global linkages, is being managed in China assists researchers' understanding of how the Chinese government maintains centralised control while promoting open innovation. The ability to maintain this policy balance between Network Sovereignty and openness conceivably affects successful innovation, and so far the evidence shows that the government has used fuzzy logic legislating and public–private petri dishes to avoid negative impacts of localisation on domestic AI innovations. When the Chinese government does not know how to regulate on hard issues, there is a reluctance to put anything in writing that might restrict the government's authority and flexibility. Therefore, in the Chinese legal system, laws often defer the specifics of key terms, and regulatory specifics and rules of implementation to more detailed documents later issued by delegated government authorities that can more easily be revised to deal with changing circumstances. China's Cyber Security Law and its impact on open-source AI is a classic case in point. Finally, 'important data' remains undefined in 2021.[1178]

10.1.2 Concluding Remark: Fuzzy Logic Is Intentional

One question that naturally arises from the conceptualisation of fuzzy logic regulatory practice presented in this book is whether the Chinese government *intentionally and purposely* applied this approach to AI and Cyber Security in order to give China a competitive advantage. Or was it

---

[1178] On 30 July 2021, five years after the Cyber Security Law became law in China, how 'critical information infrastructure' operators were designated, and what their responsibilities will be to protect the security of networks that they build and operate continued to receive some further regulatory clarity. See 《关键信息基础设施安全保护条例》 [Critical Information Infrastructure Security Protection Regulations] (People's Republic of China) State Council of the People's Republic of China, 30 July 2021.

just that the contradictions and competing interests within the various Chinese government institutions (eg, the security establishment versus innovation institutions) inevitably required compromises in technology policy, as they have with other policies in the past (eg, VIEs) – and fuzzy logic was an accidental by-product of that compromise process? Put another way, is the Chinese government really in control of the regulatory process, or is it just leaving things fuzzy because it cannot resolve its own internal (political) contradictions? The significance of this distinction will only emerge in the subsequent implementation process: an intentional fuzzy logic approach will most likely lead to more effective and coordinated development of the AI sector, whereas an accidental compromise may result in constant and unpredictable oscillation as the influence of different competing interests within the government waxes and wanes. In other words, regulators may have more flexibility to adapt laws as their effects become apparent. Yet that very discretion may also create major problems for businesses that need legal clarity to mitigate risks and navigate compliance processes.

It is difficult to give a definitive answer to this question. If one is sceptical of the coordinating ability and the knowledge and competence of governments (including China's) then the 'accidental' explanation is preferable. This would mean that China's future success and the impact on private Chinese and foreign tech firms may also remain very 'fuzzy', and unpredictable. This explanation would certainly be supported by some of the evidence and examples in this book; examples include Apple pre-emptively moving its servers to mainland China to comply with the Cyber Security Law and, more broadly, AliYun's cloud computing market share growth over the past four years.

One point that this book makes clear is that there is certainly no unified 'Chinese government' – a kind of overarching regulator – coordinating both its Network Sovereignty policies and the whole process of AI and technology regulation for the purpose of giving China a competitive edge against foreigners. If this were the case, the Chinese regulatory system would not be fuzzy at all, because this supposed single regulator would probably have already made the decision to use Network Sovereignty as an excuse to protect China from foreign competition. So-called fuzziness would become just a cloak for a unified policy of either protectionism or alternatively unrestricted innovation.

However, protectionist arguments levelled against China are too simplistic to accurately describe the complex Chinese policymaking environment. Some Chinese officials may certainly hold the narrow intention to use Network Sovereignty as a blunt tool for economic protectionism. Yet, as the book has demonstrated, there are many inconsistencies between national laws and their implementation guidelines at both central and local levels, and many of these guidelines are delayed for months, and sometimes even years, before final publication. This leaves major gaps in which technology regulators can use their discretion and adjust implementation through consultation with stakeholders.

In other words, it seems that there are elements of both accident and intention in the fuzzy logic regulatory approach, but that the intentional elements are not clearly protectionist, at least in their impacts. The fuzzy logic approach may well have originated accidentally over several decades of reform as the only practical way of dealing with competing interests within a fragmented Chinese bureaucracy. Its central objective is intentional however – namely, it is designed precisely to avoid the government committing to a single unified policy objective (eg, protectionism). Instead, it allows for a range of possibilities to be adopted over time dependent on future circumstances.

In 2020, during the Covid-19-induced economic downturn, local Chinese governments including the Shanghai and Hainan governments would still question the benefit of data localisation for their economies, offering alternate free (data) trade zone policies.[1179] The Shanghai government plan would remain unrestricted by censors online, while Hainan's plan would be swiftly censored.

This book applied the idea of intentional fuzziness to the competing interests and unforeseen issues that arose from the Cyber Security Law's implementation. Intentional and coordinated policy support for AI and open-source AI in the years since 2017 then provides the main example showing how fuzzy logic has allowed for the adjustment of apparently restrictive (but ambiguous) provisions in the Cyber Security Law to deal with the unexpected emergence of a new globally linked technology. In these rapidly changing situations, fuzzy logic regulatory practice becomes extremely convenient and useful. In the case of the Cyber Security Law, the fuzzy logic approach was certainly intentional, otherwise the law would have been clarified much earlier and key terms defined with intent at the outset.

[1179] Xiaomeng Lu, 'Is China Changing Its Thinking on Data Localization?' (*The Diplomat*, 8 June 2020) <https://thediplomat.com/2020/06/is-china-changing-its-thinking-on-data-localization/>.

10.2 Future Uncertainties

There are still numerous uncertainties surrounding the interplay between Network Sovereignty and innovation in China, which cannot be answered at this stage. How China's Cyber Security Law is eventually enforced in a world of global open innovation in AI will have a major bearing on China's progress as a potential world leader in AI technologies. China has yet to create a notable open-source ecosystem, aside from Apollo. Will the impact of Network Sovereignty and China's Cyber Security Law be that a significant and successful domestic self-contained open-source AI software framework ecosystem is developed, shutting out foreign competitors from the Chinese AI market? Thus, the following outstanding questions for further research arise:

- Will China's own open-source AI ecosystem, established through the AI National Team, succeed?
- Will developers, including Chinese developers, be drawn to these open-source platforms or will they continue to favour Google's TensorFlow?
- In onboarding partners, will the impact of Network Sovereignty and China's Cyber Security Law be such that a notable and successful domestic self-contained open-source AI software framework ecosystem is developed? Alternatively, will the Cyber Security Law and an increasingly inward-looking Chinese Communist Party eventually turn off the global open-source innovation tap for China?
- Will the final implementing regulations under the Cyber Security Law harm global open-source platform collaborations for Chinese companies?
- Would this mean that yet another domain (open-source AI platforms) is set to join a walled-off Chinese internet and protected cloud computing regime?
- Will Chinese companies be forced to keep their datasets and associated algorithms in China for Chinese developer use only?

Much depends on Chinese regulators' ability to continue to provide a space for private sector innovation without succumbing to the temptation to engage in heavy-handed restriction and control.

Crucially, Chinese government policies in Xinjiang and how surveillance technologies are deployed there, along with the changing winds of the Biden presidency in the United States will affect all of the questions above in 2021 and beyond.

10.2.1 Potential Future Developments in AI Policymaking

In addition, Federated Learning is one example of how ongoing developments in emerging technologies and business practices will pose challenges to policymaking which will require further research, such as a survey of federated learning vis-à-vis China. Federated Learning is an emerging approach to training AI with sensitive user data while protecting privacy at the same time, as distributed data remains offline and is not sent to a cloud.[1180] Rather than gathering user data in the cloud from users' training datasets, federated learning trains AI models on mobile devices in large batches, then transfers those learnings back to a global model without the need for data to ever leave the device. Open-source AI platforms TensorFlow (Google) and PyTorch (Facebook) took some steps in 2019–2021 towards data privacy with solutions that incorporate federated learning.[1181] More research will clearly be required around this area in the future, in particular on how this development affects Chinese developers' open-source AI platform preferences.

Yet, to restate this book's conclusions, despite these important ongoing uncertainties, this book has argued that based on the Chinese government's longstanding fuzzy logic regulatory practice, it is likely that the government will take account of reasonable feedback from key stakeholders, including private AI firms, and will not allow Network Sovereignty concerns to impede innovation in the technology industry. This was already to a large extent evidenced when the implementation of the Cyber Security Law's data localisation provisions were officially delayed until 31 December 2018 (and then beyond that date). Subsequent subordinate regulations in 2019, 2020 and 2021 have continued the fuzzy logic approach by indicating that for the time being

---

[1180] Google AI researcher, H Brendan McMahan (et al), first developed federated learning in 2017: see H Brendan McMahan et al, 'Communication-Efficient Learning of Deep Networks from Decentralized Data' (2017) <https://arxiv.org/abs/1602.05629>. Since then the paper has been cited more than 300 times by research scientists, according to arXiv. A team of Google AI researchers including McMahan and Ian Goodfellow also authored a heavily cited 2016 paper, Martin Abadi et al, 'Deep Learning with Differential Privacy' (2016) <https://arxiv.org/abs/1607.00133>. In March 2019, Google released TensorFlow Federated to make federated learning easier to perform with its widely used Machine Learning framework.

[1181] See Kahri Johnson, 'How Federated Learning Could Shape the Future of AI in a Privacy-Obsessed World' (*Venture Beat*, 3 June 2019) <https://venturebeat.com/2019/06/03/how-federated-learning-could-shape-the-future-of-ai-in-a-privacy-obsessed-world>.

'important data' will be interpreted to mean 'personal data' of Chinese citizens, something more closely resembling international practice (eg, Europe's GDPR) and an approach that is less restrictive for tech firms conducting cross-border AI R&D.

It must also be restated that while there are still now in 2021 constant geopolitical conversations about an AI race or a new technology-driven cold war,[1182] entrepreneurial ecosystems are globalised networks that rely heavily on cross-border trade, investment and data transfers. Chinese AI companies rely on US-made Nvidia processing chips, US investment and, increasingly, US-based research labs. Further, enterprise (or business-to-business) AI requires creating an ecosystem of partnerships. Yaqin Zhang, president of Baidu, reinforced this point in 2018 by publicly stating that it was expanding its AI technologies in traditional industries: 'For Baidu, the most important thing lies not only in product and technology, but also in partners in the ecosystem.'[1183]

Yet the Chinese government is now aware of the disruption caused by data localisation on open-source AI and open innovation in general. During 2017–2021, China's national innovation systems became increasingly globally connected. Chinese technology regulators are also aware that Network Sovereignty may hamper Chinese innovation, as no country has a monopoly on scientific discoveries and innovative advancements. In spite of that, beginning in 2019 US trade bans began to hurt the Chinese entrepreneurial ecosystem, including world class Chinese AI image recognition start-up unicorns.

China still faces challenges such as a deficit in top AI research talent, with very few AI scientists capable of producing world-leading research. According to Yu Kai, the founding director of Baidu's Institute of Deep Learning, the number of world-class AI research experts is 'between 5 and 10'.[1184] Influential Chinese academics agree with this assessment. Dong Jielin, an adjunct professor at the Research Center for Technological Innovation at Tsinghua University in Beijing, was quoted as saying: 'there's very few high-level AI talent at Chinese companies.

[1182] See, eg, Marc Champion, 'Digital Cold War' (*Bloomberg*, 17 May 2019) <https://www.bloomberg.com/quicktake/how-u-s-china-tech-rivalry-looks-like-a-digital-cold-war>; Nicholas Thompson and Ian Bremmer, 'The AI Cold War that Threatens Us All' (*Wired*, 23 October 2018) <https://www.wired.com/story/ai-cold-war-china-could-doom-us-all/>.

[1183] Zhou Mo, 'Baidu Expands Use of Its AI Tech in Traditional Industries' (*China Daily*, 31 May 2018) <http://www.chinadaily.com.cn/a/201805/31/WS5b0fe579a31001b82571d7d6.html>.

[1184] He, 'How China Is Preparing for an AI-Powered Future' (n 848).

Many are just so-so and not original'. 'They won't be able to produce first-class work without the guidance of high-level talent.'[1185] Relatedly, since 2017 Baidu has provided 15% more in compensation to AI staff willing to move to China from the United States or elsewhere.[1186]

The government's awareness of China's dependence on global talent and R&D links suggests that it will not close the door in the foreseeable future. It is more likely to continue encouraging open-source projects like Baidu's Apollo and other public–private AI initiatives, including allowing them to maintain their global linkages through selective implementation of data localisation, in order to ensure China's continued economic development and position at the forefront of advanced technology innovation. Perhaps, as one influential Chinese industry consultant suggested, '[o]pen-source [solutions and communities], in fact, can be a way to avoid tensions in the tech sector'.[1187]

The author of this book is a passionate supporter of grass-roots open-source communities, and believes they will be a great circuit breaker beyond governmental policies. Chinese coding talent is highly valued in these communities.

10.2.2 Future Impact of Fuzzy Logic Regulatory Practice on Tech Firms and Entrepreneurs

Fuzzy logic regulatory practice inevitably results in a level of uncertainty about the implementation of government laws and policies, and this also leads to uncertainty among Chinese and foreign tech firms. One of the limitations of this book is that the fuzzy nature of Chinese regulation makes it very difficult to predict its impacts in practice on these firms.

However, it is possible to make some tentative future predictions in answering an important subsidiary question that arose from this research:

[1185] Li Yuan, 'China Is Losing to the US in High-Stakes Battle for Artificial Intelligence Talent' (*Wall Street Journal*, 23 March 2017) <https://www.wsj.com/articles/baidus-loss-is-a-setback-for-ai-in-china-1490270411?mg=prod/accounts-wsj>.

[1186] Ibid.

[1187] Fang Zhixi, former global vice president at Intel and now the chairman of RISC-V Foundation's consultancy committee in China. RISC-V (pronounced 'risk-five') is a free and open ISA enabling a new era of processor innovation through open standard collaboration. Founded in 2015, the RISC-V Foundation comprises more than 275 members building the first open, collaborative community of software and hardware innovators powering innovation at the edge forward. See 'RISC-V Foundation' (*RISC-V website*) <https://riscv.org/risc-v-foundation>. Fang was quoted in Runhua Zhao, 'China Looks to Private Capital, Open Source Technology for Global Tech Game Advantage' (*Technode*, 20 December 2018) <https://technode.com/2018/12/20/china-global-tech-game-advantage>.

To what extent does the tension between data localisation laws and policies, on the one hand, and innovation in AI, on the other, reflect a broader tension in Chinese policymaking between protecting domestic firms against competition from foreign firms while promoting open innovation in AI?

Focusing first on Chinese tech firms, based on their experiences since 2016 and increasing central and local Chinese government support for AI development for solving China's governance problems, the fuzzy logic regulatory approach combined with public–private policy petri dishes can provide them with huge opportunities for rapid expansion. Providing AI solutions for governments and SOEs also allows private firms to have some influence in policy implementation debates. They can and have made clear that some aspects of Network Sovereignty and the Cyber Security Law, if strictly enforced, would impede their capacity to effectively develop advanced AI applications.

This was the case with the delay in implementing data localisation policies under China's Cyber Security Law. Partly due to input from private tech firms, the vaguely defined law was left for subsequent future implementation, and regulations have since adjusted the interpretation of the law to avoid negative impacts on AI development. This delay and adjustment process challenges the prevailing view outside China that the government is using localisation as a protectionist tool of control over Chinese data and supporting China's domestic cloud computing industry. The symbiosis of government and private firms in developing AI also supports this point, as it demonstrates that the Chinese government now has a vested interest in the success of the AI sector, and will work with private firms to ensure that Network Sovereignty does not obstruct that success.

Therefore, fuzzy logic, despite its uncertainties, is not necessarily a bad thing for Chinese entrepreneurs. Quite the opposite, it gives them the advantage of providing regulators with expert input to policymaking in an emerging and innovative, high-tech economy, in ways that greatly benefit their own business expansion.

Nevertheless, there are potential drawbacks for Chinese private tech firms in having to engage in this continuous negotiation and collaboration with regulators and the Chinese government. Alibaba's Jack Ma once famously said his policy for dealing with the government is to fall in love but not to marry.[1188] Ma's comment highlights the delicate relationship between Chinese tech companies and the government. Ant Group's delayed IPO in Hong Kong 2020 continued to further cloud the opacity

---

[1188] Shujie Leng, 'Be in Love with Them, But Don't Marry Them' (*Foreign Policy*, 31 October 2014) <http://foreignpolicy.com/2014/10/31/be-in-love-with-them-but-dont-marry-them>.

of this relationship for the world, perhaps for Ma too. This pendulum would continue to swing again towards Network Sovereignty in 2021. On 10 July 2021, CAC released a draft revision to the existing Measures for Cyber Security Review, with public comments on the revision due by 25 July 2021.[1189] This revision would be an opportunity for the Chinese government to delay or hinder foreign listings of VIEs. Specifically, 'IPO materials' would form part of that Measures for Cyber Security Review. This would dramatically affect Didi Chuxing after it listed in the United States in June 2021, as CAC announced that it was placing Didi under investigation over data security concerns and ordered app stores to remove the Didi app. CAC also prevented the company from acquiring new users.[1190] Once again, VIEs were under great scrutiny and this was seen as another example of the Chinese government seeking to dissuade companies from listing in the US.[1191]

Yet there was perhaps a precedent that could explain the new rules in late 2020. Ant Group's 'IPO materials' provided Chinese regulators with great insights into its problematic credit-lending practices.[1192] Nevertheless, personal data security would be now tied to national security and China's new Data Security Law would be cited in the proposed revision to the Measures for Cyber Security Review, leading to the belief that China is seeking to keep data locked in China.

Another major negative consequence of this complex public-private relationship for Chinese firms dependent on Western hardware had

---

[1189] 《网络安全审查办法（修订草案征求意见稿）》 [Measures for Cyber Security Review (Revised, Opinion-Seeking Draft)] (People's Republic of China) CAC, 10 July 2021.

[1190] Lucas Niewenhuis, 'Didi Drops 20% after IPO as Beijing Tightens Data Security Review' (SupChina, 6 July 2021) <https://supchina.com/2021/07/06/didi-drops-20-after-ipo-as-beijing-tightens-data-security-review/>.

[1191] Li Yuan, 'For China's Business Elites, Staying Out of Politics Is No Longer an Option' (New York Times, 6 July 2021) <https://www.nytimes.com/2021/07/06/technology/china-business-politics-didi.html>.

[1192] Ant Group's delayed dual-listing IPO on the Shanghai Stock Exchange Science and Technology Innovation Board and Stock Exchange of Hong Kong in late 2020 mystified some outsiders. While the timing of the regulatory intervention just prior to the IPO was unfortunate, there was a clear regulatory explanation, namely reporting irregularities due to recently released draft regulations requiring fintech platforms to provide higher funding to back loans and to cap loan size to borrowers, as the largest revenue stream for Ant Group is not payments but online lending. A reading of Ant Group's IPO Prospectus reveals this fact. The filing can be found at Stock Exchange of Hong Kong, *Application Proof of Ant Group Co, LTD Technology Limited* 《螞蟻科技集團股份有限公司》 (Prospectus, 27 October 2020) <https://www1.hkexnews.hk/listedco/listconews/sehk/2020/1026/2020102600165.pdf> (Ant Group IPO Filing).

already become apparent in 2019: those tech firms involved in providing surveillance and control applications to Chinese security forces for use on the Uighur population in Xinjiang have recently encountered severe restrictions on their ability to import hardware from US suppliers.[1193] Likewise, as the experiences of internet hardware firms like Megvii, Huawei and ZTE have shown, any Chinese tech firm that is perceived to have too close links with the Chinese security establishment may find its business curtailed or even brought to its knees by US export restrictions and lawsuits.[1194] Therefore, a close association between Chinese private firms and Network Sovereignty policies (in the form of government censorship and suppression of dissent) may lead to crippling economic sanctions on those Chinese firms from foreign governments.

Turning to international tech firms with business interests in China, their fears of being effectively shut out of the Chinese market in 2016–2017 due to data localisation rules were overblown. Fuzzy logic regulatory practice has already diluted the negative impact of those rules on much cross-border data transfer, and foreign firms have also pre-emptively shown a willingness to comply with the Cyber Security Law by storing at least some of their Chinese data on servers located in China. However, the implementation of some Network Sovereignty policies (eg, restrictions on licences for mapping firms) may provide a competitive advantage for Chinese firms, and would correspondingly force foreign firms developing technology in industry sectors like autonomous vehicles to collaborate with Chinese firms if they wish to benefit from the huge opportunities arising from China's public–private policy petri dishes.

Foreign tech firms in China will also continue to face a similar dilemma to that of Chinese private firms for the foreseeable future: a difficult balancing act between profiting from Chinese markets and avoiding falling into the trap of assisting the Chinese government to suppress the rights of its citizens. In the current Chinese political environment, there are no easy solutions to this dilemma.

[1193] For example, SenseTime has multiple American backers and until April 2019 was involved in a security joint venture in Xinjiang. SenseTime sold out of the venture following public pressure and states it now has very little business in Xinjiang. Christian Shepherd, 'China's SenseTime Sells out of Xinjiang Security Joint Venture' (*Financial Times*, 15 April 2019) <https://www.ft.com/content/38aa038a-5f4f-11e9-b285-3acd5d43599e>.

[1194] Tripti Lahiri and Mary Hui, 'How Huawei Became America's Tech Enemy No 1' (*Quartz*, 28 May 2019) <https://qz.com/1627149/huaweis-journey-to-becoming-us-tech-enemy-no-1>.

Thus, while fuzzy logic is a tool that enables the delicate balance between Network Sovereignty and innovation in China, it is also a tool that continues to present major obstacles for companies operating in globalised technology ecosystems. This is an ongoing, evolving and highly opaque story.

BIBLIOGRAPHY

A Journal Articles

Abadi, Martin et al, 'Deep Learning with Differential Privacy' (2016) <https://arxiv.org/abs/1607.00133>

Abrami, Regina M, William C Kirby and F Warren McFarlan, 'Why China Can't Innovate' (March 2014) *Harvard Business Review* <https://hbr.org/2014/03/why-china-cant-innovate>

Adee, Sally, 'Will AI's Bubble Pop?' (2016) 231(3082) *New Scientist* (16 July 2016)

Ahlstrom, David, Garry D Bruton and Kuang S Yeh, 'Venture Capital in China: Past, Present, and Future' (2007) 24(3) *Asia Pacific Journal of Management* 247

Ahmed, Shazeda and Steven Weber, 'China's Long Game in Techno-Nationalism' (2018) 23(5) *First Monday* <https://firstmonday.org/ojs/index.php/fm/article/view/8085/7209>

Amirahmadi, Hooshang and Grant Saff, 'Science Parks: A Critical Assessment' (1993) 8(2) *Journal of Planning Literature* 107

Ananny, Mike and Kate Crawford, 'Seeing without Knowing: Limitations of the Transparency Ideal and Its Application to Algorithmic Accountability' (2016) 20(1) *New Media and Society* 88

Arora, Ashish, Marco Ceccagnoli and Wesley M Cohen, 'R&D and the Patent Premium' (2008) 26(5) *International Journal of Industrial Organization* 1153

Baumol, William J, 'Entrepreneurship: Productive, Unproductive, and Destructive' (1990) 98(5) *Journal of Political Economy* 893

Borg, Scott, 'Economically Complex Cyberattacks' (2003) 3(6) *IEEE Security and Privacy Magazine* 64

Braman, Sandra, 'Privacy by Design: Networked Computing, 1969–1979' (2012) 14(5) *New Media and Society* 798

Cai, Dingjian, 'Development of the Chinese Legal System since 1979 and Its Current Crisis and Transformation', trans S Farhad (1999) 11(2) *Cultural Dynamics* 135

Cao, Cong, 'Zhongguancun and China's High-Tech Parks in Transition: "Growing Pains" or "Premature Senility?"' (2004) 44(5) *Asian Survey* 647

――'Zhongguancun: China's Silicon Valley' (2001) 28(3) *China Business Review* 38

Chander, Anupam and Uyen P Le, 'Data Nationalism' (2015) 64(3) *Emory Law Journal* 679

Chang, Chen-Yu and Shi Chen, 'Transitional Public–Private Partnership Model in China: Contracting with Little Recourse to Contracts' (2016) 142(10) *Journal of Construction Engineering and Management* 7

Chaudhri, Javade, 'Chinese Industrial Policies: Indigenous Innovation, Intellectual Property Rights, and the Trade Issues of the Next Decade' (2011) 34(1) *Thomas Jefferson Law Review* 1

Chen, Jia, 'China's Venture Capital Guiding Funds: Policies and Practice' (2010) 2(3) *Journal of Chinese Entrepreneurship* 292

Chen, Tain-Jy and Ying-Hua Ku, 'Rent Seeking and Entrepreneurship: Internet Startups in China' (2016) 36(3) *Cato Journal* 659

Chen, Yu-Jie, Ching-Fu Lin and Han-Wei Liu, '"Rule of Trust": The Power and Perils of China's Social Credit Megaproject' (2018) 32(1) *Columbia Journal of Asian Law* 1

Coe, Neil M et al, '"Globalizing" Regional Development: A Global Production Networks Perspective' (2004) 29(4) *Transactions of the Institute of British Geographers* 468

Creemers, Rogier, 'Cyber China: Updating Propaganda, Public Opinion Work and Social Management for the 21st Century' (2017) 26(103) *Journal of Contemporary China* 85

Deng, Jinting and Pinxin Liu, 'Consultative Authoritarianism: The Drafting of China's Internet Security Law and E-Commerce Law' (2018) 26(107) *Journal of Contemporary China* 1

Evans, Peter, 'Development as Institutional Change: The Pitfalls of Monocropping and the Potentials of Deliberation' (2004) 38(4) *Studies in Comparative International Development* 30

Fagerholm, Fabian et al, 'Onboarding in Open Source Projects' (2014) 31(6) *IEEE Software* 54

Feng, Yang, 'The Future of China's Personal Data Protection Law: Challenges and Prospects' (2019) 27(1) *Asia Pacific Law Review* 1

Feng, Zhu and Marco Iansiti, 'Entry into Platform-Based Markets' (2012) 33(1) *Strategic Management Journal* 88

Fishman, William L, 'Introduction to Transborder Data Flows' (1980) 16(1) *Stanford Journal of International Law* 1

Forte, Andrea and Cliff Lampe, 'Defining, Understanding, and Supporting Open Collaboration: Lessons from the Literature' (2013) 57(5) *American Behavioral Scientist* 535

Fraser, Erica, 'Data Localisation and the Balkanisation of the Internet' (2016) 13(3) *SCRIPTed – A Journal of Law, Technology and Society* 359

Friedewald, Michael et al, 'Privacy, Data Protection and Emerging Sciences and Technologies: Towards a Common Framework' (2010) 23(1) *European Journal of Social Science Research* 61

Fung, KC and Nathalie Aminian, 'Silicon Valley, France and China: A Comparative Study of Innovation Systems and Policies' (2017) *Journal of Chinese Economic and Foreign Trade Studies* 10(3) 194

Ganz, Frieder, Daniel Puschmann and Payam Barnaghi, 'A Practical Evaluation of Information Processing and Abstraction Techniques for the Internet of Things' (2015) 2(4) *IEEE Internet of Things Journal* 340

Gao, Zhicun and Clem Tisdell, 'China's Reformed Science and Technology System: An Overview and Assessment' (2004) 22(3) *Prometheus: Critical Studies in Innovation* 311

Goldsmith, Jack L, 'Against Cyberanarchy' (1998) 65(4) *University of Chicago Law Review* 1199

Greenleaf, Graham and Scott Livingston, 'PRC's New Data Export Rules: "Adequacy with Chinese Characteristics"?' (2017) 147 *Privacy Laws & Business International Report* 9

Hanna, Nagy K and Christine Zhen-Wei Qiang, 'China's Emerging Informatization Strategy' (2010) 1(2) *Journal of the Knowledge Economy* 128

Harwit, Eric, 'The Rise and Influence of Weibo (Microblogs) in China' (2014) 54 (6) *Asian Survey* 1059

Hawes, Colin, Alex K L Lau and Angus Young, 'The Chinese "Oppression" Remedy: Creative Interpretations of Company Law by Chinese Courts' (2015) 63(2) *American Journal of Comparative Law* 17

Hawkins, Jeff and Subutai Ahmad, 'Why Neurons Have Thousands of Synapses: A Theory of Sequence Memory in Neocortex' (2016) 10 *Frontiers in Neural Circuits* 1

Heilmann, Sebastian, 'From Local Experiments to National Policy: The Origins of China's Distinctive Policy Process' (2008) 59 *China Journal* 1

Hemphill, Thomas A and George O White III, 'China's National Champions: The Evolution of a National Industrial Policy – Or a New Era of Economic Protectionism?' (2013) 55(2) *Thunderbird International Business Review* 193

Hill, Jonah Force, 'A Balkanized Internet? The Uncertain Future of Global Internet Standards?' (2012) *Georgetown Journal of International Affairs* 49 <https://www.jstor.org/stable/43134338>

Hsu, Carolyn, 'Cadres, Getihu, and Good Businesspeople: Making Sense of Entrepreneurs in Early Post-Socialist China' (2006) 35(1) *Urban Anthropology and Studies of Cultural Systems and World Economic Development* 1

Huang, Hui (Robin), Wei Zhang and Kelvin Siu Cheung Lee, 'The (Re)introduction of Dual-Class Share Structures in Hong Kong: A Historical and Comparative Analysis', *Journal of Corporate Law Studies* (24 December 2019), <https://ssrn.com/abstract=3245885>

Hubbert, Jennifer, 'Better City, Better Life? Urban Modernity at the Shanghai Expo' (2019) 17(4) *Asia-Pacific Journal* 1

Hurwitz, Roger, 'Depleted Trust in the Cyber Commons' (2012) 6(3) *Strategic Studies Quarterly* 20

Janssen, Marijn and Jeroen van den Hoven, 'Big and Open Linked Data (BOLD) in Government: A Challenge to Transparency and Privacy?' (2015) 32(4) *Government Information Quarterly* 363

Johnson, David R and David Post, 'Law and Borders: The Rise of Law in Cyberspace' (1996) 48(5) *Stanford Law Review* 1367

Johnson, Kaitlyn, 'Variable Interest Entities: Alibaba's Regulatory Work-Around to China's Foreign Investment Restrictions' (2015) 12 *Loyola University Chicago International Law Review* 249

Junio, Timothy J, 'How Probable Is Cyber War? Bringing IR Theory Back in to the Cyber Conflict Debate' (2013) 36(1) *Journal of Strategic Studies* 125

Kania, Elsa B, 'Technological Entanglement? Artificial Intelligence in the US–China Relationship' (2017) 17(17) *China Brief* 11 <https://jamestown.org/program/technological-entanglement-artificial-intelligence-u-s-china-relationship>

Kapoor, Rahul and Joon Mahn Lee, 'Coordinating and Competing in Ecosystems: How Organizational Forms Shape New Technology Investments' (2012) 34(3) *Strategic Management Journal* 274

Karolyi, G Andrew, 'The Role of American Depositary Receipts in the Development of Emerging Equity Markets' (2004) 86(3) *Review of Economics and Statistics* 670

Khan, Lina M, 'Amazon's Antitrust Paradox' (2016) 126(3) *Yale Law Journal* 710

Komaitis, Konstantinos, 'The "Wicked Problem" of Data Localisation' (2017) 2(3) *Journal of Cyber Policy* 355

Kong, Lingjie, 'Data Protection and Transborder Data Flow in the European and Global Context' (2010) 21(2) *European Journal of International Law* 441

Krizhevsky, Alex, Ilya Sutskever and Geoffrey E Hinton, 'ImageNet Classification with Deep Convolutional Neural Networks' (2012) 25(2) *Advances in Neural Information Processing Systems* 1

Kuner, Christopher, 'Data Nationalism and Its Discontents' (2015) 64 *Emory Law Journal* 2089

Landset, Sara et al, 'A Survey of Open Source Tools for Machine Learning with Big Data in the Hadoop Ecosystem' (2015) 2(1) *Journal of Big Data* 1

Lee, Jyh-An and Ching-Yi Liu, 'Real-Name Registration Rules and the Fading Digital Anonymity in China' (2016) 25 *Washington International Law Journal* 1

Lerner, Josh and Jean Tirole, 'The Scope of Open Source Licensing' (2005) 21(1) *Journal of Law, Economics, and Organization* 20

Li, Guo, 'Chinese Style VIEs: Continuing to Sneak under Smog?' (2014) 47 *Cornell International Law Journal* 572.

Liao, Debbie and Philip Sohmen, 'The Development of Modern Entrepreneurship in China' (2010) 1 *Stanford Journal of East Asian Affairs* 27

Lin, Liwen and Curtis Milhaupt, 'We Are the (National) Champions' (2013) 65(4) *Stanford Law Review* 697

Lin, Yu-Hsin and Thomas Mehaffy, 'Open Sesame: The Myth of Alibaba's Extreme Corporate Governance and Control' (2016) 10(2) *Brooklyn Journal of Corporate, Financial & Commercial Law* 437

Lindman, Juho and Linus Nyman, 'Code Forking, Governance, and Sustainability in Open Source Software' (2013) 3(1) *Technology Innovation Management Review* 7

'The Businesses of Open Data and Open Source: Some Key Similarities and Differences' (2014) 4(1) *Technology Innovation Management Review* 12

Lindsay, Jon R, 'The Impact of China on Cybersecurity' (2014) 39(3) *International Security* 7

Liu, Wei et al, 'The Development Evaluation of Economic Zones in China' (2018) 15(1) *International Journal of Environmental Research and Public Health* 1

Livingston, Scott and Graham Greenleaf, 'Data Localisation in China and Other APEC Jurisdictions' (2016) 143 *Privacy Laws & Business International Report* 22

Mackenzie, Adrian, 'From API to AI: Platforms and Their Opacities' (2018) 22(13) *Information, Communication & Society* 1

Man, Thomas Y, 'Policy Above Law: VIE and Foreign Investment Regulation in China' (2015) 3(1) *Peking University Transnational Law Review* 217

Mishra, Neha, 'Building Bridges: International Trade Law, Internet Governance, and the Regulation of Data Flows' (2019) 52 *Vanderbilt Journal of Transnational Law* 463

Mitchell, Andrew and Neha Mishra, 'Data at the Docks: Modernizing International Trade Law for the Digital Economy' (2018) 20(4) *Vanderbilt Journal of Entertainment and Technology Law* 1073

Nguyen, Giang, Stefan Dlugolinsky and Martin Bobák, 'Machine Learning and Deep Learning Frameworks and Libraries for Large-Scale Data Mining: A Survey' (2019) 51(1) *Artificial Intelligence Review* 77

Nye Jr, Joseph S, 'Nuclear Lessons for Cyber Security?' (2011) 5(4) *Strategic Studies Quarterly* 18

Oreg, Shaul and Oded Nov, 'Exploring Motivations for Contributing to Open Source Initiatives: The Roles of Contribution Context and Personal Values' (2008) 24(5) *Computers in Human Behaviour* 2055

Parker, Geoffrey, Marshall Van Alstyne and Xiaoyue Jiang, 'Platform Ecosystems: How Developers Invert the Firm' (2017) 41(1) *MIS Quarterly* 255

Pelkola, David, 'A Framework for Managing Privacy-Enhancing Technology' (2012) 29(3) *IEEE Software* 45

Perez, Oren, 'Fuzzy Law: A Theory of Quasi-Legal Systems' (2015) 28 *Canadian Journal of Law and Jurisprudence* 343

Peterson, Dale, 'Offensive Cyber Weapons: Construction, Development, and Employment' (2013) 36(1) *Journal of Strategic Studies* 120

Phelps, Edmund S, 'The Dynamism of Nations: Toward a Theory of Indigenous Innovation' (2017) (12)1 *Capitalism and Society* 1

Posner, Eric A and E Glen Weyl, 'Property Is Only Another Name for Monopoly' (2017) 9(1) *Journal of Legal Analysis* 51

Post, David G, 'Against "Against Cyberanarchy"' (2002) 17(4) *Berkeley Technology Law Journal* 1365

Rubinstein, Ira S, 'Regulating Privacy by Design' (2011) 26(3) *Berkeley Technology Law Journal* 1409

Rubinstein, Ira S and Nathaniel Good, 'Privacy by Design: A Counterfactual Analysis of Google and Facebook Privacy Incidents' (2013) 28(2) *Berkeley Technology Law Journal* 1333

Ryan, Patrick S, Sarah Falvey and Ronak Merchant, 'When the Cloud Goes Local: The Global Problem with Data Localization' (2013) 46(12) *Computer* 54

Sargsyan, Tatevik, 'Data Localisation and the Role of Infrastructure for Surveillance, Privacy and Security' (2016) 10 *International Journal of Communication* 2221

Selby, John, 'Data Localization Laws: Trade Barriers or Legitimate Responses to Cybersecurity Risks, or Both?' (2017) 25(3) *International Journal of Law and Information Technology* 213

Shi, Serena Y, 'Dragon's House of Cards: Perils of Investing in Variable Interest Entities Domiciled in the People's Republic of China and Listed in the United States' (2014) 37 *Fordham International Law Journal* 1278

Song, Peijian et al, 'The Ecosystem of Software Platform: A Study of Asymmetric Cross-Side Network Effects and Platform Governance' (2018) 42(1) *MIS Quarterly* 121

Sum, Ngai-Ling, 'The Intertwined Geopolitics and Geoeconomics of Hopes/Fears: China's Triple Economic Bubbles and the "One Belt One Road" Imaginary' (2018) *Territory, Politics, Governance* <https://doi.org/10.1080/21622671.2018.1523746>

Tikkinen-Piri, Christina, Anna Rohunen and Jouni Markkula, 'EU General Data Protection Regulation: Changes and Implications for Personal Data Collecting Companies' (2018) 34(1) *Computer Law & Security Review* 134

Von Krogh, Georg and Eric von Hippel, 'Editorial: Special Issue on Open Source Software Development' (2003) 32(7) *Research Policy* 1149

Von Krogh, Georg, Stefan Haefliger and Sebastian Spaeth, 'Carrots and Rainbows: Motivation and Social Practice in Open Source Software Development' (2012) 36(2) *MIS Quarterly* 649

Wang, Cassandra C, George C S Lin and Guicai Li, 'Industrial Clustering and Technological Innovation in China: New Evidence from the ICT Industry in Shenzhen' (2010) 42(8) *Environment and Planning* 1987

Wu, Guohua et al, 'The Return of VIE-Structured Enterprise to China's Domestic Capital Market: A Brief Legal Analysis and Other Factors to Be Considered' (2015) 3(1) *Peking University Transnational Law Review* 211

Xing, Yijun, Yipeng Liu and Sir Cary L Cooper, 'Local Government as Institutional Entrepreneur: Public–Private Collaborative Partnerships in Fostering Regional Entrepreneurship' (2008) 29(4) *British Journal of Management* 670 <https://doi.org/10.1111/1467-8551.12282>

Yoo, Youngjin, Ola Henfridsson and Kalle Lyytinen, 'Research Commentary: The New Organizing Logic of Digital Innovation: An Agenda for Information Systems Research' (2010) 21(4) *Information Systems Research* 724

Yoo, Youngjin et al, 'Organizing for Innovation in the Digitized World' 23(5) (2012) *Organization Science* 1398

Zadeh, Lotfi A, *Outline of a New Approach to the Analysis of Complex Systems and Decision Processes* (1973) 3(1) *IEEE Transactions on Systems, Man and Cybernetics* 28

Zdziarski, Jonathan, 'Identifying Back Doors, Attack Points, and Surveillance Mechanisms in iOS Devices' (2014) 11(1) *Digital Investigation* 3

Zeng, Jinghan, Tim Stevens and Yaru Chen, 'China's Solution to Global Cyber Governance: Unpacking the Domestic Discourse of "Internet Sovereignty"' (2017) 45(3) *Politics & Policy* 432

Zhao, Hui and Haoxin Dong, 'Research on Personal Privacy Protection of China in the Era of Big Data' (2017) 5 *Open Journal of Social Sciences* 139

Zhou, Minghui and Audris Mockus, 'Who Will Stay in the FLOSS Community? Modelling Participant's Initial Behaviour' (2015) 41(1) *IEEE Transactions on Software Engineering* 82

Zhou, Tianshu and Mathias Siems, 'Contentious Modes of Understanding Chinese Commercial Law' (2015) 6 *George Mason Journal of International Commercial Law* 177

Zhu, Sheng and Yongjiang Shi, 'Shanzhai Manufacturing – An Alternative Innovation Phenomenon in China' (2010) 1(1) *Journal of Science and Technology Policy in China* 29

Ziegler, Samuel Farrell, 'China's Variable Interest Entity Problem: How Americans Have Illegally Invested Billions in China and How to Fix It' (2016) 84(2) *George Washington Law Review* 539

陈禹 [Chen Yu] «小岗村'生死契约'幕后» [The Story Behind the 'Life and Death Contract' in Xiaogang Village] 档案春秋 (2018) 1 *Memories and Archives* 10

何根源 [He Genyuan] and 刘昱影 [Liu Yuying], «微创新与突破性创新分类梳理» [Micro-Innovation and Breakthrough Innovation Classifications] 合作经济与科技 (2018) 12 *Cooperative Economy and Technology* 57

周汉华 [Zhou Hanhua], «探索激励相容的个人数据治理之道: 中国个人信息保护法的立法方向» [Exploring Incentive-Compatible Personal Data Governance: The Legislative Direction of China's Personal Information Protection Law] (2018) 2 *Law Research* 3

王冲鹬 [Wang Chongyan] and 陈丝 [Chen Si] «人工智能开源平台发展态势研究» [Researching the Development of AI Open Source Platforms] (2018) 8 *ICT and Policy* 56

谢 耘 [Xie Wei], «中国企业技术产品创新中的 几个问题分析» [Analysis of Several Problems in the Innovation of Chinese Enterprise Technology Products] 中国计算机学会通讯 (2009) 5(4) *China Computer Society Newsletter* 60

B Books

Agrawal, Ajay, *Joshua Gans and Avi Goldfarb, Prediction Machines: The Simple Economics of Artificial Intelligence* (Harvard Business Review Press, 2018)

Armstrong-Taylor, Paul, *Debt and Distortion: Risks and Reforms in the Chinese Financial System* (Palgrave Macmillan, 2016)

Austin, Greg, *Cyber Policy in China* (Polity Press, 2014)

Bellman, Richard, *An Introduction to Artificial Intelligence: Can Computers Think?* (Boyd & Fraser, 1978)

Belohlavek, Radim, Rudolf Kruse and Christain Moewes, 'Fuzzy Logic in Computer Science' in Edward K Blum and Alfred V Aho (eds), *Computer Science* (Springer, 2011) 385

Brandt, Loren and Thomas G Rawski, 'China's Great Economic Transformation' in Loren Brandt and Thomas G Rawski (eds), *China's Great Economic Transformation* (Cambridge University Press, 2008) 1

Brynjolfsson, Erik and Andrew McAfee, *The Second Machine Age: Work, Progress, and Prosperity in a Time of Brilliant Technologies* (WW Norton, 2014)

Bygrave, Lee A, *Data Privacy Law: An International Perspective* (Oxford University Press, 2014)

Chesbrough, Henry, Wim Vanhaverbeke and Joel West (eds), *Open Innovation: Researching a New Paradigm* (Oxford University Press, 2006)

Clark, Duncan, *Alibaba: The House That Jack Built* (HarperCollins, 2016)

Clarke, Donald, Peter Murrell and Susan Whiting, 'The Role of Law in China's Economic Development' in Thomas Rawski and Loren Brandt (eds), *China's Great Economic Transformation* (Cambridge University Press, 2008) 375

Clarke, Richard A and Robert K Knake, *Cyber War: The Next Threat to National Security and What to Do about It* (Ecco, 2010)

DeNardis, Laura, *Protocol Politics: The Globalisation of Internet Governance* (MIT Press, 2009)

Dickson, Bruce J, *Wealth into Power: The Communist Party's Embrace of China's Private Sector* (Cambridge University Press, 2008)

Dunne, Michael, 'The Dark Horse: Will China Win the Electric, Automated, Shared Mobility Race?' in Daniel Sperling (ed), *Three Revolutions:*

Automated, Shared and Electric Vehicles, Steering Automated, Shared, and Electric Vehicles to a Better Future (Island Press, 2018) 176

Evans, Peter B, *Embedded Autonomy: States and Industrial Transformation* (Princeton University Press, 1995)

Fairbairn, John and T Mark Hall, *The Go Companion: Go in History and Culture Intelligence* (Slate & Shell, 2009)

Freeman, Chris and Luc Soete, *The Economics of Industrial Innovation* (MIT Press, 3rd ed, 1997)

Freeman, Christopher, *Technology Policy and Economic Performance* (Pinter, 1987)

Ge, Jiangqiu, *A Comparative Analysis of Policing Consumer Contracts in China and the EU* (Springer, 2019)

Gilpin, Robert, *Global Political Economy* (Princeton University Press, 2001)

Goertzel, Ben and Casio Pennachin (eds), *Artificial General Intelligence* (Springer, 2007)

Goodfellow, Ian, Yoshua Bengio and Aaron Courville, *Deep Learning* (MIT Press, 2016)

Greenwald, Glenn, *No Place to Hide: Edward Snowden, the NSA, and the US Surveillance State* (Metropolitan Books, 2014)

Gu, Xin, 'The Paradox of Maker Movement in China' in Jeremy Hunsinger and Andrew Schrock (eds), *Making Our World: The Hacker and Maker Movements in Context* (Peter Lang, 2019) 271

Hastie, Trevor, Robert Tibshirani and Jerome Friedman, *The Elements of Statistical Learning* (Springer Science & Business Media, 2013)

Hobsbawm, Eric J, *Industry and Empire from 1750 to the Present Day* (Penguin, 1969)

Hong, Yu, *Networking China: The Digital Transformation of the Chinese Economy* (University of Illinois Press, 2017)

Hsu, Stephen C, *Understanding China's Legal System* (New York University Press, 2003)

Inkster, Nigel, *China's Cyber Power* (Routledge, 2016)

Jovanovic, Boyan and Peter Rousseau, 'General Purpose Technologies' in Philippe Aghion and Steven N Durlauf (eds), *Handbook of Economic Growth* (North-Holland, 2005) vol 1B, 1181

Kelly, Kevin, *The Inevitable: Understanding the 12 Technological Forces That Will Shape Our Future* (Penguin Books, 2017)

Lakhani, Karim R and Robert G Wolf, 'Perspectives on Free and Open Source Software' in Joseph Feller et al (eds), *Perspectives on Free and Open Source Software* (MIT Press, 2005) 1

Lee, Kai-Fu, *AI Superpowers: China, Silicon Valley, and the New World Order* (Houghton Mifflin Harcourt, 2018)

Lefebvre, Carol, Eric Manheimer and Julie Glanville, 'Searching for Studies' in Julian Higgins and Sally Green (eds), *Cochrane Handbook for Systematic Reviews of Interventions* (Wiley-Blackwell, 2008) 106

Liebman, Benjamin and Curtis Milhaupt (eds), *Regulating the Visible Hand? The Institutional Implications of Chinese State Capitalism* (Oxford University Press, 2015)

Liebman, Benjamin L, 'China's Law and Stability Paradox' in Jacques DeLisle and Avery Goldstein (eds), *China's Challenges* (University of Pennsylvania Press, 2015) 157

Lubman, Stanley (ed), *China's Legal Reforms* (Oxford University Press, 1996)

(ed), *The Evolution of Chinese Law Reform: An Uncertain Path* (Edward Elgar, 2012)

MacKinnon, Rebecca, *Consent of the Networked: The Worldwide Struggle for Internet Freedom* (Basic Books, 2013)

Mahony, Tarrant, *Foreign Investment Law in China: Regulation, Practice and Context* (Tsinghua University Press, 2015)

Mayer-Schönberger, Viktor and Kenneth Cukier, *Big Data: A Revolution That Will Transform How We Live, Work, and Think* (John Murray, 2013)

McMahon, Dinny, *China's Great Wall of Debt: Shadow Banks, Ghost Cities, Massive Loans, and the End of the Chinese Miracle* (Houghton Mifflin Harcourt, 2018)

Minzner, Carl, *End of an Era: How China's Authoritarian Revival Is Undermining Its Rise* (Oxford University Press, 2018)

Naughton, Barry, *Growing Out of the Plan: Chinese Economic Reform, 1978–1993* (Cambridge University Press, 1996)

The Chinese Economy: Transitions and Growth (MIT Press, 2007)

Needham, Joseph (ed), *Science and Civilisation in China* (Cambridge University Press, 1954–2016) vols 1–7

North, Douglass C, *Institutions, Institutional Change and Economic Performance* (Cambridge University Press, 1990)

Peerenboom, Randall, *China Modernizes* (Oxford University Press, 2007)

China's Long March Toward Rule of Law (Cambridge University Press, 2002)

Perez, Oren, 'Law in the Air: A Prologue to the World of Legal Paradoxes' in Oren Perez and Gunther Teubner (eds), *Paradoxes and Inconsistencies in the Law* (Hart Publishing, 2005)

Phelps, Edmund S, *Mass Flourishing: How Grassroots Innovation Created Jobs, Challenge, and Change* (Princeton University Press, 2013)

Potter, Pitman B, *The Chinese Legal System: Globalization and Local Legal Culture* (Routledge, 2001)

Rattray, Gregory J, *Strategic Warfare in Cyberspace* (MIT Press, 2001)

Reinert, Eric, *How Rich Countries Got Rich and Why Poor Countries Stay Poor* (Constable & Robinson, 2007)

Russell, Stuart J and Peter Norvig, *Artificial Intelligence: A Modern Approach* (Pearson, 2016)

Schumpeter, Joseph A, *The Theory of Economic Development: An Inquiry into Profits, Capital, Credit, Interest, and the Business Cycle*, trans Redvers Opie (Transaction Books, 1983) [trans of *Theorie der wirtschaftlichen Entwicklung* (1911)]

Seppänen, Samuli, *Ideological Conflict and the Rule of Law in Contemporary China* (Cambridge University Press, 2016)

Shalev-Shwartz, Shai and Shai Ben-David, *Understanding Machine Learning: From Theory to Algorithms* (Cambridge University Press, 2014)

Shao, Guosong, *Internet Law in China* (Elsevier, 2012)

Sheng, Jin, *China's Listed Companies: Conflicts, Governance and Regulation* (Kluwer Law International, 2015)

Simon, Denis F and Cong Cao, *China's Emerging Technological Edge* (Cambridge University Press, 2009)

Sperling, Daniel (ed), *Three Revolutions: Automated, Shared and Electric Vehicles, Steering Automated, Shared, and Electric Vehicles to a Better Future* (Island Press, 2018)

Spinello, Richard A, 'Google in China: Corporate Responsibility on a Censored Internet' in Alfreda Dudley, James Braman and Giovanni Vincenti (eds), *Investigating Cyber Law and Cyber Ethics Issues, Impacts and Practices* (IGI Global 2011) 244

Townsend, Anthony M, *Smart Cities: Big Data, Civic Hackers, and the Quest for a New Utopia* (WW Norton, 2013)

Tse, Edward, *China's Disruptors: How Alibaba, Xiaomi, Tencent, and Other Companies Are Changing the Rules of Business* (Penguin, 2015)

Ursic, Helena et al, 'Data Localisation Measures and Their Impacts on Data Science' in Vanessa Mak, Eric Tjong Tjin Tai and Anna Berlee (eds), *Research Handbook in Data Science and Law* (Elgar, 2018) 322

Walcott, Susan M, *Chinese Science and Technology Industrial Parks* (Ashgate, 2003)

Walton, Douglas, Chris Reed and Fabrizio Macagno, *Argumentation Schemes* (Cambridge University Press, 2008)

Xiaobo, Wu, *The Story of Tencent: Evolution of Chinese Internet Companies from 1998 to 2016* (Zhejiang University Press and China CITIC Press, 2017)

Yang, Guobin, *The Power of the Internet in China: Citizen Activism Online* (Columbia University Press, 2011)

'Social Dynamics in the Evolution of China's Internet Content Control Regime' in Monroe E Price, Stefaan Verhulst and Libby Morgan (eds), *Handbook of Media Law* (Routledge, 2012) 293

Yau, Nathan, 'Seeing Life in Your Data' in Toby Segaran and Jeff Hammerbacher (eds), *Beautiful Data: The Stories behind Elegant Data Solutions* (O'Reilly, 2009) 3

Yip, GS and B McKern, *China's Next Strategic Advantage: From Imitation to Innovation* (MIT Press, 2016)

Zhang, Lin, *China's Venture Capital Market: Current Legal Problems and Prospective Reforms* (Elsevier, 2015)

Zhou, Yu, *The Inside Story of China's High-Tech Industry: Making 'Silicon Valley' in Beijing* (Rowman & Littlefield, 2008)

Zhou, Yu, William Lazonick and Yifei Sun (eds), *China as an Innovation Nation* (Oxford University Press, 2016)

C Reports

«App 个人信息泄露情况调查报告» [App Personal Information Disclosure Report] (*Chinese Consumer's Association*, 29 August 2018) <http://www.cca.org.cn/jmxf/detail/28180.html>

«全球 AI 领域人才报告» [Global AI Talent Report] (*LinkedIn*, 2017) <https://business.linkedin.com/content/dam/me/business/zh-cn/talent-solutions/Event/july/lts-ai-report/%E9%A2%86%E8%8B%B1%E3%80%8A%E5%85%A8%E7%90%83AI%E9%A2%86%E5%9F%9F%E4%BA%BA%E6%89%8D%E6%8A%A5%E5%91%8A%E3%80%8B.pdf>

«报告 2017 凯度中国社交媒体影响报告» [2017 Kantar China Social Media Impact Report] (*Kantar Research*, 6 June 2017) <https://cn.kantar.com/媒体动态/社交/2017/2017 凯度中国社交媒体影响报告>

Atha, Katherine et al, *China's Smart Cities Development* (US–China Economic and Security Review Commission, 20 January 2020) <https://www.uscc.gov/sites/default/files/2020-04/China_Smart_Cities_Development.pdf>

Bauer, Matthias et al, *Data Localization in Russia: A Self-Imposed Sanction* (ECIPE Policy Brief No 6/2015) <http://www.ecipe.org/app/uploads/2015/06/Policy-Brief-062015_Fixed.pdf>

The Costs of Data Localization: Friendly Fire on Economic Recovery (ECIPE Occasional Paper No 3/2014) <http://www.ecipe.org/app/uploads/2014/12/OCC32014__1.pdf>

Unleashing Internal Data Flows in the EU: An Economic Assessment of Data Localisation Measures in the EU Member States (ECIPE Policy Brief No 3/2016)

Beraja, Martin, David Y Yang and Noam Yuchtman, 'Data-Intensive Innovation and the State: Evidence from AI Firms in China' (NBER Working Paper No. w27723, 21 January 2021), <https://papers.ssrn.com/sol3/papers.cfm?abstract_id=3679716>

Blackman, Colin and Simon Forge, *Data Flows – Future Scenarios: In-Depth Analysis for the ITRE Committee* (*European Parliament*, November 2017) <http://www.europarl.europa.eu/RegData/etudes/IDAN/2017/607362/IPOL_IDA%282017%29607362_EN.pdf>

Castro, Daniel, *The False Promise of Data Nationalism* (ITIF, 1 December 2013) <http://www2.itif.org/2013-false-promise-data-nationalism.pdf>

Cory, Nigel, *Cross-Border Data Flows: Where Are the Barriers, and What Do They Cost?* (Information Technology and Innovation Foundation, May 2017) <http://www2.itif.org/2017-cross-border-data-flows.pdf>

Du, Shanshan, *China Integrated Circuit Ecosystem Report* (SEMI Industry Research and Statistics, October 2018) <http://www1.semi.org/en/china-ic-ecosystem-report>

European Chamber of Commerce in China, *China Manufacturing 2025: Putting Industrial Policy Ahead of Market Forces* (March 2017)

Ezell, Stephen and Robert Atkinson, *The Good, the Bad, the Ugly, and the Self-Destructive of Innovation Policy* (ITIF, October 2010) <http://www.itif.org/files/2010-good-bad-ugly.pdf>

Ezell, Stephen et al, *Localization Barriers to Global Trade: Threat to the Global Economy* (ITIF, 2013) <http://www.itif.org/publications/localization-barriers-trade-threat-global-innovation-economy>

Future of Humanity Institute et al, *The Malicious Use of Artificial Intelligence Forecasting, Prevention, and Mitigation* (Research Report, February 2018) <https://arxiv.org/ftp/arxiv/papers/1802/1802.07228.pdf>

Global Artificial Intelligence Software Market Research Report 2017, *IT Intelligence Markets*

Hannebauer, Cristoph and Volker Gruhn, 'Motivation of Newcomers to FLOSS Projects' (12th International Symposium on Open Collaboration, 2016)

IETF, 'A Survey of Worldwide Censorship Techniques' (*IETF*, 22 October 2018) <https://tools.ietf.org/id/draft-hall-censorship-tech-06.html>

Lee, John, *The Connection of Everything: China and the Internet of Things* (Report, China Monitor, 24 June 2021) <https://merics.org/en/report/connection-everything-china-and-internet-things>

Maisog, Manuel E, *Making the Case against Data Localization in China* (IAPP, 20 April 2015)

McKinsey Global Institute, *Global Flows in a Digital Age* (April 2014) <http://www.mckinsey.com/insights/globalization/global_flows_in_a_digital_age>

National Science and Technology Council, Networking and Information Technology Research and Development Subcommittee, *The National Artificial Intelligence Research and Development Strategic Plan* (Report, October 2016) <https://www.nitrd.gov/PUBS/national_ai_rd_strategic_plan.pdf>

Navigant, *Navigant Research Leaderboard: Automated Driving Vehicles* (Report, January 2018) <https://www.navigantresearch.com/reports/navigant-research-leaderboard-automated-driving-vehicles>

Sacks, Samm, *China's Emerging Data Privacy System and GDPR* (CSIS, 9 March 2018) <https://www.csis.org/analysis/chinas-emerging-data-privacy-system-and-gdpr>

Sacks, Samm and Manyi Kathy Li, *How Chinese Cybersecurity Standards Impact Doing Business in China* (Report, CSIS Briefs, 2 August 2018) <https://www.csis.org/analysis/how-chinese-cybersecurity-standards-impact-doing-business-china>

Sacks, Samm and Robert O'Brien, *What to Make of the Newly Established CyberSecurity Association of China* (CSIS, 25 May 2016) <https://www.csis.org/analysis/what-make-newly-established-cybersecurity-association-china>

UNCTAD, *Information Economy Report 2013: The Cloud Economy and Developing Countries* (3 December 2013) <http://unctad.org/en/PublicationsLibrary/ier2013_en.pdf>

World Investment Report 2013: Global Value Chains: Investment and Trade for Development (2013) <https://unctad.org/en/PublicationsLibrary/wir2013_en.pdf>

US Congressional Committee, *Encryption Working Group Year-End Report* (20 December 2016) <https://judiciary.house.gov/wp-content/uploads/2016/12/20161220EWGFINALReport.pdf> (the link is no longer active)

Wu, Tim, *The Curse of Bigness: Antitrust in the New Gilded Age* (Columbia Global Reports, 2018)

Xiaomeng, Lu, Li Manyi and Samm Sacks, *What the Facebook Scandal Means in a Land without Facebook: A Look at China's Burgeoning Data Protection Regime* (CSIS, 25 April 2018) <https://www.csis.org/analysis/what-facebook-scandal-means-land-without-facebook-look-chinas-burgeoning-data-protection>

Yang, Kelly, Aideen Clery and Domenico Di Liello, *Sector Report: Smart Cities in China* (EU SME Centre and China–British Business Council, 2016) <http://ccilc.pt/wp-content/uploads/2017/07/eu_sme_centre_report_-_smart_cities_in_china_i_edit_-_jan_2016_1_1.pdf>

王刚 [Wang Gang], «BAT, 科大讯飞, 商汤等 5 大 AI 国家队的一次 '集体工作汇报» [A 'Collective Work Report' of the Five Major 'National Team' Members – BAT, iFlytek, and Sensetime] (*Leiphone*, 11 May 2019) <https://mp.weixin.qq.com/s/ksJm980HsmfUEhI5U6UQlg?fbclid=IwAR3BGbjFtiz1UFtMRWvYPjkfWDfGf3KgsIWJtVKn_UwXjAdGyC3wE_cnZ-I>

D Other Secondary Sources: English Language

'The 2020 State of Octoverse' (*GitHub Octoverse*, 2021) <https://octoverse.github.com/>

'26 Organizations Join the Linux Foundation to Support Open Source Communities with Infrastructure and Resources' (*Linux Foundation*, 23 May 2018) <https://www.prnewswire.com/news-releases/26-organizations-join-the-linux-foundation-to-support-open-source-communities-with-infrastructure-and-resources-300653177.html>

'4Paradigm (第四范式) national team' (*Tech in Asia website*) <https://www.techinasia.com/companies/4paradigm>

'Accenture Forms Strategic Alliance, Invests in Chinese AI Start-up Malong Technologies' (*Businesswire*, 13 August 2018) <https://www.businesswire.com/news/home/20180812005014/en/Accenture-Forms-Strategic-Alliance-Invests-Chinese-AI>

'Airbnb Tells China Users' Personal Data to Be Stored Locally' (*Reuters*, 1 November 2016) <http://www.reuters.com/article/us-airbnb-china/airbnb-tells-china-users-personal-data-to-be-stored-locally-idUSKBN12W3V6>

'Alibaba's September Cloud Computing Conference' (*Alibaba website*, September 2018) <https://www.alibabacloud.com/the-computing-conference-2018>

'Amazon Launches Another Innovation Center in China' (*Xinhua*, 24 May 2018) <http://www.xinhuanet.com/english/2018-05/24/c_137203869.htm>

'Another Chinese City Admits Releasing "Fake" Economic Data' (*South China Morning Post*, 17 January 2018) <https://www.scmp.com/news/china/economy/article/2128629/another-chinese-city-admits-releasing-fake-economic-data>

'Application Proof of Ant Group Co, LTD Technology Limited' «螞蟻科技集團股份有限公司» (*Stock Exchange of Hong Kong Limited*, 27 October 2020)<https://www1.hkexnews.hk/listedco/listconews/sehk/2020/1026/2020102600165.pdf>

'Apollo Data Sharing' (*Apollo website*) <http://apollo.auto/docs/promise.html>

'Apollo Governance' (*Apollo website*) <http://apollo.auto/docs/manifesto.html>

'ApolloAuto' (*GitHub*) <https://github.com/ApolloAuto/apollo>

'Baidu Jumps to Apollo 2.0' (*China Daily*, 17 January 2018) <http://www.chinadaily.com.cn/m/beijing/zhongguancun/2018-01/17/content_35529002.htm>

'Bytedance Partners with Berkeley Artificial Intelligence Research Lab to Foster Future AI Innovators and Entrepreneurs' (*PR Newswire*, 3 April 2018) <https://www.prnewswire.com/news-releases/bytedance-partners-with-berkeley-artificial-intelligence-research-lab-to-foster-future-ai-innovators-and-entrepreneurs-300623346.html>

'Can China Innovate? *McKinsey on China* (Podcast, McKinsey & Co, 28 November 2011) <https://podcasts.apple.com/us/podcast/can-china-innovate/id409735817?i=1000226536419>

'CBS News Poll: Americans Split on Unlocking San Bernardino Shooter's iPhone' (*CBS News*, 18 March 2016) <http://www.cbsnews.com/news/cbs-news-poll-americans-split-on-unlocking-san-bernardino-shooters-iphone>

'China Delays Data-Onshoring Rules until after US Trade Talks (*Regulation Asia*, 23 April 2019) <https://www.regulationasia.com/china-delays-data-onshoring-rules-until-after-us-trade-talks>

'China Headlines: China Unveils "Internet Plus" Action Plan to Fuel Growth' (*State Council of the People's Republic of China*, 4 July 2015) <http://english.gov.cn/policies/latest_releases/2015/07/04/content_281475140165588.htm>

'China Money Network's China Unicorn Ranking' (*China Money Network*, July 2018) <https://www.chinamoneynetwork.com/china-unicorn-ranking>

'China Outnumbers Other Countries in Smart City Pilots' (*Xinhua*, 16 September 2018) <http://www.xinhuanet.com/english/2018-02/20/c_136987058.htm>

'China Releases First Strategy on Cyberspace Cooperation' (*Xinhua*, 1 March 2017) <http://news.xinhuanet.com/english/2017-03/01/c_136094734.htm>

'China's AI Business Ready to Lead the World' (*China Daily*, 1 June 2017) <http://www.chinadaily.com.cn/business/tech/2017-06/01/content_29576692.htm>

'China's Biggest User Data Theft Exposes 3 Billion Traces of Online Data into the Wrong Hands' (*Yicai Global*, 21 August 2018) <https://www.yicaiglobal.com/news/china-biggest-user-data-theft-case-exposes-3-billion-traces-of-online-life-in-wrong-hands>

'China's Cybersecurity Law Enacted' (*ChinaTechNews*, 7 November 2016) <https://www.chinatechnews.com/2016/11/07/24439-chinas-cybersecurity-law-enacted>

'China's Social Media App WeChat Demands More Info from Users' (*Radio Free Asia*, 14 June 2018) <https://www.rfa.org/english/news/demands-06142018124702.html>

'China's Stats Chief Defends Quality of Data' (*Bloomberg*, 21 August 2018) <https://www.bloomberg.com/news/articles/2018-08-20/china-s-statistics-chief-defends-data-quality-as-doubts-linger>

'Chinese Company Apologizes over Flight Passenger Data Leaks' (*Ecns.cn*, 13 June 2018) <http://www.ecns.cn/news/society/2018-06-13/detail-ifyvfaqz8675561.shtml>

'CNNIC Hosts "Promote Internet Development through Technology and Standards" Session of WIC Wuzhen Summit' China Internet Network Information Center, 2 February 2016 <https://cnnic.com.cn/IC/Events/201602/t20160204_53402.htm> (the link is no longer active)

'Crunchbase: "Megvii" (*Crunchbase*)' <https://www.crunchbase.com/organization/megvii-technology/company_financials/>

'Declassified: Apartheid Profits – China's Support for Apartheid Revealed' (*News24*, 31 October 2017) <https://www.dailymaverick.co.za/article/2017-10-31-declassified-apartheid-profits-chinas-support-for-apartheid-revealed>

'DEF CON China 2.0 Is Cancelled' (*DEF CON Organisation*) <https://www.defcon.org/html/defcon-china-2/dc-cn-2-index.html>

'Draft Law Strengthens China's Cyber Security Legislature' (*Tech 2*, 27 June 2016) <http://tech.firstpost.com/news-analysis/draft-law-strengthens-chinas-cyber-security-legislature-322671.html>

'Driverless Street Sweepers Employed for Trial Run in Shanghai' (*Xinhua*, 13 June 2019) <http://www.xinhuanet.com/english/2018-04/18/c_137120453.htm>

Editorial, 'Delay to Ant IPO Shows Beijing's Desire to Get the Rules Right' (*South China Morning Post*, 10 November 2020) <https://www.scmp.com/com

ment/opinion/article/3109261/delay-ant-ipo-small-price-pay-getting-new-rules-right>

'Evernote Will Set Up a Data Centre in China' (*BBC*, 7 May 2012) <http://www.bbc.com/news/technology-17981737>

'EZDL Custom Sound Recognition' (*Baidu AI website*) <http://ai.baidu.com/ezdl/sound>

'Facebook Sets Up Subsidiary in China According to Filing' (*CNBC*, 25 July 2018) <https://www.cnbc.com/2018/07/24/facebook-sets-up-subsidiary-in-china-according-to-filing.html> (the link is no longer active)

'Full Text: Special Address by Chinese President Xi Jinping at the World Economic Forum Virtual Event of the Davos Agenda' (*Xinhua*, 25 January 2021) <http://www.xinhuanet.com/english/2021-01/25/c_139696610.htm>

'GitHub and Export Controls' (*GitHub Help*, May 2019) <https://help.github.com/en/articles/github-and-export-controls>

'Hikvision Launches Source Code Transparency Center' (*Ciston PR Newswire*, 8 March 2018) <https://www.prnewswire.com/news-releases/hikvision-launches-source-code-transparency-center-300610397.html>

'Home' (*NDRC website*) <http://en.ndrc.gov.cn>

'Home' (*ZF website*) <https://www.zf.com/mobile/en/homepage/homepage.html>

'Huawei Enterprise – Big Data' (*Huawei website*) <https://e.huawei.com/au/solutions/cloud-computing/big-data>

'iFLYOS Open Source' (*GitHub*) <https://github.com/iFLYOS-OPEN>

'ISC 360' (*ISC website*) <http://isc.360.cn/2018/en/index.html> (the link is no longer active)

'Israeli Firm "Helped FBI Crack San Bernardino Gunman's Cell Phone without Apple's Help"' (*Daily Mail*, 30 March 2016) <http://www.dailymail.co.uk/news/article-3514875/Israeli-firm-helped-FBI-crack-San-Bernardino-gunman-s-cellphone-without-Apple-s-help.html>

'Japan, US and Europe Push Back on China's Data Controls' (*Nikkei Asian Review*, 13 December 2017) <https://asia.nikkei.com/Politics-Economy/International-Relations/Japan-US-and-Europe-push-back-on-China-s-data-controls>

'The Keys to Data Protection' (*Privacy International*, August 2018) <https://privacyinternational.org/sites/default/files/2018-09/Data%20Protection%20COMPLETE.pdf> (the link is no longer active)

'Lawmakers Weigh China's Draft Anti-Terrorism Law' (*China Daily*, 25 February 2015) <http://www.chinadaily.com.cn/china/2015-02/25/content_19653472.htm>

'A Legal Vulnerability at the Heart of China's Big Internet Firms' (*The Economist*, 16 September 2017) <https://www.economist.com/news/business/21728984-variable-interest-entities-are-their-weakest-link-legal-vulnerability-heart-chinas?fsrc=scn/tw/te/bl/ed/alegalvulnerabilityattheheartofchinasbiginternetfirms>

'Lincoln MKZ Platform' (*AutonomouStuff website*) <https://autonomoustuff.com/>

'Linux Foundation Members' (*Linux Foundation*) <https://www.linuxfoundation.org/join/members/>

'A Look Back at KubeCon + CloudNativeCon Shanghai 2018' (*Cloud Native Computing Foundation*, 5 December 2018) <https://www.cncf.io/blog/2018/12/05/a-look-back-at-kubecon-cloudnativecon-shanghai-2018>

'The March toward Data Localization' (*Endgame*, 10 January 2018) <https://www.endgame.com/blog/technical-blog/march-toward-data-localization>

'MIT and SenseTime Announce Effort to Advance Artificial Intelligence Research' (*MIT News*, 28 February 2018) <http://news.mit.edu/2018/mit-sensetime-announce-effort-advance-artificial-intelligence-research-0228>

'More High-Tech Zones in China' (*Xinhua*, 27 March 2017) <http://www.chinadaily.com.cn/china/2017-03/27/content_28692439.htm>

'The New War over Open Source Licensing' (*Angel List*, 21 February 2019) <https://angel.co/newsletters/the-new-war-over-open-source-licensing-131>

'North Korean Hackers behind Global Cyberattack?' (*CBS News*, 16 May 2017) <http://www.cbsnews.com/news/cyberattack-wannacry-ransomware-north-korea-hackers-lazarus-group>

'OpenAtom Project List' (*OpenAtom Foundation*)<https://www.openatom.org/#/projectList>

'RISC-V Foundation' (*RISC-V website*) <https://riscv.org/risc-v-foundation>

'Renault–Nissan–Mitsubishi and WeRide.ai to Increase Presence in Chinese Autonomous Vehicle Services' (*PR Newswire*, 19 October 2018) <https://www.prnewswire.com/news-releases/alliance-ventures-leads-strategic-investment-in-weride-ai-864897996.html>

'Robert Bosch Venture Capital Backs the Evolution of Automated Driving with Investment in UISEE' (*Bosch Media Services Press Release*, 26 February 2020) <https://www.bosch-presse.de/pressportal/de/en/robert-bosch-venture-capital-backs-the-evolution-of-automated-driving-with-investment-in-uisee-208768.html>

'Seizing Opportunity through License Compliance', BSA Global Software Survey, May 2016 <http://www.bsa.org/~/media/Files/StudiesDownload/BSA_GSS_US.pdf> (the link is no longer active)

'Siemens Inks Deal with Alibaba to Launch Digital Products in China' (*Reuters*, 9 July 2018) <https://www.reuters.com/article/us-siemens-alibaba/siemens-inks-deal-with-alibaba-to-launch-digital-products-in-china-idUSKBN1JZ22U>

'Sinovation Ventures' (*Sinovation website*) <https://www.sinovationventures.com/>

'Sizing the Prize: What's the Real Value of AI for Your Business and How Can You Capitalise?' (*PWC*, June 2017) <http://www.pwc.com/gx/en/issues/analytics/assets/pwc-ai-analysis-sizing-the-prize-report.pdf>

'Strategic Emerging Industries Likely to Contribute 8% of GDP by 2015' (*People's Daily*, 19 October 2010) <http://en.people.cn/90001/90778/90862/7170816.html>

'Strengthening AI R&D among China's 2018 Innovation Goals' (*Synced*, 7 March 2018) <https://medium.com/@Synced/strengthening-ai-r-d-among-chinas-2018-innovation-goals-dee468e95abb>

'Student Suffers Fatal Cardiac Arrest after Telephone Scam' (*China Daily*, 25 August 2016) <http://www.chinadaily.com.cn/china/2016-08/25/content_26591216.htm>

'Tencent and Why Open Source Is about to Explode in China' (*Linux Foundation*, 19 February 2016) <https://www.linuxfoundation.org/blog/2016/02/tencent-and-why-open-source-is-about-to-explode-in-china>

'Tencent Open Source' (Tencent Open Source) <https://opensource.tencent.com>

'Toyota Created a Robot That Shoots Hoops Better than the Pros' (*CNBC*, 15 March 2018) <https://www.cnbc.com/video/2018/03/15/toyota-created-a-robot-that-shoots-basketball-better-than-the-pros.html>

'Trio of China's Big State Banks Invest in 4Paradigm AI' (*Synced*, 20 January 2018) <https://medium.com/@Synced/trio-of-chinas-big-state-banks-invest-in-4paradigm-ai-72f444ad5e8b>

'UPS Invests in Autonomous Trucking Company, Tests Self-Driving Tractor Trailers' (*UPS Pressroom*, 16 August 2019) <https://www.pressroom.ups.com/pressroom/ContentDetailsViewer.page?ConceptType=PressReleases&id=1565871221437-794>

'Welcome to Apollo' (*Apollo website*) <http://apollo.auto>

'Westpac Partners with Surf Life Saving Australia to Put More Eyes in the Sky over Aussie Coastline This Summer' (*Surf Life Saving*, 17 December 2018) <https://sls.com.au/westpac-life-saver-drones-program-launches>

'What is CNCF?' (*Cloud Native Computing Foundation website*) <https://www.cncf.io>

'What Is "Fuzzy Logic"? Are There Computers That Are Inherently Fuzzy and Do Not Apply the Usual Binary Logic?' (*Scientific American*, 21 October 1999) <https://www.scientificamerican.com/article/what-is-fuzzy-logic-are-t>

'What You Need to Know About Baidu's Apollo Go Robotaxi in Beijing' (*ApolloAuto Medium Page*, 28 October 2020) <https://techcrunch.com/2020/12/02/self-driving-trucks-startup-tusimple-raises-350m-from-u-s-rail-retail-and-freight-giants/>

'Why Are Standards Important for Artificial Intelligence?' (*JTC1*, 30 May 2018) <https://jtc1info.org/jtc1-press-committee-info-about-jtc-1-sc-42>

'Why China Keeps Bailing Out Ailing Heavy Industries' (*South China Morning Post*, 25 January 2017) <https://www.scmp.com/news/china/economy/article/2065332/why-china-keeps-bailing-out-ailing-heavy-industries>

'World Intelligence Congress Gathers Discussion on AI' (*Xinhua*, 17 May 2018) <http://www.xinhuanet.com/english/2018-05/17/c_137184327.htm>

'XDATA' (*DARPA*, 2019) <https://www.darpa.mil/program/xdata>

'Xilinx Announces the Acquisition of DeePhi Tech' (*Xilinx*, 17 July 2018) <https://www.xilinx.com/news/press/2018/xilinx-announces-the-acquisition-of-deephi-tech.html>

'Yitu Technology Opens AI R&D Centre in Singapore; To Add Some 70 Staff over 3 Years' (*Straights Times*, 31 January 2019) <https://www.straitstimes.com/business/companies-markets/yitu-technology-opens-ai-rd-centre-in-singapore-to-add-some-70-staff-over>

'Yutong' (*Yutong Website*) < https://en.yutong.com/>

Allen, Gregory C, 'Understanding China's AI Strategy' (*Center for a New American Security*, 6 February 2019) <https://www.cnas.org/publications/reports/understanding-chinas-ai-strategy>

Amadeo, Ron, 'Huawei's HarmonyOS: "Fake It till You Make It" Meets OS Development' (*ArsTechnica*, 2 March 2021) <https://arstechnica.com/gadgets/2021/02/harmonyos-hands-on-huaweis-android-killer-is-just-android/>

Andelman, David A, 'How China Out-Innovates: A Chat with Alibaba's Strategy Chief Ming Zeng' (*Forbes*, 25 July 2018) <https://www.forbes.com/sites/forbesasia/2018/07/25/how-china-out-innovates-a-chat-with-alibabas-strategy-chief-ming-zeng/#73ab38221a90>

Arkenberg, Chris, 'China Inside: Chinese Semiconductors Will Power Artificial Intelligence' (*Deloitte Insights*, 11 December 2018) <https://www2.deloitte.com/insights/us/en/industry/technology/technology-media-and-telecom-predictions/chinese-semiconductor-industry.html>

Asay, Matt, 'MongoDB's New License Won't Solve Its China Problem' (*Techworld*, 19 October 2018) <https://www.techworld.com.au/article/648494/mongodb-new-license-won-t-solve-its-china-problem/?fp=16&fpid=1>

'Why China Is the Next Proving Ground for Open Source Software' (*Tech Republic*, 20 September 2016) <https://www.techrepublic.com/article/why-china-is-the-next-proving-ground-for-open-source-software>

'Why Critics Who Bash Musk's Open Source Tesla Security Project Are Wrong' (*Tech Republic*, 14 August 2018) <https://www.techrepublic.com/article/why-critics-who-bash-musks-open-source-tesla-security-project-are-wrong>

Au, Lavender, 'China's New Encryption Law Takes Effect' (*TechNode*, 2 January 2020) <https://technode.com/2020/01/02/chinas-new-encryption-law-takes-effect/>

Banjo, Shelly and Mark Bergen, 'The Trade War Didn't Stop a Google and Huawei AI Collaboration' (*Bloomberg*, 1 April 2019) <https://www.bloomberg.com/news/articles/2019-04-01/the-trade-war-didn-t-stop-a-google-and-huawei-ai-collaboration>

Battelle, John, 'How GDPR Kills the Innovation Economy' (*New Co Shift*, 25 May 2018) <https://shift.newco.co/how-gdpr-kills-the-innovation-economy-844570b70a7a>

Beattie, Alan, 'Data Protectionism: The Growing Menace to International Business' (*Financial Times*, 13 May 2018) <https://www.ft.com/content/6f0f41e4-47de-11e8-8ee8-cae73aab7ccb>

Beavis, Gareth, 'Huawei Ban: The Global Fallout Explained' (*Techradar*, 28 May 2019) <https://www.techradar.com/au/news/googles-huawei-android-restrictions-heres-what-it-means-for-you>

Beddor, Christopher, 'The Alibaba IPO and How Chinese Companies Bypass Foreign Investments Restrictions' (*CKGSB Knowledge*, 1 September 2014) <http://knowledge.ckgsb.edu.cn/2014/09/01/china/the-alibaba-ipo-and-how-chinese-companies-bypass-foreign-investment-restrictions>

Bell, Ganesh, 'Why Countries Need to Work Together on AI' (*World Economic Forum*, 16 September 2018) <https://www.weforum.org/agenda/2018/09/learning-from-one-another-a-look-at-national-ai-policy-frameworks>

Bhargava, Yuthika, 'No Right Answer Yet to "Privacy vs Security" Parley' (*The Hindu*, 10 December 2017) <http://www.thehindu.com/opinion/interview/no-right-answer-yet-to-privacy-vs-security-parley/article21386236.ece>

Bishop, Todd, 'Chinese Tech Powerhouse Baidu Opens Seattle-Area Office, Expanding Its Reach in AI and the Cloud' (*Geek Wire*, 9 October 2017) <https://www.geekwire.com/2017/chinese-tech-powerhouse-baidu-opens-seattle-area-office-expanding-reach-ai-cloud>

Borak, Masha, 'China's AIChain is Decentralizing Artificial Intelligence' (*Technode*, 29 June 2018) <https://technode.com/2018/06/29/aichain-artificial-intelligence-blockchain>

'Chinese Developers Fear Losing Open Source Tech to Trade War' (*Abacus* [*South China Morning Post*], 25 May 2019) <https://www.abacusnews.com/digital-life/chinese-developers-fear-losing-open-source-tech-trade-war/article/3011463>

'Chinese Hackers Are Selling Personal Information for as Little as $0.01' (*TechNode*, 22 December 2017) <https://technode.com/2017/12/22/chinese-hackers-selling-personal-information-little-0-01>

'Meituan Dianping Launches Autonomous Food Delivery System' (*Technode*, 26 July 2018) <https://technode.com/2018/07/26/meituan-dianping-autonomous-delivery>

'Qualcomm Opening an AI Lab in Beijing, Joining Hands with Baidu's PaddlePaddle' (*Technode*, 24 May 2018) <https://technode.com/2018/05/24/qualcomm-ai-lab-china-baidu-paddlepaddle>

'We Went to Suzhou to Find AI's Biggest Breakthroughs and Bottlenecks' (*Technode*, 12 May 2018). <https://technode.com/2018/05/12/suzhou-global-ai-product-application-expo>

'WeChat Denies Reading Users' Private Messages to Train Its AI' (*TechNode*, 2 January 2018) <https://technode.com/2018/01/02/wechat-denies-reading-users-private-messages-train-ai>

Bradford, Laurence, 'How Open-Source Development Is Democratizing the Tech Industry' (*Forbes*, 26 March 2018) <https://www.forbes.com/sites/laurenceb radford/2018/03/26/how-open-source-development-is-democratizing-the-tech-industry/#7bce96c13bb6>

Bradley, Joseph, Joel Barbier and Doug Handler, 'Embracing the Internet of Everything to Capture Your Share of $14.4 Trillion' (Cisco White Paper, 2013) <http://www.cisco.com/c/dam/en_us/about/ac79/docs/innov/IoE_Economy.pdf>

Brokaw, Alex, 'This Startup Uses Machine Learning and Satellite Imagery to Predict Crop Yields' (*The Verge*, 4 August 2016) <https://www.theverge.com/2016/8/4/12369494/descartes-artificial-intelligence-crop-predictions-usda>

Brooks, Rodney, 'The Seven Deadly Sins of AI Predictions' (*MIT Technology Review*, 6 October 2017) <https://www.technologyreview.com/s/609048/the-seven-deadly-sins-of-ai-predictions>

Busvine, Douglas, 'Exclusive: China's Huawei Opens Up to German Scrutiny Ahead of 5G Auctions' (*Reuters*, 23 October 2018) <https://www.reuters.com/article/us-germany-telecoms-huawei-exclusive/exclusive-chinas-huawei-opens-up-to-german-scrutiny-ahead-of-5g-auctions-idUSKCN1MX1VB>

Byford, Sam, 'How China's ByteDance Became the World's Most Valuable Startup' (*The Verge*, 30 November 2018) <https://www.theverge.com/2018/11/30/18107732/bytedance-valuation-tiktok-china-startup>

Caiyu, Liu, 'China Eyes New Cyber Security Watchdog' (*Global Times*, 2 February 2017) <http://www.globaltimes.cn/content/1031517.shtml>

'China Sets Cross-Border Data Flow Rules' (*Global Times*, 13 June 2019) <http://www.globaltimes.cn/content/1154091.shtml>

'Companies Collect Personal Info, Sell Data Despite China's New Cyber Security Law' (*Global Times*, 24 December 2017) <http://www.globaltimes.cn/content/1081849.shtml>

Campanella, Edoardo, 'The Real Payoff from Artificial Intelligence Is Still a Decade Off' (*Foreign Policy*, 9 August 2018) <https://foreignpolicy.com/2018/08/09/the-solution-to-the-productivity-puzzle-is-simple-robots-ai>

Campbell, Charlie, 'Baidu's Robin Li is Helping China Win the 21st Century' (*Time*, 18 January 2018) <http://time.com/5107485/baidus-robin-li-helping-china-win-21st-century>

Cao, Yin, 'Rule to Protect Security "On the Way This Year"' (*China Daily*, 22 January 2015) <http://www.chinadaily.com.cn/china/2015-01/22/content_19373572.htm>

Carrington, Daisy, 'Yinchuan: The Smart City Where Your Face Is Your Credit Card' (CNN, 11 October 2016) <http://edition.cnn.com/2016/10/10/asia/yinchuan-smart-city-future/index.html>

Champion, Marc, 'Digital Cold War' (*Bloomberg*, 17 May 2019) <https://www.bloomberg.com/quicktake/how-u-s-china-tech-rivalry-looks-like-a-digital-cold-war>

Chan, Tara Francis, 'The Chinese Government Confirmed That It Can Access Deleted WeChat Conversations – and People Are Terrified' (*Business Insider*, 1 May 2018) <https://www.businessinsider.com.au/chinese-government-accessed-deleted-wechat-messages-2018-5?r=US&IR=T>

Chen, Celia and Li Tao, 'Tencent CEO Pony Ma Says China Risks Falling Behind without Strong Base in Scientific Research' (*South China Morning Post*, 28 May 2018) <http://www.scmp.com/tech/tech-leaders-and-founders/article/2148112/tencent-ceo-pony-ma-says-china-risks-falling-behind#FDgmYwXu4Vh04pcB.99>

Chen, Celia, 'Huawei Aims to Deploy Harmony OS on 400 Million Devices in 2021, Going beyond Smartphones to Reach Many IoT gadgets' (*South China Morning Post*, 13 January 2021) <https://www.scmp.com/tech/article/3117573/huawei-aims-deploy-harmony-os-400-million-devices-2021-going-beyond>

Chen, George, 'Can Li Keqiang's Internet Plus Strategy Really Save China?' (*South China Morning Post*, 8 March 2015) <http://www.scmp.com/business/china-business/article/1732704/can-li-keqiangs-internet-plus-strategy-really-save-china>

Chen, Laurie, 'Why China's Tech-Savvy Millennials Are Quitting WeChat' (*South China Morning Post*, 22 July 2018) <https://www.scmp.com/news/china/society/article/2156297/how-growing-privacy-fears-china-are-driving-wechat-users-away>

Chen, Lulu Yilun, 'Tencent-Backed Internet Giant Probes Massive User-Data Leak' (*Bloomberg*, 3 May 2018) <https://www.bloomberg.com/news/articles/2018-05-03/tencent-backed-meituan-will-probe-reports-of-huge-user-data-leak>

Chen, Qiheng, 'China's New Data Protection Scheme' (*The Diplomat*, 2 July 2019) <https://thediplomat.com/2019/07/chinas-new-data-protection-scheme>

Chen, Stephen, 'Elderly Chinese Toilet Paper Thieves Face Up to Their Crimes' (*South China Morning Post*, 19 March 2017) <http://www.scmp.com/news/china/society/article/2080272/elderly-chinese-toilet-paper-thieves-face-their-crimes>

Chin, Charlene, 'South Korea to Build Smart Highways for Driverless Cars' (*GovInsider*, 2 September 2016 <https://govinsider.asia/smart-gov/south-korea-to-build-smart-highways-for-driverless-cars>

Chin, Josh and Liza Lin, 'China's All-Seeing Surveillance State Is Reading Its Citizens' Faces' (*Wall Street Journal*, 26 June 2017) <https://www.wsj

.com/articles/the-all-seeing-surveillance-state-feared-in-the-west-is-a-reality-in-china-1498493020>

Chow, Stacey, 'How Will China's Innovation Change the World?' (*World Economic Forum*, 16 July 2015) <https://www.weforum.org/agenda/2015/07/how-will-chinas-innovation-change-the-world>

Clover, Charles, 'China Impedes Foreign Carmakers' Autonomous Tests' (*Financial Times*, 14 December 2017) <https://www.ft.com/content/2ba4366c-e08c-11e7-a8a4-0a1e63a52f9c>

Creemers, Rogier (ed), 'Outline of the National Informatisation Development Strategy' (*China Copyright and Media*, 30 July 2016) <https://chinacopyrightandmedia.wordpress.com/2016/07/27/outline-of-the-national-informatization-development-strategy>

Cushman & Wakefield (law firm), 'Data Centre Risk Index 2013' <http://www.cushmanwakefield.com/~/media/global-reports/data-centre-risk-index-2013.pdf>

Custer, C, 'State IDs of China's Rich and Powerful, Including Jack Ma, Leaked in Apparent Privacy Protest' (*Tech in Asia*, 12 May 2016) <https://www.techinasia.com/state-id-numbers-chinas-rich-powerful-including-jack-ma-fang-binxing-leaked-apparent-privacy-protest>

Dai, Sarah, 'China Adds Huawei, Hikvision to Expanded "National Team" Spearheading Country's AI Efforts' (*South China Morning Post*, 29 August 2019) <https://www.scmp.com/tech/big-tech/article/3024966/china-adds-huawei-hikvision-expanded-national-team-spearheading>

'China's National AI Champion Baidu to Test Driverless Delivery Vans in US with Udelv for Walmart' (*South China Morning Post*, 9 January 2019) <https://www.scmp.com/tech/big-tech/article/2181214/chinas-national-ai-champion-baidu-test-driverless-delivery-vans-us>

'Didi Rocked by Second Passenger Killing in Three Months Despite Additional Security Measures' (*South China Morning Post*, 25 August 2018) <https://www.scmp.com/tech/article/2161341/didi-rocked-second-passenger-killing-three-months-despite-additional-security>

'One of the World's Top Coders, Known as Godfather, Is Backing a Chinese Self-Driving Car Start-Up' (*South China Morning Post*, 7 February 2018) <https://www.scmp.com/tech/start-ups/article/2132420/one-worlds-top-coders-known-godfather-backing-chinese-self-driving>

'This Beijing Hub Is Home to 10 Major AI Labs Driving China's Tech Ambitions' (*South China Morning Post*, 8 February 2019) <https://www.scmp.com/tech/big-tech/article/2184987/beijing-hub-home-10-major-ai-labs-driving-chinas-tech-ambitions>

Dean, Jeff and Rojat Monga, 'TensorFlow: Google's Latest Machine Learning System, Open Sourced for Everyone' (*Google AI Blog*, 9 November 2015) <https://ai.googleblog.com/2015/11/tensorflow-googles-latest-machine.html>

Dean, Sam, 'Open Source AI for Everyone: Three Projects to Know' (*Linux Foundation*, 10 May 2018) <https://www.linuxfoundation.org/blog/2018/05/open-source-ai-for-everyone-three-projects-to-know>

Dedrick, Jason and Kenneth L Kraemer, 'Intangible Assets and Value Capture in Global Value Chains: The Smartphone Industry' (World Intellectual Property Organization Working Paper, November 2017) <https://www.wipo.int/edocs/pubdocs/en/wipo_pub_econstat_wp_41.pdf>

Del Bello, Lou, 'Scientists Are Closer to Making Artificial Brains That Operate Like Ours Do' (*Futurism*, 28 January 2018) <https://futurism.com/artificial-brains-operate-like-humans-close>

Delaney, Robert, 'Encouraging Signs for US–China Business Ties in Cloud Computing Access Talks' (*South China Morning Post*, 12 April 2019) <https://www.scmp.com/news/china/diplomacy/article/3005809/encouraging-signs-us-china-business-ties-cloud-computing>

Delval, Galaad, 'Old Rules, New Specification for Data Protection in Mainland China' (*International Association of Privacy Professionals*, 3 May 2018) <https://iapp.org/news/a/old-rules-new-specification-for-data-protection-in-mainland-china>

Deng, Iris, 'Tencent Releases Open Platform to Help Drive AI Projects at Other Companies' (*South China Morning Post*, 19 September 2018) <https://www.scmp.com/tech/big-tech/article/2164765/tencent-releases-open-platform-help-drive-ai-projects-other-companies>

Denlinger, Paul, 'What Will Data Rights for the Individual Look Like in China?' (*Pandaily*, 10 September 2018) <https://pandaily.com/what-will-data-rights-for-the-individual-look-like-in-china>

Dickinson, Steve, 'China's New Cryptography Law: Still No Place to Hide' (*Harris Bricken* (law firm)), 7 November 2019) <https://harrisbricken.com/chinalawblog/chinas-new-cryptography-law-still-no-place-to-hide/>

'China VIEs are Dead. Done. Over. Stick a Fork in Them' (*China Law Blog*, 22 January 2015) <http://www.chinalawblog.com/2015/01/china-vies-are-dead-done-over-stick-a-fork-in-them.html>

'SaaS in China: The 101' (*China Law Blog*, 10 October 2016) <https://www.chinalawblog.com/2016/10/saas-in-china-the-101.html>

Dickinson, Steve and Grace Yang, 'China's Cybersecurity Law and Employee Personal Information' (*China Law Blog*, 8 January 2017) <http://www.chinalawblog.com/2017/01/chinas-cybersecurity-law-and-employee-personal-information.html>

Dou, Eva, 'Global Tech Companies Call on China to Delay Cybersecurity Law' (*Wall Street Journal*, 15 May 2017) <https://www.wsj.com/articles/global-tech-companies-call-on-china-to-delay-cybersecurity-law-1494837117>

'Microsoft, Intel, IBM Push Back on China Cybersecurity Rules' (*Wall Street Journal*, 1 December 2016) <http://www.wsj.com/articles/microsoft-intel-ibm-push-back-on-china-cybersecurity-rules-1480587542>

Dou, Eva and Rachel King, 'China Sets New Tone in Drafting Cybersecurity Rules' (*Wall Street Journal*, 26 August 2016) <http://www.wsj.com/articles/china-moves-to-ease-foreign-concerns-on-cybersecurity-controls-1472132575>

Duhigg, Charles, 'The Case against Google' (*New York Times*, 20 February 2018) <www.nytimes.com/2018/02/20/magazine/the-case-against-google.html>

Dwyer, Colin, '"Like A God" Google AI Beats Human Champ of Notoriously Complex Go Game' (*NPR*, 23 May 2017) <https://www.npr.org/sections/thetwo-way/2017/05/23/529673475/like-a-god-google-a-i-beats-human-champ-of-notoriously-complex-go-game>

Evangelho, Jason, 'Amazon Alexa and Huawei Team Up for AI Cube Smart Speaker + 4G Router' (*Forbes*, 31 August 2018) <https://www.forbes.com/sites/jasonevangelho/2018/08/31/amazon-alexa-and-huawei-team-up-for-ai-cube-smart-speaker-4g-router/#2095d09cba73>

Farrell, Nick, 'US Might Have Control of Open Source' (*Fudzilla*, 28 May 2019) <https://www.fudzilla.com/news/48769-us-might-have-control-of-open-source>

Feng, Venus, 'World's Most Valuable Startup Is Home to a Complex Fortune' (*Bloomberg*, 24 March 2018) <https://www.bloomberg.com/news/articles/2019-03-24/the-complex-fortune-growing-inside-world-s-most-valuable-startup>

Finley, Klint, 'How GitHub Is Helping Overworked Chinese Programmers' (*Wired*, 4 April 2019) <https://www.wired.com/story/how-github-helping-overworked-chinese-programmers>

'What Exactly Is GitHub Anyway?' (*TechCrunch*, 14 July 2012) <https://techcrunch.com/2012/07/14/what-exactly-is-github-anyway>

Fish, Tom, 'AI to Bring "Mankind to Edge of APOCALYPSE" – With Robots a Bigger Risk than NUKES' (*Daily Star*, 15 July 2018) <https://www.dailystar.co.uk/news/latest-news/716305/ai-artificial-intelligence-autonomous-weaponry-arms-race>

Freund, Karl, 'Is NVIDIA Unstoppable in AI?' (*Forbes*, 14 May 2018) <https://www.forbes.com/sites/moorinsights/2018/05/14/is-nvidia-unstoppable-in-ai/#357f711a759e>

Gan, Nectar, 'Father of China's Great Firewall to Lead New Cybersecurity Association' (*South China Morning Post*, 26 March 2016) <https://www.scmp.com/news/china/policies-politics/article/1930959/father-chinas-great-firewall-lead-new-cybersecurity>

Gerbert, Philipp, Jan Justus and Martin Hecker, 'Competing in the Age of Artificial Intelligence' (*BCG*, 16 January 2017)

Gibbs, Samuel, 'AlphaZero AI Beats Champion Chess Program after Teaching Itself in Four Hours' (*The Guardian*, 7 December 2017) <https://www.theguardian.com/technology/2017/dec/07/alphazero-google-deepmind-ai-beats-champion-program-teaching-itself-to-play-four-hours>

Groll, Elias, 'Why Apple – and Not Google – Is in the FBI's Crosshairs' (*Foreign Policy*, 18 February 2016) <http://foreignpolicy.com/2016/02/18/why-apple-and-not-google-is-in-the-fbis-crosshairs>

Hanley, Blair, 'Baidu COO Says China's Government Will Help the Country Dominate AI' (*Venturebeat*, 9 January 2018) <https://venturebeat.com/2018/01/09/baidu-coo-says-chinas-government-will-help-the-country-dominate-ai>

Hawkins, Andrew J., 'Toyota Steers $400 Million to Self-Driving Startup Pony.ai' (*The Verge*, 30 March 2020) <https://www.theverge.com/2020/2/25/21152817/toyota-pony-ai-self-driving-car-investment-valuation-china-silicon-valley>

He, Laura, 'Baidu's Seismic Shift towards AI Must Start Delivering the Goods' (*South China Morning Post*, 8 June 2017) <https://www.scmp.com/business/companies/article/2097495/baidus-seismic-shift-towards-ai-must-start-delivering-goods>

He, Yujia, 'How China Is Preparing for an AI-Powered Future' (*Wilson Briefs*, 20 June 2017) <https://www.wilsoncenter.org/publication/how-china-preparing-for-ai-powered-future>

Hempel, Jessi, 'Facebook Launches M, Its Bold Answer to Siri and Cortana' (*Wired*, 26 August 2015) <https://www.wired.com/2015/08/facebook-launches-m-new-kind-virtual-assistant>

'Inside Baidu's Bid to Lead the AI Revolution' (*Wired*, 12 June 2017) <https://www.wired.com/story/inside-baidu-artificial-intelligence>

Hersey, Frank, 'Almost 80% of Chinese Concerned about AI Threat to Privacy, 32% Already Feel a Threat to Their Work' (*Technode*, 2 March 2018) <https://technode.com/2018/03/02/almost-80-chinese-concerned-ai-threat-privacy-32-already-feel-threat-work>

'Baidu Launches Their Open Platform for Autonomous Cars – And We Got to Test It' (*Technode*, 5 July 2017) <https://technode.com/2017/07/05/baidu-apollo-1-0-autonomous-cars-we-test-it>

'Pony.ai Q&A: Having a China Background Will Be Key to Autonomous Driving Success' (*TechNode*, 26 April 2018) <https://technode.com/2018/04/26/pony-ai-autonomous-driving-success-needs-china>

'Qihoo 360 Shuts Down Surveillance Camera Live Streaming Platform' (*Technode*, 20 December 2017) <https://technode.com/2017/12/20/shuidi-shutdown-qihoo-360>

Hickert, Cameron and Jeffrey Ding (trans), 'Read What Top Chinese Officials Are Hearing about AI Competition and Policy' (*New America*, 29 November 2018) <https://www.newamerica.org/cybersecurity-initiative/digichina/blog/read-what-top-chinese-officials-are-hearing-about-ai-competition-and-policy>

Horwitz, Josh, 'Analysis: China's Would-Be Chip Darling Tsinghua Unigroup Bedevilled by Debt and Bad Bets' (*Reuters*, 20 January 2021) <https://www.reuters.com/article/us-tsinghua-unigroup-strategy-analysis-idUKKBN29P0C2>

'China Is Rapidly Making Robots That Will One Day Manufacture Everything You Buy' (*Quartz*, 3 March 2017) <https://qz.com/922742/china-is-rapidly-making-robots-that-will-one-day-manufacture-everything-you-buy>

'China's Bewildering New Cybersecurity Law Is Keeping Foreign Tech Firms Out of the Country' (*Quartz*, 7 November 2016) <http://qz.com/829248/chinas-new-cybersecurity-law-is-so-vague-that-its-keeping-foreign-tech-firms-out-of-the-country>

'Why the Semiconductor Is Suddenly at the Heart of US–China Tech Tensions' (*Quartz*, 25 July 2018) <https://qz.com/1335801/us-china-tech-why-the-semiconductor-is-suddenly-at-the-heart-of-us-china-tensions>

Horwitz, Josh and Nikhil Sonnad, 'Meet Shadowsocks, the Underground Tool that China's Coders Use to Blast through the Great Firewall' (*Quartz*, 20 September 2017) <https://qz.com/1072701/meet-shadowsocks-the-underground-tool-that-chinas-coders-use-to-blast-through-the-great-firewall>

Hua, Nan, 'Roadstar.ai: A Promising Autonomous Driving Startup Wrecked by Infighting' (*CompassList*, 25 July 2019) <https://www.compasslist.com/insights/roadstarai-a-promising-autonomous-driving-startup-wrecked-by-infighting>

Huang, Echo, 'China Keeps Finding Millions of People Who Never Officially Existed' (*Quartz*, 27 March 2017) <https://qz.com/941240/china-keeps-finding-millions-of-people-who-never-officially-existed>

'Taobao Is Banning Merchants from Selling Foreign Media in China – Even Media Approved by Censors' (*Quartz*, 10 March 2017) <https://qz.com/929540/selling-foreign-media-in-china-even-media-approved-by-censors-is-being-banned-alibaba-baba-groups-online-shopping-platform-taobao>

Huang, Kristin and Zhou Xin, 'Fake Data: The Disease Afflicting China's Vaccine System' (*South China Morning Post*, 30 July 2018) <https://www.scmp.com/news/china/policies-politics/article/2157341/fake-data-disease-afflicting-chinas-vaccine-system>

Huang, Xuedong, 'Microsoft Computational Network Toolkit Offers Most Efficient Distributed Deep Learning Computational Performance' (*Microsoft Research Blog*, 7 December 2015) <https://www.microsoft.com/en-us/research/blog/microsoft-computational-network-toolkit-offers-most-efficient-distributed-deep-learning-computational-performance/>

Huang, Zheping and Jane Zhang, '200 Million Resumés of Chinese Jobseekers Leaked, Cybersecurity Researcher Says' (*South China Morning Post*, 11 January 2019) <https://www.scmp.com/tech/big-tech/article/2181709/200-million-resumes-chinese-jobseekers-leaked-cybersecurity-researcher>

Isbitski, David, 'Introducing the Alexa Skills Kit, Enabling Developers to Create Entirely New Voice Driven Capabilities' (*Amazon Developer*, 25 June 2015) <https://developer.amazon.com/blogs/post/Tx205N9U1UD338H/

Introducing-the-Alexa-Skills-Kit-Enabling-Developers-to-Create-Entirely-New-Voic>

Ives, Jaqueline and Anna Holzmann, 'Local Governments Power Up to Advance China's National AI Agenda' (*MERICS*, 26 April 2018) <https://www.merics.org/en/blog/local-governments-power-advance-chinas-national-ai-agenda>

Jacobs, Harrison, 'Chinese People Don't Care about Privacy on the Internet – Here's Why, According to a Top Professor in China' (*Business Insider*, 27 June 2018) <https://www.businessinsider.com.au/why-china-chinese-people-dont-care-about-privacy-2018-6>

Jing, Dong and Liu Xiao, 'Divided among Departments, Big Data Eludes Government' (*Caixin Global*, 16 April 2018) <https://www.caixinglobal.com/2018-04-16/divided-among-departments-big-data-eludes-government-101235107.html>

Jing, Meng and Sarah Dai, 'China Recruits Baidu, Alibaba and Tencent to AI "National Team"' (*South China Morning Post*, 21 November 2017) <https://www.scmp.com/tech/china-tech/article/2120913/china-recruits-baidu-alibaba-and-tencent-ai-national-team>

Jing, Ming, 'China's Cybersecurity Laws May Be Used to Block US Tech Firms on National Security Grounds, Says Expert' (*South China Morning Post*, 24 May 2019) <https://www.scmp.com/tech/policy/article/3011655/chinas-cybersecurity-laws-may-be-used-block-us-tech-firms-national>

Joffe, Benjamin, 'What Sequoia's Mike Moritz Doesn't Understand about Startups in China' (*Venturebeat*, 11 February 2018) <https://venturebeat.com/2018/02/11/what-sequoias-mike-moritz-doesnt-understand-about-startups-in-china>

Johnson, Kahri, 'How Federated Learning Could Shape the Future of AI in a Privacy-Obsessed World' (*Venture Beat*, 3 June 2019) <https://venturebeat.com/2019/06/03/how-federated-learning-could-shape-the-future-of-ai-in-a-privacy-obsessed-world>

Jordan, Michael I, 'Artificial Intelligence: The Revolution Hasn't Happened Yet' (*Medium*, 19 April 2019) <https://medium.com/@mijordan3/artificial-intelligence-the-revolution-hasnt-happened-yet-5e1d5812e1e7>

Kania, Elsa B, 'Battlefield Singularity: Artificial Intelligence, Military Revolution, and China's Future Military Power' (*Center for a New American Security*, 28 November 2017) <https://www.cnas.org/publications/reports/battlefield-singularity-artificial-intelligence-military-revolution-and-chinas-future-military-power>

'China May Become the World's Leader in AI: But at What Cost?' (*China File*, 30 July 2018) <http://www.chinafile.com/conversation/china-may-become-worlds-leader-ai-what-cost>

Kharpal, Arjun, 'Chinese Driverless Car Firm Pony.ai Valued at $5.3 Billion after New Cash Injection' (*CNBC*, 6 November 2020) <https://www.cnbc.com/2020/11/06/china-driverless-car-firm-ponyai-valued-at-5point3-billion-after-funding.html>

Knight, Will, 'China and the US Are Bracing for an AI Showdown – In the Cloud' (*MIT Technology Review*, 31 January 2018) <https://www.technologyreview.com/s/610140/china-and-the-us-are-bracing-for-an-ai-showdownin-the-cloud>

'Paying with Your Face: 10 Breakthrough Technologies 2017' (*MIT Technology Review*, May 2017) <https://www.technologyreview.com/s/603494/10-breakthrough-technologies-2017-paying-with-your-face>

Knockel, Jeffrey, Sarah McKune and Adam Senft, 'Baidu's and Don'ts: Privacy and Security Issues in Baidu Browser' (*Citizen Lab*, 23 February 2016) <https://citizenlab.ca/2016/02/privacy-security-issues-baidu-browser/#analysis>

Knockel, Jeffrey, Adam Senft and Ron Deibert, 'Privacy and Security Issues in QQ Browser' (*Citizen Lab*, 28 March 2016) <https://citizenlab.ca/2016/03/privacy-security-issues-qq-browser>

Koetse, Manya, 'Weibo's Revival: Sina Weibo Is China's Twitter, YouTube and InstaGram' (*What's on Weibo*, 20 November 2016) <http://www.whatsonweibo.com/weibos-revival-sina-weibo-chinas-twitteryoutubeinstagram>

Korosec, Kirsten, 'Autonomous Truck Startup TuSimple Hits Unicorn Status in Latest Round' (*TechCrunch*, 13 February 2019) <https://techcrunch.com/2019/02/13/autonomous-truck-startup-tusimple-hits-unicorn-status-in-latest-round>

'Daimler Deepens Ties with China's Baidu on Automated Driving' (*TechCrunch*, 25 July 2018) <https://techcrunch.com/2018/07/25/daimler-chinas-baidu-automated-driving>

'Self-Driving Trucks Startup TuSimple Raises $350M from US Rail, Retail and Freight Giants' (*TechCrunch*, 3 December 2020) <https://techcrunch.com/2020/12/02/self-driving-trucks-startup-tusimple-raises-350m-from-u-s-rail-retail-and-freight-giants/>

Kovar, Joseph F, 'Accenture Invests in China-Based AI Firm' (*CRN*, 13 August 2018) <https://www.crn.com/news/channel-programs/accenture-invests-in-china-based-ai-firm?itc=refresh>

Krazit, Tom, 'AWS re:Invent 2018' (*Geek Wire*, 21 November 2018) <https://www.geekwire.com/special-coverage/aws-reinvent-2018>

'Building a Wall around the Cloud: Why China Will Soon Be a Very Important Cloud Computing Market' (*Geek Wire*, 13 January 2019) <https://www.geekwire.com/2019/building-wall-around-cloud-china-will-soon-import ant-cloud-computing-market>

Lahiri, Tripti and Mary Hui, 'How Huawei Became America's Tech Enemy No 1' (*Quartz*, 28 May 2019) <https://qz.com/1627149/huaweis-journey-to-becoming-us-tech-enemy-no-1>

Lau, Fiona and Julie Zhu, 'China's Xiaomi Raises $4.72 Billion after Pricing HK IPO at Bottom of Range: Sources' (*Reuters*, 29 June 2018) <https://www.reuters.com/article/us-xiaomi-ipo/chinas-xiaomi-raises-4-72-billion-after-pricing-hk-ipo-at-bottom-of-range-sources-idUSKBN1JP0EC>

Lee, Amanda, 'World Dominance in Three Steps: China Sets Out Road Map to Lead in Artificial Intelligence by 2030' (*South China Morning Post*, 21 July 2017) <http://www.scmp.com/tech/enterprises/article/2103568/world-dominance-three-steps-china-sets-out-road-map-lead-artificial>

Lee, Cyrus, 'Daily Active Users for WeChat Exceeds 1 Billion' (*ZDNet*, 9 January 2019) <https://www.zdnet.com/article/daily-active-user-of-messaging-app-wechat-exceeds-1-billion>

Lee, Emma, 'China Launches Mobile ID Authentication Chips to Rein in Personal Data Theft' (*TechNode*, 17 April 2018) <https://technode.com/2018/04/17/id-authentication-chips-data-theft>

'Sale of WeChat Accounts Prompts Concern over Fraud' (*TechNode*, 16 January 2019) <https://technode.com/2019/01/16/wechat-accounts-sale-online-fraud/>

'Updated: Toutiao and Intel Set Up Joint AI Lab' (*Technode*, 22 August 2018) <https://technode.com/2018/08/22/bytedance-intel-ai-lab>

'Updated: WeChat's Privacy Policy Update Draws Attention to Information Shared with the Government' (*TechNode*, 19 September 2017) <https://technode.com/2017/09/19/now-its-official-wechat-is-watching-you-1>

Lee, Kai-Fu, 'What China Can Teach the US about Artificial Intelligence' (*New York Times*, 22 September 2018) <https://www.nytimes.com/2018/09/22/opinion/sunday/ai-china-united-states.html>

Lee, Kai-fu and Matt Sheehan, 'China's Rise in Artificial Intelligence: Ingredients and Economic Implications' (*Hoover Institute*, 29 October 2018) <https://www.hoover.org/research/chinas-rise-artificial-intelligence-ingredients-and-economic-implications>

Leng, Shujie, 'Be in Love with Them, But Don't Marry Them' (*Foreign Policy*, 31 October 2014) <http://foreignpolicy.com/2014/10/31/be-in-love-with-them-but-dont-marry-them>

Lennighan, Mary, 'China to Have 10BN Connected Devices by 2020' (*Total Telecom*, 24 February 2016) <https://www.totaltele.com/view.aspx?ID=492917>

Lentino, Amanda, 'This Chinese Facial Recognition Start-Up Can Identify a Person in Seconds' (*CNBC*, 19 May 2019) <https://www.cnbc.com/2019/05/16/this-chinese-facial-recognition-start-up-can-id-a-person-in-seconds.html>

Levine, Sergey et al, 'Learning Hand-Eye Coordination for Robotic Grasping with Deep Learning and Large-Scale Data Collection' (*arXiv.org*, 28 August 2016) <https://arxiv.org/pdf/1603.02199.pdf>

Lew, Linda, 'Airbnb China Notifies Hosts They May Begin Sharing Their Information with the Government' (*TechNode*, 28 March 2018) <https://technode.com/2018/03/28/airbnb-china-host-data-privacy>

Li, Gabriel, 'Jack Ma Talks about Manufacturing Woes, Alibaba Cloud, and the DAMO Academy at the Computing Conference 2018' (*Pandaily*, 20 September 2018) <https://pandaily.com/jack-ma-talks-about-manufacturing-woes-alibaba-cloud-and-the-damo-academy-at-the-computing-conference-2018>

Li, Jane, 'Chinese Citizens Are Racing against Censors to Preserve Coronavirus Memories on GitHub' (*Quartz*, 3 March 2020) <https://qz.com/1811018/chinese-citizens-use-github-to-save-coronavirus-memories/>

'Chinese Internet Users Who Uploaded Coronavirus Memories to GitHub Have Been Arrested' (*Quartz*, 27 April 2020) <https://qz.com/1846277/china-arrests-users-behind-github-coronavirus-memories-page/>

Liao, Rita, 'China Opens Nasdaq-style Board to Lure Tech Firms Back Home' (*TechCrunch*, 13 June 2019) <https://techcrunch.com/2019/06/13/china-new-tech-board/>

'Chinese Autonomous Driving Startup WeRide Bags $200M in Funding' (*TechCrunch*, 23 December 2020) <https://techcrunch.com/2020/12/22/weride-200-million-funding/>

'Horizon Robotics, a Chinese Rival to Nvidia, Seeks to Raise Over $700M' (*TechCrunch*, 22 December 2020) <https://techcrunch.com/2020/12/21/horizon-robotics-700-million-funding/>

Liao, Shannan, 'Alibaba Made a Driverless Robot That Runs 9 mph to Deliver Packages' (*The Verge*, 31 May 2018) <https://www.theverge.com/circuitbreaker/2018/5/31/17413836/alibaba-driverless-robot-deliver-packages-speed>

Liping, Gu, 'Didi Chuxing Refuses Data Supervision: Transport Official' (*Ecns.cn*, 28 August 2018) <http://www.ecns.cn/news/cns-wire/2018-08-28/detail-ifyxikfc9645161.shtml>

Lipton, Zachary C, 'The AI Misinformation Epidemic' (*Approximately Correct*, 28 March 2017) <http://approximatelycorrect.com/2017/03/28/the-ai-misinformation-epidemic>

'OpenAI Trains Language Model, Mass Hysteria Ensues' (*Approximately Correct*, 17 February 2019) <http://approximatelycorrect.com/2019/02/17/openai-trains-language-model-mass-hysteria-ensues/#more-875>

Liu, Coco, 'My China Dream Is Moving to the United States: Chinese Chatbots Censored after Going Off Script' (*South China Morning Post*, 3 August 2017)

<http://www.scmp.com/week-asia/politics/article/2105338/my-china-dream-moving-united-states-chinese-chatbots-censored>

Liu, Frank, 'OpenStack Development Will Accelerate Rapidly in China Market in 2015' (*Forrester*, 24 December 2014) <https://go.forrester.com/blogs/14-12-24-openstack_development_will_accelerate_rapidly_in_china_market_in_2015>

Liu, Jack and Zen Soo, 'China's Alibaba, Baidu and Tencent Join Hands to Promote "Internet Plus" Strategy' (*South China Morning Post*, 16 December 2015) <http://www.scmp.com/news/china/policies-politics/article/1892180/chinas-alibaba-baidu-and-tencent-join-hands-promote>

Liu, Jiefei, 'Alipay Introduces New Feature Allowing Parents to Trace the Vaccines Their Children Are Receiving' (*TechNode*, 24 July 2018) <https://technode.com/2018/07/24/alipay-introduces-new-feature-allowing-parents-to-trace-the-vaccines-their-children-are>

Livingston, Scott, 'Beijing Touts "Cyber-Sovereignty" in Internet Governance: Global Technology Firms Could Mine Silver Lining' (*China Law Blog*, 19 February 2015) <http://www.chinalawblog.com/2015/02/beijing-touts-cyber-sovereignty-in-internet-governance-global-technology-firms-could-mine-silver-lining.html>

Lohr, Steve, 'Is There a Smarter Path to Artificial Intelligence? Some Experts Hope So' (*New York Times*, 20 June 2018) <https://www.nytimes.com/2018/06/20/technology/deep-learning-artificial-intelligence.html>

London, Ingrid, 'China's Pony.ai Nabs $102M at Nearly $1B Valuation to Take Its Self-Driving Platform Up Another Gear' (*TechCrunch*, 11 July 2018) <https://techcrunch.com/2018/07/11/chinas-pony-ai-nabs-102m-at-nearly-1b-valuation-to-take-its-self-driving-platform-up-another-gear>

Lu, Xiaomeng, 'Is China Changing Its Thinking on Data Localization?' (*The Diplomat*, 8 June 2020) <https://thediplomat.com/2020/06/is-china-changing-its-thinking-on-data-localization/>

Lucas, Louise and Richard Waters, 'China and US Compete to Dominate Big Data' (*Financial Times*, 1 May 2018) <https://www.ft.com/content/e33a6994-447e-11e8-93cf-67ac3a6482fd>

Ludlow, Randy, 'Ohio Tries to Pull Ahead in Transportation Tech Race' (*Government Technology*, 19 January 2018) <https://www.govtech.com/fs/transportation/State-Creates-DriveOhio-to-Capture-Smart-Transportation-Research.html>

Luo, Yan and Phil Bradley-Schmieg, 'China Issues New Personal Information Protection Standard' (*Inside Privacy*, 25 January 2018) <https://www.insideprivacy.com/international/china/china-issues-new-personal-information-protection-standard>

Mac, Ryan, 'Alibaba Claims Title for Largest Global IPO Ever with Extra Share Sales' (*Forbes*, 22 September 2014) <https://www.forbes.com/sites/ryanmac/

2014/09/22/alibaba-claims-title-for-largest-global-ipo-ever-with-extra-share-sales/#548cc3518dcc>

Maçães, Bruno, 'China's Black Box Superiority' (*Politico*, 11 December 2018) <https://www.politico.eu/blogs/the-coming-wars/2018/11/china-black-box-superiority-cybersecurity-artificial-intelligence-ai>

Marcus, Gary, 'Deep Learning: A Critical Appraisal' (*arXiv.org*, 19 April 2018) <https://arxiv.org/pdf/1801.00631.pdf>

Markoff, John, 'AI Reemerges from a Funding Desert' (*New York Times*, 13 October 2005) <https://www.nytimes.com/2005/10/13/business/worldbusiness/ai-reemerges-from-a-funding-desert.html>

Markoff, John and Matthew Rosenberg, 'China's Intelligent Weaponry Gets Smarter' (*New York Times*, 3 February 2017) <https://www.nytimes.com/2017/02/03/technology/artificial-intelligence-china-united-states.html>

Marr, Bernard, 'AI in China: How Uber Rival Didi Chuxing Uses Machine Learning to Revolutionize Transportation' (*Forbes*, 26 November 2018) <https://www.forbes.com/sites/bernardmarr/2018/11/26/ai-in-china-how-uber-rival-didi-chuxing-uses-machine-learning-to-revolutionize-transportation/#11b7bc6f6732>

Marri, Shridhar, 'Can Super Intelligence and Emotional Intelligence Co-exist?' (*Forbes*, 27 June 2017) <https://www.forbesindia.com/blog/technology/can-super-intelligence-and-emotional-intelligence-co-exist/>

Marshall, Arian, 'To Save the Most Lives, Deploy (Imperfect) Self-Driving Cars ASAP' (*Wired*, 11 July 2018) <https://www.wired.com/story/self-driving-cars-rand-report>

Martina, Michael and Cate Cadell, 'Amid Industry Pushback, China Offers Changes to Cyber Rules: Sources' (*Reuters*, 19 May 2017) <http://www.reuters.com/article/us-china-cyber-law-idUSKCN18F1VZ>

McCall, Rosie, 'This App Can Detect Cancer Better than Doctors Can' (*IFLScience*, 29 May 2018) <https://www.iflscience.com/health-and-medicine/artificial-intelligence-can-now-detect-skin-cancer-better-than-humans>

McCarthy, John, 'What Is Artificial Intelligence?' (Formal Reasoning Group Stanford, revised 12 November 2007) <http://jmc.stanford.edu/articles/whatisai/whatisai.pdf>

McDuling, John, 'LinkedIn Is Doing What Facebook, Google, and Twitter Can't: Expanding in China' (*Quartz*, 24 February 2014) <https://qz.com/180755/linkedin-is-doing-what-facebook-google-and-twitter-cant-expanding-in-china>

McMahan, H Brendan et al, 'Communication-Efficient Learning of Deep Networks from Decentralized Data' (*arXiv*, 28 February 2017) <https://arxiv.org/abs/1602.05629>

Mengfan, Chen, An Limin and Han Wei, 'Is WeChat Snooping on Your Chats?' (*Caixin Global*, 4 January 2018) <https://www.caixinglobal.com/2018-01-04/is-wechat-snooping-on-your-chats-101193014.html>

Metz, Cade, 'A Mystery AI Just Crushed the Best Human Players at Poker' (*Wired*, 31 January 2017) <https://www.wired.com/2017/01/mystery-ai-just-crushed-best-human-players-poker>

Millman, Gregory J, 'Alibaba's IPO Puts VIE Structure in the Spotlight' (*Wall Street Journal*, 2014) <https://blogs.wsj.com/riskandcompliance/2014/09/22/alibabas-ipo-puts-vie-structure-in-the-spotlight>

Millward, Steven, 'China Now Has 731 Million Internet Users, 95% Access from Their Phones' (*TechinAsia*, 23 January 2017) <https://www.techinasia.com/china-731-million-internet-users-end-2016>

'Seven Years of "China's Twitter"' (*TechinAsia*, 14 August 2016) <https://www.techinasia.com/7-years-of-weibo-china-social-media>

Mishra, Neha, 'Data Localization Laws in a Digital World: Data Protection or Data Protectionism?' (*Public Sphere*, 2016) <http://publicspherejournal.com/wp-content/uploads/2016/02/06.data_protection.pdf> (the link is no longer active)

Mo, Zhou, 'Baidu Expands Use of Its AI Tech in Traditional Industries' (*China Daily*, 31 May 2018) <http://www.chinadaily.com.cn/a/201805/31/WS5b0fe579a31001b82571d7d6.html>

Moritz, Michael, 'Silicon Valley Would Be Wise to Follow China's Lead' (*Financial Times*, 18 January 2018) <https://www.ft.com/content/42daca9e-facc-11e7-9bfc-052cbba03425>

Mozur, Paul, 'China, Addicted to Bootleg Software, Reels from Ransomware Attack' (*New York Times*, 15 May 2017) <https://www.nytimes.com/2017/05/15/business/china-ransomware-wannacry-hacking.html>

'China Said to Quickly Withdraw Approval for New Facebook Venture' (*New York Times*, 25 July 2018) <https://www.nytimes.com/2018/07/25/business/facebook-china.html?emc=edit_mbau_20180725&nl=&nlid=8467969320180725&te=1>

'Internet Users in China Expect to Be Tracked. Now, They Want Privacy' (*New York Times*, 4 January 2018) <https://www.nytimes.com/2018/01/04/business/china-alibaba-privacy.html>

'One Month, 500,000 Face Scans: How China Is Using AI to Profile a Minority' (*New York Times*, 14 April 2019) <https://www.nytimes.com/2019/04/14/technology/china-surveillance-artificial-intelligence-racial-profiling.html>

Murison, Malek, 'JD.com Launches Robot Delivery in China' (*Internet of Business*, 20 June 2017) <https://internetofbusiness.com/jd-com-robot-delivery-china>

Nakanishi, Toyoki and Yu Nakamura, 'Google Seeks Better China Relations via Tencent Patent Deal' (*Nikkei Asian Review*, 20 January 2018) <https://asia.nikkei.com/Business/Deals/Google-seeks-better-China-relations-via-Tencent-patent-deal>

Niewenhuis, Lucas, 'Didi Drops 20% after IPO as Beijing Tightens Data Security Review' (*SupChina*, 6 July 2021) <https://supchina.com/2021/07/06/didi-drops-20-after-ipo-as-beijing-tightens-data-security-review/>

'Yet Another Vaccine Scandal Punctures Public Trust in Safety' (*SupChina*, 23 July 2018) <https://supchina.com/2018/07/23/outrage-over-faulty-vaccines-again>

Novet, Jordan, 'Why Tech Companies Are Racing Each Other to Make Their Own Custom AI Chips' (*CNBC*, 21 April 2018) <https://www.cnbc.com/2018/04/21/alibaba-joins-google-others-in-making-custom-ai-chips.html>

OECD, *OECD: Main Science and Technology Indicators* <https://stats.oecd.org/Index.aspx?DataSetCode=MSTI_PUB>

Ohnsman, Alan, 'Baidu Aims for "Android" of Robocar Tech with Open-Source Apollo Platform' (*Forbes*, 27 October 2017) <https://www.forbes.com/sites/alanohnsman/2017/10/27/baidu-aims-for-android-of-robocar-tech-with-open-source-apollo-platform/#2edbb5d0c799>

Osborne, Charlie, 'China Excludes Symantec, Kaspersky Lab from Approved Anti-Virus Vendors' (*ZDnet*, 4 August 2014) <https://www.zdnet.com/article/china-excludes-symantec-kaspersky-lab-from-approved-anti-virus-vendors>

Oshikiri, Tomoyoshi, 'Toyota to Join Baidu's Self-Driving Platform Apollo' (*Nikkei Asian Review*, 28 June 2019) <https://asia.nikkei.com/Business/Companies/Toyota-to-join-Baidu-s-self-driving-platform-Apollo>

Oster, Shai and Allen Wan, 'Chinese Gripe at Being Left Out of Alibaba IPO' (*Bloomberg*, 15 September 2014) <https://www.bloomberg.com/news/articles/2014-09-14/chinese-gripe-at-being-left-out-of-alibaba-s-21-billion-ipo>

Ouyang, Iris, 'Pinduoduo, China's Facebook-Groupon Mashup, Files for $1B US IPO' (*Pandaily*, 1 July 2018) <https://pandaily.com/pinduoduo-chinas-facebook-groupon-mashup-files-for-1b-us-ipo>

Pan, Che, 'Baidu's Apollo Gets Green Light to Test AD Cars in Beijing without On-board Safety Driver' (*South China Morning Post*, 8 December 2020) <https://www.scmp.com/tech/innovation/article/3113029/baidus-apollo-gets-green-light-test-ad-cars-beijing-without-board>

Pan, Yuanyuan, 'The Long-Term Implications of Ant Group's Delayed IPO' (*The Diplomat*, 20 November 2020) <https://thediplomat.com/2020/11/the-long-term-implications-of-ant-groups-delayed-ipo/>

Parmar, Tekendra, 'China: Tech Giants Push Back against Beijing's New Cyber Security Bill' (*Fortune*, 2 December 2016) <https://fortune.com/2016/12/02/cyber-security-bill-source-code/>

Patrizio, Andy, 'Baidu Takes a Major Leap as an AI Player with New Chip, Intel Alliance' (*Network World*, 11 July 2018) <https://www.networkworld.com/article/3289387/data-center/baidu-takes-a-major-leap-as-an-ai-player-with-new-chip-intel-alliance.html>

Paul, Ryan, 'Department of Defense Launches Open Source Site Forge.mil' (*Ars Technica*, 2 April 2009) <https://arstechnica.com/information-technology/2009/02/department-of-defense-launches-open-source-site-forgemil2019>

Peng, Tony, 'Fei-Fei Li at Google I/O: Humans Overestimate AI in the Short-Term, Underestimate Its Long-Term Potential' (*Synced Review*, 10 May 2018) <https://medium.com/syncedreview/fei-fei-li-at-google-i-o-humans-overestimate-ai-in-the-short-term-underestimate-its-long-term-f21d7a4a19a9>

Perez, Bien, 'China Taps Nation's Who's Who of Technology to Anchor Ownership Shakeup at Unicom's Parent' (*South China Morning Post*, 17 August 2017) <https://www.scmp.com/tech/article/2106982/unicom-shares-halted-speculation-mounts-new-investors-its-parent-company>

Perez, Chris, 'Creepy Facebook Bots Talked to Each Other in a Secret Language' (*New York Post*, 1 August 2017) <https://nypost.com/2017/08/01/creepy-facebook-bots-talked-to-each-other-in-a-secret-language>

Polk, Andrew, 'China Is Quietly Setting Global Standards' (*Bloomberg*, 7 May 2018) <https://www.bloomberg.com/opinion/articles/2018-05-06/china-is-quietly-setting-global-standards>

Prinsloo, Loni, 'Tencent's 60,000% Runup Leads to One of the Biggest VC Payoffs Ever' (*Bloomberg*, 22 March 2018) <https://www.bloomberg.com/news/articles/2018-03-22/naspers-sells-10-6-billion-of-tencent-to-fund-investments>

Purtill, Corinne, 'Your Phone Isn't Really Spying on Your Conversations – The Truth Might Be Even Creepier' (*Quartz*, 2 May 2018) <https://qz.com/1609356/your-phone-is-not-recording-your-conversations>

Qi, Frida, 'Tech Companies Prepare for Jumbo IPO Season in Hong Kong and Shanghai' (*SupChina*, 15 January 2021) <https://supchina.com/2021/01/15/tech-companies-prepare-for-jumbo-ipo-season-in-hong-kong-and-shanghai/>

Qiqing, Lin, 'Outside the Green Bubble of China's Super-App' (*Sixth Tone*, 28 June 2018) <http://www.sixthtone.com/news/1002502/outside-the-green-bubble-of-chinas-super-app>

Quakenbush, Casey, 'Three Things to Know about China's Kindergarten Abuse Scandal' (*Time*, 27 November 2017) <http://time.com/5037556/china-beijing-kindergarten-abuse-scandal>

Raby, Geoff, 'Not All Successful Markets Are Free' (*Sydney Morning Herald*, 7 August 2018) <https://www.smh.com.au/politics/federal/not-all-successful-markets-are-free-20180806-p4zvqt.html>

Radinsky, Kira, 'Data Monopolists Like Google Are Threatening the Economy' (*Harvard Business Review*, 2 March 2015) <https://hbr.org/2015/03/data-monopolists-like-google-are-threatening-the-economy>

Ramsey, Carly and Ben Wootliff, 'China's Cyber Security Law: The Impossibility of Compliance?' (*Forbes*, 29 May 2017) <https://www.forbes.com/sites/riskmap/2017/05/29/chinas-cyber-security-law-the-impossibility-of-compliance/#580961c7471c>

Rayner, Tristan, 'What China Is Doing to Create a Tech Edge over the US' (*Android Authority*, 19 December 2017) <https://www.androidauthority.com/what-china-is-doing-to-create-a-tech-edge-over-the-us-823656>

Redrup, Yolanda, 'How Chinese e-Commerce Player JD.com Is Becoming an AI Powerhouse' (*Australian Financial Review*, 21 July 2018) <https://www.afr.com/technology/how-chinese-ecommerce-player-jdcom-is-becoming-an-ai-powerhouse-20180719-h12vph>

Reich, Robert, 'Break Up Facebook (And While We're at It, Google, Apple and Amazon)' (*The Guardian*, 20 November 2018) <https://www.theguardian.com/commentisfree/2018/nov/20/facebook-google-antitrust-laws-gilded-age>

Reisman, Dillon, 'Where Is Your Data, Really? The Technical Case against Data Localization' (*Lawfare*, 22 May 2017) <https://www.lawfareblog.com/where-your-data-really-technical-case-against-data-localization>

Rivest, Ronald L, 'The Case against Regulating Encryption Technology' (*Scientific American*, October 1998) <https://people.csail.mit.edu/rivest/pubs/Riv98e.pdf>

Rowley, Jason, 'The Well-Funded Startups Driven to Own the Autonomous Vehicle Stack' (*TechCrunch*, 27 May 2018) <https://techcrunch.com/2018/05/27/the-well-funded-startups-driven-to-own-the-autonomous-vehicle-stack>

Rudder, Alana, 'ML and AI Partner to Save Disaster Victims: How Aid Organizations Can Tap into Its Power' (*Towards Data Science*, 5 April 2018) <https://towardsdatascience.com/ml-and-ai-partner-to-save-disaster-victims-how-aid-organizations-can-tap-into-its-power-b8de67e92a09>

Russell, Chris, 'Rules of the Game: Changes in China's Foreign Investment Law' (*CKGSB Knowledge*, 1 September 2014) <https://english.ckgsb.edu.cn/knowledges/rules-of-the-game-changes-in-chinas-foreign-investment-law/>

Russell, Jon, 'China Is Beating the US on AI, Says Noted Investor Kai-Fu Lee' (*TechCrunch*, 7 September 2018) <https://techcrunch.com/2018/09/05/china-is-beating-the-us-on-ai-says-noted-investor-kaifu-lee>

Russo, Bill, Edward Tse and Alan Chan, 'Accelerating Innovation in China's Automobility Sector' (*Gao Feng Advisory*, April 2018) <http://www.edwardtseblog.com/view/accelerating-innovation-in-chinas-automobility-sector/>

Saalman, Lora, 'New Domains of Crossover and Concern in Cyberspace' (*Sipri.org*, 26 July 2017) <https://www.sipri.org/commentary/topical-backgrounder/2017/new-domains-crossover-and-concern-cyberspace>

Sacks, Samm, 'Apple in China, Part I: What Does Beijing Actually Ask of Technology Companies?' (*Lawfare*, 22 February 2016) <https://www.lawfareblog.com/apple-china-part-i-what-does-beijing-actually-ask-technology-companies>

Sacks, Samm and Lorand Laskai, 'China's Privacy Conundrum' (*Slate*, 7 February 2019) <https://slate.com/technology/2019/02/china-consumer-data-protection-privacy-surveillance.html>

Sacks, Samm and Manyi Kathy Li, 'How Chinese Cybersecurity Standards Impact Doing Business in China' (*CSIS*, 2 August 2018) <https://www.csis.org/analysis/how-chinese-cybersecurity-standards-impact-doing-business-china>

Sacks, Samm and Robert O'Brien, 'What to Make of the Newly Established CyberSecurity Association of China' (*CSIS*, 25 May 2016) <https://www.csis.org/analysis/what-make-newly-established-cybersecurity-association-china>

Sacks, Samm, Paul Triolo and Graham Webster, 'Beyond the Worst-Case Assumptions on China's Cybersecurity Law' (*New America*, Blog Post, 13 October 2017) <https://www.newamerica.org/cybersecurity-initiative/blog/beyond-worst-case-assumptions-chinas-cybersecurity-law>

Saran, Cliff, 'Why AI Success Depends on IT Picking the Low-Hanging Fruit' (*Computer Weekly*, 22 September 2017) <https://www.computerweekly.com/news/450426790/Why-AI-success-depends-on-IT-picking-the-low-hanging-fruit>

Sawers, Paul, 'Google and Huawei Partner to Bring RCS to Millions via Jibe and Android Messages App' (*Venture Beat*, 18 January 2018) <https://venturebeat.com/2018/01/18/google-and-huawei-partner-to-bring-rcs-to-millions-via-jibe-and-android-messages-app>

Schechner, Sam, Douglas MacMillan and Liza Lin, 'US and Chinese Companies Race to Dominate AI' (*Wall Street Journal*, 18 January 2018) <https://www.wsj.com/articles/why-u-s-companies-may-lose-the-ai-race-1516280677>

Schneier, Bruce, 'Should US Hackers Fix Cybersecurity Holes or Exploit Them?' (*The Atlantic*, 19 May 2014) <https://www.theatlantic.com/technology/archive/2014/05/should-hackers-fix-cybersecurity-holes-or-exploit-them/371197>

Schwartz, Oscar, '"The Discourse Is Unhinged": How the Media Gets AI Alarmingly Wrong' (*The Guardian*, 25 July 2018) <https://www.theguardian.com/technology/2018/jul/25/ai-artificial-intelligence-social-media-bots-wrong>

Segal, Adam, 'Beijing's AI Strategy: Old-School Central Planning with a Futuristic Twist' (*Council on Foreign Relations*, 9 August 2017) <https://www.cfr.org/blog/beijings-ai-strategy-old-school-central-planning-futuristic-twist>

Sha, Liu, 'Govt Takes Down Illegal Websites' (*Global Times*, 14 January 2015) <http://www.globaltimes.cn/content/901784.shtml>

'UISEE Finds a Short Cut for Driverless Cars' (*CKGSB Knowledge*, 19 June 2017) <http://knowledge.ckgsb.edu.cn/2017/06/19/automobile-industry/uisee-technology-finds-shortcut-driverless-cars>

Shafto, Patrick, 'Why Big Tech Companies Are Open-Sourcing Their AI Systems' (*The Conversation*, 16 February 2016) <https://theconversation.com/why-big-tech-companies-are-open-sourcing-their-ai-systems-54437>

Shen, Jill, 'Baidu Accelerating Automaker Deals for Car Software Deployment' (*Technode*, 12 June 2019) <https://technode.com/2019/06/12/baidu-dueros-apollo-installment>

'China Drafts Guidelines for AV Security, but Challenges Remain' (*Technode*, 14 June 2019) <https://technode.com/2019/06/14/china-icv-policy-cesa-19>

Shen, Samuel and Julie Zhu, 'Start-Ups Hopeful as China Readies Nasdaq-Style Tech Board' (*Reuters*, 6 January 2019) <https://www.reuters.com/article/us-china-markets-exchange-tech/start-ups-hopeful-as-china-readies-nasdaq-style-tech-board-idUSKCN1P00PA>

Shen, Timmy, 'China's Obsession with QR Codes' (*Technode*, 16 February 2018) <https://technode.com/2018/02/16/photo-chinas-obsession-qr-codes>

Shen, Xinmei, 'Chinese Internet Users Criticize Baidu CEO for Saying People in China Are Willing to Give Up Data Privacy for Convenience' (*Abacus*, 28 March 2018) <https://www.abacusnews.com/big-guns/chinese-internet-users-criticize-baidu-ceo-saying-people-china-are-willing-give-data-privacy/article/2139313>

Shepherd, Christian, 'China's SenseTime Sells Out of Xinjiang Security Joint Venture' (*Financial Times*, 15 April 2019) <https://www.ft.com/content/38aa038a-5f4f-11e9-b285-3acd5d43599e>

Shi, Mingli, 'Translation: Principles and Criteria from China's Draft Privacy Impact Assessment Guide' (*New America*, 13 September 2018) <https://www.newamerica.org/cybersecurity-initiative/digichina/blog/translation-principles-and-criteria-from-chinas-draft-privacy-impact-assessment-guide>

'What China's 2018 Internet Governance Tells Us about What's Next' (*New America*, 28 January 2019) <https://www.newamerica.org/cybersecurity-initiative/digichina/blog/what-chinas-2018-internet-governance-tells-us-about-whats-next>

Shih, Gerry and Paul Carsten, 'Apple Begins Storing Users' Personal Data on Servers in China' (*Reuters*, 15 August 2014) <https://www.reuters.com/article/us-apple-data-china/apple-begins-storing-users-personal-data-on-servers-in-china-idUSKBN0GF0N720140815>

Si, Ma, 'China a Pioneer in AI Innovation' (*China Daily*, 27 March 2018) <http://www.chinadaily.com.cn/a/201803/27/WS5ab9a24da3105cdcf65147e9.html>

Simonite, Tom, 'China Challenges Nvidia's Hold on Artificial Intelligence Chips' (*Wired*, 20 November 2017) <https://www.wired.com/story/china-challenges-nvidias-hold-on-artificial-intelligence-chips>

'How Health Care Data and Lax Rules Help China Prosper in AI' (*Wired*, 8 January 2019) <https://www.wired.com/story/health-care-data-lax-rules-help-china-prosper-ai/>

Soo, Zen, 'Alibaba's AutoNavi Becomes the First Chinese Maps Service to Navigate a Path to 100 Million Daily Users' (*South China Morning Post*, 5 October 2018) <https://www.scmp.com/tech/enterprises/article/2167114/alibabas-autonavi-blazes-trail-first-chinese-maps-service-cross-100>

Stevenson, Alexandra, 'US Investor Tries to Shake Up Sina, a Pillar of China's Internet' (*New York Times*, 31 October 2017) <https://www.nytimes.com/2017/10/31/business/dealbook/china-sina-aristeia-proxy-fight.html>

Stupp, Catherine, 'Carmakers Fear EU Plans to Ease Data Flows Will Help Tech Rivals' (*Euractiv*, 30 September 2016) <https://www.euractiv.com/section/transport/news/carmakers-fear-eus-plan-to-ease-data-flows-will-help-tech-rivals>

Sun, Yiting, 'China Wants to Make the Chips That Will Add AI to Any Gadget' (*MIT Technology Review*, 24 January 2018) <https://www.technologyreview.com/2018/01/24/241365/china-wants-to-make-the-chips-that-will-add-ai-to-any-gadget/>

Tai, Mariko, 'Alibaba to Buy 33% of Spinoff Ant Financial' (*Nikkei Asia*, 2 February 2018) <https://asia.nikkei.com/Asia300/Alibaba-to-buy-33-of-spinoff-Ant-Financial>

Thompson, Nicholas and Ian Bremmer, 'The AI Cold War That Threatens Us All' (*Wired*, 23 October 2018) <https://www.wired.com/story/ai-cold-war-china-could-doom-us-all>

Thurm, Scott, 'Chinese-American Elites Lament a Brewing Trade War' (*Wired*, 6 May 2018) <https://www.wired.com/story/chinese-american-elites-lament-a-brewing-trade-war>

Tobin, Meaghan, 'China Wants to Build an Open Source Ecosystem to Rival GitHub (*Rest of the World*, 19 January 2021) <https://restofworld.org/2021/china-gitee-to-rival-github/>

Triolo, Paul and Jimmy Goodrich, 'From Riding a Wave to Full Steam Ahead' (*New America*, 28 February 2018) <https://www.newamerica.org/cybersecurity-initiative/digichina/blog/riding-wave-full-steam-ahead>

Triolo, Paul and Matt Scott, 'China's AI Trajectory Is Set by Entrepreneurs and International Collaboration, not by Government Edict' (*SupChina Project*, 19 April 2019) <https://supchina.com/2019/04/19/chinas-ai-trajectory-is-set-by-entrepreneurs-and-international-collaboration-not-by-government-edict>

Tse, Edward, 'Don't Belittle China's Innovation Potential' (*Europe's World*, 14 February 2014) <https://www.friendsofeurope.org/insights/dont-belittle-chinas-innovation-potential>

Udemans, Chris, 'Chinese Care More about Data Privacy than You Think, but They Still Need Better Protection' (*TechNode*, 15 May 2018) <https://technode.com/2018/05/15/data-privacy-china>

'Didi Launches Open Platform for Smart Transportation, AI Services' (*Technode*, 9 May 2019) <https://technode.com/2019/05/10/didi-open-ai-transport>

'Second-Hand Mobile Phone User Data Is Being Sold in China for as Little as RMB 10' (*TechNode*, 1 June 2018) <https://technode.com/2018/06/01/mobile-phone-user-data>

'Tencent Enforces Real-Name Verification in "Honor of Kings"' (*TechNode*, 17 September 2018) <https://technode.com/2018/09/17/real-name-verification-honor-of-kings>

US Information Technology Office, 'TC260 Drafts New Standard for China's Cloud Security Review Regime' (*USITO*, 26 June 2015) <http://www.usito.org/news/tc260-drafts-new-standard-chinas-cloud-security-review-regime>

Vincent, James, 'AI Researchers Debate the Ethics of Sharing Potentially Harmful Programs' (*Verge*, 21 February 2019) <https://www.theverge.com/2019/2/21/18234500/ai-ethics-debate-researchers-harmful-programs-openai>

Xi Jinping, 'Remarks by HE Xi Jinping President of the People's Republic of China at the Opening Ceremony of the Second World Internet Conference' (Speech, Wuzhen, 16 December 2015) https://www.fmprc.gov.cn/mfa_eng/wjdt_665385/zyjh_665391/t1327570.shtml

Wagner, Jack, 'China's Cybersecurity Law: What You Need to Know' (*The Diplomat*, 1 June 2017) <https://thediplomat.com/2017/06/chinas-cybersecurity-law-what-you-need-to-know>

Wang, Eudora, 'Chinese AI Firm 4Paradigm Pockets $700m Led by Boyu, Primavera, Hopu' (*Deal Street Asia*, 23 January 2021) <https://www.dealstreetasia.com/stories/4paradigm-funding-224587/>

Wang, Ke, 'Xiaogang Village, Birthplace of Rural Reform, Moves On' (*China.org.cn*, undated) <http://www.china.org.cn/china/features/content_16955209.htm>

Wang, Lianzhang, 'Apps That "Unlock" Wi-Fi Investigated for Privacy Breaches' (*Sixth Tone*, 4 April 2018) <https://www.sixthtone.com/news/1002042/apps-that-unlock-wi-fi-investigated-for-privacy-breaches>

Wang, Serenitie and Daniel Shane, 'Jack Ma Endorses China's Controversial 12 Hours a Day, 6 Days a Week Work Culture' (*CNN Business*, 2 April 2019) <https://edition.cnn.com/2019/04/15/business/jack-ma-996-china/index.html>

Waters, Richard, 'Making It Big in China Requires a Large Measure of Localisation' (*Financial Times*, 20 August 2015) <https://www.ft.com/content/0d472a74-4752-11e5-af2f-4d6e0e5eda22?mhq5j=e5>

Webster, Graham and Paul Triolo (trans), 'Translation: China Proposes "Global Data Security Initiative"' (*New America*, 7 September 2020) <https://www.newamerica.org/cybersecurity-initiative/digichina/blog/translation-chinese-proposes-global-data-security-initiative/>

Webster, Graham and Samm Sacks, 'Five Big Questions Raised by China's New Draft Cross-Border Data Rules' (*New America*, 13 June 2019) <https://www.newamerica.org/cybersecurity-initiative/digichina/blog/five-big-questions-raised-chinas-new-draft-cross-border-data-ruless>

Webster, Graham et al., 'China's Plan to "Lead" in AI: Purpose, Prospects, and Problems' (*New America*, 1 August 2017) <https://www.newamerica.org/cybersecurity-initiative/blog/chinas-plan-lead-ai-purpose-prospects-and-problems/>

Wei, He, 'Ma: Embrace AI Opportunities' (*China Daily*, 21 September 2018) <http://www.chinadaily.com.cn/a/201809/21/WS5ba444dca310c4cc775e7726.html>

Wei, Lu, 'Cyber Sovereignty Must Rule Global Internet' (*Huffington Post*, 15 December 2014) <https://www.huffingtonpost.com/lu-wei/china-cyber-sovereignty_b_6324060.html>

Wertime, David, 'It's Official: China Is Becoming a New Innovation Powerhouse: The World's Factory Is Turning into an R&D Machine – And Fast Catching Up with America' (*Foreign Policy*, 7 February 2014) <https://foreignpolicy.com/2014/02/07/its-official-china-is-becoming-a-new-innovation-powerhouse>

Wharton Business School, '"Land-Grab Mentality": The Cutthroat Competition on China's Internet' (*Knowledge @Wharton*, 14 December 2010) <https://knowledge.wharton.upenn.edu/article/land-grab-mentality-the-cutthroat-competition-on-chinas-internet>

Wheatley, Mike, 'Huawei Open-sources AI Framework MindSpore to Rival Google's TensorFlow' (*Silicon Angle*, 30 March 2020) <https://siliconangle.com/2020/03/30/huawei-open-sourced-ai-framework-called-mindspore-rival-googles-tensorflow/>

Wiggers, Kyle, 'Baidu Launches EZDL, an AI Model Training Platform That Requires No Coding Experience' (*Venture Beat*, 1 September 2018) <https://venturebeat.com/2018/09/01/baidu-launches-ezdl-an-ai-model-training-platform-that-requires-no-coding-experience>

'Baidu Releases Apollo 5.0 with Upgrades for "Complex" Road Scenarios' (*Venture Beat*, 1 July 2019) <https://venturebeat.com/2019/07/01/baidu-releases-apollo-5-0-with-upgrades-for-complex-road-scenarios>

Wildau, Gabriel and Yizhen Jia, 'Collapse of Chinese Peer-to-Peer Lenders Sparks Investor Panic' (*Financial Times*, 22 July 2018) <https://www.ft.com/content/75e75628-8b27-11e8-bf9e-8771d5404543>

Williams, Greg, 'Why China Will Win the Global Race for Complete AI Dominance' (*Wired*, 16 April 2018) <https://www.wired.co.uk/article/why-china-will-win-the-global-battle-for-ai-dominance>

Wong, Sue-Lin, 'China Court Ruling Could Threaten Foreign Investments in Country' (*New York Times*, 19 June 2013) <https://cn.nytimes.com/business/20130619/c19vie/en-us>

Xiang, Nina, 'China's AI Industry Has Given Birth to 14 Unicorns: Is It a Bubble Waiting to Burst?' (*Forbes*, 5 October 2018) <https://www.forbes.com/sites/ninaxiang/2018/10/05/chinas-ai-industry-has-given-birth-to-14-unicorns-is-it-a-bubble-waiting-to-pop/#2b68965246c3>

Xiaojing, Liu and Li Rongde, 'QQ Blocks Thousands of Accounts for Selling Private Information' (*Caixin Global*, 21 February 2017) <https://www.caixinglobal.com/2017-02-21/qq-blocks-thousands-of-accounts-for-selling-private-information-101057642.html>

Xu, Wei, 'China to Further Promote Innovation and Entrepreneurship' (*State Council of the People's Republic of China*, 12 July 2017) <http://english.gov.cn/premier/news/2017/07/12/content_281475723086902.htm>

Yang, Fan, 'Tech Showcase: OpenPAI: Open Source Initiative for AI Platform in China' (*Microsoft.com*, 2 August 2018) <https://www.microsoft.com/en-us/research/video/openpai-open-source-initiative-for-ai-platform-in-china>

Yang, Hongquan, 'China – the Privacy, Data Protection and Cybersecurity Law Review – Edition 6' (*The Law Reviews*, October 2019) <https://thelawreviews.co.uk/edition/the-privacy-data-protection-and-cybersecurity-law-review-edition-6/1210009/china>

Yang, Yuan, 'China's Data Privacy Outcry Fuels Case for Tighter Rules' (*Financial Times*, 1 October 2018) <https://www.ft.com/content/fdeaf22a-c09a-11e8-95b1-d36dfef1b89a>

'China's Tech Groups Bow to Beijing Censorship Demands' (*Financial Times*, 29 June 2017) <https://www.ft.com/content/43def3ec-5c8f-11e7-9bc8-8055f264aa8b?mhq5j=e1>

'Chinese Hackers Defy Government Warnings at Beijing Def Con' (*Financial Times*, 14 May 2018) <https://www.ft.com/content/f03995de-5711-11e8-bdb7-f6677d2e1ce8?desktop=true>

Yanrong, Kang, Jeanette Whyte and Thomas Hart, 'Comparative Study of Smart Cities in Europe and China' (White Paper, EU–China Policy Dialogues Support Facility II (PDSF), March 2014) <http://euchina-ict.eu/wp-content/uploads/2015/01/Smart_City_report_draft-White-Paper-March-2014.pdf> (the link is no longer active)

Yasheng, Huang, 'China's Use of Big Data Might Actually Make It Less Big Brother-ish' (*MIT Technology Review*, 22 August 2018) <https://www.technologyreview.com/s/611814/chinas-use-of-big-data-might-actually-make-it-less-big-brother-ish>

Yeung, Karen and Eric Ng, 'China to Spearhead US$1 Trillion Autonomous Driving Revolution' (*South China Morning Post*, 13 December 2017) <https://www.scmp.com/business/china-business/article/2124042/china-spearhead-us1-trillion-autonomous-driving-revolution>

Yi, Ding, 'Baidu Wins California Permit to Test Fully Driverless Vehicles' (*Caixin*, 20 June 2021) <https://www.caixinglobal.com/2021-01-28/baidu-wins-california-permit-to-test-fully-driverless-vehicles-101657263.html>

Yingqi, Li, 'China Eyes Wider Application of AI Technologies' (*People's Daily*, 14 March 2018) <http://en.people.cn/n3/2018/0314/c90000-9437000.html>

Yu, Eileen, 'Alibaba's Fiscal 2017 Revenue Climbs 56% on Cloud, Mobile Commerce Growth' (*ZDnet*, 18 May 2017) <http://www.zdnet.com/article/alibabas-fiscal-2017-revenue-climbs-56-percent-on-cloud-mobile-commerce-growth>

Yuan, Li, 'China Is Losing to the US in High-Stakes Battle for Artificial Intelligence Talent' (*Wall Street Journal*, 23 March 2017) <https://www

.wsj.com/articles/baidus-loss-is-a-setback-for-ai-in-china-1490270411?mg=prod/accounts-wsj>

'For China's Business Elites, Staying Out of Politics Is No Longer an Option' (*New York Times*, 6 July 2021) <https://www.nytimes.com/2021/07/06/technology/china-business-politics-didi.html>

Yunxu, Qu, Liu Caiping and Han Wei, 'Alibaba, JD.com on Fast Track for Homecoming' (*Caixin Global*, 22 March 2018) <https://www.caixinglobal.com/2018-03-22/alibaba-jdcom-on-fast-track-for-homecoming-101224491.html>

Yuzhe, Zhang and Liu Xiao, 'Alipay Racks Up More Penalties for Rule Violations' (*Caixin Global*, 9 April 2018) <https://www.caixinglobal.com/2018-04-09/alipay-racks-up-more-penalties-for-rule-violations-101232168.html>

Zaagman, Elliot, 'Github Gives Chinese Developers Censor-Proof Forum' (*Technode*, 16 April 2019) <https://technode.com/2019/04/16/github-gives-chinese-developers-censor-proof-forum>

Zapotosky, Matt, 'FBI Has Accessed San Bernardino Shooter's Phone without Apple's Help' (*Washington Post*, 28 March 2016), <https://www.washingtonpost.com/world/national-security/fbi-has-accessed-san-bernardino-shooters-phone-without-apples-help/2016/03/28/e593a0e2-f52b-11e5-9804-537defcc3cf6_story.html>

Zhang, Bonnie, 'Tencent, Didi, Baidu among the Seven Companies Approved for Autonomous Car Road Tests in Beijing' (*Pandaily*, 25 September 2018) <https://pandaily.com/tencent-didi-baidu-among-the-seven-companies-approved-for-autonomous-car-road-tests-in-beijing>

Zhang, Sarah, 'China's Artificial-Intelligence Boom' (*The Atlantic*, 16 February 2017) <https://www.theatlantic.com/technology/archive/2017/02/china-artificial-intelligence/516615>

'Society Shanghai Begins Driverless Trains Trial Run on Metro Line' (*South China Morning Post*, 1 April 2018) <http://www.scmp.com/news/china/society/article/2139814/shanghai-begins-driverless-trains-trial-run-metro-line>

Zhang, Shidong, 'China's Regulator Quietly Removes Capital-Sapping CDRs as It Vows Reforms to Soothe Frayed Nerves' (*South China Morning Post*, 9 August 2018) <https://www.scmp.com/business/china-business/article/2158953/chinas-regulator-quietly-removes-capital-sapping-cdrs-it>

'US Semiconductor Makers Dwarf Chinese Peers in Market Valuation as China's Chip Dream Remains Distant' (*South China Morning Post*, 23 April 2018) <https://www.scmp.com/business/china-business/article/2142929/us-semiconductor-makers-dwarf-chinese-peers-market-valuation>

Zhang, Yan, David Ramli and Lulu Chen, 'Wanted in China: Detailed Maps for 30 Million Self-Driving Cars' (*Bloomberg*, 22 August 2018) <https://www

.bloomberg.com/news/articles/2018-08-22/wanted-in-china-detailed-maps-for-30-million-self-driving-cars>

Zhang, Yunan, 'China's Autonomous Driving Startups Join the Billion-Dollar Club' (*The Information*, 23 November 2018) <https://www.theinformation.com/articles/chinas-autonomous-driving-startups-join-the-billion-dollar-club>

Zhao, Runhua, 'China Looks to Private Capital, Open Source Technology for Global Tech Game Advantage' (*Technode*, 20 December 2018) <https://technode.com/2018/12/20/china-global-tech-game-advantage>

Zhou, Zunyou, 'China's Comprehensive Counter-Terrorism Law' (*The Diplomat*, 23 January 2016) <https://thediplomat.com/2016/01/chinas-comprehensive-counter-terrorism-law>

Zhou, Youyou, 'Four of the Top 25 Github Projects Are Written in Chinese, Six Contain No Code' (*Quartz*, 18 May 2018) <https://qz.com/1280215/four-of-the-top-25-github-projects-are-written-in-chinese-six-contain-no-code>

'Microsoft to Set Up Asia AI Research Branch in Shanghai' (*Technode*, 17 September 2018) <https://technode.com/2018/09/17/microsoft-research-asia-shanghai>

Zhu, Julie and Tova Cohen, 'China's Tech Money Heads for Israel as US Welcome Wanes' (*Reuters*, 11 May 2017) <http://www.reuters.com/article/us-china-investment-israel-idUSKBN187080>

E Other Secondary Sources: Chinese Language

«15 个部委合力 首批 4 家国家创新平台确立-聚焦我国新一代人工智能发展规划» [15 Ministries Join Forces to Establish the First Batch of 4 National Innovation Platforms – Focusing on China's New Generation of AI Development Plan] (*Gov.cn*, 23 November 2017) <http://www.gov.cn/guowuyuan/2017-11/23/content_5241718.htm>

« 47 次《中国互联网络发展状况统计报告》 [47th Statistical Report on the Development of the Internet in China] (*CNNIC*, 3 February 2021) <http://www.cnnic.cn/hlwfzyj/hlwxzbg/hlwtjbg/202102/t20210203_71361.htm>

«2018 微信年度数据报告: 00 后睡觉少, 70 后爱刷朋友圈» [WeChat Annual Data Report: Less Sleep after Midnight and 70 Love to Swipe Friends Groups] (*Sina*, 9 January 2019) <https://tech.sina.com.cn/i/2019-01-09/doc-ihqhqcis4468637.shtml>

«AI 芯片卡位战: 谁赢得自动驾驶处理器, 谁就赢得了AI 时代» [AI Chip War: Whoever Wins the Autonomous Processor Race Will Win the AI Era] (*Sequoia Exchange*, 26 April 2018) <https://mp.weixin.qq.com/s/0Th9C7pwhGU9D1vEkShZE> (the link is no longer active)

«中央网信办: 正制定个人信息收集规范标准» [CAC: Establishing a Standard for Collecting Personal Information] (*Xinhua*, 11 November 2016) <http://news.xinhuanet.com/2016-11/11/c_1119897534.htm>

«习近平: 把我国从网络大国建设成为网络强国» [Xi Jinping: Build Our Country from a Large Network Country into a Strong Network Country] (*Xinhua*, 27 February 2014) <http://news.xinhuanet.com/politics/2014-02/27/c_119538788.htm>

«人工智能国家队正式出炉 阿里云负责建设城市大脑» [The AI National Team Officially Released Alibaba Cloud to Build the City Brain] (*Sohu*, 16 November 2017) <http://www.sohu.com/a/204718930_694841>

«你的个人信息安全吗？ 工信部约谈百度蚂蚁金服今日头条?» [Is Your Personal Information Safe? MIIT Cites Baidu, Ant Financial and Jinri Toutiao's Conduct] (Sina, 12 January 2018) <http://tech.sina.com.cn/roll/2018-01-12/doc-ifyqqciz5880474.shtml>

«创新工场智能投资基金落户广州, 目标总规模 25 亿» [Innovative Workshop Smart Investment Fund Settled in Guangzhou with a Total Target of 2.5 Billion] (*Innovation Works WeChat page*, 24 May 2018) <https://mp.weixin.qq.com/s/V7MVeYST17wQKau_7GjIpg>

«印发 智能网联汽车道路测试管理规范 （试行)» [Three Ministries and Commissions: Issued the 'Intelligent Network Linked Vehicle Road Test Management Regulations (Trial)'] (*Tencent Research Institute*, 16 April 2018) <https://mp.weixin.qq.com/s/yK2G1LMKPAdGLdnGN5-BLQ>

«商汤继 BAT, 科大讯飞后成第五个国家人工智能开放创新平台» [SenseTime Follows BAT and IFlytek to Become the Fifth National Artificial Intelligence Open Innovation Platform] (*Sohu*, 20 September 2018) <https://www.sohu.com/a/254985856_115565>

«国家互联网信息办公室网络安全协调局约谈 '支付宝年度账单事件' 当事企业负责人» [National Internet Information Office Cyber Security Coordination Bureau Schedules a Meeting to Talk to the Business Leaders Responsible for the 'Alipay Annual Event'] (*CAC.gov.cn*, 10 January 2018) <http://www.cac.gov.cn/2018-01/10/c_1122234687.htm>

«国家级 '新一代人工智能开放创新平台' 怎么建» [How to Build a National New-Generation AI Open Innovation Platform] (*Xinhua*, 27 November 2017) <http://www.xinhuanet.com//tech/2017-11/27/c_1122013676.htm>

«关于 Megvii Technology Limited 公开发行存托凭证并在科创板上市 之辅导基本情况表» [CITIC Securities Co, Ltd Notice about Megvii Technology Limited Public Issuance of Depositary Receipts and Listing on the Science and Technology Innovation Board] (China Securities Regulatory Commission, 29 September 2020) <http://www.csrc.gov.cn/pub/beijing/bjfdqyxx/bjfdqyjbqk/202101/P020210112533742962617.pdf>

«我们真的在意隐私吗: 多少中国网民 '一套密码走天下'?» [Do We Really Care about Privacy: How Many Chinese Netizens 'Have a Set of Passwords to Go

Online'?] (*Qianjia Net*, 15 August 2018) <http://www.qianjia.com/html/2018-08/15_301849.html>

«揭秘个人信息交易黑市: 内部分工明确 日交易额百万» [Exposing the Personal Information Transaction Black Market: The Scheme Is Exposed, the Daily Trade Is Worth Millions] (*People's Daily*, 11 October 2018) <http://tech.qq.com/a/20181011/003346.htm>

«李彦宏称中国人愿意用隐私换便利, 你认可他的观点吗?» [Robin Li Said That Chinese People Are Willing to Trade Privacy for Convenience. Do You Agree?] (*Weibo*, May 2018) <http://vote.weibo.com/poll/138701440> (the link is no longer active)

«根据 '规划' 将形成 '1+N' 人工智能项目群» [According to the Plan the '1+N' AI Project Group Will Be Formed] (*State Council Information Office*, 21 July 2017) <http://www.scio.gov.cn/32344/32345/35889/36946/zy36950/Document/1559032/1559032.htm>

«涉嫌侵犯用户隐私 工信部约谈百度、支付宝、今日头条» [User Privacy Infringements Alleged, MIIT Cites Baidu, Ant Financial and Jinri Toutiao's conduct] (*Xinhua*, 12 January 2017) <http://www.xinhuanet.com/fortune/2018-01/12/c_1122250046.htm>

«百度推出 Apollo 3.5 和 Apollo Enterprise» [Baidu Launches Apollo 3.5 and Apollo Enterprise] (*Baidu Official Blog*, 9 January 2019) <https://www.infoq.cn/article/3NA0SmwHbeg_CaUEXgxR>

«百度用网盘、发贴、评论都得实名认证» [Those Who Use Baidu's Network, Posting or Comments Functions Must All Undergo Real-Name Certification] (*Xianji*, 11 May 2017) <https://www.xianjichina.com/news/details_35326.html>

«百度系两款 APP 未经提示开启隐私权限» [Two Baidu Apps Expand the Limits of Privacy Permission without Giving Warnings] (*Xinhua*, 28 March 2018) <http://www.xinhuanet.com/fortune/2018-03/28/c_1122600485.htm>

«百度联手北环卫发布 7 款智能环卫产品» [Baidu Teamed Up with Northern Environmental Protection Department to Release 7 Smart Sanitation Products] (*PingWest*, 28 September 2018) <https://www.pingwest.com/w/177811>

«百度 Apollo 生态合作伙伴再添新成员, 携手共建车路协同智能交通» [Baidu Apollo Ecosystem Adds New Members] (*Apollo Official WeChat Account*, 3 March 2020) <https://mp.weixin.qq.com/s?__biz=MzI5MjcyNTc1Mw==&mid=2247491018&idx=1&sn=2b83c08287e952d0badc5922aa42c5a2&chksm=ec7dab5cdb0a224ac8058d1e5916f06bc055cdde871d8cfaf408c921770b510719882743d13f&mpshare=1&scene=24&srcid=&sharer_sharetime=1583322601059&sharer_shareid=081fb2cac668f46b68cafe2e49724859#rd>

«盘点: 2018 年全国各级网信办互联网乱象规范治理工作» [Inventory: 2018 Work on Standardizing Governance by CAC at Every Level throughout China of Disorderly Online Practices] (*China Information Security*, 1 September 2018) <https://mp.weixin.qq.com/s?__biz=MzA5MzE5MDAzOA==&mid=

2664115873&idx=1&sn=29fc50a73b0b3e92260ac511ccc9d854&chksm=8b5e2c58b c29a54ee0282605911888e1153f156c77f823df938bb67bc9797d3746d47d6f74ac& scene=0&xtrack=1#rd>

«腾讯 QQ 群机器人服务调整中: QQ 小冰、Baby Q 被关闭» [Tencent's QQ Chatbot Suspended: QQ Xiaobing, Baby Q Shut Down] (*Sina*, 30 July 2017) <http://tech.sina.com.cn/i/2017-08-03/doc-ifyitamv4697563.shtml>

«谁卖了我的手机号? 手机信息被盗一年损失近千亿» [Who Sold My Mobile Number? Mobile Phone Information Stolen Worth Nearly 100 Billion in One Year] (*People's Daily*, 21 December 2017) <http://it.people.com.cn/n1/ 2017/1221/c1009-29720427.html>

«辛识平: 奋斗应提倡, 996 当退场» [Xin Zhiping: The Struggle Should be Advocated, 996 Should Be Ended] (*Xinhua*, 15 April 2019) <http://www .xinhuanet.com/politics/2019-04/15/c_1124370790.htm>

«重大预警! 多家国家机关、金融机构 Wi-Fi 密码被窃, 9 亿用户如同 '裸奔'» [Major Warning! Wi-Fi Passwords of Many State Agencies and Financial Institutions Stolen, 900 Million Users Are 'Exposed'] (*CCTV Finance*, 28 March 2018) <https://mp.weixin.qq.com/s/ZZnnyuIJRKV9vnYEHSbjAQ>

«重磅: 百度 Apollo 发布全球首个车路协同开源方案» [Heavyweight: Baidu Apollo Releases the World's First Car Road Collaborative Open Source Solution] (*Baidu Public Policy Research Institute*, 14 September 2018) <https://mp.weixin.qq.com/s/p7TWjidyZ5eN5Uhc3yx1-g>

«阿里云涉侵权被判赔 26 万: '宁输官司也要保护隐私'» [AliYun (AliCloud) Alleged Infringement: 26 Million Awarded: 'Would Rather Face a Lawsuit in Order to Protect Users' Privacy'] (*Sina*, 3 June 2017) <http://tech.sina .com.cn/i/2017-06-03/doc-ifyfuzmy1489932.shtml>

«雄安: 年» [Xiongan: After One Year] (*The Paper*, 1 April 2018) <https://www .thepaper.cn/newsDetail_forward_2048269>

«雄安新区: 周年 这座城正在如何改变?» [The First Anniversary of Xiongan: How Is the City Changing?] (*China News*, 1 April 2018) <http://www .chinanews.com/gn/2018/04-01/8480837.shtml>

«深圳星行科技有限公司关于处理周光违纪行为的公告» [Shenzhen Xingxing Technology Co, Ltd Announcement on Handling Zhou Guang's Disciplinary Behaviour] (*Roadstar.ai Official WeChat Account*, 21 January 2019) <https://mp.weixin.qq.com/s?__biz=MzU3MDA5ODkyOQ==&mid= 2247484868&idx=1&sn=5c340f0169fa3e5dc811596d9a06bcf9&chksm=fcf5d05 acb82594c13b1f0f1528a52593a586906d547714984aa7bf048cd83b5ff72df54d 5fb&mpshare=1&scene=1&srcid=0121aLVkJQh096XryqUdXhfT#rd>

«从首家无人车公司猝死, 看股权设计 7 个原则» [Beyond the Sudden Death of a Leading Autonomous Car Company, a Look at the Company's 7 Equitable Principles] (*China HRD*, 4 October 2019) <http://www.chinahrd.net/blog/ 412/469578/411740.html>

«习近平在世界经济论坛 "达沃斯议程" 对话会上的特别致辞» [Full Text: Special Address by Chinese President Xi Jinping at the World Economic Forum Virtual Event of the Davos Agenda] (*Xinhua*, 25 January 2021) <http://www.xinhuanet.com/politics/leaders/2021-01/25/c_1127023884.htm>

«工信部携 Gitee 入场, 国内开源生态建设进入快车道» [MIIT Backs Gitee, to Support the Development of the Domestic Open Source Ecosystem] (*Gitee*, July 2020) <https://blog.gitee.com/2020/08/17/gitee-gxb/>

«腊月十二, 来听互联网隐私保护界最 '硬核' 的故事» [Twelfth Day of the Lunar Month, Come and Listen to the Most 'Hardcore' Story in the Internet Privacy Protection Community'] (*Privacy Guard in the Southern Metropolis Daily*, 9 January 2019) <https://m.mp.oeeee.com/a/BAAFRD000020190109129910.html>

阿司匹林 [Aspirin – a pen name], «GitHub 汽车标星 20000+, 国产 AI 开源从算法开始突破 | 专访商汤联合创始人林达华» [20,000+ Stars on Github, a Domestically Developed AI Open Source Software Starts to Breakthrough | Interview with Lin Dahua, Sensetime Cofounder] (*CSDN*, 31 August 2020) <https://mp.weixin.qq.com/s/7LLfEEONLaVTxAQDke87xw?fbclid=IwAR30b6jkmKfnrPrQR5lww4w_3qtmBBBmlfWZT8AxDiXgetqnZ13GmJ31qTw>

刘俊海 [Liu Junhai], «网安法一周年: 网络安全筑起五道 '防火墙'» [The One Year Anniversary of the Cyber Security Law: Cyber Security Builds Five 'Firewalls'] (*China Information Security*, 2 June 2018) <https://mp.weixin.qq.com/s/cjMZ1Km4bfNjwaIvw9u5Mw>

刘迈 [Liu Mai], «GDPR 之风盛行, 美, 印, 巴接连启动数据保护立法» [The Winds of the GDPR Are Blowing, as the United States, India and Pakistan Successively Initiate Data Protection Legislation] (*Baidu Institute for Public Policy*, 29 August 2018) <https://mp.weixin.qq.com/s/ePwUquQL9gZ3EeANnGAwDA>

吴晓灵、周学东 [Wu Xiaoling and Zhou Xuedong], «吴晓灵、周学东: 建议尽快制定 '个人信息保护法'» [Wu Xiaoling and Zhou Xuedong: Recommended Formulating the Personal Information Protection Law as Soon as Possible] (*Caixin*, 16 March 2018) <http://topics.caixin.com/2017-03-16/101066803.html>

张一琪 [Zhang Yiqi], «今天, 个人该怎样保护隐私» [Today, How Do Individuals Protect Privacy?] (*People's Daily*, 16 April 2018) <https://mp.weixin.qq.com/s/rSW-Ayu6zNXw87itYHcPYA>

张朝 [Zhang Chao], «张朝: 百度隐私保护经验分享» [Sharing Baidu's Privacy Protection Experience] (*Baidu Institute for Public Policy*, 13 August 2018) <https://mp.weixin.qq.com/s/2cw5suQgwIY8augRepLjNQ>

张林成 [Zhang Lincheng], «微信官方:我们不留存任何用户的聊天记录» [WeChat Official: We Don't Keep Users' Chat History] (*TechNode*, 2 January 2018) <https://cn.technode.com/post/2018-01-02/wei-xin-yinsi>

彭云燕 [Peng Yunyan], «邓玉峰个展开幕 34.6 万武汉公民的秘密被 '公之于众'» [Deng Yufeng's Opening Ceremony: 346,000 Wuhan Citizens' Secrets

'Made Public'] (*1Shoucang*, 4 April 2018) <http://www.1shoucang.com/article-41710-1.html>

方可成 [Fang Kecheng], «搜索引擎百度已死 (以及我的几点补充)» [Search Engine Baidu is Already Dead (as Well as a Few Other Points)] (*Weibo*, 23 January 2019) <https://www.weibo.com/ttarticle/p/show?id=2309404331600992154916#_0>

李开复 [Kai-Fu Lee], «李开复: 人工智能超级大国的那些事» [Kai-Fu Lee: The Things That Are Needed to Create an Artificial Intelligence Superpower] (*Sina*, 23 August 2018) <http://tech.sina.com.cn/csj/2018-08-23/doc-ihicsiav6703902.shtml>

李诗 [Li Shi], «商汤成为第五大国家人工智能开放创新平台» [Sensetime Becomes the Fifth Company to Join the National Artificial Intelligence Open Innovation Platform] (*Leifeng*, 20 September 2018) <https://www.leiphone.com/news/201809/Xf5pNSS103T1cZMh.html>

杨鑫健 [Yang Xinyu], «独家: 51Job 百万条用户信息外泄？暗网售价 12 个比特币» [Exclusive: Millions of 51Job Users Information Leaked? The Darknet Price Is 12 Bitcoins] (*The Paper*, 15 June 2018) <https://www.thepaper.cn/newsDetail_forward_2198458>

洪延青 [Hong Yangqing], «数据出境安全评估: 保护基础性战略资源的重要一环» [Outbound Data Security Assessment: An Important Part of Protecting Basic Strategic Resources] (*CAC*, 7 August 2017) <http://www.cac.gov.cn/2017-08/07/m_1121443948.htm> (the link is no longer active)

洪延青 [Hong Yanqing], «对〈个人信息安全规范〉五大重点关切的回应和解释» [Responses and Explanations to the Five Major Concerns of the Personal Information Security Specification] 网安寻路人 *Wanganxunluren* (5 February 2018) <https://mp.weixin.qq.com/s/rSW-Ayu6zNXw87itYHcPYA>

洪延青 [Hong Yanqing], «解析'个人信息出境安全评估办法 (征求意见稿)'实体保护规则背后的主要思路» [An Analysis of the Main Ideas behind the Entity Protection Rules of the 'Measures for the Assessment of Outbound Security of Personal Information (Opinion-Seeking Draft)'] (*CAC*, 15 June 2019) <https://mp.weixin.qq.com/s/sCGZtqmQBWyH_sSan8q-Eg>

洪杉 [Hong Shan] «当顶尖的 AI 创业者济济一堂, 他们在谈些什么? 特别报道» [When Top AI Entrepreneurs Come Together, What Do They Talk About? Special Report] (*Sequoia Exchange*, 27 August 2018) <https://mp.weixin.qq.com/s/1F2IZ_DGQ318nDDQsmu8Yg>

王刚 [Wang Gang], «BAT, 科大讯飞, 商汤等 5 大 AI 国家队的一次 集体工作汇报» [A Collective Work Report of the Five Major 'National Team' Members – BAT, iFlytek, and Sensetime] (*Leiphone*, 11 May 2019) <https://mp.weixin.qq.com/s/ksJm980HsmfUEhI5U6UQlg?fbclid=IwAR3BGbjFtiz1UFtMRWvYPjkfWDfGf3KgsIWJtVKn_UwXjAdGyC3wE_cnZ-I>

王融 [Wang Rong], «TC 杭州: 王坚博士: '人工智能' 是人类傲慢的名词产物» [TC Hangzhou: Dr Jian Wang: 'Artificial Intelligence' Is a Name Resulting from Human Arrogance] (*TechCrunch*, 2 July 2018) <https://mp.weixin.qq.com/s/1jNalbynko_MtPxQ_PERBQ>

王融 [Wang Rong], «自动驾驶三件事, 安全、安全、还是安全!» [The Three Keys to Drive Autonomously: Safety, Safety, and Safety!] (*Baidu AI*, 26 July 2018) <https://mp.weixin.qq.com/s/Ro_5bJYx9WO_46JjEMPSCA>

王融 [Wang Rong], «迷雾中的新航向: 2018 年数据保护政策年度观察» [A New Direction in the Fog: 2018 Data Protection Policy Observations] (*Tencent Research Institute*, 29 December 2018) <https://www.secrss.com/articles/7496>

吴朋阳 [Wu Pengyang], «人工智能在医疗行业应用的三大场景, 信任如何建立? 前沿科技» [How to Build Trust in the Three Major Scenarios of AI Application in the Medical Industry? Frontier Technology] (*Tencent Research Institute*, 30 March 2018) <https://mp.weixin.qq.com/s/Zf5Igvkqc-N2JqW9ail1lQ>

胡喆 [Hu Wei] and 周琳 [Zhou Lin], «智能视觉国家新一代人工智能开放创新平台正式亮相» [Intelligent Vision National New Generation AI Open Innovation Platform Officially Debuts] (*Xinhua*, 20 September 2018) <http://www.xinhuanet.com/politics/2018-09/20/c_1123461737.htm>

蔡雄山 [Cai Xiongshan], «第三波人工智能发展浪潮中的顶层设计, 评《新一代人工智能发展规划》» [Top-Level Design in the Third Wave of Artificial Intelligence Development, Commenting on the 'New Generation Artificial Intelligence Development Plan'] (*Tencent Research Institute*, 27 July 2017) <https://mp.weixin.qq.com/s/vtarWQe1vZiBkJyJBvhHtw>

车宁 [Che Ning], «'个人信息安全规范' 生效在即, 金融科技从业人员应了解这些事» [The 'Privacy Standards' [author's terminology] Come into Effect Soon, and Financial Technology Practitioners Should Understand These Things] (*TC260*, 20 January 2018) <https://www.tc260.org.cn/front/postDetail.html?id=20180201201040>

陆奇 [Lu Qi], «新经济 NEO100: 陆奇, YC 中国的 01 号员工» [New Economy NEO100: Lu Qi, YC China's No 01 Employee] (*36Kr*, 15 August 2018) <https://36kr.com/p/5148299.html>

F Chinese Laws

«中华人民共和国反恐怖主义法» [Anti-Terrorism Law of the People's Republic of China] (People's Republic of China) National People's Congress, Order No 36, 27 December 2015

«中华人民共和国国家安全法» [National Security Law of the People's Republic of China] (People's Republic of China) National People's Congress, Order No 68, 1 July 2015

«中华人民共和国外国投资法 (草案征求意见稿)» [Foreign Investment Law of the People's Republic of China (Opinion-Seeking Draft)] (People's Republic of China) Ministry of Commerce, 19 January 2015

«中华人民共和国外国投资法» [Foreign Investment Law of the People's Republic of China] (People's Republic of China) Ministry of Commerce, 15 March 2019

«中华人民共和国外资企业法 (2016 修正)» [Law on Wholly Foreign-Owned Enterprises of the People's Republic of China (2016 Revision)] (People's Republic of China) National People's Congress, Order No 51, 9 March 2016

«中华人民共和国民法典» [Civil Code of the People's Republic of China] (People's Republic of China) National People's Congress, 28 May 2020

«中华人民共和国密码法 (草案征求意见稿)» [Encryption Law of the People's Republic of China (Opinion-Seeking Draft)] (People's Republic of China) Office of State Commercial Cryptography Administration (OSCCA), 13 April 2017

«中华人民共和国密码法» [Encryption Law of the People's Republic of China] (People's Republic of China) Office of State Commercial Cryptography Administration (OSCCA), 26 October 2019

«中华人民共和国测绘法» [Surveying and Mapping Law of the People's Republic of China] (People's Republic of China) National People's Congress, Order No 66, amended 27 April 2017

«中华人民共和国网络安全法» [Cyber Security Law of the People's Republic of China] (People's Republic of China) National People's Congress, Order No 53, 7 November 2016

«中华人民共和国个人信息保护法(草案)» [Personal Information Protection Law of the People's Republic of China (Opinion-Seeking Draft)] (People's Republic of China) National People's Congress, 21 October 2020

«中华人民共和国个人信息保护法» [Information Protection Law of the People's Republic of China] (People's Republic of China) National People's Congress, 20 August 2021

«中华人民共和国数据安全法(草案)» [Data Security Law of the People's Republic of China (Opinion-Seeking Draft)] (People's Republic of China) National People's Congress, 2 July 2020

«中华人民共和国数据安全法» [Data Security Law of the People's Republic of China] (People's Republic of China) National People's Congress, 10 June 2021

G Chinese Regulations, Notices, Guides and Standards

«GB/T 35273-2017 信息安全技术 个人信息安全规范» [*GB/T 35273-2017 Information Technology – Personal Information Security Specification*]

(People's Republic of China) National Information Security Standardisation Technical Committee (TC260), 29 December 2018

«GB/T 35273-2020 信息安全技术 个人信息安全规范» [GB/T 35273-2020 Information Technology – Personal Information Security Specification] (People's Republic of China) National Information Security Standardisation Technical Committee (TC260), 6 March 2020

«个人信息出境安全评估办法（征求意见稿）公开征求意见的通知» [Personal Information Outbound Transfer Security Assessment Measures (Draft for Comment)] (People's Republic of China) CAC, 13 June 2019

«个人信息和重要数据出境安全评估办法 （征求意见稿）» [Personal Information and Important Data Outbound Security Assessment Measures (Opinion-Seeking Draft)] (People's Republic of China) SIIO, 11 April 2017

«个人信息和重要数据出境安全评估办法 （征求意见稿）» 公开征求意见 [Circular of the SIIO on the Public Consultation on the Measures for the Assessment of Personal Information and Important Data Exit Security (Opinion-Seeking Draft)] (People's Republic of China) SIIO, 11 April 2017

《网络安全审查办法》 [Cyber Security Review Measures] (People's Republic of China) CAC, 13 April 2020

«中华人民共和国电信条例» [Telecommunications Regulations of the People's Republic of China] (People's Republic of China) State Council, amended 2 June 2016

«互联网信息服务管理办法» [Administrative Measures on Internet Information Services] (People's Republic of China) State Council, amended 1 August 2011

«互联网用户账号名称管理规定» [Internet User Account Name Management Regulations] (People's Republic of China) CAC, 4 February 2015

«信息安全技术 个人信息去标识化指南» [Guide for De-Identifying Personal Information] (People's Republic of China) National Information Security Standardisation Technical Committee (TC260), 1 September 2018

«信息安全技术 个人信息安全影响评估指南» [Information Security Technology – Security Impact Assessment Guide of Personal Information] (People's Republic of China) National Information Security Standardisation Technical Committee (TC260), 13 June 2018

«信息安全技术 数据出境安全评估指南» [Guide for Data Cross-Border Transfer Security Assessment] (People's Republic of China) National Information Security Standardisation Technical Committee (TC260), 1 September 2018

《关键信息基础设施安全保护条例》 [Critical Information Infrastructure Security Protection Regulations] (People's Republic of China) State Council of the People's Republic of China, 30 July 2021

《关于加强车联网（智能网联汽车）网络安全工作的通知（征求意见稿）》 [Notice on Strengthening Cyber Security Work in the Internet of Vehicles

(Smart Connected Vehicles) (Opinion-Seeking Draft)] (People's Republic of China) MIIT, 23 June 2021

《关于审理理应信息网络侵权人身权益民事纠纷按键使用法律若干问题的规定》 [Regulations Concerning Some Questions of Applicable Law in Handing Civil Dispute Cases Involving the Use of Information Networks to Harm Personal Rights and Interests] (People's Republic of China) Supreme People's Court, 9 October 2014

《关于应用安全可控信息技术加强银行业网络安全和信息化建设的指导意见》(称 317 号文) [Guiding Opinions on Applying Secure and Controllable Information Technology to Strengthen the Network Security and Informatisation of the Banking Industry (Circular 317)] (People's Republic of China) China Banking Regulatory Commission (CBRC), 26 December 2014

《关于规范政府和社会资本合作合同管理工作的通知》 [Guidance on Public-Private Partnerships] (People's Republic of China) Ministry of Finance, 30 December 2014

《最高人民法院 最高人民检察院关于办理侵犯公民个人信息刑事案件适用法律若干问题的解释》 [Explanation on Several Issues Concerning the Application of Law in Criminal Cases of Infringing on Citizens' Personal Information] (People's Republic of China) Supreme People's Court and the Supreme People's Procuratorate, 1 June 2017

《北京市移动互联网应用程序公众信息服务自律公约》 [Beijing Municipality Self-Discipline Convention on Internet Application Programmes and Public Information Services] Capital Internet Society, 26 November 2011

《即时通信工具公众信息服务发展管理暂行规定》 [Provisional Regulations for the Development and Management of Instant Messaging Tools and Public Information Services] (People's Republic of China) SIIO, 7 August 2014

《国务院关于印发节能与新能源汽车产业发展规划（2012-2020 年）的通知》 [Notice of the State Council on Printing and Distributing the Development Plan for Energy Saving and New Energy Vehicle Industry (2012-2020)] (People's Republic of China) State Council, 28 June 2012 <http://www.gov.cn/zwgk/2012-07/09/content_2179032.htm>

《国务院关于授权国家互联网信息办公室负责互联网信息内容管理工作的通知国发》 [Notice Concerning Empowering CAC to Be Responsible for Internet Information Content Management Work] (People's Republic of China) State Council, 26 August 2014

《国务院关于积极推进'互联网+'行动的指导意见》 [Guiding Opinions on Actively Promoting the 'Internet Plus' Action Plan] (People's Republic of China) National People's Congress, 4 July 2015

《地图管理条例》 [Administrative Regulation of Maps] (People's Republic of China) State Council, 1 January 2016

《数据安全管理办法（征求意见稿）公开征求意见的通知》 [Data Security Management Measures (Opinion-Seeking Draft)] (People's Republic of China) CAC, 28 May 2019

《数据安全管理办法（征求意见稿）》 [Data Security Management Measures (Opinion-Seeking Draft)] (People's Republic of China) CAC, 28 May 2019

《智能网联汽车道路测试管理规范试行》 [Intelligent Connected Vehicle Road Test Management Standards (Trial)] MIIT, the Ministry of Public Security and the Ministry of Transport, 1 May 2018

《电话用户真实身份信息登记规定》 [Telephone User Real Identity Information Registration Regulations] (People's Republic of China) MIIT, 16 July 2013

《外国的组织或者个人来华测绘管理暂行办法》 [Temporary Measures on Administration of Mapping and Surveying in China by Foreign Organisations and Individuals] (People's Republic of China) Ministry of Land and Resources, 27 April 2011

《网络产品和服务安全审查办法（试行）》 [Security Review Measures for Network Products and Services (Interim)] (People's Republic of China) CAC, 2 May 2017

《网络产品和服务安全审查办法征求意见（草案征求意见稿）》 [Measures for Security Reviews of Network Products and Services (Opinion-Seeking Draft)] (People's Republic of China) SIIO, 4 February 2017

《网络关键设备安全检测实施办法(征求意见稿)》 [Critical Network Equipment Security Testing Implementing Measures (Opinion-Seeking Draft)] (People's Republic of China) CAC, 4 June 2019

《网络出版服务管理规定》 [Network Publishing Services Management Regulations] (People's Republic of China) Ministry of Industry and Information Technology and the State Administration of Press Publication Radio Film and Television

《网络安全审查办法(征求意见稿)》 [Cyber Security Review Measures (Opinion-Seeking Draft)] (People's Republic of China) CAC, 21 May 2019

《网络安全审查办法（修订草案征求意见稿）》 [Measures for Cyber Security Reviews (Revised, Opinion-Seeking Draft)] (People's Republic of China) CAC, 10 July 2021

《网络预约出租汽车经营服务管理暂行办法》 [Interim Regulations for the Management of Network Appointed Taxi Services Operations] (People's Republic of China) Ministry of Industry and Information Technology, 28 July 2016

H Chinese Policies, Plans and White Papers

《'互联网+'人工智能三年行动实施方案》 ['Internet Plus' AI Three-Year Action Implementation Plan] (People's Republic of China) MIIT, 25 May 2016

《2015年政府工作报告》 [2015 Government Work Report] (People's Republic of China) State Council, 5 March 2015

«中国互联网状况白皮书» [China Internet Status White Paper] (People's Republic of China) State Council, June 2010

«中国人工智能开源软件发展白皮书» [White Paper on the Development of China's AI Open Source Software] (People's Republic of China) MIIT, July 2018

«国家新一代人工智能开放创新平台» [National Open Innovation Platforms for New Generation AI] (*Gov.cn*, 4 August 2019) <http://www.gov.cn/xinwen/2019-08/04/content_5418542.htm>

«中国制造 2025» [Made in China 2025] (People's Republic of China) State Council, 8 May 2015

«人工智能安全白皮书» [AI Security White Paper] China Academy of Information and Communications Technology (CAICT) (People's Republic of China), September 2018 <http://www.caict.ac.cn/kxyj/qwfb/bps/201809/P020180918473525332978.pdf>

«人工智能标准化白皮书 (2018 版)» [AI Standardization White Paper (2018)] (People's Republic of China) National Standards Management Committee Second Ministry of Industry, January 2018

«全国 PPP 综合信息平台项目库第五期季报» [National PPP Integrated Information Platform Project Library Phase 5 Quarterly Report] (People's Republic of China) Ministry of Finance, Department of Finance, 2017 <http://www.cpppc.org/zh/pppyw/4684.jhtml>

«关于开展国家智慧城市试点工作的通知» [Notice of Carrying out the National Smart City Pilots] (People's Republic of China) State Council, 6 December 2012

«十三届全国人大常委会立法规划» [Legislative Planning of the 13th National People's Congress Standing Committee] (National People's Congress, 10 September 2018)

«国务院关于加快培育和发展战略性新兴产业的决定» [Decision on Accelerating and Developing Strategic Emerging Industries] (Peoples' Republic of China) State Council, 18 October 2010

«国家中长期科学和技术发展规划纲要 (2006–2020 年)» [National Outline for Medium- and Long-Term Science and Technology Development Planning (2006–2020)] Ministry of Science and Technology, 9 February 2006

«国家信息化发展战略纲要» [Outline of the National Informatisation Development Strategy] (People's Republic of China) State Council, 27 July 2016

«国家智慧城市试点暂行管理办法» [National Interim Measures for Smart City Pilots] (People's Republic of China) State Council, 22 November 2012

«国家网络空间安全战略» [National Cyberspace Security Strategy] (People's Republic of China) CAC, 27 December 2016

«国民经济和社会发展第十二个五年规划» [Twelfth Five-Year Plan for National Economic and Social Development] National People's Congress, 14 March 2011

《国民经济和社会发展第十三个五年规划》 [Thirteenth Five-Year Plan for National Economic and Social Development] National People's Congress, 17 March 2016

《外商投资产业指导目录 (2017 年修订)》 [Catalogue for the Guidance of Foreign Investment Industries (2017 Revision)] (People's Republic of China) Ministry of Commerce, 28 June 2017

《大众创业与创新》 [Mass Entrepreneurship and Innovation] (People's Republic of China) State Council, 2014

《战略性新兴产业》 [Strategic Emerging Industries] (People's Republic of China) State Council, 19 October 2010

《战略性新兴产业重点产品和服务指导目录 (2016 版)》 [Catalogue for the Guidance of Important Products and Services in Strategic and Emerging Industries (2016 version)] (People's Republic of China) National Reform and Development Commission, 25 January 2017

《新一代人工智能发展规划》 [New Generation AI Development Plan] (People's Republic of China) State Council, 8 July 2017

《'十三五'国家战略性新兴产业发展规划》 [13th Five-Year Plan for Developing National Strategic and Emerging Industries] (People's Republic of China) State Council, 19 December 2016

《'十三五'国家科技创新规划》 [13th Five-Year Plan for National Science and Technology Innovation] (People's Republic of China) State Council, 8 August 2016

《国务院关于印发'中国制造 2025'的通知》 [Notification on the Printing and Distribution of Made in China 2025] (People's Republic of China) State Council, 8 May 2015

I Other Legislation

Australia

Telecommunications and Other Legislation Amendment (Assistance and Access) Act 2018 (Cth)

Europe

Regulation (EU) 2016/679 of the European Parliament and of the Council of 27 April 2016 on the Protection of Natural Persons with regard to the Processing of Personal Data and on the Free Movement of Such Data, and repealing Directive 95/46/EC [2016] OJ L 119/1

United Kingdom

Investigatory Powers Act 2016 (UK)

United States

US Department of Commerce, Bureau of Industry and Security, Addition of Certain Entities to the Entity List (Final Rule), Effective May 16, 2019 (16 May 2019) <https://www.bis.doc.gov/index.php/all-articles/17-regulations/1555-addition-of-certain-entities-to-the-entity-list-final-rule-effective-may-16-2019>

Addition of Certain Entities to the Entity List, A Rule by the Industry and Security Bureau on 10/09/2019 (10 September 2019) <https://www.federalregister.gov/documents/2019/10/09/2019-22210/addition-of-certain-entities-to-the-entity-list>

INDEX

4Paradigm, company 228–9, 231
AI *See* artificial intelligence
AI National Team 247, 249, 252–4, 256, 293
AI Plan *See* China's National AI Plan, A New Generation AI Development Plan
Airbnb, company, 150, 165
Alibaba
  Cloud *See* AliYun, company
  company 41, 44–9, 77, 227, 248, 284, 293–4
Alipay, product 47, 172, 178, 184, 204
AliYun, company 107, 150, 160, 249, 282–3, 333
AlphaGo 222–3. *See also* DeepMind
Amazon, company 265–6, 279, 283, 289, 291
  Amazon Web Services 281, 284, 305
Ant Financial, company 47–8, 60, 178, 339
Anti-Terrorism Law, China's (2015) 80, 86–94, 97–8, 118
Apache Software Foundation 297
Apollo, open-source self-driving platform 224, 260, 295, 313–22, 325–6, 331
Apple, company 89–91, 151, 160, 289, 305, 333
artificial intelligence (AI) 28, 32, 209. *See also* Deep Learning; Machine Learning
  definition of 215, 220–1
  future 220

government policy, Chinese 223, 238–42. *See also* China's National AI Plan, A New Generation AI Development Plan
  GPU chips 218–47
  history 215–16
  Network Sovereignty, and 256–8
  open-source *See* open-source: AI platforms
  private sector, China's 227–8
  public understanding 214–15
  public-private partnerships 247–9
  research 213–17, 223–4, 258, 278, 289
  Smart Cities, and 234
AutoNavi, a Chinese online map service 188
autonomous vehicles 254, 306, 311, 313–14, 318, 324, 341. *See also* self-driving cars
AutonomouStuff, company 318

'backdoors' 87–93, 107, 111
Baidu, company 41–2, 44, 48, 77, 172, 178, 224, 248–9, 272–3, 289, 293, 312, 318, 326, 331
  Apollo *See* Apollo, Baidu's open-source self-driving platform
  EZDL 273
  PaddlePaddle *See* PaddlePaddle, Baidu's open-source Machine Learning platform
Bank of China 59, 156
BATs (Baidu, Alibaba, Tencent) 61, 77, 177, 203, 228, 247, 250
Biden, Joe 59, 71, 335

INDEX

blockchain 32, 146, 220
bottom-up innovation 33–4
ByteDance, company 31, 55, 178–9, 290

Caffe, open-source AI platform 265, 295
Cayman Islands 39–42, 45, 48, 307
CDRs *See* China depositary receipts
censorship 1, 8, 57, 65, 69, 75, 99, 152, 161, 168, 179, 201, 208, 268, 341
   content 57, 73, 76–8, 159, 161–2
   control 99
Central Leading Group for Cyberspace Affairs and the State Internet Information Office 66. *See also* State Internet Information Office
China Association for Science and Technology 225
China depositary receipts (CDRs) 53–5, 58
China Electronics Standardisation Institute (CESI) 113, 296
China National Information Security Standards Technical Committee (TC260) 114, 181, 192
China Unicom, company 228, 272
China's National AI Plan, A New Generation AI Development Plan 223, 240–4, 246, 253, 257–9, 290
China's National AI Platforms 247, 249, 251, 259, 293–6, 321
Chinese government 28, 111, 244, 333
   AI, and 211–12, 241, 256, 301, 331
   data localisation 124, 152, 296
   data protection 155
   foreign investment, and 43, 51, 53
   fuzzy logic 7, 30, 35, 330
   Informatisation 64
   innovation policies 22, 26, 329
   open-source, and 274, 292, 327
   private sector, and 15, 78, 206, 251, 258
Cisco, company 114, 292
CLOUD Act 2018 (US) 137

cloud computing 4, 63, 82, 104, 107, 143, 148, 150, 153, 235, 240, 248, 262–3, 265, 275, 282–5, 294, 303, 333, 339
CloudWalk, company 58
Congressional Committee Encryption Working Group 91
Cook, Tim 89
'core business functions'
   definition of 190–1
'critical information infrastructure operators' 100–3, 105, 115–16, 122, 197
   definition of 101
cyber security 5, 57, 65, 68, 80, 138, 162
   community 69
   innovation 81, 125, 153
   law *See* Cyber Security Law
   meaning of 73
   open-source 274, 279, 303
   regime 6, 74, 83–5, 94, 96, 99, 118, 125, 135, 140, 164, 180, 201
   review 105–7, 113–14, 156
Cyber Security and Informatisation Leading Small Group 65, 82
Cyber Security Association of China (CSAC) 68–70
Cyber Security Law
   about 95
   Article 37
      'critical information infrastructure operators' *See* 'critical information infrastructure operators'
      'important data' *See* 'important data'
      'network products and services' 103
      about 102–3
      data exits *See* data exits (out of China)
      data localisation *See* data localisation
      backdoors 107–10. *See also* 'backdoors'
   background 96–8
Cyberspace Administration of China, and 68

Cyber Security Law (cont.)
  introduction of 94–5
  Network Sovereignty, and 72
  subordinate regulations 115–21
  third-party involvement 110
  vague rules 98–107
cyber sovereignty 5, 49, 73. *See also*
  Network Sovereignty
Cyberspace Administration of China
  (CAC) 65–8, 82, 97–8, 104, 108,
  112–13, 115, 162, 164, 196, 198,
  228

DARPA (research arm of US
  Department of Defense) 279
data breach 144, 167, 172, 176–7
'data controller' 120, 136, 181, 187, 189
data exits (out of China) 17, 94, 120,
  149, 152, 182
data localisation 3, 74, 114
  AI 243, 256, 261, 282, 296, 299,
    301–6, 330
  background 130
  cost 144–8
  Cyber Security Law, under 17, 72,
    94–6, 287, 336
  definition of 102–5, 116, 123, 133,
    301
  expansion 197–8
  privacy 166
  protectionism 138–41
  rationale 131–7, 147
  technical viability 141–4
data privacy 155, 159–60, 172, 175,
  204–5, 210
  definition of 154, 165, 196, 208
data protection 94, 120, 132, 135, 140,
  142, 145, 154–6, 180, 192
  definition of 154, 159, 165, 196, 207
  demand for 175, 205
  privacy laws, and 185
Data Security Law 157, 170, 195
data theft 104, 134, 144, 155, 167,
  169–70, 172, 175, 185, 208
Deep Learning 213, 216, 220–1, 226–7,
  251, 264, 285
  definition of 217–18
DeepMind 222, 276. *See also* AlphaGo

Def Con 273–4
Development Zones, Economic and
  Technological Development
  Zone 11, 27, 37, 237
Didi Chuxing, company 160, 188, 275,
  285, 325

eBay, company 44, 230
encryption 86, 90–1, 107, 114,
  153, 180
  keys 87, 89, 94, 96, 103
Encryption Law 157
entrepreneurs 5, 8, 22, 25, 30–2, 150,
  212, 234, 259
  operating environment 32, 36, 43, 55,
    60, 339
EU *See* European Union
European Union 18, 151, 167

Face++ *See* Megvii, company
Facebook 66, 90, 174, 202, 205, 266,
  270, 278, 336
Fang Binxing 69
FBI *See* Federal Bureau of Investigation
Federal Bureau of Investigation (FBI)
  89–90
Federated Learning 336
Fei-Fei Li 214
firmware 101
  definition of 101
Five-Year Plans 22, 32, 237–8
Foreign Investment Law 50, 55–6, 59,
  71
'forking' 268
fuzzy logic 18, 73, 108, 129, 147–8, 158,
  189, 330
  AI 32, 209, 211, 222, 256,
    305–6
  computer science, in 12–13, 189
  content control 77
  data privacy 196, 202
  data protection 200, 207
  future impact 338
  intentions 332
  legal structures 36, 39, 43, 59
  legislating 7, 38, 88, 95, 117, 152, 184,
    187, 191, 257, 261, 330
  meaning in this book 11–14

GDPR *See* General Data Protection Regulation (EU)
Geely, company 172
General Data Protection Regulation (GDPR) (EU) 135–6, 155, 187, 193, 195, 199, 205, 337
 'data controller' 187
 'purpose limitation' 190
 data classes 191
GitHub 230, 267–71, 284, 294
Google 44, 203, 265, 270, 277–8, 283, 289, 298
 Android 90, 271, 280
 Brain 276, 299
 censorship 76
 DeepMind *See* DeepMind
 Maps 323
 TensorFlow *See* TensorFlow, Google's open-source AI platform
 Waymo *See* Waymo, Google's self-driving car program
GPS mapping 315, 322–6
GPU *See* graphics processing unit
graphics processing unit (GPU) 28, 218, 267, 282. *See also* semiconductors
Great Firewall 69, 76
'guiding funds' 245, 247
Guiding Opinions on Actively Promoting the 'Internet Plus' Action Plan 70–1, 239

hacking 84, 86, 141, 155, 166, 273
Hax, hardware incubator 267
hierarchical temporal memory 220
Hikvision, company 108, 254
Hong Kong Stock Exchange 43, 59–60, 293
Horizon Robotics, company 231, 246, 250, 309–10
Huawei 108, 246, 254, 271, 287–8, 291, 341

IBM, company 114, 139, 222, 265, 277, 298, 304
ICT *See* information and communications technology

iFlytek 247, 249–50, 293
'important data' 116, 123–4, 132, 136, 157–201, 302, 323
 definition of 95, 101–5, 118, 121–2, 141, 315, 332, 337
Infervision, company 202
information and communications technology (ICT) 64, 70, 73, 138, 154, 234, 239. *See also* cyber space
 industry 6, 76, 130, 145, 147, 150
 service providers 5, 73, 124
Information Technology and Innovation Foundation (ITIF) 139, 142
Informatisation 63, 66, 77, 81, 102, 111, 201, 212, 242
 meaning of 64–5
initial public offering (IPO) 44, 49, 54, 60, 339
innovation 75, 104, 139, 149, 153, 232
 defining 7–8, 21–35
 government policies, Chinese 64, 70, 78, 81, 233, 237–8, 329
 open-source 248, 264, 277, 281, 285
Intel, company 114, 290, 317
Intellifusion, company 231
International Strategy of Cooperation on Cyberspace 75
Internet Engineering Task Force (IETF) 146
Internet of Things (IoT) 2, 4, 63–4, 83, 100, 153, 164, 228, 235, 283
Internet Plus 63, 70–2, 75, 81, 153, 237, 330
 meaning of 4–5, 63–5
Internet White Paper (2010), China's 4, 49, 62
IoT *See* Internet of Things
IPO *See* initial public offering

JD.com, company 48, 54–5, 160, 254, 271, 297, 312
Jinri Toutiao, company 31, 178

Kuang-Chi, company 228

leapfrogging 27–8
Lee Sedol, World Champion Go player 222
'legitimate legal rights and interests' 187
Li Keqiang 4, 62
Li Shufu 172
Li, Robin 202, 205, 314
LinkedIn, company 151, 278
Linux Foundation 267, 271–2
Lu Wei 49

Ma, Jack 47–8, 76, 225, 339
Ma, Pony 173, 225
Machine Learning 33, 203, 213, 220, 224, 240, 251, 263–4, 266, 273, 277, 279, 282
definition of 16, 215–17
Made in China 2025 233, 306
Malong Technologies, company 209, 229–30
Mass Entrepreneurship 8, 30, 234
Measures for Cyber Security Review, Interim *See* Security Review Measures, Draft/Interim
Megvii, company 58–60, 231, 254, 341
Meituan, food delivery service 179, 312
Microsoft
  company 108–9, 111, 114, 203, 265, 268, 279, 288–9, 298, 317
  Machine Learning 266
  Open Platform for AI 267
  Ventures 230
  Windows 84, 111
Ministry of Industry and Information Technology (MIIT), China's 162, 178, 188, 228, 238, 269, 271, 296
Ministry of Science and Technology (MOST), China's 247–8, 257, 293
Momenta, company 231, 309, 317
multi-level protection system 105

Nasdaq 37, 41, 46, 58
Naspers, company 44–5
National Cyberspace Security Strategy 82

National Development and Reform Commission (NDRC) 235
natural language processing 12, 216
network effects 275
'network operator' 73, 105, 116–17, 136, 159, 164
definition of 95, 100–2, 122–3
privacy provisions 180, 183, 199
Network Sovereignty 1, 8, 14, 16, 50, 57, 63, 66, 70, 78, 87, 115, 133, 242, 256, 297, 305, 320, 322, 327–8, 333. *See also* cyber sovereignty
definition of 5–7, 72–7
neural networks 203, 216–17, 220, 223, 285
definition of 218
Ng, Andrew 218
NOBUS 90
North Korea 84
Nvidia, company 28, 230, 246, 309, 317, 337

Obama, Barack 241
OpenAI, company 224, 279–80
open-source
  AI platforms
    benefits of 275–86
    case studies of 306–26
    definition of 263
  definition of 265
  history in China 265–75
Open-Source White Paper 296–7
Outbound Data Measures 101, 116, 121
  second version 117
  third version 119–24, 197
Outline of the National Informatisation Development Strategy 81–3

PaddlePaddle, Baidu's open-source Machine Learning platform 272–3, 287
Personal Information Protection Law 121, 124, 156–94
pilot petri dishes 8, 209, 221, 226, 258
Pinduoduo, company 55, 78
Pony.ai, company 307–9, 325

Privacy Standards (2020) 177–8, 185–6, 204
 about 181–5
 intention of drafters 187
 scope and application 187–90
proprietary data theft *See* data theft
'protected personal information' 185–6. *See also* Privacy Standards (2020)
protectionism 106, 132, 141, 147, 149, 327, 333
public-private partnerships 188, 243, 293, 316
 definition of 247, 251

Qihoo 360, company 254
QQ, instant-messaging service 170, 172, 214

ransomware attack 84
'rea-name registration' or 'real-name user registration' 136, 154, 156, 201, 207
 meaning of 161–4
Reinforcement Learning 217, 220
Roadstar.ai, company 308–9

Schumpeterian innovation 22
'secure and controllable' 73, 76, 82, 109, 112–14, 242, 257, 329
 definition of 85
Securities Regulatory Commission (SRC), China's 53–4, 60
Security Review Measures, Draft/Interim 101, 103, 112, 115
Sedol, Lee, World Champion Go player 222
self-driving cars 27, 33, 83, 151, 306, 311, 316, 321, 324. *See also* autonomous vehicles
self-learning systems *See* Deep Learning; Machine Learning
semiconductors 28, 34, 212, 245, 298. *See also* graphics processing unit (GPU)
SenseParrots, SenseTime's open-source AI platform 295, 299

SenseTime, company 58, 231, 247, 249–50, 252, 291, 298
'sensitive personal information' definition of 186, 189, 196
Sesame Credit, Alibaba's social credit product 178
Shanghai Stock Exchange Star Market (Science and Technology Innovation Board) 58–60
shanzhai 23, 267
'sharding' of data 142, 144
 definition of 143
Shenzhen Stock Exchange 52, 249, 293
Siemens, company 28, 111, 283
Sina, company 41–2, 46–8, 51, 163, 176, 310
Sinovation Ventures, venture capital firm 230
Smart Cities 4, 63, 74, 100, 254–5, 259, 321
 AI, and 212–13, 236–8, 242–3
 Alibaba, and 293–4
 defined terms under Cyber Security Law, and 100
 meaning of 236
Snowden, Edward 16, 89, 130
Social Credit System 155, 178, 242
SOE *See* state-owned enterprise
Softbank 44, 48
Standardisation Administration of China 181, 188
Standing Committee of the National People's Congress 96–7, 121, 170, 194
start-ups 22
 AI 35, 212, 220, 230, 247, 250, 295, 306, 312
 Chinese 25, 267, 284, 327
 government policies, Chinese 30, 71, 77, 124, 202
 offshore investment 50, 55
State Council 4, 50, 70, 87, 102, 105, 238
State Internet Information Office (SIIO), China's 66, 162
state-owned enterprise (SOE) 9, 38, 44, 63, 101, 206, 228–9, 250, 256, 269, 316, 339

strong internet country 4, 63
Supervised Learning 216
surveillance 58, 69, 108, 130, 197, 207, 232, 252, 291, 341
Surveying and Mapping Law 323
symbiotic relationship between the public and private sectors 8, 30, 35, 212, 231, 249, 258
synthetic data 302

TC260 *See* China National Information Security Standards Technical Committee
techno-utilitarian 202
Tencent, company 44, 52, 69, 77, 161, 170, 173, 214, 227, 249, 269, 272–3, 289, 294
TensorFlow, Google's open-source AI platform 266, 272–3, 276, 282, 284, 287, 299, 336
TikTok 31, 55, 196
top-down government signalling 33, 209, 245
Trump, Donald 123, 254, 288
trust scandals 159, 166
TuSimple, company 308–11

Uber, company 151, 285, 311
Uisee, company 311
United States 16, 28, 42, 48, 52, 55, 80, 89, 137, 225, 241, 268, 278, 288, 308
Unsupervised Learning 216

variable-interest entity (VIE) 40, 45, 50, 53, 55–6, 71, 307, 333
  activist investors, and 50
  emergence 42
  legal status 43, 56, 59
  risks 52
  structure 40–2
VIE *See* variable-interest entity
virtual private network (VPN) 72, 268
VPN *See* virtual private network

Wan Gang 225, 246, 251, 292
Waymo, Google's self-driving car program 224, 314
WeChat Pay, product 204
WeChat, app 45, 100, 144, 162, 165, 172–4, 190, 196, 204–5, 207
Weibo, company 42, 46, 163
WeRide.ai, company (formerly JingChi) 308, 310
wholly foreign-owned enterprise (WFOE) 40–1, 44, 322
World Economic Forum 18, 71

Xi Jinping 1, 5, 51, 62, 65, 71–2, 238
Xiaomi, company 26, 54, 254
Xinjiang 15, 58, 335, 341

Y Combinator, incubator 279
Yahoo, company 41, 44, 47–8
Yitu Tech, company 35, 231, 254, 278, 290

ZTE, company 272, 341

Printed by Printforce, United Kingdom